# THE DREAM OF THE POEM

THE LOCKERT LIBRARY OF POETRY IN TRANSLATION

*Editorial Advisor*: Richard Howard

*For other titles in the Lockert Library, see p. 547*

# THE DREAM
# OF THE POEM

## HEBREW POETRY

## FROM MUSLIM AND CHRISTIAN SPAIN

## 950–1492

*Translated, Edited, and Introduced by*

## PETER COLE

PRINCETON UNIVERSITY PRESS

PRINCETON AND OXFORD

LIBRARY OF CONGRESS CATALOGING-IN-PUBLICATION DATA

THE DREAM OF THE POEM : HEBREW POETRY FROM MUSLIM & CHRISTIAN SPAIN, 950-1492 /

TRANSLATED, EDITED, AND INTRODUCED BY PETER COLE.

P.  CM. — (LOCKERT LIBRARY OF POETRY IN TRANSLATION)

INCLUDES BIBLIOGRAPHICAL REFERENCES.

ISBN-13: 978-0-691-12194-9 (CL. : ALK. PAPER)

ISBN-10: 0-691-12194-X (CL. : ALK. PAPER)

ISBN-13: 978-0-691-12195-6 (PB. : ALK. PAPER)

ISBN-10: 0-691-12195-8 (PB. : ALK. PAPER)

1.  HEBREW POETRY, MEDIEVAL–SPAIN–TRANSLATIONS INTO ENGLISH.    I.  COLE, PETER, 1957-II.

SERIES.

PJ5059.E3D74 2007

892.4'12080946—DC22      2006043894


BRITISH LIBRARY CATALOGING-IN-PUBLICATION DATA IS AVAILABLE


GRATEFUL ACKNOWLEDGMENT IS DUE TO THE EDITORS OF THE FOLLOWING LITERARY
JOURNALS AND VOLUMES, WHERE SOME OF THESE POEMS FIRST APPEARED: *AGNI REVIEW, DER
BRENNER, CONJUNCTIONS, DARK AGES, FASCICLE, GRAND STREET, LVNG, PARNASSUS IN REVIEW,
PEN-AMERICA JOURNAL, POETRY, POETRY INTERNATIONAL, SCRIPSI, SULFUR, WORDS WITHOUT BORDERS,
THE MIRACLE OF MEASURE* (TALISMAN), *SELECTED POEMS OF SHMUEL HANAGID, SELECTED POEMS OF
SOLOMON IBN GABIROL* (PRINCETON UNIVERSITY PRESS), *THE DEFIANT MUSE* (FEMINIST PRESS),
AND *WORLD POETRY* (NORTON).

THE LOCKERT LIBRARY OF POETRY IN TRANSLATION IS SUPPORTED

BY A BEQUEST FROM CHARLES LACY LOCKERT (1888–1974)

*For Adina,*
*for everything*

*Andalus . . . might be here or there, or anywhere . . . a meeting place of strangers in the project of building human culture. . . . It is not only that there was a Jewish-Muslim coexistence, but that the fates of the two people were similar. . . . Al-Andalus for me is the realization of the dream of the poem.*

—MAHMOUD DARWISH

# ✢ CONTENTS ✢

PART TWO
Christian Spain and Provence (c. 1140–1492)

# ⊰ *TO THE READER* ⊱

THIS BOOK was born of a fascination that evolved into addiction. Medieval Hebrew poetry and the extensive spadework its translation involves have held me in their sway for more than two decades now, and *The Dream of the Poem* seeks to account for the effect of both that initial, unmediated encounter with the verse and the more complex but no less charged engagement that has come with time. These translations have, then, been made with an eye toward being read *without* annotation—and readers are encouraged to do just that—though I have also provided substantial notes to most of the poems and a glossary of key terms for those who would like to be taken further into the gravitational field of medieval Hebrew poetics.

The poems gathered in this volume reflect a combination of concerns: I have tried, first of all, to give a full-bodied sense of the major poets from the Muslim and Christian periods, and so have included substantial selections by Shmu'el HaNagid, Shelomo Ibn Gabirol, Moshe Ibn Ezra, Yehuda HaLevi, Avraham Ibn Ezra, Yehuda Alharizi, and Todros Abulafia. At the same time I've made every effort to bring attention to the truly surprising range of (often overlooked) writers who were active during these five centuries, and to that end have translated work by an additional forty-seven poets, including several important writers from Provence. (Southern France was, during the lifetime of these poets, under the dominion of the northern Spanish kingdoms and, so far as Hebrew culture was concerned, should be considered a cultural extension of Catalonia and Aragon.) Though many of the poems appear in Haim Schirmann's invaluable four-volume Hebrew anthology *HaShira Ha'Ivrit biSefarad uveProvans* [Hebrew Poetry in Spain and Provence], 2d ed. (1954; Jerusalem and Tel Aviv, 1959), more than half of them do not—in some instances because, in the years when Schirmann was collecting his material, they hadn't yet been retrieved from libraries and private collections scattered around the globe. My selection, therefore, reflects canonical preferences, recent findings, and my own tastes, and was made after rereading the entire corpus of the literature. My goal throughout has been to present a gathering that would do justice to the richness and evolving accomplishment of the five-hundred-plus years of this poetry. The development of that poetry is traced in the biographical introductions to the poets, while the emergence of the poetry, its cultural and literary background, and the implications of that background for translation are treated in the introduction.

For material in the biographical sketches and the notes on the period's poetics, I have relied heavily on Haim Schirmann's magisterial *Toldot HaShira Ha'Ivrit biSefarad HaMuslamit* (The History of Hebrew Poetry in Muslim Spain) and *Toldot HaShira Ha'Ivrit biSefarad HaNotzrit uveDarom Tzarfat* (The History of Hebrew Poetry in Christian Spain and Southern France), both edited, supplemented, and annotated by Ezra Fleischer (Jerusalem, 1995/97), as well as on Schirmann's Hebrew anthology. Unless otherwise noted, references to Schirmann and Fleischer in what follows refer to the two-volume history.

Throughout the volume, transliteration of both Hebrew and Arabic words avoids all diacritical marks apart from the inverse apostrophe to indicate the Hebrew 'ayin and the Arabic 'ain. The Hebrew letter *het* and the guttural, aspirated *haa* of Arabic are transliterated as *h*, as are the Hebrew *hey* and the nonguttural Arabic *haa*. Long Arabic vowels are indicated by a double English vowel (e.g., *rahiil*), except when the word has to a certain extent entered English (e.g., diwan, or qasida). When an Arabic word contains more than one long vowel, only the stressed syllable is transliterated with two vowels. Other elements of the transcription are straightforward enough. On the whole, my aim has been to help the general reader approximate correct pronunciation.

Readers who wish to consult the original Hebrew texts of these poems will find them posted with an index at www.pup.princeton.edu, under the listing for this volume. Those interested in Hebrew commentary and critical apparatus will find them in the source volumes listed in my notes for each poem.

# ⊰ ACKNOWLEDGMENTS ⊱

INTENSIVE WORK on this volume was made possible by a 2003 fellowship from the John Simon Guggenheim Foundation, to which I remain deeply grateful. The PEN-America Translation Fund provided additional support, and I would like to thank all involved in awarding that grant. For support of previous volumes from which poems have been drawn for this anthology, thanks are due to the National Endowment for the Arts, the National Endowment for the Humanities, and the Marie Syrkin Foundation. I am especially grateful to Princeton University Press, which has provided an ideal home for my collections of medieval Hebrew poetry, and to its staff, which has been gracious and welcoming from the start.

Numerous individuals have in one way or another contributed to the making of this anthology—and while it goes without saying that all choices and errors in what follows are mine, it is a pleasure and honor to thank, first and foremost, the scholars of medieval Hebrew literature and history who have given generously of their time and knowledge as they answered my many questions about the poetry of the five centuries covered in this volume. Above all I am indebted to Matti Huss of the Hebrew University, who—over the course of countless hours, and through his own exemplary scholarship—patiently brought me into the inner workings of the medieval poem and showed me how to approach problems at every level of interpretation. For their ongoing support and their work in the field, I am beholden to Ross Brann, Devorah Bregman, Mark Cohen, Andras Hamori, Moshe Idel, Ira Lapidus, María Rosa Menocal, Haviva Pedaya, Raymond Scheindlin, Jacques Schlanger, Michael Sells, David Wasserstein, Steven Wasserstrom, and Yosef Yahalom. Aurelio Major and Salvador Andrés-Ordax provided critical assistance at one important (Spanish) juncture, and Jeremy Zwelling (Wesleyan University) and Robert Schine (Middlebury College) have supported my teaching of this material at their institutions; my thanks go out to them as well. For all he has written, and what he has said, I owe an immeasurable debt of gratitude to Eliot Weinberger. Special thanks are due to Gabriel Levin for years of discussion of this poetry (out of which these translations first emerged), and for the attention he lavished on this book in manuscript. Martin Earl and Michael Weingrad read the manuscript with characteristic acuity and were helpful in the extreme. Forrest Gander, Eli Gottlieb, and numerous other writers, translators, editors, and friends—Esther

Allen, Rachel Tzvia Back, Robert Cohen, Tom Cole, Aminadav Dykman, Barbara Epler, Nomi Goldberg, Michal Govrin, Barry Goldensohn, Martin Guttmann, Yahya Hijazi, Edward Hirsch, Moshe Idel, Mark Kamine, Shirley Kaufman, Meir Mazar, Bradford Morrow, Gidi Nevo, Ruth Nevo, Phillip Lopate, Stephen O'Shea, Harold Schimmel, Aharon Shabtai, David Shapiro, Richard Sieburth, Sasson Somekh, and Leon Wieseltier— have in various ways encouraged this work for many years now. Their company is everywhere in these margins and between these lines. And finally, this book and my two previous volumes of translations of medieval Hebrew poetry from Spain would not exist in the form they do were it not for the sustained generosity and selfless encouragement of John Hollander, Yosef Haim Yerushalmi, and Lockert Library editor Richard Howard. My heartfelt thanks to all.

# THE DREAM OF THE POEM

# ❧ INTRODUCTION ❧

"The Spanish miracle—"

three words were all it took S. D. Goitein, the great historian of medieval Mediterranean society, to sum up the phenomenon that was the Golden Age of Hebrew poetry in Iberia. The emergence in the tenth century of this vibrant Hebrew literature seemed miraculous to Goitein, as it has to so many others who have come to know it well, because the poetry appeared virtually full-blown, at the far western edge of the medieval Jewish world, after more than a millennium of almost exclusively liturgical and ingrown poetic activity in the language. Suddenly, for the first time since the apocryphal Book of Ben Sira, Hebrew poets were writing with tremendous power about a wide range of subjects, including wine, war, friendship, erotic longing, wisdom, fate, grief, and both metaphysical and religious mystery. They did so in a variety of sophisticated modes, taken over for the most part from the by-then well-established tradition of Arabic verse, onto which they grafted a biblical vocabulary and a potent Hebraic mythopoetic vision.[1]

The best of that radically new secular and religious verse produced in Muslim Andalusia and Christian Spain ranks with the finest poetry of the European Middle Ages—or, for that matter, of any medieval era. Embodying an extraordinary sensuality and an intense faith that reflected contemporary understanding of the created world and its order, this curiously alloyed poetry confronts the twenty-first-century reader with a worldview and aesthetic that in many respects defy modern oppositional notions of self and other, East and West, Arab and Christian and Jew, as it flies in the face of our received sense of what Hebrew has done and can do, and even what Jewishness means.[2] At the same time, its densely woven brocade, deriving as it does from the charged culture of Spanish *convivencia*, or coexistence, can speak with startling directness to us today, when identities are increasingly compounded and borders easily crossed. For in opening their lives to the entire expanse of Greco-Arabic and Hebrew learning, the dictionally pure Jewish poets of Cordoba, Granada, and Saragossa carried out an act of profound, if paradoxical, cultural redemption. As they translated both the essence of their knowledge and the effects of Arabic poetry into an innovative Hebrew verse—and in the process risked loss of linguistic and religious self to immersion in the foreign—the Hebrew poets of Spain found,

or founded, one of the most powerful languages of Jewish expression
postbiblical literature has known.[3]


## A PARADISE GROVE

The trail of that hybrid verse leads back to the middle of the tenth cen-
tury, when a young Moroccan poet with the Berber name of Dunash Ben
Labrat arrived in Cordoba. Dunash had made his way to Iberia from
Baghdad, where he was studying with the greatest Jewish figure of his
day, Sa'adia Ben Yosef al-Fayuumi. From Sa'adia, who was the *gaon*, or
head, of the Babylonian Jewish academy of Sura from 928 to 942, Dunash
had absorbed a keen appreciation of Arabic and its notion of *fasaaha* (ele-
gance, clarity, or purity), as well as its importance for the understanding
of Hebrew—and especially Hebrew Scripture. Armed with that passion
and the learning it led to, Dunash was importing to Spain a trunkful of
new poetic strategies that would—whether he meant them to or not—
soon change the face of Hebrew literature. While the process of that
change remains obscure, the city of Cordoba clearly lay at its heart.

In wandering westward Dunash was trading one metropolis for an-
other. Over the course of nearly two centuries Abbasid Baghdad had
come to be considered the most spectacular city in the world. There, in a
cultural vortex of extraordinary force, men of letters took in through
translation the vast intellectual treasures of Greek and Persian antiquity,
along with those of India (and perhaps China). Arabic literature flour-
ished, as major poets refined their verse with a complex array of formal
and thematic modes. By the mid-tenth century, Cordoba under the blue-
eyed Umayyad caliph of Spanish-Basque descent, 'Abd al-Rahmaan III (r.
912–61), was in many ways a Western version of the Round City of Peace
on the Tigris, and a rival in splendor to Constantinople. It too was a city
of great sophistication and diversity: Jews, Muslims, and Christians con-
tributed to its prosperity, and ethnic division between and within these
communities was—for a time—held at bay. Centralized administration
constructed on Abbasid, Byzantine, and Persian models was improved—
with, for instance, a well-maintained and policed network of roads and
regular postal service (using carrier pigeons) linking the seat of the gov-
ernment and the provinces. The economy thrived, as the so-called Green
Revolution of Muslim Spain increased cultivation of the land. Advanced
irrigation techniques brought from the east led Arab chroniclers of the
day to describe the elaborate systems of canals and the thousands of

water wheels that dotted the landscape. A near-alphabet of crops were imported, including apricots, artichokes, bananas, carrots, eggplants, figs, hard wheat, lemons, oranges, parsnips, peaches, pomegranates, rice, saffron, spinach, sugarcane, and watermelon—our words for which derive, in many cases, from the Arabic: *naranj, ruzz, za'afraan, sukkar, sabaanakh*.[4]

Commerce boomed, and al-Andalus became known for the goods it produced. Paper, wool, silk, cotton *(qutn)*, linen fabrics, and much more were exported—Goitein called medieval Mediterranean trade in textiles the equivalent of the twentieth-century steel industry or stock market[5]— along with agricultural products and slaves. Imports included aromatic wood and spices from India and China; slaves from France and northern Europe; horses from North Africa and the Arabian peninsula; marble from Greece, Syria, Italy, and the Maghreb; singing girls and volumes of songs from Iraq; books and manuscripts from Cairo and Alexandria; and carpets from Persia.[6]

Power was maintained by an enormous army and fleet (the latter, it's said, the largest in the world at its time)—manned by a mix of Arabs, Berbers, Christians, and foreign mercenaries or purchased Slavs—and the kingdom was gradually enlarged. Arms factories near Cordoba reportedly produced some one thousand bows and twenty thousand arrows a month, and fortresses sprang up across the landscape as revenues from the new conquests filled the treasury.[7]

Above all, Andalusian culture flourished, having come a long way from the pioneer coarseness of the soldiers who had settled the peninsula in the early eighth century, when Taariq Ibn Ziyaad crossed the straits and landed at the rock he called Jabal al-Taariq (Taariq's mountain), the collapsed Romanized form of which yields our Gibraltar.[8] Two hundred years of Muslim rule, beginning with the stabilizing reign of 'Abd al-Rahmaan I (r. 756–88), had seen Spain develop from a provincial outpost at the ends of the empire to a major Mediterranean power.[9] The learned and pious 'Abd al-Rahmaan II (r. 822–52) established a brilliant formal court on the eastern caliphal model, expanded the city's great mosque, and built many smaller mosques, palaces, baths, roads, bridges, and gardens. He also began developing Cordoba's library, which in time would become the largest by far in medieval Europe. (Under 'Abd al-Rahmaan III's son and successor, al-Hakam II [r. 961–76], it held some 400,000 volumes.) Book buyers were sent to all ends of the Islamic empire, and back in Cordoba a team of calligraphers was maintained for "the rapid multiplication of new acquisitions." Smaller private and public libraries were common, and the bibliomaniacal capital hosted a huge book market, which employed some seventy copyists for the Quran alone—including many women. Women also worked as librarians, teachers, doctors, and lawyers. The new urban wonder acted as a magnet for poets and musicians in particular, the most prominent of whom was the Persian musician Ziryaab, who—legend has it—had fallen out of favor at the ninth-century Abbasid court and decided to try his luck in the West. With him Ziryaab brought the refinements of cosmopolitan Baghdad, including new hairstyles (showing the neck), seasonal wardrobes, the use of toothpaste and deodorants, orchestrated multi-course meals (at which asparagus was served), and, more to the point, his prodigious knowledge of music, poetry, art, and science.[10] Arabic itself spread slowly but with remarkable effect, and by the mid-tenth century Jews, Christians, North-African Berber Muslims, and Christian converts were competing with the Arabs themselves for mastery of that most beautiful of languages, which became both the lingua franca of al-Andalus and the currency of high culture.[11] Under the leadership of ʿAbd al-Rahmaan III, who saw his kingdom's diversity as its strength and managed to unite the disparate communities of al-Andalus, Cordoba's population swelled, with immigrants streaming to the clean, well-lit streets of the city that one Christian poet described as "the ornament of the world."[12]

While the Umayyad capital resembled Baghdad in almost every respect, Jewish society in al-Andalus had begun to take on a different cast from that of the socially conservative world of Babylonian Jewry.[13] Oppressed for well over a century by the Visigothic rulers of Hispania, Jews had welcomed the Muslim invaders as saviors and no doubt proved valuable allies to the conquering foreigners, who knew neither the lay nor the language of the land. Arabic sources confirm this cooperation and note that Jews were often settled in conquered towns and entrusted with their garrisons, as the Muslim army advanced. While there were still hardships to bear, life in eighth-century Muslim Spain offered Jews opportunities they could not have dreamed of under the Visigoths.[14] As people of the book (*ahl al-kitaab*), Jews—like Christians—were accorded *dhimmi*, or protected, status. Enforcement of the regulations governing *dhimmi*s, which varied throughout the Muslim world, were for the first several centuries relaxed in Spain, and the rate of Jewish conversion seems to have been quite low. Little by little Jews adopted Arab ways of dressing and speaking—as well as of shopping, eating, reading, singing, composing music, and writing—and they were allowed to practice an array of occupations.[15] They farmed and owned land, managed vineyards, olive groves, and workshops, and eventually worked in medicine, textile production, trade, and even in government service. Synagogues were built and communities prospered, and Spanish Jewry enjoyed a kind of limited autonomy within the Muslim emirate. It wasn't long before North African Jews who had fled the Visigoths began returning to their homes.[16]

By the time Dunash arrived in Cordoba, Jewish intellectual life in the city was also stirring. The driving force behind that awakening was a gifted Jewish physician, Hasdai Ibn Shaprut (c. 910–75), who is the first Spanish Jew to be mentioned by name in the Arab records of the day.[17] Born to a wealthy family that had moved to Cordoba from Jaén, on the eastern coast of Spain, Hasdai demonstrated a talent for languages, early on learning Arabic, Latin, and Romance (proto-Spanish), as well as Hebrew and Aramaic. His passion, however, was medicine, and while still a young man he acquired a measure of fame as a Cordovan physician. When, around 940, he announced that he had succeeded in compounding *theriaca*, a Roman miracle drug whose formula had been lost for centuries, he was summoned to an audience with the caliph and added to the ranks of his court physicians. Hasdai continued to impress 'Abd al-Rahmaan III with both his knowledge and his way with people, and soon he was appointed to the shipping division of the customs bureau, where he supervised the collection of duties from ships entering and leaving Andalusia's busy ports.[18] From time to time the caliph also consulted Hasdai about diplomatic affairs, taking advantage of his linguistic range and his tact, and the Jewish physician helped receive delegations from the German emperor Otto I and Ordoño III, king of León, with whom he negotiated a peace treaty and whose heir (Sancho) he successfully treated for obesity.[19]

'Abd al-Rahmaan III also appointed Hasdai to the position of *nasi*, or head of Andalusian Jewry, over which he had supreme authority. As *nasi* Hasdai engaged in foreign Jewish affairs, writing to Helena, the wife of the Byzantine emperor, asking her to protect the Byzantine Jewish community from persecution. He maintained ties with the communities of Palestine and Babylonia and sought out contact with the Khazars—the independent kingdom of Jewish converts on the plains between the Caspian Sea and the Caucasus Mountains—at one stage exchanging letters with the Khazar king. As his position in the caliph's court solidified, he began to sponsor a court of his own, which he developed along the Muslim model. He supported Jewish intellectuals in a number of fields, from religious studies to science and literature. He commissioned the copying and import of books, encouraged the immigration of scholars to

al-Andalus, and, over a period of some fifty years, catalyzed Spain's development as a center of Jewish culture—no longer reliant on the eastern
academies.[20]

Like the Arab Andalusian courts of the time, Hasdai's had its poet.[21]
Menahem Ben Saruq was born—probably around the turn of the
millennium—to a Tortosan family of modest means and came as a young
man to Cordoba, which had much more to offer an aspiring intellectual
than did the remote northeastern town of his birth.[22] He was supported
in the capital by Hasdai's father, Yitzhaq, while he pursued philological
studies and served as the aristocratic family's house poet, composing
verse to mark special occasions. In time he returned to his home in the
north, where he set himself up in business, but after Hasdai's appointment to 'Abd al-Rahmaan's service, the *nasi* wrote to Menahem and asked
him to return to Cordoba and take up a position as his Hebrew secretary.
It was, in fact, Menahem who wrote to Byzantium in 948, and to the
Khazar king several years later, on which occasion he described al-
Andalus:

> The country in which we dwell is called in the sacred tongue Sefarad,[23] but
> in the language of the Arabs . . . al-Andalus. The land is fat, and rivers and
> springs and quarried cisterns abound. Wheat and corn cover the fields, the
> yield of which is great. And pleasant groves and gardens of various sorts
> are found. All kinds of fruit trees flourish, and trees on whose leaves the
> silk worms feed, and silkworms we have aplenty. On our hills and in our
> forests the crimson worm is gathered. Saffron covers our slopes and moun
> tains. Veins of silver and gold can be found . . . and from our mountains
> copper is mined, and iron and tin and lead, along with sulfur, marble, por
> phyry and crystal . . . for which merchants come from all corners of the
> land. And from every region and the distant islands of the sea, traders
> stream to it, from Egypt and the adjacent countries, bringing perfumes and
> spices, and precious gems.[24]

The letter was prefaced by an impressive quasi-martial panegyric with
messianic overtones.[25] We also know that Menahem composed poems in
praise of Hasdai and others, and on the death of both of Hasdai's
parents—though these did little to win the affection of his patron, who
seems at best to have tolerated his poet and scribe, and failed to provide
him with the sort of remuneration he had promised.

The recent discovery and publication of several other poems by Menahem has helped scholars adjust the creation-ex-nihilo version of the story
of Hebrew poetry in Spain and draw a far more nuanced, if no less mar

velous, picture of the cultural scene just prior to the start of the Golden Age, for they confirm that Menahem had absorbed at least some of the secular elements of the Arabic literary culture that surrounded him. Although he continued to compose in the Eastern style that had dominated Hebrew poetry for the preceding several centuries in Palestine and Babylonia—a style which is Jewish through and through and admits no taint of the foreign to the verse itself—the secular social setting for the poetry of the future had in fact already begun to evolve.[26] Moreover, we now know that Menahem also wrote liturgical verse (in a still more-antiquated Eastern style), and one leading scholar has suggested that such sacred verse must have been written by Spanish-Hebrew poets for at least part of the two hundred and fifty years of Muslim rule in Spain preceding the generation of Hasdai.[27]

While he was serving as court poet and penning poems for various occasions, Menahem was working toward the completion of his major scholarly work, a Hebrew dictionary based on contemporary understanding of the system of Hebrew roots. Whether a product of his own initiative or one commissioned by Ibn Shaprut, the dictionary is an indication of the interest Jewish intellectuals in Spain were beginning to take in the study of Hebrew (and of the integral link between that study and poetry). In this too they were no doubt influenced by the Arab scholars around them—who, like their Baghdadi peers, placed supreme value on a detailed knowledge of language and its workings. As with his poetry, the substance of Menahem's philological investigations bore no *direct* trace of Arabic influence; on ideological grounds he refused to make use of what he considered degrading comparisons to the cognate Arabic, despite the fact that he spoke the language. As a result, his dictionary was—as Dunash saw it—ill informed, and the definitions he offers there of scriptural vocabulary are often problematic. Attacks, needless to say, followed.[28]

But Menahem's troubles were just beginning. While we have little in the way of reliable evidence concerning what sounds like a series of shady affairs, scholars speculate that Menahem's enemies went to Hasdai with accusations of the poet's disloyalty (possibly charging him with the heresy of Karaism, which denied the authority of the entire rabbinic tradition). Hasdai wasted no time in having Menahem stripped and beaten—on the Sabbath, no less—as his house was razed before him, and he was thrown into jail. Wounded and indignant, Menahem wrote to Hasdai, again prefacing his message with a poem of praise and then issuing a long, desperate cry composed in a cadenced and semirhymed biblical style:[29]

Is it you for whom I long?
    You for whom I shed my tears?
You for whom my soul pours out,
    to whom my heart submits?
I weep for the violence done [to] me—
    for my sentence the tears stream down,
and for this perversion of justice my bones give way.[30]

Whereas Hasdai ordered the physical attack, the assault on Menahem's intellectual work was led by Dunash, who wrote a detailed and condescending corrective to the lexicon, based, among other things, on his knowledge of Arabic and Aramaic philology.[31] This too Dunash had absorbed from Saʿadia Gaon in Baghdad. A prolific writer who "transformed almost beyond recognition the intellectual and literary agendas of the cultural elite associated with the Geonic academies,"[32] the Egyptian-born Saʿadia had mastered an impressive range of disciplines that reflected the prevalent intellectual trends in both Jewish religious culture and the wider world of cosmopolitan Baghdad. It was Saʿadia who, having looked outward to Arab culture and learning and seen what the Judaism of his day was lacking, set about filling the gaps he perceived and composing everything from a dictionary for liturgical poets to biblical commentary, linguistic tracts, a prayer book, and a systematic study of theology and philosophy (*The Book of Beliefs and Opinions*) which, after several hundred pages treating creation, doubt, God, the afterlife, and more, includes modern-sounding chapters on money, children, eroticism, eating and drinking, and the satisfaction of the thirst for revenge. Writing for the most part in Judeo-Arabic—a middle register of Arabic written in Hebrew letters—so that his young Jewish contemporaries would understand him, Saʿadia also translated parts of the Bible into Arabic and composed a number of works intended to serve as models of elegant Hebrew prose. He was familiar with Greek philosophy and wrote a good deal of meditative or polemical religious poetry in the contemporary Eastern style, though here too his independent and combative spirit resulted in a breakthrough to a new kind of verse, which the later Spanish poets admired for its clarity.[33]

In critical respects, then, Dunash was Saʿadia's student. In addition to his openness to Arabic and fondness for comparative philology, Dunash absorbed his teacher's desire to further the cause of Hebrew letters, the central expression of which, in Saʿadia's view, was devotional poetry.[34] In the introduction to his poet's dictionary, Saʿadia lamented the fact that the Jews in exile had forsaken the holy tongue:

At this our heart is appalled . . . for the sacred speech which is our redoubt has been removed from our mouths, . . . its figures are like a sealed book. . . . It would be proper for us and all the people of our God to study and understand and investigate it always, we and our children, our women and our servants; let it not depart from our mouths, for through it we will fathom the laws of our Rock's teaching and Torah, which are our lives. . . . And so [I have] written this book. . . . and they will use it to fashion literary works of various sorts, and to prepare every manner of poetry and prose, which the players and singers of songs perform, accompanied by musical instruments; and the people of God will speak in it when they come in and when they go out, and in all walks of life and work, and in their bedrooms and to their children; it will not depart from . . . their hearts.[35]

When, still in his twenties, Dunash arrived in Cordoba—perhaps at the invitation of Hasdai—this was the cultural mission he envisioned. Like Sa'adia facing the Jews of Babylonia, he was appalled at the level of intellectual life he found before him.[36] He mocked Menahem's insular thinking and introduced the Cordovan Jewish community of letters both to his far more scientific philology and, more important, to the contents of his cultural trunk, which held the seemingly innocuous method he had devised to adapt the quantitative meters of Arabic poetry to Hebrew.

"Let Scripture be your Eden," he wrote, in one of those borrowed measures, "and the Arabs' books your paradise grove."

## HALL OF MIRRORS

And so it is that we enter the hall of mirrors at the heart of this literature, where we find the first native-born Spanish-Hebrew poet (Menahem) writing in the derivative Eastern style, while the first poet in Iberia to compose according to what we *now* identify as the "Spanish" Hebrew style in fact smuggled his innovations in from afar—and wasn't Spanish at all. To this disorientation we can add the fructifying conjunction of circumstances that brought this situation about: an ideologically conservative but culturally assimilationist society (tenth-century Spanish Jewry) encountering the assimilationist ideology of a culturally conservative society (Babylonia in the time of Sa'adia Gaon).[37]

The technical aspects of Dunash's metrical adaptation are not easily unpacked in English, but the gist of his accomplishment is that, in imposing the quantitative meters of a highly developed literature onto an

emerging poetry, he did for Hebrew—some would say did *to* Hebrew—
what other writers who borrowed from Arabic did for Persian and Turk-
ish, and what the Roman poets who borrowed from Greek did for Latin.
The adaptation of the Arabic quantitative meters, based on distinctions
between the length of vowels, endowed Hebrew for the first time with
precise (if not entirely organic) criteria for measuring the pace and weave
of the line, which in turn intensified the focus on the language itself and
its lyric properties. Particularly when the poetry was sung or recited to
musical accompaniment, as often seems to have been the case when it
was performed in public, the patterns, symmetries, and series of rhyth-
mic and aural expectations that the new meters established allowed the
Arabized-accent of their Hebrew to sound like the flowing Arabic poetry
that the Jewish poets admired so. Metrics aside, Dunash's prosodic revo-
lution brought with it into Hebrew the entire history of the verse that
prosody served; that is, it set before the next generations of Hebrew po-
ets, who prized Arabic poetry and looked to it for metrical models, a fresh
and vastly broadened notion of both the possible and the beautiful in po-
etry. In addition to emphasizing the purity and clarity of scriptural diction
( *fasaaha*),[38] it made everything—from the structure and imagistic content
of the line to its music and rhyme to the texture and spiritual heart of
(Spanish)Hebrew poetry—different in Dunash's wake.[39]

These new elements of the Hebrew literary imagination precipitated
around Hasdai's court, and they were developed further in the following
generation in a poetry that was often supported by other Jewish patrons.
The Jewish version of the aristocratic "court setting" proved to be contro-
versial throughout the history of the poetry, and it has been central to
its interpretation—with later medieval and modern readers alike both
under- and overestimating its importance for the verse itself.[40]

    No matter how one views it, the social setting of Andalusian Hebrew
poetry often involved a discrete world with its own rhetorical and social
codes. It was alien to what had been and would in modern times become
mainstream Judaism, just as it is—in some respects—strange to modern
literary sensibilities. Play, for instance, even beyond the lightest verse, was
undoubtedly a part of the setting—though judging from the best poems
and prose works of the period, that play seems to have involved less di-
version and frippery than an examination of the dynamics of rhetoric and
human creation, or re-creation, what T. S. Eliot meant when he said that
poetry is "superior amusement."[41] It is true that in seeking the support of a
patron and all the perks that arrangement entailed, poets wrote numerous

lines for the usual courtly reasons: to please a friend, to make sure one's bread got buttered, to exercise one's gift, to get out a message, to bask in the limelight, and so on. "Poetry of the social lie," Kenneth Rexroth called it, in relation to the verse of medieval China. But work of this sort is rarely a poet's finest, and bodies of poetry are best judged by their exceptional rather than most "conventional" or "representative" products. The Hebrew poets' highest ideal, their notion of the good, and by extension, the good life, hardly constituted a literary country club of witty repartee, or the Andalusian equivalent of afternoon couplets, tea, and croquet. It called for *otium* (leisure) as opposed to *negotium* (absence of leisure), at the heart of which lay the artist's perennial quest for freedom, freedom *from* the business of earning a living and *for* a "relaxation" of mind into a critical, nourishing entanglement of words and the world. It involved formidable scholarship, a considerable range of affective and intellectual experience, and a demanding, self-conscious, sophisticated art.

The great figures of the Spanish-Hebrew literary renaissance were, in short, neither crumpet-munching literati in tights nor rhyme-happy rabbis with time on their hands. They were men of great learning, fierce ambition, and complex talent and spirit. They were devout, but in a manner that translates poorly into our own assumptions of faith,[42] and they were driven by conflicting motives, at once broad-minded and defensive. Openness to the foreign, the new, and the beautiful we have already touched on. But text after text, and subtext after subtext, tell us that the Hebrew poets were spurred on as well by a pride that drove them to show that Hebrew could do what Arabic could—and sometimes do it better—even as the innate superiority of the Arabic poetic tradition was acknowledged. It is the complexity of their response to that challenge that, in many ways, lends the Hebrew verse its depth and power.[43]

Dunash's revolution of metrical method and diction was, in other words, a revolution of sensibility, and it had its detractors. Menahem's students engaged in a fierce polemic with students of Dunash, and the immigrant from Baghdad was accused of desecrating the holy tongue and inviting national catastrophe. (Some two centuries later, one of the period's greatest poets—Yehuda HaLevi—would return to the essence of this early debate.)[44] Nonetheless, Dunash's innovative ways quickly caught on, and they were employed and developed (albeit with farreaching changes) for the next five centuries in Spain, tentatively in caliphal Cordoba, and then, as the caliphate dissolved, in fully realized fashion within the context of the Renaissance-like city states of the Muslim Ta'ifa kingdoms, which sprang up throughout al-Andalus, ushering in a period of great creativity in Hebrew and Arabic alike.[45] (It also took hold, at the same time, in the East, and soon thereafter in North Africa and Italy, and to a certain extent even in Ashkenaz.) This and the period that followed gave us the four giants of Hebrew verse in Spain: Shmu'el HaNagid, Shelomo Ibn Gabirol, Moshe Ibn Ezra, and Yehuda HaLevi.[46]

In 1090, both the Islamic and Hebrew courtier cultures of the Ta'ifa states were disrupted by the invasion of the Almoravids, members of a strict and reformist North African Berber movement, and these were followed some fifty years later by a second and still less tolerant group of North African reformers, the Almohads. Measures imposed by these two groups in succession would eventually bring about the destruction of Andalusian Jewry. Facing crisis and, in time, threats of forced conversion or death, the Hebrew poets, and with them Hebrew culture itself, survived by migrating: some of the poets went south to the cities of North Africa, but most moved into the expanding areas of the Christian *reconquista* and what is now known as Provence, which at the time constituted a northern extension of Aragon and for all practical purposes was part of the same culture that prevailed in Sefarad.[47] Avraham Ibn Ezra—a fifth major poet, and one who straddles both periods—would wander to Italy, northern France, and even England, where he disseminated both sacred and secular elements of his Arabized learning. In Toledo, Barcelona, Gerona, and Saragossa, in Bezier, Narbonne, and Perpignan, Jewish writers and scholars became the bearers of the Andalusian cultural legacy for Christians as well, often taking an active part in the translation from Arabic into Latin of philosophical, theological, scientific, and medical texts.[48] And as was the case in tenth- and eleventh-century Muslim Spain—where the small Jewish minority could be trusted more than the ethnic rivals to a given ruling power—at times they served in official capacities. In the cultural sphere, new forms of writing became dominant, especially the rhymed-prose narrative, or *maqaama* (also adapted from the Arabic), and telling changes were rung on the now classical Andalusian genres.

Often (and somewhat misleadingly) characterized as "epigonic," this second major period in fact included numerous significant figures, among them Yehuda Alharizi, Todros Abulafia, Shelomo DePiera, and Vidal Benveniste. While it is true that the sublime quality and overall achievements of the major poets produced by Muslim Spain are not approached by the poets that follow, the Hebrew poetry written in Christian Spain surprises again and again with its lively concretion and variety. Rather than dismissing this period as a falling off, or a ghostly recollection of an increasingly distant age of grace, one might see it—as poet and scholar Dan Pagis did—as a discrete period characterized by unique emphases, marked changes in literary taste, and a wider variety of literary centers. Extending from the mid-twelfth century into the fourteenth and fifteenth centuries, the poetry of that second period constituted a response to the new social circumstances facing the poets: Jewish patrons emerged around the secular courts of Christian kings; class conflict broke out within the Jewish community; knowledge of Arabic declined precipitously; the literature of Christian lands (troubadour poetry, fables, heroic legends, and more) began to exert an influence on the previously Arabized Hebrew; and new spiritual and philosophical trends came to bear on the poetry, including the rise of the Qabbala and controversies surrounding Maimonides' philosophy and the teaching of secular subjects. Throughout this period, Spain's Jewish communities also faced increasing discrimination leading up to and following the catastrophic events of 1391[49] and the Disputation at Tortosa some twenty-two years later.[50]

At least in part, the poetry of both periods was preserved in hand-written manuscripts that were rendered on demand for patrons or friends. At times a complete collection of a poet's work (his diwan) was prepared, but more often than not individual poems were copied out or smaller compilations were assembled. All of these circulated in literary communities throughout Spain and North Africa, reaching other parts of Europe, Palestine, Babylonia, and Yemen.[51] Trials notwithstanding, the tradition itself would be sustained up until the Expulsion, and then live on in transformed fashion in the countries of the Sephardic diaspora. While much was lost, in a few happy and, once again, miraculous instances, items were rediscovered during the modern era, and to this day new finds continue to emerge.[52]

## TRANSLATION AND TRACE OF THAT POWER

Translators throughout the Middle Ages, as we've seen, played a vital part in the emergence of medieval Arabic and Hebrew literature, beginning with the incorporation through translation of large parts of the body of Greek learning into Arabic in eighth- and ninth-century Baghdad, then moving on to Dunash's "deep translation" of Arabic literary traditions into Hebrew. The subsequent evolution of Hebrew writing in Muslim Spain, Christian Spain, and Provence continued that work of cultural transmission, extending the legacy of Arabo-Hebrew learning through Latin and the Romance vernacular, as Hebrew poets translated individual

works of belletristic and philosophical prose and, to a lesser extent, po-
etry from Arabic.[53] The methods they took up are instructive.

One classic instance of contrasting medieval approaches to translation
involves two contemporary Hebrew versions of Maimonides' philosophi-
cal masterwork, *The Guide for the Perplexed*, which, like most prose by Jew-
ish intellectuals in twelfth-century al-Andalus and North Africa, was orig-
inally written in Judeo-Arabic. Shortly after Maimonides completed the
*Guide*, his student Shmu'el Ibn Tibbon, a member of the famous family
of Hebrew translators,[54] embarked on its translation into Hebrew. He
completed his work two weeks before his teacher's death in 1204. Ibn Tib-
bon's translation was well received (and approved by Maimonides), but
Yehuda Alharizi, one of the outstanding poets of the post-Andalusian era,
set out to produce another version of this enormous work at the request
of patrons in Provence, who—like Alharizi—felt that Ibn Tibbon's trans-
lation wasn't sufficiently clear.[55] What would turn into a lifelong transla-
tion competition between Ibn Tibbon and Alharizi highlighted the famil-
iar opposition between surface fidelity and essential accuracy. The far
more learned and thorough Ibn Tibbon was credited with being closer to
the Arabic, while the literary Alharizi won out on the level of style and
overall equivalence. In a foreword to another work of his—a translation
of Maimonides' commentary to the Mishna—Alharizi is explicit about
his method: "I translate in most places word by word; but first and fore-
most, I strive for the meaning of what I've heard." That is, while he tries
as much as possible to be literal and precise, he wants above all to convey
the fundamental sense of what he is translating, and to do so in com-
pelling fashion. Scholars note that his method is indeed eclectic, and
varies within a given work.[56]

This eclecticism of Alharizi's is even more conspicuous in his transla-
tion of one of the major works of Arabic literature, al-Hariiri's collection
of *maqaama*s. Taking on a challenge as daunting as any that might face a
translator, Alharizi allows himself a considerable measure of freedom
with the surface of the text.[57] Assimilating the work into a Hebrew cul-
tural context, he Hebraicizes, for instance, the names of many characters
and places, Judaizes the cultural setting, and often substitutes passages
from the Bible for what had been quotations from the Quran. In the
rhymed prose he sometimes changes the order of passages and omits
phrases, while in the poetry that appears in the flow of the narrative he
tends to be freer still—even as he maintains the original meter and rhyme
(or something very much like them). At times, however, Alharizi allows
the Arabic itself to show through and he translates "word for word." The

result is a work that is daring and absorbing and has long been considered a masterpiece of Hebrew literature in translation.

Like Alharizi in his foreword to Maimonides' commentary on the Mishna, Moshe Ibn Ezra, one of the major poets of the Golden Age, is also clear about what he considers to be the proper way to translate the texts of his day. In his *Book of Discussion and Remembrance* he writes (in Judeo-Arabic): "And if you plan to bring a matter from Arabic into Hebrew, grasp the spirit and intention of the work, but do not transpose it word for word, for not all languages are alike. . . . And if it doesn't turn out as you'd hoped, rid yourself of it entirely, for sometimes silence is better than speech, and the speaker who pleases will please with his silence too, though the opposite is not true."[58] Elsewhere in the same book he emphasizes the primacy of hearing among the senses and the importance of the musical and aural aspects of poetry.[59] The Hebrew poets' translations from Arabic verse testify to their respect for all of the foregoing principles.

The translator of medieval Hebrew poetry into twenty-first-century English would do well to keep these examples in mind as he walks into the thicket of difficulties awaiting him, for it is thick indeed. To begin with, he has to somehow account for all of the elements Dunash brought over and adapted from Arabic: rhetorical figuration, biblical echoing, the nature of convention and identity in the work, the poems' musical and formal dimensions, and much more. He should be familiar with the history of interpretation in this field and know how the poems have been understood or not. He should have in mind the history of English translation from Hebrew and other languages and the options that tradition offers, as he gauges his own historical moment and its distance from medieval Spain. And he must be aware of the unconscious elements in his reading; that is, he has to consider the dynamics of orientalism in his work, and in the work on which he relies.

Not all of his solutions will be, or need be, audible to all readers at all times in a one-to-one fashion. With regard to ornament and form, for example, the effect of a single end rhyme (for up to 149 lines) in the original would be hilarious in English (it has been tried), and many of the puns and homonyms are not transferable, and so one has to come up with quieter and relocated acoustic effects in building up the poem's compositional fabric. In the history of translation from Greek, quantitative meters have proven impossible to carry with any substantial success into English, or at best irrelevant to the English (why hamburgers look and

taste the way they do in Bolivia is how essayist and translator Eliot Wein-
berger sums up the whole effort of mirroring the formal strategies of a
poem in another language);[60] so one has to determine which effects of
the Hebrew quantity one wants to bring over and how best to go about
that. And here there might be multiple solutions.

And what about biblical quotation in the work *(shibbutz)* and allusion?
Which Bible should one use? Tyndale, Coverdale, the King James? The
Revised Standard Version? The old or new Jewish Publication Society ver-
sion? The tension between revealed Scripture and contemporary verse
that so satisfied the medieval audience may go either totally unrecog-
nized by an English-speaking reader or, worse, might have just the oppo-
site effect of the original: it might put one off, bar entry into the world of
the poem. Integral as the biblical element is to the underlying texture of
the Hebrew, it is remarkable how much power and pleasure the poems
can afford their scripturally challenged audiences today. All this should
tell the translator something about how best to embed the classical ele-
ment in contemporary lines.

Convention, too, is a factor, and the translator must ask how elements
of a given medieval trope might be transplanted without any gross trans-
mogrification of sense. To take but one of the period's prominent con-
ventions: what is one to do with the object of erotic desire, which in
much medieval Arabic and Hebrew poetry is represented by a figure
drawn from both the Arabic tradition and the Song of Songs, and vari-
ously referred to as a "fawn," "doe," "deer," and so on? We meet him (or
her) often, and the innocent reader might well be perplexed by the fact
that, for some five hundred years, all the Hebrew poets seem to be writ-
ing about the same good-looking young thing they saw at the same party
where they drank the same wine in the same garden beneath the same
moon and had more or less the same thoughts about how they would like
to get to know this one ubiquitous gazelle. Yet, while all the gazelles
seem to be the same, the poems they prompt do not, and the translator
needs to attend to distinctions of timbre from poet to poet and poem to
poem.[61] And what is he to make of the phenomenon itself—intensely
sensuous and often homoerotic poems being written by learned and pi-
ous Jews? Furthermore, the medieval poets themselves apologize, in
places, for the "obscenity" of their work, and some seek to explain it
away as allegory or exercise (a keeping up with the literary Joneses). A
few modern scholars have accepted these explanations at face value, and
interpretations of the work vary widely, presenting it as everything from
puff and fluff to sublime idealization and on to faithful depiction of a

charged air that just might point toward penetration. Here, as elsewhere, the responsible poet-translator will have to descend into the bathyscaphe of scholarship and then make his way back to the surface of the poem as he seeks to fathom the sexual mores of a society far from his own in mindset and time.[62] Having made his descent and reemerged safely, and factored in competing perspectives, which tack will he follow?

By and large, previous English translations of Hebrew Andalusian poetry have taken up one of four approaches:

Following out a perceived, if schematic, parallel between medieval Andalusian Hebrew verse and Elizabethan or Metaphysical poetry, some translators have tried to translate into a "reconstructed" sixteenth- or seventeenth-century idiom. Behind this analogy, from which the worst versions of this poetry tend to emerge, there is an implicit assumption that Christian England is in some respect equivalent to Judeo-Muslim Spain, and, by extension, that our hearing ersatz Elizabethan verse in Baltimore today is parallel to eleventh-century Arabic-speaking Jews hearing masterful eleventh-century Hebrew verse written by a classicizing avant-garde in Berber Granada. While there are obvious points of correspondence in this analogy—which then has to be calculated along a sliding scale of the poetry's development over five hundred years—the equation is impossible to make with any certainty or control, and the result of this approach is, almost always, lifeless period pieces in verse: a wax-museum–like school of translation.

The second common strategy entails taking one's (often unconscious) cue from Edward FitzGerald's *Ruba'iyat* or Robert Browning's "Rabbi Ben Ezra" ("Grow old along with me! The best is yet to be") and translating into an ersatz Victorian poetic idiom. This is what we find in the old Jewish Publication Society versions of the 1920s and 30s, at the height of English and American literary modernism, and it is this approach that relegated the great Hebrew poets of medieval Spain to the ghetto of the Anglo- and American-Jewish prayerbooks, as one of English's greatest ages of translation passed it by. FitzGerald's "tessellated eclogue" ("I see how a very pretty Eclogue might be tessellated out of his scattered Quatrains," he wrote, in a letter to Edward Byles Cowell, his younger friend and Persian teacher) or "fantasia" (the characterization by the recent and more hard-nosed Penguin translators of the *Ruba'iyat*) is in fact the work of an extremely talented poet and reader of Persian.[63] And through its various editions and revisions, it well repays close study. But it is the "new world of feeling"[64] and the vision of the whole that were central to FitzGerald's achievement; and, as Robert Lowell once put it, quoting a high-school teacher of his, "One does not imitate Homer by rewriting the Iliad."

Other translators, noting the level of difficulty involved, and taking for granted the separation of form and content one finds in medieval Arabic literary theory, choose to translate into plain prose. This is an understandable solution: the beginning of wisdom within translation is, one might argue, the fear of distortion, and form *can* be separated from content, at least superficially. But one must ask at what cost that separation will be brought about; for apart from the rarest of instances, translation into prose does nothing to further the cause of a poetry that so wholly relies on execution, or touch, for the creation of its effect (which is in turn a critical element of its deepest content and ethos). It does little more than establish the fact of the poetry's imagistic existence. Reducing the work to a single dimension—either out of an honorable fear of misrepresentation or a cowardly abdication of interest and ambition—the gloss it offers is numb to the sense of the poem as a thing that is made.[65]

And, lastly, there is the grab-bag category of None of the Above—the school of the schoolless—wherein the overriding principle is the search for a kind of Blakean vitality, with cues taken, on the one hand, from related arts or strong versions of related literatures and on the other, from a contemporary sense of linguistic force.[66] The principal aim of translation of this sort is the identification and re-creation of a compelling, authoritative presence, one that might draw the translator and then the reader (for the translator is always first a reader) into the culture in question. This method seeks out Pound's "trace of that power which implies the man"[67]—a music that possesses the reader for a spell and brings about the transformative illusion of literature, not the "accurate" representation of an irretrievable historical moment. The successful translation here entails a listening that allows the poems to be *heard*. It leads to the preservation of spirit rather than a pickling of form, as it takes up and makes use of the original's energy. It focuses on the "pleasure" rather than the "problem" of translation, at times introducing into English new or even peculiar effects as an echo of the foreign, or employing effects available in English to bring out qualities achieved in the original language by different means. It calls for humility before both the artistry of the poets and the scholarship that allows us to read them—alongside a presumption that impels one to conjure their fictional doubles in English. In fact, behind translations of this sort one often senses, or should sense, the presence of a *dybbuk*-like force driving a necessary transfer on. To my mind the most interesting work in translation from both Arabic and Hebrew medieval poetry falls (or will fall) into this large and infinitely renewable category, and this is the path I've chosen.[68]

Theoretical considerations aside, my aim has been simple: I have worked to conduct what I perceive to be the poets' quality of emotion and movement of mind, as these are embodied in their lines. While, like Alharizi, I have sought to convey the essence of what I've heard—with an emphasis on that aural dimension—I have hewn to the phrase-by-phrase meaning of the poem and only on rare occasion added or deleted material.[69] With regard to prosody, I have made eclectic use of whatever tools English offers in order to construct these equivalent versions—that is, these versions of like (if not quite equal) valence and value. When the voice in the Hebrew is ambitious or subtle or aggrieved, or where the verse is particularly musical, inventive, or sublime, I have tried for a similar sense in the English. Above all, in approaching this work I have sought to recall that when the Jewish poets of Andalusia began turning to their Muslim (or Christian) counterparts for new poetic models, they were seeking to extend the range of their language, to renovate the weave of their poems, to equip themselves for their world.

What that world has to offer us today is a question readers will ask, and rightfully so. As the biographies of the poets that follow should make clear, Spanish *convivencia* wasn't all sweetness and light, an "interfaith utopia," or even "tolerant" as we think of that notion now.[70] For some, the elite nature of medieval literary society renders work of this sort irrelevant to twenty-first-century readers, and its poetry will seem hopelessly exotic. For others, the word *medieval* itself will be enough to drive them away (if the word *poetry* hasn't already). And for others still, the experience of Spanish Jews—like that of the Jews in Germany—is a lesson in the history of collective self-delusion, inevitably leading to conversion, Inquisition, expulsion, or worse.[71] Those who hold to the latter view, in particular, may balk at my title and its provenance, or dismiss it as simply naive.[72]

But for those who hold that all ages are contemporaneous (as Pound and, yes, the rabbis did);[73] for those who are drawn to a poetry produced by "a society where holy and profane merge into an indivisible and harmonious whole, where the borders between them essentially disappear";[74] for those who believe in the possibility of coexistence, however tenuous, between Arabs and Jews and the richness that entails; for those willing to recognize the fact that, in the eleventh century, non-Ashkenazi Jews constituted *ninety-seven* percent of world Jewry, and that the Spanish-Jewish community prior to 1391 was the largest in Europe (and left Judaism a legacy that was long ago relegated to the margins of religion);[75] or simply for those who, as citizens and siblings, writers and spouses, parents, artists, workers, teachers, lovers, and readers, seek out wisdom or beauty wherever they can—medieval Spain stands at what is literally a crucial site "in the project of building human culture" and in realizing the dream of the poem.

# PART ONE

# Muslim Spain

## c. 950–c. 1140

# DUNASH BEN LABRAT

*(mid-tenth century)*

By all accounts the founder of the new Andalusian Hebrew poetry, DUNASH BEN LABRAT reimagined the very nature of Hebrew verse and, with that conceptual and tactile shift, brought about a revolution in Jewish letters and the world onto which they open. Just how and why he did that remains something of a mystery, as we have little more than an outline of his life. Born in the first third of the tenth century in Fez, Morocco (the name Dunash is Berber in origin), he traveled to Baghdad in his youth in order to study with the greatest scholar of his day, Sa'adia Gaon (d. 940). While still in Babylonia, Dunash adapted Arabic poetry's quantitative meters to Hebrew and showed the results to his teacher, who offered up the distinctly ambiguous judgment: "Nothing like it has ever been seen in Israel." He was in Spain, it seems, by age thirty, having brought with him the new poetics and all they implied. Dunash's Arabizing method caught on, despite his arrogant manner and his scorn for what he considered the provincial ways of the backward Spanish-Jewish literati he encountered in Andalusia. And though he was accused, among other things, of "destroying the holy tongue . . . by casting it into foreign meters," and "bringing calamity upon his people," sometime around 960, he displaced Menahem Ben Saruq as the reigning poet at Hasdai Ibn Shaprut's Jewish Cordovan court. Dunash's liturgical poems were soon sung "in every town and city, / in every village and county"—according to a polemical poem by one of his students; his secular verse also gained many admirers and marked the beginning of a tradition that would last for five centuries in Spain, and continue on after that in North Africa, Palestine, Yemen, Turkey, Italy, and elsewhere. With regard to poetics, compunction, and theme, his short motto and longer, conflicted wine poem (both below) in many ways anticipate the concerns of the entire period. In a controversy about which we know almost nothing, Dunash eventually abandoned Spain, leaving behind a young wife and at least one small child. A quarrel with Ibn Shaprut appears to have been behind his departure.

Most of Dunash's output is presumed to be lost, and critical opinion of his thirteen extant poems and assorted fragments is mixed. While he was ambitious and daring, Dunash was hardly a master craftsman, and much of his work shows the strain of his labor. By and large, his figurative gifts were limited and his style awkward and stiff. Still, his innovations were major and lasting, and he goes down in the annals of Hebrew literature as one of its greatest pioneers.

FRAGMENT

Let Scripture be your Eden,
and the Arabs' books your paradise grove . . .


BLESSING FOR A WEDDING

Banish suffering
    and also wrath,
and the mute
    will break into song;

guide us on paths
    of righteous action—
and grant us the blessings
    of Aaron's sons.


DRINK, HE SAID

"Drink," he said, "don't drowse,
drink wine aged well in barrels,
near henna beds and aloes
    and roses mixed with myrrh—

in pomegranate groves
by grapevines and date palms,
with tender plants and saplings,
    and tamarisks in rows.

To the sound of coursing water,
the thrumming of the zither
accompanies the singers
    with reed-pipes and an oud.

All the trees there spread
with branches and fine fruit,
and every sort of bird
    sings among the leaves.

The pigeons coo and moan,
as though composing songs,
and turtle-doves respond
    as though they're playing flutes.

We'll drink along the beds
hedged about by lilies,
and drive away our sorrows
    with wine and songs of praise.

We'll eat the sweetest morsels,
and sip from studded bowls,
and act as though we're giants
    drinking from their casks.

Come morning I'll arise
and go to slaughter bulls,
choice, fattened creatures,
    cows and rams and calves.

Anointed then with oil,
we'll burn fragrant scents—
and before destruction's hour,
    live our lives in bliss."

"Silence!" I rebuked him.
"How could you propose this?
The Temple and God's footstool
    are held by unclean hands.

You're speaking like a fool
who chose the path of sloth;
and what you say is vain,
　　the talk of a buffoon.

45　You've left your meditation
on the Law of heaven;
you'd celebrate while jackals
　　roam on Zion's hills.

How could we drink wine
50　or even raise our eyes—
while we, now, are nothing,
　　detested and despised?"

# THE WIFE OF DUNASH

*(mid-tenth century)*

This single poem by THE WIFE OF DUNASH Ben Labrat is all of her work that has come down to us. It is, so far as we know, the only poem by a woman in the entire medieval Hebrew canon. The poem's heading in manuscript explains that it was composed on the occasion of her husband's forced departure from Spain. The reasons for his leaving remain obscure, but the last line of the poem suggests that he fell out of favor with Hasdai Ibn Shaprut, the leader of Spanish Jewry and patron of the local Hebrew revival. Apart from these lines and the crisis they treat, we know nothing about the poet, not even her name. That said, the poem's restraint and quiet dignity, along with its tenderness and subtle complication of tone—melding affection, resentment, and above all a sense of acceptance of what seems to be a tragic fate—speak for her character. A relatively recent discovery, this gentle lyric was reconstructed from torn Geniza fragments by scholar Ezra Fleischer, who hailed it as "the first fully realized personal poem in the new Andalusian style." That it emerged at such an early stage of the poetry's evolution, and from the pen of a woman, makes the find all the more remarkable.

### WILL HER LOVE REMEMBER?

Will her love remember his graceful doe,
    her only son in her arms as he parted?
On her left hand he placed a ring from his right,
    on his wrist she placed her bracelet.
As a keepsake she took his mantle from him,
    and he in turn took hers from her.
Would he settle, now, in the land of Spain,
    if its prince gave him half his kingdom?

# YITZHAQ IBN MAR SHA'UL

*(mid-tenth–early-eleventh century)*

Moshe Ibn Ezra mentions some twelve second-generation writers who, he says, "surpassed [their predecessors] in eloquence." Of that dozen, we have work by just a handful, including YITZHAQ IBN MAR SHA'UL, who lived in Lucena, where he taught Hebrew language and Scripture. Ibn Mar Sha'ul's single extant secular work is the first Spanish-Hebrew poem to employ one of the central elements of Arabic medieval poetry, the figure of the *tzvi*, or gazelle, as the object of desire, and as such it is of considerable importance. While in some cases, the gazelle can be understood as either male or female, here it is clearly male, as all the imagery relating to it is drawn from characterizations of Scripture's masculine heroes.

## A FAWN SOUGHT IN SPAIN

A fawn sought in Spain
    works wonders with desire,
and through it he controls
    all male and female creatures.
5  Formed like the moon—
    his height adds to his splendor;
his curly hair is crimson
    against his cheeks of pearl.
Like Joseph in [appear]ance,
10    with Adonijah's hair;
his eyes like Ben Yishai's
    kill me like Uriah,
and in me kindle fire
    that burns now through my heart.
15  He leaves me—when he passes—
    helpless and confused.

So weep with me, O vultures;
   every kite and buzzard!
My soul's beloved has slain me:
   Is this how justice rules? 20
[ . . . ] showed no mercy for
   my heart and left it lifeless.
My soul is sick and lost,
   moaning now it wanders,
for when he spoke his words 25
   were rain across dry fields.
Raise me from this hell—
   and let me fall no more.

# YOSEF IBN AVITOR

*(c. 940–after 1024)*

YOSEF IBN AVITOR was born in Merida into a prominent Jewish family that had lived in Spain for generations. He studied in Cordoba under the renowned Talmudist Moshe Ben Hanokh and soon became known as one of his most precocious students. Ibn Avitor went on to serve as a religious authority for many Spanish Jews, who turned to him with questions regarding *halakha*, or religious law. He is, though, best known for his poetry. Just as his *responsa* show the influence of the Babylonian academies, so, too, his liturgical poetry preserves the then six-hundred-year-old Eastern tradition that went back to the work of Yannai, Qallir, and especially Sa'adia Gaon. An archaizing religious poet of what Fleischer calls "titanic powers," Ibn Avitor was prolific and ambitious. Some four hundred of his poems have survived (most still in manuscript), and he seems to have attempted almost every sort of pre-Andalusian liturgical mode. According to Ibn Daud's *Book of Tradition*, the twenty-year-old Ibn Avitor also composed an Arabic commentary—probably an abstract—of the Talmud for the library of the Andalusian caliph, al-Hakam.

By all accounts he was difficult. Well aware of his worth, and who his forefathers in Spain had been, Ibn Avitor was haughty, rash, and—at times—fanatical. These traits appear to have cost him the position he'd long coveted: head of Cordoba's Jewish academy. The bitter intra-Jewish politics of that affair involved the caliph as well, who—after the community had "excommunicated . . . and banned him"—advised Ibn Avitor to leave Spain. "If the Muslims were to reject me," said the caliph, "in the way the Jews have done to you, I would go into exile. Now betake yourself into exile!" The disgraced poet made his way to North Africa, Egypt, and then Palestine and Babylonia, before backtracking and settling in Egypt. There he resumed his life as a teacher and religious authority. He died, it appears, in Damascus. The secular poems translated here—three of just a handful of his poems that incorporate elements of the new Andalusian style— were most likely written in Egypt. The final poem, a hymn for the New Year, gives powerful and archaic expression to the poet's cosmic, quasi-mystical perspective and his Blakean sense of majesty in creation's detail.

## LAMENT FOR THE JEWS OF ZION

Weep, my brothers, and mourn
as one for the fate of Zion,
as in the cry of Hadádrimmon,
and Josiah, son of Amón.

Weep for the tender and gentle                    5
who barefoot trample thistles;
they draw water for the people
of Cush and hew their wood.

Weep for the man in captivity,
tried before he was ready;                        10
all day he's forced to work and hurry—
but the burden is too great.

Weep for men who witness
their glorious sons oppressed;
greater than gold, they are precious,             15
and Egyptians cut them down.

Weep for the blind who wander,
defiled by the blood of the slaughter
of women with child, and elders,
ripped open along with the young.                 20

Weep for the innocent, beaten
and forced to eat what has been forbidden—
to abandon their sacred bond,
the land of their heart's desire.

Weep for women of purity,                         25
modest in their piety—
for hot seed entered their bodies,
and in their wombs it grew.

Weep for all the daughters
with finely formed figures,                       30
they who were given over to horrors,
as courtesans to shame.

Weep, wail, and keen
for houses of worship left in ruins—
35     plundered and ravaged by swine
and nests now for kites.

Weep for those who were shattered—
on a day of calamity they were gathered;
weep for the poor and wretched,
40     those enslaved and crushed.

Weep for our lives and the living,
but do not weep for our dead and dying,
because to be just like them
is always our desire.

45     And so hold off, my friend,
and spare me all your consolation
for those who were butchered in Zion
and lie without a grave.


## A CURSE

Let moaning and mourning circle his skull
and great desolation come over his pate;
may rage and rebuke wear through his brow,
and in his eyes may fire blaze;
5     may the pit and its fever shrivel his tongue,
and through his cheeks my leprosy run.
May stones and [ . . . . . . . . . ] break his teeth;
may offering and slaughter slice through his throat.
May grief and languor weigh on his arms;
10     and weakness and sorrow slacken his palms.
May forked flames burn through his fingers;
may blows batter his back and shoulders,
and may the destroyer shatter his ribs.
May sweeping and [ . . . ] rattle his windows,
15     uprooting his [ . . . ] shaking his bones.

May his liver be pierced and split;
may tyrants and enemies crush his hips.
Let rocks and arrows strike through his knees;
ravaged and torn may his buttocks bleed;
may clubs rain down on his feet till he reels.　20
May curses close in from his head to his heels.


## A PLEA

My soul, which wanders on and on,
[ . . . . . . . . . . . . . . . . . . . . . . . . . . . . . . . ]
and loosen the bands of these worthless men.
　　Let day dawn on your judgment's order.
Grant strength to one who has done no wrong
　　but is hounded. Help him, [Lord,] find shelter.
Bring your power to the aid of a man
　　pursuing goodness, as the godless gather.
I weep—and the tears on my cheeks stream
　　with blood. And grief has made me bitter.


## HYMN FOR THE NEW YEAR

Who established the heights of heaven
　　　then set out glowing orbs?
Who will tell of all He's done,
　　　and who is greater than the Lord?
　　　The peace of praise awaits you, Lord. . . .　5

Who instructed the billowing waves
　　　to swell above the deepest seas?
Who between the peaks of each
　　　put three-hundred leagues?
Who spoke and opened channels　10
　　　on high before the rushing streams?

Who said no two drops from clouds
    would fall—cut from a single mold?
Who has gathered the wind in His fist
    and bound the waters in His robe?

Who counts the ninety-nine screams
    of mountain-goats giving birth on cliffs?
Who sends eagles to catch their young
    and lift them up on wings?
Who makes serpents suddenly appear
    to bite the wombs of deer?
Who creates the claps of thunder,
    each with its path across the heavens?
Who prepares a course for storms—
    a track for thunder's lightning? . . .

Who casts five occasions of fear
    over five occasions of might?
Who in giant elephants wakens
    terror of the mosquito's flight?
Who within the mysterious whale
    arouses fear of the stickleback fish?
Who sends forth His word to show
    that over all He is?
Who has hardened himself and thrived
    against the One who rules?

Who hurls ruin upon the strong
    lest in cruelty they lash out?
Who casts fright across the lion
    before the Ethiopian gnat?
Who brings over the scorpion
    terror of the spider's poison?
Who sends fear of swallows
    into the falcon's eyes?
Who established the world's foundations
    and set them beneath the skies?

# YITZHAQ IBN KHALFOUN

## *(c. 965–after 1020)*

A key transitional writer of the second generation, Yitzhaq Ibn Khalfoun was born in Spain, c. 965, to parents who had immigrated from North Africa. His father seems to have been supported by Shmu'el HaNagid's father, as was the young Yitzhaq himself. Later on HaNagid also became Yitzhaq's patron and friend, and the two exchanged poems in times of trouble. Ibn Khalfoun is often called the first professional Hebrew poet, that is, a poet who produced poems on demand for pay. His limiting role notwithstanding, he expanded the scope of the new Andalusian Hebrew poetry, introducing a fuller range of the Arabic elements and both a lither texture and lighter tone in his verse, which was far more personal and occasional than that of his predecessors. While Cordoba was his city, he traveled constantly in search of patrons and—judging from his sometimes barbed responses to his sponsors—wasn't always happy with the compensation he received or the promptness with which he was paid. His collected work is exclusively secular.

## LOVE IN ME STIRS

Love in me stirs and I bound like a deer
    just to see my lady's eyes.
Her mother, uncle, father, and brother
are gathered around her when I arrive.

I look but turn away, as though
    she had never driven me wild,
afraid of them while I long for her—
like a woman, mourning her only child.

## A GIFT OF CHEESE

My dear friend, I've asked you gently
    and pleaded with you repeatedly.
I turned to you as a tower of strength,
    a shield and buckler before my enemy—
a hot day's shelter against the sun,
    a stove on a day that's cold and wintery:

And like Elkanah remembering Peninnah—
    may the Lord take note—you remembered me,
and sent on, bless you, a piece of cheese.
    But what good is cheese when I'm thirsty?

# SHMU'EL HANAGID

## (993–1056)

The major poets of the period emerge in the third generation, and they are masters of their art in every respect and giants in the history of Hebrew literature. SHMU'EL HANAGID, known in Arabic circles as Isma'il Ibn Naghrela (from the Latin *niger*, meaning "dark"), was a spectacular figure: prime minister of the Muslim state of Granada; leader of Spain's Jewish community; military commander; scholar of religious law; biblical exegete and grammarian; patron of the arts; and poet. He was born in Cordoba to a well-established Meridian family and raised in the capital of the crumbling Andalusian caliphate. The city was ravaged during the Berber revolt of 1010–13, and the young Ibn Naghrela fled south with a large wave of Jewish and Muslim refugees. Impoverished and on his own, he made his way to Malaga, where, legend has it, he opened a spice shop and worked as a professional scribe. Impressing a Malagan vizier—the legend continues—with his Arabic literary style in letters that he wrote for the vizier's servant (some say his concubine), who would send them on to her master in Granada, he was soon summoned to that city, where he gradually rose to power in both Muslim and Jewish spheres. He served at first as tax collector and then as the vizier's assistant at the court of the Berber king of Granada, Habuus, and later as counselor to Habuus himself. In 1027 he was made *nagid*, governor of Granada's (or all of Andalusia's) Jewish community, and ten years later he was appointed by Habuus's successor, his son Badiis, to the position of chief vizier of the kingdom and—most scholars believe—head of its Muslim army. He led Badiis's forces into battle for sixteen of the next eighteen years, serving either as field commander or in a more administrative capacity as minister of defense or chief of staff. In his various public roles he helped establish Granada as one of the wealthiest and most powerful of the Andalusian Ta'ifa or Party States, and he continued to serve both Muslim and Jewish communities until he died, in 1056, not long after having returned from yet another military campaign.

Wherever one turns in HaNagid's verse, one finds the tension between Arab and Jew woven into a peculiarly supple and at the same time metallic—and even defensive—sort of beauty. "His poems . . . are various and full of color, powerful in their contents, fine in their form, original in their ideas, and clear in their rhetoric," wrote Moshe Ibn Ezra. "All that pertains to his compositions and works and letters is known to the uttermost edges of east and west and across the land and sea, and up to the leaders of the Babylonian community and the sages of

Syria and the scholars of Egypt and the nagids of [North] Africa and the lords of the West and the Spanish nobility." Three books comprise the diwan, each of which was copied out by one of the poet's young sons, who then also appended descriptive headings to many of the poems. *Ben Tehillim* (After Psalms) is perhaps the most original of the three, as it introduces to postbiblical Hebrew poetry the full range of Arabic subject matter, complete command of the new poetics, and an unforgettably personal cast to the biblical language of the verse. This combination of subject, tone, and impulse aligns HaNagid with the martial-lyric spirit of Second Samuel and the Davidic psalms, an affiliation HaNagid makes explicit at several points. *Ben Tehillim* contains intensely sensual and erotic lyrics, well-honed satirical poems, and perhaps the most moving series of elegies in the history of Hebrew poetry, which the poet wrote when his brother died in 1041. His second collection, *Ben Mishle* (After Proverbs), comprises a large body of canny, gnomic constructions that draw on the various traditions of the poet's acquaintance and amounts to a personalized anthology of wisdom literature. Finally, *Ben Qohelet* (After Ecclesiastes) consists of piercing epigrams, stunning descriptions of natural phenomena, and powerful mortality poems of various lengths.

HaNagid's oeuvre of nearly two thousand poems—the vast majority of which had been lost for centuries—was found by chance in a crate of manuscripts in 1924 and published for the first time only in the thirties (and in an edition accessible to the general reader of Hebrew only in the fifties). "It is an incomparable treasure," poet Haim Nahman Bialik wrote to a friend, telling him of the manuscript's discovery. "A kind of light shines on the marvelous prince—upon him and his period and the poets of his day. . . . The man is unrivaled in our history. See for yourself and decide."

### ON FLEEING HIS CITY

Spirit splits in its asking,

soul in its wanting is balked—

and the body, fattened, is vital
and full,

<sup>5</sup> its precious being uneasy. . . .

So the modest man
      walks on earth,
   his thought drawn toward sky.

What good is the pulse of man's flesh
      and its favors
   when the mind is in pain?

And the friends who fray me,
   their fine physiques
      and slender thinking,
   thinking it's ease or gain
      that drives me,
   pitching from place to place,
      my hair wild, my eyes,
         charcoaled with night—
and not a one speaks wisely,
their souls blunted, or blurred,
      goat-footed thinkers.

Should someone unguilty
         hold back from
longing toward heights like the moon?
      Should he wait,
   binding its wings to his waist—
like a man winding his sash about him—
till he acts and they hear of his action,
   as he adds and then adds like the sea
         to his fame?

By God and God's faithful—
      and I keep my oaths—
   I'll climb cliffs
and descend to the innermost pit,
   and sew the edge of desert to desert,
     and split the sea
       and every gorge,
     and sail in mountainous ascent,

until the word "forever" makes sense to me,

and my enemies fear me,
    and my friends in that fear
        find solace;

then free men will turn
    their faces toward mine,
        as I face theirs,

and soul will save us,
    as it trips our obstructors.

The beds of our friendship are rich with it,
    planted by the river of affection,
        and fixed like a seal in wax,
           like graven gold
in the windowed dome of the Temple.

May YAH be with you as you love,
    and your soul which He loves be delivered,

and the God who sends salvation shield you

    till the sun and the moon are no more.

## THE MIRACLE AT SEA

Is there poise for the stumbling and fallen,
    or rest for the wandering and lost?
And for me when I've slipped, or my fault when I've failed
    will there again be offering?

By the lives of all who'd come
    to console and assist the stricken,
        by the life of each who came
when I was in need and saw me panicked,

could it be that there's never respite from anguish,
    that desolate land is desolate forever?
        But God restores what He levels,
though He keeps his secrets and erases His ways.

Listen to a word and know that not for lightness
    does the Lord sustain us on earth,
  and take your reversals with an open heart,          15
    silence, and guarded thought.

Harden your ears to the brokers of spirit
    and turn your eyes from its whores,
  from Hophni at Shilo, or Zimri and the woman
from Midyan, or Onan—and his brother's widow.       20

Listen to a word and exalt the Lord
in the house and street, when you rise and lie down;
    shudder for dread and anxiousness.
  Worry, and let awe infuse you

for the God of beginnings unborn and unbearing,      25
    of lasting life without likeness.
  Return to His grace,
and face Him forever through fear and rebuke.

I am the man who went down to the sea,
    which most of the year is loud.              30
  It was August. I chose to go
    when the waves don't break in anger;

and we worked the oars and a wind came up
    as over a field of corn,
and the sea, like a slave, did as I asked,         35
    like a maid, and the sky was sapphire—

and the water like butter or virgin oil.
And the sailors told of all that they'd seen
    of wonder on board,
    and one spoke of a marvelous creature,       40

and another called it a beast—
  and the captain answered:
None of you know of the miracle sea—
    you haven't fathomed a thing.

There exists a monster whose name is Karhah,      45
    singular among the abysmal shapes,
  it devours all who feed on each other
and kills the survivors with fright.

It overturns ships, and fleets with their crews,
in its mouth they're flipped like a chariot.
   He hadn't finished his story
when lowing and raging the creature appeared.

I heard it: thunder or the sound of a throng
   seemed still alongside it;
and I looked at its terrible form,
   wrought like a fish or book-like Leviathan,

the torturous serpent like a palm tree in stature,
   its head huge as a galley with oars,
  its face haughty, like a hill,
     its eyes like pools,

its spout like a furnace, its brow like a wall,
   its mouth wide and deep as a cave;
quenching its thirst it would empty a river
with its lips like swollen wineskin on wineskin,

and between them the hole
   as though in a coat of mail.
Its flank was white, its back—green;
its neck like a tower, its belly—a mound,

   its fin like a polished sword,
and its scales like a shield made red;
its girth to us seemed like a cliff in the heart
   of the sea. And it circled the ship

   without a sound,
and swam alongside it, then, rose on its tail,
   like a cedar or climbing vine.
And everyone's heart melted like wax,

or like water, and the whirlpool engulfed us.
   I calmed and steadied my soul,
as the lamb on the day of her slaughter goes dumb,
    and called on my Lord,

as others beside me called on their own,
   like Ashemah. And I said:
In truth, and one way or another,
transgression takes the guilty soul;

if Jonah was swallowed up by the sea
    and vomited onto dry land
  in his righteousness—what of me?
My Lord, let me live, who wakes from his sleep.

If this is reward for the work of my hands,
    may my sin be absolved . . .                      90
Then it sank in the dark of the sea,
like the army God engulfed in its parting;

    and under the ship it threatened again,
as our hearts died, our breath failing.
    But the Lord rebuked the being,                  95
which in a moment returned to its depth—

    as little worms
were saved on a pitch-covered bough.
    He'd raised the dead from Sheol
and saved the swallowed with a hand held high.              100

The nautical wizards were astonished
    and wondered how it could happen—
with their ships trapped by Karhah, the accursed!
    And I told them:

Such is deliverance for those who know                       105
    the great glory of the Lord in His fullness.
He sends salvation to those who admit Him
and vengeance to those who provoke His wrath.

The sea is His, and all its creatures,
    and the waters below, which are vast;            110
    He hangs them on nothingness.
What is a beast beside the Rock

    who shaped it and granted it breath,
    then endowed it with power?
I thank the Lord with a song of redemption                   115
    my mouth will remember,

and acknowledge the Rock beyond creation,
    without completion,
and grant the truth of the resurrection—
    that the dead will arise from dust;              120

that the Book of Moses we have in our hands
    is true and composed with perfection;
that the words of the sages are worthy
    and their study is sweet—

125     and reward for the righteous will follow,
    as the dead for their sins in secret
receive their recompense;
    that the Lord rules—over land and sea

    and the sky and Great Bear above;
130     that His fear in the lines of my face is drawn,
    as His law is drawn through my blood.

## THE APPLE

### I

I, when you notice,
    am cast in gold:
the bite of the ignorant
    frightens me.

### II

An apple filled with spices:
    silver coated with gold.
And others that grow in the orchard,
    beside it, bright as rubies.

I asked it: Why aren't you like those?
    Soft, with your skin exposed?
And it answered in silence: Because
    boors and fools have jaws.

## THE GAZELLE

I'd given everything I own for that gazelle
   who, rising at night to his
     harp and flute,
    saw a cup in my hand
    and said:
  "Drink your grape blood against my lips!"
  And the moon was cut like a D,
    on a dark robe, written in gold.


## JASMINE

Look at the jasmine, whose branches are green
   as topaz, and its stems and leaves—
while its blossoms are white as bdellium.
   With carnelian red in its shoot
it looks like a pallid boy who's shedding
   the blood of innocent men with his hand.


## IN FACT I LOVE THAT FAWN

In fact I love that fawn,
   cutting roses in your garden—
which is why I've earned your wrath.
    If you could see him,
   the others would never find you.

"Scrape me some honey
   from your hive," he said.
"I'll have mine from your tongue,"
I replied. Then he bristled
   and said to me, sullen:

"And sin before the living God?"
"The sin's on me," I answered, "my lord."

## MIXED IN SPAIN

Rouge in appearance
   and pleasant to drink,
    mixed in Spain
   and prized in Bombay;
weak in its pitcher but rising to the head it
   rules in heads that sway.
Even the mourner whose tears
fall with his heart's blood,
   disperses his grief in retreat with wine.
As though friends—passing the cup from hand to hand—
   were rolling dice, for a diamond.


## YOUR YEARS ARE SLEEP

Your years are sleep,
   their fortune's wheel a dream;
best, my friend, to shut your
eyes and ears—God
    grant you strength—
and leave the hidden things
around you    to one
   who's good with clues.

Bring me wine from a cup
    held by a girl
   who excels on the lute;
a mature vintage, made by Adam,
or new, from Noah's fields.
Its hue like living coral
and gold, its bouquet
    like calamus and myrrh—

like David's wine that queens prepared,
impeccably, or graceful harems.
The day it was put in its pitcher,
Jerimoth sang to his harp                                    20
          unsurpassably, saying:
Wine such as this should be sealed
               and stored in casks in the cellar—
for those who drink with excellent hearts
and hold their glasses wisely,                               25
and keep the laws of Qohelet,
fearing death,
               and the fury to come.


## THE HOUSE OF PRAYER

Could time turn on its scholars?
     Or have they turned on the Law—
and bequeathed it to stuffed old fools in robes
     and every boor who declares:
          "I'm Mephiboshet,"                                 5
or "Hai the renowned is like Tziba my servant"?
One needs, it seems, only fringes, a turban, and beard
     to head the Academy now. My brother,
          remember the day we passed
the House of Prayer, the Day of Willows,                     10
     and heard up close a donkey bray
          and cows cry and low? And I asked:
"Is the Lord's house now a dairy?
          This is a sin and disgrace."
And they told me: "There are no fatlings or mules            15
     in the house of the Lord; they're studying Talmud."
          Then I answered from Scripture:
"They've changed the instruction and Law;
          and as for me—whither?"
So we walked on in anger, into the house of God—             20

if only we'd strayed from that path—
    and saw the teacher and students
        bobbing their heads like fronds,
    as their mouths abused the names of the great.

And the teacher expounded at length,
    preying on every sound they made,
and I sat there enraged at the sight,
      and my soul grew sad . . .
    I asked the good teacher after his health,
      but he answered as a man of strife—
and he started reciting the hundred blessings
in a coarse voice, like an army or horde,
      and he thanked the Lord
who had made him a man and not a woman.
And I told him: "You flaunt your phallic soul,
    but the Lord will prove you hollow."

25

30

35

## THE CRITIQUE

I'd pictured your poem like the king's daughter,
    a man's delight, a woman of pleasure;
or a burning fire set by the hearth—
    in its corners calamus, cassia, and myrrh.

And I found it exquisitely copied—
    all the vowels were precisely arrayed.
In the past, I'd seen poems by your friends,
    but they were obscure, while yours amazed.

Your discourse flowed like the purest water
    for ablution—but this new one's a stain.
You've been for me like a precious son,
    whose standards I'm obliged to maintain.

So, hone your poems and their subjects,
    and know that each in its way moves toward
a day of judgment. And fear the critics,
    whose tongues are polished and sharpened like swords.

## ON LIFTING THE SIEGE

Send this pigeon, a messenger
   although she can't speak,
  with a brief letter tied to her wings,
dipped in saffron and scented with myrrh.

   And once she's off and away,          5
send on another. If one falls prey
to a falcon or net's mesh, or delay—
   the other will cover, hurrying on.

When she reaches the house of Joseph,
she'll thrum from the rafter,          10
   flutter down to his fingers,
  and humor him, like a sparrow;

he'll loosen the knot at the note
and read: Know, my son, as you hold this,
   the cursed enemy has fled          15
and scatters itself on paths and hills—

like chaff driven by wind,
   or shepherdless sheep confused—
without having seen its foe except in surmise.
On our way to the rout they fled into darkness,     20

bringing death on themselves and each other—
       in panic crossing the river.
They who had hoped were humbled,
   at a walled city held fast,

like a thief caught in the storehouse;     25
the look of disgrace like a cape to their faces;
   the shame to them clinging
  like the caul that covers the liver.

And they drank from the beaker of scandal,
   drank deep and were drunk!          30
I'd had in my heart the fear of death,
   like that of a woman's first labor—

but the Lord came across it,
  like a downpour in drought,
and my eyes brightened, as my foe's went dim.
  For gladness itself I sing,

   while he moans dirges.
Now my home is the voice of delight,
  his of bilious complaint.
To you, my Rock, my highest tower,

my soul sings out:
  in my need you had mercy prepared.
Put your heart, my son, in the hand of my God
  and bring these praises before the people.

  Make them an amulet bound to your arm—
to be cut on your heart with a stylus of iron and lead.


## THE WAR WITH YADDAYIR

Back away from me now, my friend—
  wait just a moment and hear my plan.
Would you scare me with false accusations?
What would I fear—with the Rock as my light
and salvation? You've been in my circle,
but if you persist in your slander,
I'll count you among the heathen and cruel.
No good could come of one
  who exalts himself over my family,
no peace to him who threatens my city.
If you can't keep from your mouth's evil,
and insist on rebellion, like Ezekiel's rebels—
then turn to me, friends, and listen,
  and weigh his word against mine.

He disputes my alliance with kings.     15
   This, I say, is my lot and inheritance.
He fears the face of their wrath.
   My refuge and hope, I respond, is in God.
What are these battles to you? he asks.
   And I answer: The place of my death     20
and burial is set, and the Lord who sent me
     seraphs in a dream will save me.
If I were rotting away with sin could I stop it?
   My book holds my destiny!
There are people who die before their time,     25
   like Zimri, who reigned for a week, or Tivni—
     and others who face neither struggle nor war
but are buried just like the Egyptian, whom Moses saw.

There are those who are swept away
     for want of righteousness,     30
   and others in life who go hungry, poor and alone.
Leave off me now—maybe I'll spend my days in prosperity,
   a turban above me; I'll drink still water
from my well in the cup of deliverance—
     and running water drawn from my river.     35
     Is it right to despise my inheritance,
   and not rejoice in my portion and fate?
If your heart hurts for my future,
   and refuses to fathom my wealth and splendor
because of the fire and water I come through year by year,     40
   fear, my lord, for your own as for mine,
   though you're healthy at home, and calm.

I trust in the Lord who humbled my foes
   in snares concealed for my footsteps
when the enemy came to the garrisoned city     45
   and slaughtered its vizier like a calf.
He was a foe in the line of my king—
and the evil of strangers pales
   beside the evil of kin.
     Two of the Spanish princes were there,     50
   and the Zemarite troops, and they seized the city,
then advanced like a pestilence, destroying the fortress.

We went out to stop them,
    and He broke them before us,
    and August discovered their heads on stone,
      not in the orchards and grass.

We brought them down to the ground
    like birds of the air who had raised
      their wings on high;
we chased them in clusters of four and five,
    like olives from a tree the worker has beaten.
    We slew them two against three,
    like long vowels against short in a word;
we struck them the blow that had leveled
      the armies of Og and Sihon.
The princes were stricken, reward for their obstinance,
    and all of it ended,
    except for the nine who fled—their leader a tenth,
    pursued until he was brought like a gift,
      or tribute, that summer to my king.

My friend, for me in my straits
    the Rock rose up,
    therefore I offer these praises,
      my poem to the Lord:
He recognized fear of the foe in my heart
    and erased it.
      So my song is sung to the healer:
He ravaged my enemies with pain,
      easing my own.
Someone objected:
Who are *you* to pay homage?
I am, I answered, the David of my age!
He responded: Is Saul, too, with the prophets?
    And I told him:

The heir of Merari, Sitri, and Assir,
    Elkanah, Mishael, Elzaphan, and Assaf!
How could a poem
    in my mouth be improper
      to the God who heals my wound?

From Jeduthun the singer of psalms                    90
  my father descends,
    and I from my father.
For the Lord I sweeten my song in its discourse,
  as He embitters my enemy's heart.
As He has pledged to vanquish my foes,                95
  so I've pledge my song to please Him—
  to worship Him day by day in my labor,
    until He pays my wage.


## ON THE DEATH OF ISAAC, HIS BROTHER

    First
child of my mother,
    death's
angel your specter,
    soon the sun                                5
setting will turn you,
  and by evening,
    stones divide us—
earth's dust your shroud.

Neither splendor                                      10
  nor wealth could help you
    in your affliction,
  neither capital nor cup.
    I kissed you—
your heart wouldn't have it,                          15
though you lay like a healthy
    man asleep.
  I wept,
but you wouldn't reply,
your tongue held                                      20
  from speaking.

And you slept
the sleep of forever
        the Rock
    topples
        and pours
across His design.

They'd given you wine
    in the cup of
        ancient death

    I'll drink from soon.

*

Give up, heart,
    on bringing him back—
        on ever again
    seeing his likeness:

pledge yourself now to abjectness,
    and if you'd ask for
        rest from your grief—
            to dying his death.

*

Why should I force
    what custom requires
when my heart feels
like a moth-eaten shirt?
And why mourn in the
    dirt beside him,
when all my thoughts
    are slime-filled pits?

Grief has broken my
    body's bearing;
why should I shatter
pitchers and cups?

The torn clothing
   will long be sewn,
when my heart still stings
as though ripped with thorns;        55
   and the walls of my strength
      will weaken with pain,
   after my clothes have been
      beaten and washed;

and sorrow will cling        60
   to my leaning frame,
like staves
in the rings of the ark.
But rest and happiness
   beyond my brother        65

will hover forever
   strange to my mood.

*

My language,
     I'd ask of you
in my life        70
to lift up a sound
    of lament
   for my brother and father,
who was father to all who were broken
in judgment,        75
     and the widows deceived;

who was generous and opened his doors
     to the street,
   when others were locked,
who'd herd as one the heifer and bear,      80
   while none devour,
     and none become prey.

I bathed him and dressed him
   and placed him in bed,
     and into my      85
   mouth came the voice of labor,

and I brought him to his grave,
my clothing torn,
   my family gathered,
    and I rose and went down
and helped him
   toward the world below.

They said:
   "He has taken him up."

   And I thought:
"Let Him take me instead."

And they said: "Time will
   heal your hurt and you'll rest."

And I answered in pain:

"On your balm of time
   and all rest beyond
    my brother—a curse!

Take, My Strength, my soul—
for grief such as this it can't carry."

       ★

Tell him, please,
   whom I long to see—
my hands released him
    to Lostness:
By the life of the Living
   God, for the world
he'll be in my blood
   like fire,
    until I'm dust
in the dust at his side.

       ★

Twelve months have passed—
   and you still haven't fled
    the fowler's snare.

90

95

100

105

110

115

Are the clods of earth so sweet to you now
that to us you prefer worms and decay?
    You were the best of us:           120
   Come back to your place with the elders,
and we'll talk of my battles and latest campaigns.

  Though how could he rise—
    whose flesh is rotting,
      whose bones are like dry trees?     125
   Imprisoned in earth, as his soul is in sky,
as the moth-maggots eat through his leathery shroud,
    and into his skin, like leaves.

*

A brother is in me
   whose letters          130
  were like water
when my heart was thirsty.

Now, when others' come,
  not his,
the thought of him writing        135
  within me is fire.

*

A psalm to the hearer

of prayer in my spirit forever.
  To praise Him is proper
    who metes out justice     140
   to the children of men,
like the sun for all revealed in its sky.
All who govern hard in their power,
  first He created youthful and soft,
   like grass and like labor,     145
    and the poplar and oak.

But grief He created strong in its birth,
    and weak in its growth,
and wherever it festers
150      in a thinking heart—
        heart is lost.
From God-without-name to people is grace
neither language nor speech can measure.

I'd said in my mourning despair
155      would quickly wear through my heart
        which like an alley
    had narrowed with worry,
but now with solace is wide—
    and my sorrow sheds
160      like the flesh of my brother.
If my heart is stirred and at times I weep,
and the sadness still rises within me like hosts—
    more often than not I'm calm like a man
        whose heart is empty,
165      his burden light.

So the Rock wounds
    and then heals the stricken.
May He who blankets the sky with night,
    and wraps my mother's eldest with dust,
170      forgive my brother his errors—
and in His grace remember his goodness—
    and with our fathers
who were pure and His treasure,
    count him as treasure.

## FIRST WAR

First war resembles
a beautiful girl
we all want to flirt with
and believe.

Later it's more
a repulsive old whore
whose callers are bitter
and grieve.


## I'D SUCK BITTER POISON

I'd suck bitter poison from the viper's mouth
and live by the basilisk's hole forever,
rather than suffer through evenings with boors,
fighting for crumbs from their table.


## DELAY YOUR SPEECH

Delay your speech
if you want your words
to be straight and free of deceit—

as a master archer
is slow to take aim
when splitting a grain of wheat.


## THE RICH

The rich are far from common,
and the brilliant likewise are few;
and the number of each is further reduced
when they step side by side into view.

## PEOPLE WELCOME THE RICH

People welcome the rich
  with deference, respect, and credit,
but scorn the poor and charge them
  with crimes they didn't commit.


## IF YOU LEAVE A LONG-LOVED FRIEND

If you leave a
long-loved friend
  today in disgust,

you'll be like a man
destroying a building
  that took him a year

to raise from dust.


## YOU WHO'D BE WISE

You who'd be wise
should inquire
  into the nature of
    justice and evil

from your teachers,
seekers like yourself,
  and the students
who question your answer.

## WHEN YOU'RE DESPERATE

When you're desperate ride
the lion's back
to sustenance,
but don't use others
or envy them—

the envy will weigh on
your heart, not theirs.


## IT'S HEART THAT DISCERNS

It's heart that discerns
between evil and good,
so work to develop your heart.

How many are there
who heartless destroy,
and think their destruction a start?


## HE'LL BRING YOU TROUBLE

He'll bring you trouble with talk like dreams,
invoking verse and song to cheat you;
But dreams, my son, aren't what they seem:
Not all the poet says is true.


## COULD KINGS RIGHT A PEOPLE GONE BAD

Could kings right a people gone bad
while they themselves are twisted?
How, in the woods, could shadows that bend
be straight when the trees are crooked?

## WHAT'S FAMILIAR IS SOMETIMES DISTANCED

What's familiar is sometimes distanced,
   and the distanced sometimes brought near—
and the cavalier rider in fetlock-deep water
   who falls finds it up to his ears.


## ONE WHO WORKS AND BUYS HIMSELF BOOKS

One who works
   and buys himself books,
while his heart inside them
   is vain or corrupt

resembles a cripple
   who draws on the wall
a hundred legs,
   then can't get up.


## THREE THINGS

All who'd live by
   risk and resistance
manage three things:

high-sea commerce,
   excellent enemies,
and the company of kings.


## SOAR, DON'T SETTLE

Soar, don't settle for earth
   and sky—soar to Orion;
and be strong, but not like an ox or mule
   that's driven—strong like a lion.

## MAN'S WISDOM IS IN WHAT HE WRITES

Man's wisdom is in what he writes,
good sense at the end of his pen;
and using his pen he can climb to the height
    of the scepter in the hand of his king.


## BE GLAD, SHE SAID

"Be glad," she said,
"that God has given you
        fifty years
in this world"—
though she didn't know
there is no division
    between, as I see it,
my days that have passed
and Noah's
        of which I've heard.
In the world I have nothing
but the hour I'm in,
    which stands for a moment,
and then like a cloud moves on.


## THE MULTIPLE TROUBLES OF MAN

The multiple troubles of man,
    my brother, like slander and pain,
amaze you?   Consider the heart
    which holds them all
in strangeness, and doesn't break.

## GAZING THROUGH THE NIGHT

Gazing through the
        night and its stars,

  or the grass and its bugs,

I know in my heart these swarms
are the craft of surpassing wisdom.

  Think:   the skies
     resemble a tent,
      stretched taut by loops
and hooks;

and the moon with its stars,
  a shepherdess,
  on a meadow
    grazing her flock;

and the crescent hull in the looser clouds

    looks like a ship being tossed;

    a whiter cloud, a girl
      in her garden
        tending her shrubs;

   and the dew coming down is her sister
      shaking water
     from her hair onto the path;

  as we
    settle in our lives,

like beasts in their ample stalls—

  fleeing our terror of death,
    like a dove
      its hawk in flight—

though we'll lie in the end like a plate,
hammered into dust and shards.

## EARTH TO MAN

Earth to man
   is a prison forever:

These tidbits, then,
   for fools:

Run where you will.
   Heaven surrounds you.
   Get out if you can.


## THE CHILD AT ONE OR TWO

The child at one or two
   crawls like a snake on the floor;
and at ten he skips to his father,
   like a kid among goats on the hills;

at twenty, love in his heart         5
   takes hold—and he struts for girls;
he basks in the glories of youth
   for his pride and power, at thirty;

reaching forty he ripens,
   and joins the elders, his friends;      10
at fifty the sleep of his youth
   in whiteness is brought to an end;

and the terrors of time assault him,
   when a man passes sixty;
till seventy then he sighs        15
   with age, and seems to be saintly;

but time surrounds him at eighty,
   trapped in the fowler's snare;
and at ninety he can't distinguish
   between the plough and scythe;      20

at a hundred—who gets to a hundred?—
   men in amazement approach him;

when he dies he lies with maggots,
    repulsive to one and all;

25    so it's right that I wax elegiac
    from time to time in my soul.


## I QUARTERED THE TROOPS FOR THE NIGHT

I quartered the troops for the night in a fortress
    which soldiers destroyed long ago,
and they fell asleep at its walls and foundations
    while beneath us its masters slept on.

5    And I wondered . . . What had become
    of the people who dwelled here before us?
Where were the builders and soldiers, the wealthy
    and poor, the slaves and their lords—

the mourners and grooms, sons and fathers;
10    the bereaved and the women in labor?
Great nations had come in succession
    in the course of months and years.

They settled across the back of the earth,
    but rest in the heart of the ground—
15    their magnificent palaces turned into tombs,
    their pleasant courts to dust,

and if they could lift their heads and emerge,
    they'd take our lives and pleasure.
In truth, my soul, in truth and soon,
20    I'll be like them—and these sleepers.


## LUXURIES EASE

Luxuries ease, but when trouble comes
people are plagued for the wealth they've accrued.
    The peacock's tail is spectacular—
but it weighs him down on the day he's pursued.

## WHY REPEAT THE SINS

Why repeat the sins
    you know will make you sad
and not hold back from sinning
    for sorrow—

like a dove whose brood was slaughtered
    in the nest, and yet returns
        over and over again
            until she's taken?

## AT THE TREASURY

On couches stretched out at the treasury,
where the guards' vigilance knows no relief,
you fell asleep without fear by the window
    and time came through like a thief.

## KNOW OF THE LIMBS

Know of the limbs embroidered with dust
    and covered with ashen skin,
and in these graves see the power of kings
    reduced to the powder of bone.

You whose souls on earth were exalted
    will soon rise over all—
and be remembered in the world ever after
    as a dream as it fades is recalled.

## YOU MOCK ME NOW

You mock me now in your youth
    because I've grown old and gray;
I'm old, but I've seen the carpenters
    building their coffins for boys.


## TIME DEFIES AND BETRAYS

Time defies and betrays the patricians,
    and drives all who grow proud;
and lengthens the maverick's wandering,
    and separates twins, like a shroud.


## THE MARKET

I crossed through a market where butchers
    hung oxen and sheep side by side—
there were birds and herds of fatlings like squid,
    their terror loud
5        as blood congealed over blood
and slaughterers' knives opened veins.

In booths alongside them the fishmongers,
    and fish in heaps, and tackle like sand;
and beside them the Street of the Bakers,
10        whose ovens are fired through dawn.

They bake, they eat, they lead their prey;
    they split what's left to bring home.

★

And my heart understood how it happened and asked:
Who are you to survive?
What separates you from these beasts,                    15
which were born and knew waking and labor and rest?
If they hadn't been given by God for your meals,
they'd be free.
If He wanted this instant
He'd easily put you in their place.                      20

They've breath, like you, and hearts,
which scatter them over the earth;
there was never a time when the living didn't die,
nor the young that they bear not give birth.

Pay attention to this, you pure ones,                    25
and princes so calm in your fame,
know if you'd fathom the worlds of the hidden:
THIS IS THE WHOLE OF MAN.

# YOSEF IBN HASDAI

*(first half of the eleventh century)*

Very little of Saragossan Yosef Ibn Hasdai's work survived even into the time of Moshe Ibn Ezra, who wrote that "his words were few, but sublime." His reputation was made by a single poem, which became known in the Hebrew tradition as *"HaShira HaYetoma"*—literally, the orphaned poem, though the phrase in this context derives from its Arabic cognate and means something more along the lines of the unique, singular, or unequaled ode. It also happens to be his sole surviving work. Addressed to Shmu'el HaNagid, Ibn Hasdai's qasida is a classical two-part ode: lines 1–22 constitute a highly erotic prelude, and the remainder of the poem revolves around HaNagid, lauding him in elaborate fashion and then, as Ibn Hasdai gets to the point, turning to him directly and asking for his help in finding shelter for "two brothers" who are refugees from a destroyed community. The poem appears to have been composed in 1045, when HaNagid's son Yehosef (whose virtues it also extols) was ten. Ibn Ezra has high praise for the qasida's sense of proportion, as well as for its rich ornamentation and imagery. While Haim Schirmann suggests that the density of the rhetorical figuration makes the body of the poem less appealing than the prelude to modern readers, taken on its own terms the poem offers a classic example of the Arabized Hebrew qasida: the sensual unfolding of its narrative is especially fine—embodying a complicated slippage from the "discrete" homoerotic opening to an expression of friendship and fraternity, and the responsibility they entail. The poem's transitions are surprising and graceful; and on the whole Ibn Hasdai's ode is far more integrated and refined than many of the period's conventional encomia. That said, the beloved of the prelude remains a convention—however charged—and should not be identified with the poem's addressee.

# THE QASIDA

Is that fine fawn so brave as to wrap
    himself in a veil of dark like a robe—
to shepherd the stars by night and wander
    through desert ruins in terror and fear?
Would he leave the sound of lutes for dread,         5
    for roaming and danger leave his chamber—
until he was tangled in a web of dreams
    and held fast in slumber's snare?
While he was sleeping I gladly gathered
    what when awake he denied me in anger:       10
I drank from the hand of that sweetest sleep
    the juice of his mouth in a cup of jasper.
I lay there and on my breast his curls
    against his brow wafted myrrh.
I cradled the moon in my right hand—       15
    my lips kissing the shining sun.
The bed was scented with frankincense,
    the blankets with blends of choicest herbs,
and what I saw so filled me with pleasure
    I woke—and it was gone . . .       20
except for the fragrance that soothes the spirit
    and flowing myrrh that stirs the soul,
like the name of the one and only Nagid—
    whose glory, spreading, fills the world.

He soars like a tower over Israel,       25
    raised high like a wall for his people;
renewed through him, for his tribe's devotion,
    is a place of honor over Orion.
Could it be that Shmu'el is Samuel—
    who was called to enter the Lord's Temple—       30
conjured now by the sorcerers' force
    or rising to face the End with his fate?
If not—he's worthy in righteousness,
    pure in perfection of his soul,

His lips keep watch over all learning,
    and from his mouth the Law is taught;
his glory glows just like the moon,
    his deeds are like a brook to thirst.
Virtue and merit are bound to his shoulder,
    authority's always sealed at his side.
He sought out wisdom and fathomed its secrets,
    knowledge until he knew where it was.
He's brother to counsel, a breaking dawn
    through death's shadow in troubled times.
Kings by the light of his countenance walk;
    faces are covered with shame as he passes.
Before him the viziers resemble cattle,
    and all the advisers like sheep go dumb.
My lord, whose love gives rest to my soul,
    and when it's forgotten leaves me in ruins,
I've written that love within my heart—
    from youth it has been engraved on its walls.
A noble spirit and wisdom are yours,
    knowledge and cunning you also command;
your heart's as wide as East to West,
    your hand as generous as the season's rains.
The flow of your pen is honor and grace,
    although its frame is thin and plain;
cut from the reed—when its writing is read
    glory, craft, and power reign.
Riding it's raised like a mighty warrior;
    left on the ground its hope is vain;
its two teeth are sharpened arrows—
    vengeance the spit of its mouth, or mercy;
it scatters precious gems to books
    inlaid like silk, bright with embroidery.
My love for Yehosef, the fruitful vine,
    exceeds all love in its force of feeling
for the lion's cub and child of joy,
    for one who fathoms all that's hidden.
A bud has blossomed in the Levites' camp,
    by the fountain of judgment, by wisdom's spring,
tender in years but at ease in the Law,
    young yet at home in mysterious things—

as though the men of his age were a harvest,
    and he among them the priestly portion.      75
I'd give up my life itself for him—
    to whom my own soul is bound.

Hear me, prince above my people;
    lend yours ears to what I say:      80
Take this poem, in its splendor arrayed,
    an enduring token of love that's pure,
like a bride dressed in her gown and veils,
    like a maiden adorned with all her jewels—
intended for you though forever virgin,      85
    sent by a father, but sole as an orphan.
I leave with you, my lord and prince,
    two brothers who fled for their lives;
whose inheritance now is strangeness alone,
    whose land in ruins, like Admàh, lies:      90
without the shelter of your shadow across them
    they'll wander out to the ends of the earth.
May you carry greetings of peace in your greatness
    to the noble heads of our splendid school,
those men far off, who are near to my soul,      95
    which languishes here within its longing.
And by your life, my lord, and theirs
    may our Lord soon raise the fallen.

# SHELOMO IBN GABIROL

*(1021/22–c. 1057/58)*

Philosopher, misanthrope, and spectacular fly in the ointment of the refined eleventh-century Andalusian-Jewish elite, SHELOMO IBN GABIROL, the second major poet of the period, comes down to us as one of the most complicated intellectual figures of the entire Hebrew Middle Ages. He was born in either 1021 or 1022, in Malaga, to an undistinguished family that may have fled the collapsing capital of the Umayyad caliphate, Cordoba, with the same wave of refugees that included Shmu'el HaNagid. At some point his father moved the family north to Saragossa, and Ibn Gabirol—or, in Arab circles, Abu Ayyub Sulaiman Ibn Yahya Ibn Jabirul—was raised in that important center of Islamic and Jewish learning. Ibn Gabirol's father died while the precocious son was still in his early teens, and the young man was looked after by a Jewish notable at the Saragossan court, Yequti'el Ibn Hasan al-Mutawakkil Ibn Qabrun. He was writing accomplished poems by age sixteen, important ones by nineteen, though he was ill, already suffering from a disease that would leave him embittered and in constant pain; the condition has never been precisely identified, but scholars speculate that it was most likely tuberculosis of the skin. We can infer from his poems that he was short and ugly. In 1039 Yequti'el became involved in court intrigue and was executed, and Ibn Gabirol lost his patron. Ostracized by the religious and intellectual community of the city, he left (or was forced to leave) Saragossa sometime after 1045, and most scholars assume that he went south, to Granada, in order to try his luck at HaNagid's court. Things may have worked out for a while, but the two men clashed when the young, upstart poet insulted his elder poet-patron. The meager trail we have of the poet vanishes there, with Ibn Gabirol in his mid-twenties. It is probable that later in life he supported himself by writing for the synagogue, wandering from one community to another. He was known, says Ibn Ezra, for his philosophical temperament, as well as for his "angry spirit . . . and demon within, which he was not able to control."

Employing the same set of literary tools as HaNagid, Ibn Gabirol produced a poetry that stands in stark contrast to the work of his worldlier mentor. His verse is metaphysical through and through, and his brooding, passionate nature left him as isolated a figure as HaNagid was social. Ibn Gabirol's poems are distinctive for their embodiment of complex thinking, scathing satire, and a strikingly modern, self-conscious, even defiant religious devotion. His religious lyrics are considered by many to be the most powerful of their kind in the medieval Hebrew tradition, and his long cosmological masterpiece, *Kingdom's Crown*, is acknowledged today as one of the greatest poems in all of Hebrew literature. His major philosophical opus, the Neoplatonic *Fountain of Life*, became an important work in the history of Scholastic philosophy (via the Latin translation of the original Arabic). Throughout the Middle Ages and into the nineteenth century, its author was thought to be a Muslim or Christian by the name of Avicebron, Avicembron, or Avicebrol; in 1846, a Jewish-French scholar discovered that the book was in fact by the poet Shelomo Ibn Gabirol. Also of serious interest to readers of Ibn Gabirol's poetry is his short but striking ethical treatise *Tiqqun Middot HaNefesh* (On the Improvement of the Moral Qualities). Written in Arabic when the poet was twenty-four, it graphs an undissociated sensibility in which the physical and psychological endowments, or impulses, are correlated to ethical conduct. Knowledge of the soul in this not always decipherable scheme is a prerequisite for its development, or ascent, but the soul can be known solely in a descent into physical detail. The microcosm, that is, nearly always mirrors the macrocosm. Ibn Gabirol's philosophical vision is reflected, often in sublime fashion, throughout his liturgical verse, whose surface maintains the transparent, communal register required by the occasion while encoding a far more subversive, personal, and confrontational dimension. That vision also infuses a wide variety of seemingly conventional secular works, such as "See the Sun," "The Garden," "I Love You," and "I'd Give Up My Soul Itself," as well as the poet's *sui generis* poems of crisis. More than any of the other medieval Hebrew poets, Ibn Gabirol is, above all, a conflicted poet in pursuit of Wisdom.

## TRUTH SEEKERS TURN

Truth seekers, turn to my poems
  and you who are ignorant, learn:

they'll teach you hidden wisdom
  and instruct you in all that's arcane.

Don't fall for words that are empty and vain,
  but hold to these poems and you'll hold to faith.

For the weak poem kills the soul of its author—
    while he's still alive, it dies;

where the excellent in memory endures,
    like the new moon, month by month in its rise.


## I'M PRINCE TO THE POEM

I'm prince to the poem, my slave,
    I'm harp to the court musicians,
my song is a turban for viziers' heads,
    a crown for kings in their kingdoms:

and here I've lived just sixteen years,
    and my heart is like eighty within them.


## PROLOGUE TO *THE BOOK OF GRAMMAR*

A poem of glory and power I'll offer my Maker
    who set the heavens on high with His span,
because He created the language and mouth of man
    and gave them the crown of honor and splendor,
5    causing their growth in knowledge of wonder the Lord
    works in the world and the world-to-come.
Declared the Spaniard Solomon Ben Judah the Small,
    who culled for his people the holy tongue:
Examining the Lord's congregation with all my soul,
10    I saw the exiled remnant escaped,
found among them the sacred speech destroyed,
    almost wholly in ruins or erased,
given over to languages distant from Hebrew
    and utterly strange to the lips of the Jews,
15    half of whom speak in the manner of Edom,
    and half with the darkening tongue of Qedar,

in their hopelessness drowning, engulfed by the deepening whirl,
    in their ignorance sinking within it like stone,
joining pain for my people to pain through my bones—
    trapped like a fire burning inside me.    20
Knowing the foolish were lost in their groaning, I moaned
    in my heart like a harp or the harp-like sea.
Lacking all vision, living far from their Law,
    they couldn't fathom the simplest inscription.
My Lord, who could save the blind in their drowning?    25
    Who could bring their ship into port?
"Now that your eyes are clear," my heart spoke out,
    "you see that your people are lost . . .
Only you can guide them—give voice to mouths
    gone mute. Surely the Lord will reward you."    30
Pushed, I cowered, seeing that I was still young
    and easily given to anger and fury:
Reason in youth is dismissed categorically;
    what can a boy of nineteen really do?
So said my heart, when a dream like a secret came through me,    35
    and I heard a voice from the city call me—
taunting my spirit—during the night as it told me:
    *The hand of the Lord will surely strengthen you*
*under your burden; your youth doesn't excuse you.*
    *It isn't the elders who hold up the kingdom.*    40
Viewing this image my confidence grew; and I knew
    very well in my heart what the Lord
wanted, and set my mind to make of this treatise a

    xyst as fine as my hand was able,
yearning to forge through this book of our grammar a    45
    zone of repair for the language of Cain . . .


## THEY ASKED ME AS THOUGH THEY WERE MYSTIFIED

    They asked me as though they were mystified:
        Is it true your friend's hands are like clouds?
    And I told them: They were tied for being too open,
        and for goodness of heart of hunger he died.

## SEE THE SUN

See the sun gone red toward evening
as though it were wearing a crimson dress,
　　stripping the edges of north and south
and, in violet, lining the wind from the west:

and the earth—left in its nakedness—
takes refuge in the shadow of night, and rests,
　　and then the skies go black, as though
covered in sackcloth, for Yequti'el's death.


## ON LEAVING SARAGOSSA

My tongue cleaves to the roof of my mouth,
　　my throat is parched with pleading,
my heart is loud, my mind confused
　　with pain and continual grieving.
My sorrow swells and will not bear
　　sleep's gift to my eyes:
How long will this rage and yearning
　　like fire inside me burn?

Who could I turn to for help,
　　who could I tell of my plight?
If only someone would offer me comfort,
　　someone have mercy, take hold of my hand,
I'd pour out my heart before him
　　and manage to reach but the edge of my grief—
though maybe in putting my sorrow to words
　　my heart's rushing would find release.

You who seek my peace, come near—
　　and hear the roar of my heart like the sea.
If your heart has grown hard it will soften,
　　faced with the hate that faces me.

How could you call me alive,
    when you know of my distress;
is it nothing to live among people
    who can't tell their right hand from left?

I'm buried, but not in a graveyard,                25
    in the coffin of my own home;
I suffer with neither father nor mother,
    indigent, young, and alone—
on my own without even a brother,
    not a friend apart from my mind:            30
I mix my blood with my tears,
    and my tears into my wine.

I'll be consumed in my thirst
    before my thirst for friendship is quenched,
as though the sky and its hosts were arrayed     35
    between me and all that I crave.
I'm treated here as a stranger, despised—
    as though I were living with ostriches,
caught between impostors and fools
    who think their hearts have grown wise.     40
One hands you venom to drink,
    another strokes you with words
and lies in wait in his heart,
    addressing you: "Please, my lord . . .";
people whose fathers were not fit           45
    to be dogs to my flock of sheep—
their faces have never known blushing,
    unless they were painted with crimson cheeks.

They're giants in their own eyes,
    grasshoppers here in mine.           50
They quarrel with all my teachings and talk,
    as though I were speaking Greek.
"Speak," they carp, "as the people speak,
    and we'll know what you have to say"—
and now I'll break them like dirt or like straw,     55
    my tongue's pitchfork thrust into their hay.

If your ears aren't able to hear me,
    what good could my harmonies do?
Your necks aren't worthy of wearing
60    my golden crescents and jewels.
If these boors would only open their mouths
    to the rain that descends from my clouds,
my essence would soon come through them
    with its cinnamon scent, and myrrh.

65  Have compassion for wisdom, compassion for me,
    surrounded by neighbors like these—
people for whom the knowledge of God
    is a matter of spirits and ghosts.
Therefore I mourn and wail,
70    and make my bed in ashes,
and bow my head like a reed and fast
    on Monday and Thursday and Monday.

Why should I wait any longer
    with nothing like hope in sight?
75  Let my eyes in the world wander,
    they'll never glimpse what I want:
Death grows daily sweeter to me,
    the world's gossip means less and less;
if my heart returns to that path,
80    thinking its intrigue might offer success,

whatever I do will come round,
    my scheming against me revolve;
so my soul refuses its glory,
    for its glory brings only disgrace.
85  I'll never rejoice again in the world,
    my pride will find there no pleasure,
though the stars of Orion call me to come
    and take up my station among them.

For the world has always been
90    like a yoke around my neck—
and what good does it do me to linger
    by blindness and grief beset?

My soul in my death will delight
    if it leads to the Lord and His rest—
I'd put an end to my life,              95
    an end to this dwelling in flesh.

My delight's in the day of my downfall,
    my downfall the day of my greatest delight,
and I long for heart's understanding—
    the exhaustion of sinew and strength.     100
For a sigh settles into repose,
    and my leanness leads to my meat,
and as long as I live I'll seek out in search
    of all that the elder Solomon preached:

    perhaps the revealer of depths, the Lord,     105
        will show me where wisdom lurks—
    for it alone is my reward,
        my portion and the worth of my work.


## MY HEART THINKS AS THE SUN COMES UP

My heart thinks as the sun comes up
    that what it does is wise:
    as earth borrows its light,
        as pledge it takes the stars.


## NOW THE THRUSHES

Now the thrushes have gathered
    to sing on the sprigs without thinking;
how could you hear their song in the trees
and not be glad with all you've got and start drinking?

What could be better than branches renewed
    by time, with buds peeking
into the garden? When a wind comes on
they nod to each other, it seems, as though they were speaking.

## WINTER WITH ITS INK

Winter with its ink of showers and rain,
with its pen of lightning and palm of clouds,
    wrote a letter of purple and blue
        over the beds of the garden.

No artist in his cunning could measure
    his work beside it—and so,
        when earth longed for the sky
it embroidered the spread of its furrows like stars.

## THE GARDEN

Its beads of dew hardened still,
    He sends his word to melt them;
    they trickle down the grapevine's stem
        and its wine seeps into my blood.

5    The beds blossom, and open before us
    clasps of their whitening buds,
    sending a fragrance up to our faces,
        as we wander out to the myrtles.

As you go, each flower lends you a petal—
10    a wing so you won't crush it;
    and the sun's face glows like a bride
        whose jewels shine in her glow.

Through its circuit, daily, she glides,
    though no one at all pursues her—
15    and so we think it a king's chariot
        drawn by galloping horses.

As it passes over the garden you notice
    the beds now coated in silver,
    and then when the day declines it lines
20        their border with a shimmering gold.

In its sinking, soon, you find yourself thinking
   it's bowing, before its Maker;
    as it swiftly sets it seems to be veiled
     in darkening red by the Lord.


## THE FIELD

The storm-clouds lowed above us like bulls.
Autumn was angry, and its face darkened
and put them to chase like wisps of wool,
   like a ship's captain blasting its horn.

The heavens went black in a thickening mist,
as the morning stars and their light were absorbed,
then the sun with its wing whisked them across
   the earth until they split and it burst.

The wind beat at the sheets of rain,
and the clouds were cut into threads reaching down
into the world below—drenching
   ridges, preparing the furrows for sowing.

On the hills, hidden grasses emerged
like secrets a man had long withheld;
all winter the clouds wept until suddenly
   life again swept through the trees of the field.


## THE BEE

*Hear, O Israel, the Lord is one . . .*
*that ye remember and do all my commandments*

Take, little bee, your time with your song,
   in your flight invoking the prayer called "Hear"—
declaring and stretching "the Lord is *one*,"
   raising on high the hum of *remember*
to He who put honey under your tongue
   and gave you the gall to drive out foes.

It's true, in your eyes, you're small—
    but your being transcends *the things that swarm*,
and the choicest words are yours. Your merit
    refines you: you're pure as the birds of the air.


## I'D GIVE UP MY SOUL ITSELF

I'd give up my soul itself for one
    whose light is like the sun.
He softly entreated me, saying: "Drink,
    and banish your grief and longing—"
the wine poured from the beaker's spout
    a viper in the mouth of a griffon.

And I answered: "Could one contain the sun
    within a jar that's broken?"
But my heart didn't yet know of its power
    to utterly crush its burden—
which was lying safe and secure inside it,
    like the king on his bed in Bashan.


## BE SMART WITH YOUR LOVE

"Be smart with your love," my friend chided,
"find solid ground for the circle it clears."
And while I was probing love's wisdom,
Adina beside me was poised as a queen,
saying: "How long do you think you can hide

your love, refusing to let it be seen—
when you know the harvest is gathered with hatchets,
by putting the sickle and scythe to the corn
. . . and Jesse's David, at love's extreme,
cried out and sent for Avigal while she mourned."

## ALL IN RED

All in red, and come from Edom,
    settle down and be still:
By God, I love you well—
    but not like the men of Sodom.


## YOU'VE STOLEN MY WORDS

You've stolen my words and denied it—
    lied and broken down walls;
did you think you could soar with my songs
    or use them to hide your flaws?

Could a man scale the heavens
    and eclipse the light of the world?
It's all, as I see it, quite simple:
    can the Nile be drained with a pail?


## THE ALTAR OF SONG

Your answer betrays your transgression,
your words are empty, your verse is weak—
you've stolen a few of my rhymes,
    but your spirit failed: you're meek.

Try taking on wisdom's discipline,
instead of poetry's altar and pose:
for as soon as you start your ascent,
    your most private parts are exposed.

## THE PEN

Naked without either cover or dress,
  utterly soulless, and hollow—
from its mouth come wisdom and prudence,
  and in ambush it kills like an arrow.


## IF YOU'D LIVE AMONG MEN

If you'd live among men on earth forever,
  if your soul's afraid of the steel fires of hell,
despise what the world rushes to honor
  and don't be swayed by fame, family, or wealth.

Let neither shame nor poverty distract you.
  Die childless, like Seled, Judah's kin.
And know your soul as well as you can:
  it alone will last of your sinew and skin.


## I AM THE MAN

I am the man who harnessed his spirit
and will not rest with his promise unkept:
  a man whose mind has been split by his mind,
whose soul has sickened of its dwelling in flesh.

5   From earliest youth he held to wisdom
though tried seven times in the furnace of Fate,
  which razed all that he built
    and uprooted all that he planted,

as it broke through all his defenses.
10  As misfortune burned he'd approach it—
  even as destiny hemmed him in—
seeking the limits of wisdom and discipline,

wanting the source of knowledge's treasure:
   know, however, that no one will ever
      discover the mystery's secrets     15
   until his flesh begins to give way . . .

I'd gained a grain of discernment,
when Time came on and exacted its price—
   and now for as long as I live I'll ride
      out in search of wisdom,     20

even if Fate won't saddle my mount.
My heart, I vow, won't weaken with time,
   or break its vows; it will follow them out.
And know, my friends, I've feared what was coming,

   and nothing comes that fear doesn't bring . . .   25

*

It was night and the sky was clear,
   and the moon was pure at its center
      as it led me along discernment's sphere,
teaching me by its light and direction—

though as my heart went out to that light     30
   I feared extended misfortune,
like a father's feeling for his firstborn son.
The wind sent a cover of clouds across it,

wrapping its face in a mask—
as though craving the currents inside them,     35
   it leaned on the clouds till they ran.
      And the sky was clothed in darkness,

and it seemed that the moon had died
   —its grave a vapor . . .
Then the thickened heavens wept for it,     40
   like the nation of Aram weeping

   for its prophet Bilaam,
and the night put on its mail of gloom
and the thunder stabbed it with lightning,
   which flew out toward the horizon     45

        as though it were laughing,
      obeying the thunder's commands:
      it spread its wings like a bat,
    and the ravens of darkness fled when they saw it.

50  So the Lord closed in on my thoughts
    blocking my heart's desire inside it,
        holding my heart in cords of darkness,
    like the warrior bound, who'd stir and break free.

    I no longer hope for the moon, my friend,
55  which thickest dark has replaced,
    as though the clouds had envied my soul,
        and taken its light away from me—

    but when its face appears I'll rejoice
        like a servant recalled by his lord.

                    ★

60  As a soldier in battle has his sword destroyed
        and falters as he runs, then stumbles,
    so is man who is hounded by struggle,
        though Venus be home to his shrine.

            HEART'S HOLLOW

    And heart's hollow
        and wisdom is blocked;
        the body apparent
                but soul obscured:
        those who wake in the world
            for gain come to corruption.
    On earth a man rejoices in nothing. . . .

The servant, soon, will slaughter his master,
the handmaidens turn on their mistress and queen;
a daughter will rise—against her own mother,
    a son—against his father's name.
        My eye in the world dismisses
            what others most love,
        and all is labor, a ploughing for worms.
            Slime—to slime returns.
            Soul—ascends to soul.


### I LOVE YOU

I love you with the love a man
    has for his only son—
with his heart and his soul and his might.
And I take great pleasure in your mind
        as you take the mystery on
    of the Lord's act in creation—
though the issue is distant and deep,
and who could approach its foundation?

But I'll tell you something I've heard
and let you dwell on its strangeness:
    sages have said that the secret
        of being owes all
to the all who has all in His hand:
He longs to give form to the formless
    as a lover longs for his friend.
And this is, maybe, what the prophets
meant when they said He worked
        all for His own exaltation.

I've offered you these words—
now show me how you'll raise them.

## BEFORE MY BEING

Before my being your mercy came through me,
    bringing existence to nothing to shape me.
Who is it conceived of my form—and who
    cast it then in a kiln to create me?
Who breathed soul inside me—and who
    opened the belly of hell and withdrew me?
Who through youth brought me this far?
    Who with wisdom and wonder endowed me?
I'm clay cupped in your hands, it's true;
    it's you, I know, not I who made me.
I'll confess my sin and will not say
    the serpent's ways or evil seduced me.
How could I hide my error from you when
    before my being your mercy came through me?

## THREE THINGS

Three things meet in my eyes
    and keep the thought of you always before me:

the skies, which make me think of your Name,
    as they bear faithful witness for me;

the place where I stand, which brings my mind
    back to the land you extend beneath me;

and bless, my soul, my Lord at all times
    for heart's reflection within me.

## I LOOK FOR YOU

I look for you early,
my rock and my refuge,
        offering you worship
    morning and night;
before your vastness
I come confused
        and afraid, for you see
    the thoughts of my heart.

What could the heart
and tongue compose,
        or spirit's strength
    within me to suit you?
But song soothes you
and so I'll give praise
        to your being as long
    as your breath-in-me moves.


## OPEN THE GATE

Open the gate, my beloved—
    arise and open the gate:
my spirit is shaken and I'm afraid.
My mother's maid has been mocking me
    and her heart is raised against me,
so the Lord would hear her child's cry.
From the middle of midnight's blackness,
        a wild ass pursues me,
as the forest boar has crushed me.
And the end which has long been sealed
    only deepens my wound,
and no one guides me—and I am blind.

## THE HOUR OF SONG

I've set my shelter
   with you in my awe and fear
     and in despair
established your name as a fortress;
   I looked to the right
and left and no one was near—
     and into your hands
I committed my loneness . . .

I give you my portion
   of the world's worth,
     of all my labor
you're my desire and cause;
   and here out of love
in you my mind is immersed:
     in song's hour
the work of my worship is yours.


## SEND YOUR SPIRIT

Send your spirit
   to revive our corpses,
and ripple the longed-for
   land again.

The crops come from you;
   you're good to all—
and always return
   to restore what has been.

# ANGELS AMASSING

*Holy, holy, holy is the Lord of hosts,*
*the whole earth is full of his glory.*
*Isaiah 6:3*

Angels amassing like sparks in flames,
their brightness like burnished brass in their casings,
before the exalted throne in a throng
  one to another in vision turn
  to laud their Lord the Creator in longing—   5
*O sons of strength, give glory and strength to the Lord.*

Sublime creatures beneath the throne,
charged carriers encased in light,
in four quarters acknowledge your glory
  and glow in entreaty and word and awe—   10
  on guard over day, keepers of night—
*O sons of strength, give glory and strength to the Lord.*

Leading your camps and hordes they look on,
with Michael your eminent prince at the front—
a myriad chariots set to your right—   15
  and they gather together to seek out your palace
  and bow before your partition in service—
*O sons of strength, give glory and strength to the Lord.*

The hosts of the second camp stand on the left,
and Gabriel over its army looks out:   20
thousands of seraphs, a tremendous force,
  together surround your holy throne—
  of-and-through fire on fire they roam—
*O sons of strength, give glory and strength to the Lord.*

From the third camp's ranks there rises song   25
with the Lord's prince Nuriel a turret before them,
at the sound of their rushing the heavens tremble,
  in their seeking the place of I-am the Creator,
  the reward of a vision of glory and splendor—
*O sons of strength, give glory and strength to the Lord.*   30

The fourth bears witness in majestic array,
with Raphael chanting your psalms and a prayer,
they wreathe the bud and crown of power
    and the four lift in perfect accord
35        hymns you inspired to stave off despair—
*O sons of strength, give glory and strength to the Lord.*

In trembling and fear the assembled sparks
cry out as one—their will set strong;
they plead for your faithful, a people pursued,
40        and send a thunderous noise to the void,
    three times invoking your station apart—
*O sons of strength, give glory and strength to the Lord.*


### AND SO IT CAME TO NOTHING

And so it came
    to nothing—all
that had been
    so fine to behold:
no chambers of stone,
    no palace or dwelling;
no shambles, no suet,
    no Temple or offering;
no wheels, no immersion,
    no flesh for transgression;
no altar, no wine,
    no loaves in a row;
no blood, no veil,
    no incense or coal;
no smoke, no ashes
    no splendor, no robes;
no priest, no wilderness,
    no appointment by lot;
no scapegoat, no cliff,
    no country cut off.

# HE DWELLS FOREVER

*Thy kingdom is a kingdom forever . . .*

He dwells forever, exalted, alone,
and no one comes near Him
whose kingdom is One;
from the light of His garment He fashioned His world
    within three words that are sealed.      5

He yearned, longing for the teaching's counsel;
thought to reveal the ten spheres and their circles;
and against them inscribed
ten without end—
    and five against five now depend.      10

Who fathoms the mystery is shaken with fear:
From this he discerns who's beyond all compare.
Prior to "One"—what does one number?
He's prime to all primes—
    and to all that's exalted He's higher.      15

For the ten are as
if caught in a siege;
who dwells upon them knows and sees:
*He's* the Creator and within them rules.
    His witnesses' claims are made clear.      20

And so by means of the twenty-two letters,
He stretched out fire at the uppermost border;
    at the lower extension He gathered water;
and He sent out between them the wind of measure,
    and set the twelve constellations aloft.      25

It's He who brought forth Being from Nothing,
    and then from Chaos substance was formed;
He set up huge pillars beyond comprehension,
established an azure and inlaid circumference—
    the abysmal waters flow forth from its stones.      30

He fixed six directions sealed with His Name:
From water hurled fire with heavenly strength;
He established within them
His host and His throne,
    for signs and seasons and days.

His Name which is raised and borne over all
    He placed in all with desire and labor.
The earth He hung like grapes in a cluster.
From His lofty place He's the place of all:
    The Lord is a Rock everlasting.

Exalted in spirit, He established His throne
where His kingdom's glory is eternally home;
there His dominion
over all is defined:
    for the spirit of God is Life beyond time.

High above all, and of all the strongest,
He sees the cosmos, and over all watches;
above all holds sway,
      surrounds all there is:
    By means of His Name all creatures exist.

He fashioned all with a blemishless word.
He alone leads, He's instantly heard.
The Lord carries all
    without growing weary—
    within their own wisdom He captures the wise.

He gives revolution to the belt of the skies.
It's He who suspends earth's lands where they lie.
He says: Let there be . . .
    and it is by His might:
    All that's hidden He brings to light.

It's He who parts and He who gathers;
He who enriches, then brings on disaster;
He who crushes
    and He who congeals—
    He who gives form to matter revealed.

Know that it's He who brings darkness and glow;
He who exalts
    then He who brings low;
He who swells and He who collapses
    the greatest of mountains and hills;                    70

        He who brings
        subsistence to men;
He who ripples their fields with grain;
He who gives them water to drink—
    it's He who brings down the rain;                       75

and He who gives life to men of the world;
He who gives strength
        to the frame of a child;
He who over our sinew sends skin;
    He who lengthens our bones within;                      80

He who breathes through the body His breath;
He who keeps it upright in health;
He who deep
    into earth returns it—
    and He who will wake us from sleep.                     85

## HAVEN'T I HIDDEN YOUR NAME

I seek you every evening and dawn,
    my face and palms turned up to you;
with a thirsty spirit for you I moan,
    like a beggar come to my door.

The heavens can't contain you,
    and yet my thoughts somehow do:
haven't I hidden your name in my heart
    until my love for you crossed my lips?

Therefore I'll praise the name of the Lord
    so long as His breath in me lives.

## LORD WHO LISTENS

Lord who listens and attends to the poor,
how long will you distance yourself from my soul and hide?
    I'm weary from calling all night with a faithful heart,
grateful always for your gracious mercy, which abides.

For you I hope, my king; in you I trust—
like a dreamer trusting a reader with a dream that's obscure.
    This is my prayer, hear my petition:
I ask of you nothing less, and nothing more.


## I'VE MADE YOU MY REFUGE

I've made you my refuge and hope—
    who's made me rich and then poor;
your oneness I sought at the door to the poem,
    so grace your servant, my Lord,
with the good that you've long laid in store.
    Extend your mercy across me
and my way with these words will be sure.

How could my failings distract you so—
    who fashioned the world in a void—
that the daughters of song
    should be humbled and stilled.
See now my dread, my Lord,
    I stand here before you exposed
[. . . . . . . . . . . . . . . . . . . .]

## YOU LIE IN MY PALACE

You lie in my palace on couches of gold:
   Lord, when will you ready my bed
for the one with the beautiful eyes you've foretold?
    Why, my fine gazelle,
   why do you sleep while the dawn rises
      like a flag over the hills?

Ignore the mules and asses,
   and see to your guileless doe:
I'm here for one like you—and you for one like me.
    Who enters my chambers
   finds my treasure: my pomegranate, my myrrh—
     my cinnamon, my nectar.


From *KINGDOM'S CROWN*

*Through my prayer a man might profit*
  *from the study of truth and merit,*

*and in its lines I've concisely told*
  *of the wonders of the living God;*

*over all of my hymns it deserves renown—*
  *and I call it the kingdom's crown.*


### I

Your works are wondrous and I know it acutely:

Yours, Lord, is the greatness and the power and the glory,
  the splendor and majesty.
Yours, Lord, is the kingdom exalted over all.
   Yours is all wealth and honor;
all beings above and below you bear witness
that they will perish, while you endure.

Yours is the strength within whose mystery
   our minds eventually fail;

your force exceeds their intensity.
Yours is the hidden chamber of power—

   of form's secret and matter;

yours the Name that eludes the wise,
and the might to bear the world in its void,
and the craft to bring what's hidden to light.

Yours is the kindness that infuses creation,
   and the goodness veiled
     for those who hold you in awe.

Yours is the secret no notion contains,
and life that destruction will not bring down,
and the throne raised higher than height's idea,
   and the hidden hall in the heavenly mansion;

yours is the real which becomes existence
   in light's reflection

and in whose shadow we live;

yours the two worlds and the border between them,
   one for action and one for reward . . .

yours the reward
reserved for the righteous in spirit
     for whom it was hidden:

You saw it was good and concealed it. . . .

## VII

You are the light of the upper regions,

and the eye of every soul that's pure
   will take you in—

and the clouds of sin
in the sinner's soul will obscure you.

Your invisible light in the world
will be seen in the world to come
   on the mountain of God:

You are the light everlasting the eye
   of the mind longs to behold
and may yet glimpse in extremity—

but the whole of will not see. . . .

## IX

You are wise,
and wisdom is a fountain and source
   of life welling up from within you,

and men are too coarse to know you.

You are wise,                  5
and prime to all that's primeval,
   as though you were wisdom's tutor.

You are wise,
but your wisdom wasn't acquired
   and didn't derive from another.        10

You are wise,
and your wisdom gave rise to an endless desire
   in the world as within an artist or worker—

to bring out the stream of existence from Nothing,
   like light flowing from sight's extension—   15

drawing from the source of that light without vessel,
giving it shape without tools,
     hewing and carving,
   refining and making it pure:

He called to Nothing—which split;       20
   to existence—pitched like a tent;
   to the world—as it spread beneath sky.

With desire's span he established the heavens,
as his hand coupled the tent of the planets
     with loops of skill,
    weaving creation's pavilion,

the links of his will
reaching the lowest
     rung of creation—

the curtain
at the outermost edge of the spheres . . .

25

30

### X

Who could put words to your power,
splitting the globe of earth in your making
    half of it land, and the other water?

The wheel of the wind you established
over the sea, which it circles in circuits,
    as the wheel of it rests in that circling,

and over the wind
    you established the sphere of fire.

    These foundations are four,
    though sharing a single foundation,
      source and font,
    from which they emerge renewed

and then through a fourfold font diverge.

### XIV

Who could fathom your mysteries
    in surrounding the second sphere
    with the glowing circle of Venus,
like a queen overlooking her armies,
like a bride adorned with her jewels?

In eleven months' time she traces her compass,
one thirty-seventh of earth in its mass
    as its mysteries' initiates know.

With the Lord's will in the world she renews
 quiet and all tranquility,
 gladness and winning gaiety,
  song and wordless melody—
and the wedding canopy's joy and spell.

She ripens the fruit of the land and its wheat:

the choice fruit made sweet by the sun
and the fruit brought forth by the moon.

XVI

Who could contain your magnitude
 in your setting the sun up as a sign
 to measure the days and the years,
  and the seasons' appointed times—

in sending its light to grow fruit-bearing trees   5
 which blossom beneath the Pleiades,
 and under Orion grow heavy
  with seed that ripening swells?

For six months it moves to the North,
 warming the air and water,   10
 the trees and soil and stones;
  and then it approaches its border

and the light lingers, and the season slows,
 and it reaches the place where a day
 expands for the full six months of the cycle,   15
  according to faithful accounts;

and then it moves on to the South
 in a given series of circles,
 reaching the place of night's extension
  for six months' dark—as the proofs   20

of astronomers show; and so
 the Creator is known in his aspects,
 a small part of His power in shown,
  a fraction of His strength and wondrous effect—

for the servant's greatness mirrors his master's
   to those discerning in knowledge—
   as the worker defines his castle's honor,
     for he holds the worth of his lord in his hand.

## XXIV

Who could make sense of creation's secrets,
of your raising up over the ninth sphere
   the circle of mind,
the sphere of the innermost chamber?

The tenth to the Lord is always sacred.

   This is the highest ring,
   transcending all elevation
     and beyond all ideation.

This is the place of the hidden
for your glory above in the palanquin . . .

You formed its frame from the silver of truth;
from the gold of mind you created its matter;
on pillars of justice you established its throne:
   its reality derives from your power;

   its longing is from you and for you,
   and toward you ascends its desire.

## XXVII

Who could accomplish what you've accomplished
in establishing under the Throne of Glory
   a level for all who were righteous in spirit?

This is the range of pure soul
gathered in the bond of all that's vital.
For those who've worked to exhaustion—
this is the place of their strength's renewal,
where the weary will find repose;
   these are the children of calm,

of pleasure that knows no bound in the mind:     10

    this is the World to Come;

a place of position and vision for souls
       that gaze
into the mirrors of the palace's servants,
    before the Lord to see and be seen.     15

They dwell in the halls of the king,

    and stand alongside his table,
      taking delight
in the sweetness of intellect's fruit
    which offers them majesty's savor.     20

 This is the rest and inheritance
that knows no bounds in its goodness and beauty,
    flowing with milk and honey.

    This is its fruit and deliverance.

## XXVIII

Who could uncover the things you've concealed
in fashioning chambers on high and their treasures,
    some too tremendous to speak of
    and others matters of valor—

    stores of life among them
    for those who lived in innocence;

    and also stores of salvation
    for those given over to penitence;

    and stores of sulfur and rivers of fire
    for those who break their covenant;     10

    and burning stores of gorge-like pits
      whose flames will never be smothered—
    where those abhorred of the Lord will descend;

    and stores of whirlwind and storm,
    of heavy clouds and blackness;     15

    of hail and ice, of drought and snow;
    of heat and flooding waters;

of smoke and rime and fog;
and gloom and thickened darkness.

20     All you prepare in its time
and employ for judgment or mercy—

for correction in a world you designed.

## XXIX

Who could grasp your intensity

in forming the radiance of purity
from the great glow of your glory,

from a rock the Rock has hewn,
from the hollow of a clearness withdrawn?

You sent the spirit of wisdom along it
and gave it the name of soul,
and formed it out of the fire
of intellect's ardor
whose spirit burned on inside it;

and you sent it out through the body
to serve it and guard it—

and you watch as it acts like a flame within it,
though the body isn't consumed.

It was formed from the spark of soul
and brought into being from nothing

when the Lord came across it in fire.

## XXXI

Who could return your goodness
in sending breath through the body
to invest it with life,

in revealing a way of life to guide it
and save it from evil's contrivance:

Out of the ground you formed it,
 and into the blood breathed soul—
and you sent the spirit of wisdom along it,
 which sets us apart from swine,
 and allows for ascent on high . . .

You've shut us inside your world,
while you look in from beyond and observe;

 and all that we try to conceal

 within or without you reveal.


## XXXIII

I'm ashamed, my God,
and abashed to be standing before you,
for I know that as great as your might has been,
 such is my utter weakness and failing;

as exalted as your power has been and will be,     5
 such is the depth of my poverty;
as whole as your perfection is,
 so is my knowledge flawed.

For you are one and alive;
almighty, abiding, strong and wise;     10

You are the Lord my God—
 and I am a clod of dirt and a worm;
dust of the ground and a vessel of shame;

 a speechless stone;

a passing shadow;     15

a wind blown-by that won't return;

a spider's poison;

a lying heart uncut for his Lord;

a man of rages;

a craftsman of scheming, and haughty,     20
 corrupt and impatient in speech,
perverse in his ways and impetuous.

What am I or my life?
What is my might and righteousness?
Throughout the days of my being I'm nothing
    and what then after I die?

I came from nothing and nothing pursue;

against instruction I come here before you
with insolence and impure notion—

and impulse that strays to its idols

and greed as it calls—

and a soul that hasn't been cleansed—
and a heart that's lost and alone—

and a body afflicted with swarms of desire
    ceaseless within their resistance.

## XL

I've known, my God, that those who implore you
have excellent action to speak for their fate
or virtue they've helped in creating,

while I have nothing—

am hollow and shaken out—

a ravaged vine,

and in me is neither
honor or what seems right;

affection or candor of heart;

not prayer and not supplication;

not purity, faith, or simplicity;

not fairness or honest measure;

neither repentance nor service.

Let it therefore be your merciful will,

my God and the God of our fathers,    15
Sovereign Lord of all worlds—

to be near and have mercy upon me;

to remember me in the call of your will;

to lift the light of your face across me,
and conceive for me your graciousness—    20

and not repay me for all I've done
and make me an object of scorn for the base,

or take me away in the midst of my days,

or obscure your face before me;

to cleanse me of all transgression—    25
not to cast me away from your presence;

to quicken my being with dignity,
and lead me into honor.

And then, when you withdraw me
from the life of the world we know,    30
    bring me to peace
in the life of the world-to-come,

and call me to rise;

place me among the righteous,
with men who among the living were summoned    35
    to life ever after;

and cleanse me with
the light of your countenance;
return me to life from the earth's depths

and on that day, as today, I'll say: Lord,    40

I'm grateful that when you were angry
you softened your wrath and took pity on me.

Loving-kindness is yours
in all the good you've done me,

45   and until I die will do. . . .

For all this I'm bound to thank you,
to glorify, laud, and extol you:

May you be praised in the mouth of creation
and be hallowed by words of sanctification;
50   be known as One by those
    who seek to know you in oneness;
be extolled by those who extol you
and lifted by those who would lift you
    up in song;

55   and may you be raised in the mouth of those who pray—

for among the gods none is like you,
and nothing, my Lord,
    compares with what you have done.

May the words of my mouth and my heart's meditation
60    before you be pleasing—

my rock—

and my redemption.

# YITZHAQ IBN GHIYYAT

## (1038–89)

Protected from the hot southern winds by a range of mountains and therefore cooler than much of southern Andalusia in summer, the town of Lucena—known both as "the city of the Jews" and "the city of song"—was famous for its fertile lands and thriving commerce, which included trade in slaves. It was also home to Spain's most important Hebrew academy, for many years headed by YITZHAQ IBN GHIYYAT. In temperament Ibn Ghiyyat was distant from the Arabized and progressive court of HaNagid, whose student he had been, and he was very much the moderate man devoted to the world of the synagogue and his religious community. He was highly regarded as a teacher and scholar, and was a key figure in the transmission of Hebrew learning in al-Andalus. Among his students were several important Hebrew poets, including Yosef Ibn Sahl, Yosef Ibn Tzaddiq, and Moshe Ibn Ezra. (Only the Talmud, religious law, and—to a certain extent—the Bible were taught at the academies, however; nonreligious subjects, including poetry, were pursued privately.) In his *Book of Tradition*, Avraham Ibn Daud says that Ibn Ghiyyat was well versed in "Greek wisdom" (the sciences), learning that found expression in some of his liturgical work—albeit with little of the grace and flair we encounter in Ibn Gabirol's *Kingdom's Crown*. Ibn Ezra notes that while Ibn Ghiyyat was, in his writing, more inclined than his predecessors to devotion, asceticism, lamentation, and mourning, he was less gifted than they were at metrical composition, perhaps because he was "weak in Arab wisdom," meaning literature. Still, says Ibn Ezra, his style was simple and clear.

Only a handful of Ibn Ghiyyat's secular poems have survived, but the body of his liturgical work is large, and many of his hymns were preserved in the prayer books of various communities and in the Cairo Geniza. On the whole, the hymns build on Ibn Gabirol's innovations; what was radical in one generation became standard practice in the next, particularly when it was taken up by respected figures such as Ibn Ghiyyat. Though much of Ibn Ghiyyat's liturgical work is conventional, the best of his *piyyutim*, particularly those that deal with Israel's relation to the nations of the world, capture—Schirmann suggests—the air of mystery and desire that often accompanies the congregation's middle-of-the-night recitations of penitential poems in the month leading up to the Days of Awe.

## MY WANDERING

I suffer in my wandering
　　and savor my dispersion,
and worship Him who drives me
　　and hope within despair.

Confinement is my pleasure,
　　I seek no end to censure,
I bear up through disquiet,
　　rejoicing in rebuke.
I give in to the bridle
　　and reins held by my foe—
　　　　delighting in misfortune,
　　　　　　joyful in affliction.
　　　　Torment and distress
　　　　　　are all my glory now.

The enemies of your Law
　　despise me without cause;
your covenant they slander;
　　they hound me with their god
to worship one beside you—
　　and I was nearly swayed.
　　　　But all my life I've turned
　　　　　　to you alone for strength;
　　　　I'll stand by what I am—
　　　　　　and not stray from my path.

My thoughts no longer seek
　　an end to tribulation;
my vision's gates are sealed,
　　there is no revelation.
My eyes no longer picture
　　the time of my salvation.
　　　　Foes amass before
　　　　　　the border of my home,
　　　　　　like thorns that pierce my side
　　　　　　　　when I fall in pain.

*"I will send up song,*
    *singing of redemption;*
*I'll return my love*
    *to Zion and appear.*
*Over all nations*
*in peace I'll place my chosen.*
        *My glory then they'll see*
            *adorn my house of prayer.*
        *I'll show them all my mercies*
            *and make my deliverance theirs."*

# YOSEF IBN SAHL

*(mid-eleventh century–1124)*

The small fraction of YOSEF IBN SAHL's work that has come down to us seems to bear out his friend Moshe Ibn Ezra's judgment that his poetry "joined extremes of firmness and sweetness, strength and grace" and that when he aimed his arrows at the enemies of poetry, "he made men laugh describing their ways, and gladdened their hearts revealing their lies." If not for his uncontrollable tendency toward the satire at which he excelled, says Ibn Ezra, he would have been among the front rank of men. In terms of talent, Schirmann implies, Ibn Sahl was one of the most important poets of his generation. His surprising poem about fleas is a relatively late discovery; it was found among the papers of the Cairo Geniza (alongside HaLevi's famous ode, "Won't You Ask, Zion?") and published in 1965. One of only five extant poems by Ibn Sahl, it shows the poet in a lighter mode that was still somewhat rare in the Andalusian matrix and may also give some indication of the satirical impulse Ibn Ezra notes. Three of his other surviving poems are addressed to Ibn Ezra (two are translated below) and there is also a single erotic poem. Born to a distinguished family in the second half of the eleventh century, Ibn Sahl studied in Lucena, where he was one of Ibn Ghiyyat's leading students. He died in 1124, in Cordoba, having served as a judge in that city's religious courts for the last ten years of his life.

## THE FLEAS

The fleas charge like horses at war—
    swoop in like birds to devour my skin;
they leap like goats and dance about,
    and in my bed keep me from sleeping.
I'm tired of hunting down large and small
    to wipe them out, for they know no fear—
like hard-hearted warriors charging in battle,
    they're spurred on as their brothers fall.

Although they're a little lazy by day,
    come night, like master thieves, they're ready;
and so I've loathed them always . . .
    and my hands weary of crushing them.
My flesh is covered with bright red buds
    that blossom daily from their bites.
Banish them, Lord, for I can't sleep:
    I'm fading fast—while they delight!!


## YOUR POEM, MY FRIEND

*(to Moshe Ibn Ezra)*


Your poem, my friend, is a necklace to scholars
    and its strictures painful correction to fools.
Rhymes have often been likened to pearls,
    but yours pay tribute to God, better still—
they lure the scoundrel without a hook,
    and leave no height where his heart had hills.


## A COMPLAINT ABOUT THE RICH

*(to Moshe Ibn Ezra)*


Has choice gold gone suddenly dim?
    Could precious gems lose their luster?
Poetry's rhymes are finer than jewels
    and pour forth now but have no buyer!
Has God made hearts too fat for wisdom?
    Or kept the rich man's eyes from seeing?
Daily he chases after lead,
    loading his empty chests with nothing—
despising song's crystal lines
    which hold more worth than all his wealth,

for they can tell the generations
    of grace and greatness after death.
How utterly foolish the idiot is—
    killing his spirit to fill his coffers.
He leaves his legacy to a stranger.
    His riches will not bring him honor.

# LEVI IBN ALTABBAAN

*(second half of the eleventh century)*

Saragossan Levi Ibn Altabbaan was primarily known as a grammarian, though Yehuda HaLevi has high praise for his poetry in several places. His younger friend Moshe Ibn Ezra refers to him as "the renowned teacher and exalted scholar," and he too counts him among the poets. In the early thirteenth-century Yehuda Alharizi writes that "[his] poems are greatly desired" and, playing on the consonants of his name, notes that he shook out lines of poetry as easily as the winnower of wheat shakes out piles of straw (*matben*). That said, Ibn Altabaan was extremely modest about his own gifts and may not have considered himself a "professional poet" in the classic secular mold. His single surviving secular work is a response to a poem by Ibn Ezra, who had written to complain about not having heard from him. In it he humbles himself before Ibn Ezra and admits that his own literary powers just can't compare to those of his friend: "If my soul trembles in the face of prose, / what hope could I possibly have of rhyme? // If I ascended poetry's altar, / my shame would surely be exposed." He was, it seems, more comfortable with a lower, plain-spoken register. The two liturgical poems that follow give some indication of his gentleness of spirit and piety.

## UTTER HIS ONENESS

Why wallow in blood, my soul,
    and writhe in pain for all your sins—
and pour out your heart like water before
    the Highest, riven with suffering?

Utter His oneness, morning and evening.
    And sing in praise of every living thing.

## EXPOSED

Bow before your God and go
   exposed and naked: soften his wrath.
Seek forgiveness for your wrongs,
   and let your tears pour forth like streams.

By day, my only one, and into the night—
so long as you breathe in me, bless His name.

# BAHYA IBN PAQUDA

*(second half of the eleventh century–first half of the twelfth century)*

About BAHYA IBN PAQUDA we know very little, apart from the fact that he lived in Muslim Spain and was probably a religious judge at Saragossa or Cordoba. He also composed *piyyutim*, including two long poems of petition and admonition that gained a considerable following. The short poem below comprises a verse abstract of Bahya's major prose work, the Muslim-influenced ethical treatise *Hovot HaLevavot* (Duties of the Heart), which he composed as a corrective to his predecessors, whom he felt had stressed religious observance—the duties of the body—at the expense of inwardness and the life of devotion. Bahya wrote his book in Arabic and placed this Hebrew poetic summary at its end; in 1161 Yehuda Ibn Tibbon rendered Bahya's prose into Hebrew. The translation enjoyed immense popularity, and *Duties of the Heart* is still widely read today.

## DUTIES OF THE HEART

Unite your soul with Him, my son,
declaring the Oneness of your Creator.

Gird yourself with justice and faith;
observe and seek out all His wonders.

Always keep His teaching and laws.
Fear God, so you won't falter.

Let your heart be firm, and hold
close to Him who'll be your savior.

Keep His precepts with the purest of hearts,
for Him alone—not for others.

See that all is dust, and know
you'll lie in dirt and clay. Be humble.

Fight off folly with understanding;
turn from the ways of your desire—

and through heart's wisdom take the path
of God—in your secret hour.

Put an end to childhood's whims;
release yourself from youth's pleasures:

and in your longing you'll see His face,
and be united with your Creator.

# MOSHE IBN EZRA

*(c. 1055 – after 1138)*

Balance, calm employment of ornament, clarity of presentation as well as emotion—these are the traits that characterize the poetry of the third major poet of the period, MOSHE IBN EZRA, who was often considered Andalusia's finest Hebrew craftsman. While lacking the spirit of innovation we find in the poetry of HaNagid and Ibn Gabirol, Ibn Ezra brings to his work such a thorough integration of Arabic and Hebrew literary elements that he has come to be considered the representative poet of the Spanish-Hebrew Golden Age. Often overlooked in this concentration on Ibn Ezra's technical and typical accomplishments, however, is the quietly personal aspect of his work; for the fusion of ethoi at the heart of his poetry acts in fact as ballast and keel against a deep and abiding melancholy. From his exquisite craft a distinctive, bittersweet tenderness emerges, one that is moving in its restraint, especially in his poems of exile. Ibn Ezra also excelled at short meditative lyrics and sensual verse, and he is highly regarded for his devotional poetry, where his blending of elements from the Jewish religious tradition and the secular Arabic literature of the age at times turns the latter inside out, transporting the reader, or worshiper, from a Bedouin desert encampment to a synagogue and place of deepest devotion.

Born in Granada to a family of Jewish aristocrats who had served that kingdom's Berber rulers, Ibn Ezra passed the first half of his adult life in comfortable surroundings in the city of his birth. The Granadan Jewish community rapidly recovered from the events of 1066, when the city's Muslim population rose up against Yehosef HaNagid, who had assumed his father's position as chief vizier to the Berber king but was, it seems, much less gifted and respected a leader. An Arabic chronicle of the day written by 'Abd Allah b. Buluggiin, the grandson of King Badiis, recalls Yehosef as a manipulative and selfish figure who sowed unrest and brought on his own downfall. He was assassinated, and in the riots and slaughter that followed, a large proportion of the city's Jews were killed (the precise numbers are hard to determine). The Ibn Ezra family may have taken refuge in Lucena, where Moshe studied under Ibn Ghiyyat. At some point after returning to Granada, Ibn Ezra was given the title *saahib al-shuurta* (chief of police), though the title was by then honorary alone. Like his relatives, however, he most likely held a position of distinction in the kingdom. He seems to have forged close ties with a number of poets and early on recognized the gifts of the young, northern-born Yehuda HaLevi, whom—it appears—he invited to

Granada. Ibn Ezra's Andalusian idyll ended in 1090, with the invasion of the reformist Almoravids from North Africa. His family fortune was confiscated, and his three brothers fled. For reasons that are still not clear, the poet himself remained behind with his wife and children. A few years later, again under mysterious circumstances (which may have involved a scandal of some sort with one of his female cousins), he was forced to abandon Granada and his family. He spent the rest of his life wandering in the Christian north, bemoaning the loss of his Andalusian world and its glories. Castile, Navarre, and their outer provinces represented for him a major step down on the cultural ladder. He felt himself to be surrounded by boors and suffered both materially and spiritually. Loneliness and complaint dominate these poems of the second half of Ibn Ezra's life, which are in many ways his most distinctive. He died sometime after 1138.

In addition to his large body of secular and religious poems, Ibn Ezra is the author of two prose works, both written in Arabic late in his life. The meandering, Neoplatonic *Maqaalat al-Hadiiqa fi Ma'ana l-Majaaz wa-il-Haqiiqa* (Essays in the Garden of the Figurative and Literal) deals with a variety of philosophical topics concerning the intersection of theology and figurative language. *Kitaab al-Muhaadara wa-al-Mudhaakara* (The Book of Discussion and Remembrance), which has been cited frequently in this anthology, is the only contemporary work that critically examines the Andalusian Hebrew poetry in belletristic (rather than, say, linguistic, or prosodic) fashion. Combining elements of a literary memoir, manual, biography, and meditation on the art of poetry, it comprises the poet's response to a friend in the Christian north who had asked him eight questions about the Hebrew verse of al-Andalus.

## WEAK WITH WINE

We woke, weak with wine from the party,
barely able to get up and walk
to the meadow wafting its spices—
    the scents of cassia and cloves:

and the sun had embroidered its surface with blossoms
    and across it spread a deep blue robe.

## THE GARDEN

All who are sick at heart, and whose cry is bitter:
    moan and sigh no longer.
Enter the garden of my poems and find
    balm for your sorrow, and joy in song.
Honey beside their taste is sour;
    their scent makes myrrh's the foulest odor.
Through them the deaf man hears, and speech comes to stammerers;
    the blind see and the lame race forth.
Men who grieve and despair in them rejoice—
    and all who are sick at heart and whose cry is bitter.

## BRING ME MY CUP

Bring me my cup when the shadows lengthen
    and the sun kisses darkness's hand,
and its face goes pale like a man who's ill—
    or a lover stricken by passion.

The wine will drive out legions of grief—
    although it's weak, and has no weapon.

## A SHADOW

Winter's cold has fled like a shadow—
the driving rain with its riders and troops;
and high in its circuit, the sun in the Ram
    now sits like a king at his feast.
The hills have put on turbans of blossoms,
the plain its robes of grasses and herbs,
wafting fragrances up to our faces,
    all winter they'd hidden within.

So pass the cup, which will raise my joy
and raze the grief that lies in my heart;
my tears will weaken its fire's flames,
    for anger burns in it still.
Fear fortune whose gifts are venom
mixed with a little nectar and sweetness;
deceive yourselves with its goodness by morning,
    then wait for reversal by dusk.
Drink through the day, until it turns
and the sun coats its silver with gold,
and by night until it flees like a Moor
    as dawn's hand grasps its heel.

## THE FAWN

As the cup rides his hand to his mouth,
    turn and look at that handsome fawn:
he raises it so to his face and I see
    the sun, being kissed by the moon.

## THE GARDEN, THE MISER

The world, my friend, has been remade,
and the garden beds live on after dying:
winter fed them its waters and dressed them
    in crimson and purple brocade.

The flowers rejoiced seeing the clouds
sending down their rain without end,
and swifts cry now over the treetops
    while turtledoves coo and moan.

To all this, friend, make haste—
the wine will soon drown our concerns . . .
and take what Time offers, but know
    that a miser's gifts are mistakes.

## THE PEN

The pen in the prince's hand, writing,
seems to be stitching and racing like lightning,

scattering flecks of myrrh over frost,
embedding its turquoise into white onyx—

until the book like a sapphire shines
and in the mind glows like the sun.

When it's thirsty it sucks at the nib for ink
to extend that embroidery's line through thinking,

and what it says flashes like fire
from God—and like a hammer shatters.


## HEART'S DESIRE

Heart's hope
   and delight of my eyes—
a fawn beside me,
   a cup in my hand:

Many have warned me,
   but I wouldn't listen;
come, my fawn,
   we'll overwhelm them;
Time will wear them away
   and death lead them down.
     Come, my fawn,
      come near and heal me,
    with nectar from your
     lips for which I've longed.

Why would they
   deny me your company,
as though I were being
   drawn toward sin?

5

10

15

If your beauty defeats me,
20      my Lord will be with me.
          Pay no attention
      to them who dissuade me.
      O my stubborn one,
          try me—come.

25  And so he was tempted
          and led me home,
      where he bowed his shoulder
          to the yoke of my burden—
      and all through the night
          I lay with him:
30          I stripped off all his clothes
              while he stripped mine;
          and from each other's
              lips we drank our wine.

      But once my heart
35          was trapped by his eyes,
      my trespass grew
          too great for him.
      His anger swelled
          and he complained,
40          rebuking me
              and shouting: *Stop!*
          *Enough now!*
              *You're forcing me . . .*

      Don't be so angry
45          with me, my fawn,
      that in your rage
          you nearly destroy me.
      Have mercy, my friend—
          just kiss me . . .
50          If living's what you
              have in mind, sustain me.
          But if it's death—
              be done and please just kill me!

## THAT BITTER DAY

That rash and bitter day of departure
   left me drunk with the wine of desire.
Desolate now, I dwell among mules,
where no one sees to the needs of my soul.

I call to the left—there is no answer,
then turn to the right and find—only strangers.

## LET MAN REMEMBER

Let man remember throughout his life
   he's on his way toward death:
each day he travels only a little
   so thinks he's always at rest—

like someone sitting at ease on a ship
while the wind sweeps it over the depths.

## THE DOVE

Why is that dove in the highest branches
   grieving now in a garden of spices?
His summer streams won't run dry,
   the palm tree's shade will always shield him,
and before him, in spring, his fledglings sing
   all the melodies he has taught them.
So cry, little bird, but cry for the man
   forced to wander. His sons are far.
He cannot tend their young. He sees
   no one who sees them—and sorcerers alone
can he consult. Sigh for his wandering,
   but do not bring your song to him:
Lend him your wings to fly to them
   and delight in the dust and stones of their land.

## WHY DOES TIME HOUND ME SO

Why does Time hound me so
   and wake to drive on the wandering sparrow?
Can a plundered man be plundered again?
   How could the humbled be brought any lower?
In distress it forced him up to the fortress
   where he sits alone on the rooftop now—
hearing only the wailing of jackals
   and owls mourning in sorrow below.
Before him the vulture enlarges its baldness;
   when it sees him grieving it cuts itself.
At night he lies with the constellations
   and beneath his footsteps clouds are crushed.
He's made to count the stars on high,
   or measure the vastness of heaven's breadth—
as he sighs for a land that holds no friend
   to offer him comfort, or lend him strength.


## ANCIENT GRAVES

Ancient graves weathered by time,
   where people now are sleeping forever:
they have neither hate nor envy within them;
   they know no love or fear of their neighbor.

And seeing them so, I couldn't discern
the difference between a slave and his master.

## IF YOU SEE ME

If you see me in my grave, my son,
  locked in a cell, a pit my home—
in a hole where no one goes or comes,
  held like prey in the claws of dust,
my face ravaged, its dignity gone,
  the worms like a mantle over my flesh—
you will not know then who I am,
  for darkness will have come through my skin.

How could my loved ones have been so distant
  and my brothers treated me like a stranger?
Like them, my sons have left me behind,
  as I abandoned my parents in anger.
They've only a while to live on earth;
  their fate tomorrow will be like mine:
they'll be devoured by death's first-born,
  their memory here on earth forgotten.
For a man who fathers a thousand children
  is just like one, in the end, who's barren.


## IVORY PALACES

Ivory palaces built on earth
  and mansions lined with galleries—
with marble columns on inlaid floors
  in spacious halls that filled with parties:
in a flash I saw them all as rubble
  and weathered ruins without a soul.

Where, now, are the nobles who dwelled there
  and the spirits of those who raised their walls?
What hope has a man whom the grave awaits,
  who's drawn down to the pit by his life,
as though the world were a flock of sheep—
  and Time its shepherd, and death his knife.

## THE WORLD

Men of the world have the world in their heart,
God set it in them when they were born—
it's a flowing stream that won't suffice
    though the sea becomes its source,

as though its water turned to salt
when a parched heart called out to them—
they pour it from buckets into their mouths
    but their thirst is never quenched.


## MY HEART'S SECRET

I seek the favor of the Lord alone
    and trust my heart's secret to no one.
What good is one man's strength to another?
What use to a wretch are the words of a pauper?

Scorn the World, which spurns her noblest,
    wearing thin the treasure she holds.
She's given birth to a pair of children:
the one in her belly is dead and gone—

on her back the other is dying.


## I ROUSED MY THOUGHTS FROM SLUMBER

I roused my thoughts from the deepest slumber
    to make my eyes' desire drowse,
and in my heart saw fleeting Time
    telling me what in time it would bring.
My mind told me wondrous things
    and set the marvels of my Rock before me.

It spoke of mysteries and exalted matters;
    until I thought the angels my neighbors
and saw, thinking, God Almighty,
    and knew the Lord Himself was within—      10

He whose essence is always hidden
    though shown to the mind's eye through His action.
Within my body He set a lantern;
    its glory guides my path to wisdom.
This is the light that has always shined      15
    through youth and with greater force as I aged,
and if it weren't from the source of His might,
    that light would weaken with time and fade.
With it I seek out wisdom's chamber
    and ladderless climb to the garden of pleasure;      20
my world beside it is nothing, for I
    will go where others before me have gone
and take the path my fathers followed,
    and rest where my elders came to rest.
For this the Lord will bring me to trial,      25
    and my actions will be both witness and judge.
Therefore I've turned from life in the world,
    which in its deceit increases malice,
and left it behind before it betrayed me
    and took off my shoe, and spat in my face.      30

Let it set the sun as a crown on my head,
    or make the moon my golden crescent—
Orion a bracelet around my wrist,
    its glowing children about me my necklace,
I will not come to desire its power,      35
    not for a home beyond the stars.
My longing instead is to lay my threshold
    near the threshold of learned men:
all I want is to move toward them,
    although my iniquity holds me back      40
among a people that does not know me;
    with whom I have no part or ease—
for when I greet them with kisses of peace,
    they say I hurt them with my teeth.

45 So I treasure the knowledge of those who are gone,
 with them alone I keep sweet counsel—
their books to my pain and grief are balm
 they're my choice companions, and faithful;
I swim in the sea of their minds and gather
50  pearls to adorn the neck of Time.
In them my heart and eyes rejoice,
 for them my lips in hymns sing out.
They're light to my eyes and the music I'd hear,
 and they're my palate's only sweetness.
55 Toward me like cinnamon's scent they rise
 and soon I will be lifted by them:
I'll dwell upon them as long as I live,
 for they're my hope, my source, my fountain.


## LET MAN WAIL

Let man wail whose years are consumed
and whose days have passed like smoke from a furnace,
 while his malice amasses like sand,
  and his guilt increases like locusts—

for his life is like a dream, and death his waking from it.


## ON THE DEATH OF HIS SON

### I

My heart went out seeing Jacob dead,
riding with men, held in their arms.
The world had seen nothing like it before:
 people—in earth—interring a star.

## II

I cry now for my soul's spirit—
whose home is suddenly set in the heavens,
and grieving for him, wish that I
   could, today, have died for my son.

## III

Before me the world is a binding seal,
and my home to me is a prison, my son.
After your death I'll go in fear
   no more of Time—for my terror has come.


## THE BLIND

The man whose eyes have dimmed but sees
   justice in his heart isn't blind;
the blind man is he who seeing scorns
his friends and brings them shame and trouble—
   until he resembles someone who flees
   the Lord our God for a wretched idol.


## THE GAZELLE'S SIGH

Hurry to homes of beloveds whom Time
   has scattered and left behind in ruins;
what once were the dwellings of graceful does
   are lairs now to lions and wolves.
I hear the gazelle's sigh and her wailing
   from Edom's prison, and Arabia's jail;
she weeps for the bridegroom of her youth
   and calls in pleasing song to Him:
"Sustain me with cakes of nuts and raisins;
   revive me with apples of your love."

## GOLD

Why is my beloved so haughty
   and why is He so angry with me?
Before Him why do I shake like a reed?
He's forgotten how I walked in the wilderness
after Him—and doesn't respond, though I plead.

If He kills me still I will trust in Him.
If He hides His face, to His goodness I'll turn.
The Lord's favor to His servant will not alter—
   for how could the finest gold go dim?


## THE DAY TO COME

From the day to come,
   and the fear of His being
like smoke from the furnace,
   His terror will rise.
His wrath will be grievous,
   and who could bear it—
for who will stand
   when He arrives?

Terror will shake
   the smug and complacent;
with death forgotten
   destruction will take them.
They'll lie there pleased
   when shouting will wake them—
their souls will depart
   and to dust they'll return.

This bitter day,
   like a burning kiln,
will rage like the sea,
   and like it turn;

and the foaming wine
   will confound the sober
and hasten their sleep
   which will last forever.

Blessed is he
   who sees in his mind
how the soul will leave
   the body behind
and in wonder ascend
   to Wisdom's Palace,
then with the righteous
   rest in peace.

## AT THE HOUR OF CLOSING

*Lord of wondrous workings,*
*grant us understanding—*
   *now at the hour of closing.*

A chosen few are called,
   their eyes toward you lifting—
they stand exalted in their trembling
   *now, at the hour of closing.*

They pour forth their souls;
   erase, then, their straying—
and grant them, Lord, your absolution
   *now at the hour of closing.*

Be a shelter for them
   through all their suffering;
consign them only to rejoicing
   *now, at the hour of closing.*

Show them your compassion,
   in your justice turning
on all who brought oppression to them—
   *now at the hour of closing.*

20   Recall their fathers' merit
        and count it as merit for them;
     renew their days as once they were,
        *now, at the hour of closing.*

     Call for the year of grace—
25      the remnant flock's returning
     to Oholìbah and Oholàh—
        *now at the hour of closing.*

# YOSEF IBN TZADDIQ

## *(c. 1070–1149)*

"A sage and a sage's son" is how Ibn Daud in his *Book of Tradition* characterizes YOSEF IBN TZADDIQ. About his life we know only that he was born to a family of considerable means and social standing, wrote—in addition to his poetry—at least one important work of philosophy (*Sefer 'Olam Qatan*, or Microcosmos), and was appointed to the Cordovan religious courts in 1138 as a judge, a position he held until his death in 1149. Moshe Ibn Ezra describes him as kind-hearted, gracious, and remarkably learned in matters of religious law. He maintained close ties with the leading figures of his day, including Yehuda HaLevi. Ibn Tzaddiq's friendship with Avraham Ibn Ezra is reflected in poems the two men exchanged about the delicate topic of the latter's wedding-night troubles. Some thirty-plus poems by Ibn Tzaddiq have come down to us, no doubt only a small part of his work, which was divided equally between secular and liturgical modes. Schirmann notes that more than a few of these can be considered among the finest works of the period. In particular, Ibn Tzaddiq excelled at the strophic *muwashshah*, and the fluid liturgical poem below ("Lady of Grace") is a good indication of why he was known as a master of that form. In the two poems translated here, the poet's human understanding of religious law and his knowledge of Neoplatonic philosophy, respectively, are embodied in the weave of the verse with subtlety, humor, and power.

## A WEDDING NIGHT'S CONSOLATION

Take up this poem and let it console you,
bridegroom of blood who resembles a ram
perched on a cliff above a stream,
     where its thirst can't be quenched.

Delight in the doe of your desire,
so beautifully formed and fine to behold;
look as you will, but do not touch her,
   look as you would to the stars.
Do not cross the border and spill
the blood of peace in the cause of war:
you're sad today, for the milk-like nectar
   in anger has started to rise—
but you'll be safe and secure outside her,
terror awaits you only within:
and the time will pass quickly as though
   it swept through your sleep in a dream.
Then you'll be able to do what you'd like,
freely and with the highest hand,
and all will know if your city is open
   or guarded still like a fortress—
and the day will come when you'll emerge
with the crimson clothes and salvation's dress.
My soul sighed at what it heard,
   longing for you like the sea,
distressed at the plight of my suffering brother
trapped among the high-place's priests—
he who is far away, although
   no wall divides him from me.
I remember now how we would be roused
over nothing, and needlessly—
may the Lord have mercy upon you, my brother,
   and lend you courage and might:
for when the power through you climbs,
it will lift you toward Orion's heights,
and then if you find what I have found—
   to console yourself, take up this poem.

# LADY OF GRACE

This lovely lady of grace
   is hidden from the eye—
try to fathom, masters of wisdom,
   how, and where and why.

Into the house of clay
   she descended taking on form,
and there she is concealed,
   held against her will—
bound, but not by a hand,
   sold, though not for coins,
      sent to till the body's ground,
         then sow it with glory and awe,
   and through the mind's devising
      to distance beast from man.

Your wonder's mystery grows—
   help us, Lord, to understand—
creation's strength combining
   gold and stone in man.
This is the crown of your labor—
   for what is straw to grain?—
      your hand's power joined
         my body to a soul,
   fashioning my figure
      from the dust and loam.

The lone soul seeks freedom
   from all that here enslaves her—
rest at last one day,
   release from all her labor.
For the soul herself lives on
   beyond the day of her departure,
      and, it seems, precedes
         the body that receives her—
      though she's condemned or called
         in keeping with her deeds.

35 Your glory is fallen manna,
  your word like honeyed nectar—
the might of all you've done
  bears witness to your grandeur.
Have mercy upon your people
40  in the house of prayer,
   for every mortal longs
    for you like a servant girl
   whose voice endlessly utters: Praise
   the One who forms all souls.

# SHELOMO IBN TZAQBEL

*(first half of the twelfth century)*

Rhymed prose had long existed in both Arabic and Hebrew literature, albeit in wholly independent traditions. Pre-Islamic Arabic literature made use of *saj'*, a nonmetrical mode that was employed by soothsayers and diviners for their incantations, and numerous parts of the Quran are also composed in a musical and powerfully cadenced prose employing variable rhyme. In the Hebrew tradition, liturgical poetry from Byzantine Palestine often contained passages of nonmetrical rhymed prose; the mid-eleventh-century Italian Byzantine historical chronicle *Megillat HaYuhasin* (or *Megillat Ahima'atz*) for example, employs rhymed prose throughout; and of course Ibn Gabirol's great poem *Keter Malkhut* makes magnificent use of *saj'*. It was only at the end of the tenth century, however, that the term *maqaama* was introduced into Arabic and that the literary genre of the rhymed-prose narrative took shape in its fictional mode, with a standard set of conventions that usually included a wandering narrator representing a given set of social ideals; a literarily gifted, mischievous, and socially marginal protagonist—often one who had fallen from grace and was almost always an itinerant beggar; and a loosely strung together recounting of the pair's adventures and the complex relation between them. In many ways the *maqaama* might be considered the forerunner of the picaresque novel. The term itself derives from the Arabic word for "place" (*maqaam*)—as in "place of assembly" or public gathering. In later Hebrew the *maqaama* is distinguished by its new narrative content, its artful literary style, its entertainment value, and the insertion of metrical lyric poems into the flow of the narrative itself. These poems, which are almost always in the classical monorhymed Andalusian style, serve to intensify a given element of the narrative and enhance its hero's standing by a display of his literary powers. Schirmann likens them to arias in an opera. In addition to their intensifying and illustrative functions, they provide pleasure on both the narrative and linguistic level.

SHELOMO IBN TZAQBEL is the author of the first Hebrew *maqaama*, *Mahberet Ne'um Asher Ben Yehuda* (The Book of Asher Ben Yehuda). This short tale, which is considered among the finest of its kind, tells of the bizarre experiences of its eponymous hero in his friend's harem. Courtship and notions of the cooked and the raw; desire, terror, titillation, and cross-dressing—all come together in this at-once realistic and fanciful story. Nothing is known about its author, apart from

142

the fact that he lived in Muslim Spain and wrote this *maqaama* along with one other (only fragments of which remain). The poems that follow are taken from various points in the narrative, as the hero is gradually drawn into the harem and toward the mysterious woman who, as the story opens, throws him an apple with a poem written across its skin.

### LINES INSCRIBED ON AN APPLE

You who race to hunt gazelles
across the herb-filled hills in flower—
know they're held behind high walls
in lavish cells, and secret chambers.


### NOTE TO A SUITOR NOW PERPLEXED

You who knock upon the door
I'd never barred to you before

but only to one who, erring, wasted
both my precious time and his:

If I open it—how could I forgive?
If I keep it closed, how could I live?


### A FAWN WITH HER LASHES

I'm a fawn who hunts with her lashes,
trapping valiant men with her snare;
so that the good receive their due,
I show my grace to those I'd spare.

# YEHUDA HALEVI

## (c. 1075–1141)

An unrivaled master of Hebrew and its prosody, YEHUDA HALEVI is perhaps the most famous and certainly the most revered of all the medieval poets. "The quintessence and embodiment of our country . . . our glory and leader, illustrious scholar, unique and perfect devotee," is how an 1130 letter from the Cairo Geniza describes him, and his reputation has faded little since. Born near the border between Christian and Muslim Spain (some say in Toledo, others Tudela, and still others neither of the two), HaLevi, it seems, traveled to Granada as a teenager, at the invitation of Moshe Ibn Ezra, whom he had impressed with a poem. The self-described "immigrant from Christendom" lived in the Muslim south for several years. By the time the North African Almoravids assumed control of Andalusia in 1090, bringing great hardship upon Andalusia's Jews, HaLevi had already begun to wander, and he lived, it seems, for a while under Almoravid rule in Seville, Lucena, or Cordoba. Like many other Andalusian Jewish refugees, he eventually made his way north to Castile, which was then ruled by the tolerant King Alfonso VI, who allowed Jews to take up the professions of their choosing and even participate in the administration of the kingdom. The beginning of the twelfth century finds HaLevi settled in Toledo. Earning a living as a physician, he attended to Castilian court circles, though the practice brought him little gratification: "I busy myself at an hour that is neither day nor night with the vanities of medicine," he wrote to a friend. " 'We heal Babel, but it is beyond healing' " (Jeremiah 51:9). He also engaged in trade and was active in Jewish communal affairs. Following the political murder in 1108 of the nephew of his Jewish patron, Yosef Ferrizu'el (Cidellus, or the Little Cid), who had been close to the Christian king, HaLevi became disillusioned with his situation at court. A few months later, when Alfonso himself died, anti-Jewish rioting broke out. What happened to HaLevi at this point is hard to say, but it appears that he left Toledo and again traveled from town to town before settling for a while in Cordoba with his wife and their daughter. Throughout these years he witnessed the devastation of Jewish communities by Christian and Muslim forces alike, and the events of his day shaped his emerging nationalist (or as Salo Baron has called it, "racialist") consciousness.

HaLevi is an important piece of the Spanish-Hebrew cultural puzzle not only for his achievements, which are major, but because in the course of his career he came to develop far-reaching reservations about the adoption of Arabic poetics and all they implied. By midlife he had rejected the Andalusian cultural ideal altogether, though he expressed that rejection through masterful employment of the Andalusian forms. "And don't be taken by Greek wisdom, / which bears no fruit, but only blossoms," he writes. More sanguine in temperament than any of the other major poets of the period, he seems to have kept at least the courtly dimension of his work as a poet in perspective. When Levi Ibn Altabbaan implied in a poem that he, HaLevi, was a dedicated professional poet who earned a living from his art, HaLevi replied: "If wisdom is like the expanse of the sea, / poetry's rhymes are its breakers' foam. / Writing isn't a wall to break through; / diversion for masters is the making of poems." A treatise he wrote on Hebrew meter c. 1129 shows him returning to essential questions about the Andalusian revolution that had been raised by Dunash's opponents at the beginning of the period. And in the last fifteen years of his life, even as he continued to compose in the classical Andalusian style, he began experimenting with an alternative poetics that would de-Arabize Hebrew verse and return it to exclusively Jewish sources.

In the summer of 1140, HaLevi set sail for the Holy Land, hoping to pray at Judaism's holiest places. (More than one scholar has suggested that he made his pilgrimage because Jewish life in the Holy Land, including perhaps the gathering of a group of priests to perform the cultic rites on the Mount of Olives, near the site of the former Temple, would—according to his worldview—have accelerated the redemption and brought about the revelation of the Shekhina.) Unable to free himself from the lure of the Andalusian modes, he engaged in an intensive final bout of composition on the sea and while wintering in Egypt, where he was regaled as a celebrity by the local literati and socialites, and also besieged by friends pleading with him not to risk the extremely dangerous journey to Crusader-held Palestine. All in all he spent some eight months in Alexandria and Fustat (Old Cairo), as he prepared for the second leg of his trip. Initially, it seemed, he was going to take the overland route through the desert, but when those plans were thwarted, he had to wait for the gentler spring winds that would carry him across the final stretch of the Mediterranean to the port of Acre, from which he would journey by land to Jerusalem. He was last heard from in a poem written aboard ship just outside Alexandria's port in mid-May of 1141.

His more conventional secular lyrics apart—some of which are quietly haunting—the poetry HaLevi wrote is prized for its fusion of a pure Hebrew lyricism and religio-historical concerns. It is, however, only when either crisis or loss enters his work that the secular poems rise to the level of major poetry—as in his poem of friendship to Moshe Ibn Ezra, his meditations on aging and the worth of his work in the world, and the sui generis poems he wrote on his journey away from Spain. Beyond that, some have argued that HaLevi's real greatness lies in his liturgical poetry, where his effortless command of the language comes into perfect conjunction with his subject. Throughout that sacred verse one feels the tremendous force of the poetry's currency and the spell of its fluency; at the same time, HaLevi's temperament lends his lines a combination of tranquility and clarity that is in many ways unique in the literature. Ironically, we find this most nationalistic of all the major medieval Hebrew writers incorporating Sufi or Shi'ite devotional elements, such as the notion of total surrender before the divine (*tawakkul*)—perhaps because he knew it would speak to his peers, but clearly because it spoke to him.

HaLevi is also the author of one of the period's major (and most widely read) works of prose, *The Book of the Kuzari: Defense of a Despised Faith (Kitaab al-Khazari: Kitaab al-Radd wa-l-Daliil fi l-Diin al-Dhaliil)*, which was written in Arabic and completed during the last decade or so of his life. Seeking guidance in matters of religion, a fictional Khazar king summons representatives of the three Abrahamic faiths, along with a philosopher, to present their beliefs to him. The king soon comes to the conclusion that the spokesman for rabbinic Judaism is the most convincing of the four, and the remainder of the book involves his asking questions that allow the Jewish representative to hold forth on the tenets of his faith. At the end, the Jewish scholar announces that he is leaving for the Holy Land. Recent readings of the book argue that its essential purpose was, as Ross Brann has put it, "to undermine the attachment to Sefarad among the culturally sophisticated Jews."

## THAT NIGHT A GAZELLE

That night a gazelle
    of a girl showed me the sun
of her cheek and veil
    of auburn hair,
like ruby over
    a moistened crystal brow,
she looked like dawn's
    fire rising—
reddening clouds with flames.

## A DOE WASHES

A doe washes her clothes
    in the stream of my tears
and sets them out to dry
    in the glow of her glory—

she doesn't need the spring's
    water, with my
two eyes, or the sun's
    rays with her splendor.

## IF ONLY DAWN

If only dawn would hurry along with the wind
    that kisses her lips and sways her form,
and if the clouds would carry my greetings to her—
    her heart just like her hips would soften.

My doe, who has chosen to dwell on high with the Bear,
    have mercy on one who would fly to a star.

## THAT DAY WHILE I HAD HIM

That day while I had him on my knees
    he saw himself there in my eyes and tried
to trick me. He kissed them ever so lightly—
    kissing himself, not me. . . .

## ANOTHER APPLE

You bound me, doe of delight, in your beauty
    and in that captivity worked me ruthlessly.
Since parting came between us that day,
    nothing I've seen has matched your grace.

And so I turn to an apple for succor
  whose fragrance recalls your breath like myrrh—
its shape, your breast, and its color the flush
  that races through your cheeks when you blush.


## TO IBN AL-MU'ALLIM

Gently, my hard-hearted, slender one,
be gentle with me and I'll bow before you.
I've ravished you only in looking—
my heart is pure, but not my eyes:
They'd gather from your features
the roses and lilies mingled there.
I'd lift the fire from your cheeks
to put out fire with fire,
and then when I was thirsty,
it's there I'd look for water.
I'd savor the lip that glows like ruby—
like coals in the tongs of my jaws.
My life hangs by scarlet threads;
my death is now concealed in dusk. . . .
I find that nights have no end,
where once no dark divided my days:
For Time then was clay in my hands
and Fortune—the potter's wheel.


## IF ONLY I COULD GIVE

If only I could give
  myself in ransom for that fawn
who served me honeyed wine
  between two scarlet lips . . .

I think of all that pleasure
    the best of months gone by,
a time when in my arms
    the sun's brother would lie;
my chalice was his mouth—
    I drained its ruby dry.
        And love's hand between us
        sustained me in my love;
        love's hand brought us near
        and never did me harm.

The blame then is mine,
    not his who stole my heart,
and yet my pain was great
    the day that I departed
from his tents despite
    his pleas that I stay on.
        But Time's thread led me out,
        and onward to another;
        Time despised me so,
        it saw to my departure.

The Red Sea, my friends,
    was parched beside my weeping,
and for my heart, my eyes
    had not the least compassion,
from the day my footsteps
    fell on foreign soil . . .
        Sorrow in my eye
        formed a second sea—
        I feared that it would drown me
        and no one pull me free.

In David I forgot all this,
    and thinking of his favors,
I offer up these verses
    a necklace in his honor,
rebuking Time, which hounds me,
    increasing now my power.

My sword grows drunk with Time's
    blood which leaves me thirsty—
Time would drive me out,
    but clearly doesn't know me.

A dove nesting there
    in the myrtle now is watching,        45
as I prepare my song,
    as I complain of Time;
her voice gently calls—
    like a girl who's singing:        50
        *In the end I'll win—*
            *loving once was fun;*
        *leave Time to Ibn*
            *al-Dayyeni's son.*

## EPITHALAMIUM

The stars of earth are joined today—
a pair unrivaled in the hosts of heaven.
Even the Pleiades envy this union,
for breath itself can't come between them.

The light of the East has reached the West
and among its Many has found the One.
Above us he spread a canopy of grace—
set for them, like a tent for the sun.

## WHEN A LONE SILVER HAIR

When a lone silver hair appeared on my head
    I plucked it out with my hand, and it said:

"You've beaten me one on one—
    but what will you do with the army to come?"

## IF TIME

If Time today provides you with shelter,
know it can also become your snare.
The arrow's aided by feathers from wings
that guided the eagle as it glided through air.


## INSCRIPTIONS ON BOWLS

### I

Handsome one, open your eyes and see
this fine piece of meat on which you should chew—
before it's noticed and eaten up
   by the person sitting beside you.

### II

Brother of kindness—whose hands stretch out
to guests like a cloud with your bounty:
fill me with food to warm their hearts—
   for they're extremely hungry.


## FOUR RIDDLES

### I

Evincing the infinite—
   the size of your palm—
what it holds is beyond you,
   curious, at hand.

### II

What's slender, smooth and fine,
and speaks with power while dumb,
   in utter silence kills,
and spews the blood of lambs?

### III

What's cast dead to the ground
    and buried naked with dung,
then comes to life in its grave,
    giving birth to fully clothed young?

### IV

What cries without an eyelid or eye
    and weeping makes all glad—
and when it's happy, and sheds no tears,
    with joy makes men sad?


## DEPARTURE

Night, be long and linger
    before my friends' departure:
gently spread your black
    wing across the glow
of dawn—and turn, tears,
    to rain to keep them from going.
Heart's grief, cloud
    the sky with dark so they'll
not see the light of morning.
    May my sighs then stir
the sun's flames to strike them—
    until at last they fathom
that they can leave my tents
    only once I've blessed them.

## ON FRIENDSHIP AND TIME

*(to Moshe Ibn Ezra)*

We've known you, parting, ever since we were young,
    and the river of weeping that runs between us is ancient.
What good would it do to fight against blameless Fortune,
    or quarrel with days, when they have done no wrong?
5    The heavens' spheres race along fixed courses,
    and nothing on high ever departs from its path.
Could this be news—when nothing new comes into
    a world whose laws are drawn by the hand of God?
How could its ways be blamed by us or altered,
10    when all is sealed with a signet worn by the Lord,
when each beginning circles back as an end,
    and everything under the sun has already been?
Men are brought together, but only to part,
    to yield from a single nation manifold nations:
15    earth's peoples would never have scattered across it
    if humankind had not known separation.
A thing can sometimes bring both good and harm:
    one man's potion in another's bones is poison;
men fly into a rage, cursing the day,
20    detesting each of its doomed and loathsome moments,
while elsewhere others that instant are counting their blessings,
    passing the hours in perfect peace and contentment.
Food in the mouth of a healthy man is honey;
    honey on the tongue of the sick is bitter as broom.
25    Lights go dark in the eyes of one who is troubled—
    they shine on, but he can't see through the gloom—
like mine on the day a dark cloud descended
    and Moshe left, as streams began to fall
for one who was always a fountain of wisdom for me,
30    in whose words I'd found a mine of gold.
Friendship bound my soul inside his soul,
    while parting's chariots stood at a distance unharnessed.
Fate was with us in fullness of spirit then—
    and I had yet to know departure's pain.

Though destiny brought us into the world in division,    35
   love in her household raised us together as twins,
and we grew up by beds of the sweetest spices,
   at the breast of the vine's daughter drinking our fill.
I think of you here on hills that now divide us—
   beside you once, they were mountains of herbs—    40
and with that memory, my eyelids start to moisten,
   and my eyes redden, flushed with the blood of love.
All that comes back to me . . . the years we passed
   living as if we were one inside a dream,
till Time betrayed me, and in your stead sent men    45
   who spoke of peace, but planned only for war.
I'd speak with them and find in all they said
   your precious manna replaced by garlic and straw.
Anger within me rose facing these fools—
   who put on airs as though they were truly wise:    50
challenged, they called their fraud and fickleness faith,
   and mocked my faith as a casting of spells and lies.
And so they sow and harvest their meager crop,
   taking delight in their blasted and shriveled corn—
forgetting that wisdom's exterior often resembles    55
   a vessel of clay holding precious stones.
But I have lamps to search the innermost chambers,
   and from these hidden places lift out gems;
I will not rest until I've seen their sheaves
   in their wisdom bowing down to mine.    60
I'll say to boors who seek to know the mysteries:
   What good are golden rings in the snouts of swine?
Why should I press my clouds to drop their rain
   on seedless land, whose fields have not been plowed?
My soul's need of Fortune in fact is slight,    65
   like spirit's need for bodies God designed:
so long as they contain it, it fills them with life—
   but when they weary, like husks they're left behind.

## SLAVES OF TIME

The slaves of time are slaves of a slave,
    only the servant of the Lord is free;
therefore, as others seek their portion,
    "My portion," says my soul, "is with Thee."

## HEAL ME, LORD

Heal me, Lord, and I will be healed.
    Don't let me perish in your anger.
All my balms and potions are yours
    to guide to weakness or to vigor.

It's you alone who chooses, not me;
    you know best what's flawed and pure.
It isn't my medicine on which I rely—
    I look instead toward your cure.

## TRUE LIFE

I run to the source of the one true life,
turning my back to all that is empty and vain.
My only hope is to see the Lord, my king—
    apart from Him I fear and worship nothing.

If only I might see Him—at least in a dream—
I'd sleep forever, so the dream would never end.
If I could see his face in my heart's chamber,
    I'd never need to look outside again.

## THE MORNING STARS

The morning stars sing out to you,
for their glory and splendor derive from yours;
and the angels of God stand guard above them,
forever exalting the name of their Lord.
   And the holy assembly follows in turn,
   rising to reach your house at dawn.


## HIS THRESHOLDS

Seek the Lord and His thresholds, my soul:
   offer your songs like incense before Him.
For if you're pursuing the vapors of Time
   and calling their spells and sorcery Truth,
and roaming in search of them night and day,
   and sleeping sweetly after their feasts—

know that your hand holds nothing at all
   but a tree whose branches soon will wither.
Be before your God and King,
   beneath whose wings you've come for shelter.
Let His name be hallowed and praised
   by all through whom His breath still moves.


## WHERE WILL I FIND YOU

Where, Lord, will I find you:
your place is high and obscured.
   And where
     won't I find you:
your glory fills the world. . . .

I sought your nearness:
with all my heart I called you.
And in my going
out to meet you,
I found you coming toward me.


## YOU KNEW ME

You knew me long before you formed me,
and while your spirit is in me you guard me.
Can I stand if you choose to drive me away?
Can I move if you choose to stop me?
What could I say? My thoughts are yours.
What can I do until you help me?
I seek you now in an hour of grace:
Set your favor as a shield about me.
Rouse me to seek out your holy shrine.
Wake me—to bless your name.


## A DOE FAR FROM HOME

That graceful doe so far from her home
is laughing although her beloved is angry.
Her laughter's aimed at the daughters of Edom
and Hagar—who long for him with envy.

How could desert asses compare
to a doe who leaned once on her hart?
Where are their prophecies? Where is their lamp?
Where is His Presence above the Ark?

Don't seek, my foes, to smother this love,
whose flame your envy only fans.

## A DOVE IN THE DISTANCE

A dove in the distance fluttered,
   flitting through the forest—
     unable to recover
she flew up, flustered, hovering,
   circling round her lover.           5
     She'd thought the thousand
years to the Time of the End
   about to come, but was
     confounded in her designs,
and tormented by her lover,          10
   over the years was parted
     from Him, her soul descending
bared to the world below.
   She vowed never again
     to mention His name, but deep      15
within her heart it held,
   as though a fire burning.
     Why be like her foes?
Her bill opens wide
   toward the latter rain          20
     of your salvation; her soul
within her faith is firm,
   and she does not despair,
     whether she is honored
through His name or whether      25
   in disdain brought low.
Let God, our Lord, come
   and not be still: Around Him
     storms of fire flame.

## YOU SLEPT, THEN TREMBLING ROSE

You dozed and slept, then trembling rose:
    What is this dream that you have dreamed?
Perhaps the vision showed you your foes,
    weakened and humbled, with you supreme?
Tell Hagar's son: Draw in the hand
    you raised in pride and anger over
Sarah's child—for I've seen you shamed.
    Maybe on waking you'll be ruined,
and the year of the crushing end will come
    to bring down all your grand designs—

you who were called a wild ass
    of a man—then honored for your power;
you whose mouth had spoken of greatness,
    who fought against the heavens' saints—
the creature whose feet were made of iron
    and clay, to be raised at the end of days.
Perhaps He'll strike with havoc's stone,
    and you'll be paid—for all you've done.


## LOVE'S DWELLING

From time's beginning you were love's dwelling;
    wherever you dwelled, my love would rest.
My rivals' taunts are sweet through your Name:
    they torture one whom you have tortured,
and because they learned their wrath from you
    I love them for hounding one you've stricken.
Since you scorned me I've scorned myself,
    for how could I honor what earns your disdain,
until—indignation passes . . . and you send
    redemption to a people you once redeemed.

## LORD,

all my desire is here before you,
    whether or not I speak of it:
I'd seek your favor, for an instant, then die—
    if only you would grant my wish.
I'd place my spirit in your hand,                    5
    then sleep—and in that sleep find sweetness.

I wander from you—and die alive;
    the closer I cling—I live to die.
How to approach I still don't know,
    nor on what words I might rely.                  10
Instruct me, Lord: advise and guide me.
    Free me from my prison of lies.

Teach me while I can bear the affliction—
    do not, Lord, despise my plea;
before I've become my own burden                     15
    and the little I am weighs on me,
and against my will, I give in
    as worms eat bones that weary of me.

I'll come to the place my forefathers reached,
    and by their place of rest find rest.            20
Earth's back to me is foreign;
    my one true home is in its dust.
Till now my youth has done what it would;
    When will I provide for myself?

The world He placed in my heart has kept me          25
    from tending to my end and after.
How could I come to serve my Lord,
    when I am still desire's prisoner?
How could I ask for a place on high,
    when I know the worm will be my sister?          30

How at that end could my heart be glad,
    when I do not know what death will bring?
Day after day and night after night
    reduce the flesh upon me to nothing.
35  Into the winds they'll scatter my spirit.
    To dust they'll return the little remaining.

What can I say—with desire my enemy,
    from boyhood till now pursuing me:
What is Time to me but your Will?
40    If you're not with me, what will I be?
I stand bereft of any virtue:
    only your justice and mercy shield me.

But why should I speak, or even aspire?
    Lord, before you is all my desire.


## IF ONLY I COULD BE

If only I could be
    a slave to God who made me;
though others drive me away,
    He always draws me near.

5  My shepherd, my creator,
    you formed my frame and soul,
you've understood my mind,
    you've seen all that it holds.
You circumscribe my ways,
10    my wandering and repose.
    If you came to help me,
      who could cast me down?
    And if you hold me back,
      who would set me free?

15  My heart within me yearns
    to have you draw it near,
but all my cares just drive it
    further from you still.

My road, now, has turned
   far from your own will.       20
      Lord, my God, instruct me,
         guide me on your path,
     and lead me gently into
        judgment: don't condemn me.

If I, within my youth,       25
   am slow to bring you pleasure,
what then in decline
   could I expect or hope for?
Heal me, Lord, heal me—
   my cure's with you alone.       30
      When old age roots me out
        and strength no longer knows me—
      My Rock, O my Lord,
        please, do not forsake me.

Abject and weak I'll sit,       35
   at every moment trembling,
naked, I'll go stripped,
   vain in my delusion,
bruised within my sin,
   wounded in transgression.       40
      Between us now my trespass
        has raised a great divide,
     and so I'm kept from seeing
        your light with my own eyes.

Incline my heart to offer       45
   in service of your kingdom,
and purify my thoughts
   to bring me toward your heaven.
In my hour of pain
   come quickly with your healing.       50
      Hear me, now, my Lord,
        don't withdraw or hurt me.
      Redeem me once again—
        and tell me: *Here I am.*

# WON'T YOU ASK, ZION

Won't you ask, Zion,
　　how your captives are faring—
this last remnant of your flock who seek
　　your peace with all their being?
From west and east, from north and south—
　　from those near and far,
from all corners—accept these greetings,
　　and from desire's captive, this blessing.
He offers his tears like dew upon
　　the slopes of Galilee's mountain
and longs to shed them upon your hills.
　　I wail like a jackal for your affliction,
but when I dream of your captives' return
　　I am a lute to your songs and hymns.
My heart yearns for the Lord's home,
　　for Peniel, and Mahana'im,
all the places where your pure ones appeared—
　　there the Lord's Presence dwelled,
and He who formed you opened your gates
　　and the glory of God alone was your beacon:
you needed neither the sun nor moon.
　　Where God's spirit came to your chosen
I'd pour out before you my spirit and soul—
　　for you are the kingdom's sacred foundation,
the threshold and house of God, my Lord,
　　though slaves now sit on your princes' thrones.
If only I could wander where
　　He was revealed to your heralds and seers.
Who would make me wings to go there?
　　I'd take my broken heart to your hills,
and fall, my face to your ground, with desire
　　delighting in your dust and stones.
How much more when I reach Hebrón
　　and the cave and tombs of my fathers!

I'd pass through your forests and fields;                              35
    in Gilead I would stand astonished,
on Mount Abarim and also Mount Hor
    where the two great lights taught and shone.
Your air is life to my soul, your dust
    sweeter than myrrh—your rivers are nectar.                        40
Walking barefoot over the ruins
    of your shrine, naked, would be my pleasure,
there where your ark of the law was hidden
    and the cherubs lay in your innermost chamber.
I'd cut off my hair and give up its glory,                            45
    and curse Time that deigned to defile
your saints in the holy land it profaned.
    How could eating and drinking please me
when dogs are dragging about your lions?
    How could the light of day be sweet                               50
when I see your eagles in the beaks of ravens?
    Let grief's cup be gentle with me,
let it be poured out more slowly—
    for suffering has already come to fill me.
For Oholáh, I drink down your wrath;                                  55
    with Oholíbah, I reach your dregs.
Zion, perfection of beauty,
    bound in love and the Lord's mercy,
as your souls' assembly to you were bound—
    they who were happy in your peace,                                60
then came to grief over your ruin
    and now bewail your devastation.
From captivity's well they've striven to reach you
    and bow at your gates, each in his fashion.
The flocks of your masses in exile scattered,                         65
    although your walls were not forgotten.
Those who clung to your robes strove
    to climb and touch your palm tree's branches.
Could Shinar and Patros stand by your signs?
    Could their vanity ever match your greatness?                     70
Who could be likened to your anointed?
    Who to your singers and prophets and priests?
The kingdoms of idols will utterly vanish;
    your wealth is forever, your crown endures.

You've sought to be a throne for your Lord—
    and happy are they whose place is secure,
who draw near to dwell in those courts.
    Happy is he who waits and reaches
then watches your light ascend as dawn
    breaks across his body and soul
and, as your chosen people flourish,
    rejoices—in your joy at your youth restored.


## MY HEART IS IN THE EAST

My heart is in the East—
    and I am at the edge of the West.
How can I possibly taste what I eat?
    How could it please me?
How can I keep my promise
    or ever fulfill my vow,
when Zion is held by Edom
    and I am bound by Arabia's chains?
I'd gladly leave behind me
    all the pleasures of Spain—
if only I might see
    the dust and ruins of your Shrine.


## HOW LONG WILL YOU LIE

How long will you lie asleep in childhood's dream?
    Know that youth like chaff will be cast off.
Could the black hair of boyhood last forever?
    Rise, see how the silver heralds rebuke you.
Shake off Time, as birds shake off the dew
    and damp of night. Soar and glide like a swallow
to freedom from falseness, and days that rage like seas.
    Pursue your King, at one with the souls' assembly—
which glows and towards His goodness and bounty streams.

## HEART AT SEA

Are you still chasing youth past fifty,
    your days about to take wing—
as you turn from the service of God
    and yearn for the service of men?
Would you leave the One within reach         5
    of all and seek out the Many?
Slow to prepare for your journey,
    would you sell your share for stew?
Hasn't your soul been sated
    with wanting that's always renewed?     10
Leave its counsel for God's—
    and from your senses keep far;
try to appease your Creator
    with your dwindling hours,
but don't let heart deceive you,         15
    or seek out charms and spells.
Be like a lion to please Him
    and swift as a young gazelle—
your heart at sea won't fail
    though mountains crumble and fall,     20
and the sailors' hands grow weary,
    as the soothsayers all go still.
Journeying east they're happy;
    turning back they're ashamed.
The ocean alone is your refuge;         25
    you have nowhere to turn,
as sails flap and flutter
    and the planks move swiftly along,
and the winds toy with the water,
    like threshers of wheat with straw.     30
Now they flatten it out—
    now it's raised in heaps.
Mounting it looks like a lion;
    receding it writhes like snakes.

<sup>35</sup> Without a charmer the latter
    pursues the former and kills;
and the ship nearly topples
    with weakening masts and sails.
Decks and compartments rattle,
<sup>40</sup>    stacked within the hull.
Men pull at the ropes
    in pain, while others are ill.
Sailors are wounded by wind;
    bodies give up souls.
<sup>45</sup> The mast's might is useless,
    the veteran's wiles as well.
The cedar poles are like straw;
    the cypress snaps like a reed.
Ballast of iron and sand
<sup>50</sup>    is tossed about like hay,
and all pray in their way—
    but you turn to the Lord,
remembering how He parted
    the Jordan and Moses' Sea,
<sup>55</sup> extolling Him who stills
    the waves that toss up mire—
recalling your purity's merit,
    as He recalls your fathers'.
His miracles he renews,
<sup>60</sup>    and you the Levites' song—
as spirit returns to flesh,
    and life to your dry bones.
The water then grows still,
    like flocks of sheep on hills,
<sup>65</sup> and the sun goes down as night
    ascends with its hosts and moon—
a dark woman wearing
    a gown of violet and gold.
Stars in the currents stray,
<sup>70</sup>    like exiles driven from homes;
their image is there in the light,
    in the heart of the sea, ablaze,

as the water's surface and sky
    shine like polished gems.
The abyss looks just like the heavens,       
    the two great seas are bound—
and my heart, a third, between them,
    pounds with waves of praise.


## MY SOUL LONGED

My soul longed for the house of assembly
and trembled as fear of leaving came through me;
but the heavens conspired to ease my departure,
    and I found His name in my heart to help me.

Therefore I'll offer Him thanks with each step,
and bow before Him the length of the journey.


## HAS A FLOOD WASHED THE WORLD

Has a flood washed the world to waste?
    Is there no dry land at all to be seen?
No man, no beast, no bird of the air?
    Have all perished, lain down in pain?
The sight of a hill or reef would comfort me,
    a stretch of empty desert delight me.
I gaze in every direction around us—
    nothing but ship and sky and sea,
as Leviathan churns the deep and it seems
    white hair sprouts across the abyss.
The sea's heart turns on the craft—
    pouring its waters across its boards;
and the waves rage as my soul rejoices,
    nearing the sacred shrine of her Lord.

## IN THE HEART

I tell the heart in the heart of the seas,
 as the pounding waves bring on its fear:
If your faith is firm in the Lord who made
 the sea—whose name endures for eternity—
the deep won't frighten you with its swells,
 for He who sets its bound is near.

## ABOVE THE ABYSS

Heart sinking, knees buckling, I cry
 out to God, fear coursing through me:
astonished oarsmen and sailors—helpless above
 the abyss—feel their hands failing them,
and I there on the deck of the ship in the winds
 as well, between sky and sea, dangling—

stagger and reel. . . . But all this is nothing—
beside the way I'll dance within you, Jerusalem.

## TIME HAS TOSSED ME

Time has tossed me toward Egypt's deserts,
 but tell it to hurl me further and turn
until I see the desert of Judah
 and reach that gentle northern land.
I'll wrap myself there in His name's glory,
 and beneath His sanctity's crown I'll whirl.

## BE WITH ME

At Zo'an be with me, on the mountain and sea,
 and I'll turn toward Shiloh and the shrine in ruin,
and follow the path of the covenant's ark,
 and kiss the honeyed dust of its tomb.

I'll see the fair one's forgotten nest,
 where doves were banished—and crows now rest.


## ALONG THE NILE

Has Time taken off its clothes of trembling,
 and donned its finest gown and jewels?
Is earth now wearing robes of linen,
 richly woven and threaded with gold?
The land along the Nile is checkered,     5
 as though with the priestly breastplate and vest,
and the desert oases are carpets of color;
 Ramses and Pithom in bronze are decked.
Girls wander beside the river
 just like does of gazelles but slower—   10
their hands weighed down by bracelets of brass,
 their gait constrained by bangles and anklets.

The heart, forgetting its age, is lured
 and finds itself thinking of Egypt's Eden,
its young there by the river's gardens,    15
 along its banks, and across its fields,
where the wheat has turned a reddish gold,
 as though it too had been dressed in robes,
and a breeze from the sea ripples across it,
 so it seems to be bowing—in thanks to the Lord. . . . 20

## THIS BREEZE

This breeze of yours is scented, West—
    its wings are fragrant with apple and balm;
you've clearly come from the spice-traders' chests
    and not from the heavens' stores of wind.
You spread the feathers of birds, and free me,
    like scent wafting from purest myrrh.
We've all longed and waited for you,
    prepared to ride the sea on a board,
so do not lift your hand from the sails,
    whether the day declines or dawns,
but pound the deep and rend its heart
    until you've reached the holy hills,
rebuking the East and its gales which cause
    the sea, like a cauldron, to swell and seethe.
But what could one do, held back by the Lord,
    bound today and tomorrow released?
My prayer's answer is in His hand—
    who forms the mountains, and fashions the wind.

# PART TWO

# Christian Spain and Provence

## C. 1140–1492

# AVRAHAM IBN EZRA

*(c. 1093–c. 1167)*

With the departure of Yehuda HaLevi for the Land of Israel and, several years later, the first wave of invasions by the North African Almohads, the Golden Age of Hebrew literature in Andalusia for all practical purposes comes to end. Its spirit, however, does not; instead, it moves north with many of the Jewish refugees from Muslim Spain and continues to develop, albeit along different lines, in Christian Spain and Provence. One of the most important transmitters of that Andalusian heritage was AVRAHAM IBN EZRA, who is sometimes considered a fifth major poet of the Spanish-Hebrew Golden Age. His astonishing life and literary production fall into two distinct parts. We know very little about the first, aside from the fact that he was born sometime between 1090 and 1093, in Tudela—then a border town of Muslim Spain with a large Christian population—and that he passed most of the next fifty years in the south and Toledo. (He was not related to Moshe Ibn Ezra.) While much of Ibn Ezra's work from that period has been lost, he apparently wrote many poems for patrons and friends in the conventional Andalusian modes and considered himself a professional poet. We know that he befriended Yehuda HaLevi at some point, perhaps in Toledo, or Cordoba, where they both settled, and he appears to have spent a good deal of time with the older poet, at one point even traveling with him to North Africa. His son would eventually marry HaLevi's daughter and then leave Spain with his father-in-law.

It is the work of this post-Spanish period that made Ibn Ezra's reputation. Sensing, Schirmann suggests, the imminent threat to Jewish life in Spain as he had known it, he made up his mind: by 1140, he was in Rome, where in a foreword to his commentary on Ecclesiastes he wrote: "And from his home / in Spain he fled, / descending to Rome, / his soul afraid." In another commentary he noted the persecution that he'd faced in Spain, most likely under the Almoravids: "Oppressors have driven me out of Spain." And in response to the Almohad invasion of the mid-1140s—word of which reached him in France—he wrote one of the most explicit elegies in the literature for the lost communities of Andalusia and North Africa. ("Lament for Andalusian Jewry," below.) Over the next twenty-seven years Avraham HaSefaradi (the Spaniard), as he usually called himself, earned his living by writing for the edification of Jewish communities in North Africa, Italy, Provence, northern France, and even England, where some scholars believe he died in either 1164 or 1167. (Others say he died in France or in Italy, and some suggest that he returned to Spain.) Working in Hebrew rather than Arabic—which the Jews of these northern and Mediterranean communities did not know—he composed some one hundred volumes on mathematics, astronomy, philosophy, poetics, and philology. He also translated a great deal of scientific work (treating medicine, physics, and the natural sciences) from Arabic into Hebrew and wrote a large body of innovative biblical commentary, which remains to this day among the most important of its kind.

Ibn Ezra's poetry is equally wide ranging and on the whole is distinguished by its introduction of a vivid realism into the literary matrix. Stripped of the trappings and comforts of the Jewish courts of Spain, the itinerant Ibn Ezra took his knowledge out into the world, where he faced the trials of the medieval open road. As a result of that encounter, the thematic axis of his poetry shifts, and its tone and register change as well. In addition to his elegy on the lost Andalusian communities, his newly diverse subjects include chess, flies, his torn coat, his rotten luck, his offended honor, and the presence of God in the world. In his secular poetry—which has yet to be gathered in a critical volume—a new plainspoken, humorous, and even self-ironizing voice emerges. Far from involving a decline or degradation of the Andalusian modes, Ibn Ezra's work shows him to be, as one scholar has put it, "a great rebel" who sought to save Hebrew poetry from sinking into spiritual and formal epigonism. He left behind a vast body of sacred verse and is often described as the last great liturgical poet of the age. Perhaps the most philosophical of all the Hebrew liturgical poets, he merged meditation and devotion, while also excelling at devotional verse in a more plain-spoken register that reflected some of his innovations on the secular side of the ledger. In his secular and sacred work alike, he was, first and foremost, a poet of exile.

## FORTUNE'S STARS

### I

The heavenly spheres and fortune's stars
veered off course the day I was born;
if I were a seller of candles,
    the sun would never go down.

## II

I struggle to manage and even succeed,
but I'm thwarted by the stars in the sky;
if I were a dealer in shrouds,
    no one so long as I lived would die.

## III

    If I had a scheme to profit
    from arms and going to war,
    all the foes in the world
        would be friends and fight no more.

## HOW IT IS

I get up and head to the patron's house—
    I arrive and they tell me he's gone;
and then they tell me he's sleeping,
    in the evening when I return.

Either he's out on his horse,                5
    or else he already turned in.
Pity the poor creature born
    under the sign of misfortune.

## A CLOAK

I have a cloak that's a lot like a sieve
    for sifting wheat and barley:                10
at night I stretch it taut like a tent,
    and light from the stars shines on me.
Through it I see the crescent moon,
    Orion and the Pleiades.
I weary, though, of counting its holes,          15
    which look like a saw's sharp teeth,
and dreaming they might be mended with thread
    drawn back and forth's no use.

If a fly lands there with force like a fool,
    at once it regrets what it's done:
Replace it, Lord, with a mantle of glory—
    and one that's properly sewn.


## THE FLIES

Who could I turn to in my distress?
    The flies have plundered my home;
they will not leave me a minute of peace,
    attacking me fiercely like foes.
Across my eyelids and eyes they race;
    in my ears they recite their poems;
like a pack of hungry wolves they devour
    my bread when I'm eating alone,
and as though I'd asked them over like friends,
    they take what they want on their own.
It seems they're only seeking their share
    when I offer them lamb and wine—
but that, it turns out, isn't enough:
    they also covet what's mine.
If I summon guests to come and dine,
    at the head of the table they swarm,
and so I long for winter lest
    I starve because of them.
Its cold and rain will wipe them out—
    thank God, who dwells with the cherubim.


## WORLD POETRY

The Arabs write of love in boasts,
and the Romans of vengeance and battles—
the Greeks of wisdom and cunning,
and the Persians of fables and riddles;

but Israel sings—in psalms and hymns—
of God, the Lord of hosts.

## ALL THE REST IS COMMENTARY

### I. The Flood

No man's foot would touch the ground
if my weeping ever kept pace with my sorrow—
but the covenant wasn't for Noah alone;
　for my tears, too, God sent the rainbow.

### II. Reading Exodus

Can the tyrant defying his Maker prosper?
An arrow will strike through his smugness and liver!
Observe, wise one, if you still need proof,
　what the parted sea did to Pharaoh's troops.

### III. The Miracle (at Lehi)

I'm not surprised by the average idiot
who suddenly blurts out something articulate:
Life-giving waters—it came to pass—
　once gushed from the jawbone of an ass.

## PLEASURE

Take pleasure today in the friend at your side;
tomorrow he'll leave, and the joy will die.

Could you trap a day so it couldn't move on?
Or ambush the next, so it wouldn't come?

## IN PLACE

My honor's in place although I sit to the side,
　without my seeking a place like the base in their pride,
who sit at the head table and think they're special—
　even as their place conceals what they'd hide.
I am the place I need—the Place is with me,
　while they use place to console them for all they're denied.

## THE WEDDING NIGHT, CONTINUED

*(a reply to Ibn Tzaddiq)*

You're far from me now, wisdom's perfection,
    whose friendship has always been my salvation,
and so the affliction caused by your leaving
    is greater than any other I've known.
Your sun which rises and shines for all,
    for me has set—and now is gone.
How can I bear this being apart,
    when here within my very own home
a woman holds me within her prison,
    although I barely know what for?
The rivers of Eden flow along
    gently before me, and I am thirsty,
and like a man looking up at the sky,
    all I have is what I can see.
But a poem has come to offer me comfort—
    its words woven like the finest embroidery—
and the signs it mentions are already here
    and this is what they mean for me:
hugging and kissing, thigh over thigh,
    an arm across a shoulder and nape—
though now from that place where the milk runs full
    I turn as a Nazirite turns from the grape.
For me it's enough that she is near,
    pure if not yet cleansed by the rains;
meanwhile with some guile and craft,
    I take just a little of what I crave.
And this will have to be sufficient
    until the day her gown goes crimson,
when I race and finally enter her bed
    and strike with a blow that does her in—
having enticed her just like a snake
    (and the serpent's cunning, we've seen, is great)—
and so I'll have brought the work to an end,
    knowing the job has been well done.
I send you blessings like the ocean's sands—
    O father of song, perfection of wisdom!

## AN ANCIENT BATTLE

I'll sing of an ancient and excellent battle
    devised long ago, by thinking men,
waged on a board along eight rows—
    with each then split into eight positions.

The rows are composed of a series of squares,       5
    and there the armies, massed, await:
Kings stand by, aligned with their camps,
    about to fight and determine their fate.

All look on, prepared for the struggle:
    forward they'll move, then come to a stop—      10
though none in this war will draw his sword,
    for the battle is all a matter of thought.

Each is marked by a singular sign—
    clearly displayed, and carved from its core;
a man who sees them there arrayed      15
    might think that they were Christians and Moors.

Reaching out first, the dark ones begin,
    and the red rivals follow in kind;
the foot-soldiers lead the way into battle,
    moving along their appointed lines.      20

Another comes forward resisting his foe,
    then veers to the side, springing his trap;
but as he advances he does not swerve—
    nor can he turn back on his tracks.

If he'd like, he can leap at the start      25
    three spaces in any direction;
and if he succeeds, and wanders farther,
    up to the final row progressing,

he'll be allowed like the leader to turn
    around and rejoin the developing fray.      30
To the four corners of the field he'll venture,
    watching his back, making his way.

The elephant then, advancing, approaches,
    and lies in ambush, off to the side;
35  his gait, in fact, is like his commander's,
    although his range makes him hide.

And though he charges in jagged fashion,
    the horseman's exceedingly fleet of foot;
his path is twisted and never direct—
40     three adjacent squares are his limit.

The rook can slide along the sides
    of the field of battle, back and forth;
his way is always straight and smooth;
    he never takes a circuitous course.

45  Aiding his men, the King can move
    just as he pleases, in any direction.
He's cautious when standing, and as he sets out
    fighting to hold down the battle's stations.

And should he encounter a hostile force,
50     as when the rook rebuffs him in anger,
challenged then, he has to retreat;
    pursuing his power from chamber to chamber.

He hides behind his remaining troops,
    or has to find a way to flee—
55  for the forces seek to kill one another
    and wipe out every last soldier they see.

And so the warriors all go down;
    they're slain although no blood is shed.
The dark fighters at times the victims—
60     the ones emerging triumphant are red,

and sometimes when the Christian king
    is mortally wounded, the Muslims win:
suddenly caught in their snare—he's doomed,
    for they will throw him into prison.

There is no chance of his being saved,        65
    of finding a city of refuge or shelter;
he'll be judged by his foe and done in,
    or his troops, in ransom, go down together.

Their glory begins to fade the moment
    their leader is stricken, and soon it's gone;      70
but they will fight again before long—
    for the dead on this field are always reborn.

## LAMENT FOR ANDALUSIAN JEWRY

*Calamity came upon Spain from the skies,*
*and my eyes pour forth their streams of tears.*

I moan like an owl for the town of Lucena,
where Exile dwelled, guiltless and strong,
for a thousand and seventy years unchanged—     5
until the day that she was expelled,
leaving her like a widow, forlorn,
deprived of the Scriptures and books of the Law.
As the house of prayer took folly in,
some men murdered and others sought shelter.     10
For this I weep and, mourning, wail:
    *If only my head were a fountain of water.*

I shave my head and bitterly keen
for Seville's martyrs and sons who were taken,
as daughters were forced into strangeness of faith.     15
Córdoba's ruined, like the desolate sea:
its nobles and sages have perished in hunger.
There are no Jews left in Jaén,
Majorca, Malaga, and Almería;
all traces of life are gone—     20
and those who survived were beaten down.
For this I wail in my grief and mourn—
    *for they have melted away like water.*

For Sijilmása I groan in distress—
city of sages whose light barred darkness—
its pillar of Talmud was toppled and broken;
its Mishnah was trampled, cursed, and crushed.
The upright were slaughtered and no one was spared.
Fez was razed and its brethren butchered.
Telmesen's splendor shines no more.
For Meknes and Cueta my cry is bitter.
For Der'a I put on sackcloth and mourn:
    *their blood*, on the Sabbath, *was spilled like water.*

What could I hope for or possibly say—
when this is the work of my own hand?
From God this calamity has come upon me,
and now within me my heart's aflame
for my soul which has strayed from longed-for lands
and silently grieves in her trouble and shame.
She hopes for mercy from her Rock and strength,
for refuge beneath His wing's shadow.
Whenever she thinks of His name she revives,
though she'll face the hail of her handmaiden's arrows—
    *till the Lord with compassion looks down from the skies.*


ELEGY FOR A SON

Come, father, approach and mourn,
for the Lord our God has distanced from you
your son, your one and only child—
    Isaac whom you always loved.

"I am a man who has witnessed affliction
    and watched as joy was driven away.
The fruit of my loins has been taken from me—
    words I never imagined I'd say.

I'd always envisioned him offering comfort,
 and being near me as I aged,      10
but all my labor has been in vain,
 for I've given birth to my own dismay—
  and how can I rejoice again
when Isaac has breathed his last and died?

Moment by bitter moment I weep     15
 and send up a mournful cry and lament,
thinking of how, three years ago,
 he died alone, in a foreign land,
after he'd wandered from place to place.
 And so my soul for his spirit moaned   20
until I'd be able to bring him home;
 all night and day, alone, I grieved.
  What pain and suffering I knew then!
And this is the story of Isaac, my son.

Be kind to me now—bear with me, friends!  25
 The comfort you offer adds to my grief.
So do not speak of my heart's desire,
 or even utter his name to me.
Time has quenched my final ember:
 How could it do any worse to me,    30
having decreed my ruin forever,
 and taken from me the light of my life?
  Now my flesh and heart are failing,
as Isaac's heart gave way when he died."

Lord, in whose hands all is held,     35
 whose will extends through all creatures,
speak to the heart of this grieving father
 who held your name in awe as a child.
Waken the spirit of consolation
 and let it pass through a heart now broken. 40
He taught, with his wife, his son to fear you,
 so he would follow on the path they do:
  While he was a boy, you set it before him,
for the sake of your servant, Isaac, their son.

## MY HUNGER

I'm filled in my hunger to praise your greatness;
  in my thirst to serve you, I am refreshed.
In my fear of you I rest secure—
  putting on terror, like a coat, and awe.
When I bow before you I am exalted.
  When I'm humbled you come and raise me up.
Freedom is mine, although I'm enslaved
  to cousins, for in your name I call.
The wounds and pain you bring me are balms
  that run through my heart, my spirit, my soul.


## SENT OUT FROM THE GLORY

Sent out from the glory of God, your Creator,
  over the four creatures who bear you;
within and about you are all of His wonders.
  How could you hide when He also fills you?

What would you do? He searches your chambers,
  and always hears you and knows where you are.
Before His works don't ask how—
  with Him whose discernment is pure be pure.

All you have is your word and prayer.
  Who were you till His mercy came?
Know that the heavens and earth endure
  to bless your Creator and Maker's name.


## LORD, I HAVE HEARD

Lord, I have heard of your unity's mystery,
  though I could not fathom it in my iniquity.
I've longed for the One, beside which is none,
  and despised all thought and talk of the Trinity.

Accept my prayer—ignore what I've done.
    And take no account of all I've imagined.
Come to the aid of a man in distress—
    out of your goodness, not for my actions.

Bear with a broken heart's transgression;
    it longs for your mercy, though I still sin.
Pardon my falseness, then send me word:
    "As you asked, I have forgiven."


## MY GOD,

I praise you with a heart that's pure,
    from deep within my prison:
You fashion souls from a sacred source,
    a place of brilliance and wisdom.
Your wonders are far beyond comprehension,
    too great to ever be reckoned.
He sends his servants: heat and cold,
    frost and snow, with wind—
some have the faces of eagles or bulls,
    some of lions, or men.


## TO THE SOUL

Sent down from a luminous fountain of life,
    drawn from a sacred place, and pure,
created as one, though not with form,
    and greater by far than honor or wisdom—
why were you ushered into the world
    and then in the dark of the body imprisoned?
At first its sleep seems sweet to you,
    but in the end it's hard and bitter.

Put the pleasures of Time behind you,
    unless in exile you'd always wander.
Consider your glory, for this is your Good,
    to serve the living God in awe:
listen while living within this world
    and be bound in the one-to-come with the Lord.

## BLESSÈD IS HE WHO FEARS

Blessèd is he who fears
the still voice calling
    while his soul is in him;
for just how worthy is he
who'll pass away and then not be—
    when he returns to dust?

His spirit's driven through him
and so his heart is raised—
    while the soul is in him;
but he'll be suddenly crushed
and then be taken to his grave,
    when he returns to dust.

He glides through life on high,
an angel through His skies,
    while the soul is in him;
but like a beast in death,
in the end, he's only breath—
    when he returns to dust.

He wakes and washes his face,
and thinks he's somehow chaste,
    while the soul is in him;
who then will come near
as he's defiled and left impure,
    when he returns to dust?

One day he lifts his voice                                    25
in mirth and song rejoicing,
   while the soul is in him;
but his friends will mourn,
with dirges, then, they'll keen and moan,
    when he returns to dust.                30

He seeks out sweet perfumes,
scented oils and myrrh,
   while the soul is in him;
his clothes will soon be torn
and he'll become a bed for worms,                             35
    when he returns to dust.

His trial lingers on,
and he brings honor home,
   while the soul is in him;
but then disaster comes                                       40
and leaves him holding onto nothing,
    when he returns to dust.

His power is his glory—
his speech flows forth freely—
   while the soul is in him;                       45
but brought into the pit,
his flesh and tongue begin to rot,
    when he returns to dust.

Before him splendor lies—
he sees it with his eyes,                                     50
   while the soul is in him;
but he will come to ruin
and eyes that shone will both be dim,
    when he returns to dust.

He seeks out his companions                                   55
and shares in their delusions,
   while the soul is in him;
what could he find in a world
where all is only vapor and words,
    when he returns to dust.                 60

Trusting in what's true,
he sings in praise of you,
    while the soul is in him.
His bones will rest in dirt,
65      but I ask you Lord to spare his spirit
    when he returns to dust.


## I BOW DOWN

I bow down, my face to the ground,
    for there is no place lower—
I fall before the King on high—
    sublime, beyond all splendor.
5   How could I come before Him except
    with spirit from His hand?
He set it to dwell in the heart's chamber—
    and nothing is finer in man.
His greatness has no beginning or end;
10      how could my words exalt Him,
farther from me than heavens' heights,
    and nearer than my skin?
Lord, I come before you here—
    only you can save me.
15  You formed the hosts of heaven and earth,
    just as you formed me.
What comfort could I seek from them?
    All their help is vain;
and a servant has no refuge apart
20      from the lord by whom he's retained.
What more could I learn when now I know
    that out of love you formed me?
How could I count your mercies when
    my lapses would fill the seas?
25  How could I raise my eyes toward you,
    when they too have sinned?
And if my lips presumed to speak,
    what of their transgression?

My heart's pride has done to my soul
   what no foe was able—             30
again and again, I have rebelled,
   and so with fear I tremble.
I did not intend to anger you;
   my desire led me on;
the wrong I've done harmed me alone—    35
   from you alone can mercy come.
You who've taught me all I know,
   show me the path of compassion.
My heart's burden I've uttered aloud—
   now hear it, Lord, in heaven.          40

## CHILDREN OF EXILE

We are the children of exile,
   oppressed by poverty and trial;
pinned down, weary, harassed—
we've long cried out at injustice.

From the hour our prophets departed,
   we've been besieged by despots.
We call to you for kindness:
Toward us, now, turn your goodness.

We tremble before your terror—
   for who could bear your anger?
We ask with the prayer of Moses:
*Why does your wrath blaze forth at us?*

## I CALL TO HIM

I call to Him who has chosen song—
   May His name be always exalted!

I look and He has graced the world.
I sing to the things that He has numbered,
for He fashioned man from the dust of earth—
    and in his heart He placed the soul,
        a king within his fortress.

He lies in all and all is from Him.
No one could ever do anything like Him,
for all before Him becomes as nothing—
    and what could I offer when every creature
        born is too feeble to know Him?

His wonder's sublime, and His fiery hosts
serve His presence, beside His throne.
Throughout His circles His terror roams—
    He fills the upper chambers with waters;
        the heavens are calmed by His winds.

Awe is His, He's in all places;
it's seen by all who witness His greatness.
To prophets the Lord reveals His secrets—
    for He teaches the precious soul before Him
        to follow Justice's course.


## YOU WHOSE HEARTS ARE ASLEEP

You whose hearts are asleep,
    why don't you look within?
Know your own beginning—
    and what you'll be in the end.
Fathom, first, your soul;
    plumb it last as well—
and then you'll know your Maker,
    and see Him from your skin.
For the form of the world is within you,
    a likeness of all there is,
and in your heart His hand
    has set the soul that breathes.

Your head is the house He dwells in.
   His palace is your brain.
Your soul is in the body,              15
   reigning like a king.
Your eyes are like its scouts;
   your ears stand at its gates.
Its servants are your hands;
   its stewards your legs and feet.     20
Your nostrils take in scents;
   the tongue gives voice to heart.
Your lips taste your food,
   as teeth grind your meat.
Mind—your minister—rules,         25
   as desire waits within.
The liver helps with food,
   and kidneys flame your passion.
This is the whole foundation—
   which serves the good of man,    30
though four elements battle,
   struggling to prevail.
See when the heart's heat fails,
   how quickly royalty flees;
how what was high is toppled,     35
   and homes that towered fall—
as the body, utterly ruined,
   is then devoured by worms.
For once the King departs,
   he will not return.           40
Be smart then with your lives,
   for if you do not know Him,
you'll become like beasts—
   better off not having been.
Remember this, be wise,         45
   and keep it before you always:
Who brought you spirit?
   By whom could it be freed?
Use the heart's endowment
   to see how all was made,     50
and know the Creator's ways—
   for who like Him can lead?

# YITZHAQ IBN EZRA

*(c. 1109–mid-twelfth century)*

Peculiar, vulnerable, hypersensitive, and arrogant are some of the adjectives scholars have used to describe YITZHAQ IBN EZRA. And, indeed, both his poems and the often obscure letters by him that have emerged from the Cairo Geniza's mountain range of correspondence suggest that Avraham Ibn Ezra's son was a difficult and gloomy man. We know little more about his life in Spain than we do about his father's during that period, and none of Yitzhaq's poems from those early years have survived. He seems to have spent part of his childhood in Seville and lived in both Cordoba and Almería, though the precise dates and places of his birth and death are unknown. Fleischer proposes that he was born around 1109. The Geniza letters also indicate that the young Ibn Ezra was engaged in commerce of various sorts with Yehuda HaLevi's friend Halfon Ben Netanel. By age eighteen he seems to have been a poet of considerable stature on the Andalusian cultural scene. Some scholars question his relation to Yehuda HaLevi, but all the available evidence would appear to confirm that he was in fact HaLevi's son-in-law. That said, for one reason or another—perhaps involving the younger poet's gradual drift away from his family, friends, and faith—they had a falling-out in Egypt, and Yitzhaq decided not to accompany his distinguished father-in-law on the voyage to Acre. He didn't even make the trip from Fustat (Old Cairo) to the port in Alexandria to see him off. Instead, he remained behind for the better part of a year—writing an elegy for HaLevi when news of his death reached Egypt—and later on he set out for Babylonia. We find him near Damascus in 1142, and a year later he was in Baghdad, studying with the leading Jewish intellectual of the East at the time, Natanel Ben 'Ali, who was also known as Abu al-Barakat. When, some twenty years later, Natanel converted to Islam, Yithzaq appears to have followed him. Scholars have long suggested that the poem "Conversion" (below) was written by Yitzhaq about his having become a Muslim, perhaps under duress, and after he'd already reembraced Judaism. We have, however, no proof of any return to the fold, and such a move on the poet's part would have been extremely dangerous, especially in the East, as the penalty for abandonment of the faith by a Muslim was execution. This and other strong evidence leads Fleischer to conclude that the poem is not by Yitzhaq Ibn Ezra. We also have contradictory evidence regarding Ibn Ezra's death, which most likely occurred in the East.

On the whole, Yitzhaq Ibn Ezra's poetry is powerful and accomplished in a classical Andalusian manner, though entirely lacking his father's wit and humor. Stylistically, he was also far more conservative than his father. His tendency toward quotation of other poets and conventional application of the standard modes was pronounced, something that might be a reflection of his immaturity as a poet, and also of his activity in the East, where literary tastes had not evolved, and where he may have been leaning on his knowledge of the Andalusian tradition and, like his father, trying to keep it alive. Still, this approach led to accusations of plagiarism, and it also leaves one feeling that his work is derivative. Of the three poems and excerpts attributed to him and translated here, only the lines about HaLevi can be credited to Ibn Ezra without hesitation.

## ON THE DEATH OF YEHUDA HALEVI

I am the man who was left alone
    when friends drifted off like dreams.
Departure's fires continually burn
    deep within me, and my eyes stream
with tears, sprouting trees in a desert,            5
    as the blood in my weeping strengthens the rains.
Grief has long since plowed my back
    and wandering in me gathered its grain.
At the sound of the swift and dove I start:
    so how could my heart bear thunder's roar?      10
Wherever I go, I find no rest;
    Fate sets death upon me, and terror.
How could I mix the flowing myrrh?
    There are no herbs, the ointment has turned;
Time has slipped the rings from my wrists      15
    and from my coffers taken gems.
It kept the light of the sun from me—
    my eyes are blind, though they're still young—
the father who has no peer is gone,
    and the world below extends its arms      20
to welcome him who was fêted by men
    as sages took pride in his presence among them.

After his death, wisdom went still
   and song's gates were shut and sealed;
25    the vine vowed to drink no more
   and wine was bitter and could not heal.
He raised me when I was young like a father—
   he cast my lines in pleasant places;
every day I heard from him,
30    and with him all my fears were allayed.
All good things and grace were ours,
   as though a blessing had filled my barns.
I'd gathered manna from his hands,
   but the roots of broom are now my share.
35    To whom could I turn, and what would I say,
   when all the world is a net and snare?

## OVER HIS BOY

Wail from the top of the highest mountain
   and I'll wail from the desert plain,
and offer a bitter mournful lament
   like a jackal along the road.
5    With great sorrow now I speak,
   with grief and a broken heart—
of a friend to whom friendship always came
   with base men he met.
He abandoned a man who had trusted in him,
10    hoping for his friendship;
his actions were an abomination,
   arousing anger and wrath—
they made him the object of derision to all
   and brought him as low as he'd soared.
15    Now everyone talks of his shame alone
   and scandal wherever he goes.

I was walking home one day on my own
   when I saw the bursar's servant
laughing and calling me over. She asked
20    if I'd heard about my old

friend who was living under some roof
  behind an attic grating—
"the one whose face looks like a loaf
  of black bread," she said.
"Well, we found him over his boy—                                    25
  sucking on his mouth.
With his beak against that face he looked
  like a crow devouring a mouse."


CONVERSION

They contend against me for having abandoned
  the Lord's covenant for godless injustice—
but Amram's son in anger destroyed
  the Law's tablets in his disgust.
And the Lion, Judah, went to Tamar,
  and Amnon to his sister, a virgin;
and David was tried by the Lord and erred
  beside Bathsheba, like Delilah's Samson.

I never tasted impure food,
  I always thought it a rotting carcass—
and if I tell you, "The Prophet's mad,"
  but acknowledge him with every blessing,
my mouth speaks, but my heart replies:
  "You're lying again, and bearing false witness."
I've sought the shadow of the Presence's wing
  and ask of you now, my Lord, forgiveness.

# YOSEF QIMHI

*(c. 1105–c. 1170)*

Born in southern Spain, YOSEF QIMHI was father to a famous line of sons who distinguished themselves in various fields of learning, particularly Hebrew grammar and biblical commentary. Sometime during the 1140s, he came to Provence in order to flee the Almohad invasion. He settled in Narbonne—some forty miles north of Perpignan—where he played a major role in the dissemination of Andalusian culture. Yosef Qimhi's primary fields of interest were the same as his sons', though he also wrote liturgical and didactic poetry, including *Sheqel HaQodesh*, medieval Hebrew's largest compilation of epigrammatic poetry next to Shmu'el HaNagid's *Ben Mishlei*. These epigrams, Qimhi tells us in his introduction, are drawn from a variety of sources, Arabic and Hebrew alike, especially *Mivhar HaPeninim* (The Choice of Pearls; some 367 of the 431 poems in *Sheqel HaQodesh* derive from that collection of prose aphorisms, which is often—and, it appears, erroneously—attributed to Shelomo Ibn Gabirol). He arranged these poetic adaptations into twenty-two categories according to their subject matter: Wisdom, Silence, Truth, Friends and Friendship, and so on. Most scholars agree that Qimhi's literary gifts were limited and that, on the whole, his epigrams are awkward and make for tedious reading. Nevertheless, I find more poetry in the best of them than others have, though Qimhi's diction is, as Schirmann notes, far less polished than that of the better writers of the day and one often senses that the poem is struggling to express itself within the metrical formulation. Still, the poetry is there—with a certain straightforward charm and insight; and that struggle for articulation embodied in these epigrams is very much like the balancing process and mechanism alluded to by the name of the volume. Qimhi's title comes from a pun in his introduction, where he notes that he has weighed (*shaqal*) and put into meter (or scanned—also *shaqal*) the words of the wise according to the standard and currency of the sacred tongue (*sheqel lashon haqodesh*)—this so that these maxims and the wisdom they contain would be easier to recall. In biblical and rabbinic usage, the term *sheqel haqodesh* refers to a unit of weight or coin measured out by the sanctuary scale: its worth was double that of the ordinary *sheqel*. A critical and constant value in Judaism has been the linkage of the profane and the holy, and the driving force behind the concept of the holy *sheqel* was just that: the investment of sacrality into one of the most profane dimensions of social existence. This is precisely what Qimhi's ethical epigrams aim for—and the result, when it works, is a quiet sort of ordinary mysticism linking language and moral example.

## LOVE FOR THE WORLD

Man in his love for the world is like
a dog gnawing on bones:
He sucks the blood between his lips
and doesn't know it's his own.

## ALWAYS BE VIGILANT

Always be vigilant not to take
anyone lightly, no matter their size—
lest you end up holding your throat
as you gag on the smallest of flies.

## CONSIDER THIS

I'm always amazed by intelligent people
who never consider this:
How is it that man grows so proud
when he comes from the place where we piss?

## SUFFER YOUR SORROW

Suffer your sorrow to soften the pain.
Try to resist and the sorrow remains.

## ON WISDOM

### I

In seeking wisdom, be willing
to ask and look like a fool;
but once you have it within you—
    guard it like a jewel.

### II

One without wisdom who tries to be wise
in his folly resembles a mule at a mill:
he walks for hours day after day—
going no farther than one who stands still.

## IF YOU HEAR SOMEONE INSULT YOU

### I

If you hear someone insult you,
walk away from it all—
lest you hear still harsher words
    and wounded have to crawl.

### II

Don't respond to the fool's slight,
for he's more vile than what he says.
Silence here is the proper response—
as *he* fades into its haze.

## WAIT AND BE SAVED

Wait—and be saved like a bird from a snare;
hurry and usher your soul to despair.

## WEALTH

### I

Ask the man who's amassed great wealth
if he's also managed to acquire health.

### II

Delight in the riches that you accrue,
so long as all you've neglected you rue.

## SILENCE AND SPEECH

### I

The less said, the fewer mistakes;
the greater the talk, the greater the headache.

### II

See, creature, what the Creator
   in heaven for you devised:
your legs and hands are doubled,
   and so are your ears and eyes—
your knees along with your nostrils,
   your buttocks and your thighs.

But you have just one tongue—
   never a pair in its cave:
and two high walls surround it,
   with teeth and lips arrayed;
therefore twice consider
   all that you might say—
and treat your tongue as a treasure
   to guard till your dying day.

# YOSEF IBN ZABARA

*(c. 1140–late twelfth century)*

YOSEF IBN ZABARA was the first Hebrew poet who was raised in the Christian north and then lived there for most of his life; some scholars, therefore, mark the beginning of the Christian period of Hebrew Poetry in Spain with his—and not Avraham Ibn Ezra's—work. Born in Barcelona, where he was educated by his physician-father, Yosef too became a doctor, possibly having gone to study at the Hebrew school of medicine in Narbonne in his mid-twenties. Sometime after that he returned to Barcelona and practiced medicine there for several years. In the early eighties he began traveling but soon returned to the city of his birth.

In addition to medicine, Ibn Zabara was well-versed, it seems, in several fields, including Talmud, translation from Arabic, religious thought, philosophy, and more. Little of his writing survives, apart from a long anatomical poem, *Batei HaNefesh* (Homes/Stanzas of the Soul), employing a non-Andalusian rhyme scheme; one accomplished liturgical poem; several medical prose volumes of uncertain attribution (including *On the Analysis of Urine*); and *Sefer Sha'shu'im* (The Book of Delight), the volume on which Ibn Zabara's fame rests. The latter was dedicated in Barcelona no later than 1209 and comprises a book-length, rhymed-prose narrative of the author's wanderings with another physician whom he comes to despise, one 'Einan HaNatash ben Arnan HaDash—essentially an acronym for Einan the Devil, son of the Demon. While the specific setting of the body of the narrative is never mentioned, at least not by names that we can identify, the book begins and ends in Barcelona, and its fictional landscape appears to be based on Muslim Spain and Provence. A series of moral tales set within a frame story, it is the first structurally complex Hebrew narrative in the tradition and among the most entertaining. Although the book makes use of the usual scriptural and rabbinic elements, its emphases are worldly and—in keeping with Ibn Zabara's training and profession—corporeal (and often moral).

Israel Davidson, who edited the critical edition of the work, describes it as a "veritable storehouse of medieval lore . . . built in the Arabian style, decorated with fables and riddles of India, inlaid with the choicest products of Greek science, and illumined with the wisdom and maxims of the Orient. The whole," he says, "is a magnificent monument to the zeal for secular learning among the Jews of the Middle Ages." With its lean, pragmatic, and often nonbiblical language, its generally subversive treatment of misogynistic tales, and its reluctance to make use of interspersed poems, Zabara's work departs from the "classical" standard of the Andalusian poems and even from that of the later *maqaamas*. Schirmann calls it one of the earliest efforts in the direction of a Hebrew novel—at a time when similar work was being done in European languages—though in the proper sense of the word, it isn't a *maqaama* at all. Its high quality notwithstanding, *Sefer Sha'ashu'im* was for one reason or another very slow to gain a readership, and for hundreds of years there was little mention of it or its author. The book was printed for the first time in Constantinople in 1577, and interest in Zabara's work was not renewed until the nineteenth century, when *Sefer Sha'ashu'im* appeared in a Hebrew journal. Davidson's critical edition was published in 1914. The poems translated here are drawn from the twenty-two contained in the body of the book. Just three or four of them are believed to be by Ibn Zabara; the others remain unattributed, but may well be his.

## SWEET AND SOUR

Gall when it helps is good,
 even if it's bitter;
but sweetness once it starts
 to harm will soon devour.
Therefore, the wise at heart
 eat the bitter that's better,
and keep their distance from
 the sweet that makes them sour.

## MY EX

A demon was drawn in that woman's face
and her beauty cut into my organs and limbs;
whenever she spoke, my hair stood up straight—
as the intricate links of my heart wore thin.

She shut the gates of affection and peace—
opened the door to strife and we fought;
she set her dwelling on a hill of complaint,
pitching her tent, and stretching it taut.

She weighed on my heart like the sands of the sea,
and as though she were cooking—boiled my belly.


## LOOK AT THESE PEOPLE

Look at these people so wise in their eyes,
who sneer at others as though from the skies;
pride has built a nest in their hearts,
although they put on modesty's disguise.
Their bellies are full of fraud and deceit—
like skins bloated with milk and wine;
and as they address you with gentle words,
they're holding weapons of war in their minds.
Their piety's all in prayers that are vain—
prolonging their ONNNNE, in ONE IS HIS NAME;
Lord may my life by you be sustained,
until they're like Abel—and I like Cain.


## THE PHYSICIAN

Be a physician, said Time to the fool,
and murder men in exchange for a fee;
you'll have it better than the angel of death,
who has to kill them for free.

# ANATOLI BAR YOSEF

### *(c. 1130?–c. 1213)*

Although he spent the majority of his life outside Provence, ANATOLI BAR YOSEF is considered the first of the properly Provençal Spanish-Hebrew poets. He is also a major contributor to the southern extension of the Andalusian school of poetry into the mid-Mediterranean. Born in Marseille and, it seems, raised there, Anatoli lived for a considerable period of time in Lunel, where he became known as an outstanding scholar and serious poet. For reasons that remain elusive, at some point in his life Anatoli decided to leave Provence and make his way to Egypt. As was customary for travelers sailing from Marseille, he stopped along the way in Norman (and still Arabized) Sicily, staying most of the time in Palermo, Mazzara, Termini, and Messina. Many of his extant poems were either written while in Sicily or derive in one way or another from his stay on the island, which had an ancient Jewish community whose members were well-versed in Spanish-Hebrew culture. They welcomed Anatoli and embraced him for his learning. How long he remained in Sicily we do not know, but the attachments he formed there were strong. He engaged in poetic correspondence with many of the island's leading men of letters, and Sicilians were still writing to him to inquire about halakhic matters after he reached Egypt (c. 1190), where he served as a judge on the religious court of Alexandria. Anatoli's poems are entirely Spanish in character and evince the direct influence of the period's Andalusian masters. "The Test of Poetry," for example, echoes HaNagid's "The Critique" (above). On the whole, Anatoli's poems are well crafted and compelling in their way, even if they lack both the power and surprise of work by the major poets.

## THE TEST OF POETRY

Put your poems to discernment's test—
 refine them, then, in quality's furnace;
scrutinize what they say and don't,
 and ask if their images suit their sense.

5 Draw your ideas from deep within,
　　then weigh them out on a trustworthy balance,
and don't race after others' notions.
　　sharpen yours alone with your wits.
Keep your language crisp and cunning,
10　　and consider it all with an eye to its fate,
for too many words will weary the reader:
　　out of each eighty, choose only eight—
and know that when its figures are flimsy,
　　a poem's like clay that hasn't been shaped.

15 You've rushed me one that's extremely thin;
　　no thinking person could let it go by—
it's wheat that hasn't yet yielded fruit,
　　and I found that its soil was far too dry.
Not long ago your coin was pure,
20　　but now it's debased and can't be excused:
there's new dross in the mix this time,
　　when the old mold of the money's not used.
What I'm saying seems harsh, I know,
　　but don't start throwing one of your fits,
25 for I do what I do out of love alone—
　　hidden away in my heart though it is.
So search out instruction instead of silver,
　　and rather than treasure, seek wisdom's gifts.


MOTTO

Gently, verses, as though you were waiting—
　　remember you have my heart in tow.
With soul and spirit, my pledge of love,
　　I'll line your walls, then tell you: Go.

# YEHUDA IBN SHABBETAI

*(1168/88–after 1225)*

Misogyny is by no means an uncommon theme in medieval literature, and a vast corpus of work on the defects of women was produced in both Muslim and Christian lands. Numerous misogynistic elements can be found in Scripture, in the Talmud, and throughout rabbinic literature; and while hardly in keeping with the refined courtly ethos of classical Andalusian Hebrew poetry, misogyny surfaces at times in poems by the major poets of the period as well. It is, moreover, everywhere in the background of that literature, literally and allegorically. The topic doesn't emerge as an explicit subject in the literature, however, until the mid-twelfth century, when a debate in northern Spain took shape around a work entitled *Minhat Yehuda Sonei Nashim* (The Offering of Yehuda the Misogynist), by YEHUDA IBN SHABBETAI. Little information about the author has come down to us. He seems to have been affiliated with the courts of several prominent Jewish notables—for whom he wrote poems of praise or scorn as the occasion demanded—and we know that he also lived in Burgos and Saragossa. The initial draft of his *maqaama* was written when its author was twenty years old and then edited some two decades later. It was dedicated to a local Jewish aristocrat, Avraham Al-Fakhaar, himself a talented poet (in both Hebrew and Arabic) attached to the Toledan court of Alfonso VIII. Ibn Shabbetai's work aroused opposition in its own time, and in its wake several *maqaamas* were written in defense of women and in unambiguous praise of marriage and family life. As Matti Huss has observed, *Minhat Yehuda* could have emerged only in a Christian cultural context, where asceticism was prized; moreover, says Huss, the principal subject of this entertaining and complex work is in fact not "women" or "misogyny" at all (though it *is* often misogynistic, or at least conflicted in its treatment of women) but the institution of marriage. The author's actual position on the subject remains unclear, and modern scholars have read the work in a wide variety of ways, seeing in it everything from a harmless diversion, to a satirical and ultimately egalitarian presentation of a *mundus inversus*, to a complete denigration of women. Whatever *Minhat Yehuda* was trying to say, it was extremely popular, and numerous manuscripts are extant.

Ibn Shabbetai's subsequent work is perhaps less compelling for the modern reader, but another *maqaama*, *Milhemet HaHokhma veHa'Osher* (The Battle of Wisdom and Wealth), which was written in 1214 as an answer to the responses to

*Minhat Yehuda*, caught on with his peers and was admired by generations of readers after them. (Only a few manuscript copies survive, but the work was printed ten times from the early sixteenth century on.) Toward the end of his life Ibn Shabbetai became embroiled in a bitter controversy surrounding a historical book he'd written about prominent Jewish sages, poets, and community leaders, and several Christian kings. That chronicle has not come down to us: for reasons that remain obscure, the sole copy of the book was burned by the Jewish community, and its author was driven out of town (like Ibn Gabirol before him, and Shelomo Bonafed two centuries later). Ibn Shabbetai responded with a vituperative work called *Divrei Ha'Alah veHaNidu'i* (The Curse and Ban), which castigates the leaders of the Saragossan Jewish community. Both *Minhat Yehuda* and *Divrei Ha'Alah veHaNidu'i* are indicative of the distance the Hebrew literary tradition had come from classical Andalusian decorum.

## From *THE OFFERING OF YEHUDA THE MISOGYNIST*

### I. PHARAOH'S WISDOM

Pharaoh's wisdom was great when he sought
    to subject the people of learning to slaughter:
he hardened their burden, increasing their grief,
    killing their sons—but not their daughters.

### II. THE MISOGYNIST IN LOVE

My love for you, and my desire,
have eaten through my bones and skin;
a small fly could cover me now,
I've grown so very weak and thin.

If I lived on an ant's eyelid,
it wouldn't know if I was out or in.

### III. A Raised Offering

My terrible, beautiful, perfect doe
fine as Tirzah, and the sun in the sky:
come to bed and give yourself to me
with a raised offering of breast and thigh.

### IV. Two Things

Two things embitter my being,
and I'll warn of them throughout my life:
a scholar who places his hope in a fool,
and a man enslaved to his wife.

### V. The Sage Lies

The sage lies in the finest of graves
beside saints, sharing their destiny.
His statute was set for his people to see:
Let no man ever marry!

# YEHUDA ALHARIZI

## (1165–1225)

In all of the extant documents pertaining to medieval Jewish life in Spain and the Eastern rim of the Mediterranean, there is just a single physical description of an important Hebrew poet by another writer. "A tall, silver-haired man with a smooth face" is how the Arab biographer Ibn al-Sha'ar al-Mawsili (1197–1256) describes YEHUDA ALHARIZI, whom he refers to by his Arabic name, Yahya Ibn Suleimaan Ibn Sha'ul Abu Zakhariyya Alharizi al-Yahudi. From al-Mawsili's short biography we also learn that Alharizi's masterpiece, the collection of maqaamas known as Sefer Tahkemoni, was written in the East, for which the poet had set out in 1215. Alharizi is, nonetheless, an Andalusian writer through and through, though the classical Andalusian ethos seems in his writing, as Ezra Fleischer has put it, to be reflected in a warped mirror. Dictional purity, pictorial density, sophistication of form, and loyalty to Arabic literary models remain, but the high seriousness, sublimity, profundity, and lyric innocence of the classical poetry are gone. In keeping with the requirements of the maqaama, they are replaced by the elements of humor, picaresque narration, and at times a more popular register, tone, and choice of subject. While the details about the first half of his life are not quite clear, it seems that Alharizi was born in Toledo, to a family that—as his name implies—originally came from Jerez. He was educated in the Arabized Christian capital of Castile, and it appears that most of his adult life was spent in Provence, where he translated a number of important Arabic and Judeo-Arabic works, including Maimonides' Guide for the Perplexed and part of his commentary on the Mishna. He also produced an impressive Hebrew version (or adaptation) of one of the most important maqaamas in the history of Arabic literature, al-Hariiri of Basra's Maqaamaat (c. 1054–1112), which the modern editor of that work called Mahberot Iti'el (The Book of Iti'el).

Driven by a combination of economic, political, and perhaps even spiritual factors, Alharizi set out for the East c. 1215, stopping in Alexandria, then taking the overland route via Fustat to Jerusalem. From there he continued on to Jewish communities in Palestine, Syria, and Iraq, transforming his impressions of the places and people he encountered into what is perhaps the greatest achievement of Hebrew literature during the Christian-Spanish period. A book of staggering verve and virtuosity, Sefer Tahkemoni artfully blends rhymed prose narratives and metrical poems to provide a hilarious and often scathing account of the communities through which he passes. Alharizi's sharp tongue spares no one, as it passes judgment on officeholders, religious leaders, poets, pretenders, and patrons. While the author's introduction places the work in a religio-philosophical frame, the book is overwhelmingly secular, and his subject matter ranges from nature, war, morality, and the history of the Hebrew language to erotic encounter, drunkenness, homosexuality, and fraud. (Alharizi also wrote a more straightforward account of his travels in an Arabic work called *Al-rawda al-'aniiqa*—The Pleasant Garden—which reveals him to be an excellent poet in that language as well.) As an Andalusian, Alharizi had high expectations of his visit to the cradle of Arabic civilization, but he was deeply disturbed to find that Jewish life in the East was very different from what he had known in Spain and even Provence, where Hebrew literature had blossomed in the context of some two centuries of court life. Appalled at the state to which Eastern Hebrew culture had fallen, and also angered by the fact that Hebrew had not been able to produce anything original to rival the splendors of al-Hariiri's *Maqaamaat*, he set out to compose *Sefer Tahkemoni* to redeem—he says—the language itself. The work may also reflect, Fleischer notes, a crisis in the Jewish circles of northern Spain, which were increasingly dominated by a growing class of nouveau-riche Jews who had little connection to Hebrew culture and Judaism as a vital faith. In a culture defined by this essentially vulgar class of people, poetry's place was marginal at best. Read in this light, *Sefer Tahkemoni* can be seen as a part of a larger battle for survival that Alharizi was waging in the face of cultural decline. Alharizi died in Aleppo, Syria, in December of 1225. The selection here is taken from the metrical poems found in various chapters of *Sefer Tahkemoni*.

## BORN TO BASENESS

Born to baseness, a brother to greed,
  within him all is deceit—
in two languages I praised his name,
  and clearly fell on my face in each.

When I looked for him, he couldn't be found—
　　they told me he'd gone, and it stung;
and though he thinks he's safely hidden,
　　his name to the tip of my pen has clung—
like a mouse that fled to its hole but left
　　its tail on the house cat's tongue.


## THE HYPOCRITE

Look at the lecher who stands there praying,
his mind full of wicked things and sin.
He's wrapped in white, like a cote for pigeons:
　　spotless without and filthy within.


## THE JERK

A turban above the jerk's face,
I thought a vessel filled with disgrace;
pompous and set over nothing at all—
　　a world hung over empty space.


## A MISER IN MOSUL

In Mosul I praised a miserable man
　　with a poem that was sheer invention;
and he made me a vow as full as my song
　　of wind and utter pretension.
From Baghdad to Spain, I've never known
　　an oath even half as vain—
and when his friends objected, "Lord,
　　your hands were taught to be open!"—

he answered them: "I've got nothing left,
　　and don't know what I can say."

Every day I've bills to pay
    and so, it seems, I'm stuck:
I've got a boy who does my will
    —our bed is always fresh—
but I'm obliged by law to provide him
    with clothing, food, and a fuck."


## THE MISER

### I

Closed to the seeker, your hand
is a virgin no man has known;
if this is how your mother had been,
    there'd be no flaw in her son.

### II

I'm amazed how the clouds of your goodness closed
and waters that flowed through your hands froze.

You're like the pipe that emits a great sound,
though in it there's nothing—only wind.

### III

I met a miser among the patrons
who thought himself supreme among them.

But he'll attain philanthropy's degree
when a ladder is mounted by a donkey.


## ON ZION'S HOLY HILL

A corrupt man is in charge in Zion,
and the plague is creeping across his skin.

He spreads his legs for all who pass,
and so they call him: Mount My Ass.

## BOYS: TWO POEMS

### I. If Amram's Son

If Amram's son had seen my friend
drinking his wine when the flush came on—
his beauty and curls would have compelled him
  to cancel the law about lying with men.

### II. An Answer

The man who desecrates Moses' law
with filthy things he likes to recall,

and opens himself to all who come—
on all fours, defiled by men—

will have his flesh parted by death,
as a farmer's plow cuts through earth.

## MASTERS OF SONG

While sages retreated from poetry's sound,
wise men in Spain made their choice:
In the East they couldn't hear the song,
while the Western prophets gave vision voice.

## MEASURE FOR MEASURE

That gorgeous gazelle destroyed me with beauty,
  and sent up flames of longing through me.

But measure for measure, against what he'd done,
  I made him consume the fruit of his sin.

I held up a mirror before his eyes—
  so those same flames through his heart would rise.

## A LOVER WANDERED

A lover wandered down to the stream—
    desire's pain like a wound through him,
and there he saw a woman washing
    the soiled shirt of his friend by the spring.

He kissed it in honor of the one who'd worn it,
    not because its fabric was fine—
for there are men who'd gladly drink
    vinegar so as to remember wine.

## HOW LONG, MY FAWN

How long, my fawn, will you torture me,
    like a woman sold to you as slave?
If only I'd see an end to your anger
and the plague of your distance finally stayed.

You set a fountain of tears in my eyes,
    and in my heart, a conflagration—
and the Torah says that now you're obliged,
as the fire's starter, to pay compensation.

## CURSES' COMPOSITION

### I

"Curses" composes poems like shit
    and thinks the shit in his mouth honey.
His judgment only highlights his shame:
    he's wholly exposed in his lines of poetry.
His father was always villainy's slave,
    his mother was bound to her disgrace;
both were then gathered and taken up,
    their infamy left for us to face:
for the father's filth in the son can be seen—
as the stench makes it easy to find the latrine.

II

"Curses" came and gave me his poems—
and the next day returned, and took them home.

Giving and taking, coming and going—
a dog that returns to its vomit I thought him.


A FLASHING SWORD

*A flashing sword in a warrior's hand—*
*a flame sent out among them.*
Friends asked me what it was.
Word, I answered, from a sage's tongue.


PALINDROME FOR A PATRON;

OR, CAUTION: THIS DOOR SWINGS BOTH WAYS

Master, yours is righteousness. No evil
do you grasp. All mercy. Yours are morals
empty of obloquies. This God did—for,
truthfully, you are joy without dishonor.

*

Dishonor without joy are you, truthfully.
For did God this—obloquies of empty
morals are yours. Mercy! All grasp
you do evil. No righteousness is yours, Master.

## A POEM NO PATRON HAS EVER HEARD:
## WITH THE LETTER *R* IN EVERY WORD

Precious progeny. Splendor's facture.
  Our era's lord. Glory's honor.
Creation's fruit. Luster's power.
  Mirror for our Maker's grandeur.
Ruling through fear before our Lord—
  pursuing our Master, nature's Creator,
your precious brow crowned secure,
  over other viziers our victor.
Rock, raise our protector. Guard
  our fortress through trouble's trial forever.


## ADMIRATION FOR THE PATRON AGAIN I'LL PROVE,
## AND THE LETTER *R* I'LL NOW REMOVE

God's companion, Good's diadem,
  his mind a ceaseless fountain of wisdom,
he leads His chosen, unique in existence,
  and so we laud him above all men.
He builds bastions of kindness and justice;
  his line's value sets the foundation.
And because what he does is so beloved,
  his name is exalted in the holy nation.


## TWO POEMS ON KARAISM

### I. FOR

I believe in the faith of Moses alone,
  and not in what dreamers think they've known.
Why should I listen to your sages' talk,
  which alters the law of the Lord we were shown?

I rely on the teachings of God who exalts
    him who obeys them, I take no chances—
like a man who trusts in the trunk of the tree,
    but will not risk his life on its branches.

## II. Against

Men who believe in Moses' law
    and dismiss the sages' words in anger,
resemble people who say: "I'll obey
    my king—but not his commander."

## VIRTUE

Humility's best among virtues,
    and suits every thinker and cause.
It arouses love in the hearts of foes
    and hides from others one's flaws.

## I'LL SET OUT A VERSE AND LAY THE FOUNDATION; THEN YOU'LL ADD ONE FOR THE STANZA'S COMPLETION

### I

*Young Man:*
The writer's pen across the scroll
lays down darkness in its wrath—

*Old Man:*
like a snake that slithers across the dust
and leaves behind it a leveled path.

### II

*Young Man:*
The hawk downs eagles high in the skies,
spreading its pinions against the heavens—

*Old Man:*
its eyes are cut from precious gems,
its flashing wings from bolts of lighting.

### III

*Young Man:*
The waters slowly flow in the stream,
just like delicate chains of silver—

*Old Man:*
and the hand of the wind like a craftsman comes
and turns that elegance into armor.

### IV

*Young Man:*
Hidden from men and always veiled,
the pomegranate's cheeks are just like girls—

*Old Man:*
once they're opened, it seems they contain
coffers loaded with gold and pearls.

### V

*Young Man:*
The fruit of the nut is sweet in its shell,
but until it's broken, it can't be eaten—

*Old Man:*
much like those who seek like fools
and learn not a thing until they're beaten.

# YA'AQOV BEN ELAZAR

## (1170–c. 1233)

When Ya'aqov Ben Elazar began writing, his home town of Toledo had already been in Christian hands for over a century. While European vernacular and Latin traditions formed part of the city's cultural heritage, Toledo was still very much informed by all things Arab and Arabic, and Castile's kings often maintained courts there that preserved the cultural legacy of Andalusia. Ben Elazar's *Sefer HaMeshalim* (literally, The Book of Parables, though it is also known as *The Love Stories of Ya'aqov Ben Elazar*), completed around 1233, is a wonderful example of a possible fusion of elements from both European and Eastern traditions—so much so that it has at times left scholars baffled. Some have argued that several of the book's narrative elements and themes most likely derive from European sources, though it is hard to identify precisely which ones. The *Roman de la Rose*, a thirteenth-century French tale known as *Aucassin and Nicolette*, various romances, or the Provençal poetry of the troubadours have been proposed as likely candidates. The problem is that many of these same elements could just as easily be traced to Eastern sources, as *Sefer HaMeshalim* has much in common with, for instance, the romantic stories of *A Thousand and One Nights*, or the suffering-lover motif of the Majnun Layla ('Udhri) tradition. Less ambiguously, the book's form and poetics—rhymed prose laced with metrical poems—are based on the *maqaama*, and its narrator is even named Lemu'el Ben Iti'el, that is, Lemu'el the son of Iti'el, who was the narrator in al-Hariiri's classic, as translated by Alharizi. The question of an Eastern source, then, remains a distinct possibility, as Ben Elazar did know Arabic quite well. He wrote at least one work (on Hebrew grammar) in Arabic, and—using an Arabic intermediary text—produced a Hebrew translation of the Sanskrit tales of Kalila and Dimna. He also wrote liturgical poems and philosophical works.

Like *Sefer Tahkemoni* by Alharizi, *Sefer HaMeshalim* was written in response to the challenge posed by Arabic literature, and it too is driven by a desire for cultural redemption. But unlike the *Tahkemoni*, Ben Elazar's collection was soon forgotten, and just a single, problematic copy of the work has survived. A series of unrelated stories bound only by the presence of the narrator, who is for the most part identified with the author (he tells us so at the outset), *Sefer HaMeshalim* contains a high percentage of metrical poems for a work of this sort, and they employ a wide range of meters. "The Hypocrite's Beard" (below) comes from the one story in the collection that contains specifically Jewish elements. According to Haim Schirmann, the entire chapter is unique in Hebrew literature and very likely reflects the corrupt state of affairs in the Jewish community at the time. And other scholars have suggested that Ben Elazar's satirical treatment may involve an element of protest against the "ultra-Orthodox" Jews of his day (the anti-Maimonideans), who demonstrated their zealousness by growing their beards long. Contemporary readers—especially those aware of the charged secular–religious relations in Israel—will find it hard not to draw the compelling, if anachronistic, connection to the long beards of today's ultra-Orthodox community, which many associate with anything but virtue. Elsewhere in *Sefer HaMeshalim*, Ben Elazar writes that "a beard and a belly are half of the rabbinate."

## THE HYPOCRITE'S BEARD

The hypocrite's beard has branches extending,
    just like his cant in every direction.
Its length reaches down, deep into hell,
    after it's worn itself out with exertion.
Within it small creatures are creeping about.
    Are monkeys, I wondered, also hidden
where fleas bequeath their places to lice
    and once I saw a night-bird flying?
They told me his beard's in fact like a forest,
    where all sorts of beasts and foxes have dens;
there the arrow-snake builds her nest,
    and rabbits, too, have found a haven.
All dwell there, safe and sound,
    each beneath its grapevine resting.
And their young in the shadows of fig trees are reared,
    plump and fresh, in the hypocrite's beard.

# FOUR POEMS ON SUBTLE LOVE

## I. The Doe

Take in, my eye, that beautiful doe,
    for this is all of her you'll know.
Tell your mouth to try to kiss her—
    in her eyes you'll then find favor—
for this is the teaching of wisdom's call;
    for brothers in learning, this is the law.
The doe's departure is always bitter.
    And harder still is lament for her.

## II. A Kiss

I sent him a kiss with the Envoy of Friends.
"My lips," he answered, "are far more faithful!
Should I be content with a kiss from afar?
Is *this* how lovers learn to be tasteful?"

## III. A Lover's Transgression

This lover's transgression is too great to bear
    and there is no pardon for his sin;
so I'll turn my passion into his jail
    and make my heart's cage his prison—

ignoring his pleas for me to appear,
    pretending suddenly I can't hear.

## IV. Spats and Squabbles

Day after day, spats and squabbles;
Time stands still, and still we wobble.

Are we alone in this torturous state?
Do *all* lovers share this fate?

"Love like a neighbor for his neighbor,"
says a friend, "lacks all savor.

Without the tension, without the tussle,
love and poems alike are dull."

# AVRAHAM IBN HASDAI

*(first half of the thirteenth century)*

AVRAHAM IBN HASDAI's major belletristic work, *Ben HaMelekh veHaNazir* (The Prince and the Monk), reflects the deep if not always conscious curiosity about foreign literature that characterized the Hebrew readership of the day: it adapts and Hebraicizes a Sanskrit tale that was transmitted through Arabic, via old Persian, and tells the story of the life of the young Buddha. The original tale was popular among Muslims, Jews, and Christians alike, and was also translated into Greek (in the seventh century, at the Mar Saba Monastery near Jerusalem), and it eventually made its way into numerous other European languages as well. In the almost entirely universalist worldview of the Hebrew version—with what may well be Sufi influences—we read that once upon a time there was a pagan king in India who persecuted a cult of monotheistic monks, which he soon expelled from his kingdom. When a son was born to the king and astrologers warned that the striking-looking child was destined to become one of these monks, the king banished the son to a tower on a distant island; his guards and servants there were ordered not to utter a word about death or the afterlife, or anything that might encourage the boy to begin thinking of final things. The plan ran aground as the adolescent son began to grow curious about the world beyond the island and asked to see it; at the advice of his wise men, the father relented, allowing the boy a single expedition to the kingdom. Despite the guards' efforts to shield him, the son saw things during the expedition that caused him to reflect on the nature of existence—an old man and the effects of aging, for instance—and so he began to despair. Word of the prince's crisis spread through the kingdom and beyond, eventually reaching the expelled monks, one of whom decided to come to the rescue. The monk made his way to the island, where he engaged the prince in extended conversation, educating him through tales told in rhymed prose studded with metered poems and epigrams, all the while preparing him to become a just and wise king for his people. Both the prose frame stories (which are warm and direct) and the poems (which are a tad more awkward than first-rate Spanish-Hebrew verse) seem to rely heavily on their original materials. The translator weaves into his work numerous biblical citations and allusions, though without involving specifically Jewish subject matter. Schirmann notes that it's doubtful Ibn Hasdai would have undertaken this adaptation had he known of its provenance; but, he adds, the Hebrew alters the original Indian nature of the text much less than did the Christian versions, which in time made their way into

European literature as well and are evident in *Everyman* and in works by Boccaccio, John Gower, Shakespeare, Lope de Vega, Calderon, and others. In medieval Christian versions of the story the main characters are known as Barlaam and Josaphat (distortions of the original Indian names, Blodar and Budassaf—the latter preserving the name Bodhisattva, the Buddha's herald).

A resident of Barcelona during the first half of the thirteenth century, and one of the leaders of the Jewish community there, Ibn Hasdai was also a translator of key philosophical works (by Jewish and Muslim writers alike, including Maimonides and al-Ghazaali) and an ardent supporter of Maimonides in the controversy that took shape around his *Guide for the Perplexed*.

## WATCH OUT

Watch out for the man who lies to you
more than for one who steals your gold.
The thief runs away with your wealth,
    but the liar loots your soul.


## PROPORTION

The fool hurts for the little pleasure
    he loses, and trembles for what remains;
the wise man is always content with his portion
    and adds in the end to his good name.


## AGE AS AUTHOR

Writers write in black on white—
but age in white on black's extension.
    As the latter records, it has to wipe out,
and what good's an author who writes by erasing?

## WHICH IS MORE BITTER

My soul's seen much, though I still don't know
which is more bitter of what I've been through:
serving friends who betrayed me or being
a traitor to one who was always true.

## THE LYING WORD

Prefer death to a lying word,
for the ripple-effect of its plunder is worse.
    When a man dies, he dies alone—
but many are slain with the lie and its curse.

## THE MONK'S ADVICE

Seekers of wisdom don't eat their fill
and forgo the pleasure that wine can give.
They don't just live so they can eat:
    they eat a little so they can live.

## ADVICE FOR A FUTURE KING

### I. Wisdom's Mantle

As long as a man seeks out wisdom,
wisdom will have him hold sway over men;
but once he thinks he's wearing its mantle—
    know it has just been taken from him.

## II. Don't Believe

Don't believe all who plead
before you—or trust in talk that's smooth:
Joseph's brothers sold him, remember,
then went to his father with tears, not truth.

## III. The Hyssop and the Cedar

Always be humble and don't go around
with men who are puffed up with pride in their power;
look at the hyssop, which hangs from the wall
and holds in the wind that topples a cedar.

# MEIR HALEVI ABULAFIA

## *(1170–1244)*

MEIR HALEVI ABULAFIA opposed Avraham Ibn Hasdai in the debate that took shape around the *Guide for the Perplexed* and reached its height in the 1230s. Abulafia admired the Rambam, but differed with him profoundly on philosophical and religious matters, and he was the first European rabbi to publicly denounce the great philosopher. Born in Burgos and raised in Toledo, Abulafia was the most renowned Jewish religious leader of his time. He was also known for his extensive talmudic commentary, his role in the administration of Spain's Jewish communities, his writings on the *masora* (the body of notes relating to the transmission of the authorized biblical text), and his poetry. The stylistic influence of Moshe Ibn Ezra is evident in Abulafia's poetry, which concentrates on abstract spiritual concerns even as it reflects the poet's involvement in social affairs. Distinctly occasional, it is often addressed to members of the Castilian-Jewish aristocracy. While this community no longer participated in the sort of court life that gave rise to the Hebrew literature of Muslim Spain, the art of composition in the secular Andalusian style was prized in the north, if circumscribed. Religious poetry in Christian Spain had also been greatly reduced in its scope, as by the early thirteenth century the canon of the Spanish-Hebrew prayer book was for all intents and purposes closed, except when it came to marginal genres that didn't attract many of the important poets. This, notes Ezra Fleischer, might explain why so few liturgical poems have come down to us by the key figures of Toledo's religious community. Only four liturgical poems by Abulafia, for example, are extant.

In addition to several long, powerful elegies (for Maimonides and on the death of his sister, who speaks from the grave), Meir HaLevi Abulafia wrote a lengthy philosophical poem and several epigrams, including the one translated here, where he appears to be asking, in poetic fashion, for a tax break from a minister. The selection below also includes a rare translation from the work of an Andalusian Arabic poet. By and large, the Hebrew poets tended to translate the major poets of the East.

## PLEA FOR A TAX BREAK

My hope's ship sails on the sea of evil
    Time, which spreads its net before me.
Guide it, my prince, safely to port—
    on the wings of your grace and mercy.


## (L)ATTITUDE

The Lord's counsel will stand forever,
    and his judgment come forth into the light;
therefore, my brother, want what there is—
    if you can't have what you'd like.


## FIGHTING TIME

Tell our rivals we're fighting Time,
because the strong alone are its foe.
Go now, gaze at the sea where corpses
float while pearls are lying below.

The hosts of heaven are endless—true.
But eclipses only come over two.

# YITZHAQ HASNIRI

### *(c. 1170/75–after 1229)*

While the Spanish liturgical canon left little room for new material, it seems that greater opportunity for expression was offered by the tradition of sacred verse in Provence, where links were maintained to other Jewish communities in France and Ashkenaz. YITZHAQ HASNIRI was the first Provençal religious poet who, in the eyes of the period's leading scholars, bears comparison to the Spanish liturgical poets, and he is perhaps the most important of the Provençal *paytanim*. He was active during the turbulent years of the Albigensian Crusade; though that campaign was not aimed at the Jewish community, the Jews of Provence suffered in its wake, and the aggressive policies of Pope Innocent III also made life difficult. In his poetry, HaSniri was by far the most outspoken critic of the Church's harsh policies. His somber temperament was further darkened by these circumstances, at times to the point of morbidity. In his famous, long *tokheha* (admonition) he walks the worshiper through his own burial, visualizing the scene in disturbing detail. The poem translated here, which is unusually direct in its ridicule of the Church and Islam, should be read in the light of the talmudic dictum: "All sneering is forbidden except the ridiculing of idols" (*Avodah Zarah* 25b). The fact that it was intended for recitation as part of the Passover liturgy—in other words, in close proximity to a *yom hahesger*, a day near the Easter holiday on which Christians traditionally hurled stones at the Jews and their property—may account for the extended mockery of the cross.

The poet's name, which alludes to the snow-capped biblical Mount Snir (Hermon [Deuteronomy 3:9]), indicates that he came from the region of Mont Ventoux (meaning, in Provençal, the mountain of snow), near Malaucène. In 1195 (or 1190), he met Yehuda Alharizi, who praises him in Gate 46 of his *Tahkemoni* ("in his poems he puts the stars to shame"). From this we can deduce that HaSniri was already considered a formidable poet by then. We also know that he was active during the years 1208–29, the latter date marking the conquest of Jerusalem by the Crusaders, an event that figures in one of his poems. No secular poems by HaSniri have survived.

## ON THE WORSHIP OF WOOD AND A FOOL

The sons of Qedar turn to a fool,
and two pieces of hewn wood
joined by a craftsman are Edom's shelter.
 They send up hymns before false gods,
5  worship and bow before their boards—
 as Sheba's gold covers their idol.

Vermilion anoints it and various hues
lend it an air of the almost-human;
it's kept in place, hanging by nails.
10 So the work was completed and perfectly done,
 and hovering over the hall, it's dumb.
 Seekers approach it and leave in shame.

Arabia trusts in a madman's mind,
while Edom in wood's delusion is calm.
15 To the living God alone I turn
 here at the outer edge of their border,
 a slave subject to all of their orders—
 knowing the Lord will reward them in kind.

Jeshurun, still, is fresh and strong,
20 although the Exile has lasted long—
for its heart has been touched by the Lord's splendor.
 And so as one in praise they proclaim:
 *Blessèd be God, our Maker, forever.*
 *Blessèd be His glorious name.*

# MESHULLAM DEPIERA

*(early thirteenth century–after 1260)*

MESHULLAM DEPIERA lived his entire life in northeastern Spain and never experienced Muslim rule. Born, it seems, and raised in Gerona, he was also known by the Catalan name of Envidas and most likely spoke the regional language, which was close to Provençal. He was one of the most daring and innovative of the Spanish-Hebrew poets, and his poems indicate that the man was every bit as difficult as his work: "I admit there's a little strangeness in me," he confesses in one poem, but adds, "though my heart goes out to my friends in need." Perhaps because he was marching to the sound of a distinctly un-Andalusian drummer, his poems enjoyed only minimal circulation after his lifetime (among some of the later poets) and then disappeared after the seventeenth century. They were rediscovered in the 1920s and published in a critical edition in 1939.

The fifty poems of Meshullam that have come down to us are characterized by their density and at times obscurity, their supple manipulation of the qasida form, their innovative use of rabbinic as opposed to biblical diction, their complication of perspective, and—in their polemical mode—their subtle satiric strategies. It is possible that the torque of Meshullam's verse was influenced by the troubadour poets of Provence and their *trobar clus* style; others suggest that some of his abstruseness can be traced to his qabbalistic training. (Meshullam was a member of Spain's first qabbalistic circle, which took shape around Nahmanides in Gerona, though his poetry rarely mentions the other members of his group or their mystical doctrine.) Not all his work, however, is obscure; on the contrary, some consider him the first Hebrew medieval poet to break free of the Arabic literary conventions and speak "freely" in his verse. Unburdened by the literary protocol of the court context, Meshullam was writing to please himself alone. And where he does preserve the classical conventions, he often significantly extends their range or undermines them, so that their surface can be deceptive. There is, for instance, a pronounced antisecular strain throughout his verse: he wrote many poems against Maimonides' Aristotelian *Guide for the Perplexed*, which he considered blind to the mysteries of Scripture; and in "How Could You Press for Song" he pours forth scorn for the grammarians. Fleischer notes that this marks a sea change in Hebrew literature, as the study of Hebrew had always been prized and poems were often written in praise of the language and its intricacies. That said, Meshullam was not at all averse to worldly pleasures and, while without doubt a God-fearing man, he was perfectly willing to give vent to his impatience with excessive piety. Schirmann notes lines such as: "Jewish faith is ablaze in me, / though I do not weaken my heart with fasts" and "My prayer is pure, though it isn't long, / and I offer it softly, not with a cry."

It is difficult to make a selection of Meshullam's work that does him justice: most of his poems are long, and choosing one over another would exclude critical elements of his poetry and its vision. Included here, then, are three short poems and excerpts from a number of other poems treating topics such as the nature of poetry, its power and mystery, the limits of linguistics, and the true goal of study.

## THE POET

They asked me: Wise one, who is it who doesn't
distinguish between what's right and wrong,
and sings in praise of his day's elect
while his heart has long seen through his song?

And I answered them: My friends, it is I—
I am the poet who lies.

## ON A NEW BOOK BY MAIMONIDES

Silence, *Guide*, and keep your mouth from speaking,
for these are things unheard of and extreme.
They will be punished who say the Book of the Lord
is all a parable, and its prophesy only a dream.

## BEFORE YOU TAKE UP YOUR PEN

Before you take up your pen to write
take a good look at your heart and life—
and know that words are sharpened arrows,
and what one puts in a book is a knife.

# HOW COULD YOU PRESS FOR SONG

How could you press for song from me,
    when my tongue is tied and I'm unworthy,
and pleasure now is gone from poetry,
    until Time restores it to me.
And since my flute's music was halted,           5
    my mind has settled on the Talmud's mystery;
the Midrash is what I seek out instead,
    and the Mishnah's become a shelter to me:
I study the rules of prayer before standing,
    bequeathal's laws in the Order of Owning,       10
confronting the Book of Creation's secrets
    and probing the seven letters' doubling.
What good is the verb's declension and pattern?
    Do conjugations make things happen?
Can quadrilateral forms of the verb         15
    teach us of arcs and expanses of circles?
Has grammar ever made a man wise?
    Are pedants appointed to lead the people?
All their distinctions just weary the spirit.
    There's nothing of worth within their linguistics     20
(though morphology's known to the masters of Scripture),
    and so they come to the greatness of prophets
with the wisdom of letters—hard and soft—
    hoping that grammar might cut through their haze,
or the comments of Qimhi, of blessed memory,     25
    and the wise one of Fez, whom they all praise.
The fight over roots and the weaving of words
    is the sole achievement of the winged-one's age.
With dots and lines they live out their days;
    their hearts heavy, they labor in vain—     30
for seeing the word's form is sufficient
    to know its gender and how it should change.
What are these shifting verbs to me—
    full and hollow, weak and strong?
Only eternity, and with it my honor,     35
    moves through me with dance-like song.

## AS ONE WITH THE MORNING STARS

Singing as one with the morning stars,
 singing as night drew near to its end
and the light around me came up and drove
 the darkness out, and my sun rose—
5 as I roused my thoughts from the deepest sleep
 and woke my limbs as they lay in slumber,
I sought to waken the dawn with a tune
 and went to meet the morning with song.
I held my precious lute in hand—
10 my left was skilled at making it quiver;
my timbrel and flute were tied to my shoulder
 by cords I knotted and then let go.
And so I broke out in song to compose,
 to see if my poems would soon find favor,
15 and comfort me there in the fields as I roamed
 through wandering's country, which is my home.
I sang, but my flute wouldn't reply,
 and nothing was heard from among the branches.
O brothers in mystery, have you ever known
20 a pipe or lute to refuse my entreaty,
while birds fell silent among the boughs,
 and from my roof not a sparrow called?
But I send them greetings, for without a sound
 they've warned me to put my songbook away
25 and keep its lines from the eyes of men—
 and hide my secrets, as well as I can. . . .

# MOSHE BEN NAHMAN (NAHMANIDES)

## (1194–1270)

The central personality of the "Catalan renaissance" of the early thirteenth century and an important writer in diverse fields that included Qabbala, biblical commentary, religious law, philosophy, poetry, and communal affairs, MOSHE BEN NAHMAN—HaRamban, Nahmanides, or, to his fellow Catalans, Bonastruc de Porta—was one of medieval Spanish Jewry's outstanding figures.

Nahmanides was born to a distinguished family in Gerona and lived most of his adult life there and in Barcelona, where he was involved in the major controversies of his day. The first of these involved the debate over Maimonides' work, when Ben Nahman sought, without much success, to mediate between the anti-Maimonidean French rabbis—whose pupil he was—and the Spanish Jews, for whom Greek philosophy was a central part of a proper education. In 1263, in the wake of the antiheretical movement that had taken hold in southern Europe, he was called upon to appear before the king of Aragon and defend Judaism and its central texts against the claim put forth by a Jewish convert to Christianity by the name of Pablo Christiani that the Bible and Talmud and other writings contained proof of the messianic claims of Jesus. While the king was impressed by Ben Nahman's performance over the course of the five-day debate known now as the Disputation at Barcelona, Christian writers insisted that Pablo had the upper hand; Pope Clement IV intervened, and soon Jewish books were confiscated in Aragon and all so-called anti-Christian references were blotted out. Whether because he was facing threats and certain punishment, or for some other, altogether unrelated reason, Nahmanides fled to either southern France or Castile in 1265, and two years later he left for Palestine, landing in Acre and traveling to Jerusalem. There he witnessed the destruction wrought by the Mongols, whose forces had invaded the country eight years earlier: "Israel is not to be found [in Jerusalem]," he wrote in a letter to his son, "for when the Tartars came, they fled, and some were killed." He did what he could to help revive Jerusalem's Jewish community, and within a year Jews were returning. He then moved to Acre, where he served for a short while as the spiritual leader of that community. About his private life we know little, apart from the fact that he had both sons and daughters, and lost at least one son.

Like Meshullam DePiera, Ben Nahman was part of what Ezra Fleischer has called the Gerona school of poetry. With their "counter poetics," he notes, the

234

writers of that school "sought to uproot secular poetry from its historical ground and transplant it to another, more fertile soil. In Gerona, for the first time in the history of Spanish Hebrew literature, poetry was performed far from the main centers of Jewish political life, and by poets lacking any but oppositional contacts with the Jewish oligarchic upper class." The poetics of this new "oppositional aristocracy" eliminated much of the ornamental, metaphorical richness and conventional practice of the Andalusian school and shunned the humor and frivolity of the *maqaama*. As a result, says Fleischer, "poetry became poetry again"—that is, it returned to verse and regained its serious, contemplative aspect.

Though Nahmanides' poetic output was slim, poetry for him was neither a diversion nor window dressing. On the contrary, his eighteen extant poems give every indication of considerable literary gifts and, as in the magisterial hymn below, they contain full-bodied expression of his thought, including—some say—his immersion in the mystical doctrine of the new Qabbala, which had entered Gerona from Provence.

## BEFORE THE WORLD EVER WAS

*My work, I say, is concerning a king.*

From the beginning, before the world ever was,
I was held on high with his hidden treasures.
He brought me forth from nothing and in
    the end I will be withdrawn by the King.

My being flowed from the spheres' foundation,
which endowed it with form in evident fashion.
The craftsmen's hands weighed its creation,
    so I would be brought to the vaults of the King.

He appeared to reveal what once he concealed,
on the left and on the right as well.
He sent me down the stairway leading
    from Siloam's pool to the groves of the King.

I was formed from dust, though your breath in me burns.
You've known this stranger's thoughts in these lands.
How long, my soul, until you return          20
    and meet with approval before the King?

You set a lamp at my feet on the path
and searched to see if my spirit was willing.
As I set out before you, you warned me, repeating:
    Fear, my child, the Lord and King.          25

My heart was given balance and choice:
if it brings me to goodness—in that I'll rejoice.
But if it brings evil, derision will reign,
    for this is not the will of the King.

Trembling I hasten to confess my transgression          30
before my life is brought to its end.
My name will testify for me then—
    and who could deny the decree of the King?

I was drawn to a land of drought and starvation
and nearly buried in wanting's tomb;          35
but I turned back, feeling contrition:
    I had not kept to the words of the King.

He set great love in my heart for the world.
I pursued its pleasures, and vanity's whirl;
and so I'll be judged for all I have hidden          40
    and go in fear of my Lord and King.

Knowing iniquity, trembling in guilt—
knowing its fortune will wane, heart waits
in terror for mercy, for how can man's spirit
    corrupted come before the King?          45

In weighing out wrong that a servant admits,
place your mercies on the scales with his merit,
as against his will, he offers account
    before the Master, my Lord and King.

Yours is the grace of benevolence, Lord;          50
with it alone is refuge secured.
Yours is forgiveness with which he is rescued—
    its portion determined by the King.

I've trusted you and not my power,
55   and know your compassion endures forever!
Before I call, somehow you answer.
    I'm ashamed to bring my requests to the King.

Your ways are a comfort, you crush all baseness,
so soul in its refuge will know no disgrace.
60   The body interred will surely be vanquished—
    but soul ascend through the halls of the King.

She knows you will plunge me into the mire,
knows you'll take as pledge her attire—
that you will restore her, once she has suffered
65     the judgment soon to be made by the King.

Strengthen the weak one, so she will be firm—
and when things to their former state are returned
bring her forth from the palace's garden
    through the paradise groves that belong to the King.

*From* "ONE HUNDRED VERSES"

My friends, lamenting, gathered to ask me:
    "Where are the days that rejoiced in the glory
of Time, then came to an end and vanished
    utterly? What do they mean?" And another
wondered: "Could they ever return,          5
    if Time chose to restore that bounty,
returning the treasure of its precious vessels,
    its joy and laughter, its stolen memories?
For desire granted is sweet to the soul,
    and the pleasure we once knew is gone. . . ."    10
But they had rejoiced in nothing and grieved
    for an empty notion—a vanity.
Listen to soul's counsel, I said,
    you in your pain, for this is destiny:
At appointed times the days are against us.      15
    This is justice, and ordered rightly.
Youth and its season of song are empty:
    they drive nothing—are driven only.
Time came to youth with its wind
    and overwhelmed you, painting your eyes. . . .   20
So many have faltered at its hand,
    and stumbling fallen prey to confusion;
they hoped to see silver appear on their head,
    then perished in smoke, at the Lord's raging.
But age is fine to those who hold         25
    to virtue, and above all fear transgression—
lifting their souls toward contrition,
    although they bear no guilt or sin,
fasting often, and mixing their food
    and drink with water from their weeping. . . .   30
For the heart will raise age on its throne,
    and the reverent be shown the glory on high—
where seraphim walking among the coals
    are not consumed within the fire.
With angels bearing banners of love,      35
    they stroll—the paradise grove their shelter:

Trusting they'd see in the world of souls
 the hidden place and His shining splendor,
they stream in Eden to the garden's goodness,
<sub>40</sub>  although they're shaken and go in terror
of climbing toward the Tree of Knowledge
 where visions are seen, and men grow wise—
and toward the Tree of Life and the living
 angels ministering in its branches' shade.
<sub>45</sub> For there they sing to the Lord above
 and there his servants in service are gathered,
their souls in righteousness resting and sated—
 filled by the glory of God's great love.
Still to be bound in the chain of life,
<sub>50</sub>  for adornment and luster, in beauty's perfection,
they will be borne, returning to bodies,
 as through the rocks and caverns they roll.
So men in dispersion bear their indenture,
 in God's name, and do not suffer.
<sub>55</sub> They know shame, and exile's burden,
 but reap honor within their abjection—
their legs' fetters like anklets to them.
 And though they witness the wicked secure,
their steps hold fast to their chosen paths
<sub>60</sub>  and their hearts never stray from their borders.
They do the will of the Lord, their Maker,
 although it often means disaster,
taking their first-born out to die,
 as tears of joy well up in their eyes—
<sub>65.</sub> for the fruit of their loins at heart is yours,
 Lord, and so they do not mourn.
Those who die by your sword aren't "slain."
 Do not keen or wail for them
who say: "Through our blood, we live!"
<sub>70</sub>  for wallowing in that blood they're saved.
These, Lord, are men of your hand.
 They are your portion and will not leave you,
whose vision will sate them when they awaken,
 for then your presence will take them in.

For them justice will pour from the skies,                                    75
    and the dew of life—and so they'll rise,
their youth renewed, their flesh made tender
    once again, as the dew descends,
and they'll be crowned with glory and splendor,
    who in their entreaty did not seek them.                      80
The sun will be shamed by the light of their faces,
    confounded and made to seem dark at their side,
as the world of life everlasting devours
    death, which over all abides.
A fountain of life is the King's light,                                       85
    by which they'll walk and always be guided,
for He is a God of account, repaying
    evil with vengeance, and good in kind—
and the world will be renewed as the heavens,
    trembling, together, are rolled like a scroll:               90
for the Lord is God, a rock everlasting.
    May His works forever be praised and extolled.

# SHEM TOV IBN FALAQERA

## *(c. 1225–after 1290)*

The attack on the old secular poetry and all it implied is taken up more directly by SHEM TOV IBN FALAQERA. In the introduction to his major work, *Sefer HaMevaqesh* (The Book of the Seeker), Ibn Falaqera resolves to turn his back on his youthful literary ways and, instead of flattering the wealthy and impugning misers, and pursuing vain songs of desire, "to compose a treatise to teach [men] the proper path." First, however, he would have to divorce the Muse, something he does explicitly, in verse: "I'll send the daughters of song away—and with this tract our bonds I'll sever—and take instead the daughter of wisdom and reason—to be my wife, forever." Noting that he has already composed some twenty thousand lines of verse, Falaqera then proceeds to write a belletristic ethical work in rhymed prose (interspersed with poems—to help the reader remember!) that will serve as a conclusion to his poetic project and the beginning of a life without song and all it implies. The "ritual exorcism" of *The Book of the Seeker* records a young man's encounters with a variety of types, including a wealthy man, a soldier, a craftsman, a physician, a pietist, a linguist, and more—all of whom he seeks out on his quest for knowledge. At the end of the first, rhymed-prose half of the book, he turns his attention to the poet, whom he finds wanting with respect to truth and morality. Having dispensed with poetry as a worthy endeavor, Falaqera abandons the rhymed prose and metrical verse of part 1, as he continues his exploration of other (scientific) disciplines in the second half of his book.

Its confessional nature notwithstanding, *The Book of the Seeker* reveals little in the way of hard facts about its author's life, and Falaqera's other sixteen volumes treating science, philosophy, medicine, psychology, biblical studies, Maimonides' work (he was a disciple), and ethics barely add to our knowledge of him. He seems to have come from a prominent family and lived in Tudela—then a Christian town that preserved much of its Arabic heritage. He received a traditional education in the secular sciences and humanities, as well as in Jewish religious studies, and may have been trained as a physician. He also translated numerous philosophical works from Arabic to Hebrew. Apart from *The Book of the Seeker* and a collection of epigrams called *Iggeret HaMusar* (The Epistle of Morals), he is best known for his abstract of Ibn Gabirol's *Fountain of Life*, which figured prominently in the discovery of that work in the nineteenth century. He was married, it seems, and had at least one son.

## CAREER COUNSELING

If you like being among the elect
who know the secrets of all the patricians,
and crave long looks at the unveiled doe—
    be a physician.

## A MYSTERY

The mind's a mystery far beyond man,
as is the Creator's work in creation—
and the soul's path when the body's consumed—
and the growth of an infant's bones in the womb.

## ON POETS AND POETRY

Many will praise you, including the wealthy,
when poetry comes your way and you sing.

You'll offer them flattery and in exchange
they'll give you gifts that are just as vain.

## WHY GOD MADE YOU

To avoid sin speak no more
than half of what you hear;
and know that this is why God made you
with just one mouth, but a pair of ears.

## THE FOOL THINKS

The fool thinks wisdom's honey is bitter
and folly's gall much sweeter to lick—
like a patient who's tired of cures from his doctor
and craves a dish that will make him sick.

## POVERTY'S WAR

Poverty strikes powerless people
and kills them soon enough like a sword.
The soldier's battle at least brings honor;
disgrace is the end of poverty's war.

# YITZHAQ IBN SAHULA

*(late thirteenth century)*

YITZHAQ IBN SAHULA was a resident of Guadalajara, a town that was close to
the centers of the Spanish mystical movements that came to full flower toward
the end of the thirteenth century. He appears to have known Moshe de Leon, the
principal author of *The Zohar*, and he himself wrote a qabbalistic commentary
on the Song of Songs. There is, however, nothing esoteric about his best-known
work, *Meshal HaQadmoni* (An Ancient Tale), which is grounded in the scientific
learning of his day and addressed to the broadest possible readership rather than
the limited audience of the Qabbala.

A physician by training and learned in the natural sciences as well as philoso-
phy, Ibn Sahula had been drawn toward secular poetry in his youth, but in his
thirty-seventh year, as he notes in the introduction to *Meshal HaQadmoni*, "a spirit
came across him and he saw the evil of his ways . . . and he said: I have sinned,
and my sins have been written with an iron pen / where now can I turn?" He
composed his tale in that spirit of contrition, couching his stories in the guise of
ancient lore in order to enhance their appeal for an audience which, as he saw it,
had only a tenuous link to Jewish tradition and was, instead, drawn to the foreign
literature of the day (both European and Arabic). His aim, he wrote, was "to re-
move the books of Homer, heretics, and aesthetes from their hearts."

Ibn Sahula did, however, make use of foreign elements to sweeten the pill,
and he based *Meshal HaQadmoni* on Arabic, Persian, and Indian models, such as
*Kalila and Dimna* and *Tales of Sendebar (The Seven Sages of Rome)*. As in those
works, his characters are animals, but throughout the five parts of the book—
which treat Wisdom and Knowledge, Repentance, Good Counsel, Humility, and
Awe—they deliver sermons drawing on traditional Jewish sources. Despite the
contempt for the reader that sometimes comes through Ibn Sahula's work, *Me-
shal HaQadmoni* soon became extremely popular and was even published in Yid-
dish, in nine editions, beginning in the seventeenth century.

Part and parcel of Ibn Sahula's principled rejection of the foreign was, per-
haps, the author's choice to include very few metrical poems in his narrative—as
he saw the use of quantitative meters as alien to the spirit of Hebrew. *Meshal
HaQadmoni* contains just twelve poems, five of them in the preface; all are far
inferior to the poems found in earlier collections of rhymed Hebrew prose by

Alharizi, Ben Yaʻaqov, and others. Ibn Sahula's Hebrew prose, on the other hand, is vivid and lithe.

## THE CYNIC SPEAKS

Why bow down, mortal man,
before the power of wisdom and learning?

Whenever you're right you're ruined, and when
you're clever you wither in your perfection.

Pity the heart in its weakness and failings,
and the eye, weeping, as it gives in.

Better to offer joy your portion—
the song of girls heard in the garden;

you'll gain wealth and soon be wound
in the turban of Time's bounty and fortune.

## ON HUMILITY

They lie in the darkness of earth, sleeping—
    a city stricken, in an instant brought down.
The world and all who dwell there are dreams.
    Its joy is drawn toward grief in time.

Look at the merit of the humble about us,
    whose path in lowliness always wends—
and see how birds whose soul is low
    live on high, and offer song.

Blessèd is he who hears and learns
in wisdom—and in the Kingdom, lives on.

# AVRAHAM ABULAFIA

*(1240–c. 1291)*

Avraham Abulafia is known as one of the major figures in the history of the Hebrew mystical tradition. Born in Saragossa in 1240, and raised in Tudela, he was orphaned at the age of eighteen and two years later began a life of wandering that would take him to Palestine, Greece, mainland Italy, and Sicily. His first trip was to the Land of Israel, when he was twenty, in search of the ten lost tribes and the mythical river Sambatyon, beyond which, legend had it, large parts of these tribes had been exiled by the Assyrian king Shalmanaser. Abulafia believed that finding them would help usher in the Messianic age. He made it no farther than the port town of Acre, however, and headed home, passing through Greece and Italy, where he spent some ten years. In 1271, in Barcelona, a mystical experience led him to believe that he had attained prophetic inspiration, and he began preaching his sometimes Christian-seeming doctrine to a select circle of disciples in Spain, some of whom converted to Catholicism. Three years later he left his native country once again, returning to Greece and Italy. In 1280, he experienced another mystical vision and set out for Rome, where he planned to take Pope Nicholas III to task for Christianity's treatment of the Jews in their exile and then persuade the pontiff to convert to Judaism. This foolish adventure nearly cost Abulafia his life; he was condemned to hang, and only because of the pope's sudden death was the poet spared. After a month in prison, he was released and returned to Sicily. His troubles continued, however, and he was attacked within the Jewish community for his messianic speculation. When in the midst of that controversy the most influential rabbinic authority of the time called him a "charlatan," Abulafia was forced to flee to the desolate island of Comino (near Malta). There, in 1288, he wrote the apocalyptic—even hallucinatory—fourteen-hundred line *Sefer Ha'Ot*. (The Book of the Letter—or Sign), the only surviving example of several prophetic works he composed late in his life. Abulafia also wrote many language-centered mystical texts and manuals of ecstatic meditation, whose aim was, as he put it, "to unseal the soul, to untie the knots which bind it."

While much of the excerpt from *Sefer Ha'Ot* translated here involves the esoteric use of numerology (on which, see the notes to the poem at the back of this volume), the prophetic thrust of the work is self-evident. Blood and ink in Abulafia's thought stand, respectively, for imagination (soul) and intellect (spirit), and the ongoing battle between them involves an effort to raise imagination to the power of the Active Intellect, which is the conduit to eternal life and the divine. This transformation is brought about through—among other things— manipulation of the letters of the divine name. The poet likens their combination to the combination of sounds in music. Abulafia's prophetic vision involves a synthesis of these and other often-conflicting forces through a kind of *psychomachia*, or war for the soul, wherein the inner processes are externalized through imaginative vision and its figures. In another work, *Gan Na'ul* (A Garden Enclosed), Abulafia writes: "When the Name, whose secret is in blood and ink, began to move within him . . . it began to move him from potentiality to actuality." While the lines of *Sefer Ha'Ot* are neither metrical nor rhymed, the cadence throughout is pronounced, and the poem's various sections at times make use of regularized stanzas and a generally consistent number of words per line. Both in style and form the poem is unique in the literature.

Curiously, Abulafia's *Sefer Ha'Ot* is one of the few strong, explicitly qabbalistic works in the canon of medieval Hebrew poetry from Spain. There are of course other powerful poems by qabbalists (Nahmanides' poem on the soul, for example), and many first-rate mystical poems (by Ibn Gabirol and others); and there are poems about *The Zohar* or the Qabbala in general (by Todros Abulafia and Meshullam); in almost all cases, however, there is considerable controversy over the extent to which these works are, at root, "qabbalistic." With Avraham Abulafia, there is no doubt.

## From *THE BOOK OF THE LETTER*

And the letter is longing,
and sky desire
to know the will
that moves Him and lends
grace to spirit                                                    5
and mercy to power
to rectify action,
Kingdom now foremost
and Law behind,
now Law foremost                                                   10
and Kingdom behind—
and the letter and vowels
and song reveal
the mystery of blood . . .

                              *

And YHVH spoke to me when I saw His name                           15
spelled out and merged with the blood in my heart,
separating blood from ink and ink from blood:
and YHVH said to me: Behold,
blood is the name of your soul, and ink the name of your spirit:
your father and mother are vessels for my name and a sign.        20
And then I fathomed the tremendous difference between
my spirit and soul, and a great joy came through me.
For I knew my soul was dwelling in the redness as blood,
and my spirit was dwelling in the blackness as ink.
And there raged a war in my heart between                          25
the blood and ink: the blood from the wind
and the ink from dust, and the black ink
over the blood was victorious—
as the Sabbath subdues all the days of the week.

And so my heart rested within me—and I offer                      30
praise to the Lord, to the Name in my heart forever.

                              *

And the Lord showed me a new vision with a name
renewed and a spirit revived, on the fourth day
of the seventh month, the first moon at the start
of the eighteenth year from the onset of my visions:
I was watching, and behold a man came up from the west
with a great force, and the number of men in his camp
was twenty-two thousand: that man's glory and strength
of heart and splendor shook the earth's foundations,
and the hearts of his soldiers trembled; strong-armed riders
were with him, and men on foot, and the line of those men
came to no end, and his forehead was marked with blood
and ink in both its corners, and the image of a letter
like a staff determined between them, and this is the sign
deeply occulted: black was the color of blood
and went red, and the ink's color was red and behold
it blackened, and the color of the letter determining between
the two colors was white: He shows us wonders—
the sign, the key, within the forehead of he
who comes, and in accordance with it the whole
of his army gathers its forces, setting out:
and I, when I saw his face, was alarmed at the sight,
and my heart withdrew within me, was moved from its place,
and I longed for it to speak, to call on the name
of the Lord for help, but the matter fled from my spirit:

And it came to pass, when I saw that man, my terror
mounted and my dread increased, and he opened his mouth
and spoke, and I answered him in kind, and with
those words became another man. . . .
                                        And from
the bow of knowing they shot arrows of learning,
sending insight toward the target of wisdom,
for the power of blood in the heart is signed and sealed,
and the heart of he who is wise at heart is whole,
knowing his blood is alive and the slime is dead
within him, and so—slime and blood are enclosed
in his heart; more bitter than death is slime,
his power is sunken within it, and sweeter than honey
is blood, and his spirit dwells in the heart's shrine:

and the soul of every creature of mind must journey 70
from slime's tent toward the tent of blood
and from blood's tent toward the shrine of the heart
of heaven it travels, and there it dwells for all
the days of its life: . . .
                       And I lifted up my eyes 75
and I saw three warriors pursuing each other and racing
one after the other, at a bow-shot's distance,
and each turned to his friend and said: "Run
and fight against me," and I saw and behold, the first
ran out toward the second, who fled before him 80
and fleeing, turned, and shot a sharpened arrow
and the arrow fell at his feet by the stone that drew it
and turned it there from side to side as it struck
his foot, and clung to it, and the man let out
a tremendous, bitter, powerful shout and cry, 85
"Lord, God of my fathers, let this arrow
which has struck me now bring on death with its poison."
And while he was speaking, behold, his foot puffed up
like a goatskin full of wind, the pain mounting
and spreading through every inch of his body until 90
his limbs and joints were swollen, like yeast risen:

When I heard his cry my heart was stirred, and I ran
toward him, drawing near, and bent down,
and whispered into his ear, and his pain abated
before my whisper. . . . And it came to pass, when the warrior 95
who'd struck his foot with the arrow saw how the other
was cured by the whisper, he ran out to him holding
his spear and struck him through the navel, and drove
the blade deep into his belly, and there spilled
forth to the ground his guts . . . and he fell to the ground 100
and died:
          And when the third saw that the second
had fallen at the hand of the first, he ran
out after the first with his sword drawn,
once, and again, and then a third time, 105
ten blows and he died [ . . . ] on the tenth
and I went up toward the dy[ . . . ] and greeted him
saying, "[ . . . ] with you the warrior soldier

[ . . . ] tell me, my lord, if you will,
110    the meaning of this battle, which I have seen
in the v.i.s.i.o.n"—and he showed me an old man
seated upon a throne of judgment, his robes
were purple and blue: "Go and ask," he said,
"that man upon the Hill, and he will tell you
115    what these battles mean, and what they will bring,
for he is one of your people." And I went up toward
the Hill of Judgment, approaching the old man,
and I bowed down and put my face to the ground
before his feet, and he set his hands upon me
120    and lifted me up to my feet before him and said:
Blessed, my son, is your coming. Peace be upon you,
and all who love you, for from the battle you
were saved, and all my battles you have waged
and won: and now, know that these many days
125    and years I have waited for you here,
until you came, and now I will reveal
the meaning of the battles you have seen:
The three warriors pursuing each other are kings . . .

The name of the first warrior-king is Qadari'el,
130    and the name of the second is Magdi'el; and the name of the third
is Alfi'el; and the name of the warrior-king you saw
at the beginning of that vision is Turi'el.
And I, I am Yeho'el. For I have been willing
to address you now these several years, therefore
135    your name in Israel shall henceforth be—forever—
Roi'el, the Seer of God, son of the living
source of God, Maqor El HaHai,
for you came from the source of life, and life you chose,
and so with life you'll live, as Abraham's children
140    live—Isaac, Israel, and all our fathers,
and all who hold to them will hold to Truth
and with us thrive now, see the fifth
warrior is from the Messiah, the one who will reign
at the end of the kingdoms' days—this is the meaning
145    revealed to all, though only one who knows
within his knowing will fathom the hidden meaning.
And here, my son, this is what the Lord

of Israel told you: Write what you have seen
in a book, and call that book *The Book of the Letter,*
and it shall be a sign to all who see it,                    150
so they will know the Lord is good to the people
of Israel—already he has brought them salvation
and seen fit to send this book to Spain;
go in fear of no one, and be not ashamed
before any man, for you see that the Lord is God;            155
in him alone you've trusted, who raises your arm
so it may tell of his Name to the ends of the earth.
And I did all that the old man told me to do
in the name of the Lord, and I wrote this book, and here
have sent it to you this day as [ . . . ] a savior           160
to say the Lord is with you in your returning
to him in this year of the mind
with a heart that is whole."

# AVRAHAM BEN SHMU'EL

*(second half of the thirteenth century?)*

Virtually nothing is known of AVRAHAM BEN SHMU'EL's life and work apart from the one powerful penitential poem included here, which Haim Schirmann ranks among medieval Hebrew poetry's finest creations. Schirmann has suggested that it might be possible to identify its author as Avraham Ibn Hasdai (of *The Prince and the Monk*), but there is no evidence of Ibn Hasdai's ever having displayed the gifts possessed by the writer of this poem. Likewise some have sought to identify the poet as the qabbalist Avraham Abulafia (above), whose father was in fact named Shmu'el—but again, the extant evidence argues against this, as Abulafia left behind only ecstatic hymns and other poems that bear no resemblance to the poem signed "Avraham Ben Shmu'el."

The poem first surfaced in a manuscript from 1300 and later appeared in various Spanish prayer books. Its prosody is somewhat unusual: the lines are built on a sequence of parallelisms that employ neither meter nor rhyme and suggest a return to the biblical form of the prophetic mode. Most likely the poet had Avraham Ibn Ezra's "I Bow Down" before him as a model (above). A similar inventory of body parts and their attendant sins or flaws can be found in *Genesis Rabbah* 18: "I will not create her [Eve] from the head, so she will not think too much with her mind, and not from the eye, so she will not become too curious, and not from the ear, so she won't be inclined to eavesdrop, and not from the mouth, lest she talk too much, and not from the heart, so she won't be jealous." Avraham Ben Shmu'el's poem was, in all probability, composed to accompany the liturgy.

# TO WHOM AMONG THE AVENGERS OF BLOOD

To whom among the avengers of blood can I cry,
    when my blood has been shed by my own two hands?

The hearts of those who despised me I've tried,
    and none have despised me more than my heart.

The enemy's blows and wounds have been mighty,      5
    and none have wounded or struck like my soul.

The corrupt have beguiled me into destruction,
    but what like my own two eyes beguiles?

From fire to fire I've passed alive,
    and nothing has burned like my own desire.      10

In nets and snares I have been trapped,
    but nothing has trapped me like my tongue.

Snakes and scorpions have bitten and stung me,
    but my teeth bite into my flesh more fiercely.

Princes pursued me swiftly on horseback,      15
    but none have pursued like my own two feet.

My anguish has swelled and long overwhelmed me,
    but stubbornness brings me much greater grief.

My heart's sorrows are many—
    and greater still are my sins . . .      20

To whom, then, could I cry—and who could I condemn?
    My destroyers emerge from within me.

Nothing I've found in life surpasses
    seeking refuge in your compassion.

Cast your mercy on hearts that are weary,      25
    O Lord, my king on the Throne of Mercy.

# YOSEF GIQATILLA

*(1248–c. 1325)*

Praised by Avraham Abulafia as his finest student, YOSEF GIQATILLA was greatly influenced by the prophetic Qabbala of his teacher, and he went on to become one of the major qabbalists of the thirteenth century. His most well-known book, *Sha'arei Ora* (Gates of Light, which was written before 1293), demonstrates a marked departure from Abulafia's thought and shows Giqatilla to be immersed in theosophical qabbalistic teachings treating the *sefirot* and qabbalistic symbolism. Though no direct link has been established, he seems to have been close to Moshe de Leon, and generally speaking his approach to his subject in his later work falls somewhere between the Geronese school of Nahmanides and the school of *The Zohar*. His other work—much of which remains in manuscript—includes a qabbalistic commentary on the Passover Haggada, two commentaries on the Song of Songs, a book about the *mitzvot* (observance of the commandments), and some twenty liturgical poems, and proverbs. While Giqatilla is not considered a poet per se, and isn't among the poets treated in Haim Schirmann's definitive four-volume anthology, *Hebrew Poetry in Spain and Provence*, his handful of extant hymns and didactic poems are of interest for their qabbalistic content and the author's desire to cast it in Andalusian verse forms. The poem below is taken from the opening section of Giqatilla's first extant composition, *Ginat Egoz* (The Nut Garden), which he wrote in 1274, at the end of his two-year period of study under Abulafia. The first word of the title is an acronym standing for *gematria* (numerology), *notarikon* (acrostics), and *temura* (permutation—of the letters, as in anagrams). Comprising an introduction to the mystical symbolism of the alphabet and the divine names, *Ginat Egoz* is studded with short didactic poems introducing each chapter and epitomizing some of the points made in the prose. Born in Medinaceli, Castile, Giqatilla lived for many years in Segovia.

## THE NUT GARDEN

The Nut Garden holds things felt and thought,
and feeling for thought is always a palace—

Sinai with flames of fire about it,
burning though never by fire devoured.

On all four sides surrounded so,
entrance is barred to pretenders forever.

For one who learns to be wise, however,
its doors are open toward the East:

he reaches out and takes a nut,
then cracks its shell, and eats. . . .

# TODROS ABULAFIA

*(1247–after 1300)*

A distant relative of Meir HaLevi Abulafia, but no relation to Avraham, TODROS BEN YEHUDA ABULAFIA was born in Toledo in 1247 and spent most of his life in that city, where Arabic was still in use some one hundred and fifty years after it had been retaken by Christians. Todros studied Arabic early on and commanded both the language and its literature; he was probably also familiar with Christian vernacular literature. An ambitious poet who was anxious to make his way in the culturally rich court of King Alfonso X (the Wise), of Castile (r. 1252–84), Todros managed to attach himself to a wealthy and influential Jewish courtier, dedicating numerous poems to him and being rewarded in turn with—among other things—clothes, funds, chickens, goats, and a donkey. He was even granted an audience with the king himself (see "Before the King," below). Apart from his work as a poet in the context of the Jewish courts, Todros served as a senior tax collector and diplomatic envoy. His luck turned in 1279, when the increasingly religious king ordered Todros's patron to raise an extravagant amount of money from the Jewish community in order to support a military campaign. The king's son, however, diverted the funds for his own purposes, and the troops were stranded; Alfonso's anger led to the execution of the patron (along with another leading tax collector). Two years later most of Castile's Jews—Todros among them—were rounded up while at synagogue and put in prison, where they were held for ransom. Todros wrote numerous poems during this period of imprisonment and was released later that year. Somewhat subdued by his time in jail and his fall from grace, he managed to regain a measure of prominence in the court of Alfonso's son and successor, Sancho IV (d. 1295), and his ambition once again took hold. Though contemporary documents complain of the slack standards of religious observance at the time and a general trend toward assimilation among the upper classes, Todros maintained his faith, and this despite his wild ways and clear predilection for Christian and Arab women—a preference that finds powerful and colorful expression in his poetry.

We have scant information about Todros's later life, and firm evidence of him vanishes after 1298, when he collected his poems into a diwan, which he called *Gan HaMeshalim veHaHidot* (The Garden of Parables and Riddles). He gave the poems descriptive headings in traditional fashion (though for the most part in Hebrew rather than Arabic) and introduced the entire collection with an apology that echoes similar statements in HaNagid's diwan and Ibn Ezra's criticism. After the poet's death, his poetry is rarely mentioned in the literature for another six hundred and twenty-five years. We now know that the diwan was copied in the seventeenth century in Egypt, and that the manuscript then passed from hand to hand among antiquarian collectors in Iraq and India. At some point Sha'ul 'Abdullah Yosef, an Iraqi businessman and an amateur but extremely learned scholar of Hebrew poetry, got hold of that seventeenth-century manuscript while he was working in Hong Kong (!) and made a handwritten copy of Todros's treasure trove for his own research. Yosef died of blood poisoning in 1906, and the manuscript came into the possession of one of the leading scholars of medieval Hebrew poetry at the time, David Yellin. Yellin prepared a critical edition which was published in three volumes from 1934 to 1937. With that publication, some twelve hundred poems were added to the medieval Hebrew canon.

Critical evaluation of the poems in *Gan HaMeshalim* has varied widely. Todros has been looked upon as everything from "one of the greatest poets of whom the Jews can boast," to an egocentric graphomaniac who lacked national consciousness and was of interest primarily to historians, to "a mediocre epigone" whose work is "repetitive and superficial." Taken on its own terms, his large oeuvre reveals Todros to be among the liveliest of the Silver Age Spanish-Hebrew poets. He constantly widened the boundaries of the art and, in addition to his many accomplished poems in the familiar Andalusian modes, composed concrete or pattern poetry and some verse that was likely influenced by the troubadour tradition. Two of his poems treat the concept of "spiritual love." Above all, Todros's work is distinguished by its freshness and candor: he managed to introduce a vivid (though not always straightforward) personal dimension into his verse that went well beyond anything medieval Hebrew poetry had seen before him. He filled the classical conventions with irony, turned them on their heads, or did away with them altogether and created new poetic space in which to work. His one hundred and thirty–plus *Todrosi'ot*, as scholars have come to call them, establish what is virtually a new hybrid genre. Short poems constructed along a five-letter acrostic of the poet's first name, they ground the poet's intimate conversation with his God in the most profane circumstances. Perhaps the most unusual of all the "sacred" poems in the Hebrew canon, they lack any liturgical function whatsoever. In short, Todros Abulafia is easily one of the most surprising poets of the entire period, though his work is not often read by nonspecialist Hebrew readers and is almost completely unknown to readers of poetry in English.

## I'VE LABORED IN LOVE

I've labored in love and brought nothing forth,
   and I'm trapped in the trap of that fawn
      of an Arab girl.
              My soul
    so craves a kiss from her mouth,
that I long to turn myself into a woman:
    for women she'll kiss—
but I'm lost as long as I'm male.

## SHE SAID SHE WANTED

She said she wanted to run when she saw
   the gray scattered with white in my hair:
"Dawn's already come up on your head
   and I'm the moon—you'll drive me away."
"It isn't true," I said, "you're the sun—
   and can't, by nature, hide by day."
"You've lost your power to run after love,"
   she replied. "What good would it do to stay?"
"Nothing's changed," I told her, "except
   for the gray. I've got the heart of a lion
to do your will." And she offered: "OK,
   you're a lion. . . . Then I'm a gazelle.
Would I lie down in the lion's den,
   bright gazelle that I am?"

## THE DAY YOU LEFT

The day you left was bitter and dark,
   you finest thing, you—and when I think of it,
it feels like there's nothing left of my skin.
   Your feet, by far, were more beautiful,
     the day they mounted
     and wrapped my neck in a ring . . .

## THAT FINE GAZELLE

That fine gazelle, that fawn sent
to torture lovers with endless grief,
    heard me complain my soul was faint
with desire for her, and offered: "My saint,

if inside me you feel it's too tight for you—
loosen up and you'll find your relief."


## THEY FIGHT WITH ME OVER DESIRE

They fight with me over desire,
and think I'm sleeping when I'm wide awake;
they do what they can to smother my love,
    or slowly drive it away with spirit.

But it's all fire, and their words are wind:
and wind just fans the fire that's near it.


## THAT GIRL EMERGED

That girl emerged from her lover's soul—
    not from any rib or bone.
And from her heart comes honey. Amazing!
    How could honey come from stone?


## MAY MY TONGUE

May my tongue cleave to the roof of my mouth
    if I, girl, forget your sigh
the day you whispered to me: "Hold me,
    and put your hand upon my thigh."

## THERE'S NOTHING WRONG IN WANTING A WOMAN

There's nothing wrong in wanting a woman,
and loving girls is hardly a sin—
but whether or not they're pretty or pure,
Arabia's daughters are what you should look for.
Stay far away from the Spanish Christians,
although they're fair and bright as the sun,
for they'll provide neither comfort nor ease,
even with shawls and silken sleeves:
their dresses are always covered with mud,
as their hems are dragged through dung and crud.
Their minds are empty from heartless whoring—
when it comes to seduction, they know not a thing.
But the Arab woman's grace is her glory,
ravishing spirits, banishing worry.
And whether or not she's wearing her clothes,
she looks as though she's decked out in gold.
She'll give you pleasure when the day arrives,
for in lewdness's ways and desire she's wise,
her legs gripped tightly around your head,
crying out *Lord!!*—and raising the dead.
The lover who opts for the Christian feast
is just like a man who'd lie with a beast.

## STRONG POET, WEAK POET

Your song, friend, is born of a woman,
and the heart of a girl is what it has.
My poems take it daily to bed,
  and drive their standards up its ass.

## PLASTER AND PEARLS

All you compose is plaster and chalk,
    while I—I fashion genuine pearls!
How could you even compare what we do?
    Can worthless pebbles be likened to jewels?
The stream of your song is about to go dry;
    along it thistles have started to crowd.
So open its rut to my currents and watch
    my springs fill it, if they're allowed—
for the sea of my song is wide, my friend,
    and from it come the heavy clouds.

## NOTHING LEFT TO SAY

Have you really nothing left to say?
Are your poems' pockets completely empty?
Has a cat suddenly got your tongue
while mine's like a sword, with which I slay?

Come to the threshing floor of my poems;
I'll leave some gleanings for you to take home.
I'll lend you a stanza, or at least a line—
a bed in the corner, a table to write on.

But take this advice as well with the song:
Weaklings like you shouldn't take on the strong.

## TEACHERS AND WRITERS

Your reason resembles the braying of mules.
Have asses begun competing with stallions?
You comment but get the meaning all wrong,
    teaching the Law just like a heathen.

Your folly's revealed by my knowledge's light—
the contrast affords us an excellent look:
Refusing to learn from the writers themselves,
    you've gleaned nothing at all from their books.

## BEFORE THE KING

Faith's vengeance on falsehood was taken
the day Alfonso was crowned as King—
and so, coming to serve you, I bring
a cup for your glory, with this small hymn.

For the Lord commanded in Scripture: Ascend
    to sacred feasts with a gift in hand.

## MY KING

Make my king regard me with mercy
and incline his heart toward favor for me.
Lord, bring my distress to an end,
and in your way, judge me gently—
so I can say: "A voice has been heard,"
and the sentence will be a comfort to me.
The master will order those who serve him
to give me his riches, and then I'll see
ministers coming from every direction
to fill my bags to the brim with money.

## POEMS FROM PRISON

### I. As Love Lives

As love lives, fly—O birds—to lovers
with greetings from suffering men, held in the ground,
and tell the world, I beg you, they're hungry and thirsty,
though bread of their tears and blood of their hearts abound.

They're cast like unwanted births, deep in dungeons,
where lice and fleas and mosquitoes feast on their flesh,
and tiny creatures that have no names yet jostle
against one another, like lovers in frenzies of lust.
Flies buzz at the bees, the rodents gnaw,
their teeth attacking body and soul exposed—
and jailers and soldiers harry the prisoners, as ordered,
and no one brings them a morsel, not even the crows.

## II. Treacherous Time

Treacherous time has put me in prison
where I've chirped away like a bird in a snare.
How pure and fine my inspiration
is, and was, and will be there.

## III. The Filthy Lay In Darkness with Me

The filthy lay in darkness with me,
    their legs in shackles, just like mine;
Time has twisted my paths—unjustly.
    My jailers are cruel. I've done no harm.

A willing spirit upheld me, Father,
    but scoundrels put that spirit to shame;
greatness was taken from its masters,
    and what they lost won't be regained.

Have mercy, Lord, and free the prisoners.
    Raise the fallen in your name.

## IV. My Rings Have Fallen

My rings have fallen off, but I still have fingers,
    and rings don't determine my glory.
I still have honor, and faith and a noble soul,
    bequeathed to me—my fathers' legacy.
My heart and mind are able to do many things,
    but I'm useless so long as my pockets are empty,
and so I hope for the Lord who was and is,
    and will, again, make Time serve me.
Brace me, Lord, uphold me—your will is mine.
    But how much longer will fools control me?

### V. Is It the Lord

Is it the Lord who brought on this stammering?
  Before Him what have I done wrong?
I no longer have the power to sing,
  and my father's legacy to me was song.

Heal me, Lord, and I'll be healed,
  forgive me in my sin and transgression.
I hope still to serve my God,
  if He'll release me from this prison.

Then when I call, he'll answer me.
I'll pray—and the Lord will hear my entreaty.


### TIME TRIES AS I DRIFT

Time tries as I drift across it
to sink me by mixing my nectar with poison:
against my body it raised its hand,
after taking my wealth and son.

But I will foil all its plans.
I'll praise my Maker, with endless song.


### THE SEA CASTS UP MIRE AND MUD

The sea casts up mire and mud,
  but sinks its pearls to the ocean's floor,
and Time's way is to raise the vile—
  demeaning the precious, exalting the boor.
Good and evil it turns on their heads,
  while fools think their state will endure,
but the wise toy with Time in their way,
  finding in *maybe* and *if* some pleasure.
In the end, there's a balance in heaven whose pans
  the pure will lower, as the empty ascend.

## ON A BIBLE WRITTEN BY SHMU'EL HANAGID

The Lord gave me to Amram's son—
and the Nagid Shmu'el wrote me down,
weaving me with Betzalel's wisdom
in the year Ten Twenty-Five in his hand.

No one knew my worth. And so
from person to person, unwanted, I passed—
then Todros Ben Yehuda, the Levite,
in Thirteen Hundred, redeemed me at last.

## TIME SPREADS ITS NETS

Time spreads its nets at death,
 and all under its spell are swayed:
it gathers every creature there.
 One is lowered and another raised.
Day after day, to all alive,        5
 it acts the custodian for orphans' affairs,
slipping poison into its pot—
 and setting out snakes by furrows of herbs.
Although on occasion its path seems smooth,
 most of its days are cursed with pain.   10
For clouds vanquish every brightness,
 and thunder and lightning come with rain.
Who can avoid its trial and fear?
 In it no man is ever consoled.
It offers righteous men no rest,      15
 not even Noah, whose heart was whole.
What happens to one, happens to all.
 The fool fades along with the wise,
and the Lord whose actions are weighed is awesome;
 his workings are wondrous and vast as the skies. 20
His ways' mystery no one can fathom,
 the womb, for example, filling with bones.
And a secret scroll shouldn't be opened,
 or sealed words ever be known.

## OLD AGE IS DOUBLE-EDGED

Old age is double-edged,
    and this—to me—is how it appears:
like precious oil anointing the head,
    and drivel dripping into beards.


## PERVERSION'S PIGEONS

Perversion's pigeons descend on eagles of truth
    in this generation's twisted ways—
and Time, in anger, draws its bow and shoots
    at men of learning, day after day.
Fools have risen, as men of understanding
    who teach wisdom are brought low,
while *Hear, O Israel* and *Happy is the man*
    the age's children do not know.

Scripture and legend they seek no more,
let alone the knowledge of things obscure.


## MY THINKING WOVE

My thinking wove a song of purple and blue
for God, as manna and nectar were spun on my tongue.
I strung pearls of verse in His name, like a necklace
or links in a chain, the work of a skillful craftsman.
For He is full of compassion. There is no end
to His pleasing things, and who could ever count them?
And so with a grieving heart, I cry—and He answers:
Here is a sign, in faith, it shall be done.
Your fear is over, Todros. Rise, and know
your Time and day and hour soon will come.

## THE LORD IS GOOD AND SO I'M TORMENTED

The Lord is good, and just, and so I'm tormented,
 for I have not done as I was commanded.
My actions alone twisted the path to redemption:
 I've hated the good, and loved transgression,
and run, craving Time's vapor and vanity
 until I was weakened and wholly undone.
Now, as I come to take my leave of this world,
 may I exit just as I entered:
I've only songs—to offer you who forgive.
 I bring these lines, in which I live.


## DEFILED AND PURE ARE ONE

Defiled and pure today are one,
 and the age has given into corruption.
The noble ranks have long been thinned.
 The order has changed. Hell is Heaven.
Calamities mount and this is your sign—
 saved from the trap, you enter the dungeon.
Seeing this in my mind's eye,
 I said to my soul: "Look—it's clear:
All in the end is in God's hand.
 Be strong, Todros, and do not fear."


## ON HEARING CHURCH BELLS

Could young men sing to pagan demons,
 and I not praise the Lord in heaven?
Could they rise to pray in the dark of night
 or at dawn for other gods, for nothing,
and I not wake for the Living God,
 the source and secret of all things?
Rise, heart, and praise the Lord,
 God of worlds on high and below,

5

and come to the land of song's nectar—
10    crossing the honeyed sea of poems.
Send up psalms by night and day,
    with great delight, thank Him with hymns;
for all who hear them bear clear witness
    they're worth more than precious gems.
15  Serve Him with a heart that's pure,
    and He'll bend kings toward your desire.
Fear Him and trust His kindness and grace,
    and in distress He'll show you favor.
But do not put your faith in Time.
20    Time is only chance—not Truth:
for it contains both bitter and sweet,
    and in its way, does what bees do.


## I TAKE DELIGHT IN MY CUP AND WINE

I take delight in my cup and wine
and go down to the garden and spring—
and hearing the song of doves and swifts,
    I, too, begin to sing . . .

5   I tell plainly of all my loves,
despite my jealous friends' concern.
I sing with a beautiful doe whose cheek
    is like the crescent moon—
the melody rises up in the groves
10  and my lips there in the garden move
    and like the birds above me call,
    as from the branches they respond.

I hold the goblet in my hand—
a graceful girl is at my feet;
15  I take in the fragrance of the cinnamon's scent
    and eat thin slices of roasted meat.
I taste her lips and drink the wine,
and waken my flute, as desires rise—
    and drink my fill of nectar with her,
20    until my thirst is wholly quenched.

My friends speak and plead with me
to loosen myself from the grip of that girl:
"How could you let that daughter of Canaan,
　　hold you in desire's spell?"
And I, in turn, answer them:　　　　　　　　　25
"If love of that girl is a burden to me,
　　I'll wear it on my head like a crown—
　　or around my neck like a string of pearls."

Now like a miser, she holds back.
In my largesse, I scatter tears.　　　　　　　30
I look at my plight, and think "Just maybe,
　　she'll have mercy and see my ordeal."
I'm wearing away in my desire—
if only I would grow so thin
　　that to these spies I'd disappear,　　　　　35
　　and never be seen by them again.

Come back, my doe, and sit by my side.
With the balm of your mouth, heal my pain.
"I can't," she says, "I'll be rebuked
　　if they see us," and I respond:　　　　　　40
"Within my illness I've been consumed
and so no longer possess a body—
　　*and in my thinness if a man*
　　*stared at me he wouldn't find me.*"

# NAHUM

*(second half of the thirteenth century)*

Since the mid-nineteenth century scholars have speculated as to the identity of the talented liturgical poet who signed his poems NAHUM. Some have identified him as the fourteenth-century Moroccan writer Nahum HaMaʿaravi, who wrote poetry and translated several important commentaries from Arabic to Hebrew, and whose epithet (HaMaʿaravi—the Westerner, or Maghrebi) appears to be alluded to at the end of the poem below. All the other extant evidence, however, seems to argue against that attribution. Another source mentions a penitential poem by one Nahum of Castile, from the second half of the thirteenth century. Whoever our Nahum was, subsequent poets particularly admired two of his hymns—including the *me'ora*, or "poem of light," translated here—and they often sought to imitate them. (For more on the *me'ora* see the glossary at the back of this volume.) Both employ a delicate music to create sensuous and seemingly secular surfaces, extolling the virtues of spring and its delights. They do this with such grace and deftness that only at the end, and in the subtlest fashion, is the liturgical—and messianic—dimension of the poem revealed. Just twelve of Nahum's poems have come down to us, some of them in manuscripts dating from around 1300. A number of his poems have been included in Sephardic prayer books.

## WINTER HAS WANED

> Winter has waned
> and with it my sorrow,
>    the fruit trees flower
>     like my joy.
> 5  Spikenard and myrrh
>    send up their scents,
> and orchards of treasures
> blossom and thrive—
> within them hearts
> 10    of friends delight.

Far-flown hart,
fled from my walls,
　　come back and drink
　　　my milk and wine;
for grief recedes
　　as the beds fill out,
embroidered like robes,
and trimmed with vines—
so worry flees
　　in a flash and is gone.

Fragrances waft
from the furrows of spices,
　　and the nut tree's branches
　　　above me are spread;
precious trees
　　sway in the shadows—
behind me cassia,
and aloe ahead.
My crystal cup
　　is ringed with gold,

my garnet wine
is mixed with dew,
　　and I let go
　　　of all my cares.
What made the beloved
　　grazing with roes,
leave the city
to dwell in groves?
Come to your lover
　　who longs with song,

and raise the western
　　lamp, my pure one:
Through you, my cherub,
　　my flame burns on.

# AVRAHAM HABEDERSHI

*(mid-thirteenth century–after 1290)*

Born to a prosperous, well-established family in the Provençal town of Beziers (the medieval name of which was Bedris), AVRAHAM HABEDERSHI was raised in the home of his wealthy grandfather. When the grandfather died, the young Avraham moved to Perpignan—at the time part of Aragon—where he was educated and went on to work in finance and moneylending. He was also a professional letter writer, known for his flowery style. His financial success allowed him to establish himself in Perpignan as a literary patron and arbiter of poetic taste, someone who determined which poets received support and which did not. Bestowal of that support, of course, was contingent upon acknowledgement of HaBedershi's superior literary gifts, and he has many poems and epistolary works attacking writers who challenged him. At times these literary wars involved "staged" contests between friends, like the Provençal *tenso*, but at other times the line was crossed and real animosity took hold.

HaBedershi's first work addressed the confiscation of Jewish books that was ordered in Aragon in the wake of the Disputation at Barcelona. In 1275 he met with Jewish members of Alfonso X's papal delegation, as it passed through Perpignan, and he made a particularly strong impression upon the Jewish dignitary Todros Ben Yosef HaLevi Abulafia (not the poet in this anthology); the two engaged in literary contests and exchanged many poems, including parodies of both the Passover Haggada and somber liturgical hymns. In 1285, as part of a larger attack on the kingdom of Aragon, much of Aragonese southern France was overrun by the French king Philip III and his son (Philip IV), and the Jewish community suffered heavy losses. Suddenly impoverished and friendless, HaBedershi fled to Narbonne; there, between 1285 and 1290, he composed his longest and most complicated work, *Herev HaMithappekhet* (The Revolving Sword), the second half of which incorporates a "lament for the makers," among whom he counts the Provençal poets Peire Cardenal and Folquet de Marseille. (HaBedershi knew no Arabic and was apparently unfamiliar with its literature.) No more is known about HaBedershi's life, except that he had three sons. Two died while he was alive; the third, Yedaya, went on to become an important Hebrew poet as well (see Yedaya HaPenini, below).

HaBedershi's poetry is, on the whole, mannered and tedious, though at its best it can be quite forceful. His most focused work was written in the context of his poetic battle with Yitzhaq HaGorni, a competition that gave full expression to his combative nature. While it is impossible to get to the bottom of HaBedershi's quarrel with his younger rival, since we have only HaBedershi's side of the exchange, all indications are that the hostility between the two poets was real, and not part of the roles played in a literary correspondence. As the editor of HaBedershi's poems tells it, HaGorni, most likely having failed to find support elsewhere, arrived in Perpignan and sent HaBedershi an endless stream of poems, hoping to gain his favor. In some of these poems, however, HaGorni's boasts appear to spill over into a direct challenge to HaBedershi's literary supremacy. At first, HaBedershi refrained from engaging the desperate HaGorni, but in time he sent him a few lines of verse out of pity. The exchange soon heated up. Eventually HaGorni surrendered to the banker-poet, and HaBedershi softened and sent HaGorni some money to keep him going; but that, it seems, just made matters worse. The first three epigrams translated here register the development of their quarrel, with HaBedershi ratcheting up the level of sarcasm in his replies.

### WHY THE POET REFUSES TO FIGHT

As he went out to fight the Amazons,
    Alexander was warned by them to disperse:
"If you beat us you'll only have beaten girls.
    And if we win—the shame will be worse."

### YOUR MUSE

Your muse would have been a lady if
    you'd taken your time, like a troubadour;
but leaving her lessons behind you rushed
    to find the throng. Now she's a whore.

## LAMENT FOR A FOE

When he dies his neighbors will jump for joy,
though Bedershi will weep, deep in his debt.
For with Isaac gone, where will he find
jokes for his poems and his arrows' target?


## THE POET'S DISTRESS

I've weighed out the world's evil and good
   on the scales of night and day and the seasons—
but the worst thing I've found is the poet's distress
   when he's filled with hatred, and can't get even.

# YITZHAQ HAGORNI

*(second half of the thirteenth century)*

HaBedershi may not have given him the time of day, or bothered to save his po-
ems, but close readers of Hebrew literature are in agreement that YITZHAQ
HAGORNI was by far the more gifted poet. Born in the small and remote town of
Aire, in Gascony—closer to the Atlantic than to the Mediterranean—the poet
added the Hebrew translation of his hometown (*goren*, meaning threshing floor)
to his name. Though he held Aire in high esteem, he was forced to leave it in
search of work and spent most of his adult life wandering through southern
France, stopping in Perpignan, Luz en Barège, Lucq, Manosque, Carpentras, Ar-
les, Narbonne, Aix, and Draguignan. HaBedershi describes him as "a meander-
ing man who measured the land." Lacking anything in the way of a stable home,
HaGorni suffered from the elements, poverty, and the contempt of people
through whose towns he passed. He often settled his accounts in verse, and
many of his poems begin by mentioning the town he is writing about and the
treatment he received there. He was, in other words, a poet very much in the
mold of the peripatetic troubadour—one who sang for his supper and often
went to bed hungry. And as with the troubadour poets (and Meshullam De-
Piera), music and musical instruments figure prominently in HaGorni's art. At
least at the start, his poetry seems to have been integrally linked to its musical ac-
companiment.

HaGorni's somewhat adolescent clash with HaBedershi we have already wit-
nessed. Again, HaGorni's side of the quarrel hasn't survived, though we do have
his initial poem of entreaty to the man he hoped would be his patron; it was, ap-
parently, far too self-involved to open HaBedershi's wallet or heart. From this
poem we know that HaGorni saw himself as the leading Hebrew poet of his day,
whose mission was to carry the banner of the Hebrew language. In his zeal he
was willing to put up with considerable humiliation at the hands of his compatri-
ots, who seem to have considered him a bohemian beggar and a nuisance. One
poet called him "a drinker and a dancer in taverns," and he was accused in vari-
ous towns of having relations with local women—charges he at first denied but
later admitted (also in verse).

Given the poet's energy and the occasional nature of much of his work, it
isn't unreasonable to assume that he must have been a prolific poet and that
the lion's share of his writing has been lost. Only eighteen poems by HaGorni

have come down to us. While these employ a familiar Andalusian prosody, and contain the standard self-inflation and mannerism of the time, their spirit and content are, in the Hebrew context, exceptional in every way, and it stands to reason that they were influenced by the Provençal poetry that surrounded the poet. At its best, HaGorni's poetry is characterized by a singular directness and wholly individualistic power, as in what may have been his final poem, "HaGorni's Lament."

## WOULD YOU TELL ME

Would you tell me, friends, how I should sing?
    How to treat and tune my lute, then play?
Then why have you gone and snapped the strings
    which I'd set out in perfect array?

Go, Gorni, bellow and bray
    like a mule longing for grass—like a bull.
They're telling me how I should handle the spindle!
    How could I work with the distaff's wool?!

## HAGORNI'S LAMENT

For desire, now, I begin this lament,
    as my drum has long since ceased to sound—
transgression, friends, has kept me from favor:
    my errors are legion, my sins renowned.
5    And so my lute has turned to mourning,
    its flute to weeping, and sorrow's wail—
for love's pleasure came to nothing,
    as passion faded, then finally failed.
The day is dying, the shadows fleeing,
10    the breeze no longer stirs in the garden.
Fear of death is settling in me:
    What hope could there be for the ass I've been?

Clouds will hover over my grave,
    as my lust kindles earth's foundations;
and if I die while I'm still young,              15
    complaints will follow me into the dust,
for year after year I pursued desire—
    likened in towns to Hell's blaze.
But all of that has come to corruption,
    for in that love there was no faith.         20

Peddlers will come from afar to gather
    the earth of my grave for women's balm;
and from the planks of my coffin they'll fashion
    cures for the barren, to bring forth sons.
Worms' mouths through me will make       25
    the mute speak in seventy tongues,
and across lutes my hair will be strung
    and give forth song without being strummed.
My belt will hold back the lecher's lust,
    and keep adulterers from their whores;     30
my timbrels will serve in sacred processions;
    in mystery's rites my robes will be worn.
Who, then, will crush my bones,
    before they're made into amulets' eyes?
May my words give wisdom to fools and the young,     35
    and increase knowledge for even the wise.

# YEDAYA HAPENINI

## *(c. 1270–after 1306)*

Avraham HaBedershi's son YEDAYA HAPENINI was born in Perpignan, then edu-
cated in Beziers, like his father. (While he sometimes called himself HaBedershi,
more often than not he used the epithet HaPenini—the source of which isn't
clear.) After his time in Beziers, Yedaya returned to Perpignan and perhaps lived
in Montpelier as well. He was a precocious student and wrote with authority in a
number of disciplines while still in his teens. His philosophical commentaries
were heavily influenced by the Muslim philosopher Ibn Rushd, and he played an
active role in the second Maimonidean controversy in 1305, siding with those
who defended the place of secular and philosophical training in Jewish educa-
tion. He may have worked as a physician. After 1306 we lose all trace of him—
apart from the date of his death, which some scholars posit as 1340.

Yedaya is known for his *Baqashat HaMemim* (Petition of the *Mems*), a liturgical
hymn in which all one thousand words begin with the letter *mem*. (He wrote it
when he was fourteen, in imitation of his father's famous *Baqashat HaAlephim*.)
Yedaya's two principal claims to fame, however, are *Ohev Nashim* (Defender of
Women), a rhymed-prose response to Yehuda Ibn Shabbetai's *Minhat Yehuda Sonei
Nashim* (The Offering of Yehuda the Misogynist, above) and his far more famous
ethical work, *Behinat 'Olam* (Investigation of the World). One of the most popu-
lar Hebrew belletristic works of its kind, *Behinat 'Olam* went through numerous
editions and exists in some seventy-five manuscript sources, many with commen-
tary. It was also translated into several languages and was familiar to figures such
as Goethe and Lessing from a mid-eighteenth-century German translation. For
modern readers, that popularity has been hard to comprehend, as this ethical es-
say is gloomy and unoriginal. Fleischer, for example, calls it "banal and boring,"
though he praises its energetic style. The work's formal dimension, as well, may
have drawn readers to it early on, for the Hebrew of *Behinat 'Olam* employs nei-
ther rhyme nor meter—and the removal of those constraints involved something
of an innovation in a belletristic context. Also contributing to its popularity was
the work's moralistic emotional thrust: *Behinat 'Olam* treats Fate, the tragic ten-
sion between body and soul, the traps of temptation, and the vanity of passing
things. HaPenini's themes resonated powerfully against what scholars take to be
at least part of the historical background of the work: the corruption of the Jew-
ish elite who served in, and benefited from, the French financial administration

of the day, and the eventual expulsion of Jews from French territory by King Philip IV (the Fair) in 1306. Its prose mold notwithstanding, *Behinat 'Olam* is generally treated in the context of medieval Hebrew poetry, since scholars believe that Yedaya may have been modeling his work on biblical prosody, which made conspicuous use of parallelism and cadence. Others suggest that perhaps it was influenced by Sa'adia Gaon's long *baqashot*. What in fact emerges in *Behinat 'Olam* is, in Haim Schirmann's opinion, a hodgepodge of styles that only on occasion feel integrated into a powerful poetic field. The following passage constitutes one of these peak moments in the work, and it has regularly (and rightfully) been included in collections of Hebrew poetry. In Schirmann's anthology, for example, it is set out in free-verse, parallelistic lines, which, to a large extent, I have followed.

## THE WORLD IS A RAGING SEA

The world is a raging sea
whose depth and width are vast,
and Time is a rickety bridge extending across it.
Anchored in bonds of absence
    preceding its existence,            5
it leads one toward eternal bliss
by the light of the countenance of our King.
The bridge is wide as the span of man—
along it there is no railing;
and you live on, son of man,            10
    against your will—
and from the day that you were born,
you've always walked across it.
Seeing the narrow path before you,
without any room to the left or right,           15
    will you boast of what you are?
With death and destruction like a wall
on either side,
        will your heart hold out—
    and will you still be strong?           20

You pride yourself on all you've amassed,
and what you earn with the work of your hands—
seeking it out on your own,
   and trapping it in your nets and snares.
25 What will you do with the sea's rage
and its rising waves,
as they swell and crash across your home,
   until it's about to give way?
For this is the powerful sea,
30    in the midst of which you are:
Are its breakers the source of your glory and splendor?
Are these the soldiers you'd bring down?
Go out, now, to battle against it:
stagger and lunge about as you will,
35    in drunken pride;
you'll be subdued in time
by the wine of your contempt and scorn,
   which will soon deceive you.
To and fro, in danger you'll reel,
35 then suddenly plunge
into the frightening depths,
   with no one near to avenge your blood.
From abyss to abyss you'll descend,
whirled within the sea's deep springs,
40 and not a soul will cry out then—
   *Save him!*

# AVNER [OF BURGOS?]

*(1260/70–c. 1340)*

Toward the end of the thirteenth century, pietistic and mystical trends took hold of Spanish Jewry and Christianity: the central work of the Qabbala, *The Zohar*, was composed between 1280 and 1286 in central Castile, and like contemporary Christian mystical movements, it espoused humility, poverty, and closeness to nature. In addition to advancing an implicit critique of the Spanish-Jewish aristocracy, which the qabbalists—and some of the Hebrew poets of the day—considered arrogant and corrupt, *The Zohar* and other related mystical texts of the time spoke of the imminent spiritual triumphs of a messianic age, against the backdrop of Christian persecution. Great fervor followed in the Jewish community, though not always along lines the qabbalists had envisioned. In the summer of 1295, at the urging of a self-styled prophet from Avila, Jews dressed in white and gathered in synagogues—as on the Day of Atonement—hoping to hear a blast from the Messiah's *shofar*, or ram's horn, which would signal the start of the End. Instead, as Christian tradition has it, a hail of crosses fell from the sky, appearing on the worshipers' garments and in their homes. Some of the people who had seen the vision of the crosses came for treatment to a prominent local physician by the name of Avner. Already troubled by the theological implications of Jewish suffering in exile, Avner, like many members of the Jewish community, was greatly disturbed by the mysterious events and for the next twenty-five years he wrestled with his belief in Jewish teachings. Finally, in 1320, writing in Hebrew, he professed his Christian faith in a work that was then translated into Spanish, and Avner was baptized and given the name Alfonso of Valladolid. He spent the rest of his life as a minor church official, launching a series of vitriolic attacks on Jews and Judaism as a whole, though his particular brand of Christianity incorporated many Jewish, and even qabbalistic, elements.

His polemics (all of which were conducted in Hebrew, even after the conversion) reveal Avner/Alfonso to be a sharp thinker and a gifted writer. In 1961 a manuscript was discovered that included a long and highly unusual poetic confession—technically a *baqasha*—by a *paytan* named AVNER. The work's peculiar intensity and embodiment of an acute sense of guilt, evident in the excerpt translated here, have led scholars to attribute the poem to Avner of Burgos, prior to his conversion.

## THE LAST WORDS OF MY DESIRE

These are the last words of my desire—
speech sufficient to wholly consume
one who brings an offering to idols
    arousing anger;
5    an utterance of one
raised over every misfortune and ruin,
the anointed of alien gods of Sidon,
the sweet strangeness of what's not real
    to sons of whoring's children.
10   "Make your cakes for the Queen of Heaven,
    not for the God of Israel."
So desire spoke in me, saying:
"The Rock to you will be a thorn and snare.
Bring down the stone of Israel the builders rejected;
15  you'll be a brother to me and my friends
    in groves where we will gather.
What need do you have to declare
statutes fit for an ancient age?
Choose the new from what is near,
20  and lately come—
    the gods of Moab and Amon.
Take for yourself one of their daughters,
and give us children from impure women,
    forbidden whores.
25  For this you'll plant gardens of pleasure.
Your portion is with the adulterers,
with well-fed mares—
and a man's wife, who can find her?
    Her price is far above pearls.
30  By daylight rise
and trample the wretched and poor.
Among your brothers send rebellion,
    and be a friend
to all who pursue riches in greed.

Revel in gifts and bribery, 35
devouring every unclean thing
that lives, like the dead, in darkness.
　　Let your soul delight in luxuries.
Set your table with the richest fare,
chief among them creeping things 40
that crawl and gnaw,
come of a nation that is not strong—
　　of rats, and badgers, and hares.
Drink in turn, and stagger, and be made bare."

# QALONYMOS BEN QALONYMOS

## *(1286–after 1328)*

One of the most versatile Hebrew translators of the middle ages, QALONYMOS BEN QALONYMOS was responsible for the rendering of at least thirty works from Arabic into Hebrew—many by Ibn Rushd—and he also translated from, and at times into, Latin. Born in Arles in 1286 to an illustrious family that saw itself as descended from the biblical King David, he was raised in relative comfort. Later in life, however, he suffered along with the rest of the Jewish community during the reign of Philip the Fair, who exploited the Jews in every way for financial gain. In 1316 Qalonymos completed his translation of the *Iggeret Ba'alei HeHayyim* (The Epistle of the Animals), by the Iraqi scholars known as the Brethren of Purity, and during the following years he seems to have traveled around Provence and Catalonia. In the late fall of 1322 he finished his major work, *Even Bohan* (Touch-stone). He was thirty-five years old. Shortly thereafter he was summoned to Italy, where Robert Manjou, duke of Provence and king of Naples, had assembled a school of translators. Qalonymos spent several years in the king's employ in Naples and Rome, translating scientific works from Arabic and Hebrew into Latin. (He was known there as Maestro Calo.) While in Italy he met the greatest Italian-Hebrew poet of the day, Immanuel of Rome, who, in his *Mahberot Immanu'el*, writes admiringly about Qalonymos's tremendous learning and the accomplishment of his rhymed prose. By 1328, Qalonymos was back in Arles.

*Even Bohan* reflects both the poet's arrival at midlife (the age of account) and the historical events through which he lived. Its death-obsessed later chapters are accordingly dark, gloomier even than Yedaya's *Behinat 'Olam*. The first part of Qalonymos's work, though, consisting of a series of descriptions of the Jewish community and its "types," contains an unusual mix of humor, biting satire, and resigned acceptance of the writer's situation. *Even Bohan* is written in rhymed prose, and Qalonymos is explicit about his desire *not* to be considered a poet. In fact he singles out poets for some of the harshest treatment in his sketches:

> There are those who take pride in poems they've made—which make them brave—as they're filled with subjects abstruse and grave. Before the people's eyes they rise, then strut about with their heads held high, speaking in riddles—and twisting the lessons of the wise. . . . On streets and alleys throughout the town, toe to heel, they prance around, like gilded doves, because they've found . . . in rhetoric's ways some strange innovation to let

them speak as no one has done. . . . And if they're praised—to their faces—their eyes beam and give off rays. And then one says: 'Blessed are you to the Lord! You've understood my every word!' . . . And so I've observed: O you deep ones, over your heads in law and religion, you fritter away your days in a mission that's neither a trade nor yields any wisdom. You dive through the depths, and work so hard, only to surface with worthless shards.

Also included in the first part of *Even Bohan* is a section in which the writer—who had been in the midst of a long confession of his sins and a Job-like indictment of the day he was born—suddenly breaks off and offers the surprising prayer translated below. Again, while the Hebrew original is in rhymed prose rather than lines of metrical poetry, or even the quasi-biblical parallelistic free verse we've seen elsewhere, it is offered here because of its excellence and its prominence in the Hebrew canon. Scholars have struggled in their reading of this section, seeing it as an "odd," "amusing," or "parodistic" insertion; in fact, grappling with the passage in the context of Qalonymos's work as a whole reveals it to be part of *Even Bohan*'s quasi-carnivalesque critique of the author's own culture.

## ON BECOMING A WOMAN

Lord in heaven,
who brought forth wonders
by fire and water for our fathers,
cooling Abraham's Chaldean kiln,
    so in its flames he'd not be burned;          5
who altered Dina's fate in the womb,
and made a serpent of Moses' wand;

who whitened with illness Miriam's hands
and turned the Sea of Reeds into land—
10 transforming the muddy bed of the Jordan
    into passable sand,
and making from stone and shale
a pool whose springs would not fail—
    *if only you would make me female!*

15 If that alone might be done,
how wondrous then would be my fortune!
Spared the arduous labor of men,
    I'd settle down and raise my children.
But why complain and bitterly whine?
20 If my Father in heaven is so inclined
as to fashion me with a lasting deformity,
    how could I ask that He take it from me?
Worry about what just can't be
is incurable pain and endless misery;
25 empty condolence is hardly an answer.
"I'll just have to bear it," I said, "though I'll suffer
    until I wither away and die."
And since long ago I learned from tradition
that both good and bad deserve benediction,
30 in the faintest of whispers I'll mutter each morning:
*Blessed art Thou, O Lord—who has not made me a woman.*

# YITZHAQ POLGAR

*(first half of the fourteenth century)*

When Avner of Burgos converted to Christianity and mounted his attacks against the Jews of Castile, his considerable literary skills rendered the assault all the more effective and cast a shadow across the Jewish community, which had few leaders capable of responding in kind. One Jew who did take on the challenge was Avner's disciple, YITZHAQ POLGAR, about whom we know very little. (His name also appears as Polqar, Pulgar, or Poliqar.) In answer to Avner/Alfonso's initial assault—in which he claimed to find proof of Christian doctrine in talmudic and other rabbinic texts, and argued for determinism—Yitzhaq sent on a pamphlet of biting ad hominem epigrams, which Avner later referred to as *Iggeret HaHarafot* (The Epistle of Blasphemies). Avner responded with a hasty defense of the faith. Some twenty years later, revising his earlier epistle, Polgar set out to write a comprehensive work that would present Judaism in the proper light and serve as a corrective to Alfonso's distortions. *Ezer HaDat* (Support of the Faith) consists of five dialogues in lively and forceful (often rhymed) prose that is illustrated by several accomplished metrical poems. Perhaps the most successful dialogue, "The Man of Faith and the Philosopher"—from which the poems translated here are taken—examines the value or validity of philosophical understanding in the context of religious faith. The debate, which is set in a fictive Jerusalem, is at first hostile in the extreme. By the end of the argument, however, the judgment is put before the community, which turns to the author, who concludes that the two modes can coexist. While Polgar avoids explicit mention of Avner/Alfonso in these dialogues all but once, he clearly frames the work as a response to his adversary's doctrine.

## FAITH'S PHILOSOPHY, PHILOSOPHY'S FAITH

### I. THE PHILOSOPHER SEEN BY THE MAN OF FAITH

Behold a man whose way is corruption,
    betraying the Law God handed down.
He drives out honest men and sways them
    with alien faith, like Moab's son.
Stay, therefore, far from his doctrine;
    wash with lye and keep yourselves clean.
But gather together to pelt him with stones,
    lest his faith live on and he flee.
Then burn the body in sulfurous flames,
    till nothing is left—not even his name.

### II. THE AUTHOR'S DECREE

Cleanse your soul with faith if it's tainted,
    earn it merit, observe the Law,
and you'll emerge like a polished mirror—
    wholly pure, without any flaws.

Wash your transgressions away with lye,
    as faith's path is the route you've sought;
prepare your soul to perceive God's actions,
    all of which can be found through thought.

If your soul seeks out wisdom with faith,
    and acts in kind, to preserve their bond,
you'll rejoice, seeing the pleasures
    of God, the Lord, as faith lives on.

But faith without wisdom means not a thing—
    a feast prepared, with no one eating.
And without the Law, wisdom is worthless:
    lacking Scripture, its knowledge is thin.

So join the two if you'd pursue
    the strength and power of the purest soul;
wisdom, then, will serve all men—
    and in its glory, destroy its rebels.

# SHEM TOV ARDUTIEL (SANTOB DE CARRIÓN)

## *(late thirteenth century–after 1345)*

Shem Tov Ardutiel is best known as the author of a marvelous collection of Spanish epigrams, *Proverbios morales*, written under the name Santob de Carrión. The modern Spanish poet Antonio Machado—who, like Shem Tov, spent formative time in Old Castile's stark highlands, which he described as being "so sad, they have a soul"—has testified to the potency of Santob's wise, doubt-ridden, and down-to-earth "spiritual autobiography," modeling his own moral proverbs after them. Shem Tov's Hebrew *Milhamot HaEt veHaMisparayim* (The Battles of the Pen and the Scissors, 1345) has received much less attention, in part because it adopts a minor mode, but also because it has proven so slippery: modern scholars have had a hard time determining what the work is "about." Its fluid rhymed prose and interlaced metrical poetry tell the story of a writer who, in utter isolation, sits down at his table one very cold winter's day to write; after boasting of his skill in verse and singing the extended praises of his pen, he tries to dip his pen into the ink and finds that the latter is frozen solid. An elaborate scene follows, with the author trying to break the ice, as it were, without success. Praise gives way to scorn, the pen defends itself, and then suddenly a voice is heard suggesting, again in highly figurative fashion, that there are other ways to solve this problem. One might, for instance, write with scissors!—by cutting the shapes of the desired letters into parchment. There ensues a debate between the pen and the scissors over which way of writing is preferable. Finally a judge called in from the street issues the verdict that the pen is indeed best suited for writing, the scissors for clipping hair and nails, and order is restored—though we also learn in the end that this story itself has been, it seems, written with scissors. And here it is important to point out that several Andalusian Arabic poems from the early thirteenth and mid-fourteenth centuries refer to the practice of scissor writing, and that both Hebrew and Arabic etymology link story (*sippur*), telling or counting (*le-sappeir*), and scissors (*misparayim*)—all of which are derived from the *s-p-r* root, just as in Arabic we find *qissa* (story) and *miqass* (scissors).

Interpretations of Shem Tov's narrative have varied. Some readers have seen it as an allegory of Avner's apostasy (above); others suggest that it refers to Gonzalo Martinez, the Christian advisor to Alfonso XI who was responsible for the jailing and eventual execution in 1333 of two Jewish officials, which in turn led to the imprisonment of all of Castile's Jews and their release in exchange for a considerable ransom. It has also been seen as a light-hearted diversion (perhaps for Purim). The most immediate and powerful impression a close reading yields is that the work, at least at some basic level, is about writing, obstacles to writing and isolation in writing, and ways to overcome both. It appears to be cast in the mode of a literary entertainment, possibly a parody of serious debates in the Jewish community (e.g., over the Qabbala, Maimonides' writing, or the Oral Tradition), or perhaps a send-up of the medieval literary debate itself (between, for instance, the pen and the sword). None of these interpretations, of course, rules out the incorporation of historical or autobiographical echoes, though a straight one-to-one allegorical reading seems to be inconsistent with the details of the story itself.

Shem Tov was born in the town of Carrión de los Condes (west of Burgos on the Santiago de Compostela pilgrimage route) and composed his *maqaama* while living in Soria. He seems to have served at the court of Alfonso XI, most likely participating in state affairs, where use could be made of his fluency in the three languages of Spanish cultural *convivencia*. In addition to *The Battles of the Pen and the Scissors* and his *Moral Proverbs*, Shem Tov also composed a penitential prayer in Hebrew, a poem of petition (*Yam Qohelet*—The Sea of Ecclesiastes) consisting of two thousand words beginning with the letter *mem*, and a qabbalistic treatise called *Sefer HaPe'er* (The Book of Glory). He also translated a halakhic work from Arabic into Hebrew.

From *THE BATTLES OF THE PEN AND THE SCISSORS*

I. Writer, You Hold

Writer, you hold a flame in your hand,
    or is it the blade of a sword or a spear—
the tree of knowledge of good and evil,
    or a staff to make wondrous signs appear?

## II. To Praise the Pen

Are there words enough in all of song
   to praise the pen? Who else could bear
the burden of bringing back the past
and preserving it then as though with myrrh?

It has no ear with which it might hear,
   or mouth with which to offer answers;
and yet the pen, in a single stroke,
at once does both—observes and remembers.

## III. Tomorrow I'll Write

At night he says: "Tomorrow I'll write,"
but there's nothing at all to back up his words;
the heaven's frost laughs in his face,
and the cackling of mocking ice is heard.

Don't pride yourself on tomorrow's prize,
when you have no notion of what it hides.

## IV. Enter the Scissors

A body fully drawn and rotted through,
like clothes eaten by moths—but this one's written:
a man with his hand in wisdom brought it forth,
   forming hole after hole in its skin.

## V. Work I Was Cut Out to Do

I'm precious to every soul and man,
and lacking matter am only form.

I'm purest spirit—my body's nothing,
riding clouds and wings of the wind.

### VI. THE PEN FIGHTS BACK

If only someone would shut you up,
    or that might be your wisdom's will;
for hope deferred you'll finish writing
    just makes the heart and soul feel ill.

Your languor casts us into a torpor—
then leaves us holding shreds of paper.

### VII. THE SCISSORS LONGED

The scissors longed to be joined at last,
leaving nothing in the way of division—
so that its two might then be one,
to cut through what might come between them.

# SHMU'EL IBN SASSON

*(first half of the fourteenth century)*

Scholars agree for the most part that the historical value of SHMU'EL IBN SASSON's poetry far outweighs its literary worth, and they read it for the light it sheds on the cultural situation of mid-fourteenth-century Castile. About the poet himself we know very little, apart from the fact that, unlike nearly all the other Hebrew poets of Spain, he spent most of his adult life in provincial towns (Carrión de los Condes and Fromista, both west of Burgos). Even in those provincial outposts, however, he was able to maintain a literary circle of sorts, albeit a small and inferior one. Two noteworthy poems (below) tell respectively of the plight of "poets who are not rich" and of the hardships that Jewish communities endured after Alfonso XI promoted his anti-Semitic counselor Gonzalo Martinez to a position of higher influence in 1336. "They Will Be Tried" is part of Ibn Sasson's 164-line *maqaama*, which begins with the rhymed-prose heading: "And I made this at the time of the debate between R. Yehoshu'a and R. Avner, for at this time trials increased and the labor was great in the Land, and the enemy would have devoured us had it not been for the Lord, our God, who was with us." R. Yehoshu'a has not been identified, but R. Avner is Avner of Burgos (the modern editor of Ibn Sasson's diwan describes the *maqaama* as "an imitation of Avner's vision"), and the trials he mentions refer to the increased tax burden borne by the Jewish community at the time. The local nouveau-riche and boorish Jewish tax collectors—whom the poet despised and attacked in a series of poems—worked for the authorities and were often the worst of the oppressors. The *maqaama* notes that during this period the Jews were also sometimes imprisoned, forbidden from conducting public prayers, paraded naked, or forced to convert. At the beginning of the section presented here, the poet has just been cast into a deep sleep, through which he hears a prophetic voice telling him: "Son of man, why are you sleeping? Do you wonder at the trials that have come . . . heavily upon the Jews?" The voice explains that the trials are God's means of punishing his people for their evil ways, and the poem—spoken by this voice from the skies—sums up the situation. Ibn Sasson also exchanged poems with Shem Tov Ardutiel and Yitzhaq Polgar.

## MAN'S PERIL

*Once I was sitting among my friends, when a pretty*
*young woman passed by us. They challenged me*
*to condemn her ways, and I said: "Even as praise."*

Once when I saw a beautiful girl,
    pure as any gem or pearl,
I said in scorn, "Within your face
    Hell sparkles—and man's peril."


## WHY MOST POETS ARE POOR

Why are poets hounded so
and always assaulted by forces from heaven,
whose blows rain down on them alone,
    until that seems their only mission?
5  And when it's decided to lighten men's load,
why is the poets' burden increased—
making them run a gauntlet of trials
    and battle Fate as if fighting a beast?
At this I marvel, and my heart grieves
10  whenever I think of all their suffering.
Why did I choose to become a poet,
    when Time reserves its malice for them?
All mankind harvests their crops,
and the heaven's hosts to their vineyards hasten;
15  yet Time has set them to guard the abyss—
    to show how full its faith in them is.
Maybe the heavenly spheres and hosts
conspired to bring the singers down:
discovering their plans, the bards grew sad,
20    and now they hide their faces in shame.
For fools thrive—in their stead—
trading in favors and gaining money,
finding their standing at once improved,
    as with astrologers they keep company.

They're given assistance, their worth soon swells;          25
their steps, it seems, are guided by Fortune,
which when it comes to the aid of men
    on earth always comes to them.
But poets never see the rich,
just as chicks aren't fed by ravens.                        30
How could fools be honored so,
    daily defying wisdom's lessons?
Learning and intellect, too, they scorn,
sneering whenever they hear a poem:
"This man, it seems, like his friends,                      35
    longs for madmen, and so he invents them."

Alas, there's little they comprehend,
for how could goats impart any wisdom;
and so the Lord has blocked the path
    before them lest they start to sing.                    40
This state of which I speak resembles
a war where leopards are vanquished by puppies;
for all the sons of song were chosen
    to sing the praises of God Almighty,
just as at His shrine they served                           45
before Him once with the Levite's Psalter.
By song alone is God extolled,
    and Psalms, we know, are filled with splendor.
And so the poets deserve the honor
of serving as guardians over our treasures,                 50
for they bring laughter and grace to men:
    they're a source of continual pleasure
and should take pride—over viziers,
who constantly seek out their wisdom's wonders.             55
May those who keep His faith be kept
    by the mercies of He who keeps His creatures.
And may their station soon be raised,
at least above these boorish men—
and may the Lord of the world desire
    to make the spheres help them again.                    60

## THEY WILL BE TRIED

They will be tried for leaving the Lord
who formed them to serve in a sacred bond;
but they sought instead to amass a fortune,
    trusting only in wealth, not Him.

They've offered no help to the hearts of the poor,
lest they lose any coins from their hoard;
for this their trials are now renewed
    and foes assail them by way of reward.

And so His house is surrendered to strangers
for their forefathers' many transgressions and sins;
but when they loved their God with spirit,
    the Lord appeared in the Land before them—

as once in Goshen, when Pharaoh was cruel,
they cried to the Rock, who heard their call.

# MOSHE NATAN

*(mid-fourteenth century)*

When the Black Plague wreaked havoc through Spain in 1348, Jews were accused of having poisoned wells and of helping the epidemic spread. Popular uprisings against them further diminished Aragon's Jewish communities. In Saragossa, for example, the combination of plague and pogrom destroyed four-fifths of the Jewish population. Elsewhere Jews had their houses demolished, were tortured and forced to confess to false charges, or worse. In 1354, Jewish notables gathered at a conference in Barcelona to address the situation and, it was hoped, reorganize Jewish life in Aragon.

One of the speakers at the Barcelona gathering, and among the four signatories to its concluding declaration, was MOSHE NATAN. A wealthy merchant and rabbi from Tarrega, he was in good standing at the royal court and was known for his philanthropy and learning. He was also a Hebrew poet and apparently composed at least some verse in Catalan as well. As a poet, his preferred form was the didactic or moral epigram, and his work—which was gathered in a collection called *Totza'ot Hayyim* (The Issues of Life)—in many ways resembles that of Yosef Qimhi in *Sheqel HaQodesh* (above). Though Qimhi's proverbs are superior in every respect, Natan's Hebrew is fluid, and the best of his work is characterized by its clarity and common sense. Given the state of Hebrew letters at the time, *Totza'ot Hayyim* represented a considerable achievement, and it was greeted as such by the poet's contemporaries.

## PRISON

Dig a grave in your heart for your secret.
    Tellers of secrets don't know what they do.
Your secret's your hostage so long as it's kept—
    but once you reveal it, the prisoner is you.

*From* "THE TEN COMMANDMENTS"

## I

Despise the swindler and do not steal—
happy is he whose path has been straightened.
    For I've seen a man with his hands cut off:
He took what he lacked. What he had was taken.

## II

    Do not murder, for a man's blood cries
        from the ground after he dies.

    The shedder of blood finds his spilled,
        as one who kills in time is killed.

## III

Fear your God but don't fear people;
    be free in your worship, that is, and brave.
For if you're not devout in your service,
    you will be a slave to slaves.

## CLOTHES MAKE THE MAN

The chosen people were doomed to scorn,
from the day they wandered into exile;
but once they put on the locals' clothes—
    the banishment in them was final.

# SHELOMO DEPIERA

*(1340s–after 1417)*

The first seventy years of the fourteenth century, according to Haim Schirmann, marked a low point in the history of Hebrew poetry in Spain. Things began to stir again only with the appearance on the scene of a group of Saragossan poets who called themselves, among other names, '*Adat Nognim* (The Minstrels' Circle). The senior and perhaps most important member of the group was Shelomo DePiera. Born sometime between 1340 and 1350, in Catalonia, Shelomo seems to have been a distant relative of Meshullam DePiera, possibly his great-grandson or great-great-grandson. For much of his life he worked for one of the community's most distinguished families, the Ben Lavis. In sharp contrast to members of the materialistic Jewish upper class at the time, Don Shelomo Ben Lavi turned his attention to cultural matters, and in many ways he was the driving force behind this late Saragossan renaissance. In addition to writing work of their own, Don Shelomo, his son Benveniste, and some of his grandsons supported Hebrew scholars, funded translations of scholarly works into Hebrew, and employed the period's most prominent poet—Shelomo DePiera—as a Hebrew secretary and tutor in the Ben Lavi household. DePiera's curriculum naturally included verse, and it seems that gifted friends of the Ben Lavi children also studied the art with his group. At least two of DePiera's students (Vidal Benveniste and Yosef Ben Lavi—Don Shelomo's grandson) went on to write serious poetry. In time, as DePiera became known as an important cultural figure, various aspiring poets began sending him work and soliciting his opinion.

The year 1391 brought cataclysmic changes to the Jewish community. After more than a decade of anti-Jewish preaching by Archdeacon Ferrant Martinez, violent disturbances broke out in Seville and soon spread throughout the peninsula. Incidents of murder, plunder, and forced conversion (as well as martyrdom) were widespread, and in their wake, the Jewish population—especially of Catalonia—was decimated. Barcelona's days as an important Jewish center came to an end, and the violence threatened the Jews of Saragossa as well. The Ben Lavi family seems to have secured a refuge for themselves and DePiera outside the city, which, it turned out, was spared. The poet's own children, though, were taken by "the angels of death," as he wrote in one poem, and either slaughtered or sold. DePiera spent the rest of his life under the cloud of that loss, and he sought revenge or at least an outlet for his anger in his poetry.

Eventually DePiera returned to Saragossa, where he resumed his work in the service of the community's leaders. "The spine of Spanish Jewry," however, notes Schirmann, "had been snapped."

The last period of DePiera's life—after the death of his patron Benveniste Ben Lavi in 1411—was particularly grim, and it's from this period that the vast majority of his poems come down to us. His diwan contains some three hundred poems. Neglected by his former students, DePiera lived out his remaining days in bitterness and poverty, plagued by the infirmities of old age, including illness, blindness, and arthritis (about which he writes in verse—below; he also writes about a sore throat, a toothache, and the inadequately heated living quarters in which he was holed up through the winter). Further suffering was brought on by a wave of proselytizing by Vincente Ferrer and the subsequent Disputation at Tortosa (1413–14), where circumstances worked against the Jewish delegation and brought about a massive wave of conversion that—as with the events of 1391—in many cases wiped out entire Jewish communities. Among the new converts were members of the Ben Lavi family (including Yosef, who had been part of the delegation to Tortosa), and with them the desperate septuagenarian poet. Even after his conversion, Shelomo, like many other *Conversos*, maintained relations with his Jewish friends and colleagues, often exchanging Hebrew letters and poems with them. The last we hear of him is in a short poem complaining about the bad wine produced in 1417 in his adopted hometown of Monzón (in northeast Aragon).

The monotony of much of DePiera's poetic output has been described by one leading scholar as "frightening"; the poet also had little sense of proportion and could write endlessly in mannered and often ridiculous prose and verse alike: "Your song's soul dozes, and the dust / of my poems is tossed in your noses, and you sneeze!!" His long-windedness and fustian notwithstanding, the poet was devoted to the Hebrew language, something that could by no means be taken for granted in his day, when cultural assimilation and conversion were the norm. (DePiera also wrote prose in Spanish.) He clearly saw himself as an important link in the transmission of Hebrew Andalusian culture, though his poetic models were postclassical rather than classical: he singles out Meshullam, Alharizi, HaBedershi, and others for mention, rather than the major poets of the eleventh and twelfth centuries. From poets like HaBedershi (in his longer poems) came DePiera's fondness for mannerist contortions and perhaps also his prolixity. That said, there are numerous places where the poetry comes to life and impresses. His poems of complaint about old age are among his strongest, along with his satirical epigrams—though the latter are less representative of his work and sensibility on the whole. In addition to his secular work, DePiera left behind some forty-one technically accomplished liturgical poems, which in the estimation of their twentieth-century editor speak with a dignified simplicity and quiet, noble feeling.

## THINKERS WITH THINKING

At times the fool in his folly fathoms
what thinkers with thinking cannot grasp:
    the angel of God came to Bálaam,
who missed him—although he was seen by his ass.

## THE BEE AND THE GRUMBLER

When the bee stings, it hurts like a thorn—
though the wound can be dressed with its honey and calmed.
But you, complaining, strike with an arrow
    that's sharpened—and your mouth yields no balm.

## MEDIEVAL ARTHRITIS

My hips hurt so much, I fear,
that I can neither see nor hear.
The pain today was the worst I've known—
like a woman's giving birth on stones.

As Scripture, O my Lord, enjoins:
"Sigh for the breaking of my loins."

## WINTER IN MONZÓN

The sound of the rain coming down and the clouds'
　　breaking has weakened and wearied my soul—
and so she withdraws into her chamber
　　and curls up between the brazier and stove.
She only wants to be warmed by the coals,
　　but the heavens send down storms upon her,
and Time sends ice across her spark,
　　and so she mixes fire and water.
She piles on blankets but isn't warmed,
　　for she, it seems, has been led astray,
and so she sits inside her home,
　　trembling and shivering the winter away.
She sleeps in the bed of her lair and consumes
　　her food around the consuming fire,
forlorn in the pit as the snow comes down,
　　like a lazy man who's always tired,
bound where the wood is stacked for the blaze—
　　her heart as cold as the slaughterer's blade.

No light at all will shine for her now,
　　apart from the glow of the candle's flame.
She'll ask her friends: Did you see the sun
　　at the edge of the sky—has it gone down?
Is its brightness gone? Is it clothed in dark?
　　Is it only my tent that it won't illumine?
Has the sun plunged into the deep?
　　Or maybe the morning stars have fallen,
or the Lord has come and stricken the spheres,
　　removing their dominion from them.
She sits until the thoughts of her heart
　　seem like those of a fool to her,
and sleep is taken from her eyes,
　　as into her thinking she sinks further.
She fears for her future: What if she isn't
　　saved from the freezing season's prison?
But what can one do who lies alone—
　　his ailing soul wearied and weakened? . . .

## AFTER CONVERSION

*(to Vidal Benveniste)*

Friends have forgotten you now, my soul—
for I've strayed from the truth they think they own;
and the seventy years of my life are erased
like Tyre's daughter, who sang to be known.

So take up your lyre and roam through the city,
and sing to be recalled in poems.

## TABERNACLES: A PRAYER

Recalling the years he dwelled alone,
he roars and his roar like water pours.
He wearies, astonished at his distress—
and apart from your name, there is no cure.

Be a balm to the wound in his heart,
and say when he suffers, "The illness will fade."
For now he laments the blaze of Time.
Be to him a booth and shade.

## A PRAYER FOR RAIN AND SUSTENANCE

The nation's king has asked the Lord
to set the table with food for the poor.
May his words be pleasing before Him
so that the living waters pour.

## THIS YEAR'S WINE: 1417

Distress and despair have made me drunk, not wine:
    I've downed serpent's venom—the heat of this wine.
The grape gladdens the heart, but this one it saddens—
    and my stomach alone, it seems, is smitten with wine.
5  If this is what they'd known when religion began,
    Nazarites now would not abstain from wine,
nor would the Temple priests have been commanded
    daily to ready their drink-offerings of wine.
No band of gluttons and drunks would have been tempted
10  long ago to sell any girl for wine;
the wise at heart wouldn't have cautioned their children
    not to be like "those who guzzle wine."
They wouldn't have had to utter words of reproof:
    "Woe to one who tarries long over wine!"
15  Not for the likes of this would it have been said:
    "The priests and seers have been confused with wine."
Nor would Time's fools have heard false prophets
    saying: "I will preach to you of wine."
Here my face is red and my eyes have dimmed—
20  but just from smoke from the hearth and not from wine!

# VIDAL BENVENISTE

*(c. 1380–before 1439)*

Shelomo DePiera's student VIDAL BENVENISTE was the most talented member of *'Adat Nognim,* though his gift, it seems, often gave rise to tension with his teacher. Benveniste has several harsh characterizations of the elderly DePiera, whose poetry, he says, "speaks in secret then raises its voice, / answering softly but gnashing its teeth, / provoking quarrels as it calls for peace; / it flirts with combat and then retreats." At one point he makes it clear that he doesn't consider the older poet his teacher at all, or even an important influence on him: "How could you think I draw from your well, / or drink the waters of your poetry's spring? // One whom HaLevi and Gabirol raised / spits out the milk of Meshullam's son." His 156 poems are, on the whole, marked by their variety, concision, and overall grace and appeal.

Given the personal nature of much of his work, we know surprisingly little about the poet's life. How he supported himself remains a mystery, but on the evidence of his poems he seems not to have had, or needed, a patron; and at times he appears to be contributing to Shelomo DePiera's support. So far as we know, he held no official office, nor do his poems relate to events of the day, not even the cataclysmic trials and tribulations of the Jewish community. Unlike his good friend Yosef Ben Lavi and his teacher DePiera, Benveniste did *not* convert to Christianity in the wake of the disputation at Tortosa, and he was far less understanding of his colleagues who did so than was, say, Shelomo Bonafed (below).

Vidal Benveniste's major work, *Melitzat 'Efer veDina* (The Tale of 'Efer and Dina) is a rhymed-prose narrative laced with metrical poems that tells the tragicomic tale of a rich and lascivious (but impotent) old man named 'Efer. His immoral behavior brings great grief to his wife, who tries to return him to the straight and narrow, but fails and dies from grief. Immediately upon the conclusion of the seven days of mourning, the widower decides to marry a beautiful young virgin named Dina. His condition, however, prevents him from consummating the marriage. When this humiliating fact becomes public, one his of loyal employees advises him to use an aphrodisiac made from the navel of a certain fish. The servant warns his master to take just a very small amount of the aphrodisiac, but 'Efer can't restrain himself. He takes more than he should and dies an agonizing death. A city official accuses 'Efer's employees of having

306

poisoned their master, and he throws them in jail, tortures them, and confiscates all their property. At the end of the story the narrator turns to the reader and explains that the tale is in fact allegorical; it depicts the rational soul's fate in the recalcitrant human body, which is given over to the pursuit of worldly pleasures. As a result, body and soul alike are doomed to burn in the fires of hell. The moral of the story is then proposed: Be upright, trust in God, and abandon faith in the world and its values. Opinions differ as to the nature of the allegorical section, with some scholars feeling that it is an integral part of a unique, hybrid composition and others arguing that it was tacked on by the author. Be that as it may, Benveniste's tale is masterfully told, and it ranks with the best of the medieval Hebrew narratives. Its metrical Andalusian-style poems are also accomplished, though difficult to excerpt from the narrative. The selections here, therefore, concentrate on the equally impressive body of metrical poems from the poet's diwan and emphasize the works in which his individuality is most distinct.

## ADVICE FROM WIVES

Don't listen, men, to advice from your wives,
　or let your hearts be moved by their ways.
Ask them, if you'd know what's wise—
　and do the opposite of what they say.

## WHAT GIRLS WANT

Girls—like camels in heat—run every which way.
They stray from the straight and narrow, on paths that wind.
　They'll follow a lover even into captivity,
and often, of course, their love turns out to be blind.

They softly draw those who know how to love,
and only young men can bring that delight to their eyes;
　they long for lovers whose hands are nimble and burn
for the touch of those who'll lie between their thighs.

## TO A POET-FRIEND TOO MUCH IN NEED

*(a reply to Shelomo DePiera)*

Tyre's forgotten whore of a daughter
wandered and drummed so men would remember—
   just as your soul betrayed her Lord
and strayed in its way, like a headstrong heifer.
Therefore after seventy years,
her friends now treat her like a stranger.
   Rise, whore, take up your lyre—
and sing your songs, if you can, for hire.


## POEMS FOR A DOE IN A GARDEN

### I

This beauty's cheek is the ruby's color
and her talk crushes the hearts of lovers;
her two lips are redder than blood
from hearts her love's arrows sever.

She takes their blood with talk that's smooth—
and sets it on her cheeks, like rouge.

### II

I held you, doe, deep in my thoughts,
and saw you in my dream last night.
Has the order of nature, I wonder, changed?
It was pitch dark, but the sun was bright.

III

A doe who wears her grace like a gown
called though I was loath to come.
And so she readied desire's arrow—
my heart her target, her eye the bow.

And with that grace, like a snare,
she trapped me like a bird of air.

## A THANK YOU NOTE

Your hand is like the sky above,
and the scroll it fills is like your flourishing land;
and the inkwell's mouth is the river from which
  your pen's cloud draws the rains you send.

## THINK ABOUT THIS

God's blessing alone can make you rich;
so in your stinginess, think about this:

One man gives and always has more,
while the miser withholds and ends up poor.

## BEYOND WORDS

The coarse tried to compose their poems,
but only extended the line of confusion.
They thought they'd make the purest songs,
and still don't know where they went wrong.

## MY SON, BEFORE YOU WERE BORN

My son, before you were born
I longed with all my heart—
through prayer and with petition,
I sought you from the Lord.

But now I wish I'd asked
to die, since you are gone.

## TO ONE WHO SAID HIS HEART
## FOR VERSE WAS ADAMANT

Sit with me, friend, and watch what I do;
don't turn to things best left alone.
If your heart is adamant, my word is fire—
which like a hammer, shatters stone.

## CLARITY

The glass was clear and fine, and so was the wine,
and every eye that saw them grew confused—
for it seemed the wine stood there all on its own,
or the cup was empty and hadn't yet been used.

## WHAT GOES AROUND COMES . . .

My enemy shames me, although the shame
will surface soon in him by surprise.
His mind is blinded and he can't see
beyond the view from his own eyes.

# THE TONGUE SPEAKS AND THE HAND RECORDS

*(to a friend who slandered my good name)*

The tongue speaks and the hand records—
  from mountains of thought, quarrying words—
quarrying words from crags in the mind,
  with neither a hammer nor spike to hold.
Still the tongue like an axe is taken
  to the forest of speech, whose cedars are felled;
and lines are hewn from the rifts of Time,
  as hearts of men with pride are filled.
It opens doors without a hand
  and like a lion, lies where it will. . . .

Your soul, though, is wounded with age,
  and by my verse your heart has been cowed.
Time's trials have wearied your spirit,
  and in your infirmity, now it's bowed.
Age has spread its net of years
  and waited in ambush to hunt you down.
The days of your youth and strength are gone,
  and gray like an enemy threatens your crown.
Your eyes are dim with vexation's trial;
  you sigh as Time wears at your bones;
the years and disasters have taken their toll,
  and so you seek a rest for your soul.
Therefore in silence I've held back my thoughts
  and in answering you my muse has been slow.
Out of respect for you I've been still—
  refusing the urge to speak my mind—
for friends have told me that you've been saying
  the sea of my song has begun to go dry.
I heard their words and from my mouth
  there came forth flames of devouring fire.

Wrath stretching from Heaven to Hell
  is kindled within me like a blaze,
and the poem that yesterday sang your praises,
  in anger puts you today in your place.

The smoke of complaint to its nostrils has risen,     35
    and your barking calls for rebuke of its own.
Have I ever scavenged on floors where you threshed,
    like a gleaner come to pile up straw;
or asked at all for your assistance
    or said my verse was hungry for yours?     40
From all your fields have my poems ever gathered
    so much as a handful of food for a stanza?
But my storehouse is full and my heart is wide
    with poetry's spirit, and growing still.
My strength isn't fading, my branch is green;     45
    my words are fresh, my lines are lithe;
my soul sings, as breezes of song
    across my fields are sent by the Lord.
For God works through me and so He created
    a tongue that speaks and a hand that records.     50

# SHELOMO HALEVI (PABLO DE SANTA MARIA)

## (c. 1351–1435)

The wave of converts to Christianity at the end of the fourteenth century included, as we have seen, members of the Jewish cultural elite. While some maintained close ties with their Jewish friends and colleagues, others took to their new religion in zealous fashion. Among the latter was SHELOMO HaLEVI, who was born in Burgos to a wealthy family. A respected community leader and tax collector, he was extremely learned in Jewish law, maintained strong connections to scholarly circles, and was a competent writer of verse. He was also, it seems, drawn to Christian philosophy and "the hidden treasure of Christian books . . . things not discerned by the Jewish scholars," as his friend Yehoshu'a Lorqi put it in a letter to him at one point. No doubt under the spell of those books, and perhaps under the influence of his townsman Avner, to whose works he was also drawn, on July 21, 1391—just several weeks after the outbreak of the disturbances that held most of Spain in their grip—Shelomo HaLevi was baptized, along with his children, taking the name Pablo de Santa Maria. Initially he went to Paris to study Christian theology, and he then served for a period in Avignon, where he became close friends with Cardinal Pedro de Luna (who would in time become Pope Benedict XIII). Shelomo/Pablo rose rapidly through the ranks of the Church to become bishop of Burgos. Like Avner, whom he often quoted, he was one of Castilian Jewry's major oppressors, and among the instigators of the Disputation at Tortosa, which proved disastrous for what was left of Spain's Jewish communities. (The events of 1391 alone had reduced the number of the country's Jews by over two-thirds.) Pablo's bishopric was inherited by his son, who is buried in a major chapel near the entrance to the Burgos cathedral. Don Shelomo/Pablo himself was interred at the Convent of San Pablo, along the Río Arlanzón. While the convent has since been destroyed and the tomb has disappeared, this is the only known burial site of any of the medieval Hebrew poets of Spain, apart from the vague information we have regarding the graves of Shmu'el HaNagid and his son Yehosef in Granada.

Not long before his conversion, still a believing Jew and community leader, Shelomo was—as Schirmann tells it—imprisoned in London when he was included on a list of sixty aristocratic Jewish and Christian hostages sent by King Juan I of Castile as a pledge against a large outstanding debt owed to the English duke of Lancaster. According to historian Yitzhak Baer's version of the story, however, HaLevi was actually part of a 1389 Castilian delegation to Aquitaine (in

southern France, then controlled by England), which had been sent to help nego-
tiate a truce between the French and British crowns, as the former was allied po-
litically with Castile. Finding himself unable to properly celebrate the Purim hol-
iday, and longing for companions, Shelomo HaLevi wrote the following poem,
which he then sent on as part of a letter to his friend Meir Alguades, who was
court physician to a series of Castilian kings and the chief rabbi and justice of the
Jewish community. Traditionally, the Purim holiday is marked, among other
things, by sending gifts of food to neighbors and the poor, as well as by obliga-
tory drinking. The talmudic injunction is to imbibe until one can no longer dis-
tinguish between the hero and the villain in the Purim story, which is told in the
Book of Esther. If Baer's account is accepted, the poem was written in jest, and
the "imprisonment" mentioned in the letter is figurative and refers to the service
of the king and being surrounded by Gentiles. If Schirmann's reading is fol-
lowed, the poem is an elegiac expression of HaLevi's longing for Spain and antic-
ipation of his return there.

## MEMORY'S WINE

These are days when gifts should be given
    and delight in the cup's color taken,
but friends and favors are far from me now:
    there are no poor, and I'm alone.
In their stead I'd find consolation
    if only I could meet my companion,
for there has never been one like him—
    ever since the world began.
Because of his absence the Flood flowed forth
    in the time of Enosh and Tubal-Cain,
and if not for Noah's legacy to us,
    fear of another would still plague man.
Today, however, I'm on my own,
    and my soul sighed when I went to the fountain.
The party's pleasure and joy have been dimmed;
    the sun above my feast won't shine.
Memory alone can comfort me now—
    and so from my heart I draw up wine.

# SHELOMO BONAFED

*(final third of the fourteenth century–after 1445)*

The youngest member of *'Adat Nognim* was SHELOMO BONAFED. A prolific poet, he wrote with apparent ease about everything he encountered, and his work is marked above all by its individuality, vitality, density, and poignancy. Far more than the other poets of the Saragossan circle, Bonafed reacted in his poems to the events of his day and the hardships faced by the Jewish community. He saw himself as both a defender of the faith in troubled times (on which see, "World Gone Wrong," below), and, eventually, the last Hebrew poet of Spain: "When I die," he wrote, conjuring the most famous musicians and singers of the Psalms, "Yeduthun and Heman will pass away with me. / When I disappear, my generation will be silent as a widower." The Golden Age of Andalusian poetry was a distant memory, having come to an end in the mid-twelfth century with the emigration of Yehuda HaLevi to the east and the Ibn Ezras to the north; the Catalan-Provençal school of the thirteenth century had no heirs; Todros Abulafia's work (unknown to Bonafed) was a thing of the past; and the founders of *'Adat Nognim* were dying out. As the self-perceived last poet of a late renascence, with his potential audience evaporating (through conversion) before him, Bonafed bore a heavy burden. Though hardly a major figure, he responded valiantly, and the extant manuscripts of his work contain several hundred poems, only a handful of which have been published. Of these, fewer still have been presented with a critical apparatus that would make his work accessible to the general reader.

Bonafed ranged widely in his studies and seems to have known both Latin and Spanish (and sometimes written in the latter). His philosophical work suggests that he was familiar with Christian Scholastic philosophers, from Thomas Aquinas to Raymond Lull. On the Hebrew and literary side of the ledger, Bonafed identifies, as did Vidal Benveniste, with the major Andalusian writers, as well as with the important poets of Provence and Aragon, including Meshullam DePiera, Avraham HaBedershi, and Yedaya HaPenini. Apart from the time he spent in Tortosa during the Disputation, Bonafed seems to have lived and taught for most of his life in the small towns of Aragon and Catalonia: Cerezo, Mora, Tarrega, Ixar, and Belchite. He also lived for a considerable period of time in Saragossa, though at the end of his life he entered into a harsh confrontation with the leaders of the Jewish community there. Like his eleventh-century namesake—Shelomo Ibn Gabirol—and the poet Yehuda Ibn Shabbetai, Bonafed was forced out of the city and wrote a scathing series of poems and prose sketches attacking his oppressors. Midway through the longest poem in this series (excerpted below), which imitates Ibn Gabirol's "On Leaving Saragossa" in both form and content, the earlier poet appears to him (like Milton appearing to Blake) as a giant angel who confirms their common greatness. In actuality, the two poets shared little beyond their hot temper and contempt for what they perceived to be the fraudulence of the Jews who controlled the cultural and religious scene in Saragossa.

Curiously, Bonafed addresses the poem to his former friend, the new Christian Yosef Ben Lavi, who had converted, along with Shelomo DePiera, after the Disputation at Tortosa. Bonafed attended that sad event ("where most of the Kingdom's poets gathered") and was deeply marked by it—though he did find time for an exchange of poems with another writer, who in the midst of this most fateful of trials had criticized Bonafed's meter in certain verses; the insulted Bonafed responded with characteristic zeal, defending his metrical honor. Following the Disputation, Bonafed and other members of the Jewish community continued to write to converted colleagues, sometimes praising their wisdom and talent and lamenting their having abandoned the faith and entered the "bitter waters" of baptism. Some wrote back, in Hebrew. One of these exchanges across the religious divide resulted in the poem "Wherever You Go" (also below) which was sent to Astroq Rimokh, a formerly Jewish poet who had converted and assumed the name Francesc de Sant Jordi. While Rimokh's conversion may have been partly a matter of fashion, he soon took it to heart. In a letter to one Shealtiel Bonafos, the erstwhile Jew tries to persuade Bonafos to follow suit and leave his Judaism behind. Francesc ends that letter by describing himself as "your faithful soul, formerly of Israel's fold, which knew not God. Francesc de Sant Jordi." Shelomo Bonafed eventually saw Francesc's letter and—having decided that his friend Bonafos's reply had been too forgiving—he wrote back in defense of the faith. The conciliatory tone of the second half of the poem, and its encomium, are surprising, given that this poem was appended to Bonafed's far harsher prose reply.

## WORLD GONE WRONG

> Horses like lightning streak through the sea,
>   ships sail through the markets' streets,
> a flaxen cord shatters iron,
>   and water burns like wood from a tree.

From goats and lambs the leopard flees;
　　foxes race, pursuing lions;
so wonder not at a world gone wrong
　　and nature's course betraying seasons.
Believe this when you see the circles
　　of twisted leaders crushing men—
when wisdom's left for dead, forgotten,
　　or taken up and tortured by children.
Preparing to marry they ask about money,
　　and not if the groom is a scholar or wise.
The tailor sets out wielding his needle,
　　thinking he'll topple the sons of giants—
and the fabric around his neck a necklace,
　　the thread in his mouth sweet as nectar.
The silversmith scorches his beard in the kiln,
　　his eyes go red from the sparks and fire;
he's envied for his money or gold,
　　although, in fact, he's a worker for hire.
And the weaver considers his loom a lyre;
　　warp and woof he likens to Scripture;
the tanner's filthy lips kiss women—
　　he whose teeth has pulled at skins.
The mean in their wealth give impudent answers;
　　their pride and power stretch toward heaven.
Therefore, my pure one, let's walk for a while
　　into the country, among the flowers;
brothers breathing the air of meadows,
　　we'll sit in gardens, and not with stones,
our bower surrounded by furrows in bloom,
　　the valley's lily, the crocus and rose.
The birds of the air will be our companions,
　　beasts of the fields, and streams, and doves.
There we won't be disturbed by betrayal.
　　We'll pay no attention to Time's contortions:
now we'll mock the ways of our day,
　　and now look into mysterious notions—
Slowly we'll drink down wisdom's wine,
　　tasting song's choicest portions,
till Time comes round to repair its distortions
　　and then sets out to rebuild on ruins

and sort the gold from tin as it hastens                45
   to separate locusts from giants again.
Come, friend, our troubles will fade;
   I'll sing and the mute will break into song.
Come, lest the envious draw their bows—
   and those who hold all lovers in scorn.       50
Whether you're near, my cherub, or far,
   with your friendship I'm always busy;
and if you find I've chosen another,
   horses like lightning will streak through the sea.

## A VISION OF IBN GABIROL

And while I was speaking, behold, I saw
   Gabirol rising up before me—
awesome in might, he stood like an angel
   revealed there in the heights to me,
a sword in his hand, while from his mouth        5
   lightning flashed as he approached me.
His voice exploding with thunder and grandeur,
   he spoke to me of victory:
"Greetings to you, Reuben's son,
   friend of my delight and pleasure.            10
Do not fear, for I have come
   to help you with my strength and power.
Have villains here conspired against you—
   the wicked among my people, my friend?
For every man whose heart is pure                15
   they lie, like foes, in ambush again.
Their fathers' roots of bitterest broom
   sought to uproot my tender plants,
and now they think that I am with you,
   and hate you just because I am.               20
They saw that you were in fact my brother
   in song's worth, for your words were fine;
my name is in you, and in this time
   you've done great things, as great as mine—

25        so that they thought I'd returned from the dead
        and from the world below had climbed.
        Soon, my friend, I'll take my revenge
        and pay these people back in kind.
        So flee, my brother, before I destroy
30        this wicked nation in your time.
        Could the valley's lily remain with thistles,
        or pearls be left to lie with slime?
        And who could compare the moth to an eagle?
        Or today's fools to the stars of Orion?

## WHEREVER YOU GO

*(for the convert Francesc de Sant Jordi)*

Wherever you go, letter, wherever you wander,
        empty of truth but lined with grace's figures,
the world will always know of your dishonor.
        What good, then, is grace to you as a stranger?

5        For you were like the girl in the window watching,
        casting her passion's lance from on high, then hiding.
You'd break a heart stronger than that of a lion—
        speaking softly, but bearing the lion's weapon.

Your words are honey, but at their heart hold poison,
10        an owl suddenly breaking out in song;
your lines were woven as though by stars' constellations,
        but they're full as well of moths and devouring worms.

So speak, please, to the heart of your lord, whose anger
        against a broken vessel now has turned.
15        And it answers: "One who's white and ruddy has come
        from Edom, and in high places has set his throne.

A nursling raised in faith, his folly's his learning—
        and so he's hostile toward you in his shame.
In his high station his poor he has forgotten,
20        remembering only the glory of his own name.

His anger is roused, for he cannot fathom
    that a portion of his people still remains.
The staff of the pious man became a serpent,
    and the purest, clearest, brightest light a stain."

And so I groan for this giant of wisdom and luster,     25
    for his people in him had long seen splendor's crown,
as souls of wisdom's leaders entering the gates
    of his vast knowledge basked in his renown.

To bless his poems the kings of song would come,
    for then he brought honor to heights of song.     30
To bless such music once Barak rose up,
    and with such words Deborah sang in turn.

He stood guard lest the world be vanquished,
    and all that was most precious come to ruin.
Ceasing to write, he could make evening fall;     35
    and with his might he'd move the doors of dawn.

His moon crept to set his glow on high,
    and the sun before him cancelled darkness and gloom.
My anger's aimed only at treacherous Time,
    whose trials' abyss is like the sea's in a storm.     40

His soul which traded once in wisdom and grace
    was on the ship of his will when it went down.
The nectar of his learning now is bitter,
    and so his reason can't by men be found.

Whether he's stricken and cured, recovered or ill,     45
    my sorrow's joy is still to sing of his glory.
My soul still is wholly given to serve him;
    I wear his memory like a crown above me.

For I am a prisoner of desire—my heart
    is drawn by threads of mercy from his home.     50
If only, scroll, you'd make your way and speak
    of justice and my love, so he would know—

and send greetings from Shelomo Ben Reuben to him,
    wherever you wander, letter—wherever you go.

# YITZHAQ ALAHDAB

*(mid-fourteenth century–after 1429?)*

Conversion or hardship weren't the only options for Jews after the disturbances of 1391; large-scale emigration also followed. Some of the refugees headed for Muslim North Africa, some for the Land of Israel, and some for Sicily, which at the time belonged to the crown of Aragon and had a substantial Jewish population. Among the émigrés who settled in Sicily was YITZHAQ ALAHDAB, who had been raised in Castile and acquired considerable learning in the fields of astronomy, mathematics, Scripture, translation, and—to an extent—poetry. Between the years 1391 and 1426, Alahdab lived in Syracuse and Palermo, where he wrote books in all the aforementioned fields, and also invented what seems to have been an upgraded astrolabe. Throughout this period Alahdab also composed verse, nearly all of which remained in manuscript until the late 1980s. His output is limited in quantity (some eighty-five poems) and accomplishment, but his poetry is of interest for its humor, sharpness, and concretion. His marvelous long poem on the trades, for instance, has numerous lively sections and offers a vivid, if caricatured, sense of the working class at the time. Like Bonafed, Alahdab looks back nostalgically to the Golden Age of Hebrew poetry, which he contrasts with the sorry state of the art in his day.

## INFLATION

Money easily mounts and so
   whatever you have, hurry and trade.
And when you sell, buy at once.
Don't keep your funds at home where they'll fade.

## ANOTHER FLEA

Who's as bold as the delicate flea,
　　who bites the lion at will in the wild?
Miniscule things, they have at kings
　　and before their viziers are not riled.


## SECURITY

The sellers of glass worked in peace
and paid no attention to the sounds of the mouse,
　　until to protect them they brought in a cat—
who shattered all their wares when he pounced.


## THE ELDERLY ASKED IF THE DOCTORS

The elderly asked if the doctors were able
to straighten their backs, which were all out of line.
The doctors replied: "The years have bent them,
　　and who could ever try to fix Time?"


## AS SORCERERS SPREAD

As sorcerers spread through Egypt and Goshen,
　　frauds, now, are filling the land.
They tell you they're having a castle put up.
　　In fact, they're building a shack by hand.

## BEING POOR

The yoke of hunger and plunder
　　in war is hard on the will;
and heart's sorrow is grievous and bitter;
　　but being poor is harder still.


## STATE OF THE ART; OR, POETRY WAILS

Poetry wails at its downfall now,
　　its robes of glory having been stripped—
for once long ago, it built up its kingdom,
　　and with its hand, ruled like a prince.
Its meaning and worth were instantly fathomed
　　by scholar, sage, and skillful enchanter—
upright, honest men of account,
　　during its watch, standing together.
Shelomo led in Spain at the start
　　with sacred currency and figures of splendor.
Poetry crowned his kingdom and rule.
　　His pen and ink were a powerful mirror.
And Ibn Ghiyyat's thinking was swift:
　　he carved out lines that we still hear.
How deep they were, and how they soared,
　　taking their place on high with the spheres!
And the poems of HaLevi are milk and honey,
　　with manna beside them, a sheer delight—
smooth and pleasing, precious vessels,
　　their discourse sweet, their texture tight.
The Ibn Ezras were like commanders
　　who harnessed their chariots in armies of song—
verse their vehicle, they were riders,
　　bearing bows along with their swords.
All these in each generation
　　were viziers of song, whose bread was words.
But then it all came crashing down
　　to a level below its own tombstone:

now every idiot, and every fool,
    spreads his net in the hunt for poems.       30
Bizarre formulations with plaintive sounds
    are sent up from within their homes.
All sing songs that are battered and bruised,
    severed and torn, from the tops of trees,
and the listeners take in the clamor and stench—      35
    as each comes forth with his trough and kneads.


## RENAISSANCE MAN

    I'm skillful as skillful ever comes,
    and so I've mastered numerous trades,
    I know about spinning and weaving on looms,
        and how, with warp, the weft is made.

    When I was a boy, I dreamed of becoming      5
    a soldier on horseback, a man of war,
    and with my helmet charging on stallions
    whose snorting terrified all who saw—
        wearing a coat of armor and mail,
        bearing a bow, bringing down walls.      10
    But when I beheld what the battle entailed—
    how soldiers pursuing became the pursued
    and fled at the sound of a wind-driven leaf—
        I settled down to till the soil.

    I planted gardens and tended vines,      15
    and plowed my fields with pairs of oxen;
    beans, garlic, pumpkin, and squash . . .
    I sowed all sorts of greens and onions.
        But then the rains stopped in the heavens,
        and from my labor I earned not a thing.      20
    And so I decided to take up construction,
    and build myself magnificent homes—
    towers filled with wondrous paintings,
        high on hills, set in stone. . . .

25     I also knew the secrets of numbers,
and the work of observing and charting the skies:
I counted the grains of sand and dust
and accurately measured the waters' rise.
    With ease I fathomed the new moon's phase,
30     whether it lasted a day or two days.
I saw when I put the scope to my eye
the stars in their orbits, moving on high:
their zenith and nadir, ascent and decline,
    and when they'd cast an eclipse with their line. . . .

35     To sell fruit and bread in the market,
and dry goods, too, I opened a store—
garlic, scallions, melons, legumes,
herbs, greens, and beans galore.
    To help out my brothers I went back to school
40     and learned how to weave blankets for mules.
In time, though, I became a cantor,
for my voice is good and I can sing:
I chanted prayers and recited psalms,
    the Song of the Sea and all the hymns. . . .

45     And I can translate from every tongue,
and swiftly turn the wheels at the mill:
I know how to properly sift the flour
and winnow wheat with tremendous skill.
    I toiled to learn the secrets of glass—
50     through which sunlight would perfectly pass.
I laundered, bleached, and traded wares,
and also in Scripture instructed boys.
Better than all, I could cut hair
    and knew how to press and filter oil. . . .

I've searched through all the lands of the West,
and to the East I've also turned,
calling—*Come, whoever it pleases!*
*Try to outdo me if you can!*
   In France's regions, and Arabia's lands,
   no one could ever keep up with my plans.
And though I tired, then I departed
for Assyria, Babylon, and Istanbul's shores,
and it became known that without my advice
   no one could finish the simplest of chores!

# MOSHE REMOS

*(c. 1406–c. 1430)*

Born in Majorca and educated in Rome, MOSHE REMOS lived the few years of his adult life in Sicily. He was working there as a doctor when, at the age of twenty-four, he was charged by either government officials or officers of the Inquisition with poisoning Christian patients during their treatment. He was sentenced to death and executed sometime around 1430. A poet neither by nature nor training, Remos was, like all the educated men of his time, reasonably skilled at verse composition, and he left behind a handful of poems, both secular and liturgical. His place in Hebrew literary history, however, was guaranteed with the composition of a sui generis elegy for himself just before his execution. A poem of 188 lines, its achievement is not sustained, but the best of it (excerpted here) is extremely powerful and startling in its directness.

The poem's heading reads: "I keened on that Sunday, for they told me that I would die the following day. Woe unto me! May it be God's will that my death serve as atonement for my iniquity. And with bitter tears and without deliberation or reflection, I, Moshe Remos, have taken up the pen, weeping as I write. . . ." The poet implores anyone who reads the poem to copy it and send it on to others until it reaches his family. Opening with a cry to the various dimensions of existence, as they were known from medieval (Greek) philosophy and the Qabbala, the poet then conjures a bizarrely digressive and at times curiously elaborated parade of the various elements, realms of nature, and fields of knowledge that will mourn for him once he is gone. This list includes the ten *sefirot*, the Active Intelligence, the heavens, the twelve signs of the zodiac, the planets, the four elements, the five senses, the sciences he studied, and the books he read, including what amounts to a full library of Greek and medieval Jewish learning. At line 144, the poet breaks off and confronts his death directly.

## LAST WORDS

Who could believe that a doctor and scholar
    who'd sought God would die such a death,
and like a lamb being brought to slaughter,
    Moshe the man of God would be led?

Judgment's aspect against me is roused—            5
    the Impatient One and the One Who Forbears.
The glow of the Shining Face is obscured;
    the Ancient of Days no longer hears.

Absolute Being and Substanceless One,
    Enactment, Form, End, and Eternity;          10
Wise, Willing, Able, Unchanging:
    How, my God, could you forsake me? . . .

The skies will don sackcloth and darkness,
    and the spheres, too, begin to mourn;
on the day I die the heavens will cease          15
    their longing in turn for the sons of the Lord.

Be stunned, O heaven, by death's barbarity:
    the Zodiac's wheel will tilt as it spins,
and like the Bull or Ram they'll take me—
    my arms and legs bound like the Twins.          20

And like the Crab, backwards I'll stumble,
    my neck bent, my hands in chains,
and at my right, my judge, like Satan—
    his face like a Lion's pursuing its prey.

I'll send up a cry and complaint like the Virgin          25
    to justice's Scales, but hear no reply—
lashed with ropes, while the Scorpion stings,
    and the Archer aims his bow at my eye.

As a Goat is rent, I will be torn—
    and pity the eyes that witness the torment;          30
they'll need a Pail for the tears that stream
    till even Fish could swim in them. . . .

Death has seized me and shakes me with fury—
    grieving is over, the word has come down.
35  "Tomorrow you'll die!" the jailer tells me.
    A mule's burial awaits me now.

My storm-tossed mother, in your distress,
    what will you do when the envoy appears?
Light of my eyes, and crown to my head,
40    you'll mourn for me with a fountain of tears.

And you, father, whose house has fallen,
    what will become of your old age?
Forgive me, I pray, my debt and transgression
    if I've not honored you with my days.

45  Stamping fiercely, Satan accuses—
    he's found a debtor from whom to collect;
but know, my friends, that I will be killed
    for horrible crimes I did not commit.

They say I prescribed a deadly potion
50    for some of my patients, a cup of poison.
It wasn't my fault—though now they crush me
    with false accusations of killing Christians.

The Lord's secret is known in fear;
    yet when I saw I'd die without cause,
55  I'd have collapsed, if not for Akiva.
    The Lord is just in all He does.

The tyrant's vizier offered to save me
    if I would abandon my Lord for his;
but better to die in body than spirit
60    and give my portion to the God who lives.

Now I'm despised, and to all I'm dross—
    for death's brutality I am destined.
Who'd have believed this for Moshe Remos?
    I am a man who has seen affliction.

65  Here in the prime of my life I'm bitter:
    death and disaster are already near.
A man who is whole and full of desire,
    I have lived for twenty-four years.

The end of the matter—God is good,
    and I confess that I have sinned.        70
I've acted with malice, but He is just.
    May I, Lord, be forgiven—

and may my dying be expiation.
    Help me, Lord, and in my faith
may my soul in the bundle of life        75
    be bound with you till the end of days.

# ʿELI BEN YOSEF [HAVILLIO?]

## *(second half of the fifteenth century?)*

Some eleven poems by a poet named ʿELI BEN YOSEF were discovered in the archives of the Cairo Jewish community and brought to Jerusalem in the early 1950s. Their author may well be ʿEli Ben Yosef Havillio, of Monzón, who lived in the second half of the fifteenth century and was known as a philosopher and translator of Christian philosophical works by writers including Thomas Aquinas, Duns Scotus, and William of Occam. Considered an important figure in the revival of philosophy in the Jewish circles of his time, Havillio was not known as a poet.

The poem translated here appears to be one of several addressed to a single unidentified individual, and it is distinguished by its self-deprecating image and tone. While the Hebrew poets of Christian Spain, and particularly the later poets of that period, no longer had the supreme confidence in their poetic powers that characterized the poets of the Golden Age, it is still somewhat unusual to find such direct expression of genuine modesty in the Hebrew poetry of the day.

## WHO SOARS

Who soars through air without being stricken
is a fly soon crushed in a net or prison;
    and the ant lifting its limb is a sign:
its fall is near, for an arrow will strike him.

My songs, friend, sought to rise—
but fell toward Hell like a stillborn child.

# MOSHE IBN HABIB

*(second half of the fifteenth century)*

Portugal's small Jewish community played virtually no part in the renaissance of Hebrew poetry in Iberia. The first evidence of a Portuguese dimension to the canon comes at the beginning of the fourteenth century, when David Ben Bilieh writes a treatise called "How to Rhyme." After the Expulsion we find Yehuda Abravanel (Leone Hebreo), perhaps the most famous of Portuguese Jewish writers, in Italy composing a long poem of complaint about his Iberian trials. Also of interest among the part-time Portuguese-Hebrew poets is MOSHE IBN HABIB, who was known primarily as a grammarian and philosopher. Born and raised in Lisbon, at some point he left Portugal for Italy. (The Jews were expelled from the country in 1497, but Ibn Habib, it seems, emigrated no later than the middle of the 1480s.) The impoverished writer settled in the Apulian town of Bitonto, and then moved on to Naples and Otranto. While hardly a poet of note, he composed a valuable, if distorted, guide to verse; *Darkhei No'am* (Pleasant Paths), written in Bitonto, surveys the poetics of the Spanish Hebrew school—which, as he sees it, derive from the Bible. In it Ibn Habib demonstrates the prosodic practice of the period through short didactic poems of his own, two of which are translated here. Of the six types of poetry that he says existed previously, he is willing to discuss just three: uplifting sacred verse, poetry of reproof, and poetry of moral guidance. "Of the other three [types]," he says, "it is forbidden to speak, let alone write them down in a book, for only a person whose soul has been sullied with such things and whose mind is muddied would employ them."

## ACCOUNT

I came to make account for my soul
and see if its merit outweighed its debt—
but panic struck me when from the figures
there shot forth only flames of regret.


## YOU COME TO THE HOUSE OF GOD

You come, man, to the house of God
and chirp away all the time like a bird:
How could you cleanse your heart of its sins,
or your soul find freedom through your words?

With all your heart then, bless the Lord:
Your prayer will rise like the scent of myrrh.

# SAʿADIA IBN DANAAN

*(mid-fifteenth century–1505)*

The final poet in our selection brings us full circle, back to the south and Muslim Spain. Saʿadia Ibn Danaan was born and raised in the last remaining Muslim territory on the Iberian peninsula, the kingdom of Granada, which at that time would have had a Jewish population of perhaps one thousand souls. After the city fell to the Christian Reconquest and the sentence of Expulsion was pronounced over all of Spain's Jews in 1492, Ibn Danaan fled to North Africa and settled in Morocco, where he became a leading transmitter of the Andalusian legacy and a religious authority known for his *responsa* literature and his wide learning. Apart from religious law and poetry, he wrote on history, linguistics, philosophy, biblical commentary, and poetics. He died in 1505.

Living in fifteenth-century Granada, Saʿadia developed outside the mainstream of Hebrew literature in the Christian north, and his work preserved a natural, though anomalous relation to the Arabic tradition out of which Hebrew poetry in Spain had evolved. In addition to his numerous epigrams, he wrote secular and religious poems, most of which are still in manuscript. But Ibn Danaan is best known for his 1468 composition about the Spanish-Hebrew meters, which has been called the most detailed work of its kind written in the Middle Ages. Here, at the tail end of the period, we find a Jewish poet—writing in Arabic prose and translating himself into Hebrew—for the first time systematically comparing the Hebrew meters to their Arabic models. Like Moshe Ibn Habib, Ibn Danaan demonstrated the meters in both versions with classical (though far more accomplished) Hebrew epigrams of his own. In the Hebrew version of his treatise, Ibn Danaan presents didactic proverbs dealing with faith and morals. As the examples below demonstrate, the didactic poems stand in curious tension with the erotic epigrams that serve as illustrations in the original Arabic version of his work. The latter are distinguished by their extraordinary lightness of touch, and it's on a grace note, with selections from Saʿadia's primer—linking ethics, desire, and meter—that this remarkable period comes to an end.

## ENMITY SMOLDERS

Enmity smolders and wakens quarrels
    among fools and evil men.
Among the wise, however, love
    covers nearly all transgression.


## HORDES OF READERS

I see hordes of readers abandoning grammar
as with their language they indict us all;
and so the sons of 'Ever consider them strangers,
and their words wait in ambush for the soul.


## MIXED MESSENGER

You've nectar on your lips, my fawn,
    but shoot sharp arrows with your eyes;
your mouth comes from Judah's sons,
    your gaze—from Ishmael's line.


## SHE TRAPPED ME

She trapped me with temptation's bread;
with stolen waters she hunted me down.
    Her angel's eyes looking at me
    were archers slowly taking aim.

Now her cheeks are the breaking dawn.
Now her hair brings evening on.

## CHIASMUS FOR A DOE

In my lap—a doe,
    and in her lap—a harp;
she plays it with her fingers,
    and kills me with her heart.

# NOTES

# ⊰ INTRODUCTION ⊱

1. S. D. Goitein, *A Mediterranean Society: The Jewish Communities of the World as Portrayed in the Documents of the Cairo Geniza* (Berkeley, Los Angeles, and London, 1988), 5:425. Goitein, who writes, "then 'the Spanish miracle' occurred" puts the phrase between quotation marks but doesn't cite a source, though he seems to be alluding to R. Kayser's *The Life and Times of Judah Halevi* (New York, 1949), p. 50. Kayser notes that "it is like a historical miracle that . . . the people of Israel in southern Europe enjoyed a golden age, the like of which they had not known since the days of the Bible," while "orgies of persecution" were occurring not far to the north. My thanks to Mark Cohen for pointing out the link to Kayser. The varying conclusions drawn from the lesson of Spain are treated in succinct fashion by Cohen in *Under Crescent and Cross* (Princeton, 1994), especially pp. 1–14 and 195–99. The leading modern scholar in the field, and in many respects its founder as a serious academic discipline, the late Haim Schirmann also refers to the miraculous nature of the period (below, n. 44, and *Toldot* [1995], pp. 15–16), as does Shulamit Elitzur in *Shirat HaHol Ha'Ivrit biSefarad HaMuslamit* [Secular Hebrew Poetry in Muslim Spain] (Ramat Aviv, 2004), p. 45. Likewise Ezra Fleischer, with regard to the poem by Dunash's wife ("Will Her Love Remember," below), writes: "For if in Dunash's generation women were already writing poems of this quality, one has to wonder if the secular Hebrew poetry of Spain wasn't born in miraculous fashion, at a single stroke, as a mature and fully-formed entity in every respect, a perfect being brought forth from absolute emptiness" ("'Al Dunash Ben Labrat veIshto," in *Mehqerei Yerushalayim beSifrut 'Ivrit* 5 [1984]: 202). Ismar Schorsch notes that the term "Golden Age" was first applied to this period by the Lutheran Hebraicist Franz Delitzsch in Leipzig in 1936. (See Ismar Schorsch, "The Myth of Sephardic Supremacy," *Leo Baeck Institute Yearbook* 34: 61.) Schorsch examines what he calls the "Sephardic mystique" that was promulgated by German-Jewish scholars. For more on the question of historical distortion in scholarship, see note 70. The "insular poetry" of the first postbiblical millennium includes epithet-laden talmudic elegies and the enormous corpus of hymns from late antiquity and the middle ages; while these hymns can sometimes be quite forceful, they are also limited in their liturgical range and at times wound down to hyper-mannered, coded concoctions that were mocked by the later Spanish poets. Raymond Scheindlin refers to the diction of that liturgical verse as "a special poetic dialect . . . merely degenerate forms of a classical language" ("The Influence of Muslim Arabic Cultural Elements on the Literature of the Hebrew Golden Age," *Conservative Judaism*, Summer 1982, p. 64). By contrast, the poetry of Spain has been described by one scholar as "a rich and full expression of the poet's self" (Elitzur, *Shirat HaHol*, p. 67). See below, on *fasaaha* (note 36).

2. The word—cosmos—in many ways takes us to the core of this poetry, which is often spoken of in terms of its "ornament." "Cosmos" derives from the Greek *kosmein*, that is, to order, and secondarily, to ornament. It is from this cluster of meanings that we get our "ordered world" (as in the pseudepigraphic *Prayer of Manasseh*: "He who made the heaven and the earth with all their embellishment [*kosmo*] . . ."), as well as our word "cosmetic." For more on this important nexus, see *Selected Poems of Solomon Ibn Gabirol*, trans. Peter Cole (Princeton, 2001), pp. 11–13; hereafter Cole, *Selected Ibn Gabirol*.

Historian Yom Tov Assis describes the culture of the Christian period as "*a brand of Judaism* [italics mine] that emerged as a result of the fusion of Jewish tradition with elements of Greco-Arabic civilizations and elements from Romance culture brought by the *Reconquista*. . . . Sefarad was no less authentic or Jewish than Ashkenazi pietism" ("Sefarad: A Definition in the Context of a Cultural Encounter," in *Encuentros and Desencuentros: Spanish Jewish Cultural Interaction throughout History*, ed. A. Doron [Tel Aviv, 2000], p. 35). His notion of Andalusian Jewish culture as "a brand of Judaism" applies all the more to the Muslim period. For more on *convivencia*, see note 70, below, and the glossary at the back of this volume.

3. In contrast with, say, nineteenth-century Jewish intellectuals of the European Haskala (Enlightenment), the Spanish-Jewish elite did *not* succumb to assimilation in the wake of exposure to the foreign. Conversion among the poets was rare in the Andalusian (Muslim) period and became a problem only in Christian Spain. That said, some scholars feel that the destruction of the Jewish community in Spain was an inevitable, even organic outgrowth of that exposure. Surveying the various "apologetic and ideological tendencies" that have informed readings of this poetry since the nineteenth century, Ross Brann notes that the tide has swung from the early modern understanding of the secular Hebrew poetry of Spain as a "model of enlightened Jewish culture" to more recent, and conservative, perspectives that present "challenging critiques that minimize the historical relevance of the Andalusian school and depreciate the 'Jewishness' of its poetry." "According to this revisionist view," Brann continues, "secular poetry may be relegated to an isolated corner of Hebrew literary history for two reasons: first, because the poets' obsession with literary elegance and social manners barely found its way to other strata of Andalusian Jewish society; and second, because Golden Age secular poetry had no lasting impact on the course of Hebrew literature, in contrast, say, to the Andalusian piyyut" (*The Compunctious Poet* [Baltimore and London, 1991], p. 16). While the argument can be made that Spanish-Hebrew secular poetry occupied a marginal position with regard to the mainstream of Hebrew and Jewish culture in post–Spanish-Hebrew history, that detracts only from its *historical* relevance and in no way diminishes its power or its value for the present and future. And here it is also important to recall that Andalusian accomplishments in the secular and devotional spheres were integrally linked.

4. As one writer has remarked, "One wonders what the Visigoths ate!" (Stephen O'Shea, *Sea of Faith* [New York, 2006]), p. 85. O'Shea follows by noting that the seventh-century polymath Isadore of Seville was already singing the praises of Iberia's fertile lands. Anticipating modern Spain's enormous fleet, Isadore also singles out the fish. Information for this paragraph comes from the following sources: Dimitri Gutas, *Greek Thought, Arabic Culture: The Greco-Arabic Translation Movement in Baghdad and Early Abbasid Society* (London, 1998), pp. 1, 11–12, and 14 (where he notes the possible link to China); Joseph F. O'Callaghan, *A History of Medieval Spain* (Ithaca and London, 1975), pp. 117, 141; Richard Fletcher, *Moorish Spain* (Berkeley, 1992), p. 53; and S. M. Imamuddin, *Muslim Spain 711–1492: A Sociological Study* (Leiden, 1981), pp. 75–99. Gutas notes that certain paper was named for the patrons of the translation movement, an indication of that activity's importance. 'Abd al-Rahmaan III's mother was Frankish and his grandmother a Basque princess. He is described in contemporary chronicles as being "handsome . . . and equally at home in Arabic and in the emerging Romance tongue." He reportedly dyed his hair black to make himself look more Arab.

The new Muslim population was deeply divided along ethnic and tribal lines: the conquering troops from North Africa comprised soldiers from rival Yemeni Arab clans (Beni Qalb and Beni Quraysh), both of which looked down on the soldiers drawn from the crude Berber tribes of the Maghreb. The conquered Iberians were also diverse. While the Mozarabs, or Arabized Christians, adopted Arab customs and the Arabic language, they continued to worship in their churches and for the most part were subject to the rule of their own officials and Church law. Many Christians, however, converted to Islam. These converts (*musaalima*) and their children born into the new faith (*muwalladun*) occupied yet another tier in this ethnically charged society-in-formation. There was also a large population of fair-haired slaves (Slavs), brought from the north, as well as darker servants purchased from Africa. Many of the Slavs were eunuchs and took on a range of domestic, administrative, and military functions in the caliphate.

5. Goitein, *Mediterranean Society*, 1:101ff. He notes that textiles of the day were especially durable, variegated, and expensive, and that "clothing formed part— sometimes a considerable part—of a family's investment, being transmitted from parents to children." He also comments on what he calls the "color-intoxication" of the age, quoting from orders for textiles and descriptions of trousseaus: "Five fine covers, one gazelle blood, one pure violet, one musk-colored, one silvery, one intense yellow; two others pure, clean white, inclining to yellow. . . . Eight pairs of small prayer carpets, two white, two indigo blue, two green, two red. . . . Please, my lord, the red should be as red as possible, likewise the white and the yellow should be exquisite. . . . The siglaton [gold brocade] robe is of the utmost beauty, but not exactly what I wanted, for it is white and blue, while I wanted to have . . . onion color, an 'open' color. The lead-colored [i.e. bluish gray] robe is superb." According to the Geniza records, Spain was the leading Mediterranean country in the production of silk.

Paper had been produced in the Islamic world from the eighth century on, at first in Baghdad—with the secrets of production having been taken, it seems, from the Chinese. In al-Andalus, Játiva, near Valencia, was a major center for paper production. See Richard Fletcher, *The Cross and the Crescent: Christianity and Islam from Muhammad to the Reformation* (New York, 2003), pp. 56–57, who notes that "among the various grades of paper listed by an encyclopedist of technology was a special lightweight type known as 'birds' paper' because it was thin enough to be sent by carrier pigeon: the earliest known airmail paper." See also Jonathan Bloom, *Paper before Print* (New Haven and London, 2001), p. 88.

6. Imamuddin, *Muslim Spain*, pp. 130–34; B. Reilly, *The Medieval Spains* (Cambridge, 1993), pp. 61–67.

7. Robert Hillenbrand, "Medieval Cordoba as a Cultural Center," in *The Legacy of Muslim Spain*, ed. Salma Khadra Jayyusi (Leiden, 1994), p. 117. Fletcher, *Moorish Spain*, pp. 60–61.

8. The Berber chieftain Taariq Ibn Ziyaad led a legion of some 7,000 men (6,000 of them Berbers) across the straits on April 27/28, 711. A second wave of support troops brought the strength of his army to 12,000 men, and on July 19, Taariq's Muslim army routed the Visigothic king Rodrigo. The mission's success notwithstanding, Taariq's Arab commander Muusa Ibn Nusayr was angered by his lieutenant's insubordination—since the Umayyad caliph in Damascus had cautioned Ibn Nusayr to limit their mission to intensive *explorations* of the area—and the following spring he gathered a mixed Arab, Syrian, Egyptian, and Berber force of 18,000 and crossed the straits as well, occupying towns Taariq had passed by. Within three years the two armies had secured control of most of the peninsula, before both conquerors were recalled to Damascus. Some years later, another 30,000 troops were dispatched from Damascus to help quell civil unrest.

9. In 749, following several military victories over the Umayyad army, Abu-l-ʿAbbaas, a descendant of the Prophet's uncle (who was known as al-Saffaah, "the spiller of blood"), was named the first Abbasid caliph. The following year, the Umayyad caliph, Marwaan II, was murdered, and all members of the royal family—except ʿAbd al-Rahmaan—were hunted down wherever they were and killed. The new Abbasid caliphate was soon moved eastward, and in 762 the city of Baghdad was founded as its capital. ʿAbd al-Rahmaan, whose mother had been a Berber slave, fled to his mother's homeland, before settling in al-Andalus.

10. In fact, we don't know why Ziryaab went west, but the story of his falling out at court appears to be a "later invention" (H. Kilpatrick, in *The Encyclopedia of Arabic Literature*, ed. J. S. Meisami and P. Starkey [London and New York, 1998], p. 826). For the other information here, see Fletcher, *The Cross and the Crescent*, p. 59; María Rosa Menocal, *Ornament of the World* (New York, 2002), pp. 32–33. Some estimate that al-Hakam's library held 600,000 volumes. By comparison, the library of King Charles the Wise, of France, in the mid-fourteenth century held a mere 900 books, two-thirds of them treating theology (S. M. Imamuddin, *A Political History of Muslim Spain* [Dacca, 1961], p. 97). The Andalusian private libraries also

stood in stark contrast with the situation outside the Arab world. In eighth- and ninth-century Byzantium, "a very modest private library of a few dozen books was beyond the means of most, if not all, rich intellectuals" (Gutas, *Greek Thought, Arabic Culture*, pp. 176–77). See also Thomas F. Glick, *Islamic and Christian Spain in the Early Middle Ages* (Princeton, 1979), pp. 38ff.; O'Callaghan, *History*, pp. 107, 158; Hillenbrand, "Medieval Cordoba," pp. 117–21. On the subject of women's roles in Andalusia, see Shirley Guthrie, *Arab Women in the Middle Ages* (London, 2001), p. 176. María J. Viguera makes it clear that Andalusian letters and literary culture generally yield a somewhat distorted picture of women's level of freedom in Muslim Spain, and that the majority of Andalusian women by no means enjoyed "genuine freedom" ("On the Social Status of Andalusi Women," in Jayyusi, *The Legacy of Muslim Spain*, pp. 709–24).

11. In an effort to assimilate, some of the new converts faked an Arabic lineage. Alvarus, the ninth-century bishop of Cordoba, complains that Christian youth were "intoxicated with Arab elegance" (*Encyclopedia of Arabic Literature*, p. 730). The precise linguistic situation in al-Andalus is not known with any certainty and no doubt varied from community to community. "The language of the fields and streets might be that Romance which had devolved from the old late-vulgar Latin," writes Bernard Reilly, referring to the largely peasant class of Romance speakers (*The Contest of Christian and Muslim Spain: 1031–1157* [Cambridge and Oxford, 1992], p. 21). David Wasserstein explains that poetry in particular attracted the youth of the day. And Moshe Ibn Ezra's twelfth-century book also testifies to the Spanish Jews' admiration for Arabic verse (*Sefer Ha'Iyyunim ve-HaDiyyunim: al-Kitaab al-Muhaadhara wa-'l-Mudhaakara* [*The Book of Discussion and Remembrance*], trans. and ed. A. S. Halkin [Jerusalem, 1975], p. 57; hereafter *The Book of Discussion*). The Jewish population, Wasserstein adds, would have spoken and written Latin prior to their adoption of Arabic, using Romance as their vernacular; both were probably spoken during an interim period. In time, however, Arabic proved dominant, and spoken Arabic became their only vernacular. Most written expression was in a middle-register Judeo-Arabic, which was written in Hebrew characters. Only poetry and a few other "prestige texts" were composed in Hebrew (David Wasserstein, "The Language Situation," in *Studies in the Muwashshah and the Kharja* [Oxford, 1991], pp. 3–4 and 15). Some Jews probably also spoke Berber.

12. Menocal, *Ornament of the World*, p. 12. The famous characterization is by the tenth-century writer Hrotsvit of Gandersheim, who had never seen the city. Writing from her home in lower Saxony, she based her account on reports that reached her. Her topic was in fact a Christian martyr, Palagius, who (reportedly) died holding out against the homosexual advances of the caliph of Cordoba, 'Abd al-Rahmaan III (Katherina Wilson, *Hrotsvit of Gandersheim: A Florilegium of Her Work* [Cambridge, 1998], pp. 6,10; also John Boswell, *Christianity, Social Tolerance, and Homosexuality* [Chicago and London, 1980], pp. 198ff). Scholarly estimates of the city's population vary widely, from 90,000 to 1 million. (See, for example,

O'Callaghan, *History*, p. 155; Haim Schirmann, *HaShira Ha'Ivrit biSefarad HaMuslamit* [Jerusalem, 1995], p. 100; and Hugh Kennedy, *Muslim Spain and Portugal: A Political History of al-Andalus* [London and New York, 1996], p. 107: "Cordoba was vastly more developed than any of the muddy market towns of northern Europe.") Figures offered for the population of tenth-century Spain as a whole are also unreliable. It is often given by scholars as between 6 million and 9 million residents. The Jewish population is estimated to have been some 1 percent of that—though concentrations of Jewish population were generally considered to have been much higher in the major cities (S. D. Goitein, "Jewish Society and Institutions under Islam," in *Jewish Society through the Ages*, ed. H. H. Ben-Sasson and S. Ettinger [New York, 1971], p. 173; Reilly, *Contest*, pp. 191–92, n. 3). David Wasserstein, however, regards these estimations with considerable skepticism, commenting that "there is no information at all which would make it possible to offer such an exact estimate" ("Jewish Elites in al-Andalus," in *The Jews of Islam: Community, Society, and Identity*, ed. D. Frank [Leiden, 1995], p. 107; also pp. 108–10). He assumes that the number of Jews in eleventh-century Spain was in fact very much smaller than is generally assumed. To the extent that one can get a rough sense of the size of the Jewish population, he concludes, the numbers "show how very much the Jewish people today owes to a very small absolute number of medieval inhabitants of the Iberian Peninsula" (p. 110). See also Eliyahu Ashtor, *The Jews of Moslem Spain* (Philadelphia, 1973/92), 2:190–300.

13. Self-mythologizing Spanish-Jewish tradition traces Jewish settlement in Spain back to the exile of Jewish families from Jerusalem in 586, in the wake of the First Temple's destruction. Scholars assume that the migration of Jews throughout the Roman diaspora (from the second century B.C.E. through the second century C.E.) brought them to Spain as well, as traders, and then as slaves, following the destruction of the Second Temple in Jerusalem in 79 C.E.; additional waves of Jewish immigration came from North Africa, Italy, and Provence.

14. Assis, "Jews of Spain," p. 11; Ross Brann, "The Arabized Jews," in *The Literature of al-Andalus*, ed. María Rosa Menocal, Raymond Scheindlin, and Michael Sells (Cambridge, 2000), pp. 435–38. The Arian (non-Trinitarian) Christian and Latin-speaking Visigoths at first treated the Jewish communities they found with relative tolerance, but the situation deteriorated with their conversion to Catholicism in the late sixth century. Harsh legislation was passed, ranging from mandatory observance of Sunday as the day of rest, to the banishment of Jewish children to monasteries (where they were to be raised as Christians), to forced baptism of the entire community, confiscation of Jewish property, and the enslavement of all Jewish wives and children. While this and other legislation wasn't always enforced, conditions in Spain were by no means conducive to communal development, and in fact many Jews fled to areas of Gaul and North Africa that were still controlled by Roman nobility (Jane Gerber, *The Jews of Spain: A History of the Sephardic Experience* [New York, 1994], p. 8). See Gerber for the early history of Jewish presence in Iberia (pp. 2–25). For more

on the Visigothic documentation, see *Medieval Iberia: Readings from Christian, Muslim, and Jewish Sources*, ed. Olivia Remie Constable (Philadelphia, 1997), pp. 12–23.

15. These regulations were known as the Pact of 'Umar, an English translation of which appears in N. Stillman, *The Jews of Arab Lands* (Philadelphia, 1979), pp. 157–58. See also *The Jew in the Medieval World*, ed. Jacob R. Marcus (1938; Philadelphia and New York, 1960), pp. 12–15. Marcus notes there that, by and large, "this pact, like much medieval legislation, was honored more in the breach than in the observance." For a detailed discussion of the pact and its application, see Cohen, *Under Crescent and Cross*, pp. 54ff.

Regarding the overall Arabization of the Spanish Jews, Brann notes, "Before the emergence of their literary culture in the mid-tenth century, the Jews of al-Andalus had been speaking Arabic for generations and thereby came to think in and view the world through the medium of that language" ("Arabized Jews," p. 441). By the time the Hebrew renaissance was underway, in the eleventh century, it could be assumed that the state of Hebrew letters was such that Jews could also converse in Hebrew, though it is not at all clear whether that was ever done. The spoken language of the Jews of Muslim Spain was without doubt a middle register of Arabic (S. Morag, "HaMoreshet HaLeshonit Ha'Ivrit biSefarad," *Pe'amim* 53 [1992]: 6). See also note 11, above. Wasserstein adds: "In economic life there were scarcely any real restrictions on Jews, or *dhimmis*. . . . In religious life real constraints on Jewish practice were minimal" ("Jewish Elites," p. 103). The status of Jewish elites, he adds, was "slightly different" from the status of Arab elites.

16. Ashtor, *The Jews of Moslem Spain*, 1: 30–35; Schirmann, *Toldot* (1995), pp. 100–101; Brann, "Arabized Jews," pp. 435–54.

17. Schirmann, *Toldot* (1995), p. 102.

18. The tenth-century Arab geographers and chroniclers Ibn Hawqal and al-Muqaddasi comment on the "remarkable sea ports" of Andalusia and the extensive network of trade routes they serve. See Olivia Remie Constable, *Trade and Traders in Muslim Spain* (Cambridge, 1994), p. 17. The appointment was hardly honorary, and the job brought with it a great deal of responsibility.

19. For more detailed accounts of Hasdai's life, see Ashtor, *The Jews of Moslem Spain*, 1: 155–263; Schirmann, *Toldot* (1995), pp. 102ff.; Haim Beinart, *The Sephardic Legacy* (Jerusalem, 1992), 1: 15; and D. Wasserstein, *The Rise and Fall of the Party Kings: Politics and Society in Islamic Spain, 1002–1086* (Princeton, 1985), p. 196.

20. See also Moshe Ibn Ezra's *Book of Discussion*, pp. 56–57, where he describes the cultural awakening around Hasdai and his gathering scholars and works from faraway places. Among other things, Hasdai was interested in the Khazars' conversion and also asked if they had any knowledge about the reckoning of the end of days. See Beinart, *The Sephardic Legacy*, 1: 16.

21. S. M. Stern notes that while the Hebrew poets themselves "had no standing at all in Muslim society [as poets] . . . some of their Jewish patrons did occupy

positions there, though mainly minor ones. Smaller figures in the outer world, they loomed large in Jewish society: like minor planets in the system of some Muslim court, they formed centers around which their Jewish courtiers (among them the Hebrew poets) moved like so many satellites" ("Arabic Poems by Spanish-Hebrew Poets," in *Romanica et Occidentalia*, ed. M. Lazar [Jerusalem, 1963], p. 254).

22. Schirmann, *Toldot* (1995), p. 101; Fleischer, "LeQadmoni'ut Shirateinu biSefarad," *Asufot* 2, (1988): 231–33; Ashtor, *The Jews of Moslem Spain*, 1: 244ff.

23. Hasdai's use of the term is straightforward here. Generally speaking, however, the word "Sefarad" meant much more than just "Spain." As Yosef Haim Yerushalmi has pointed out, "*Sefarad, Tzarfat,* or *Ashkenaz* were not merely fabricated Jewish equivalents for Spain, France, or Germany; they were Hebrew place names lifted out of their biblical contexts and superimposed over the map of contemporary Europe" ("Exile and Expulsion," in *Crisis and Creativity in the Sephardic World: 1391–1648*, ed. Benjamin R. Gampel [New York, 1997]), p. 13. "Sefarad is not Spain," declares Yom Tov Assis, who describes the trilateral Jewish–Greco-Arabic–Romance cultural symbiosis, rather than any single geographical entity, as its essence ("Sefarad," pp. 31 and 35).

The term itself appears in Obadiah 20: "And the exile of Jerusalem that is in Sefarad"—though modern scholars understand the word there to refer to Sardis. It is taken to mean Spain for the first time in the Peshitta—the Syriac translation of the Hebrew Bible, which was begun in the first century of the Common Era—and shortly thereafter in Targum Jonathan, one of the Aramaic translations of the Old Testament (made in Babylonia during the early centuries of the Common Era). From the eighth century on Sefarad is generally taken in Hebrew and Jewish literature to mean Spain. Targum Jonathan to Obadiah 20: " 'And the exile of Jerusalem that is in Sefarad'—and the exile of Jerusalem that is in Spain." See also *Seder 'Olam Zuta* (a sixth- or seventh-century Babylonian midrash): "Vespasianus came and destroyed the Temple and exiled Israel and many families from the House of David and Yehuda to Espamya [Spain], which is Sefarad" (*Seder 'Olam Zuta*, ed. A. Neubauer, in *Seder HaHakhamim VeQorot HaYamim*, vol. 1 [Oxford, 1887], p. 71).

24. Hasdai's letter is curiously reminiscent of Isadore of Seville's seventh-century description in the prologue to his *History of the Goths, Vandals, and Suevi* (624 C.E.), wherein he sings the praises of Iberia: "Of all lands from the west to the Indies, you, Spain, O sacred and always fortunate mother of princes and peoples, are the most beautiful. . . . Indulgent nature has deservedly enriched you with an abundance of everything fruitful. You are rich with olives, overflowing with grapes, fertile with harvests. You are dressed in corn, shaded with olive trees, covered with the vine. Your fields are full of flowers, your mountains full of trees, your shores full of fish. You are located in the most favorable region in the world; neither are you parched by the summer heat of the sun, nor do you languish under icy cold, but girded by a temperate band of sky, you are nourished by fertile

west winds. You bring forth the fruits of the fields, the wealth of the mines, and beautiful and useful plants and animals. Nor are you to be held inferior in rivers, which the brilliant fame of your fair flocks ennobles" (translated from Latin by Kenneth B. Wolf, in *Medieval Iberia*, p. 3). Hasdai and Menahem's letter is quoted in Schirmann *Toldot* (1995), p. 100; the translation is mine. The letter, which begins with the sort of mythologizing referred to above (note 13)—"I, Hasdai, son of Isaac, belonging to the exiled Jews of Jerusalem in Spain"—was written some time between 956 and 961. The full letter, with King Yosef's answer, can be found in F. Kobler, *Letters of Jews through the Ages* (Philadelphia, 1978), pp. 100–101.

25. Into the spine of his poem Menahem embeds an acrostic that reads: "I am Hasdai, son of Yitzhaq, son of Ezra, son of Shaprut, Menahem Ben Saruq." Acrostics of this sort were normally used only in liturgical poems.

26. Based on one of the recently discovered poems by Menahem, Fleischer writes, "it is possible to see what the Hebrew poetry of Spain would have looked like . . . if Dunash's innovations hadn't come to pass. The poem is Jewish to its marrow: all the ideas it embodies are originally Jewish" ("LeQadmoni'ut Shirateinu biSefarad," p. 253). Menahem's version of that style appears to be influenced by Sa'adia Gaon's poetry. His work has not been included in this anthology for that reason: in most respects it belongs to the older style of Eastern poetry, though it was composed in the west, and in a very different social context.

27. See Fleischer, "LeQadmoni'ut Shirateinu biSefarad," pp. 249–69. Apart from the poem to the Khazar king and the prefatory poem to the epistle to Hasdai (see below), three other poems, all panegyrics, are extant. They were published by Ezra Fleischer in 1988. Fleischer characterizes these, too, as impressive examples of a courtly application of the Eastern style exemplified by Sa'adia, and on the whole he considers Menahem "an extremely talented poet." Examples of Menahem's cadenced prose in English translation can be found in T. Carmi, *The Penguin Book of Hebrew Verse* (New York, 1981), pp. 277–79, and Raymond Scheindlin, "Hebrew Poetry in Medieval Iberia," in *Convivencia*, ed. V. Mann, T. Glick, and J. Dodds (New York, 1992), p. 45. In addition to the three "new" secular poems, Fleischer has also uncovered evidence for the composition of liturgical poetry in Spain prior to Dunash's arrival. The two very brief liturgical poems he published alongside the secular finds clearly demonstrate, he says, that liturgical poetry in the Eastern manner was known to Menahem and the Spanish congregations. Beyond that, he notes, it is hard to imagine that for the 250 years of Jewish life in Muslim Spain prior to Dunash's arrival, the Spanish cantors sang only foreign liturgical poems and never tried their hand at the various liturgical genres. There are, however, no extant *piyyutim* from this period, apart from the eight lines that Fleischer quotes. That said, there were other poets writing during this initial phase, including the students of Menahem and Dunash. In his *Tahkemoni* (ed. Y. Toporowski [Tel Aviv, 1952], p. 43), Yehuda Alharizi also mentions two other poets by name, Avun and Shmu'el, as well as "many others apart from them, of whose work there is no trace—/for their matter was weak and therefore erased."

For more on the development of Hebrew verse and the other poets who were active at the start of the Spanish period, see Fleischer, "LeToldot Shirat HaHol Ha'Ivrit biSefarad beReshitah," in *Asufot, Tarbut veHevrah beToldot Yisrael beYamei HaBenayim*, ed. M. Ben-Sasson et al. (Jerusalem, 1989), pp. 197–225.

28. In Menahem's scheme, Hebrew words were composed of one-, two-, or three-letter roots. (The correct understanding of the three-letter root—common to Hebrew and Arabic—would come about only in the next generation, with the work of Yehuda Ibn Hayyuj and, after him, Yona Ibn Janaah.) Menahem does, though, repeatedly demonstrate an appreciation of linguistic elegance and purity. Dunash felt that Menahem wasn't qualified to undertake a dictionary of this sort as he lacked the tools for systematic analysis—though as Schirmann points out, Dunash too had misconstrued the root system (S. Morag, "Mahloqet Menahem veDunash veTehiyyat Ha'Ivrit," *Pe'amim* 56 [1993]: 9 and 13–14). See also Schirmann, *Toldot* (1995), p. 129.

29. Accounts of Menahem's troubles vary from scholar to scholar. Schirmann, for one, casts doubt on the accusation of Karaism; but whatever the charge was, he says, it had to be serious enough to warrant Hasdai's violation of the Sabbath (*Toldot* [1995], pp. 113–14). Ashtor presents a slightly different version of his catastrophe from the one related here (*Jews of Moslem Spain*, 1: 241ff.).

30. Epistle to Hasdai, in *HaShira Ha'Ivrit biSefarad uveProvans*, 2d ed. (Jerusalem and Tel Aviv, 1959), p. 14, lines 81–85.

31. Morag, "Mahloqet Menahem veDunash veTehiyyat Ha'Ivrit," p. 14. See also E. Rosenthal, *Judaism and Islam* (London and New York, 1961), pp. 73–76.

32. Robert Brody, *The Geonim of Babylonia and the Shaping of Medieval Jewish Culture* (New Haven and London, 1998), pp. 37–38, 236–37, 239. For Sa'adia's poetry, see Brody, pp. 323ff., and Menahem Zulay, *Ha'askula HaPaytanit shel Rav Sa'adia Gaon* (Jerusalem, 1964), pp. 13–40. "Gaon" was the official title of the head of the academy and signified, literally, eminence and great learning.

33. Ezra Fleischer, "Meqomo shel Rav Sa'adia Gaon beToldot HaShira Ha'Ivrit," *Pe'amim* 54 (1993): 10. His polemical poetry treating religion was notable because it was independent of any liturgical station and as such involved a kind of proto-secular verse.

34. Fleischer, "Meqomo shel Rav Sa'adia Gaon," p. 7.

35. Nehemia Allony, *Sefer Egron* (Jerusalem, 1969), pp. 158–59. The extended quotation cited here is from the Hebrew introduction to the first edition. The translation is, for the most part, mine, but see also Brody, *The Geonim*, pp. 247–48. Fleischer comments that Sa'adia's elevation of poetry to this central role was unheard of in Jewish letters since the age of Scripture ("Meqomo shel Rav Sa'adia Gaon," pp. 6–8).

36. Fleischer, "Hirhurim beDavar Ofyah shel Shirat Yisrael biSefarad," *Pe'amim* 2 (1979): 17.

37. Both observations are Fleischer's, in "LeQadmoni'ut Shirateinu HaSefardit," pp. 229–30, and "Hirhurim," p. 18. A simpler, if cruder, way of putting this

is that the Jews of the early to mid-tenth century in Spain were not open to the ideas of the people around them, although they easily mixed with those people and adopted much of their cultural style; the Jews of Babylonia, on the other hand, were very much open to the ideas of the people around them, but did not easily mix with their neighbors or absorb much of their cultural style.

38. The notion of dictional purity, or clarity (*fasaaha*), based in Scripture comes from the Arabic tradition, where the Quran served as the model. (*Fasaaha* derives from the Assyrian and Aramaic words meaning, among other things, "radiant" or "bright.") Purity here is a relative term. The lexicon of the Spanish-Hebrew poets wasn't frozen, and they would ring certain changes on it to increase its range and flexibility. But it almost entirely removed the obscurantism and mannerism of the "special dialect" that characterized the Eastern liturgical verse of the preceding five or six centuries. Yerushalmi has commented that it wasn't just the biblical register that the medieval Hebrew poets adopted but a biblical mindset. This is demonstrated by the biblical typology of HaNagid, for example, who calls his enemy in Almeria by the biblical name "Agag" (1 Samuel 15:8) and refers to his Slavic army as "Amaleq." See Yerushalmi, "Exile and Expulsion," pp. 13–14. See HaNagid's poem "The War with Yaddayir," and *Selected Poems of Shmuel HaNagid*, trans. Peter Cole (Princeton, 1996), pp. xiii–xiv, 39–47, and 65–68; hereafter, Cole, *Selected HaNagid*. For a detailed discussion of biblical typology in this work, see Brann's *Compunctious Poet*, pp. 23–58.

39. That is, the monorhymed Arabic ode, or qasida, along with the shorter lyric and epigrammatic fragment known as the *qita'*, would determine the contours of the Hebrew poem. Jewish life would flow through their lines, as the poets employed these forms for erotic, elegiac, didactic, epistolary, satirical, gnomic, and panegyric poetry, as well as for their most intimate prayers. In time, other forms (e.g. the *muwashshah* and additional strophic modes) would be added to the repertoire, drawn from the Arabic, Eastern Hebrew, and Romance traditions of Spain and Provence. Likewise, various changes in the meters were introduced, with, in some cases, syllabics, word-count, biblical-style cadenced verse, and other measures replacing the quantitative system. With regard to the relation between the quantitative meters and music, see Amnon Shiloah, "Development of Jewish Liturgical Singing in Spain," in Beinart, *The Sephardic Legacy*, 2:426–27. For more detailed discussion of all the forms mentioned above, as well as of the genres and the rhetorical figures that the poets employed, see the glossary at the back of this volume.

40. See the introduction to Cole, *Selected Ibn Gabirol*, under the entry "Gentility, the Good, the Good Life," pp. 26–27, and in particular the reference there to the canonical 1947 essay by Joseph Weiss, which reads in part: "Wherever a 'court' exists, there you will find 'style'. . . . The pleasures of society, such as play, laughter, music, literature and of course the bonds of love and friendship, all pass through the crucible of subtle stylization until the social life of the court becomes entirely a game of art . . . poetry, song, entertaining rhymes and riddles, laughter, and light, cultured conversation." The problem here is tonal as much as anything else.

In this respect, it is critical in reading medieval Hebrew poetry to have a sense of how the poetry of other courtly traditions has been treated in English translation and in modern scholarship. Shulamit Elitzur offers a balanced assessment of the situation: "Most of the important Hebrew poets active in Spain were financially and spiritually independent, and even if the stamp of court poetry is in various places impressed on their work, *they can by no means be defined as court poets* [italics mine]" (*Shirat HaHol*, p. 50). Moreover, a good deal of the encomia and occasional poetry that precipitated around the court involved poets writing to friends and fellow poets, rather than patrons. In other words, the poetry that evolved from the aristocratic background of Spanish-Muslim and Spanish-Jewish court society involved an elite element of the society, but it is an independent literature which, for the most part, is not dictated by the demands of any court or by financial considerations. (In this respect it is like much of the best medieval poetry from other cultures, including Japan and China.) See also Elitzur, *Shirat HaHol*, pp. 63–64. For more on this topic, see "encomia" in the glossary at the back of this volume.

41. Quoted in Frank Kermode's introduction to *Selected Prose of T. S. Eliot*, ed. with an introduction by Frank Kermode (New York, 1975), p. 19. In many ways this is akin to poet and artist David Jones's conception of art as an extra-utile and gratuitous act (*Anathemata* [London and Boston, 1952], pp. 23 and 29).

42. Abraham Ibn Daud, *Sefer Ha-Qabbalah: The Book of Tradition*, translation and notes by Gerson Cohen (Philadephia, 1967), especially pp. 276–77 and 286–87. The representation of "court poets" as prissy poetasters does, however, have its place in the literature, particularly later on. Qalonymos Ben Qalonymos (1286–after 1328) mocks poets he considered epigones as precisely the embodiment of that sort of effete figure—prancers and dancers on tiptoe and heel. See the biography preceding his poem in this anthology. The main point in Qalonymos's portrait is that these deluded figures represent a plummet from the grace and sublime stature of the great poets of an earlier age. "The sons of elegance have passed away," he writes, "the daughters of song are bowed, and only a carcass remains, unfit for an offering of man." See Schirmann, *Toldot* (1997), pp. 529 and 539. This opposition to poetry was entirely new, and characteristic of later developments in Christian Spain. On the characterization of this period as a "renaissance," see Joel Kramer, "The Culture Bearers of Humanism in the Renaissance of Islam," Dr. Irene Halmos Chair of Arabic Literature Annual Lecture, Tel Aviv University, 1984.

43. "The Jews of al-Andalus," writes Raymond Scheindlin, "adopted the classicizing concept of *'arabiyya*—the Arabic view of the preeminence of classical Arabic—but . . . made biblical Hebrew the equivalent of classical Arabic and accorded their language a new status as a cultural monument above and beyond its traditional status as the 'holy tongue' " ("Hebrew Poetry in Medieval Iberia," pp. 43–45). And Brann comments: "The stimulus for the poets' linguistic ideology and literary practice came from the dynamic Arabo-Islamic host culture, yet their conscious objective was nationalistic. Golden Age Hebrew poetry . . . must

be seen, therefore, as literary discourse designed to mediate cultural ambiguity" (*Compunctious Poet*, p. 24). Throughout *The Compunctious Poet* Brann is alert to the way in which the often-contradictory concerns of the Jewish poets gave rise to "compunction," which would manifest itself in a variety of modes. See also *Compunctious Poet*, pp. 69 and 88, and Ibn Ezra on the superiority of Arabic poetry (*The Book of Discussion*, pp. 29ff.), as well as Avraham Ibn Ezra's "World Poetry," below. Yehuda Alharizi also makes it clear that he composes his great work, *Tahkemoni*, in order to demonstrate Hebrew's power (e.g., *Tahkemoni*, pp. 11–12, 22) and redeem the language from its fallen state, in which it had become the object of mockery and scorn. He states that he was driven to write the *Tahkemoni* by the example of that greatest of *Arab* authors, al-Hariiri, whom he himself had translated—also, in a sense, out of shame—though here he notes that al-Hariiri stole his material from Hebrew sources. The charge of "plagiarism" was of course false, but par for the contemporary course.

In his book on Hebrew poetics and literary history, Moshe Ibn Ezra also laments the fact that the richness of Hebrew had been lost long ago (when it was by no means inferior to Arabic), and that it was being rediscovered only in the new Hebrew poetry of Spain. He explains that the supremacy of the Sephardic poets is due to both their descent from illustrious Jerusalem families and their absorption of the sweetness of the Arabic poetry, which in turn derives from climatic and geographical circumstances (*The Book of Discussion*, pp. 28–31, 35, 43, and 54–55). Accounting for Sephardic supremacy, Alharizi expresses the common medieval belief in favorable geographical influence, which was based on the theories of Hippocrates. See *Tahkemoni*, p. 183, and 'Eruvin 53a, which enumerates the virtues of the Judean Jews as opposed to the Galilean Jews: "The Judeans, who cared for [the beauty of] their language, retained their learning, but the Galileans, who did not care for [the beauty of their language], did not retain their learning." The passage goes on to mention "precision" as one of the other virtues that preserved the Judean tradition.

María Rosa Menocal describes Cordoba and the culture it stands for as "a first-rate place" in the sense of F. Scott Fitzgerald's formula: "the test of a first-rate intelligence is the ability to hold two opposed ideas in the mind at the same time." "In its moments of great achievement," Menocal writes, "medieval culture positively thrived on holding at least two, and often many more, contrary ideas at the same time" (*Ornament of the World*, pp. 10–11).

44. "He destroyed the holy tongue,/which is our remnant,/by casting Hebrew/in foreign meters"; "and he sought . . . to bring down his people with him" (*Teshuvot Talmidei Menahem Ibn Saruq*, facsimile ed. [Vienna, 1870], p. 7, lines 43–44; p. 20, lines 1–3. The response to Dunash was written by a student of Menahem, Yitzhaq Ibn Qapron, who composed his attack in one of the quantitative meters (in imitation of a poem by Dunash) in order to demonstrate that his opposition to them didn't derive from the difficulty of writing in the these new meters. Ibn Qapron added a good deal of fuel to the fire by inserting an ad

hominem dimension to the debate: he said that Dunash had clothed himself in spider webs, appealed to the young and ignorant, made himself a laughingstock every time he opened his mouth, and was driven by a desire for fame. In many ways the debate remains unresolved: to this day there is a good deal of disagreement over how this poetry should be recited, or sung, what much of it means, and—by extension—what the worth of it is.

On HaLevi's return to the debate, see his statements in *The Kuzari*, 2:63ff. and Schirmann's characterization of his position in *Toldot* (1995), pp. 443ff.

45. *Ta'ifa* means "party" or "faction" in Arabic. David Wasserstein comments that the increased opportunities that the rise of the decentralized Ta'ifa states brought about for Jews also resulted in increased exposure and risk. He points out that the Jewish cultural renaissance might be looked upon as part of the larger trend toward *shu'ubiyya*, "a form of national self-assertion, in cultural terms, by non-Arabs against Arab domination and Arab claims to superiority" (*The Rise and Fall of the Party Kings*, pp. 169, 181–83, 191–93, and 220). Arabic literature, too, saw something of a renaissance, as new poetic forms and modes were developed, especially the dialect- or vernacular-based *zajal*. Andalusian Arabic poetry experienced its golden age during this time (from the late tenth through the eleventh century). Some of the major poets of that period include Ibn 'Abd Rabbihi, Ibn Darraaj al-Qastali, Ibn Shuhayd al-Andalusi, Ibn Hazm, and Ibn Zayduun. That tradition continued on through the period of Muslim presence in Spain and produced other major poets as well, such as the Sufi Muhyaddin Ibn al-'Arabi. For more on this work see Salma Khadra Jayyusi, "Andalusi Poetry: The Golden Age," in Jayyusi, *The Legacy of Muslim Spain*, pp. 316–66. For effective selections of the poems in English translation, see *Andalusian Poems*, trans. Christopher Middleton and Leticia Garza-Falcón (Boston, 1992); also A. R. Nykl, *Hispano-Arabic Poetry* (Baltimore, 1946).

46. The appearance of these four major poets (to be followed by Avraham Ibn Ezra) in rapid succession in the eleventh and twelfth century was also described by Schirmann as partaking of the miraculous.

47. The Almoravids originally came to Spain at the request of the Spanish Muslims, who were unable to ward off the armies of the Christian Reconquest on their own. (Toledo had been retaken by the Christians in 1085). In time they turned against their Andalusian co-religionists, whom they regarded as excessively worldly, weak, and corrupt, and they attempted to spread their reductive doctrine through the region, imposing as well heavy taxation to fund their military efforts. The Jewish community suffered at the hands of both the Christian and the Berber forces. As Yehuda HaLevi wrote, in a poem beginning "Aqonen 'al mar tela'otay": "Between the hosts of Seir [the Christians] and Qedar [the Muslims], my host is lost. . . . They wage their wars and we fall when they fall— thus was it ever in Israel!" (in Yitzhak Baer, *The History of the Jews in Christian Spain* [Philadelphia, 1961/92], p. 70). The Almohads arrived on the scene in order

to reform what they considered to be the corrupt ways of the Almoravid rulers. Eventually the practice of any other religion except Islam was forbidden in Almohad Andalusia. The father of Maimonides, for example, fled Cordoba during the Almohad invasion and, after much wandering, settled his family in Fez in 1160. The family may have converted to Islam for a period of time, though this is by no means clear. See C. Roth, *A History of the Marranos* (New York, 1931), pp. 9–12; *Encyclopedia Judaica*, 11:754. "Almoravid" in Arabic is *al-muraabit*, deriving from the word for the fortified monasteries *(ribaat)* where the warrior-monks of this sect were stationed, or with which they identified spiritually; the Almohads were the *al-muwahhidun*, those who profess the unity or Oneness *(wahda)* of God. See in Menocal et al., *The Literature of al-Andalus*, J. Dodds, "Spaces," p. 9, and P. Heath, "Knowledge," pp. 112–13, Brann, *Power in the Portrayal*, pp. 17–18; Ronald A. Messier, "North Africa, Islam and the Mediterranean World," *Journal of North African Studies* 6/1 (Spring 2001): 65, 67, and 72–74; and *The Encyclopedia of Islam*, under "Almoravid" (P. Chalmeta) and "Almohad" (M. Shatzmiller).

48. The dissemination of (and hunger for) Arabic learning went on, Scheindlin notes, even as the creators of that culture were being subjugated ("Hebrew Poetry in Medieval Iberia," pp. 51–52).

49. One writer has described these events as "the Spanish equivalent of Kristallnacht" (Rabbi Jonathan Sacks, commentary in *Covenant and Conversation*, August 26, 2005, reprinted in *Sephardic Heritage Update*, ed. David Shasha no. 175 [September 21, 2005]). For more details of the events of 1391, see the biographical introduction and notes to Shelomo DePiera's poems.

50. Raymond Scheindlin divides the five centuries of composition into three (rather than two) periods: the period of Arabic ambience (c. 900–c. 1150); a transitional period (c. 1100–c. 1300); and "a period when most Jewish literary figures inhabited a Christian ambience" (c. 1250–1492) ("Hebrew Poetry in Medieval Iberia," pp. 39–40, 50, and 53). As Hebrew poetry moved into Christian Spain it entered what he calls "a period of literary experimentation stimulated by new cultural circumstances." Elsewhere Scheindlin notes how the Hebrew writers of the fifteenth century seemed to be working toward a new synthesis of Hebrew and Romance culture, though that synthesis was, for a number of reasons, never fully realized. The characterization of the later poetry as "epigonic" is reflected in remarks by Schirmann (*HaShira*, 4:530) and others. Dan Pagis comments on the way in which scholars and ordinary readers have mistakenly read the period's poetry as though it were all cut from a single cloth. In doing so, they have failed to appreciate its variety and the essential nature of the change that came with the later work (*Hiddush uMasoret beShirat haHol* [Jerusalem, 1976], pp. 1–2 and 180). See also Scheindlin, "Secular Hebrew Poetry in Fifteenth-Century Spain," in *Crisis and Creativity in the Sephardic World: 1391–1648*, p. 34.

51. In this pre-print society, poems were also memorized and disseminated through an oral tradition, albeit to a lesser extent. Numerous texts illustrate the value placed on this poetry and the manner in which it circulated. In a damaged

and not altogether decipherable late eleventh- or early twelfth-century Arabic letter retrieved from the Cairo Geniza, we find a Palestinian Jew named 'Ali writing somewhat frantically to his friend, the cantor of the Egyptian port city of Damietta, quoting Arabic proverbs, passages from the Bible, rabbinic sayings, and contemporary poetry as he asks him to send on a list of items, in particular articles of clothing, which he'd left in Damietta. "I also need," he tells him, "[the collection of] Ibn Khalfoun's poems. Either send it on and I will copy it, or have it copied for me. I beg of you!! For someone borrowed the [ . . . ] from me . . . and then was embarrassed to return it and took it with him to Yemen. Please do not forget under any circumstances to do this for me" (S. D. Goitein, "LeQorot Shirato shel Yitzhaq Ibn Khalfoun," *Tarbiz* 29 [1960]: 357–58).

Likewise, Ammiel Alcalay in his *After Arabs and Jews*, which extends this poetry's links beyond the medieval world of the Geniza and into the living legacy of a modern and contemporary Levantine sensibility and community, finds in the maze of Goitein's Geniza documents an eleventh- or twelfth-century estate agent's inventory of a Spanish-Jewish coppersmith's belongings, which lists—in addition to the tools of his trade and his clothes—a small chest containing two prayer books (including the one compiled by Sa'adia Gaon), part of the Book of Psalms, and "a book of poetry in Arabic characters." The latter, Goitein comments, reflects "the infatuation of Spanish Jews with Arabic poetry," and the prayer books, as Alcalay puts it, serve "the double function of ritual guide and [liturgical] poetry anthology" (Goitein, *A Mediterranean Society*, 4:338; Alcalay, *After Arabs and Jews: Remaking Levantine Culture* [Minneapolis and London, 1993], pp. 142ff.). Goitein also comments elsewhere on the impressive level of learning displayed by the letters of middle-class Jews in the Geniza documents (in Alcalay, pp. 151–52; Goitein, 2:195).

Finally, Dan Pagis notes that Moshe Ibn Ezra, at the end of his chapter on the Spanish-Hebrew supremacy in poetry (*Book of Discussion*, p. 87), explains that he hasn't quoted from the master poets and their choice pearls because these were already "famous and constantly recited by the *rawis*"—or, "regularly in the mouths of the reciters of poetry" (Pagis, *Hiddush uMasoret*, p. 43). For Ibn Ezra's comments on the dissemination of HaNagid's work from Spain to Babylonia, see the biographical introduction to HaNagid's work in what follows.

See also "diwan" in the glossary.

52. In time some of the poetry would make its way to India, and in one case even to Hong Kong. With regard to the often-astonishing recovery and reconstruction of the poetry from the Cairo Geniza and other sites in Iraq, Syria, Egypt, and most recently from the archives of the St. Petersburg Library, see Goitein's *Mediterranean Society*, 1:1–6; Stefan C. Reif, *A Jewish Archive from Cairo: The History of Cambridge University's Genizah Collection* (Cambridge, 2000), pp. 1–22; Paul Kahle, *The Cairo Geniza* (Oxford, 1959), pp. 3–13; A. M. Habermann, *HaGeniza veHaGenizot* (Jerusalem, 1971); and especially, Solomon Schechter, *Studies in Judaism*, 2d ser. (Philadelphia, 1908), pp. 1–30, which offers a vivid

account of his experience in Cairo and a marvelous description of what he found there:

> It is a battlefield of books, and the literary productions of many centuries had their share in the battle, and their *disjecta membra* are now strewn over its area. Some of the belligerents have perished outright, and are literally ground to dust in the terrible struggle for space, whilst others, as if overtaken by a general crush, are squeezed into big unshapely lumps, which even with the aid of chemical appliances can no longer be separated without serious damage to their constituents. In their present condition these lumps sometimes afford curiously suggestive combinations; as, for instance, when you find a piece of some rationalistic work, in which the very existence of either angels or devils is denied, clinging for its very life to an amulet in which these same beings (mostly the latter) are bound over to be on their good behavior and not interfere with Miss Jair's love for somebody. The development of the romance is obscured by the fact that the last lines of the amulet are mounted on some I.O.U., or lease, and this in turn is squeezed between the sheets of an old moralist, who treats all attention to monetary affairs with scorn and indignation. . . . All these contradictory matters cleave tightly to some sheets from a very old Bible. This, indeed, ought to be the last umpire between them, but it is hardly legible without peeling off from its surface the fragments of some printed work, which clings to old nobility with all the obstinacy and obtrusiveness of the *parvenu*. ("A Hoard of Hebrew Manuscripts," in *Studies in Judaism*, pp. 6–7.)

For the story surrounding the recovery of the manuscript that came to be known as "Schocken 37," which was, at the very last moment, saved from the flames and found to contain some four thousand poems by most of the period's major poets along with work by a host of lesser-known writers, see Cole, *Selected Ibn Gabirol*, "Deaths, Diwans, Detectives," pp. 9–11. The tale of HaNagid's retrieval from oblivion is sketched in my *Selected HaNagid*, pp. xiv–xv. In certain instances—HaNagid is one—the twentieth-century discovery brings about an Emily Dickinson–like entry of a poet from an older era into the mix of the evolving modern literature (though in this case the eras are nearly a millennium apart). The late Israeli poet Yehuda Amichai, who as an undergraduate studied with Haim Schirmann, often spoke of Shmu'el HaNagid as his favorite poet; and the first great modern Hebrew poet, Haim Nahman Bialik, devoted a good deal of his life to the "ingathering" of the medieval Hebrew poetry. Likewise poet Leah Goldberg's connection to the poetry was strong. The history of the retrieval of this work is, in other words, at times as fascinating as the work itself.

53. While less common, the cases in which poets translated individual poems are also instructive, as the Hebrew writers often transformed them in telling ways. Yehuda HaLevi has two marvelous instances of translation from heteroeroticism to homoeroticism and profane to sacred (in this volume, "That Day while I Had

Him" and "Love's Dwelling"). Shmu'el HaNagid's virtuoso improvisation on a bowl of apples begins with an impromptu translation of Arabic lines (see Cole, *Selected HaNagid*, pp. 12–13, and in this anthology, "The Apple"). Meir HaLevi Abulafia, a major religious figure from Toledo, has one of the few Hebrew translations from an Andalusian (rather than Abbasid) Arabic poem—"Fighting Time"—and of course Alharizi's *Iti'el* (below) involves the translation or adaptation, of numerous individual poems as well as many passages of prose. A number of the later Hebrew poets also wrote in Spanish, with one of them—Shem Tov Ardutiel, a.k.a. Santob de Carrión—becoming an important writer in the Spanish literary canon.

All the Hebrew poets of Muslim Spain wrote their prose in Judeo-Arabic or in Arabic proper. Some also wrote poems in Arabic, and at least one—Ibrahim Ibn Sahl (d. 1259/60), who seems to have converted to Islam early in his life—became an important Arab poet. His diwan is "one of the finest specimens of Andalusian poetry" (*Encyclopedia of Islam*, vol. 3). See also Qasmuna bint Isma'il in the note to The Wife of Dunash's "Will Her Love Remember?" (below).

54. The family was from Granada and then moved to southern France. According to Assis, this "one Andalusian family . . . changed the outlook and the character of . . . Provence. . . . Four generations of translators and scholars provided Provencal Jewry and in a sense the whole of Europe with [an entire] library of books on Jewish philosophy and books of arithmetic, geometry, trigonometry, astronomy, medicine, general philosophy, and other branches of science and thought" ("Sefarad," p. 33).

55. Schirmann, *Toldot* (1997), pp. 148–53 and 180–84.

56. *Toldot*, (1997), pp. 146–53 and 177–84; and Matti Huss, "HaMagid be-Maqamot HaQlasi'ot—leVeiruro shel Munah," *Tarbiz* 65/1 (1996): 164–72. Elsewhere in the world of translation at the time, Alharizi's method was known as *sensus de sensu* (or *ad sensum*, according to sense); Ibn Tibbon's method was referred to as *verbum et verba* (or *ad verbum*, according to the word, i.e., literally). What is unusual here is that Alharizi chooses a method *(sensus de sensu)* that is usually associated with societies in which the "target language" is dominant. As Huss points out ("HaMagid," pp. 170–71), Ibn Tibbon saw Hebrew as inferior to Arabic, at least with regard to its capacity to absorb philosophical discourse. Alharizi, on the other hand, made it clear elsewhere in his work (*Tahkemoni*, pp. 12, 21) that he considered Hebrew superior (though it was not culturally dominant at the time).

57. Not unlike the young Nabokov translating *Alice in Wonderland* into Russian and replacing Carroll's French mouse, come over with William the Conqueror, with one that Napoleon left behind him in Russia. See Wyatt Mason, "Swann's Ways," *New Republic*, January 12, 2005.

58. Moshe Ibn Ezra, *The Book of Discussion*, p. 177.

59. Moshe Ibn Ezra, *The Book of Discussion*, p. 143. "For by the ear will the work be tested, and the ears are the gates to the mind." He also quotes an Arab

poet: "Poetic meter [or cadence] is something natural, found in the senses [in a sense for it]" (p. 137).

60. Weinberger is one of our finest writers on, among other things, the art and importance of translation. His comments appear in "Mislaid in Translation" (*Written Reaction: Poetics, Politics, Polemics* [New York, 1996], p. 166). An expanded and updated version of that essay appears in *Fascicle* 1 (2005), at http://fascicle.com/issue01. The best discussion of the problem of employing quantitative meters in English is by John Hollander. See "Observations in the Art of English Quantity," in *Vision and Romance* (New York, 1975), pp. 59–70. Also Paul Fussell, *Poetic Meter and Poetic Form* (New York, 1965/79), pp. 68–69.

61. Again, medieval Hebrew poetry, as Pagis notes, has long been treated by scholars as "a collective accomplishment rather than a variety of distinctly individual achievements." While the poets shared, as it were, a single toolbox and set of materials, and while it is critical to become familiar with the tools contained in that box and the materials with which the poets worked, it is just as important to learn to differentiate between their various ways of employing those tools and molding their material. In fact, the work they produced with that equipment is remarkably varied and expressive. Pagis's revisionist statement is perhaps the most eloquent articulation of the situation: "I now believe," he writes, with characteristic modesty and reconsidering a long and distinguished career during which he held to a somewhat different view, "that the Hebrew-Spanish school as a whole allowed much more room for individuality than is generally supposed, and that modern scholars have been sometimes more conventional in their views than medieval poets were in their work" (*Hebrew Poetry of the Middle Ages and the Renaissance* [Berkeley, 1991], pp. 6–23).

62. For a fuller treatment of the challenges facing the translator of medieval Hebrew Poetry, see Peter Cole, "Real Gazelles in Imaginary Gardens: Art, Scholarship, and the Translation of Medieval Hebrew Poetry from Spain," *Yale Review*, Winter 2007.

63. *The Ruba'iyat of Omar Khayyam*, trans. Peter Avery and John Heath-Stubbs (London, 1979/81), pp. 42–43.

64. T. S. Eliot, *The Use of Poetry/The Use of Criticism* (Cambridge, 1961), p. 24.

65. One could dwell for the length and depth of a long career on this form/content controversy. A person who has done just that is Jaroslav Stetkevych, one of the leading scholars of medieval Arabic literature, who says: "Instead of looking for signs of dichotomy of form and content, one could, with equal ease, reverse the lens and see in Arabic poetry the closest possible—or the will to the closest possible—marriage between form and content, precisely because the poetry is so highly formalistic. . . . Poetic content not only survives [there] but flourishes, albeit in unaccustomed ways, [extracting] out of [its] predicament a strange power and solidity of imaginative impact" (*Zephyrs of Najd* [Chicago and London, 1993], pp. 4–5).

66. In particular, the parallel with the Islamic arts is instructive. The central role of ornament in the visual arts sheds considerable light on the use of the rhetorical figures, or poetic ornaments, taken over to Hebrew verse from Arabic. I have written about this aspect of the poetry in *Selected Ibn Gabirol*, pp. 11–13, and *Selected HaNagid*, pp. xix and xxii. See also Julie Meisami, *Persian Court Poetry* (Princeton, 1987), pp. 315–17, and Oleg Grabar, *The Mediation of Ornament* (Princeton, 1992), pp. 24–27 and *The Formation of Islamic Art* (New Haven and London, 1973/87), especially "The Idea of the Arabesque," pp. 178ff.

67. Ezra Pound, *Translations* (New York, 1963), p. 24.

68. See Cole, *Selected HaNagid*, pp. xxi–xxiv and *Selected Ibn Gabirol*, pp. 11–13, 16–18, 22–30, 35 and 37; also Weinberger, *Written Reaction*, pp. 164–65, and *Outside Stories* (New York, 1992), pp. 59–61.

69. This applies both on the level of line-by-line readings and with regard to the poems as a whole. That is, if I have included a poem in this volume, I have generally translated all of it—or at least self-standing sections of a composite work—in order to demonstrate how the parts of the poem come together (or don't). In a few instances, however—especially where long poems are involved— I have made do with excerpts, in which case the notes explain precisely what has been taken from what. Excerpting of this sort was, as it happens, a common practice in medieval Arabic anthologies. See "epigram" in the glossary.

70. Schorsch ("The Myth of Sephardic Supremacy") and Jane Gerber ("Towards an Understanding of the Term 'Golden Age' as an Historical Reality," in *The Heritage of the Jews of Spain* [Tel Aviv, 1995]) discuss the ways in which the political motives of eighteenth- and nineteenth-century German-Jewish scholars distorted their portraits of the period. Distortion of another sort is examined by María Rosa Menocal in *The Arabic Role in Medieval Literary History* (Philadelphia, 1987). In *Under Crescent and Cross* Mark Cohen discusses the "myth of an interfaith utopia" as well as Muslim outbursts of violence against the Jews (pp. 3–14 and 163ff.). He also places the term "tolerance" in context, noting that "tolerance, at least as we in the West have understood it since John Locke, did not [in the Middle Ages] constitute a virtue. . . . Monotheistic religions in power throughout history have felt it proper, if not obligatory, to persecute nonconforming religions. . . . When all is said and done, however, the historical evidence indicates that the Jews of Islam, especially during the formative and classical centuries (up to the thirteenth century), experienced much less persecution than did the Jews of Christendom" (p. xix). Scheindlin, in "Hebrew Poetry in Medieval Iberia" (pp. 49–50), notes that little mention of Jewish cultural activity is made in Muslim sources. That said, as another writer put it, "the question of cross-fertilization of cultures, of a *convivencia* of Muslims, Christians, and Jews, is not merely a modern-day fashion. It is indeed the central issue in the history of al-Andalus, for its political fortunes rose and fell in relationship to its ability to minimize ethnic factionalism and forge a spirit of common enterprise" (L. Alvarez, "Spain," in *Encyclopedia of Arabic Literature*, p. 729). A detailed comparative study of the way in

which relations between Jews and Muslims fluctuated between tolerance and hostility—and how that is reflected in the poetry and the literature that surrounds it—is offered by Brann in his *Power in the Portrayal* (Princeton, 2002). See also David Nirenberg, *Communities of Violence* (Princeton, 1996), pp. 3–10 and 245–46, and "What Can Medieval Spain Teach Us About Muslim–Jewish Relations?" *CCAR Journal* (Spring/Summer 2002), pp. 17–36; Alex Novikoff, "Between Tolerance and Intolerance in Medieval Spain: An Historiographical Enigma," *Medieval Encounters* 11/1–2 (2005): 7–36; and *"convivencia,"* in the glossary.

71. The "neo-lachrymose" school of historians. See Cohen, *Under Crescent and Cross*, pp. 9–11. Also Assis, "Sefarad," p. 34, and N. Stillman, "Myth, Countermyth, and Distortion," (*Tikkun,* vols. 6:3–4, 1991).

72. Darwish's comments are from an interview he gave to *Hadarim* (no. 12), a prominent Israeli literary journal in 1996, in Amman. The journal's editor, Helit Yeshurun, had asked Darwish about the meaning of al-Andalus for him, since the term figures prominently in his work in several places. As for Darwish and his dream, the cultural vision at its heart is—notwithstanding the changes brought about by recent events—shared by at least a few. The Syrian poet Adonis ('Ali Ahmad Sa'id) recently wrote: "Andalusia was in human and cultural terms . . . a mosaic of different yet harmonious elements, numerous yet one. It was a sort of hybridization of the world in form as well as in essence. In everything Andalusia produced, whether philosophical, scientific, or artistic, three horizons converged, Jewish, Christian, in addition to the foundational horizon, the Arabic-Islamic constituent. It therefore transcended all that was bounded by a language or by a particular national or cultural affiliation. . . . It was the homeland of the self and the Other. As such, it was the originator of the avant-gardist idea of stripping the concept of the homeland of boundedness and constructing it in the space of freedom. . . . Thus, in the light of the Andalusian nucleus, we can see how a culture with intertwining borders and languages, a culture that transcends politics and geographic-national boundaries, might emerge in today's world. It is a culture of hybridization, a culture that finds its identity in diversity, a culture in which Otherness is an organic and constituent dimension. Thus Andalusia seems a viable project, not only for the present, but also for the future" (lecture at Dartmouth College, 2002).

73. "It is dawn at Jerusalem while midnight hovers above the Pillars of Hercules. All ages are contemporaneous" (Ezra Pound, "Praefatio Ad Lectorem Electum, 1910," in *The Spirit of Romance* [New York, 1952], p. 6); "There is no earlier and later in the Torah" (*Pesahim* 6b). This is not to say that one shouldn't account for the differences between the medieval world and our own; one should. At the same time, it is important not to lose sight of the dimensions of experience that are shared across time. The fact is that poets themselves live the contemporaneity of all ages, as do readers who turn to poetry for nourishment, for what poems can tell them about being alive. Yosef Haim Yerushalmi writes at eloquent length about the ways in which this non-chronological dimension finds

expression in the Jewish historical imagination: "Unlike the biblical writers the rabbis seem to play with Time as though with an accordion, expanding and collapsing it at will. . . . In the world of *aggada* Adam can instruct his son Seth in the Torah, Shem and Eber establish a house of study, the patriarchs institute the three daily prayer-services of the normative Jewish liturgy, Og King of Bashan is present at Isaac's circumcision, and Noah prophesies the translation of the Bible into Greek. . . . There is something rather compelling about that large portion of the rabbinic universe in which ordinary barriers of time can be ignored and all the ages placed in an ever-fluid dialogue with one another" (*Zakhor* [Seattle and London, 1982], p. 17; see also pp. 31–52).

74. Yom Tov Assis writes that Spanish-Hebrew poetry introduces us to this society. Considering its sexual mores, he notes the gap that existed between reality and theory in Muslim and Christian communities—the influence of which Jews were exposed to: "On both sides of the ever-changing border in the Iberian peninsula, [Spanish Jews] were more deeply involved in the social, economic, cultural and political life of the land than was any other mediaeval Jewish community." As a result, he says, "[Hispano-Jewish society], torn between extreme and contradictory trends, found itself characterized by sexual laxity to an extent unknown elsewhere in mediaeval Jewry" ("Sexual Behaviour in Mediaeval Hispano-Jewish Society," in *Jewish History: Essays in Honour of Chimen Abramsky*, ed. Ada Rapoport-Albert and Steven J. Zipperstein [London, 1988], p. 27).

75. Yosef Haim Yerushalmi, "Assimilation and Racial Anti-Semitism: The Iberian and the German Models," Leo Baeck Memorial Lecture 26 (New York, 1982), p. 8; Daniel Elazar, *The Other Jews: Sephardim Today* (New York, 1989), p. 45. Jane Gerber cites the figure of 90 percent and notes that they were "an absolute majority in medieval times. . . . By the twentieth century, an absolute reversal had occurred: in 1930 Sephardim were less than 10 percent of world Jewry" (*The Jews of Spain*, p. xxiv). At the time of the Expulsion, which was signed on March 31, 1492, and gave Jews until the end of July to convert or leave the kingdom, the Jewish community had been greatly reduced through conversion, emigration, and slaughter. Reliable numbers are, once again, hard to come by, and estimations offered by scholars range from some eighty thousand to triple that (with the former more likely). Many of the remaining Jews—perhaps more than half—chose conversion over emigration. The last Jews left Spanish soil on July 31, or the seventh of the Hebrew month of Av; because it fell so close to the day marking the destruction of the First and Second Temples, the Expulsion itself was added by Jewish tradition to the commemoration of those catastrophic events in Jewish history. For a description and analysis of the Expulsion and the events that led to it, see H. Beinart, "Order of the Expulsion from Spain: Antecedents, Causes, and Textual Analysis," in *Crisis and Creativity*, pp. 79–94. See also Gerber, *The Jews of Spain*, p. 140, and H. Kamen, *The Spanish Inquisition: An Historical Revision* (London, 1997), pp. 23–24.

# ⊰ *NOTES TO THE POEMS* ⊱

THESE NOTES contain the following items: (1) the poet's name; (2) comments referring to the biographical notes; (3) the English title of the poem—which I have added, as the Hebrew poems have no titles; (4) the poem's provenance (print volumes of the poet's work are listed first, and then, for convenience, the citation from Haim Schirmann's four-volume *HaShira HaIvrit biSefarad uve-Provans*, 2d ed. [Jerusalem and Tel Aviv, 1959], hereafter *HaShira*, if in fact the poem was included in that anthology); (5) comments on the poem, treating formal elements, copyists' headings (where they are of interest), biblical citations, allusions, as well as other textual and cultural background. The "neutral *shibbutzim*" (on which, see the glossary at the end of this volume) are listed in abbreviated fashion and do not generally have implications for the meaning of the poem that would warrant the wearying process of looking up each citation. I offer the abbreviated listings here, erring perhaps on the side of excess, in order to concretize the reader's sense of the biblical substratum of the work. In some cases, these neutral *shibbutzim* are listed in full, particularly when they occur in key positions in the poem (such as the end) or when, for any number of reasons, they might be of interest to the English reader. Unless otherwise noted, all the poems below are, in the original Hebrew, monorhymed and written in the quantitative meters adapted from Arabic poetry. Other forms—such as the *muwashshah* and other strophic patterns—are generally indicated. For an explanation of these forms and the various genres they involve, see the glossary. Most biblical citations are from the Jewish Publication Society (JPS) version of 1929. The new JPS version (NJPS) is occasionally cited as well. Square brackets in the translations indicate that the manuscript is corrupt. At times guesses have been hazarded by scholars in order to fill in the missing material, in which case the translation follows suit. If the missing material has not been reconstructed, ellipses are inserted between the brackets. In the longer poems, ellipses without brackets generally indicate that I have omitted material. Details of these excerpts are always mentioned in the notes; if the notes do not mention the omission, the ellipses constitute punctuation.

## MUSLIM SPAIN

### DUNASH BEN LABRAT

Moshe Ibn Ezra states that Dunash was born in Baghdad and educated in Fez. Sa'adia Gaon's comments were reported by Dunash himself, who of course considered them high praise. The characterizations of Dunash's manner and temperament are Schirmann's, based on *Teshuvot Talmidei Menahem Ibn Saruq*, facsimile ed. (Vienna, 1870), part 1, p. 29, where the students of his rival, Menahem, describe him as haughty and full of contempt for the local (Cordovan) culture.

## FRAGMENT

*Dunash Ben Labrat: Shirim*, ed. N. Allony (Jerusalem, 1947), p. 93; *Teshuvot Yehudi Ibn Sheshet*, ed. S. G. Stern (Vienna, 1870), p. 37. This fragment has survived as Dunash's intellectual credo; his attempt to blend Hebrew sources with Arabic forms was, as the biographical note suggests, more fully realized by subsequent poets.

## BLESSING FOR A WEDDING

*Shirim*, p. 60. Most likely composed as a *piyyut* to the priestly blessing, this short hymn in time came to serve as an extension of the grace after meals at weddings. **Lines 3–4:** Isaiah 35:6. **5–6:** Psalms 23:3; Genesis 24:27. **7–8:** Numbers 6:22–27. Aaron's blessing reads: "The Lord bless thee, and keep thee; The Lord make His face to shine upon thee, and be gracious unto thee; The Lord lift up His countenance upon thee, and give thee peace." Schirmann (*Toldot* [1995], pp. 127–28) notes that Dunash was characteristically daring here, composing several short religious hymns (including the now-popular "Dror Yiqra," which is not translated) in the new meter as well, even though introducing them into the arena of the sacred was bound to prove far more controversial and revolutionary than the introduction of Arabic elements into the secular literary realm.

## DRINK, HE SAID

*Shirim*, p. 64; *HaShira*, #4. In several respects one can say that medieval Hebrew secular poetry in Spain begins with the wine poem, since the first well-known poem in the canon of the new, Arabic-inspired quantitative verse is this one by Dunash. The invented patron (or courtier) of his poem extends an invitation (to a garden party) that continues for some fifteen lines before it is interrupted by the "I" of the poem, possibly Dunash himself—though the characterizations here appear to be ambiguous by design. Schirmann suggests that, for someone who is setting up a rejection of what he sees, Dunash seems to be enjoying his description of the party and its pleasures a great deal. Fleischer states plainly that the poem confronts the libertine court of Hasdai with the conservative social mores of the Babylonian-trained Dunash, who is represented in the poem by the shocked interlocutor. Although the poem expresses the ambivalent feelings that a poet like Dunash may have had, the device of the interlocutor is also common in Arabic poetry, so that in some respects even the "compunction" here might be conventional. At any rate, and in conflict, this is where it all begins. It is interesting in this regard to note—as Raymond Scheindlin does—that the medieval copyist who preserved the poem assumed in the heading he composed for it that the poem's central subject was in fact the pleasures of the party and its atmosphere and not the compunction of the second speaker (*Wine, Women, and Death* [Philadelphia, 1986], pp. 43–44). Scheindlin also comments that the meter of this poem "represents an experimental stage in the adaptation of Arabic prosody to Hebrew," and may have sounded somewhat mechanical to listeners who were accustomed to hearing accomplished and flowing Arabic verse (*Wine, Women, and Death*, p. 45). The Hebrew rhymes *aaab, cccb, dddb*, etc.; while the translation echoes that scheme in places, it highlights instead the rhythmic and aural emphases of the original. **Heading:** "Another poem by Dunash of blessed memory, about drinking at evening and dawn . . . accompanied by musical instruments, the sound of water courses and strings, and the birds chirping from the branches, with the scent of all sorts of herbs—all this he described at a party by Hasdai, may he rest in peace." **Lines 1–4:** Parties of this sort were often held just before dawn. Aloe here is the tall aromatic Indian tree (Song of Songs 4:14), not the succulent houseplant. **9:** Psalms 42:8, though here it refers to the channels of water and fountains in the garden. **12:** Psalms 150:4. **15–16:** Ezekiel 17:23. **20:** Jeremiah 48:36. **26:** Amos 6:6. **28:** Judges 5:25. **33:** 2 Kings 20:13. **35:** Isaiah 28:2. **36–40:** *Baba Batra* 60b: "Since the day of the destruction of the Temple we should by rights bind ourselves not to eat meat nor drink wine." **39:** Lamentations 2:1. **40:** Jerusalem was, at the time, held by the Muslims. **44:** Ecclesiastes 4:5, 2:14; Proverbs 19:25. **45–46:** Psalms 19:16.

## THE WIFE OF DUNASH

### WILL HER LOVE REMEMBER?

E. Fleischer, "ʿAl Dunash Ben Labrat veIshto uVeno," *Mehqerei Yerushalayim beSifrut Ivrit* 5 (1984): 196. See also Fleischer, "LeToldot Shirat HaHol HaʿIvrit biSefarad beReshitah," in *Asufot/Tarbut veHevrah beToldot Yisrael beYamei HaBenayim*, ed. M. Ben-Sasson et al. (Jerusalem, 1989), pp. 205–6 and 216–18. Women poets hold a place of esteem in medieval Arabic literature and numerous women poets are prominent in the Christian tradition, but the wife of Dunash is the only Hebrew woman poet we know of from the Middle Ages. Moreover, as Tova Rosen points out, "not only is she the first identifiable woman poet in the Hebrew language since the biblical poetesses Miriam and Deborah, she is also the only one for centuries to come" (*Unveiling Eve: Reading Gender in Medieval Hebrew Literature* [Philadelphia, 2003], p. 2). Goitein explains the near-total absence of woman in the Spanish-Hebrew literary context by noting that the composition of poetry as the Andalusian Jews understood it required extensive knowledge of Scripture, as well as familiarity with rabbinic literature. Men spent their entire childhood studying such texts, which were reinforced by worship and ongoing study. Most woman were illiterate, and—for the most part—even educated women (for whom, like the men, Arabic was their spoken mother tongue) would not have been exposed to Scripture in the manner necessary for the composition of Hebrew verse. Still, upper-class Jewish women, at least, would have received a serious education, and the Geniza records indicate that there were exceptional women who were teachers and copyists. In the Arabic context, a daughter's relationship with her father was, as Shirley Guthrie points out, "crucial to her future in society, since his views of women in the wider world, their education, his assessment of her suitability and worth and so on would be honed from early childhood" (*Arab Women in the Middle Ages* [London, 2001], p. 175). When it came to poetry by Jewish women, apart from Dunash's wife, only Qasmuna bint Isma'il al-Yehudi is reported to have written poems, though in Arabic:

### ON SEEING HERSELF IN THE MIRROR

I see an orchard where
the time has come for harvesting,
    but see no gardener
reaching out a hand . . .

Youth passes, vanishing—
    and there remains,
alone,
one I will not name.

### AH, GAZELLE

always grazing
here in this garden—
I'm dark-eyed just
like you, and lonely.

We both live far
from friends, forsaken—
patiently bearing
our fate's decree.

Several scholars have identified the author of these Sappho-like lyrics as the daughter of the great Hebrew poet Shmu'el HaNagid (who was known in Arabic as Isma'il Ibn Naghrela). For more on her and the problem of identification, see S. D. Goitein, *A Mediterranean Society* (Berkeley, 1969–88) 5:468–69, 2:183–85, and 3:321–22; J. Nichols, "The Arabic Verses of Qasmuna bint Isma'il," *International Journal of Middle East Studies* 13 (1981): 155–58; James Bellamy, "Qasmuna the Poetess: Who Was She?" *Journal of the American Oriental Society* 103 (1983): 423–24; David Wasserstein, "Samuel Ibn Naghrila ha-Nagid and Islamic Historiography in al-Andalus," *al-Qantara* 14 (1993): 109–25; M. A. Gallego, *Miscellania de estudios Arabica y Hebraica* 48 (1999): 63–75; and Abdullah al-Udhari, *Classical Poems by Arab*

*Women* (London, 1999), pp. 178–80. **Line 1:** Proverbs 5:19. **2:** Fleischer notes that the involvement of a young child in the tableaux of the poem is extremely unusual in the medieval Hebrew context, where children are mentioned only when they are born and when they die ("LeToldot Shirat HaHol," p. 217). **3–4:** Song of Songs 8:6. The bracelet around the upper arm was worn as a sign of strength and dignity. **6:** Men sometimes wore the outer garments of their wives. Song of Songs 5:7; Song of Songs 8:6–7. **7:** *Eretz Sefarad*. **8:** Esther 5:3. According to Goitein the final lines, which he acknowledges are confusing, should read: "Will there remain in the entire land of Spain its lord Dunash, even if he takes one half of the kingdom with him?" (Literally, "one half of the prince's [*nagid's*] kingdom with him.) *Nagid* in this context would have referred to Hasdai, and been a general title. My translation follows Fleischer's explication. It isn't clear why his wife couldn't have joined Dunash in exile, but judging from the tone and content of the poem, that was out of the question. She may have been bound to her family in Spain, or Dunash may have had to flee at once.

Part of Dunash's far less impressive (though tender) reply is extant as well. He begins by quoting what appears to have been either another poem sent on by his wife's relatives, or a letter by them or by Dunash's wife: "Were you seeking the day of my death when you wrote:/'Have you betrayed and abandoned your vows?'/Could I ever betray a woman as wise as you are,/given to me by the Lord from youth?/If my heart had ever thought to leave you/I would have torn it into pieces./For those who betray their beloved companion,/God brings down with the trials of foes./Lions soon will devour his flesh,/and eagles suck up his blood./Who resembles the stars of dawn. . . ." The poem is cut off at this point in the manuscript. Fleischer writes: "The pathos and garrulousness of this fragment are very much in line with what we know from his other poems, and they are, it needs to be said, the opposite of what we find in the poem attributed to his wife." Fleischer goes on to note the "professional" nature of Dunash's response, moving from the particular to the general. It is entirely possible, he adds, that Dunash returned to Spain at some point. (See Fleischer, "'Al Dunash veIshto," pp. 199–200.) A still more recent discovery arising from the documents found in the Geniza (and possibly from Hasdai's archive) confirms that in fact Dunash did "betray and abandon" his vows. In the upper-left corner of what appears to be a poem of complaint by Dunash addressed to Hasdai, after their break, Fleischer has noted the following lines: "Grapes I will not glean, and I will not gather the corn./I've betrayed a young wife and sent her a writ of divorce./I've abandoned my home and left the son she bore." In the preceding lines Dunash complains, says Fleischer, of the conditions of his service under Hasdai, of the pressures he faced in that job, and of the heavy price he had to pay for it in the end: the destruction of his family ("LeToldot Shirat HaHol," p. 218).

## YITZHAQ IBN MAR SHA'UL

Ibn Mar Sha'ul is primarily known for his liturgical verse, including the famous poem of petition that begins "Lord, do not judge me for my sins" (not translated here). Among his most distinguished students at the Lucena academy was Yona Marwaan Ibn Janaah, the great linguist.

### A FAWN SOUGHT IN SPAIN

*Shirim Hadashim min HaGeniza*, ed. Haim Schirmann (Jerusalem, 1965), pp. 157–58; Ezra Fleischer, "Hadashot beYitzirato shel R. Yitzhak Bar Levi (Ibn Mar Sha'ul)," in *Mehqerei Lashon Mugeshet leZe'ev Ben-Haim*, ed. M. Bar Asher, A. Dotan, D. Tenna, and D. Ben 'Ami (Jerusalem, 1983), p. 450. For more on the figure of the *tzvi*, and on erotic and homoerotic poetry generally, see the glossary at the back of this volume under "gazelle" and "desire, poems of." On homoeroticism in medieval Arab society, see also James Bellamy, "Sex and Society in Islamic Popular Literature," in *Society and the Sexes in Medieval Islam*, ed. Afaf Lutfi Al-Sayyid-Marsot (Malibu, 1979), 23–42; J. W. Wright and Everett Rowson, *Homoeroticism in Classical Arabic Literature* (New York, 1997); and John Boswell, *Christianity, Social Tolerance, and Homosexuality*, pp. 194ff. On homoeroticism in Jewish society, see Jefim Schirmann, "The Ephebe in Medieval Hebrew Poetry," *Sefarad* 15 (1955): 55–68; S. D. Goitein, "The Sexual Mores of the Common People," in Lufti, *Society and the Sexes*; Yom Tov Assis, "Sexual Behaviour in Mediaeval Hispano-Jewish Society"; Norman Roth, "Deal Gently with the Young Man: Love of Boys in Medieval Hebrew Poetry of Spain," *Speculum* 57 (1982): 20–51; and, in Hebrew, articles by Matti Huss and Yosef Na'eh (cited in the notes to Yitzhaq Ibn Ezra's "Over His Boy," and Alharizi's "On Zion's Holy Hill," respectively). **Line 1:** The poet uses the term "Espamya"— which was common up until the time of Shmu'el HaNagid. **2:** Jeremiah 32:19. **7–8:** Song of Songs 7:6. **9:** Genesis 39:6. **10:** Adonijah here probably comes instead of Absalom, who was noted for his long hair; the substitution in the Hebrew maintains the meter. **11–12:** 1 Samuel 16:12. **20:** Isaiah 28:7. **21–22:** Part of this line is corrupt. The other part was copied incorrectly in the manuscript found in the Cairo Geniza and printed as such by Schirmann (it repeated previous lines from the poem). In 1983, Fleischer published an article (above) on new findings relating to Ibn Mar Sha'ul's work, including another copy of the poem that contained what appears to be the correct wording. **27–28:** Psalms 55:24; and Psalms 86:13, where "nethermost pit" and sheol (or netherworld) are identified. The lines might also read, literally: "Raise me from this grave, lest I fall into Hell."

## YOSEF IBN AVITOR

"Avitor"—Arabic for "father of the ox"—was an epithet; the family name Ibn Shatnas, or al-Shatnas (some say Satnas), seems to be Spanish in origin. In the controversy around the directorship of the academy, Ibn Avitor sought to displace his former teacher's son (Hanokh Ben Moshe). For the caliph's comment, see Ibn Daud, *The Book of Tradition*, trans. Gerson D. Cohen (Philadelphia, 1967), p. 67.

### LAMENT FOR THE JEWS OF ZION

*HaShira*, #12. This *qina*, or elegy, the first Spanish-Hebrew poem of its kind relating to specific historical circumstances, is considered to be among Ibn Avitor's finest works. It is one of the few poems of his written in the Arabic-influenced meter introduced by Dunash. (Another follows below.) Fleischer notes that this is clearly a very late poem for Ibn Avitor—written after the disturbances in Palestine of 1024, during which Jews were attacked by Bedouin from the tribe of Bnei Jaraakh—and may have constituted either an appeal for support or merely a lyric expression of the poet's response to the events of his day. It is written in the Spanish-Hebrew *marnin* meter but employs a traditional Eastern strophe and rhyme scheme (*aaaa/bbbb/cccc*). It was clearly not intended for use in the liturgy, though for a while it may have been recited on the Ninth of Av. See detailed notes in Fleischer, "Behinot beShirato shel R. Yosef Ibn Avitor," *Asufot* 4 (1990). See also commentary in M. Cohen, *Under Crescent and Cross*, pp. 261–62; Ross Brann, "Tavni'ot shel Galut baQinot Ivri'ot ve'Aravi'ot biSefarad," in *Sefer Yisrael Levin* (Tel Aviv, 1994), p. 49; Goitein, *Mediterranean Society* 5: 58–59; M. Gil, *A History of Palestine* (Cambridge, 1992), pp. 385–97. **Line 3:** Zechariah 12:11: "And there shall be a great mourning in Jerusalem, as the mourning of Hadadrimmon in the valley of Megiddon." Also 2 Kings 23:29. **15:** Lamentations 4:2. **17–18:** Lamentations 4:14. **20:** Hosea 14:1. **30:** Psalms 144:12. **36:** Isaiah 34:15. **41–42:** The previous stanzas all treat suffering and tormented Jewish communities in the wake of the disturbances; they, says the poet, are the ones who need and deserve our pity. Jeremiah 22:10: "Weep ye not for the dead, neither bemoan him; but weep sore for him that goeth away, for he shall return no more, nor see his native country." See also the short talmudic poem in *Mo'ed Qatan* 25b: "Weep for those who mourn,/not for what is gone./For the dead at last find rest,/while we're left in distress." **45–48:** The Hebrew is somewhat uncertain here; Schirmann suggests that it means, 'My friend, don't turn to me with words of consolation' "[or mourning]," i.e., for the dead.

### A CURSE

Fleischer, "Behinot beShirato shel R. Yosef Ibn Avitor," p. 163; *Ginzei Schechter* (New York, 1928), 3:320. Schirmann and Fleischer suggest that this poem is either a generalized curse, to be applied to any enemy, or may have been written for a specific occasion—perhaps Ibn Avitor's banishment from Spain. Ibn Avitor was no stranger to bans of this sort, and he seems to have made use of his own authority to impose such punishment, especially later in life. The original involves a defective alphabetical acrostic. There are several places where the manuscript is corrupt; these are indicated here by ellipses. This poetic formulation of the ban involves considerable elaboration of the standard formulation, Fleischer notes, and as such is of serious interest. (For that standard formulation, see *Asufot* 4: 165, n. 130, and the sources Fleischer cites there.) While the poem was used in a religious context, it was not, properly speaking, liturgical. Its categorization by Fleischer as a "secular poem" bears witness to the wide range of social situations that term covers. **Line 1:** Isaiah 29:2: "And there shall be mourning and moaning." **2:** Nahum 2:11: "She is empty, void, and waste."

## A PLEA

Fleischer, "Behinot beShirato shel R. Ibn Avitor," p. 182. The manuscript containing the poem (in Avitor's own handwriting) is damaged and part of the poem is indecipherable. The poem is written in what would become one of the more common Andalusian meters and maintains the classical monorhyme. **Line 3:** Isaiah 58:6. **7:** Hosea 12:1. **9–10:** Lamentations 1:2. Fleischer sees this sui generis poem as a continuation of the "tradition of [uncategorizable] personal, intimate poems," along the lines of the lyric by the wife of Dunash, and he again notes the counterpoint of grief 's pressure in the speaker and the poem's expressive restraint. He speculates that it emerges from one of the many arguments that the high-strung and perhaps overly sensitive poet engaged in with his Andalusian and Egyptian peers. This, too, is most likely a late work and along with the previous poem testifies, says Fleischer, to the degree of acceptance the Spanish prosody achieved, for here we have a major figure who had long resisted these innovations suddenly taking on the new style late in life in order to give voice to powerful emotions in a personal fashion.

## HYMN FOR THE NEW YEAR

*HaShira*, #9; S. Bernstein, "Selihot Bilti Yedu'ot leR. Yosef Ibn Avitor," *Sura: Sefer HaShana* 1953. A hymn to be recited as part of the liturgy for the Jewish New Year, a *pizmon*. Acrostic: An alphabetical acrostic (*aleph* through *tav*, excepting the final line of each stanza) is woven through the second word of each Hebrew line after the opening stanza; this is followed with the poet's name, *Yosef HaMeridi* (of Merida). Each stanza ends in a biblical quotation. The translation is an excerpt rendering the Hebrew lines 1–3, 14–23, and 29–38 (the end of the poem). Much of the poem alludes to talmudic passages from *Baba Batra* and *Shabbat*, and on the whole it is modeled on Job 38–41. The former glosses verses

from Job, some of which are also alluded to in the poem. The hymn is desig-
nated for the New Year because according to rabbinic tradition, the world was
created in the Hebrew month of Tishrei, the first day of which is celebrated as
the Jewish New Year. The renewal of the year and its festival, then, also cele-
brates the renewal of Creation, as cosmic time is aligned with the calendar. The
opening stanza was most likely recited as a refrain. **Lines 1–4:** Isaiah 59:9. **5:** The
biblical line alluded to here—Psalms 65:2—has been translated in strikingly dif-
ferent ways: the Hirsch Psalms translation seems most relevant: "Peace of soul is
an emanation of Thy mighty acts." JPS has "Praise waiteth for thee, O God, in
Zion"; NJPS has "praise befits You." The Soncino Psalms comments, noting the
similarity between this verse and Psalms 62:2: "The probable meaning is: 'Praise,
like prayer, is often truest when in deep and still devotion it waits in the presence
of God.'" **6:** The translation skips to line 14 of the Hebrew. Jonah 2:4. **5:** *Baba Ba-
tra* 73a, where Rabbah tells of seafarers' legends. A note to the talmudic text ex-
plains that the legend probably involved social and political allegories. **10–11:** Job
38:5. **12–13:** *Baba Batra* 16a: "Many drops have I created in the clouds, and for
every drop a separate mould, so that two drops should not issue from the same
mould, since if two drops issued from the same mould they would wash away
the soil, and it would not produce fruit." **14–15:** Proverbs 30:4. **16–19:** *Midrash
Tanhuma, Tazri'a* 4: "Our Rabbis said: A woman sends forth one hundred
screams when she is giving birth; ninety-nine are for death, and one for life."
Also *Baba Batra* 16a–b: "The wild goat is heartless towards her young. When she
crouches for delivery, she goes up to the top of a mountain so that the young
shall fall down and be killed, and I prepare an eagle to catch it in his wings and
set it before her, and if he were one second too soon or too late it would be
killed." **20–21:** *Baba Batra* 16b: "'Canst thou mark when the hinds do calve?' [Job
34:35] This hind has a narrow womb. I prepare a serpent which bites her at the
opening of the womb, and she is delivered of her offspring; and were it one sec-
ond too soon or too late, she would die." **24–25:** Job 38:25. **26–31:** The translation
skips to line 29 of the Hebrew. The five examples or kinds of fear are cited in
*Shabbat* 77b, with Rashi's commentary there. "Our Rabbis taught: There are five
instances of fear [cast] by the weak over the strong." The elephant fears that the
mosquito will enter its trunk (according to the commentary) or its ear (according
to legend); the whale fears that the stickleback fish (according to the commen-
tary) will enter its ear. **32:** Job 9:4. **36–37:** Amos 5:9: "It is He who hurls destruc-
tion upon strongholds, so that ruin comes upon fortresses." **38–43:** Other exam-
ples of the five fears, from *Shabbat* 77b. The "Ethiopian gnat" is taken from the
Soncino commentary. Other commentaries to the passage have "the plague." Ac-
cording to Rashi the passage refers to "a small animal that terrifies the lion with
its loud cry"; he also comments that the spider is reported to enter the scorpion's
ear. "Poison" is not in the Hebrew. The word for "falcon" in the translation is
generally rendered, in the Bible for instance, as "eagle." Rashi comments that
the swallow creeps under the larger bird's wings and hinders it from spreading

them. **44–45:** The final line in the Hebrew is a direct quote from Proverbs 30:4: "Who established the ends of the earth [NJPS: foundations of earth]?" The final English line does not appear in the Hebrew, but echoes Isaiah 42:5.

## YITZHAQ IBN KHALFOUN

Ibn Khalfoun's reputation lasted through the early thirteenth century, after which his poetry was lost until fragments of it were discovered, along with some of HaNagid's work, in the late nineteenth century. Examination of the Cairo Geniza documents, along with other finds, revealed several more fragments, and finally in 1942 mention was found in the Geniza papers of an entire diwan by Ibn Khalfoun, which seems to have been in wide circulation. A critical edition of his work was published in 1961.

### LOVE IN ME STIRS

*Shirei R. Yitzhaq Ibn Khalfoun*, ed. A. Mirsky (Jerusalem, 1961), #1; *HaShira*, #14. One of the earliest Andalusian poems involving a seemingly "erotic" situation, this short but cunningly constructed lyric has generated considerable scholarly debate, and as such demonstrates the elusive nature of this literature. (See also Moshe Ibn Ezra's "Heart's Desire,"; Yitzhaq HaGorni's lament, and Shelomo HaLevi's "Memory's Wine," which have also given rise to strikingly different readings.) Some readers have understood the poem as a tragic romantic episode, others seen it as entirely comic or "lightly ironic," and still others have viewed it as tragicomic. By the same token some consider it an inarticulate expression reflecting an early stage of literary development (anticipating the courtly lyric), while others think of it as a sophisticated departure from courtly expectations (as established in the Arabic tradition). Finally, scholars disagree about both the autobiographical and erotic dimensions of the poem: some read the first person of the poem as a conventional figure, while others feel it represents the poet; some understand the poem as an embodiment of "chasteness and restrained desire," while others suggest it reflects the standard hedonism of the Arabic erotic poem. Tova Rosen's feminist reading rejects all of these interpretations (by men) and treats the poem instead as a self-portrait of the poet as a man "writing like a woman." In that reading, both the poet and his beloved are "victims of patriarchy." The poem's ambiguity, it seems to me, permits all of these interpretations, though I find it hard to read the poem without recognizing in it at least some element of comedy and self-mockery. See *Prooftexts* 16/1 (1996): 5–13, and *Unveiling Eve*, pp. 61–62. **Line 1:** Song of Songs 2:8: "Hark! My beloved! Behold, he cometh, leaping upon the mountains, skipping [NJPS: bounding] upon the hills. My beloved is like a gazelle or a young hart. . . . Behold, he . . . looketh in through the windows." **2:** Literally, "to see the eyes of my glorious one *(kevuda)*." The word *kevuda* is drawn from Psalms 45:14, which is often translated as "All *glorious* is the king's daughter within the palace"; in medieval literature the word came to represent the young woman or lady whose honor was guarded ("within") by her (patriarchal) family. Hence the "uncle, father, and, brother." "Uncle," which appears last in the series in the Hebrew, can also be understood as "beloved" or "betrothed." See also Psalms 27:4: "To gaze upon the beauty of the Lord" (NJPS). **6:** Literally, "as though I were not her beloved." **8:** Or, "her only son," as in the story of the sacrifice of Isaac.

## A GIFT OF CHEESE

*Shirei Ibn Khalfoun*, #23; *HaShira*, #16. **Line 2:** 1 Kings 8:28. **3:** Psalms 61:4; Jeremiah 16:19; Judges 9:21. **4:** Psalms 91:4. **5:** Isaiah 4:6. **7–8:** The allusion is ironic; whereas Elkanah (1 Samuel 1:2–4) gave Peninnah a single portion, he gave a double portion to the childless Hannah. **10:** Some read the final line as "What good is cheese when I'm suffering?"

## SHMU'EL HANAGID

Muslim chroniclers of the day describe HaNagid with a mixture of admiration and condescension, singling out, among many other qualities, his tremendous learning, wisdom, courtesy, energy, and political savvy—along with his excellent command of classical Arabic—but noting as well his ignorance when it came to his choice of religion. At least one text by the famous Arab writer Ibn Hazm (who engaged the young Shmu'el in a religious debate) is far more scathing about what he calls his materialism, arrogance, and religious backwardness. More detailed discussion of HaNagid's role in the Muslim administration and how he was perceived by Muslim writers can be found in Ross Brann, *Power in the Portrayal* (Princeton, 2002). For excellent analysis of his identification with biblical characters and his use of biblical typology, see Brann's *The Compunctious Poet* (Ithaca, 1991), pp. 46ff.

## BEN TEHILLIM

The 222 poems of *Ben Tehillim* were originally copied out by HaNagid's son Yehosef, when he was eight and a half and continuing until 1056. Yehosef also added descriptive headings to the poems, possibly as dictated in Arabic by his father. For an English translation of the full preface, see my *Selected Poems of Shmuel HaNagid* (Princeton, 1996)—hereafter Cole, *Selected HaNagid*—which also contains more detailed notes and an introduction to the work. The preface also indicates that the shorter poems were recited to musical accompaniment, though we know very little about the nature of that music or its relation to the words themselves. In addition to D. Yarden's edition of these poems, *Ben Tehillim* (Jerusalem, 1966/85), hereafter *BT*, I have also consulted the earlier edition prepared by A. M. Habermann, *Diwan, veKalul bo Sefer Ben Tehillim* (Tel Aviv, 1947).

## On Fleeing His City

*BT*, #67; *HaShira*, #23. HaNagid fled the battle of 1013 when, after three years of ethnic unrest in the region, Berbers under the leadership of Suleiman al-Mustai'in stormed the city and massacred its population, including some sixty scholars. HaNagid eventually made his way from Cordoba to Malaga, normally a four-day journey of some ninety miles to the southeast, but probably double that in this instance; we know from another poem of his ("Pass of Sand," #19) that HaNagid took an indirect route, passing through Ecija, Osuna, and Morón, all of which are southwest of Cordoba. Malaga (directly to the south) was safe because it was ruled by a Slavic governor who had made a pact with the Berbers. **Heading:** "And this in his youth, on leaving Cordoba." **Lines 1–2:** Literally; "Soul from that which it desires is cut off, and soul from that which it wants is blocked." The verb in the first line of the Hebrew has two variant readings. Yarden reads *geru'a* (deriving it from Exodus 5:8); Schirmann reads *gedu'a*, "cut down," or "distanced." My somewhat free translation reflects Schirmann's text. **3–4:** Deuteronomy 31:20; Isaiah 30:23. **4–5:** "Precious being" in the original reads, literally, "honorable soul." Ecclesiastes 6:7. *Ecclesiastes Rabbah* 6:6: "If you bring [the soul] all sorts of worldly delights, they mean nothing to it. Why? Because it is from the most high." Bernard Septimus comments that the longing in the poem is neither religious nor philosophical so much as aristocratic or high-minded. "He'erot leDivrei HaZa"L beShirat Sefarad," *Tarbiz* 53 (1984): 608. He compares it to Aristotle's notion in the *Ethics* (1123a–1125b): "A person seems to be magnanimous in thinking himself worthy of great things when he is worthy." **9:** "pulse of man's flesh"—literally, "flesh of man's flesh." **12–15:** The Hebrew here has an intricate weave, picking up on the sound (*ra'a*) at the end of line 3 in the original. The roots involved in this sound can mean either evil/trouble, or companion/friend. The Hebrew reads: *vehanefesh b'ra'ah/veyesh re'im meree'im*. The English mirrors the effect of the Hebrew sound and syntax. **19:** Jeremiah 4:30. **20:** Job 34:35. **22:** Deuteronomy 14:7. **23–25:** The Hebrew contains a play on the words for "white" (as in purity or innocence) and "moon," which in Hebrew are both *levana*. So the line might also read as follows: "Should someone whose soul is white [or "a moon," or "moonlike"] . . . ?" **26–28:** Psalms 139:9. **29–31:** 1 Kings 10:7; 2 Chronicles 9:5–6. **37:** The Passover Haggada: "If he had only split the sea for us . . . ," from the Seder song "Dayenu," a hymn that dates to the second century B.C.E. **38:** The Hebrew is unclear. Yarden understands the line to read: "with every twisting swimmer [sail]." My reading in this case is based on Schirmann's text, which says: "and split the sea and every twisted trench." **39–40:** Literally, "and sail [roam] in ascent to the peak, which only eternity knows." **44–46:** Exodus 21:5–6. Literally, "And I will bore with an awl through the ear of free men [i.e., they will choose to be faithful to me out of love], and as for me an ear to my friends will be pierced." **47:** Literally, "and for me soul will hold fast to friends, and for me soul will avoid obstructors." Here and in the following lines the English collapses several of the Hebrew lines and the rendering is free. **49–53:** Esther 3:12; Song of Songs 8:7; Exodus 39:6; Psalms 68:14; Jeremiah 22:14. **54–55:** Schirmann reads: "your soul, which God loves." Yarden reads: "your soul, which I love." Job 33:24. **56–57:** Psalms 68:21. **58:** I.e., forever. Psalms 72:7: "In his days let the righteous flourish, and abundance of peace till the moon be no more."

## THE MIRACLE AT SEA

*BT*, #108; *HaShira*, #22. Tova Rosen calls this "in many respects the strangest poem in the diwan . . . and in medieval Hebrew poetry at large." She argues that the poem reflects the conventions of a typical medieval poem about a "fantastic voyage" rather than a simple representation of the poet's experience. HaNagid may, however, have taken such a trip in his youth. In particular, Rosen suggests that HaNagid drew from *The Seven Voyages of Sinbad* or something like it. (See T. Rosen-Moked, "A Hebrew Mariner and the Sea Monster," *Mediterranean Historical Review* 1/2 [1986].) Some scholars feel that HaNagid's journey—if in fact the poem is based on an actual voyage—occurred while he was still a student in Cordoba, possibly as part of a business apprenticeship; others suggest that it took place after he settled in Malaga. **Heading:** "And he sailed the sea in his youth with merchants and they encountered a beast called *tina* by those who know the creatures of the sea, and they have established that no one who met this creature at sea has ever escaped in peace, and God saved them from its assault, and he recited this poem in which he described what happened." **Line 1:** Literally, "Is there a power to stand [or recover] for one who stumbles?" Leviticus 26:36–37. **3:** Psalms 38:1: "When my foot slippeth, they magnify themselves against me"; 2 Samuel 22:37; Psalms 18:37. **5–8:** Amos 6:8. The meaning of these lines in the Hebrew is uncertain, and Yarden and Schirmann differ in their readings here. Schirmann reads: "By my soul, the All [God] will come to help and comfort the afflicted soul. By their souls, there is none who would come on the day of my confusion, and they saw me confused." The translation reflects Yarden's text. **10:** Ezekiel 29:11–12. **11:** 1 Samuel 2:8; Psalms 113:7; Isaiah 25:12. **15–16:** *Sefer Yetzira* 8: "Keep your mouth from speaking and your heart from its speculation." **17–18:** Proverbs 24:21; Isaiah 33:15. **19–20:** 1 Samuel 2:12–34; Numbers 25; Genesis 38:8–10. **21–22:** Deuteronomy 6:7. From the daily liturgy, the Shema'. **23–24:** Numbers 22:3; Psalms 22:24; Deuteronomy 32:27, 1:17; 1 Samuel 18:15; Job 41:17, 19:29. **25–26:** The Quran 112:3: "In the Name of God, the Merciful, the Compassionate, Say: He is God, One God, the Everlasting Refuge, who has not begotten, and has not been begotten, and equal to Him is not anyone" (Arberry translation). **33–34:**

Ezekiel 27:6. **37:** Job 20:17 and 29:6. **45:** "Karhah": Yarden notes that the animal was also referred to as a *tina*, which is drawn from a Spanish word *(tiña)* indicating a condition that causes baldness. The creature's name recalls the Hebrew *keireyah*, or bald. Schirmann suggests that the name comes from the Greek *karharias*, "shark" (in Hebrew, *karish*). *Baba Batra* 73–77 mentions a number of sea monsters and offers a variety of wild narratives and descriptions; 74a in particular mentions *karisa*, probably shark (see note to lines 71–72). Rosen notes that the name does not exist in related literatures, in contemporary books on zoology and seafaring, or in dictionaries. She agrees with Schirmann and points out that a large shark could easily have upended the typical sailing vessels of the time, which were small. **46:** Ezekiel 31:8. **49–50:** Isaiah 33:21. Literally, "gallant ships" or "mighty craft." **56:** Psalms 139:15. **57:** Job 40:25; Isaiah 27:1; Song of Songs 7:8. **58:** Isaiah 33:21. **62:** Song of Songs 7:5; Song of Songs 4:15; Job 41:12; Exodus 19:18; Ezekiel 23:32; Job 40:23. **63–66:** Psalms 119:83; Judges 4:19; Ecclesiastes 10:12; Exodus 28:32; Exodus 39:23. **67–70:** Song of Songs 7:3–5 (as above, lines 60–62); Psalms 91:4; Nahum 2:4. **71–72:** Literally, "And its girth to those looking on was like Tyre in the midst of the sea or Dumah"—which refers to the two cities. The English plays off the word for Tyre (Tsor), akin to the Hebrew *tzur*, meaning cliff, rock, fortress, or refuge. The biblical passage this verse is based on can be read in a number of ways. Ezekiel 27:32 (old and new JPS versions): "Who was there like Tyre fortified in the midst of the sea?" "Who was like Tyre when she was silenced in the midst of the sea?" Also, *Baba Batra* 73b: "Rabbah b. Bar Hana further stated: Once we were traveling on board a ship and saw a fish whose back was covered with sand out of which grew grass. Thinking it was dry land we went up and baked and cooked upon its back. When, however, its back was heated it turned, and had not the ship been nearby we should have been drowned." **73:** Isaiah 10:14. **74–75:** Job 40:17. **76–77:** Ezekiel 21:12; Micah 1:4; Psalms 22:15; Psalms 69:3. **78:** Psalms 131:2; Isaiah 53:7. **82:** 2 Kings 17:30. The Hebrew name Ashemah suggests "guilt" *(ashma)*. **83:** Judges 18:4. **84:** Proverbs 5:22. **85–86:** Jonah 2:1–11. **87–88:** Judges 9:16; Isaiah 3:10–11. **91–92:** Exodus 15:1: "The horse and his rider hath He thrown into the sea"; Exodus 15:4: "And his chosen captains are sunk in the Red Sea." **94:** 1 Samuel 25:37. **95:** Zechariah 3:2: "The Lord rebuke thee, O Satan." **97–98:** Psalms 22:7; Job 25:6; Judges 9:48; Ezekiel 37:6. **100:** Isaiah 9:16; Exodus 14:8. **103:** Fleischer reads "angered" or "aroused" instead of "accursed." **108:** Job 12:6. **109–12:** Job 26:7: "He . . . hangeth the earth over nothing"; Psalms 95:5: "The sea is His, and He made it"; Isaiah 51:10. **112–14:** Isaiah 44:10; Proverbs 8:23; Psalms 68:36. **115:** *Berakhot* 54b: "Rab Judah said in the name of Rab: There are four [classes of people] who have to offer thanksgiving: those who have crossed the sea. . . . Let them give thanks unto the Lord for His mercy, and for His wonderful works to the children of men." **115–16:** Deuteronomy 31:19. **117ff.:** Isaiah 26:19; Daniel 12:2: "And many of them that sleep in the dust of the earth shall awake." The passage from here through to the end resembles Maimonides' Thirteen Articles of Faith (twelfth century) and several precursor lists of "principles," beginning with Philo's. **121–23:** Ecclesiastes 12:10–11;

*Baba Batra* 64a: "And I heard them say, 'Moses and his law are truth and we are liars.'" **124–25:** Proverbs 3:17. **126–28:** Ecclesiastes 12:14; Psalms 90:8. **131:** Exodus 20:17; Jeremiah 31:33: "I will put my Law in their inward parts, and in their heart will I write it."

## The Apple

*BT*, #114, 116. **Composite Heading:** "And he mentioned being at this house where one of the poets recited a poem [in Arabic] about a bowl of fine and beautiful apples which were brought before him. One of the company translated the poem into Hebrew. And then they implored him to respond with a version of his own, and he improvised the following." These two riddlelike poems are taken from the series of fifteen that HaNagid improvised in various classical meters; they seem to be about the aesthetic and ethic of the Andalusian court. **Line 5:** Song of Songs 4:14.

## The Gazelle

*BT*, #183; *HaShira*, #52:19. For more on the figure of the gazelle, and on erotic and homoerotic poetry generally, see the glossary at the back of this volume under "gazelle" and "desire, poems of." Cf. also the introduction (under, "Translation and Trace of That Power") and Scheindlin, *Wine, Women, and Death*, pp. 77–89. **Line 6:** Deuteronomy 32:14: "And of the blood of the grape thou drankest foaming wine." **7:** Literally, "cut like a *yod* [the tenth letter of the Hebrew alphabet: a crescent]," possibly for *yayyin* (wine). I have translated it as "D," for "Drink" (or "Death"—according to *Genesis Rabbah* 13:10, God made the afterworld from the letter *yod*) and for the shape of the half-moon as it curves to the right. The image of the moon like a letter is also common in Arabic poetry of the time: "The air was clear, and the moon was bound in brightness, which shone toward the west, like a blue page with a silver dot of a golden N." For *shahar*, see Joel 2:2: "as blackness spread upon the mountains," and Shulamit Elitzur, *Shirat HaHol Ha'Ivrit biSefarad HaMuslamit*, p. 133.

## Jasmine

*BT*, #129; *HaShira*, #49. **Line 2:** Exodus 28:17.

## In Fact I Love that Fawn

*BT*, #162; *HaShira*, #51b. **Lines 1–2:** Song of Songs 6:2: "My beloved is gone down to his garden, to the beds of spices, to feed in the gardens, and to gather lilies." (The words for "lily" and "rose" are often confused.) **3:** Exodus 15:7. **4–5:** Literally, "If you could see the one I love with your eyes/your lovers would pursue you but you would not be there." Job 7:21. **6–7:** Judges 14:9: "But he told them not that he had scraped the honey out of the body of the lion." **11:** Joshua 3:10: "Hereby ye shall know that the living God is among you." **12:** 1 Samuel 25:24: "And she fell at his feet, and said: 'Upon me, my lord, upon me be the iniquity.' "

Mixed in Spain

*BT*, #146; *HaShira*, #52:7. **Lines 3–4:** "Prized" is per Schirmann's reading. Others understand, "mixed in Espamya, its scent [or bouquet] reaches India." Esther 1:1. *Espamya* is a rabbinic term for Spain. See *Niddah* 30b: "A person sleeping here [in Babylonia] might see a dream in Espamya." **5–6:** Literally, "weak in its goblets [or vessel]." Song of Songs 7:3; Abu Nuwas: "Its power rises to heads and temples; as for its taste, it is like butter." **7–8:** Deuteronomy 32:14; *Erubin* 65a: "R. Hanin observed: Wine was created for the sole purpose of comforting mourners and rewarding the wicked; for it is said, 'Give strong drink unto him that is ready to perish, and wine unto the bitter in soul (Proverbs 31:6–7).' " The tenth-century Damascene poet Abu Alfaraj al-Wa'wa' writes: "Drink, by the flowers of the gardens, wine which banishes all worry with instant joy." **9–10:** Joel 4:3; Obadiah 1:11; Nahum 3:10.

Your Years Are Sleep

*BT*, #130; *HaShira*, #52:1. **Line 1:** Arabic literary tradition attributes a similar saying to the prophet Muhammad. Other versions of this idea appear in two Indian story collections, *The Prince and the Monk*, in Ibn Hasdai's Hebrew translation— "As the wise man said: men while they live are asleep, and when they die, they wake"—and in *Kalila and Dimna* (see note to Ibn Hasdai's "Luxuries Ease"): "My soul, my soul, do not distance the morrow and rely on today; for your tomorrow is your awakening, and this day is your dream." **5:** Psalms 68:36. **6–8:** *Hagigah* 13a: "And R. Aha b. Jacob said: There is still another Heaven above the heads of the living creatures, for it is written: 'And over the heads of the living creatures there was a likeness of a firmament, like the color of the terrible ice, stretched forth over their heads above' (Ezekiel 1:22). Thus far you have permission to speak, thenceforward you have not permission to speak, for so it is written in the Book of Ben Sira: 'Seek not things that are too hard for thee, and search not out things that are hidden from thee. The things that have been permitted thee, think thereupon; thou hast no business with the things that are secret.' " **9:** Whereas the poem begins in a moralistic vein, by line 9 it seems to be clear that this is merely a strategy of misdirection, or complication, and the theme of *carpe diem* is now brought out more fully. **11:** 1 Samuel 16:17; Ezekiel 33:32; Psalms 46:1. The meaning of *alamoth* is uncertain. "Lute" is based on Yarden's reading: "an ancient musical instrument." It might also refer to one "who loves to sing [a certain kind of melody]." **12–13:** Genesis 9:20–21: "And Noah, the husbandman, began and planted a vineyard." Abu Nuwas writes: "I asked the wine merchant: 'How long has it been since the presser pressed [them]?' He answered: 'This is beyond my powers of computation. They've told me that my grandfather's father chose it, from Adam's cellars, or Eve's.'" Another poem of his describes wine as follows: "This wine saw Noah, who was already old and gray; and it saw hundreds of years before Noah." **14:** Job 28:18. **20:** 1 Chronicles 25:1–6. Jerimoth, the son of Heman the Levite, whom David appointed to serve with his sons as Temple singers. **22:** I.e., all such (excellent) wine, or, in keeping with *Berakhot* 34b, a reference to the wine made during the six days of Creation, which was stored up and held for the righteous in the afterlife. **24–26:** Ecclesiastes 9:7: "Go thy way, eat thy bread with joy, and drink thy wine with a merry heart." Qohelet is the preacher of Ecclesiastes and the Hebrew name for the book itself. (Also *Nedarim* 10b and the Jerusalem Talmud *Qiddushin* 66b, which allude to the talmudic ideal that a person will be judged after his death for the pleasures foregone in life.) As Dan Pagis notes (*HaShir Davur 'al Ofnav*, ed. E. Fleischer [Jerusalem, 1993], pp. 29–49), the poem is based on the assumption common to the *memento mori* tradition, i.e., that one should remember the day of one's death and that the soul will live on, but it rejects that tradition's conclusion and its call for restraint or even asceticism. On the other hand, the poem rejects the assumption of the *carpe diem* tradition, i.e., that the soul won't last and there is no life after death, but accepts its conclusion: drink and take pleasure in life while you can. In fact, the poet sees it as a commandment, just as he sees the rejection of God's gifts as a transgression. Pagis therefore links the conclusion of this poem not only with Ecclesiastes 9:7 but with Ecclesiastes 11:9: "Rejoice, O young man, in thy youth, and let thy heart cheer thee in the days of thy youth, and walk in the ways of thy heart, and in the sight of thine eyes; but know thou, that for all these things God will bring thee into judgment." Also *Berakhot* 51a: "Whoever says the blessing over a full cup is given an inheritance without bounds [i.e., the world to come]."

### THE HOUSE OF PRAYER

*BT,* #83; *HaShira,* #45. **Line 1:** Literally, "Is time behaving insolently against [bullying] Rabbi Judah HaNasi, [the redactor of the Mishna in the third century C.E.] and Rava [a Babylonian *amora*, or teacher, who died in 352 C.E.]?" Isaiah 3:5. **5–6:** Mephibosheth was Saul's grandson and Jonathan's son. Tsiba was Saul's servant. 2 Samuel 9:6–13. Also *Berakhot* **4a:** "Why then was he called Mephibosheth? Because he humiliated David in the Halakha." (*Me-phi-bosheth* means "Out of my mouth humiliation.") **6:** Rav Hai HaGaon was the last of the Babylonian *gaonim*, or leaders of the Yeshivot there. The leading talmudist of HaNagid's time, he died in 1038. **7:** Numbers 15:38. **10:** The allusion is to the holiday of Hoshana Rabba, on the seventh day of Sukkot, when willow sprigs are beaten in the synagogue.

Margoliooth's *Sefer Hilkhot HaNagid*, which collects HaNagid's halakhic commentary, contains an entry on the beating of willow sprigs. **11:** HaNagid is referring to the sound of a crowd one often hears coming from a synagogue or house of study. **17–19:** Genesis 37:30: "And as for me, whither shall I go?"; Isaiah 8:20. Literally, "They've changed the testimony and Torah." **17–19:** Literally; "like a tamarisk in the wilderness." The students were moving their bodies in traditional fashion during study and prayer. Jeremiah 17:6. **21:** There are variant readings for this line. My reading is based on Habermann's texts. **23:** Literally, "In their mouths they abused Hillel and Shammai and struck on the cheek Rabbi Akiva." 2 Kings 19:22; Micah 4:14. Hillel and Shammai are the two major authorities cited in the Mishna. Akiva is one of the great heroes of postbiblical Judaism. One of the most important *tannaim*, or scholars of the first generation, he died while being tortured by the Romans during the Bar Kokhba rebellion, circa 132 C.E. **25:** The teacher would take whatever noise they made as a sign of comprehension and agreement and go on with his nonsense. **30–31:** Daniel 10:6; *Menahot* 43b: "R. Meir used to say, A man is bound to say one hundred blessings daily, as it is written, "And now, Israel, *what* doth the Lord thy God require of thee?" (The Hebrew word for "what" (*ma*) is interpreted as though it were *me'ah*, which means "a hundred") **32–33:** *Menahot* 43b: "R. Judah used to say, A man is bound to say the following three blessings daily: '[Blessed art Thou . . . ] who hast not made me a heathen,' '. . . who hast not made me a woman'; and . . .'who hast not made me a brutish man.'" The prayer 'who hast not made me a woman' is part of the morning liturgy. See the fourteenth-century poem on this topic by Qalonymos Ben Qalonymos, below. **34–35:** Literally, "Would you put your soul among the males [or masculine], when the Lord will testify against you that you are feminine?" The word for "feminine" (*neqeva*) is akin to the words for "punctured" or "holed" (*naquv*), "anus" (*naquva*), and "to blaspheme" (*naqav*).

## THE CRITIQUE

*BT*, #82. **Heading:** "In which he responds to someone who sent him a weak poem." **Line 1:** Psalms 45:14: "All glorious is the king's daughter within the palace; her raiment is of chequer work wrought with gold." **2:** Ecclesiastes 2:8. **3:** Isaiah 10:16. **4:** Psalms 45:9; Exodus 30:23–24. **8:** Literally, "while yours were white [as hail]." **9–10:** Numbers 31:23. Literally, "but this poem is impure." **11:** A line from the Hebrew has been omitted here. Literally, "I weighed it against your poems, which were as grooms, but this one among them would be outlawed." Jeremiah 31:20. **16:** Psalms 57:5: "and their tongue a sharp sword."

## ON LIFTING THE SIEGE

*BT*, #11; *HaShira*, #34. Located some 120 miles northeast of Granada, on the slopes of the Sierra del Cano, Lorca was one of the most famous fortresses in

Andalusia. HaNagid's troops were sent to aid the city, which was under siege by Ibn Abi 'Ammaar, the ruler of neighboring Almeria after the death of Zuhair. **Heading:** "When those who were laying siege to Lorca heard that the troops were approaching the city, they quickly fled, and our army sped toward Lorca and camped there, where he wrote me the following." **Line 1:** Carrier pigeons had been used by the Greeks since the fifth century B.C.E., and references to them are not unusual in medieval Spain. **4:** Song of Songs 3:6: "perfumed with myrrh and frankincense"; also Song of Songs 4:14. **10:** Literally, "from the beam over the entrance." Proverbs 9:3. **12:** Job 41:5: "Wilt thou play with him as with a bird?" **16–18:** 1 Kings 22:17: "I saw all Israel scattered upon the mountains, as sheep that have no shepherd." **17:** Hosea 13:3: "They shall be . . . as the chaff that is driven with the wind out of the threshing floor." **19:** Psalms 54:9, 58:11, 118:7. **20:** Psalms 63:7, 90:4. **23–25:** Psalms 69:7; Job 6:20: "They were ashamed because they had hoped; they came thither, and were confounded"; Jeremiah 2:26: "As the thief is ashamed when he is found"; Leviticus 25:29; Exodus 22:1. **26–28:** Psalms 71:13, 109:29: "Mine adversaries shall be clothed with confusion, and shall put on their own shame as a robe"; Exodus 29:13. **29–30:** Job 34:7; Ezekiel 23:33–34; Isaiah 51:17: "Thou hast drunken the beaker, even the cup of staggering, and drained it." **31–32:** Jeremiah 4:31; Psalms 55:5; Jeremiah 6:24. **35:** 1 Samuel 14:29. **36–37:** Isaiah 65:14. **38–39:** Isaiah 22:4. **40:** 2 Samuel 22:2–3; Psalms 18:3: "The Lord is my rock . . . my high tower." **45–46:** Deuteronomy 6:6–8: "And these words which I command thee this day, shall be upon thy heart; . . . thou shalt bind them for a sign upon thine hands [arms]"; Proverbs 3:3: "Write them upon the table of thy heart"; Job 19:24: "With an iron pen and lead they were graven in the rock forever."

## The War with Yaddayir

*BT*, #7; *HaShira*, #31. Yaddayir (the Hebrew vocalization is Schirmann's; the name is pronounced "Yiddiir" in Buluggin's Arabic chronicle, *The Tibyaan*) was a cousin of Granada's King Badiis and aspired to his throne. The battle took place at Argona, which is east of Cordoba and north of Granada. Almunekar, where Yaddayir was eventually imprisoned, is south of Granada, on the coast. **Heading:** "And Yaddayir the commander came to the place known as Argona in the year 4801 [1041], and with him were Waasil and Muwaafaq, both of them well-known officers among the Andalusian leaders, and they overcame Argona and killed the commander of the city. Afterward they marched to a place known as Samantin and overcame most of the castles there. And then our forces went out against them and the hand of God was with them and they killed Waasil and Muwaafaq. And Yaddayir fled until he was trapped at Cordoba and he was taken from there and imprisoned in the castle of Munekar. And my lord, my father, spoke of what happened to him and how he fared, praising God for having granted him this great victory." **Line 1:** Psalms 39:14, Job 14:6. **2:** Proverbs 4:20, 2:2. **3–4:** Psalms 27:1. **7:** Proverbs 5:9–10. **8–10:** Jeremiah 33:9; Exodus 9:17. **12:** Ruth 1:18; Ezekiel

2:8: "Be not thou rebellious like that rebellious house"—where God instructs the prophet to listen to Him and accept His word, and not to be like those who have rebelled against Him; 2 Chronicles 13:7. **16:** Psalms 16:5. **18:** Psalms 62:8. **22:** Cf. "A Day of Distress and Anguish" (in Cole, *Selected HaNagid*) in which the archangels Gabriel and Michael appear to HaNagid. Also Exodus 18:4. **23:** Leviticus 26:39. **24:** Literally, "My fate is decreed from the heavens." **26:** Literally, "there are people in life who never rule, like Tivni who died before his time, and Zimri." 1 Kings 16:10, 15–22. **28:** Exodus 2:11. **29–30:** Proverbs 13:23. **32:** Job 7:16, 10:20, and 21:13: "They spend their days in prosperity." **33–35:** Ezekiel 24:23; Proverbs 5:15: "Drink waters out of thine own cistern, and running waters out of thine own well"; Psalms 23:2, 116:13. **36–37:** Psalms 16:5 (as in line 16, above); Job 10:3. **38:** Ezekiel 23:25. **40:** Psalms 66:12. **43–44:** Psalms 17:11; Jeremiah 18:22; Psalms 9:16. **43–49:** Isaiah 11:6. This stanza tries to mirror the complex weave of the Hebrew: *Ani evtah be'el hepil ashurai betoh pahim temanum le-ashuri/beyom ba tzar le'ir meevtzar, vetavah/betoho sar kemo egel v'kheemri/vetzar zeh m'she'air malkhi— v'ra'at/rehoki tehsar mai'ra she'airi.* **50:** Waasil and Muwaafaq were the two princes. **51:** Cf. Genesis 10:18 for the Zemarites, who were a Canaanite people. In this context, they stand for the Slavs. The city they seized was Argona. The Slavs were for the most part of Christian origin and from territories in Europe that were ruled by non-Muslims. The name derives from the Greek *sklavas,* for slave. Often mercenaries, they were a distinct population within the Andalusian mix and maintained their own communities. **52:** The fortress (or forts) at Samantin, near the city of Jaén, fifty miles due north of Granada. Psalms 91:5–6; Deuteronomy 32:24. **57–61:** Hosea 7:12; Isaiah 51:20; Job 39:18; Isaiah 17:6: "Yet there shall be left therein gleanings, as at the beating of an olive tree, two or three berries in the top of the uppermost bough, four or five in the branches of the fruitful tree, saith the Lord." **62:** Isaiah 17:6. The long Hebrew vowel referred to here (*tzeri*— pronounced *ai*) has two dots side by side beneath a letter while the short one (*segol*—pronounced *eh*) has three dots arranged in an inverted triangle beneath a letter. **65:** Deuteronomy 1:4. **66:** Leviticus 26:27. **69:** Isaiah 18:7. **71:** "My friend"— the same skeptical acquaintance to whom the opening of the poem is addressed. **82:** 1 Samuel 12:11; Psalms 99:6; and *Rosh Hashana* 25b: " 'Moses and Aaron among his priests and Samuel among them that call on his name.' Jepthah in his generation [of his age] is like Samuel in his generation [of his age], to teach you that the most worthless, once he has been appointed a leader of the community, is to be accounted like the mightiest of the mighty." **83:** 1 Samuel 10:11: "Is Saul also among the prophets?" **85–86:** Exodus 6:16, 22–24. All of the people mentioned in these lines are descendants of Levi and therefore among the cult of the Temple musicians. HaNagid reminds his listeners (as he does even more forcefully in the wine poem "Have You Heard How I Helped the Wise?" [Cole, *Selected HaNagid,* p. 65]) that he too is a Levite and of a lineage befitting a poet. **89:** Hosea 5:13. **90:** Psalms 39:1: "For Jeduthun. A psalm of David." **93–96:** *Numbers Rabbah* 19: " 'Then sang Israel'—Israel reasoned thus: It is Thy duty to perform miracles for us, and our duty to bless and praise Thy name." Also Psalms 55:15; Jeremiah 8:22. **97–98:** Deuteronomy 24:14–15.


## On the Death of Isaac, His Brother

The poems included under this title are taken from a series of eighteen elegies that HaNagid composed in the wake of his older brother Isaac's death. Isaac was forty-eight at the time. The order of the poems here in some cases departs from that of the diwan. A fuller selection from the sequence can be found in Cole, *Selected HaNagid*, pp. 21ff.

*First child of my mother:*

BT, #91; *HaShira*, #30:2. **Heading:** "And he recited this in which he describes his going in to see him and his kissing him while he was lying on his bed." **Line 1:** Literally, "Firstborn of my mother, the first of death [the angel of death] has stolen you." The English has departed from this somewhat to maintain a semblance of the Hebrew's weave and the tension between "firstborn" and "first of death." Job 18:13: "Yea, the firstborn of death shall devour his members." **9:** Literally, "curtain." **12:** Literally, "on the day of your affliction [or misfortune]." **13:** *Eruvin* 65b: "R. Ila'i said: By three things may a person's character be determined: By his cup (*koso*), by his purse (*keeso*), and by his anger (*ka'aso*)." Also Psalms 16:5. **22–27:** Isaiah 29:10: "For the Lord hath poured out upon you the spirit of deep sleep, and hath closed your eyes." **28–30:** Job 5:26, 30:2, and *Bereshit Rabbah* 79:1: "And you will come fresh toward the grave."

*

*Give up, heart:*

BT, #88. **Heading:** "And then he said." **Line 1:** Ecclesiastes 2:20. **5–8:** Literally, "Live after him in misery, and if you'd request respite from his grief [the grief of his death], die like him."

*

*Why should I force:*

BT, #89. **Heading:** "And he said when he tore his clothes in mourning for him." **Lines 1–4:** Literally, "Why should I tear my clothes and garments [as a traditional sign of mourning]?" 1 Samuel 4:12; Job 13:28: "Though I am . . . like a garment that is moth-eaten"; Joel 2:13. **5–8:** Literally, "Why put dirt on my robes [or dress]?"—another traditional sign of mourning. "Slime-filled pits" allude to the biblical Vale of Siddim, as in Genesis 14:10: "Now the vale of Siddim was full of slime pits, and the kings of Sodom and Gomorrah fled, and they fell there." The line is saying, "I do not need the (literal) dirt of his grave on my robe to show that I am mourning—the thoughts (of my heart) are so dark." **11–12:** Breaking cups was another sign of mourning. **13–16:** The Hebrew plays on the words for "walls" or "sides" of my heart (*tzeedei levavi*) and "thorns" (*tziddim*) and its melic weave is again conspicuous. Acoustic correspondences in the English function here in place of the puns. Judges 2:3; and *Mo'ed Qatan* 22b: "For all dead [except for one's father and mother], one tacks the rent together after seven [days] and [completely] reunites [the edges] after thirty [days]." **17–18:** Literally, "the walls of my heart." Jeremiah 4:19. **19–20:** In other words, the pain will continue well after the official display of mourning is over. Ecclesiastes 9:8. **21–24:** Exodus 25:15: "The staves shall be in the rings of the [holy] ark; they shall not be taken from it." **27–28:** Literally, "from my soul [my life] will forever be distant."

*

*My language:*

   BT, #92; *HaShira*, #30:3. **Heading:** "And he said, describing his being wrapped in the shroud and lowered into his grave, may God have mercy upon him." **Line 1:** Literally, "My tongue [or language]." The Hebrew carries the double meaning that the contemporary English "tongue" strains for. Judges 8:24. **3:** The translation is literal, but idiomatically conveys, "by my life." **6–7:** The Hebrew here means that Isaac was like a father to HaNagid and others. He was a friend who looked out for them. **9:** Hosea 5:11 (where the Hebrew is uncertain). **10–12:** Job 31:32. **13–15:** Psalms 78:72; Isaiah 11:7–9: "And the cow and the bear shall feed; their young ones shall lie down together." **19:** Jeremiah 4:31: "For I have heard a voice as of a woman in travail, the anguish as of her that bringeth forth her first child." **21–22:** 1 Samuel 4:12. See note to "Why should I force" (above), lines 1 and 13. *Mo'ed Qatan* 22b and 24a: "For all [other] dead, if he desires, he bares [his shoulder—and also bares his heart] and if he does not desire he does not bare it." "Samuel said, Any rending [of clothes] not done in the flush [of grief] is not a [proper] rending." A line of the original has been omitted here: "my face covered." **28–29:** 2 Samuel 19:1: "Thus [King David] said: 'O my son Absalom . . . would I had died for thee." **36:** "My soul" is a literal reading. The expression often means "my life." Psalms 22:20: "O Thou my strength"; 1 Kings 19:4: "O Lord, Take away my life, for I am not better than my fathers."

*

*Tell him, please:*

   BT, #95. **Heading:** "And afterward he said." **Line 4:** Proverbs 27:20. "Destruction" in the Hebrew plays on the root for lost. **10:** Literally, "Until I'm laid by his side." The repetition of "dust" mirrors the repetition of the *esh* sound in the Hebrew, which runs through the poem and, on its own, means "fire."

*

*A brother is in me:*

   BT, #101. **Heading:** "And he recited this when his letters stopped and others' arrived instead." **Lines 3–4:** Jeremiah 2:25.

\*

*Twelve months have passed:*

BT, #103; *HaShira*, #30:6. **Heading:** "And he recited this after a year had passed since his death." **Lines 2–3:** Psalms 91:3: "He will deliver thee from the snare of the fowler, and from the noisome pestilence." **4:** Job 21:33: "The clods of the valley are sweet unto him." **7:** Psalms 107:32. **9–10:** Zechariah 14:12: "Their flesh shall consume away . . . and their eyes shall consume away in their sockets." **11:** Ezekiel 37:11; Isaiah 56:3: "Behold, I am a dry tree." **13–14:** Literally, "eats along his skin." Isaiah 50:9: "They all shall wax old as a garment; the moth shall eat them up."

\*

*A psalm to the hearer:*

BT, #104. **Heading:** "And when his grief had passed and he was consoled in his mourning, he recited the following." This poem is also found in *Ben Qohelet* (Abramson, 395), with several variants. **Lines 1–2:** Psalms 65:3: "O Thou that hearest prayer, to Thee doth all flesh come." **3:** Psalms 33:1. **5:** Psalms 49:3. **7–9:** Yarden notes the parallel in the Arabic poetry of Abu 'Ali al-Qali al-Baghdadi: "God, may He be magnified and exalted, created everything small, and after a time they grow large, except for grief, which he created large and which becomes smaller with time." **9** The Hebrew word for "labor" might also be translated as "creation" or "production." **11:** Hosea 4:13; Isaiah 6:13. **14–16:** Literally, "And if grief remains in a heart as at the outset." **16:** Literally, "From God (*elohim*)." **20–22:** Numbers 22:24: "like a lane between the vineyards," which alludes to Balaam, who is about to have his foot crushed against the wall of the lane. **23–24:** Literally, "And my worry runs out." **26:** Ezekiel 1:24. **31:** Job 5:18. **32–33:** Job 38:9. **36–38:** Literally, "And with the fathers who were righteous and his treasure, may he be counted as treasure." Exodus 19:5; Ecclesiastes 2:8: "I gathered me also silver and gold and treasure." Also Ibn Janaah, *Sefer HaShorashim* (Berlin, 1896), p. 333, under "s-g-l."

### Ben Mishle

HaNagid's collection of Hebrew epigrams, *Ben Mishle* (pronounced MISH-lay), contains 1,197 Hebrew poems. *Ben Mishle* was originally copied and arranged by HaNagid's youngest son, Eliasaf, who was born in 1049. In 1056, when Eliasaf was six and a half years old, HaNagid instructed him to begin work on the book. (According to Abramson, Eliasaf could read Torah by the age of three and a half.) It is not clear how long it took him to complete the task, though there is some indication that he may have finished before his father died (also in 1056). Along with D. Yarden's edition, *Ben Mishle* (Jerusalem, 1983), hereafter *BM*, I have also consulted S. Abramson's, *Ben Mishle*, (Tel Aviv, 1948).

The preface to the book (translated in Cole, *Selected HaNagid*) tells us that many of the poems are taken from other languages and traditions. This was a common practice at the time and was not considered plagiarism, since the essence of the poem was in the poet's *treatment* of his conventional material. There was, however, engaged consideration of the problem of plagiarism in medieval Arabic and Hebrew literary criticism.

## First War

*BM*, #1034; *HaShira*, #42:21. This poem is based on the Arabic epigram attributed to Imru' al-Qa'is (500–42 C.E.): "War [at first] is a beautiful girl urging young men to sign away their lives. As the fire breaks into flames she becomes a headless hag who offers a broken promise and an [unkissable] stinking corpse" (Trans. A. al-Udhari). Andras Hamori cites similar lines by al-Kumayt: "When, after having seemed a delicate young girl, / war shows itself a graying old woman, quarrelsome and shrill . . . ," in *The Art of Medieval Arabic Literature* (Princeton, 1974), p. 49.

## I'd Suck Bitter Poison

*BM*, #58. **Lines 1–2:** Job 20:14–15; Isaiah 11:8. **3–4:** Proverbs 23:6; Deuteronomy 2:28; Numbers 20:19; Proverbs 17:1; 2 Samuel 12:3.

## Delay Your Speech

*BM*, #54. **Line 1:** Genesis 24:56. **3:** Proverbs 4:25; Job 5:24. **4:** Job 41:20; 1 Samuel 31:3; 1 Chronicles 10:3. **6:** Judges 20:16; Deuteronomy 8:8. The poem plays on the similarity between *yehtei* (to sin) and *hitta* (wheat). *Berakhot* 61a: "Samuel said: [The evil inclination] is like a kind of wheat [*hitta*], as it says, sin [or deceit, *hattat*] circleth at the door" (Genesis 4:7). This may be in connection with the notion that the forbidden food of which Adam ate was wheat. See *Berakhot* 40a.

## The Rich

*BM*, #178.

## People Welcome the Rich

*BM*, #118. **Lines 1–4:** Proverbs 14:20; Ben Sira 13:21–23. **3–4:** Job 34:6.

## If You Leave a Long-Loved Friend

*BM*, #126.

## You Who'd Be Wise

*BM*, #195. **Lines 1–2:** *Avot* 4:1: "Who is wise? He who learns from every man." *Berakhot* 63b: "R. Ishmael says, One who desires to be wise should occupy himself with money judgments, since no branch of Torah surpasses them, for they are like a perpetual fountain [of instruction]." **3–4:** Proverbs 10:8–9, 11:5.

## When You're Desperate

*BM*, #198; *HaShira*, #42:3. **Line 1:** Judges 6:6. **6:** Psalms 78:40.

## It's Heart That Discerns

*BM*, #231. **Line 1:** Kings 3:9. **3:** Proverbs 15:32, 19:8. **5–6:** Jeremiah 1:10. *Megillah* 31b: "R. Simeon b. Eleazar says: If old men say to you, 'throw down,' and young men say to you, 'build up,' throw down and do not build up, because destruction by old men is construction, and construction by boys is destruction."

## He'll Bring You Trouble

*BM*, #632; *HaShira*, #42:7. **Line 1:** Kings 9:11. **2:** Psalms 137:3. **3:** Zechariah 10:2; Ecclesiastes 5:6. **4:** Cf. Aristotle (*Metaphysics* 982b and *Poetics* 24:9), to whom Ibn Ezra refers when he says, "the image [metaphor] is completely false [a lie]" (*The Book of Discussion*, p. 119). The version in HaNagid's poem plays on the three-word Arabic proverb, "The best of a poem is its falseness" (*ahsan al-shi'ir akdhabuhu*), which was central to the poetics of the Spanish-Hebrew writers of the period as well. Ibn Ezra refers to this Arabic formulation in 62a and 64a: "The poet is he who most skillfully draws a form that will astonish the eye and yet not have substance." The English parallel to this, of course, is Shakespeare's "the truest poetry is the most feigning." It's important to keep in mind here that the question is being considered in Aristotelian (epistemological) rather than moral terms.

## Could Kings Right a People Gone Bad

*BM*, #382. **Line 1:** Proverbs 4:25; Habakkuk 1:4. **2:** Deuteronomy 32:5; 2 Samuel 23:20. **3:** Numbers 23:27; Ecclesiastes 1:15: "That which is crooked cannot be made straight." **4:** Lamentations 3:9.

## What's Familiar Is Sometimes Distanced

*BM*, #962. **Line 2:** Ben Sira 13:10: "Do not push forward lest you be repulsed, and do not remain at a distance lest you be forgotten." **3:** Proverbs 13:13; Leviticus 11:4; Ezekiel 32:13. **4:** Proverbs 20:5.

### ONE WHO WORKS AND BUYS HIMSELF BOOKS

*BM*, #24. **Line 4:** Ruth 1:21; Deuteronomy 15:13; Nehemiah 5:13; *Pesahim* 4:5 (64a). **6:** Ezekiel 23:14; *Berakhot* 10a; Ezekiel 8:10 (Targum). Cf. Ibn Khaldun's introduction to the study of history, *The Muqaddimah* (trans. N. J. Dawood), chapter 6, section 55: "A person who is ignorant of the composition of speech and its methods, as required by the (Arabic) linguistic habit, and who unsuccessfully attempts to express what he wants to express, is like an invalid who attempts to get up but cannot, because he lacks the power to do so."

### THREE THINGS

*BM*, #1129; *HaShira*, #42:20. Based on the Arabic of Ibn Hamdun. **Line 1:** *Berakhot* 11a. **2:** 2 Chronicles 17:6. **4:** Isaiah 45:14.

### SOAR, DON'T SETTLE

*BM*, #1097. **Line 1:** Psalms 57:12; 2 Samuel 18:9; Jeremiah 51:9. **2:** Literally, "soar to the Bear" (i.e., the constellation). **3:** Deuteronomy 31:7; 1 Kings 18:5. **4:** Isaiah 53:4; Job 4:11.

### MAN'S WISDOM IS IN WHAT HE WRITES

*BM*, #1194; *HaShira*, #42:14. **Line 3:** Esther 5:2–3.

### BEN QOHELET

*Ben Qohelet* contains 411 poems. The poems are presented without a preface, and their editor is unknown. In his introduction to the Oxford edition of HaNagid's diwan (*Diwan Shmu'el HaNagid*, ed. D. S. Sassoon [Oxford, 1934]), Sassoon proposes that HaNagid himself arranged the poems. Habermann suggests it was HaNagid's older son, Yehosef. Abramson (*Ben Qohelet*, ed. S. Abramson [Tel Aviv, 1953], hereafter *BQ*), says that we do not know enough to suggest an editor, and that perhaps the copyist simply omitted the preface at some point. He leans, however, toward HaNagid as the most likely candidate.

Several poems appear in both *Ben Qohelet* and *Ben Tehillim* or *Ben Mishle*, or as parts of poems in those books. The date of the book's completion is not known. Whereas the superscriptions to *Ben Tehillim* often include the date of a given poem, there are neither superscriptions nor dates in the extant manuscripts of *Ben Qohelet*. The first mention of this book in later literature is by Moshe Ibn Ezra in *The Book of Discussion* 32b: "And it [*Ben Qohelet*] is the most sublime and admirable of HaNagid's compositions, and it is more beautiful and more profound than *Ben Tehillim* and *Ben Mishle*, because it was written after its author reached middle age."

## Be Glad, She Said

*BQ*, #35; *HaShira*, #41:5. **Lines 8–9:** Cf. HaNagid's contemporary Ibn Hazm (994–1064): "Having seen the hoariness on my temples and sideburns, someone asked me how old I was. I answered him: I consider all my life to have been but a short moment and nothing else" (trans. J. Monroe).

## The Multiple Troubles of Man

*BQ*, #24. See also the later (unfinished) edition by D. Yarden, *Ben Qohelet* (Jerusalem, 1992). **Lines 1–2:** Exodus 18:8; Psalms 71:20; *Hagigah* 5b. The Hebrew has *betzarot* ("in trouble" or "in pain"); Abramson suggests *ketzarot* ("like troubles" or "like pain"), which I have followed. **3:** Genesis 43:33.

## Gazing through the Night

*BQ*, #22; *HaShira*, #41:22. This poem appears in both *Ben Qohelet* and *Ben Tehillim*. In the latter it is incorporated into a poem of friendship that begins: "It's upon you, sons and supporters of the Law, it's upon you to reveal its secrets, because humankind upon earth is in darkness, and you are its sun." **Lines 1–5:** Psalms 8:4; Psalms 104:24; *Berakhot* 10a: "He came out into the open air [of the world] and looked upon the stars and constellations and broke into song." **3–4:** Literally, "the earth and its creeping things." Genesis 1:25–26: "every thing that creepeth upon the ground." Rashi's annotation to Genesis 1:25 reads: "It [*remes*] means creeping swarms that creep low upon the ground; they appear as though they are dragged along, for how they move is not discernible." Genesis 6:7: "Man and beast and creeping things, and fowl of the air." Also, Ibn Hazm: "If I should come to possess [love], then all the earth will [seem like] a senile camel and mankind motes of dust, while the land's inhabitants will [seem like] insects" (trans. J. Monroe). **8:** Isaiah 40:22; *Baraita de Shmu'el HaQatan* 1: "The heavens are made like a tent." **9:** Exodus 26:4ff., which describes the sanctuary in the desert: "And thou shalt make loops of blue upon the edge of the one curtain"; *Shabbat* 99a: "the clasps in the loops looked like stars set in the sky." Similar images abound in Arabic poetry. **10:** Psalms 8:4, as above, lines 1–5. **11–13:** Ibn Gabirol, "KeShoresh Etz" (*Shirei HaHol, Shelomo Ibn Gabirol*, ed. Brody and Schirmann, [Jerusalem, 1974] #203); "The Tree," in Cole, *Selected Ibn Gabirol*, pp. 100–103: "He scatters his stars about like a shepherd,/sending his flock across a field." This is also a common image in Arabic poetry. **14–15:** Jeremiah 10:13; Proverbs 25:14. Schirmann reads "clouds"; Yarden, "clouds carried by wind." The biblical reference alludes to "vapors." Ibn al-Mu'tazz compares the moon to a ship of silver loaded with amber incense; other poets use the image of a ship as well. **19–21:** Isaiah 18:4. "Shaking water": the Hebrew plays on the root *n-a-r—na'ara tena'ir* (a girl [*na'ara*] will shake out [*tena'ir*])—then alludes to Song of Songs 5:2: "For my head is filled with dew, my locks with the drops of the night." I have taken several liberties here to establish a similar weave in the English. **22:** Some versions of the text have two extra lines here. See *BT*, #41. Isaiah 18:3. **24:** The Hebrew (*hayyah*) is in dispute, and Abramson discusses the matter in his notes to *Ben Qohelet*. Both he and Yarden read "troops," alluding to 2 Samuel 23:13. The word might also mean "beast." Schirmann does not comment here. A literal version of the entire passage would read: "And dwellers on earth are like beasts falling off to sleep [or troops pitching camp for a night], our yards/courts their stalls." **27:** *Mekhilta beShalah* 3: 86, line 86: "To what can the Israelites at that moment be compared? To a dove fleeing from a hawk." **28–29:** Isaiah 30:14: "And He shall break it as a potter's vessel is broken, breaking it in pieces without sparing; so that there shall not be found among the pieces thereof a shard"; 2 Kings 21:13: "And I will wipe Jerusalem, as a man wipeth a dish"; *Baba Batra* 16a: "Raba said: Job sought to turn the dish upside down [to declare all God's works worthless]"; *Pesahim* 50a: "Rabbi Joseph the son of R. Joshua b. Levi became ill and fell into a trance. When he recovered, his father asked him, 'What did you see?' 'I saw a topsy-turvy world, the upper [class] was underneath and the lower on top.' 'My son,' he observed, 'you saw a clear world.'" The image of the broken plate is common in Arabic poetry, e.g.: "Death will smash us into pieces as though we were glass" (Abu al-'Ala al-Ma'arri).

## EARTH TO MAN

*BQ*, #38. **Line 2:** Jeremiah 37:4, 52:31. Al-Ma'arri: "We're surrounded by a place from which escape is impossible, and time is running out on its souls [residents]."

## THE CHILD AT ONE OR TWO

*BQ*, #79; *HaShira*, #41:7. A classic "stages of life" text. *Avot* 5:1: "He would say: At five to [the study of] Scripture, ten to Mishna, thirteen to the commandments, fifteen to Talmud, eighteen to the [wedding] canopy, twenty to pursuit [of a livelihood], thirty to [fullness of] strength, forty to understanding, fifty to counsel, sixty to old age [maturity], seventy to grey hair, eighty to extended strength, ninety to [a] bending [figure]. At one hundred he is as though he were dead, and had passed away and faded from the world." Cf. *As You Like It*, act 2, scene 7: "All the world's a stage" and the seven ages of man. **Line 2:** Jeremiah 8:17; *Ecclesiastes Rabbah* 1:4: "R. Samuel b. R. Isaac taught in the name of R. Samuel b. Eleazar: The seven 'vanities' mentioned by Qoheleth correspond to the seven worlds a man beholds. At one year old he is like a king seated in a canopied litter, fondled and kissed by all. At two and three he is like a pig, sticking his hand in the gutters. At ten he skips like a kid. At twenty he is like a neighing horse, adorning his person and longing for a wife. Having married, he is like an ass. When he has begotten children, he grows brazen like a dog to supply their food and wants. When he has become old, he is [bent] like an ape." **3–4:** Song of Songs 2:8. **7:** Ecclesiastes 11:10. **9:** Literally, "he becomes righteous (blameless) and joins his friends the elders," i.e., he matures and comes to completion of character. Psalms 18:26. **13–14:** Job 24:17. **15–16:** Genesis 48:10. Abramson notes that the manuscript here is hard to decipher and he reads *nireh* (seems/appears) rather than *nikheh* (broken as in Psalms 109:16). **17–18:** Job 18:10; Hosea 9:8; Psalms 91:3, 124:7. **20:** Literally, "He won't know the harvest [season] from the ploughing [season]." Genesis 45:6. **22:** *Pesahim* 72b: "All your words are . . . naught but mysteries." **23–24:** Literally, "And at a hundred he is brother to the worm, repulsive to people, his raiment stained." Isaiah 14:19.

### I Quartered the Troops for the Night

*BQ,* #131; *HaShira,* #41:8. Cf. Latin poetry's *ubi sunt,* especially the twelfth-century poem by Bernard of Morlay: "Where now is your glory, Babylon, where is the terrible Nebuchadnezzar, and strong Darius and the famous Cyrus? Where now is Regulus, or where Romulus, or where Remus?" (For more on the *ubi sunt* tradition and excerpt of Bernard's poem, see Johan Huizinga, *The Autumn of the Middle Ages,* trans. R. J. Payton and U. Mammitzsch (Chicago, 1996), pp. 156ff. Or Villon's "Where are the snows of yesteryear?" in his "Testament." Helen Waddell comments: "The [Latin] hymn of the great age, 1150 to 1250, has secret springs, and scholars have made a good, if non-proven case for Celtic and Arabic" (*Mediaeval Latin Lyrics,* trans. H. Waddell [Harmondsworth, 1952], p. 7). **Lines 5–7:** Genesis 4:9. **9–10:** *Shabbat* 114a. **20:** In the original "these sleepers" is "these crowds" or "these masses," which I understand as referring both to HaNagid's own troops and to the "masters" who "slept on."

### Luxuries Ease

*BQ,* #210. **Lines 1–2:** Ecclesiastes 5:12. **3:** Isaiah 52:7; Song of Songs 1:10; 1 Kings 10:22. **4:** Isaiah 17:13 and *Kalila and Dimna,* a fourth-century c.e. Indian cycle of fables which was available to HaNagid in an Arabic translation. The cycle was translated into Hebrew in the twelfth century: "For like it was the male of the peacock which, when it was pursued by a hunter, grew weary from the weight of its tail and was snared; and the weight of its tail was its misfortune and sorrow. Riches kept by its owner thereof to his hurt."

### Why Repeat the Sins

*BQ,* #144. **Line 2:** Psalms 78:40. **6:** Genesis 8:3.

### At the Treasury

*BQ,* #296. Cf. The Arabic of Dik al-Jinn al-Himsi (d. circa 850): "Time watches people in their sleep/A thief waiting for his chance" (trans. A. al-Udhari, in

*Fireflies in the Dark* (London, 1934). **Line 1:** Amos 6:4. **2:** Song of Songs 2:9. **4:** Exodus 22:1.


## KNOW OF THE LIMBS

*BQ*, #365. **Line 1:** Ezekiel 37:6. The Hebrew of lines 1–4 sets up a weave that links *atzamot* (bones), *ha'rekumot* (embroidered, decorated), *krumot* (covered), and *atzumot* (powerful, great) on the one hand, with *efer* (ash) and *'afar* (dust) on the other. I have tried to work this play into the English with the cross-weave of "know" and "bone," "limbs" and "skin," "dust" and "reduced," "power" and "powder."


## YOU MOCK ME NOW

*BQ*, #388. **Lines 3–4:** *Pesiqta deRab Kahana* 26:9: "Many a young ass has died and had its skin turned into saddlecloths for its dam's back." Also, *Sanhedrin* 52a: "Moses and Aaron once walked along, with Nadab and Abihu behind them, and all Israel following in the rear. Then Nadab said to Abihu, 'Oh that these old men might die, so that you and I should be the leaders of our generation.' But the Holy One, blessed be He, said unto them: 'We shall see who will bury whom.' R. Papa said: Thus men say: 'Many an old camel is laden with the hides of the young.'"


## TIME DEFIES AND BETRAYS

*BQ*, #169. **Line 1:** Deuteronomy 21:8. **2:** Literally, "haughty and proud." Numbers 32:13. **3:** Literally, "lengthens the wandering of the separated." **4:** Literally, "and it comes between twins as between north and south."


## THE MARKET

*BQ*, #314; *HaShira*, #41:9. Several poems in the diwan begin like this one and employ the same form and locutions. The Hebrew end rhyme (and often the internal rhyme at the hemistich) throughout the poem is on the syllable *dahm*, which by itself means "blood." **Line 1:** *Hullin* 9a: "Rab Judah stated in the name of Samuel, one may not eat of the slaughtering of any butcher who does not know the rules of *shehita* (ritual slaughter)." **3–4:** Literally, "and fatlings [or beasts] as many as the fish of the sea, and much poultry, their day of great fear come." Ezekiel 47:10; Jeremiah 46:21: "Their day of calamity was come upon them." **5:** Exodus 15:8. **23–24:** The texture and weave of these extremely slippery lines is wonderfully complex and in many respects misleading, in a sense epitomizing the aural and thematic effects of the poem as a whole. The Hebrew sounds like this: *lo nimtza et lo met bo met o et lo yolid molidahm*, which would translate literally as "there is never found a time in which a dead [or mortal] thing didn't die, or a time that does not give birth to those that bear them." In other words, as with beasts, so with people: they are being born and dying all the time, and at the same time. At first it appears that HaNagid is talking about people, but in fact he is still talking about the beasts of the previous lines, which are likened to people. (See Elitzur, *Shirat HaHol*, pp. 235–40.) **28:** Ecclesiastes 12:13. Translations of the line in the biblical text vary from "This is the whole duty of man" to "This is the end of man" to "This is the whole person" to "For this applies to all mankind." "This" refers to "keeping the commandments," though HaNagid angles the verse at the preceding lines of his own poem, which liken this world to the bustling market and allude to Ecclesiastes 3:19–21: "Man has no pre-eminence over a beast, for all is vanity." Avraham Ibn Ezra's commentary on Ecclesiastes (which postdates HaNagid by nearly a century) resembles HaNagid's approach in this poem.

## YOSEF IBN HASDAI

The poet's son is also of interest, since he served as a high-ranking vizier under three Saragossan rulers and became an accomplished poet in Arabic. He may have converted to Islam.

### THE QASIDA

*HaShira*, #54; *BT*, #51\*. HaNagid replies in a similarly lavish poem (*BT* #51, not translated here) that he will take care of the refugees, whom he refers to as the poet's nephews. **Lines 1–11:** The first part of the qasida, the erotic prelude, has often been treated as a wholly independent unit by poets and critics. Recent scholars, especially of Arabic poetry, have put forth more integrated (and more persuasive) theories of the qasida, demonstrating how its seemingly autonomous parts interact—though, again, this shouldn't imply an identification of addressees in the various sections of the poem. See, for example, J. Meisami, *Structure and Meaning in Medieval Arabic and Persian Poetry* (London, 2003), pp. 13–14, and *Persian Court Poetry*, pp. 30–39; J. Stetkevych, "Arabic Poetry and Assorted Poetics," in *Islamic Studies: A Tradition and Its Problems*, ed. M. Kerr (Malibu, 1980), pp. 103–23; M. Sells, "The Qasida and the West: Self-Reflective Stereotype and Critical Encounter," *Al-'Arabiyya* 20 (1987): 305–57; S. Stetkevych, *The Mute Immortals Speak* (Ithaca, 1993), pp. 3ff. **2:** Psalms 104:2. **3–4:** Micah 1:6; Jeremiah 26:18. **7–8:** The figure of the fawn (the young man) is, as Ezra Fleischer notes, subtly developed here and restored to its original meaning—a wild animal—through the metaphor of the snare. It is this sort of subtle linkage, says Fleischer, that, along with the powerfully sensual opening and transition, won the hearts of Ibn Hasdai's contemporaries and makes the poem one of the period's finest. **21–24:** Fleischer rightly calls this transition—in which a dream leaves behind it a palpable fragrance, which is felt in the texture of the verse itself—"a tour de force." The passage to the body of the poem is enacted by means of the *takhallus* (the transition), i.e., line 23, in which a distant scriptural association (Song of Songs 1:3: "Thy name is as ointment poured forth") links the subject's name and reputation with a pleasant fragrance's effect on those whom it reaches. Again, the poem's energy is modulated and transformed through the rhetorical device, or "ornament," though the allusion does not involve direct quotation. Also Song of Songs 5:5. **26:** 2 Samuel 23:1. **29–30:** That is, Samuel the prophet, of Scripture. This second and main part of the poem comprises the "ode" itself—praise of its recipient and the values he embodies. In keeping with the polythematic nature of the qasida, however, numerous subjects and themes are treated within the ode. This poem takes up—in addition to the eroticism of the opening and the encomium of the body of the poem—description (of the pen), friendship, and, a final "message." The lines involve an elaborate return through allusion to the association of fragrance and Scripture, on a literal level, in order to praise HaNagid hyperbolically. **31–32:** Isaiah 47:9; Daniel 12:12 (NJPS): "arise to your destiny [at the end of days]." **37–38:** Job 29:3; 31:26. **39–40:** Isaiah 8:16: "Bind up the testimony"; 9:5: "and the government is upon his shoulder." **49–50:** I.e., when my soul was actively engaged with yours, I was happy; when all I have left is the memory of that love, I am empty and like a desert landscape. **61:** Riding the hand or fingers, i.e., writing; when it's lying flat, unused, it's worthless. Ibn Hasdai is most likely alluding to the importance of writing in HaNagid's rise to power and glory, and of course to his talent as a poet. **63:** Two teeth—the nib, which is usually forked; its spit—the ink. **67:** Yehosef is HaNagid's son, who later replaced him as the prime minister of Granada. Genesis 49:22. **70:** Genesis 41:45: "Pharaoh then gave Joseph the name Zaphenath-paneah" [Egyptian for "God speaks; he lives" or "creator of life"]. Literally, "[for] one who solves all hidden things." **71:** HaNagid was a Levite, a descendant of Qehat (Numbers 3:17). **73:** *Avot* 5:24: "At ten [one is ready for] Mishna." **75–76:** Jeremiah 2:3. The priestly portion is the portion of the harvest reserved for the high priest. Yehosef is likened to the best portion given to God. **77:** I.e., I'm prepared to do anything for him, even die. **79–98:** While technically part of the body of the ode, this "conclusion" or "message" might be understood as an echo of the pre-Islamic qasida. **85–86:** "Intended" as in both "betrothed" and "addressed." In the medieval intellectual context, "virgin," referring to a poem or its ideas, means new or original. "Orphaned," as explained above, also indicates a unique status. Literally, "though it has a father, it is an orphan (*yetoma*)," i.e., unique. **88–92:** Two brothers: apparently refugees. **90:** Literally, "whose lands lie, like Admah, in ruin." Admah is a biblical land laid waste (Deuteronomy 29:22; Hosea 11:8). **94:** Schirmann says this refers to the heads of the yeshiva in Granada, i.e., the city's scholars, who are physically far from the poet, but close to his heart. **98:** I.e., the congregation of Israel (the phrase in the Hebrew is feminine).

# SHELOMO IBN GABIROL

As with Shmu'el HaNagid and Todros Abulafia, the discovery of the poet's work seems to partake of the "miracle" Goitein invokes in his description of the entire period (see introduction). For while many of his liturgical poems were preserved in prayer books and recited as part of the daily and festival liturgies throughout the Jewish world, the nonliturgical poems were harder to come by and clearly not in great demand. Nor—prior to the discovery of the Cairo Geniza and its scrap heap of Scripture, scrolls, shopping lists, recipes, letters, and assorted literary gems—was there any mention of there ever having been a complete diwan of Ibn Gabirol's poems. That we have a full selection of the poet's work is only thanks to the stubborn devotion of Iraqi-Jewish poet David Zemach—who, in the 1920s, discovered the manuscript containing Ibn Gabirol's "collected poems" beside a fireplace in northern Iraq, where it was about to become fuel for the week's laundry—and the great modern Hebrew part Haim Nahman Bialik, who assembled an edition of Ibn Gabirol's poems from manuscripts scattered in libraries throughout Europe and North America. (See Cole, *Selected Ibn Gabirol*, pp. 9–11.) I have consulted Yarden's edition of the secular poems, *Shirei HaHol leR. Shelomo Ibn Gabirol* (Jerusalem, 1984), hereafter *SH*, and his edition of the liturgical poems, *Shirei HaQodesh leR. Shelomo Ibn Gabirol* (Jerusalem, 1971/72), hereafter *SQ*, as well as *Shelomo Ibn Gabirol: Shirei HaHol*, ed. H. Brody and H. Schirmann (Jerusalem, 1974), hereafter Brody-Schirmann, and *Shirei Shelomo Ben Yehuda Ibn Gabirol*, vols. 1–6, ed. H. N. Bialik and Y. Ravnitzky (Tel Aviv, 1928–30), hereafter Bialik-Ravnitsky.

## Truth Seekers Turn

*SH*, #108. Added by a later editor or copyist, the Arabic heading reads: "A poem about one who doesn't know the craft of poetry." **Line 1:** The Hebrew has "poem," singular, and might also be understood collectively as "song." **2:** Psalms 94:8. **5:** Deuteronomy 32:47: "For it is no vain thing for you; because it is your life," and Isaiah 30:7. **7–9:** "Kills the soul", i.e., it destroys him. The line alludes to the frequently anthologized lines of the Arabic poet Di'ibel Ibn 'Ali, "the devil of poets," quoted in Ibn Ezra's *Book of Discussion* 47a: "The bad poem will die before its author, whereas the good poem will live even if its speaker dies." **10:** Exodus 12:2. The Hebrew calendar is lunar, hence the prominence of the moon in the regulation of the social and natural order. According to *Sanhedrin* 42a, "Whoever pronounces the benediction over the new moon in its due time welcomes, as it were, the presence of the *Shekhina*" (the feminine aspect of the divine).

## I'm Prince to the Poem

*SH*, #109; *HaShira*, #61. Written when the poet was sixteen. By then Ibn Gabirol had already written poems to Shmu'el HaNagid in Granada and been commissioned to write four elegies for Hai Gaon, the great Eastern rabbi and head of the academy in Pumbedita. **Line 1:** There are two variant readings for "prince"—"singer" and "song"—and Schirmann uses all three at different points in his career. Ecclesiastes 10:7, Proverbs 19:10, Esther 1:3 (NJPS), 2 Samuel 19:7. **2:** The instrument in the Hebrew is *kinnor*, indicating, generally, "a string instrument played by hand," probably a lute or a kind of lyre or small harp. 1 Samuel 16:16 (NJPS); 1 Samuel 16:23; Psalms 68:26. **3:** 2 Samuel 12:30. **5:** Literally, "Here I am," which echoes the young Samuel's reply to God, when he is called to prophecy. Samuel 3:4, 8. **6:** The English image departs some from the Hebrew, for which there are two variant versions. Schirmann reads: "My heart understands (*ban*) like the heart of [a man of] eighty," or "my heart is like eighty with wisdom." Yarden has: "My heart within me (*bi*) is like the heart of [a man of] eighty." The Jerusalem Talmud, *Berakhot* 7:4: "And they went on to appoint Rabbi Elazar ben Azariah to the Yeshiva at the age of 16 and his head was covered with silver." Also, the Haggadah: "R. Elazar ben Azariah said: 'Lo, I am like a man of seventy.'"

### Prologue to *The Book of Grammar*

*SH*, #226. Drawn from Ibn Gabirol's *Sefer Ha'Anaq*, a long poem about Hebrew grammar that the poet wrote when he was nineteen. All that remains of the poem is the prologue (the beginning of which is translated here) and the first forty lines of the book itself. The prologue follows an *alef-bet* acrostic, duplicated in the translation, with the final three letters of the English (though not the Hebrew) set off in a triplet at the end. The Hebrew breaks the acrostic at one point, and the English follows suit. **Line 1:** Psalms 68:35 and 96:6. **2:** Isaiah 40:12. **3:** Isaiah 59:19; Exodus 4:11. **4:** Song of Songs 3:11. **5–6:** I.e., God gave man language and the power of speech, along with the crown of honor (the soul), which lead to our knowledge of God's remarkable work in this world and the next. Ecclesiastes 12:9; Isaiah 40:14. **6:** Job 37:14. **7:** *Hullin* 60b, where "the Small" is added to a man's name to indicate humility. Ibn Gabirol called himself Shelomo HaQatan, Solomon the Small (i.e., this Lesser, or Younger). **9:** Numbers 27:17. **10:** 2 Kings 30:6: "and the remnant that is escaped." **11:** Cf. Sa'adia Gaon's introduction to *Sefer HaEgron*, lines 27–44, ed. N. Aloni (Jerusalem, 1969), pp. 158ff., where Sa'adia tells of Israel's exile. The Jews, he says, spoke "Ashdodi," Greek, and the languages of Persia and Egypt, but not the holy tongue. Ashdod was a Philistine town on the Mediterranean coast of biblical Palestine, today the Israeli town of the same name, between Gaza and Jaffa. **12:** Isaiah 59:16. **13–14:** Nehemiah 13:24; Job 19:13. **15–16:** "Edom" in the world of Andalusian Hebrew poetry is Rome. "Edomite" in this case is probably the Romance precursor to Spanish. "The tongue of Qedar" is Arabic. Song of Songs 1:5; Isaiah 21:16. **17:** Literally, "in the enclosures of their heart sinking into the depths of the abyss." **18:** Literally, "sinking like lead." Exodus 15:10. **19–20:** Jeremiah 45:3 and 20:9. **21–22:** Jeremiah 48:36; Isaiah 16:11. The Hebrew plays on the root *k-n-r* in *kinnor* (harp) and *yam kinneret* (the Sea of Galilee, or the harp-shaped sea). **23–24:** Literally, "They didn't know prophecy [the books of the Prophets] or the Book [Torah], or how to read a letter or scholarly composition." Isaiah 29:11–12. **25–26:** Exodus 15:4; Jonah 1:13: "The men rowed hard to bring it to the land, but they could not." **27–28:** Isaiah 42:7 **29–30:** Exodus 4:11; Psalms 63:12, 38:14; Ruth 2:12. **31–32:** Job 32:6; Isaiah 51:20; Deuteronomy 28:20. **33:** Deuteronomy 30:17; Job 4:12–16. **34:** Proverbs 8:1–3. **36:** Psalms 119:173. **37–38:** Literally, "Get up and do not say, I am only a youth." Jeremiah 1:5–7: "I have appointed thee as a prophet unto the nations [said the Lord]. Then said I: 'Ah, Lord God! behold, I cannot speak; for I am a child.' But the Lord said unto me: Say not: I am a child"; Job 32:9. **39–40:** Literally, "My horn was exalted." 1 Samuel 2:1; Genesis 24:50. **41:** Ecclesiastes 2:3. A xyst (pronounced *zist*) was, in ancient Rome, a garden walk lined with trees. It prefigures images in the poem's second section (not translated), where Ibn Gabirol describes his *'Anaq* as a garden full of myrtle, roses, and tall trees (lines 30–31 in Yarden). It also points ahead to the extended and highly charged descriptions of gardens later in the diwan. "In Spain," says James Dickie, who has written extensively on gardens and garden architecture in Andalusia, "one can never get very far away from Ancient Rome." (*The Legacy of Muslim Spain*, ed. S. Jayyusi [Leiden, 1994], p. 1024). **42:** The "language of Cain" is, literally, "the holy tongue"; I've sought to avoid the repetition of the phrase (from line 8) and freely interpolated this epithet. It was generally believed in the medieval world that Hebrew was the language given to Adam.

### They Asked Me as though They Were Mystified

*SH*, #51. **Line 1:** "Like clouds," i.e., like clouds that bestow rain generously over the land. **3:** Isaiah 14:17. **4:** Exodus 35:22; Jeremiah 11:22. In medieval Arabic poetry, the liberal man is likened to clouds, rain, and rivers.

### See the Sun

*SH*, #158; *HaShira*, #68. An elegy for the poet's patron Yequti'el, who was murdered by rivals at the Saragossan court in 1039, at the age of ninety-nine. The loss was catastrophic for Ibn Gabirol, who had little means of his own and had held Yequti'el in the highest esteem. This is one of his more famous short poems, distinctive in part for its merging of a private sensation of loss with a larger, cosmic response to that loss. **Line 1:** Genesis 27:27. **2:** Isaiah 1:18. The Hebrew word for "crimson" is *tola'a*, which also means a worm, from which a red dye was made. Crimson, then, carries overtones of Yequti'el's glory, of the blood shed in his murder, and of the worms that "eat through the shrouds" of the dead in the earth. Also Isaiah 14:11: "Thy pomp is brought down to the nether-world; and the noise of thy psalteries: The maggot is spread under thee, and the worms cover thee (*oomekhasekha tolei'ah*)." **3:** The Hebrew verb employed here *(tifashet)* is used in Scripture only with regard to the dead. 1 Samuel 31:8; 2 Samuel 23:10. For "edges," see Numbers 35:5, 24:17. **4:** Daniel 8:8. **6:** Isaiah 16:3; Psalms 91:1, 36:8: "And the children of men take refuge in the shadow of Thy wings." **7:** The progression of colors is often central to the effect of Ibn Gabirol's poetry: here the movement is from implied daylight to red to violet to grayish black. Isaiah 50:3; Jeremiah 4:28. **8:** 2 Kings 19:1.

## On Leaving Saragossa

*SH*, #111; *HaShira*, #74. The Arabic heading reads: "Another of his poems, from the time he was leaving Saragossa." While the poet at first appears to be emotionally out of control, in fact the poem is cunningly built through a series of paradoxes and mirroring devices that lend it a particular brilliance. The shift from self-praise or boasting (*fakhr*) to mockery of others is characteristic of the poet's Arabic models. It is also one of the many binary oppositions that characterize his work. **Lines 1–2:** Psalms 69:4; Lamentations 4:4; Psalms 137:6. **3–4:** Psalms 38:11; Deuteronomy 26:14. **5–6:** Psalms 132:4. **7–8:** Job 6:11; Psalms 79:5, 89:47. **9–10:** Jeremiah 6:10. **11–12:** Lamentations 1:21; Psalms 73:23. **13–14:** Psalms 142:3, 62:9; Numbers 23:13. **15–16:** Job 32:20; *Yoma* 75a. **17–18:** Psalms 122:6; Isaiah 60:5; Psalms 65:8. **19–20:** Zechariah 7:12; Isaiah 74:4. **23–24:** Numbers 16:9; Jonah 4:11. **25–26:** 1 Kings 2:34: "He was buried in his own house in the wilderness"—there is an internal rhyme of *niqbar* (buried) and *midbar* (wilderness, desert), with *midbar* also being a common term in medieval discourse for a graveyard. **27–28:** Psalms 69:30, 25:16, and 119:141: "I am small and despised." **29–30:** A play of roots in the Hebrew between *re'a* (friend) and *ra'ayoni* (my idea) leads into the complex patterning of the entire poem: the poet longs for a friend and finds only his mind; in his mind is wisdom. By wearing away his existence (his body) he can come closer to the object of his desire (wisdom and friend), whom he finally finds in himself-not-himself, Solomon the elder (of Ecclesiastes' wisdom literature), not Solomon the Younger, or the Small (see "Prologue to *The Book of Grammar*," note to line 7). **31–32:** Psalms 102:10, 90:6. The mingling of blood and tears is a standard image in Arabic poetry. **33–34:** Ezekiel 5:12. **35–36:** *Yebamot* 112a: "Three [classes] of women must be divorced. . . . One who declares . . . 'Heaven is between me and you'"; Nehemiah 9:6. **37–38:** Genesis 23:4; Job 30:29; Lamentations 4:3, a verse that is followed by the allusion of line 1: "The tongue of the suckling cleaves." **39–40:** Proverbs 26:12. **41–42:** Jeremiah 8:14; Job 20:16. **43–44:** Jeremiah 9:7; Genesis 43:20: "If you please, my Lord, said [Joseph's brothers]" (NJPS). **45–46:** Job 30:1. **47–48:** Isaiah 1:18. **49–50:** The verse here involves a characteristic reversal of the terms involved in the scriptural allusion to Numbers 15:33: "And there we saw the Nephilim, the sons of 'Anak [the giant], and we were in our own sight as grasshoppers and so we were in their sight." **51–52:** Literally, "When I take up my parables [or images] they quarrel." Job 27:1; Joel 4:6–8. **53–54:** Literally, "this language [of yours] is the language of Ashqelon"—a non-Hebrew coastal city in Scripture, near Ashdod, likewise non-Israelite. Joshua 13:3; Nehemiah 13:24. Jeremiah

5:15; 2 Kings 18:25. See "Prologue to the Book of Grammar," note to line 11. **55–56:** The Hebrew of line 56 involves another of the poem's striking internal rhymes (see note to lines 25–26, 97–98, and 101–2): *qilshoni* (my pitchfork) *leshoni* ([is] my tongue/language). 2 Samuel 22:42; Psalms 64:4; Jeremiah 9:7. Expressing this sort of contempt for one's rivals and other people in general, in the context of self-praise, is a rhetorical strategy taken over from Arabic poetry, though, again, it seems particularly suited to Ibn Gabirol. **57–58:** Jeremiah 6:10; Hosea 10:3. **59–60:** The primary allusion is to Judges 8:21: "And Gideon arose . . . and took the crescents that were on their camels' necks." But the camels in the poem may also be associated with the Arabic pre-Islamic qasida, in which these noblest of animals take the poet/hero across the desert (see lines 25–26). There the camels are contrasted to the other animals also alluded to in the early qasidas; here the other "animals" are the people—snakes, oxen, ostriches, creatures lower than dogs, and so on. **61–64:** Job 29:23: "And they opened their mouths wide as for the latter [spring] rain."—"Latter rain"—in the Hebrew, *malqosh*—echoes the pitchfork (*qilshoni*) of lines 55–56. Also Exodus 30:23. **65–66:** Nega'aim 12:6; Psalms 120:5. **67–68:** Hosea 4:1; Proverbs 2:5; Deuteronomy 18:11; Leviticus 20:27. **69–70:** Micah 1:8; Jeremiah 4:8; Joel 1:13. **71–72:** Isaiah 58:5; *Ta'anit* 2:9: "The first three fasts are on Monday, Thursday, and Monday." **73–74:** Ecclesiastes 9:4. **75–76:** Zechariah 4:10. **77–78:** Jonah 4:3; Psalms 116:15: "Precious in the sight of the Lord is the death of His saints." **79–80:** Proverbs 7:25; Job 31:33. **81–82:** Psalms 7:17, 35:13. **83–84:** Habakkuk 2:16. **87–88:** Ruth 4:1. The constellation referred to specifically is the Great Bear (the sons of the bear). **89–90:** Genesis 27:40. **91–92:** Hosea 14:9; Deuteronomy 28:28. It isn't clear whether "blindness" is being used metaphorically or refers to an extension of Ibn Gabirol's illness. **93–94:** Job 7:15; Psalms 71:3. **95–96:** Genesis 27:46. **97–98:** Another instance of the conspicuous word play referred to above. This time the two terms involved are *sesoni* (my joy) and *asoni* (my downfall or disaster, i.e., death), which is then reversed in the following hemistich. The English resorts to a more conspicuous alliteration. **99–100:** Ecclesiastes 2:21; Proverbs 5:11; Psalms 71:9. **101–2:** Yet another two conspicuous consonant shifts, the former appearing at least two other times in Ibn Gabirol's diwan, and once in HaNagid. In line 101 the terms are *anaha* (sigh) and *hanaha* (repose/rest/assumption); in 102 *rezoni* (my leanness—from his asceticism or perhaps his illness) and *mezoni* (my food, nourishment—implying spiritual nourishment and/or the world to come). **103–4:** Ecclesiastes 1:13; Proverbs 2:3–5: "Yea, if thou call for understanding, lift up thy voice for discernment; if thou seek her as silver, and search for her as for hid treasures, then shalt thou understand the fear of the Lord, and find the knowledge of God." **105–6:** Job 12:22; Psalms 119:18. **107–8:** Ecclesiastes 2:10: "This was my portion from all my labor."

## My Heart Thinks as the Sun Comes Up

*SH,* #193. **Line 1:** Isaiah 10:7. **4:** Genesis 38:18; Exodus 22:25.

## Now the Thrushes

*SH*, #199. **Lines 1–2:** The Hebrew has a general term for "songbirds," drawn from Isaiah, *benot 'agur*. "Thrush" picks up on that bird's distinction for song, as the prosody of the translation enfolds an homage to Hardy and his sense of the line. Isaiah 13:21; Isaiah 38:14; Psalms 48:5: "For, lo, the kings assembled themselves"; Ezekiel 17:6; Jeremiah 31:18. The gist of the Hebrew is that the birds sing naturally, without having been taught. The implicit contrast is with the court singers and, by extension, the poets who would likely be in attendance at the garden gatherings. **3–4:** It's natural for birds to sing and men to drink, though the learned among the latter need some coaxing. Song of Songs 6:11; Exodus 18:9. **5–6:** Zechariah 9:18. **7–8:** The natural (untaught) approaches the courtly (taught), and the circle comes round. *Genesis Rabbah* 13:2: "All the shrubs of the field and trees were as though speaking to one another." See also L. Ginzberg, *Legends of the Jews* (Philadelphia, 1925/53), 2:60–61: "Hippolytus . . . explicitly states . . . that according to the Jewish view 'all things in creation are endowed with sensation, and that there is nothing inanimate'"; Exodus 12:27: "And the people bowed the head and worshipped"; 1 Kings 22:24: "Which way went the spirit [*ruah*, which also means 'wind'] of the Lord from me to speak?"; Psalms 103:16: "For a wind passeth over it, and it is gone"; Numbers 5:14; Job 37:21.

## Winter with Its Ink

*SH*, #189; *HaShira*, #79. **Line 1:** The tight musical weave of the Hebrew throughout the poem, but especially at the start, matches the look of the letter and the garden. Winter implies the Mediterranean rainy season, as in Song of Songs 2:11: "For, lo, the winter is past, the rain is over." Generally it can be taken to refer to the months October–March. See Targum Onqelos to Genesis 8:22; Psalms 72:6; also *Pirqei Rabbi Eliezer* 5:23: "But when the Holy One, blessed be He, wanted to bless the growth of the earth . . . he opened his treasure of good in the heavens and sent down rain to the earth; these rains were masculine waters and the earth immediately conceived, as a bride is made pregnant by her first husband. There grew there the seeds of blessing." **2:** I.e., as the lightning comes through the clouds, the pen runs through (is held in) the palm or hand. Psalms 45:2: "My tongue is the pen of a ready writer." **5–8:** The vocabulary of craft-work is drawn from accounts in Exodus of the building of the tabernacle by Bezalel. Also 2 Chronicles 26:15. **5–6:** 1 Samuel 2:3. **7:** Scheindlin reads *hamda* as "longed for," though he notes that most editors explain that the word in this context meant "envied." "Longed for" (as in "coveted") seems to me to convey the more complicated overtones of *hamda*, which implies both envy and desire, and maintains the erotic elements of the personification. **8:** Literally, "like its (the sky's) [or his] stars." The larger harmony between the heavens and the earth exists in the mind, or in the art, of the poet, who likens the flowers to stars and seeks an explanation for the correspondence he senses. Other writers have suggested a

slightly different, but convincing reading, in which the sky (male) writes a love let-
ter to the earth (female) with its rain. In response to the calligraphy of the sky, the
earth embroiders a message of longing along its furrows, reflecting or represent-
ing the stars. Regardless of how one reads it, the central dynamic is between up-
per world and lower world, and the so-called ornamental arts are central to its
equation. (For more on the role and nature of ornament in this poetry, see the in-
troduction to this volume, note 66 and the text: for more on the image of the pri-
mal calligrapher, and the calligraphed manuscript–garden comparison in poetry,
see A. Schimmel, *Calligraphy and Islamic Culture*, (New York, 1984), p. 4 and pp.
121–23.)

## THE GARDEN

*SH* #181. While this poem is classified by Yarden as a descriptive nature poem,
Ibn Gabirol characteristically transcends the limits of the convention, as the
poem also powerfully embodies the poetics of *badii'a*, which Ibn Qutayba says
"makes meanings subtle and speech delicate" (Adonis, *Arab Poetics*, trans. Cather-
ine Cobham [Austin, 1990], p. 50). For more on *badii'a*, see the glossary at the end
of this anthology.

The heading to the poem in Brody-Schirmann reads: "In which the various or-
naments (*badii'a*) are employed in the supplest fashion, with power and original-
ity; a poem that describes the garden beds and the changing conditions of the
sun in relation to them." **Line 1:** Song of Songs 5:2; Exodus 16:8: "The floods
stood upright as a heap"—Ibn Gabirol uses the scriptural figure from Moses'
"Song of the Sea" (celebrating deliverance from Israel's Egyptian oppressors) to
describe the miraculous solid state of the water; Scripture refers to "floods," Ibn
Gabirol to "dew"; Psalms 33:7. **2:** Psalms 147:18: "He sendeth forth His word and
melteth them." **3–4:** Literally, "it trickles through me." The Hebrew uses the
same word (*yitfu*—literally, "drip") to characterize the action of the dew and the
"juices" of the vine. Joel 4:18; also Amos 9:13, and the great Muslim prose writer,
al-Jaahiz, on *nabiidh*, date wine: "When *nabiidh* soaks into your bones, spreads to
every organ and suffuses into your brain, it clarifies your mind, redeems your
spirit [from care], relaxes you in body and soul . . . it seeps into your soul and
mingles with your blood" (*The Life and Works of Jahiz*, ed. Charles Pellat, [Berke-
ley, 1969], p. 54); Abu Nuwas: "[Wine] flows through their limbs like healing
through a sick body" (*'Abbasid Belles-Lettres*, ed. J. Ashtiany et al. [Cambridge,
1990], pp. 230–31). **6:** Exodus 26:11, where "clasps" are part of the ornamental
equipment of the sanctuary. **7:** Ezekiel 8:17; Deuteronomy 33:10. The Hebrew for
"fragrance" recalls the myrrh of the Song of Songs (3:6) and the incense offered
on the altars of Exodus (30:7). **8:** Zechariah 1:8, 10, 11: "I saw in the night and be-
hold a man riding upon a red horse and standing among the myrtles." In contrast
to the messianic associations of myrtle in Zechariah, Yarden suggests that "myr-
tle" is simply a generic term for "flowers," or that one is walking among the

flowering myrtle trees or bushes. In classical literature the myrtle is sacred to Venus and an emblem of love. **9–10:** Psalms 58:9. There is some dispute over how to read the word *tzitz*, which is used twice. The first time it means "flower" or "blossom" (Isaiah 40:6 and Numbers 17:23; 1 Kings 6:18: "And the cedar on the house [the Temple] . . . was carved with knops and open flowers"). In interpreting the second usage, most editors draw from the reference to Ibn Janaah and Jeremiah 48:9: "Give wings unto Moab." The line says that one who walks about in the garden will be lifted into the air on a petal—or the wing of a petal—so as not to crush the flower beds. Other scriptural allusions are at work as well and establish an association with the ornament of the high priest: Exodus 28:36–38; Leviticus 8:9. **11–12:** Isaiah 61:10: "As a bride adorneth herself with her jewels"; Isaiah 3:18. The great Arab poet al-Mutanabbi writes: *wa-fi 'anaq al-hasnah yithasan al-'iqd* ("On the neck of the beautiful woman the necklace is made more beautiful"), which has a similar subject and chiastic structure. The image of the sun as a bride is taken from Arabic poetry. **14:** Leviticus 26:17. **15–16:** 2 Kings 23:11: "And he took away the horses that the king of Judea had given to the sun . . . and he burned the chariots of the sun with fire." The combination of images in these lines recalls *Kingdom's Crown*, particularly cantos 14 and 16. E. Zemach suggests the source of the image is the Greek myth of Apollo, the sun god, who gallops with chariots of fire across the sky. The story, he says, might have reached the Jewish poets through Arabic sources, but he also notes related images in *Pirqei Rabbi Eliezer* 6 and other Jewish sources that show Greek influence. See E. Zemach, *KeShoresh Etz* (Tel Aviv, 1973), pp. 109ff. **17:** Yarden has "as you pass through the gardens." **18:** Proverbs 26:23. **20:** Psalms 68:14: "The wings of the dove are covered with silver, and her pinions shimmer with gold." **21–22:** Isaiah 60:14; Isaiah 49:23; *Sanhedrin* 91b: "Antoninus said to Rabbi: 'Why does the sun rise in the east and set in the west?' He replied, 'Were it reversed thou wouldst ask the same question.' 'This is my question,' said he. 'Why does it set in the west?' He answered: 'In order to salute its Maker.'" Also *Kingdom's Crown*, canto 15. **24:** Zemach notes that in the Jewish wedding ceremony the groom marks the taking of the bride into the sphere of his protection by drawing her in under a *tallit* or a hat or a coat (which is red in some communities)—biblical precedents for which are found in Ruth 3:9 and Ezekiel 16:8. Other readers have commented on the associations of the image with death, adding that the poem in many ways echoes the myth of Persephone.

## The Field

*SH*, #182. The heading in Schirmann reads: "And he offered this description of the abundant rainfall and the appearance of the first grasses." Once again the poem registers an "upper world/lower world" correspondence; again the poet depicts a battle between darkness and light, and brings about a stunning reversal of polarities. **Line 1:** 2 Samuel 22:12; Job 6:5; 1 Samuel 6:12. **2:** Genesis 40:6–7;

Nehemiah 2:2–3. **3:** Some editors read this line as "like the masts of a ship." The translation is based on Brody-Schirmann and refers to the difference between the heavy storm clouds of line 1, *'avei-shehaqim*, and lighter cirrus clouds implied by the word *'anan*. **4:** Again there are variant readings for this line: Zemach reads "like hunters blasting at rams' horns." The Hebrew alludes to Joshua 13:3 ("lords") and Joshua 6:4–9 ("blast with the ram's horn"). **5:** Jeremiah 4:28; Isaiah 5:30. **6:** Job 38:7 and 6:3. **7:** Malachi 3:20; Psalms 139:9. **8:** Job 26:8; Genesis 7:11–12; Proverbs 3:20. **9–10:** Some versions of the poem have another two lines here. Schirmann, however, says they are a later addition, and he omits them. The lines refer to the heavy clouds and read: "How they stood, massed against it, while swift as an eagle they once had fled." Exodus 39:3: "And they did beat the gold into thin plates and cut it into threads to work it in the blue and the purple and the scarlet." **11:** Deuteronomy 32:22; Psalms 38:3. I.e., the rain penetrated the field. **12:** Psalms 65:10–11. **13–14:** Proverbs 27:25; Job 40:20; Deuteronomy 29:28: "The secret things belong unto the Lord, but the things that are revealed belong unto us." **15:** The Hebrew has the same *stav* here, the idea being that the poem traces the progress of the seasons. **16:** Isaiah 55:12.

## THE BEE

*SH*, #184; *HaShira*, #220. This poem treats the recitation of the most important prayer in the Jewish liturgy, the Shema', whose first part reads in the JPS translation as follows (from Deuteronomy 6:4): "Hear, O Israel; the Lord our God, the Lord is one." Following the dictates of the Midrash and the Talmud, the final syllable of the word "one" (*ehad*) and the end of the first syllable of the word "remember" (*tizkeru*) in a later part of the prayer are emphasized, for reasons outlined below. In the Brody-Schirmann edition the poem is categorized as of uncertain authorship. **Line 1:** Judges 5:12: "Awake, awake Deborah,/Awake, awake, utter a song." The line employs the wording from the "Song of Deborah"—"utter a song"—as it puns on the name Deborah (Devorah), which also means "bee." **2–3:** *Berakhot* 13b: "It has been taught: Symmachus says: Whoever prolongs the word *ehad* (one), has his days and years prolonged. R. Aha b. Jacob said: [He must dwell] on the [letter] *daleth*. R. Ashi said: Provided he does not slur over the [letter] *heth*." Cf. *Berakhot* 15b and 61b. Also *Pirqei Rabbi Eliezer* 4: "One unifies his name . . . and recites the Shema' Yisrael." The line reads, literally, "uniting and extending in 'one.'" Shulamit Elitzur suggests the image of the *daleth* may refer to an old pronunciation of the soft *daleth*, which may have sounded like the Arabic equivalent, closer to a hard *th*, as in the word "the" (*Leshonenu La'am* 397–8), and hence like the buzz of the bee. **4:** "Remember" appears in the third paragraph of the prayer: "So that you may remember and perform all my commandments." The Jerusalem Talmud, *Berakhot* 2:4: "One needs to stress [the letter *zayin*] so as to remember." The play is on the Hebrew *tizkeru*, "remember" (Numbers 15:40), and *tiskeru*, "to lease/hire/bribe", with which of course it should not be confused. Emphasizing the *z* brings the worshiper back to the the proper intention of the prayer and commandments. **5:** Song of Songs 4:11: "Honey and milk are under thy tongue." **6:** Much like Ibn Gabirol's play on Deborah/*devora* (bee), *Deuteronomy Rabbah* 1:6 contains an extended play on *devarim* (words) and *devorim* (bees): "Just as the honey of the *bee (devora)* is sweet and its sting is sharp, so too are the *words (devarim)* of the Torah; any one who transgresses them receives his punishment. . . . But any one who fulfils the Torah merits long life. . . . Another explanation: . . . Just as the *bee* reserves honey for its owner and for the stranger its sting, so to Israel the *words* of the Torah are the elixir of life, but to the other nations the poison of death." Also Deuteronomy 6:19: "To thrust out all thine enemies from before thee"; Job 20:12,14: "Though wickedness be sweet in his mouth, though he hide it under his tongue." **7:** 1 Samuel 15:17: "And Samuel said [unto Saul]: 'Though thou be little in thine own sight, art thou not head of the tribes of Israel?'" **8:** Deuteronomy 21:17: "The right of the first-born is his," where Ibn Gabirol plays on the Hebrew phrase and bends it toward meaning "the choicest sentence/portion is yours." **9:** The images relate to the question of food that is kosher, or pure. *Bekhorot* 7b: "The Divine Law expressly permitted honey. For it was taught: R. Jacob says: *Yet these may ye eat of all the winged swarming things:* . . . An unclean fowl that swarms you must not eat, but you may eat what an unclean fowl casts forth from its body. And what is this? This is bees' honey." Also Daniel 10:11, where Daniel is referred to as a "precious" man, and Ibn Janaah, *Sefer HaShorashim*, under *h-m-d*, where the reference to Daniel is explained as meaning "a man of great virtues [merit] and good qualities." **10:** Deuteronomy 14:11: "Of the clean birds you may eat."

## I'd Give Up My Soul Itself

*SH*, #197. This poem involves another classic instance of the poet's lifting a poem in a lighter genre (the wine poem, which initially seems to be an erotic poem as well) into a much more resonant and evocative mythopoetic register. **Lines 1–2:** Exodus 21:28–30: "If an ox gore a man . . . If there be laid on him a ransom, then he shall give for the redemption of his life whatsoever is laid upon him"; Psalms 49:8–9; Job 9:7. Here the speaker is (figuratively) willing to pay with his life for the serving boy's beauty (or the wine he offers), and the redemption takes on the menacing associations of the biblical context. **3–4:** Proverbs 7:21, 31:6–7: "Give strong drink unto him that is ready to perish, and wine unto the bitter in soul;/Let him drink, and forget his poverty, and remember his misery no more"; Isaiah 46:2. **5–6:** Proverbs 23:31–32: "Look not thou upon the wine when it is red, when it giveth its color in the cup, when it glideth down smoothly; at the last it biteth like a serpent and stingeth like a basilisk"; Leviticus 11:13. The griffon is a kind of vulture and the name, by design in this translation, carries overtones of the griffin, the mythological creature. **7–8:** The Hebrew has a homonym here: "Can a *heres* (sun) be put in *heres* (clay/potsherd)?" The English intensifies the rhyme and alliteration but doesn't attempt to reproduce the pun. Isaiah 45:9; Psalms 22:16; Job 9:7. There is also a possibility that Ibn Gabirol is alluding to Deuteronomy 28:27, where *hares* indicates "the itch whereof thou canst not be healed"— i.e., his own skin disease. **9–10:** The slippery syntax of these lines (where the referent of "its" is twice suspended and initially unclear in the Hebrew) extends and complicates the allusion of the first stanza, wherein the wine poses a threat with its smooth talk. Psalms 13:3; Proverbs 31:6–7, above, lines 5–6. **11–12:** Bashan appears in Deuteronomy as a region in what is today northern Jordan and southern Syria. Hosea 2:20. Og's sixty fortified cities were legendary. Deuteronomy 3:4–11: "And we took all [of Og, King of Bashan's] cities. . . . All these were fortified cities, with high walls, gates, and bars. . . . For only Og, King of Bashan, remained of the remnant of the Rephaim, and behold his bedstand was a bedstand of iron . . . nine cubits [fifteen feet] was the length thereof, and four cubits [six-and-a-half feet] the breadth of it." *Rephaim* means, literally, ghosts, though in this biblical verse it refers to a race of giants. To appreciate the powers of the wine in this poem, it helps to recall the figure of Og in the Oral Tradition. There we read that "Og was born before the Flood and was saved from it by Noah on the promise that he and his descendants would serve Noah as slaves in perpetuity. Sihon and Og were giants, their foot alone measuring eighteen cubits. . . . During his reign he founded sixty cities, which he surrounded with high walls, the lowest of which was not less than sixty miles in height" (*Encyclopedia Judaica* [1972], 12:1341–42).

### Be Smart with Your Love

*SH*, #211. Schirmann suggests that while Ibn Gabirol's other love poems involve the young poet trying his hand at the genre and embracing its "ideal," this poem, precisely because it breaks with the conventions of erotic verse, might accurately reflect the poet's experience. **Line 1:** Literally, "Consider and love," with the Hebrew word for "consider"—or in this translation, "be smart"—also meaning "set limits" or "check." Deuteronomy 13:15. **2:** Literally, "find scale [balance] for your love and a circle [boundary]." Proverbs 4:26. Also, Proverbs 16:11: "A balance and just scales." **3:** Literally, "while I looked into the limits [or 'that which has been searched out' or 'the deep things'] of love"—using the same roots (*h-q-r/a-h-v*) as line 1. Job 8:8, 11:7; Psalms 145:3. The poet is cautioned to be moderate, and his own inclination, as we know, is to inquire and seek out the metaphysical dimension in things. The essential word play on the root *h-q-r* pivots on the double-edged nature of "be smart" and involves a measure of self-irony, which becomes clear in the following lines. **4:** Adina, in Isaiah 47:8, means, literally, "a woman given to pleasure" or "the gentle," though it is also a name. **5:** Proverbs 27:5: "Better is open rebuke than love that is hidden." **7–8:** Psalms 74:6; Joel 4:13. **9:** Literally, "in the might of love." **10:** 1 Samuel 25:39: "And when David [the son of Jesse] heard that Nabal [the husband of Abigail] was dead, he . . . [David] sent and spoke concerning Abigail, to take her to him to wife." In Hebrew, Abigail is *Avi-guy'il*; in this poem Ibn Gabirol uses *Avigal*, for the rhyme.

ALL IN RED

*SH*, #268. The heading reads: "A clever stanza of his." **Lines 1–2:** "Red" might re-
fer to the clothes or the color of the young man's hair. The English reverses the
order of the first two lines, which are somewhat obscure in the original and in-
volve a play on the syllable *dom*, which on its own means "silent" or "mute." Isa-
iah 63:1–2: "Who is this that cometh from Edom, with crimsoned garments from
Bozrah? . . . Wherefore is Thine apparel red, And Thy garments like his that
treadeth in the wine vat?"; Genesis 25:14, Targum Jonathan, which involves a play
on the names of Ishmael's sons. While normally an epithet for Christianity,
Edom was also traditionally associated with the Messiah (see Ibn Gabirol's litur-
gical poem "You Lie in My Palace," (below), and *admoni* in the notes to that
poem). For the Hebrew reader, then, religious associations are raised in the dic-
tion of the first three lines, only to be punctured with the final line's explicitly
sexual allusion. This combination of allusions might suggest that the poem is ad-
dressed to, or about, a Slav wine-server or *saqi*, that is, a fair-haired European
convert to Islam, whom Ibn Gabirol is reassuring—he (the poet) is harmless.
Also Jeremiah 47:6; Psalms 37:7: "Resign thyself (*dom*) unto the Lord." **3–4:** Liter-
ally, either "By God" (*l'el*) or "It is in my hand to"; it appears that he is maintain-
ing the religious overtones, playing on the idiom *l'el yadi* (it is in my power).
Genesis 31:29: "It is in the power of my hand to do you hurt"; Genesis 19:1–5 for
the "men of Sodom."

YOU'VE STOLEN MY WORDS

*SH*, #126; *HaShira*, #86:1. **Line 1:** Leviticus 19:11: "Ye shall not steal; neither shall
ye deal falsely"; also Joshua 7:11; Jeremiah 23:30: "Therefore, behold, I am against
the prophets, saith the Lord, that steal My words." **2:** *Berakhot* 63a; Psalms 80:13,
89:41. **4:** Literally, "Did you hope to find [through stealing my poems] help in
trouble?" **5:** Deuteronomy 30:12. **7:** 2 Kings 3:18. **8:** Daniel 12:5, and David Qimhi's
*Sefer HaShorashim* (Berolini, 1847), p. 131, on *ye'orot*, where he explains that the
word normally means "channels," but also refers to the Nile and the Tigris
rivers. In Daniel it is "rivers."

THE ALTAR OF SONG

*SH*, #132; *HaShira*, #86:2. **Heading:** "About one who claimed for himself some
of the poet's work." **Lines 1–2:** Hosea 14:5; Job 16:19; Genesis 41:19. **3–4:** Literally,
"your knees are weak." Isaiah 35:3. **5–6:** Proverbs 1:2–3. Line 6, literally, is: "Don't
ascend on the altar of poetry by degrees [steps]." **7–8:** Exodus 20:23: "Neither
shalt thou go up by steps unto mine altar, that thy nakedness be not uncovered
thereon"; Deuteronomy 25:11: "If the wife of one draweth near to deliver her
husband out of the hand of him that smiteth him, and putteth forth her hands
and taketh him by the secrets [the private parts]."

## The Pen

Brody-Schirmann, #5. **Lines 1 and 4:** Jeremiah 9:7. The first word of the Hebrew, *'arom* (naked), puns on *'aroom*, which means clever (like the snake in the garden of Eden). For more on the use of martial imagery and writing in Arabic poetry see Schimmel, *Calligraphy*, pp. 118–19.

## If You'd Live among Men

*SH*, #176; *HaShira*, #92. G. Bargebuhr (*The Alhambra: A Cycle of Studies on the Eleventh Century in Moorish Spain* [Berlin, 1968]) calls this "an Islamic poem in the Hebrew language" and quotes "the pessimistic and somewhat gnostic" al-Ma'arri, the poet he feels had the greatest influence on Ibn Gabirol: "I see but a single part of sweet in the many parts sour/and wisdom that cries: Beget no children, if thou art wise." (trans. Nicholson). **Line 1:** The first line is deceptive in the Hebrew, as it appears to say, "if you want to live among [with] men of this world (*heled*)." The ambiguity is maintained in the English. Schirmann glosses: "to be among men who live eternal life" (relying, it would seem, on the Arabic *khuld*, i.e., eternity). Yarden reads: "If you want, among men of this world, to live [on] in eternity in the world to come." Psalms 17:14–15: "[Deliver my soul from the wicked . . . ], from men, by Thy hand, O Lord, from men of the world, whose portion is in this life, and whose belly Thou fillest with Thy treasure; Who have children in plenty, and leave their abundance to their babes. As for me, I shall behold Thy face in righteousness; I shall be satisfied, when I awake, with Thy likeness." Also Psalms 49:2; Psalms 96:48; Job 11:17. **2:** Isaiah 33:14; Nahum 2:4. **3–4:** Line 3 might also read: "Take lightly what the world . . ." Isaiah 23:9; Psalms 49:13; 2 Kings 19:10; Psalms 49:17; Proverbs 3:13–16. **5:** Genesis 16:4 (the story of Hagar and Sarah); Proverbs 13:18. **6:** This line is heretical in the Jewish tradition, where the commandment is to "be fruitful and multiply" (Genesis 1:28). See also *Nedarim* 64b, and notes to Moshe Ibn Ezra's "If You See Me," lines 17–18. 1 Chronicles 2:30: "But Seled died without children." Seled was in the line of Judah (see 1 Chronicles 2:3f.). **8:** That is, while you're alive, soul infuses your flesh; but after you die, the body will wear away and only soul will remain. Psalms 78:27; 1 Samuel 16:11; Job 16:15.

## I Am the Man

*SH*, #102; *HaShira*, #56. **Heading:** "And he was up late one Friday night and was looking about. And the light of the moon guided his way until the clouds thickened in the air and the horizon grew dark. As the rain began falling, the moon disappeared and he couldn't see it. Then he described this situation and recited a poem that became famous." Yehuda Ratzhaby reads the heading differently: "He went out to read by the light of the moon"—since it was the Sabbath and reading by lamplight was forbidden (*Leqet Shirim Metequfat HaZohar HaSefaradit*, ed. Y. Ratzhaby [Tel Aviv, 1994], p. 59). **Line 1:** The elaborate rhetorical opening alludes to Lamentations 3:1 and, by implication, to what follows there: "I am the man that hath seen affliction." The second half of the first line reads literally: "girded up his loins" [or "belt"] and alludes to 1 Kings 18:46: "And the hand of the Lord was on Elijah, and he girded up his loins." Also Job 38:3 and 40:7, where the Lord says to Job, out of the whirlwind: "Gird up now thy loins like a man." **2:** Numbers 30:16. **3:** Literally, "whose heart [mind] was frightened by his heart [mind]." Schirmann glosses: "whose drive." Ratzhaby comments: "when his old heart, the seat of wisdom, saw what his new heart had vowed, it trembled in fear." Song of Songs 5:2. Septimus suggests that the line alludes to several rabbinic sources (*Yalqut Shim'oni* 296, *Midrash Tehillim* 14:1), where man is described as having two hearts, i.e., two impulses, one to good, one to evil, and that what appears to be the presentation of a modern "divided self" is in fact a standard medieval figure (Dov Septimus, "He'arot leDivrei HaZaL beShirat Sefarad," *Tarbiz* 53 [1983/84]: 1). It might also simply mean that his body and spirit were at war. **4:** Job 7:15–16. **6:** Isaiah 48:10; Psalms 12:7: "The words of the Lord are pure words, as silver tried in a crucible on the earth, refined seven times." **7–8:** Ecclesiastes 3:2–3; Jeremiah 1:10; Isaiah 5:5. **10:** Or, "as misfortune surrounds him." **11:** Literally, "And the children of the daughter of days." The tenses in English depart from the Hebrew, and some commentators understand these lines to read: "He'd have made it to the limits of wisdom and right conduct if it hadn't been for misfortune, which surrounded him, and fate, which shut him in." **12:** Proverbs 1:7. **13:** Jeremiah 31:37. **16:** Psalms 73:26. **21:** I.e., "Even if the day (fate, time) doesn't help me." Genesis 22:3: "Then Abraham rose up early and saddled his ass"—to climb the mountain as God had commanded. **23:** Numbers 30:15–16. **25:** Job 3:25: "For the thing which I did fear is come upon me, and that which I was afraid of hath overtaken me"; Proverbs 10:24. **26–27:** For Yarden's and Bialik-Ravnitzky's "it was night," Schirmann has: "While I was resting [sleeping, staying over for the night]"—opening the possibility that this might have been a dream-vision. Psalms 24:4. **29:** Isaiah 59:13: "conceiving and uttering." This line in the Hebrew, like its biblical precedent, has proven hard to decipher, and the English maintains the ambiguity. The implication is that Ibn Gabirol saw the moon as a powerful, even magical, guide. **32:** Malachi 3:17. **34:** 1 Kings 20:38. **36:** Jeremiah 6:7. **37:** Isaiah 50:3. **39–40:** 2 Samuel 22:12. **41–42:** Numbers 22:6, 31:8 and Deuteronomy 23:5 for the story of Bilaam (Balaam) and the circumstances of his death. **43:** 1 Samuel 17:38: "And [Saul] clad [David] in a coat of mail"—before he went out to face Goliath. **48:** Jeremiah 48:40. **49:** The image of darkness as a raven appears often in Arabic poetry, from pre-Islamic verse on. Here it is lightning that sends the ravens up into the air. There are various interpretations of the referents in this line; the English maintains the ambiguity of the Hebrew. **53:** As a warrior (the allusion is to Samson) breaks free from his chains, so the poet's thoughts, will, and heart would free themselves from the prison of the body. Judges 15:13–14. Also Psalms 78:65. My reading here, in many other instances, draws on Devorah Bregman's detailed study of the poem ("Tznefat Hur," *Mehqerei Yerushalayim beSifrut 'Ivrit* 14, part 2 [1988]:460). **54–55:** The transition and recapitulation of the poem's earlier images here is not altogether clear, but it seems to be saying that "this is the state of mankind," to be torn from within, and shackled and bound from without, and therefore the poet had best reconsider his ambition and accept the given state of things with humility. Job 30:26; Proverbs 20:20. See also Coleridge's "Dejection," lines 45–46: "I may not hope from outward forms to win/The passion and the life, whose fountains are within." **59:** Psalms 123:2. **60:** Literally, "has his spear beaten" (or "broken"), as in Isaiah 2:4, "into plowshares." **64:** The line might also read, literally, "though he put his holy of holies [dwelling] in the house of [among] the brightest stars [splendor]." The word in question is *noga*, which most likely refers to Venus. (See *Kingdom's Crown* 14, where Venus is associated with mirth and well-being.) At least one scriptural association, however, also suggests the moon: Isaiah 60:19. See also Proverbs 4:18–19.

## HEART'S HOLLOW

*SH,* #173; *HaShira,* #91. The Arabic heading from Brody-Schirmann reads: "And this which speaks in dispraise of Time." **Lines 1–4:** Job 11:12, "A hollow man shall get understanding" (NJPS). Bialik-Ravnitzky comments: "Man's heart is hollow and empty, and wisdom [philosophy, thought] is obscured [or blocked] to him, and only his body and its affairs are visible and apprehensible, and people are drawn to them." In short, one is trapped in the world and in the body, and only death will offer release. **6:** Literally, "find evil [or trouble]," "Corruption" picks up on Schirmann's gloss to the previous lines. **7:** This line might also be understood as "Man in the ground rejoices in nothing." **8–9:** The implied metaphor of rebellion and struggle is that of body/servant versus master/soul (or master of the world, i.e., God). Proverbs 30:22–23; 1 Kings 16:9–10; 2 Kings 9:31. **10–11:** Micah 7:6–10: "For the son dishonoreth the father, a daughter riseth up against her mother. . . . A man's enemies are the men of his own house. But as for me, I will look unto the Lord . . . He will bring me forth to the light. . . . Who said unto me: Where is the Lord thy God? Mine eyes shall gaze upon her; Now shall she be trodden down as the mire of the streets." The English reverses the order of the Hebrew images in these lines. **14:** Ecclesiastes 8:15; Job 7:5: "My flesh is clothed with worms and clods of dust." **15–16:** Ecclesiastes 3:20–21: "All go unto one place; all are of the dust, and all return to dust. Who knoweth the spirit of man whether it goeth upwards, and the spirit of the beast whether it goeth downward to the earth?" Also Ecclesiastes' closing words: "And the dust returneth to the earth, and the spirit returneth unto God who gave it. Vanity of vanities, all is vanity." The original has "dust returns to dust," or "clay returns to clay"; "slime" in the penultimate line picks up on Micah 7:10 (above, line 10).

I Love You

SH, #74. Line for line one of the most thoroughly discussed works in all of post-biblical literature. Essentially the debate concerns the nature of the poem and its philosophical or theological implications. According to the Arabic super-scription it is "an answer to a student who has asked about the nature of existence." Bialik-Ravnitizky refers to another source wherein it is described, by R. David Qimhi, as a poem about "the mysteries of creation." It is important to note in this context that there is also a legend according to which Ibn Gabirol created a golem: "They said of R. S[helomo] Ben Gabirol, that he created a woman, and she waited on him. When he was denounced to the authorities, he showed them that she was not a perfect creature, and [then] he turned her to her original [state], to the pieces and hinges of wood, out of which she was built up" (from Shelomo del Medigo, *Matzref leHokhma*, in Moshc Idel, *Golem* [Albany, 1990] p. 233). Comparing this poem to the philosophical treatise *The Fountain of Life*, scholar Yehuda Liebes notes that "in the relationship between the teacher and the pupil the secret of creation is given expression" ("The Book of Creation in R. Shelomo Ibn Gabirol and a Commentary on His Poem 'I Love You'" [Hebrew], *The Proceedings of the Second International Congress on the History of Jewish Mysticism*, 1987, in *Mehqarei Yerushalayim* 63–4 (1987): 73–123.) For detailed English discussion of the poems' particulars and its background, see Cole, *Selected Ibn Gabirol*, pp. 261–64. **1:** Genesis 22:2: "Take now thy son, thine only son, whom thou lovest, even Isaac, and get thee into the land of Moriah"; Isaiah 43:4. **3:** Deuteronomy 6:5, from which the Shema' is taken. (See "The Bee.") **5–7:** Ecclesiastes 1:13, 7:25; Psalms 72:6. Liebes points out that Sa'adia Gaon in his introduction to the *Sefer Yetzira* also describes the first principle and the secret of creation as "far off and deep." Sa'adia raises the issues again in his major philosophical work, *The Book of Beliefs and Opinions*, where he notes that King Solomon was able to understand the issue only because he ascended from the level of philosophy to that of prophecy. As we have seen, Ibn Gabirol often identified with his biblical namesake and was also familiar with Sa'adia's influential book. **8:** Isaiah 44:18; Psalms 82:5. **11–13:** The Hebrew is particularly difficult to paraphrase, and the English is woven accordingly. Liebes suggests that the "sages" of the poem are in fact the sages of the Neoplatonic, Gnostic gospels, in particular the *Gospel of Truth* ("The Book of Creation and R. Shelomo Ibn Gabirol," pp. 120–23); Schlanger is also quoted as suggesting that the lines refer to thinkers "with gnostic tendencies." (See Ya'aqov Schlanger, *HaPhilosophia shel Shelomo Ibn Gabirol*, trans. from French by Y. Ur [Jerusalem, 1979]). "Owes all" in line 12, is based on a reading by Zemach, but is usually understood to mean "for the sake of." Proverbs 16:4; 1 Chronicles 29:11–16. Also, *Berakhot* 6:8: "He who drinks water to quench his thirst recites [the blessing]: 'For all was created at his word.'" The Hebrew for "word" in this blessing and in the poem is *davar*, one of the more complex or overloaded terms in the language; from the same root we derive "commandments," "thing," "a matter of importance," and the verb "speak." It appears three times in this poem by Ibn Gabirol. See also *Fountain of Life*, 410: "Unity [oneness] overcomes (the) all and extends through (the) all, and sustains (the) all." Line 13 might also be understood as saying that the secret, or mystery, of all creation resides in each person (in all), in their power to create. This individual aspect of "all" is used in Isaiah 43 (verse 7), a chapter Ibn Gabirol alludes to several times in the course of the poem. **14:** Literally, "He longs to appoint (or place, establish) there-is as [like] there-is," or "being as near-being." Bialik-Ravnitzky comments: "'Primary matter,' which in *The Fountain of Life* is called 'foundation,' has no true existence of its own, but is 'like-existence,' and longs to couple with 'form,' so that the Creator will give it true existence; and this desire of matter to take on form is very great . . . and according to the ancients is the reason for the eternal movement in creation." Numbers 24:23. Yarden glosses: "All things long for God to establish them in being that resembles the true being, which is the Lord." **16–18:** Isaiah 43:7: "Everyone that is called by My Name whom I have created for my glory, I have formed him, yea I have made him." **19–20:** There are two readings of the last line and numerous interpretations of their meaning. Literally, "Now, get (*qnei*) a sign to set it [him] up aright" and "Now, offer (*tena*) a sign to set it [him] up aright." Sachs, Bialik-Ravnitzky, and Liebes prefer the latter, all others—including all extant manuscripts—have the former. Arguing that the next word in the poem, *mofet* (sign, example), appears numerous times in Scripture after the verb *natan*, from which *tena* is formed, Liebes suggests that a copyist's error may have changed *tena* to *qnei* (in Hebrew only the initial letter is different)—but that in the Gabirolian context, the thrust is similar: create or form signs with your behavior that will embody what you have learned from the teacher. Exodus 97:9: "Show a wonder"; 1 Kings 13:3: "And he gave a sign the same day"; Deuteronomy 13:2.

Both readings further allude to *Sefer Yetzira* 1:4: "And put the matter straight and set the creator in his proper place." Cf. also Ezra 2:68 (which appears in *Sefer Yetzira* 1:4): "And some of the heads of the fathers' houses, when they came to the house of the Lord which is in Jerusalem, offered willingly for the house of God to set it up in its place" (or the NJPS: "to erect the House of God in its site"), where the subject of the Hebrew is one that Ibn Gabirol returns to repeatedly: a "second creation."

In distinction to other scholars who stress the passive philosophical aspects of the poem, in which the student is expected to find proof or support, perhaps in the literature, for the teacher's claims, Liebes is convinced of the fundamentally erotic nature of the final line, in which the religious pursuit is embodied. As God's love leads to the creation of the world, the teacher's love leads to the development of the student's knowledge and the alteration of his action in the world. In both cases the flow must be reversed along the ladder of being, and "spirit" raised or returned to "spirit."

BEFORE MY BEING

*SQ*, #126; *HaShira*, #96. Schirmann says this poem's genre isn't known, but that it may be a *baqasha* (poem of petition), as the first line is repeated at the end of the poem. Yarden suggests that it may be a *reshut* to the *nishmat*. (See the glossary for all three terms.) Scheindlin describes it as a poem about the creation of the human species, not just the individual person (*The Gazelle: Medieval Hebrew Poems on God, Israel, and the Soul* [Philadelphia, 1991], pp. 209–13). As in many of Ibn Gabirol's poems, examination of the microcosm of the "I" leads to contemplation of the macrocosm, and what appears to be a naive expression of religious faith is actually a complex formulation of a much less comforting philosophical understanding. One should keep in mind as well that the poem was possibly part of the liturgy. See also Yehuda HaLevi's "You Knew Me." **Line 1:** Jeremiah 1:5: "Before I formed thee in the belly I knew thee"; Psalms 119:41. **2:** *Sefer Yetzira* 2:5: "He created from utter chaos and made of the void existence." Ibn Gabirol uses this image at least five other times in his poems, including the famous instance of *Kingdom's Crown* (canto 9). Scheindlin notes the ambiguity of the Hebrew syntax, maintained in the English here, which establishes the ironic reading of the poem: the line implies that God destroys existence—brings existence or being to nothing—and also creates existence from nothingness. In this reading, the existence of the pure soul is sullied by its descent into the world of the body. **3–4:** Psalms 139:15: "My frame was not hidden from Thee, when I was made in secret, and curiously wrought in the lower parts of the earth"; Job 10:10. **5:** Genesis 2:7: "He breathed into his nostrils the breath of life." *Neshama* in the biblical citation and the poem is both "breath" and "soul." Scheindlin quotes George Herbert on prayer: "God's breath in man returning to his birth." **6:** Jonah 2:3: "Out of the belly of the netherworld cried I"; also Psalms 139:15 (lines 3–4 above). Following the Targum to the verse in Psalms, Yarden glosses: "out of the belly of my mother." Scheindlin: "The workshop in which this flesh of man was made is not Eden but Sheol." **7:** 2 Samuel 7:18; Psalms 71:17. **9:** The central prayer of the liturgy, the *'amida*: "O favor us with knowledge, understanding, and discernment. Blessed art Thou, O Lord, gracious Giver of knowledge." The line literally reads: "Who taught me understanding and made me wondrous [more than other creatures]?" **9–10:** Isaiah 64:7; Jeremiah 18:6; Job 10:9; Ezekiel 29:3. **11–12:** Psalms 32:5; Genesis 3:13. **13:** Job 27:11. **13–14:** See line 1, though now the "mercy" and act of God have taken on an ironic cast. Calling the confession of line 13 "not the humble expression of that feeling of being transparent before God . . . [but] a taunt," Scheindlin notes the possible use in line 14 of the Hebrew *hesed*, "mercy" or "kindness," as a homonym, meaning "shame," from Leviticus 20:17: "If a man shall take his sister . . . and see her nakedness, and she see his nakedness: it is a shameful thing (*hesed hu*)." I.e., the poet may be saying, "I am a sinner, but you in your so-called kindness created me as such."

## THREE THINGS

*SQ*, #138; *HaShira*, #97:2. Acrostic: *Shelomo*. Scheindlin comments: "Of all of Ibn Gabirol's poems, this miniature masterpiece most clearly, succinctly and beautifully evokes the inward-looking character of his religious thought and experience" (*Gazelle*, 191–93). He notes the poem's progression from far-off sky to earth to mind, adding that "the author of the Psalms might very well have been inspired by sky and earth to praise God; but that the mind of man should also be a source of inspiration is a distinctively medieval contribution to religious thought." Also characteristic is the opposition of first person and second person throughout the poem—so that a poem in praise of God is in fact held intact compositionally by the (on the face of it odd) repetition of the first-person pronouns referring to the speaker. **Line 3:** Isaiah 26:8; Psalms 8:4–10. On the use of God's name, see note to "The Hour of Song," lines 3–4. **4:** Psalms 19:2, 45:18; Isaiah 8:2. **5–7:** Isaiah 42:5; Job 38:4–5. **8:** Psalms 34:2, 104:1. In lines 7–8 there is an elusive play on *adanai* ("foundations")—as in "the extender of my foundations" (line 7, literally)—which is juxtaposed with *adonai* ("my Lord"), the name of God (line 8). Psalms 39:4, 5:2, 19:15.

## I LOOK FOR YOU

*SQ*, #24; *HaShira*, #97:4. A *reshut* to the *nishmat* for the Day of Atonement, and one of the more famous poems in the liturgy, as it appears in many prayerbooks. Acrostic: *Shelomo*. **Lines 1–4:** Psalms 62:7, 5:4. Line 4 might also be understood as "my morning prayer and my evening prayer." **6:** Literally, "afraid"—without "confused." Job 28:9. **7–8:** Lamentations 3:60; 1 Chronicles 28:9; Jeremiah 20:12; Genesis 615. **9–10:** Judges 8:3. Scheindlin points out that the source of the idea here is the Arabic maxim *innamaa 'l-insaan al-qalb wa-'l-lisaan* ("The being of man is the heart and tongue"). **11–12:** Job 6:11; Isaiah 26:5. **13–16:** Psalms 69:31–32, 104:34; 2 Samuel 22:50; Job 27:2–3: "As God liveth, who hath taken away my right . . . all the while my breath is in me and the spirit of God is in my nostrils." As is customary in this type of poem, the final line of the poem leads into the powerful Sabbath-morning *nishmat* prayer.

## OPEN THE GATE

*SQ*, #145; *HaShira*, #99:7. A *reshut*. Acrostic: *Shelomo*. Addressed by the congregation of Israel to God. **Lines 1–2:** The poem begins with a reversal of the situation in the Song of Songs 5:2, where the woman waits in her room and hears her beloved: "Harken! my beloved knocketh: 'Open to me, my sister, my love.'" In this poem the terms are reversed, and the feminine congregation of Israel is asking her lover, the Lord, to open the gate and come to help her. This is somewhat misleading, however, as the poem is in fact a complaint concerning Israel's condition in exile. Bialik-Ravnitzky comments: "The poet is knocking at the gates of heaven, of mercy." **3**: Psalms 6:3–6; Ezekiel 27:35. **4**: "My mother's maid" refers to Hagar, Sarah's handmaid. Genesis 16:1–4 tells the story of Hagar and her child, Ishmael, whom she bore to Abraham, and who is considered the ancestor of the Arabs in the Jewish tradition. After Hagar conceived, "her mistress was despised in her eyes." **5–6**: After Isaac was born to Sarah and Abraham, Sarah had her husband send Hagar and Ishmael away into the "wilderness of Beersheba." Genesis 21:15: "And the water in the bottle was spent, and she cast the child under one of the shrubs. And she went, and sat her down over against him . . . and lifted up her voice, and wept. And God heard the voice of the lad." Also Ezekiel 31:10. **7–9**: The allegorical vocabulary is extended here. "Midnight's blackness" is the exile from the Land of Israel; "wild ass" is a traditional epithet for Islam—Scripture having noted that Ishmael would be a "wild ass of a man" (Genesis 17:11–12), while Christianity is called a "wild boar" (*Leviticus Rabbah* 13:5, on Leviticus 11:7: "'and the swine': 'the swine,' this is Edom"). Also Psalms 80:14. Scheindlin links the use of "middle" and "midnight" to Ibn Gabirol's (and others') attempts to calculate precisely the time of the redemption, noting the scriptural context in the Book of Daniel, which also alludes to a "specific date for the redemption" (*Gazelle*, p. 107). **10**: Daniel 12:4: "But thou, O Daniel, shut up the words, and seal the book, even to the time of the end." **11**: Jeremiah 45:3. **12**: Literally, "there is no one to understand for me—and I am ignorant" ("brutish"). Daniel 8:27: "I was appalled at the vision, but understood it not"; Psalms 142:5, 73:22: "I was brutish and ignorant; I was as a beast before Thee." The English "blind" departs somewhat from the Hebrew, which is like that of the Psalms: "brutish and ignorant." I've let the music bring the English in a slightly different direction, one that picks up on trapped aspects of Ibn Gabirol's character that are made explicit in other poems.

### THE HOUR OF SONG

*SQ*, #150; *HaShira*, #97:7. A *reshut*. Acrostic: *Shelomo*. **Lines 1–4**: Psalms 31:2–6. **5–8**: Literally, "there is no helper." Psalms 142:4: "Look on my right hand and see, for there is no man that knoweth me"; Isaiah 63:5; Psalms 31:6, above (lines 1–4). "Loneness" is an epithet for the soul, as in Psalms 22:21. **9–12**: Ecclesiastes 2:10; Psalms 142:6; Ecclesiastes 2:20–21. **13–16**: "I'm immersed" for *eshgeh* is based on Yarden's note, which reads "I occupy myself," and also on Proverbs 5:19: "A lovely hind and a graceful doe, let her breasts satisfy thee at all times; with her love be thou ravished (*tishgeh*) always. Why then wilt thou, my son, be ravished with a strange woman?" Job 35:10. "Worship" and "work" in Hebrew are identical.

### SEND YOUR SPIRIT

*SQ*, #107. A *mehayyeh* for Passover, the Prayer for Dewfall. Acrostic: *Shelomo*. **Lines 1–2**: Literally, "to revive our bodies." Psalms 104:30: "Thou sendest forth thy spirit"; Nehemiah 9:20. **3–4:** *Eretz hatzvi* ("the land of desire," or "the land of glory") in the original is an epithet for the Land of Israel, as in 2 Samuel 1:19: "Thy glory [beauty], O Israel, upon thy high places is slain." The word *tzvi* here means, literally, "that which is desired."(See "gazelle" in the glossary.) Jeremiah 3:19. **5:** Hosea 14:9. **6:** Psalms 145:9: "The Lord is good to all." **7–8:** Psalms 85:7: "Wilt Thou not quicken us again?"

ANGELS AMASSING

*SQ,* #28; *HaShira,* #106. An *ofan* for the Day of Atonement. Acrostic: *Shelomo.* **Lines 1–2:** The English opening to a certain extent reflects the heavy alliterative effect of the Hebrew, which is characteristic of the genre and, as it were, imitates the sound the angels make. *Shinannim* means "thousands" and is an epithet for "angels." It is drawn from Psalms 68:18: "The chariots of God are myriad, even thousands upon thousands." Also Ezekiel 3:13: "Then a spirit lifted me up, and I heard behind me a great rushing: . . . also the noise of the wings of the living creatures as they touched one another, and the noise of the wheels beside them, even the noise of a great rushing." One might also read the angels as thoughts, and see the poem as a whole as the Vision of a Loud Mind. (See note to lines 7–11 below.) **2:** Ezekiel 1:7. **3:** Isaiah 6:1–2; 1 Kings 22:19. **4–5:** Like the fourth and fifth lines of each stanza, these directly anticipate the important liturgical station that will follow the poem. Isaiah 6:3: "And one called unto another and said: Holy, holy, holy is the Lord of hosts; the whole earth is full of his glory." **6:** Psalms 29:1: "Ascribe to the Lord, O ye sons of might, ascribe to the Lord glory and strength." The Targum reads "divisions of angels" for "sons of might"—*bnei elim*—which is one of the more common biblical terms for angels. Other terms for angels that appear in the poem include *serafim, erelim, hashmalim,* and *hayot.* The terms are elusive in the original, and in the poem usually only their associations are translated. **7–8:** The specific kinds of angels referred to in these lines allude to Ezekiel 1:4: "Behold . . . a great cloud with a fire flashing up, so that a brightness was round about it . . . as the color of electrum," and *Hagigah* 13b: "What does [the word] *hashmal* mean?—Rab Judah said: Living creatures speaking fire." Also Ezekiel 1:14: "And the living creatures ran and returned as the appearance of a flash of lightning"—a phrasing that figures in *Sefer Yetzira,* chapter 1, where it refers to the heart's (or mind's) activity and risks. **9:** "The angels consist of fire and water, or according to another account, of four heavenly elements: mercy, strength, beauty, and dominion, corresponding to the four earthly elements: water, fire, earth, and air" (*Encyclopedia Judaica,* 2:956ff.). Avraham Ibn Ezra recalls the intellectual aspect of the angels as well, in his biblical commentary to Genesis 28:12 (Jacob's ladder): "And R. Shelomo the Spaniard [Ibn Gabirol] said that a ladder alludes to the upper soul, and the angels of god—wisdom's thought." **10:** Isaiah 29:23. Also the Sabbath Qedusha; see note to line 16 below. **14:** Daniel 12:1. **15:** Psalms 68:18. **16:** Genesis 1:9; *Sefer HaBahir* 11: "Michael the prince on the right of the Holy One, Blessed Be He, is water and hail"; the Sabbath Qedusha of the (Mussaf for additional service): "We will reverence Thee and sanctify Thee in the mystic utterance of the holy Serafim. . . . His ministering angels ask one another, 'Where is the place of His glory?'" **17:** "Partition" is the word used for the cover or curtain before the Holy Ark in the synagogue, *pargod*. *Pirqei Rabbi Eliezer* 4: "Seven angels created in the beginning serve Him before the veil which is called *pargod*." **19–23:** The language of this stanza in the original is drawn both from that of the tent of meeting (Exodus 40:22) and Gabriel's coming to overturn Sodom (*Baba Metzia* 86b and Genesis 18:16). **20–21:** The word *serafim* derives from *saraf*, burned. *Sefer HaBahir* 11b: "And Gabriel the prince on the left of the Holy One, Blessed Be He, is fire"; 2 Kings 2:18, 18:17. **26:** Song of Songs 4:4. I.e., Nuriel was a picture of strength and power. **27:** Jeremiah 47; Job 26:11, 22:14. **28:** Exodus 3:14: "I am that I am"—the Lord's answer when Moses asks Him what His name is. Literally, "I-am, the creator of the heavens and the netherworld." **31:** Job 16:19. **33:** *Hagigah* 13b: "Sandalfon . . . stands behind the chariot and wreathes crowns for his Maker"; Job 31:36; *Sefer Yetzira* 3:7: "He made the letter *alef* king over breath and bound a crown to it." **38:** *Pirqei Rabbi Eliezer* 4: "And the creatures stand in fear and terror." "Will set strong": literally, "their feet were straight" (Ezekiel 1:7). **41:** In the Qedusha prayer the word "holy" is repeated three times, as in the quote from Isaiah 6:3. "Holy" in Hebrew denotes separation.

## And So It Came to Nothing

*SQ*, #81. A *piyyut* for the Additional Prayers of the Day of Atonement. An alphabetical acrostic is embedded in the Hebrew, with *Shelomo* following. This poem recalls earlier (c. fifth-century c.e.) *piyyutim* such as Yossi Ben Yossi's "Ain lanu kohen gadol lekhapeir be'adeinu" (We have no high priest to atone for us), as it contrasts the ritual glories of the past with the ruins of the exilic present. The list that follows in lines 5–20 is drawn from a combination of scriptural and talmudic sources. On occasion I depart from the order and literal meaning in the interest of sound and comprehension in English. **Lines 1–4:** Isaiah 64:10. **5–6:** *Yoma* 2a: "There was a place on the Temple mount called *Birah*. Resh Lakish said: The whole sanctuary is called *Birah*, as it is written: 'And to build the *Birah* [palace] for which I have made provision' [1 Chronicles 29:19]"; *Middot* 5:3–4: "Six offices were in the courtyard [of the Temple] . . . the office made of hewn stone, there the great Sanhedrin of Israel was in session." **7–8:** *Sanhedrin* 94b: "That wicked man [Sennacherib] said: First will I destroy [His] nether abode [the Temple on earth], and then the upper"; *Tamid* 3:5: "The shambles was located at the north of the altar, and on it were eight short pillars, and square blocks of cedar wood were on them. And iron hooks were set into them . . . on which they would suspend [the slaughtered beasts]"; Leviticus 9:19–20; Isaiah 44:28. **9–10:** 1 Kings 7:32: "And the axletree of the wheels were in one base"; *Yoma* 3:3: "Five acts of immersion . . . does the high priest carry out on that day"; Leviticus 16:15–21: "Then shall he kill the goat of the sin-offering, that is for the people . . . when he goeth in to make atonement in the holy place . . . for himself, and for his household, and for all the assembly of Israel." **11–12:** Leviticus 23:37: "an offering by fire unto the Lord . . . a burnt-offering, and a meal-offering . . . and drink-offerings"; Leviticus 24:5–6: "And thou shalt take fine flour and bake twelve cakes. . . . And thou shalt set them in two rows, six in a row, upon the pure table before the Lord"; Exodus 40:22: "And he put the table in the tent of meeting, . . . and he set a row of bread in order upon it before the Lord." **13–14:** *Yoma* 5:4: "He slaughtered [the goat] . . . and he sprinkled some [of its blood] . . . like one who cracks a whip"; Leviticus 16:12: "And he shall take a censer full of coals of fire from off the altar before the Lord, and his hands full of sweet incense beaten small, and bring it within the veil." **15–16:** Leviticus 4:12: "The skin of the bullock, and all its flesh . . . shall he carry forth without the camp unto a clean place, where the ashes are poured out"; *Yoma* 7:5: "The high priest serves in eight garments: tunic [robe] . . ."; Exodus 28:2: "And thou shalt make holy garments for Aaron . . . for splendor and for beauty." **17–18:** Leviticus 16:10, 21, where the ritual sending of the scapegoat into the wilderness is discussed. The scapegoat is chosen by lot, Aaron confesses over the goat the iniquities of the people, and a man is appointed to lead it into the wilderness—"And the goat shall bear upon him all their iniquities unto a land which is cut off." Mishna *Yoma* 6:3 says that a priest was sent out with the goat to make sure that it didn't return to a settled area; 6:6–8 mentions the later practice of hurling the scapegoat from a cliff. The Hebrew refers to "Azazel," whose precise meaning is uncertain, but which seems to imply a goat-demon of sorts, a ruler of the wilderness, into whose realm the scapegoat was sent (Baruch Levine, *Leviticus, JPS Torah Commentary* [Philadelphia, 1989], pp. 102–3).

### He Dwells Forever

*SQ*, #6. A *mustajaab l'malkhuyot*. Triple acrostic: *Shelomo HaQatan Bar Yehuda*. This poem is recited during the New Year service in the Sephardic liturgy, as part of the additional prayers dealing with the kingdom *(malkhut)* of God. It picks up on the line from Psalms 145:13: "Your kingdom is the kingdom of eternity" [or in the NJPS: "Your kingship is kingship for eternity"—literally, "of all worlds" or "all times"], which acts as a choral refrain (rhyming with the last line of each quatrain), then weaves together numerous motifs drawn directly from *Sefer Yetzira*. The refrain has not been factored into the translation. **Lines 1–5:** Isaiah 57:15; *Sefer Yetzira* 1:1; *Sefer Yetzira* (long version) 6:1; Isaiah 2:11; Psalms 148:13; Ecclesiastes 4:8; *Sefer Yetzira* 1:5; *Pirqei Rabbi Eliezer* 3: "From what place were the heavens created? From the light of the Holy One, blessed be His garment"; *Sefer Yetzira* 1:1: "He created His universe with three books *(sefarim)*," or three words with the *s-f-r* root: *sefer, sefar, sippur*—text, number, telling or story. **6–10:** "Against them inscribed ten without end . . . five against five"—literally, "are aligned" or "in agreement." Moshe Idel argues that this refers to the qabbalistic notion of the existence of ten additional, supernal *sefirot* [spheres] above the standard ten. *Pirqei Rabbi Eliezer* 3: "The Holy One, blessed be He, consulted the Torah . . . to create the world"; *Genesis Rabbah* 1:1: "*Amon:* pedagogue . . . So the Holy One, blessed be He, looked in the Torah and created the world"; Genesis 31:30: "Thou sore longest for thy father's house"; *Sefer Yetzira* 1:1–2: "The ten *sefirot* of Nothingness . . . their measure is ten which have no end . . . ten like the number of ten fingers, five opposite five." **11–15:** *Sefer Yetzira* 1:5; *Sefer Yetzira* 6:1: above, lines 1–5. **16–20:** "Caught in a siege"—*Sefer Yetzira* 1:5: "Their end is embedded in their beginning and their beginning in their end"; *Sefer Yetzira* 1:5, lines 11–15 above; *Sefer Yetzira* 6:3. **21–25:** *Sefer Yetzira* 2:1: "Twenty foundation letters"; *Sefer Yetzira* 3:3: "Fire is above and water is below, and breath [wind] is the decree dividing between them"; *Sefer Yetzira* 5:3: "Twelve elementals . . . with them He formed twelve constellations [the zodiac] in the universe." **26–30:** *Sefer Yetzira* 2:5: "From Chaos He formed substance, and He made that which was not into that which is. He carved great stones [pillars] out of air that cannot be grasped"; *Sefer Yetzira* 1:12: "Chaos is an azure line that surrounds all the world; Void consists of the spongy rocks that are established in the abyss, between which water emanates." **31–35:** *Sefer Yetzira* 1:14: "He selected three letters from among the Elementals, and fixed them in His great Name, YHVH; with them He sealed the six directions"; *Sefer Yetzira* 1:12: "Four is fire from water. With it He engraved and carved the throne of Glory, *serafim, ofanim*, and the holy *hayyot* [creatures] and the ministering angels"; Genesis 1:14: "let [the lights be] for signs, and for seasons, and for days and years." **36–40:** *Sefer HaRazim* 7:29: "He hung the world like a cluster of grapes"; *Genesis Rabbah* 68:9: "The Holy One, blessed be He, is the place of the world and the world is not His place"; Isaiah 26:4. **41–45:** "Life beyond time"— literally, "eternal life." *Sefer Yetzira* 1:9; Psalms 93:2, 145:11; 1 Chronicles 29:12; Genesis 1:2. **46–50:** Psalms 113:4. **51–55:** The Prayer for the New Moon: "Who with His word creates the heavens, and their hosts with the breath of His mouth"; Psalms 33:6; *Sefer Yetzira* 6:1: "Exalted *(nasa)* . . . because He supports *(nosei)* and sustains the entire universe [world]"; Isaiah 46:4, 4:28; Job 5:13. **56–60:** Job 26:7; Amos 9:6; Genesis 1:6–7; Job 28:11: "And the thing that is hidden bringeth He forth to light." **61–65:** Job 11:10; 1 Samuel 2:7; Job 16:12: "He hath taken me by the neck and dashed me to pieces"; Isaiah 2:14. **66–70:** Proverbs 30:8; Ezekiel 34:26. **71–75:** 1 Samuel 2:6; Psalms 17:14; Ezekiel 37:8; Job 10:11. **76–80:** Genesis 2:7, 3:19; the *nishmat* prayer: "Thou arouseth those who sleep and awakeneth men from their slumber"; Daniel 12:2: "And many of them that sleep in the dust of the earth shall awake, some to everlasting life, and some to reproaches and everlasting abhorrence."

## Haven't I Hidden Your Name

*SQ*, #135; *HaShira*, #97:5. A *reshut*. Acrostic: *Shelomo*. **Lines 1–4:** Psalms 63:2–3; Job 11:13; Psalms 55:17–18. The speaker moans/longs for the Lord, not like any beggar come to any door, but like one come to the speaker's door—so that the speaker is, as it were, begging from himself. In other words, the speaker is like a beggar before the Lord, and like a lord before the beggar at his door (which is also the door—*delet*—to his poem; see "Line" in the glossary and Ibn Gabirol's "I've Made You My Refuge," below). He seeks admission to his own reflection, wherein God is somehow contained (lines 5–6). Similar paradoxes are set out in the following lines, and this seemingly conventional poem of praise becomes a powerful poem of experience. **5–6:** 1 Kings 8:27: "Behold, heaven and the heaven of heavens cannot contain Thee; how much less this house that I have builded." Scheindlin notes the presence of the pun on *ve'ulam*, a homonym which means "and yet" in the poem and "a temple" in the allusion to the verse from 1 Kings. The paradox evident here, he says, is the gist of the poem, and it resembles both the rabbinic saying, "The world is not His place, but rather He is the place of the world," and the Sufi tradition attributed to Muhammad according to which God said, "My earth and My heaven contain me not, but the heart of my faithful servant containeth Me." **7–8:** Psalms 119:11; Job 10:13, 27:3; Jeremiah 20:9: "And if I say: 'I will not make mention of Him, Nor speak any more in His name,' then there is in my heart as it were a burning fire shut up in my bones, and I weary myself to hold it in, but cannot"; Psalms 17:3: "Thou hast tested me and Thou findest not that I had a thought which should not pass my mouth."

## LORD WHO LISTENS

*SQ*, #93. A *reshut* for the *qaddish* of the first day of Sukkot, the Festival of Booths. Acrostic: *Shelomo*. **Lines 1–2:** Psalms 22:25, 34:7; Genesis 25:21, 13:2, 10:1. **3–4:** Literally, "calling day and night." Psalms 102:1, 61:3, 57:8, 112:7–8, 86:12–13. **5–6:** Psalms 28:7, 5:3; Genesis 41:15. **7–8:** Psalms 27:4, 61:2, 86:6; *Shabbat* 19:5: "An infant is circumcised on the eighth, ninth, tenth, eleventh or twelfth days [after birth], never sooner [less], never later [more]."

## I'VE MADE YOU MY REFUGE

Sigi Ben-Ari, "HaMeshorer u'Venot HaShir—Reshut Hadasha le Shelomo Ibn Gabirol," *Mehqerei Yerushalayim beSifrut 'Ivrit* 14 (1993):109. A *reshut*. Acrostic: *Shelomo*. This poem was recently discovered among the texts and scraps of texts that comprise the Cairo Geniza collection. Ben-Ari offers the interpretation that the poem deals with Ibn Gabirol's fear that the "daughters of song" (the Muses) have deserted him at the start of a poem. Moshe Ibn Ezra, in his book of poetics (83a), comments on the phenomenon as well: "As for the poet, his fortune shifts, and his muse [literally, 'the daughter of his song'] sometimes attends to him and sometimes rebels. . . . When his heart turns away, the poem starts to stray. Therefore one of them said: 'When the pain starts, there is no poem [song] in the heart.' And one of the best poets has stated: 'I am considered by people to be a great poet, but it sometimes happens to me that it's easier to pull out one of my molars than to write a single couplet [line].'" **Line 1:** Psalms 73:28. **2:** 1 Samuel 2:7. **3:** Literally, "I rose to declare your oneness with the first few words of the poem." Again, in the context of the Hebrew-Andalusian poetics, "door" also refers to the first hemistich in a given line. The slight awkwardness in the symmetry of the lines and their off rhymes (poor/lord, store/sure) seek to account for a similar difficulty in the Hebrew, which Ben-Ari suggests was due to the poet's difficulty in composition. **5:** Psalms 31:20. **8–9:** Literally, "What is my sin to you?" **10–11:** Ecclesiastes 12:4: "And one shall start up at the sound of a bird, and all the daughters of song shall be brought low." Standard rabbinic interpretations of this biblical passage say that it is describing the effects of aging on a person. In this vein Avraham Ibn Ezra comments as follows on the same verse from Ecclesiastes: *And all the daughters of song shall be brought low*—this is the throat, which once gave song, though now its voice is bowed low." Ben-Ari, however, interprets the lines metaphorically, with the "daughters" of song here being the muses, or inspiration. **14:** The final line of the poem is missing. Ben-Ari points out that it would likely provide the link to the poem's specific place in the liturgy.

### You Lie in My Palace

*SQ*, #131; *HaShira*, #99:4. A *reshut*. Acrostic: *Shelomo*. Scheindlin observes that this is one of the more obscure poems on redemption by Ibn Gabirol (there are thirteen in all), and that the text at some point might be corrupt (*The Gazelle*, pp. 93–103). In any event, in its ambiguous current form, it appears that *Knesset Yisrael* (the congregation of Israel—grammatically feminine) is asking a complacent God (who is resting, as the allusion would have it, between the cherubim of the ark) to prepare her bed for the *admoni*, the "ruddy one"—an expression that alludes to 1 Samuel 16:12 and implies the Messiah, the "anointed one." In the second stanza God is addressed as the lover, not the go-between. Finally, the logistics of the poem are somewhat confusing, as God is, at the beginning of the poem, inside the palace but inactive, but at the end of the poem the congregation of Israel calls Him to enter the palace. (Another possibility is that the address shifts to the "ruddy one," the Messiah, whom the poet longs for, calling him "my fine gazelle.") The final call to the lover to drink at dawn, Scheindlin notes, "echoes countless Arabic and Hebrew wine poems." **Line 1:** 1 Samuel 4:4: "The Lord of hosts, who sitteth upon the cherubim"; Exodus 25:18; Amos 6:4; Esther 1:6. **3:** 1 Samuel 16:12: "And Samuel said unto Jesse: 'Send and fetch [David] . . .' And he sent and brought him. Now he was ruddy and withal had beautiful eyes, and was goodly to look upon." The Hebrew uses the characteristic "ruddy," which would be awkward in the English; I've shifted the allusion to the next term of the *shibbutz*. See also Song of Songs 5:10: "My beloved is white and ruddy," which the Targum explains as: "Then the ecclesia of Israel began to speak about the praise of the Lord of the World, saying, 'It is God I desire to worship, for by day He wears a robe white as snow . . . and His face is radiant as fire from the greatness of his wisdom' " (trans. Scheindlin). **4:** Song of Songs 2:9: "My beloved is like a gazelle." **5:** Psalms 44:24. **6:** Isaiah 13:2: "Set ye up an ensign upon the high mountain." The Hebrew specifies Mount Hermon and (or) Senir, from which the Land of Israel can be seen. **7:** Numbers 16:26; Genesis 16:12: "And he [Ishmael] shall be a wild ass of a man." **8:** Proverbs 5:19: "A lovely hind and a graceful doe, let her breasts satisfy thee at all times." **9:** Song of Songs 6:3: "I am my beloved's and my beloved is mine." **10–12:** "Chambers" is actually "palace" in the original, the same word that appears in line 1. Song of Songs 8:2: "I would lead thee, and bring thee into my mother's house, that thou might instruct me; I would cause thee to drink of the spiced wine, of the juice of my pomegranate."

## From *Kingdom's Crown*

*Keter Malkhut*, ed. Y. A. Zeidman (Jerusalem, 1950); *SQ*, #22; *HaShira*, #108. *Kingdom's Crown* is essentially a *baqasha*, or poem of petition, though its hybrid composition renders it in many ways unique in Hebrew literature. While it is doubtful that the poem was originally intended for synagogue use, its powerful religious emphases have led to its incorporation into the rite for the Day of Atonement, on which it is uttered quietly by individual worshipers. Current practice varies from community to community.

There are three parts to the poem: part 1 opens with an address to the Creator that gives poetic expression to the philosophical thought of *The Fountain of Life* (cantos 1–9); part 2 is a detailed (Ptolemaic) cosmology (cantos 10–32); and part 3 is a percussive confession *(vidu'i)* of human failings that returns the speaker/reader to God (cantos 33–40). My rendering of the poem takes its cue from the graphic arrangement of Y. A. Zeidman's definitive, and out-of-print, 1950 edition *Keter Malkhut* (Jerusalem, 1950). Zeidman's great innovation was to set the poem out in lines that highlight the rhyme and rhythmic movement of the cantos (whose prosody differs considerably from that of the monorhymed and metrical lyrics in this volume). Zeideman's method emphasizes the symphonic nature of the work—something that the standard and prayer book editions obscure. For more on the formal aspects of the poem, as well as translation of the poem in its entirety, see *saj'*, in glossary at the back of this volume, and Cole, *Selected Ibn Gabirol*, pp. 137–95, 289–90.

*

*Epigraph*
   **Lines 1–2:** Job 2:21, 24:9; *Pirqei Avot* 2:2: "For the merit of their fathers is their support." **5–6:** Literally, "I've set it over [at the head of] all my hymns, and called it *Kingdom's Crown*, [or 'the crown of the kingdom']." With this translation of the title I have tried to emphasize the overall and abiding sense of majesty-in-creation—God's, but also the poet's—while maintaining the abstract aspects of

the register and its esoteric implications. Possible sources for the title include *Pirqei R. Eliezer* 23 and Esther 2:17.

*from Part I: Prologue*

**Canto I. Line 1:** Psalms 139:14. **2–5:** *Netzah* has been variously translated as "triumph," "victory," "glory," and "eternity." 1 Chronicles 29:11; 1 Samuel 19:29. I have followed the medieval commentator David Qimhi in his *Book of Roots*, where he says it implies "authority and might [or glory]." **6–7:** Psalms 102:27. **8–9:** Literally, "within whose counsel our ideas cannot stand"—Jeremiah 23:18. **11–12:** Habakkuk 3:4; Proverbs 25:2. Zeidman points out that *sod* and *yesod*—literally, "mystery/secret" and "foundation"—here stand for "form" and "matter," key terms in Ibn Gabirol's philosophical scheme. **13:** I.e., the four letters of the Name of God. *Qiddushin* 71a for the rabbis on Exodus 3:15, where a change of vocalization in "This is my name forever (*l'olam*)" turns "forever" into "to be kept silent [secret] (*l'alem*)"; also *Exodus Rabbah* 3:9. The knowledge of how to pronounce the four letters no longer resides with the wise. **14:** Job 26:7. **15:** Job 28:11. **16–17:** I.e., "your creatures." Psalms 31:20. **18–21:** Psalms 102:27–28; Isaiah 6:1. See part 2, canto 24 for the location of the throne in the tenth sphere. **22–25:** The translation follows Zeidman's gloss, especially "light's reflection." Lamentations 4:20; *Fountain of Life* 5:41: "And the impression of form in matter, when it reaches it from the Will, is like the return of the form of the one who gazes into a mirror at his reflection there." Literally, "the hidden dwelling in the secret heavenly place." **26–30:** This world and the world-to-come. *Pirqei Avot* 2:21: "He used to say: The work is not upon thee to finish, nor art thou free to desist from it. . . . Faithful is the master of thy work who will pay thee the wages of thy toil. And know that the giving of the reward to the righteous is in the time to come." Also the *Epistles of the Brethren of Purity* 1, which Yarden cites (p. 43): "And they have said in the books of wisdom: This world is a bridge. Cross over it into the world-to-come [the Hereafter]. . . . For this world is a house of action, the one to come a house of reward." **31:** Exodus 2:2: "And when she saw that he [Moses] was a goodly child, she hid him"; here the words refer to God and the reward to come. See also *Hagigah* 12a, which glosses the verse from Genesis, "And God saw the light, that it was good"—this being the primary light that could be seen from "one end of the world to the other," but which, after witnessing the corrupt generation of the flood and the dispersion, God hid and reserved for the righteous.

**Canto VII. Line 1:** Psalms 36:10. **2–5:** Isaiah 59:2; Lamentations 3:44. **6–8:** The reading follows Zeidman; other Hebrew editions read: "will be revealed in the upper world of beauty." Genesis 22:14. Also *Ta'anit* 31a. **9–12:** Isaiah 60:19: "The Lord shall be unto thee an everlasting light"; Numbers 23:3: "Thou shalt see but the uttermost part of them and shalt not see them all."

**Canto IX.** This entire section reverberates against the "autobiography of wisdom" as it is set forth in Proverbs 8, especially 22–31: "The Lord made me as the beginning of His way, the first of His works of old." **Lines 1–4:** Proverbs 16:22;

Jeremiah 10:14; Psalms 36:10, which also explicitly mentions the "fountain of life" that gives the poet's major philosophical work its title. **7:** Proverbs 8:30; **8–10:** Isaiah 40:14. **11–13:** Shelomo Pines calls these and the following lines "among the most remarkable" of the poem ("'He Called to Nothing, Which Split': On *Keter Malkhut*" [Hebrew], *Tarbiz* 50 (1980): 339–47). *Genesis Rabbah* 1:2: "I was an instrument of the artistry of the Holy One, blessed be He"; Zeidman adds: "like a workman and artist [or artisan] with whose help the Holy One, blessed be He, created the world." See note to lines 20–22. **14–15:** *Sefer Yetzira* 2:6: "He formed substance out of chaos, and made nonexistence into existence." "According to Empedocles, vision was occasioned by particles continually flying off the surface of bodies which met with others proceeding from the eye" (*Selected Religious Poems of Solomon Ibn Gabirol*, trans. I. Zangwill, ed. I. Davidson [Philadelphia, 1923], p. 178). **16–19:** In the Hebrew the active agency and grammatical subject of these lines is God's desire (line 12) or will. Emanating from God, this desire works like an artist, or artisan, to give shape to the world. Zeidman cites (p. 23) the *Epistles of the Brethren of Purity*: "And know, my brother! Every flesh-and-blood artist has need of six things in order to complete his work. . . . Primary matter, place, time, tool, vessel, and movement. . . . ; whereas the exalted Lord has no need of any of these, all of which are his creations and works." Proverbs 9:1; *Sefer Yetzira* 1:12: "Fire from water, with it He engraved and carved the throne of glory"; Malachi 3:3. **20–22:** The interruption of part 1's anaphora—"you are the . . ."—by "He called" signals the transition to part 2 of the poem, the cosmology. **23–26:** The imagery here is taken from the description of the wilderness sanctuary in Exodus. Exodus 26:4; Isaiah 44:24; Exodus 36:17: "And he made fifty loops upon the edge of the curtain that was outmost in the first coupling [set]," where "coupling" is understood, by Zeidman, as referring to the system of the spheres. In the scheme laid out here, God's desire or will—literally, "the power [of his/its hand]" (Ibn Gabirol identifies God's will as "the power of unification")—reaches from the highest "innermost chamber" of the tenth sphere (canto 24) to the "outermost edge" of the lower creation, with earth at its center. See also Isaiah 40:12: "Who has . . . meted out the heavens with his span."

*from Part II: The Cosmology*

Readers of *Kingdom's Crown* have long had a certain prejudice against this section of the poem. The rabbis of the Middle Ages were concerned about its confusion of science and religion; twentieth-century teachers have suggested that students would be more interested in the emotionalism of parts 1 and 3, and that the detail of part 2 was something of an acquired taste. To my mind, it is precisely the musical and physical detail of part 2 that establishes the palpable sense of grandeur and kingdom that are central to the poem.

**Canto X. Line 1:** Part 2 begins at the center of the Ptolemaic universe, with the sublunary sphere—the globe of earth and water surrounded by air and fire. The poem then begins its ascent up through the ten spheres of the moon,

Mercury, Venus, the sun, Mars, Jupiter, Saturn, the fixed stars (the zodiac), the all-encompassing (diurnal) sphere, and the sphere of intelligence (the source of angels). Above this tenth sphere is the "place of the souls of the righteous after death," universal matter, the Throne of Glory, and the "Effulgence of Divine Glory: the Source of Soul" (see R. Loewe, *Ibn Gabirol* [New York, 1989], p. 114). Psalms 106:2. **2:** Zeidman notes that the notion of the earth as a sphere appears in the Jerusalem Talmud (*Avodah Zarah* 3:1): "It is said: The earth is made like a ball . . . R. Yonah said: Alexander of Macedon, when he asked to ascend on high and ascended on high, rose until he saw the earth as a ball and the seas as a bowl"; the full term "ball of earth," he notes, was renewed in Hebrew by Ibn Gabirol. Prior to that it appears, of course, in Pythagoras, and the Muslim cosmographers drew on earlier Greek sources. *The Epistles of the Brethren of Purity* (cited in Loewe, *Ibn Gabirol*, p. 181): "The parts of the water were lighter than the parts of the land and the water stood over the land. And since the parts of the wind were lighter than the water the wind was set over the water." **3:** For more on Ibn Gabirol's treatment of the elements, see his early ethical treatise *The Improvement of the Moral Qualities*. **4:** In an effort to establish a sense of motion and dimension, and to maintain the musical flow of the poem, I have varied the English for *galgal* throughout—here "wheel," but a few lines later "circle," or "circuit," and elsewhere "sphere." **5:** Ecclesiastes 1:6. **10:** Ibn Gabirol, *Fountain of Life* 1:5: "The universal essence . . . is not unified, however, . . . it is reduced to two principles . . . the universal matter and universal form." **11:** Hosea 2:2: "And the children of Judah and the children of Israel shall be gathered together, and they shall appoint themselves one head, and shall go up out of the land." The *shibbutz* again employs the biblical phrase in a different context entirely. **13:** Genesis 2:10: "And a river went out of Eden to water the garden; and from thence it was parted, and became four heads." Avraham Ibn Ezra's commentary (M. Friedlander, *Essays on the Writings of Abraham Ibn Ezra* [London, n. d.], p. 40) reads as follows: "And now I will reveal to you by allusion the secret of the garden and the rivers. . . . And I have not found this matter discussed by any of the sages except R. Solomon Ibn Gabirol, who was a great sage and saw into the matters of the soul's mystery. . . . And the 'river'—is like a mother (which is to say, the universal natural common matter) to all bodies; and the 'four heads' [fonts]—are the roots [the elements of fire, wind, water, dust]." In the standard editions of his commentary Ibn Ezra writes: "And he who understands this mystery will understand how the river diverges."

　　**Canto XIV. Lines 1–5:** Isaiah 61:10. **6–8:** As Raphael Loewe has demonstrated, the measurements Ibn Gabirol refers to are remarkably close to modern computations throughout the poem. For precise figures see Loewe's *Ibn Gabirol* and the notes to the poem in Cole, *Selected Gabirol*. **9:** *Baraita de Shmu'el HaQatan* 9: "Venus is appointed over charm and grace and love, and over passion and desire and fruitfulness and over increase of humankind and beasts, and over the fruit of the land and the fruit of the tree"; *Ketubah* 8a: "Blessed art Thou, O Lord, . . . who hast created joy and gladness, bridegroom and bride, rejoicing and song, mirth and delight." **15–16:** Deuteronomy 33:14: "precious things of the fruits of the sun . . . and the precious things of the yield of the moon."

**Canto XVI. Lines 1–4:** This canto is still about the sun. Genesis 1:14. **4–8:** Genesis 1:12; Job 38:31; *Genesis Rabbah* 10:6: "R. Simon said: There is not a single herb that does not have a constellation in heaven which strikes it and says, 'Grow,' . . . R. Hannina b. Papa and R. Simon said: Pleiades binds the fruit and Orion draws it out between knot and knot, as it is written, *'Canst thou lead forth the constellations in season?'* (Job 38:32). R. Tanhum b. R. Hiyya and R. Simon said: The constellation which ripens the fruits." **24:** Psalms 78:4. **26:** Daniel 1:4. **28:** Genesis 24:10: "All the goods of his master [Abraham] were in his hand." Ratzhaby notes the Arabic proverb from which the line might also derive: "The power of the servant [derives] from the power of his lord."

**Canto XXIV. Line 4:** 1 Kings 6:17: "The house, that is, the Temple, before [the Sanctuary]"—where the Hebrew for Temple is *heikhal,* and might also be translated "palace" or "chamber." **5:** Leviticus 27:32: "Every tenth . . . shall be holy to the Lord." **9:** Habakkuk 3:4. **10–13:** Song of Songs 3:9–10. "Throne" (*matzava*) or "base" has a variant reading, *misba,* "couch" or "table"—Song of Songs 1:12: "while the king sat at his table." **15–16:** Genesis 4:7: "unto thee is its desire."

**Canto XXVII. Lines 1–3:** *Shabbat* 152b: "R. Eliezer said: The souls of the righteous are hidden under the Throne of Glory." **4–6:** 1 Samuel 25:29. **7–9:** Isaiah 40:31; Job 3:17; *Genesis Rabbah* 9:7, Esther 9:16. The verse involves a play on Genesis 9:19: "The sons of Noah"; *no'ah* also means "rest" in Esther 9:16. **11:** *Berakhot* 17a on the pleasures of the world to come; cf. below (line 16). **14:** Exodus 38:8. **16–20:** Descriptions of the world to come and its pleasures abound in rabbinic literature. See, for an elaborate example, *Yalqut Shim'oni* to Genesis (in Zeidman). A more concise description is found in *Berakhot* 17a: "In the future world there is no eating nor drinking nor propagation nor business nor jealousy nor hatred nor competition, but the righteous sit with their crowns on their heads feasting on the brightness of the divine presence, as it says, *And they beheld God, and did eat and drink* (Exodus 24:11)." Also Avraham Ibn Hasdai's *Ben HaMelekh veHaNazir,* chapter 35, on the pleasures of the "world of intelligence and mind, which have absolutely nothing in common with any other kind of pleasure." **21–24:** Numbers 13:27: "A land [that]. . . . floweth with milk and honey, and this is the fruit of it."

**Canto XXVIII. Lines 1–4:** The translation follows Zeidman's commentary. **5–6:** *Hagigah* 12b: "'Araboth* is that in which there are Right and Judgment and Righteousness; the treasures of life and the heavens of peace and the heavens of blessing, the souls of the righteous and the spirits and the souls which are yet to be born." **7–8:** Isaiah 59:20. **9–10:** Isaiah 30:33; Ezekiel 38:22; Hosea 6:7; *Yalqut Shim'oni,* Ecclesiastes, 976: "He created the Garden of Eden [beside] Gehinnom so that one could be saved from the other, and what is the space between them? R. Haninah said: A wall the width of a hand-breadth." **11–13:** Proverbs 22:14. **14–19:** Zechariah 14:6; Job 24:15; Deuteronomy 4:11; Genesis 15:17; *Hagigah* 12b.

**20–23:** Habakkuk 1:2: "O Lord, Thou hast ordained them for judgment, and Thou, O Rock, hast established them for correction"; Job 37:13: "They are turned about by His guidance. . . . Whether it be for correction, or for His earth, or for mercy, that He cause it to come."

**Canto XXIX. Lines 1–5:** Ezekiel 28:7, 28:17; Isaiah 51:1. **6–10:** Numbers 11:17. **11–14:** Psalms 29:7; Isaiah 30:33; Genesis 2:15; Exodus 3:2: "The bush burned with fire, and the bush was not consumed." **15–16:** See note to canto 9, line 14; Exodus 19:18: "Now Mount Sinai was altogether in smoke, because the Lord descended on it in fire."

**Canto XXXI. Lines 4–5:** Proverbs 15:22; Jonah 4:6. **6–7:** Job 33:6; Genesis 2:7. **8:** Numbers 11:17. **11–12:** Literally, "you've shut him [man]." Likewise in the following two lines, where the translation continues the first person plural. **13–14:** Exodus 25:11: "Within and without shalt thou overlay it," where Ibn Gabirol plays both on *titzapenu* ("thou shalt overlay it")—taking it to mean "thou shalt see it" (also *titzapenu*)—and on "within" (the body / the home) and "without."

*from Part III: Confession*

**Canto XXXIII.** Having ascended as high as one might ascend, and mapped the cosmos, the poem now picks up where the final cantos of part 2 left off, with the link between God, man, and man's conduct in the world. **Lines 1–4:** Ezra 9:6; Jeremiah 22:22. Also *Berakhot* 17a: "Raba on concluding his prayer added the following: My God, before I was formed I was not worthy [to be formed] and now that I have been formed I am as if I had not been formed. I am dust in my lifetime, all the more in my death. Behold, I am before Thee like a vessel full of shame and confusion." **12–13:** Job 7:5; Genesis 2:7. **14:** Habakkuk 2:19: "Woe to him that says to the wood 'Awake!'; to the dumb stone, 'Arise!' " **15:** Psalms 144:4. **16:** Psalms 78:39. **17:** Psalms 140:4. **18:** I.e., a heart uncircumcised, as in Jeremiah 9:25. See also Jeremiah 17:9. **19:** Proverbs 19:19. **20–22:** Proverbs 6:18, 14:12, 19:2, 28:18; Isaiah 6:5; Psalms 101:5. **23–26:** *Yoma* 87b: "What are we, and what is our life?"; Isaiah 40:17; Deuteronomy 31:27. **27:** *Pirqei Avot* 3:1: "Know whence thou camest, and whither thou art going, and before whom thou art destined to give account and reckoning." **28–29:** Esther 4:16. *Ta'anit* 7b: "Any man who is insolent stumbles in the end." **30–33:** Ezekiel 6:9, 22:24. **34–35:** *Pirqei Avot* 1:13: "A name that is widespread loses its fame; one who does not add [to his knowledge] causes [it] to cease."

**Canto XL. Line 4:** Cf. The liturgy for the Day of Atonement, *Avinu Malkeinu*: "Our father, our King, be gracious unto us and answer us, though we have no worthy deeds." **5–10:** Nehemiah 5:13; Isaiah 24; Hosea 10:1; Esther 8:5; 1 Kings 8:38. **14ff.:** The liturgy for the Day of Atonement—"May it be Thy will . . . again in Thine abundant compassion to have mercy upon us and upon Thy Sanctuary." The syntax in the Hebrew is somewhat unusual as well. **17:** Genesis 45:10. **18:** Zeidman has: "Remember me in the order of peace." **19–20:** Psalms 4:7; Numbers 6:25–26, and the Priestly Blessing: "The Lord make His face [to] shine upon thee, and be gracious unto thee, the Lord lift up His countenance to thee and give thee peace." **21–22:** Psalms 103:10, 39:9. **23–24:** Psalms 102:25, 27:9. **25–26:** Psalms 51:4, 51:13. **27–28:** Psalms 71:20, 73:24. **29–33:** Genesis 15:1; Hosea 11:7. **34–36:** Psalms 17:14. **37–39:** Job 33:30; Psalms 89:16, 71:20. **41–42:** Isaiah 12:1. **43–45:** Psalms 62:13. **46–47:** The morning liturgy for Shabbat and festivals, *U'bemaqhalot*: "For this is the duty of all creatures towards Thee, O Lord . . . to give thanks unto Thee, to laud, adore, and praise Thee." **48–55:** The morning liturgy for Shabbat and Festivals, *Shokhen 'ad*: "It is befitting for the upright to praise Him . . . ," etc. The lines of the poem follow the outline of the prayer. "Hallowed in the mouth of the holy" is, literally, "the mouth of those who hallow (sanctify) you," i.e., the holy ones, as in the prayer. **56–57:** Psalms 86:8: "For there is none like unto Thee among the gods, O Lord, and there are no works like Thine." **58–61:** These lines incorporate elements of the end of the *'amida* prayer and Psalms 19:15: "Let the words of my mouth and the meditation of my heart be acceptable before Thee, Lord, my Rock and my Redeemer."

## YITZHAQ IBN GHIYYAT

### My Wandering

*Shirei R. Yitzhaq Ibn Ghiyyat*, ed. Y. David (Jerusalem, 1987), #98; *HaShira* #127. A *ge'ula* in the form of a *muwashshah*. Schirmann, who calls this "a remarkable poem," notes that it takes to an extreme the notion that the hardships forced on the people of Israel are in fact its greatest source of pleasure and hope. As such, it echoes the *'Udhri* tradition of Arabic love poetry, where suffering in love is central. (See Yehuda HaLevi, "Love's Dwelling" and the commentary there.) Line **3:** Exodus 6:5. **6:** Proverbs 23:13. **8:** Proverbs 3:11. **9–10:** Isaiah 52:2. **13:** Lamentations 3:19. **18:** Literally, "they incense me with no-god," as in Deuteronomy 32:21. **33–34:** Numbers 33:55; Isaiah 17:11. **35:** God is the speaker in the final stanza. **40:** The pronoun in the Hebrew is "it" (or "him")—literally, "I'll place him." Schirmann comments that it refers to "my love," or "he who loves me," i.e., the people of Israel, which the Lord will set over all other peoples. I have inserted the third-person plural for clarity, as both "it" "him" would be confusing. **44:** Deuteronomy 28:65.

## YOSEF IBN SAHL

### The Fleas

*Schirmann, Shirim Hadashim min HaGeniza*, p. 212. This is the first of several highly entertaining flea (or fly) poems in the medieval Hebrew tradition. See also Avraham Ibn Ezra's "The Flies" and Alahdab's "Another Flea," as well as Alharizi's hilarious prose passage about fleas in the *Tahkemoni* (Gate 4—not translated here). Line **6:** Isaiah 8:12. **10:** 2 Samuel 5:24. **14:** Song of Songs 6:11.

## YOUR POEM, MY FRIEND

*Sefunei Shira*, ed. D. Yarden (Jerusalem, 1967), p. 24; *BeLashon Qodmim*, ed. S. Abramson (Jerusalem, 1965), p. 76. The heading indicates that this poem was one of three written in response to Moshe Ibn Ezra's having asked Ibn Sahl for his opinion about a new poem of his (of Ibn Ezra's). The Hebrew contains an odd use of the plural in an incomplete construct state, which contributes to its light tone. Abramson suggests that its final rhyme be read as *sie* (rhymes with "high") rather than *say* (rhymes with "day"). Yarden adjusts the Hebrew to read *soe* in each case, but Abramson says this is incorrect. **Line 1:** Song of Songs 4:9. **2:** Proverbs 7:22. **4:** Numbers 31:28. **5:** Job 40:25. **6:** Isaiah 40:4; Psalms 31:21.

## A COMPLAINT ABOUT THE RICH

*HaShira*, #142, lines 1–8. Another response to the poem Ibn Ezra had shown him. Ibn Sahl begins with a complaint about the state of cultural affairs in their day. That complaint continues for another four lines in the Hebrew, and the remainder of the poem (another twenty lines) praises Ibn Ezra's poem, which Ibn Sahl says saved him from the boors that surround him; he then exhorts his friend to be strong, although he too is surrounded by people he can't bear. **Lines 1–4:** Lamentations 4:1. With the somewhat ironic quotation, the poet implicitly likens the cultural situation to the ruin of Jerusalem. **10:** Proverbs 8:18. **14:** Psalms 49:18. **15–16:** Lamentations 5:2; Obadiah 1:11.

## LEVI IBN ALTABBAAN

Ibn Altabbaan's poems were so accomplished in their way that they were often confused with HaLevi's. See, for example, HaLevi's "If Only Dawn."

## UTTER HIS ONENESS

*Shirei Levi Ibn Altabbaan*, ed. D. Pagis (Jerusalem, 1967), #2; *HaShira*, #130:1. *Reshut* to the *nishmat*. Acrostic: *Levi*. The poet calls to the soul to put the agony of ceaseless contrition behind it for now and take up instead the path of devotional delight. **Line 1:** The image of the blood alludes to Isaiah 59:3: "For your hands are defiled with blood, and your fingers with iniquity." Schirmann suggests that it derives from the conventional image (in secular Arabic verse) of the weeping tears mingled with blood, indicating that they come from the heart. Also 2 Samuel 20:12. **2:** Psalms 51:7. **3:** Lamentations 2:19. **4:** Isaiah 59:15; Psalms 76:6. **5–6:** Psalms 150:6, 146:1.

EXPOSED

*Shirei Levi Ibn Altabbaan*, #3; *HaShira* #130:2. *Reshut leBarekhu*. Acrostic: *Levi*. **Line 1:** Isaiah 51:23. **2:** Ezekiel 16:22: "when you were naked and bare, and lay wallowing in your own blood." **4:** Lamentations 2:18. **6:** Literally, "so long as your spirit is in your nose." Psalms 104:33: "Bless the Lord, O my soul." And from the liturgy: "As long as the soul [*neshama*—like 'breath,' *neshima*] is in me, I offer my thanks before you"; "Bless the Lord, O my soul, and all that is within me, bless His holy name."

## BAHYA IBN PAQUDA

Ibn Tibbon's less than felicitous translation of *Duties of the Heart* was so popular that it displaced the Arabic original, and the book has since been translated into numerous languages, often multiple times. It was one of the first Hebrew books to be printed (1489, in Naples).

DUTIES OF THE HEART

Bahya Ibn Paquda, *Hovot HaLevavot* [Duties of the Heart], trans. from the Arabic into the Hebrew by Yehuda Ibn Tibbon, ed. A. Tzafroni (Tel Aviv, 1964), p. 584. See also Menahem Mansoor's English translation, *The Book of Direction to the Duties of the Heart* (London, 1973), p. 447. The ten couplets of the poem summarize the ten chapters of the book, so that the poem acts as both a table of contents and mnemonic device for meditation on its themes, with its acrostic spelling out the poet's name: *Bahya Bar Yosef*. The chapters are (1) The Unity of God; (2) Creation and God's Grace Which Is Revealed in It; (3) The Obligations of Service and Obedience; (4) Trust in God; (5) Pure Devotion; (6) Humility; (7) Repentance; (8) Spiritual Accounting; (9) Asceticism; and (10) True Love of God.

## MOSHE IBN EZRA

While in the north, notes Raymond Scheindlin, the poet "diverts the language of Jewish aspiration for national restoration to his personal longing for al-Andalus, the home of the Judeo-Arab synthesis." For a detailed discussion of Ibn Ezra's life and work, see Scheindlin's cogent article on him in *The Literature of al-Andalus*, ed. M. R. Menocal, R. Scheindlin, M. Sells (Cambridge, 2000), pp. 252–64.

WEAK WITH WINE

*SHIE*, #116; *HaShira*, #145:1. **Heading:** "And he wrote, describing a meadow where violets were growing." **Lines 1–2:** Literally, "weak with the wine of love" or "the wine of friendship," implying the party, and in line 2, "lacking the power to get up and walk." Isaiah 28:1; 1 Samuel 17:39. **3–4:** Song of Songs 7:13, 4:16; Exodus 30:24, 34. **5–6:** Numbers 4:6. The Hebrew has *tekhelet*, which can stand for any number of shades; in this case it appears to be a deep blue bordering on violet.

## The Garden

*Moshe Ibn Ezra: Shirei HaHol*, ed. H. Brody (Berlin, 1935), #1 (hereafter *SHIE*). This poem opens the standard Hebrew edition of Ibn Ezra's work, edited by Haim Brody. It employs the Arab rhetorical figure of the boast *(fakhr)*, but in a particularly gentle manner. **Lines 1–2:** Lamentations 5:17; Zephaniah 1:14; Jeremiah 48:36. **3–4:** Isaiah 14:7. **5–6:** Ink and paper were sometimes scented, especially when used for poems that were dispatched to friends. Scripture also associates sweetness and scent with what is written, as in God's ordinances (Psalms 19:11). **7–8:** Isaiah 35:5–6, 32:4.

## Bring Me My Cup

*SHIE*, #226; *HaShira*, #145:5. **Lines 1–2:** Jeremiah 6:4; Song of Songs 2:17 and 4:6. **3–4:** Brody notes in one place that "its" refers to the sun, which changes color as it sets, and in another place that it refers to the cup, which is changed by the addition of the wine. Schirmann says it refers to the sun. Nehemiah 2:2.

## A Shadow

*SHIE*, #19; *HaShira*, #145:2. **Lines 1–2:** Job 14:2; Song of Songs 2:11. Literally, "with his horsemen and chariots," as in Exodus 14:23. **3–4:** Psalms 19:7; Song of Songs 1:12. **5–6:** Exodus 29:9. **7–8:** Job 31:33. **11–12:** Esther 1:12; Isaiah 10:16. Wine was usually mixed with water, to reduce its potency; here the tears replace the water. **13–16:** Jeremiah 37:9. **17–18:** Jeremiah 6:4; Proverbs 26:23. **19–20:** Genesis 25:26: "And after that came forth his brother, and his hand had hold on Esau's heel."

## The Fawn

*SHIE*, #136.

## The Garden, the Miser

*SHIE*, #34. **Lines 1–2:** Genesis 39:11, which emphasizes the festive nature of the occasion, singling out this day as special. Literally, "My friend, the time/season has been made new, and the flower beds live on as the day after death." **4:** Exodus 26:1. **6:** Lamentations 3:49. **7–8:** Isaiah 38:14; Jeremiah 8:7; Ezekiel 7:16; Isaiah 59:11. **10:** Literally, "the vine's daughter."

### THE PEN

*SHIE*, #196. **Lines 1–2:** Nehemiah 2:5; Isaiah 10:11 **6:** The mind of one who sees it. **7:** The paper seems to suck at the pen out of thirst. **9–10:** Jeremiah 23:29, 5:13.

### HEART'S DESIRE

*SHIE*, #249; *HaShira*, #143:1. A *muwashshah*. Ibn Ezra's erotic poems are especially sensual, and this poem has one of medieval Hebrew poetry's more explicit depictions of the sex act itself (lines 27ff.)—or at least what sounds like the sex act. There is considerable disagreement about the tone, nature, and fundamental meaning of this poem. In this way it resembles Ibn Khalfun's "Love in Me Stirs," HaGorni's "Lament," and Shelomo HaLevi's "Memory's Wine"—all of which, again, highlight the elusive aspect of this poetry. Scheindlin suggests that it involves a "frivolous" treatment of philosophical notions about an ideal, Platonic plane of pleasure, and notes that the seduction was not successful. Schirmann states that the poem is in fact quite explicit about the pleasures of love and its consummation (and that the fawn then regrets what he did). Perhaps because of the allusion to the heterosexual situation of the Song of Songs 3:4 in lines 25–26, Pagis, Schirmann, and Fleischer say the love interest in the poem is most likely a woman, even though the poem presents the *tzvi* as masculine. Matti Huss, however, takes the designation at face value. In his *Book of Discussion*, Ibn Ezra expresses the standard regret over having composed "obscene" and "frivolous" poems when he was young. He says he wrote such poems rarely and without great enthusiasm and that in any event doing so was wrong (57a and 143a–b). **Lines 1–4:** Psalms 21:3; 1 Kings 20:6. **5–10:** Psalms 49:15. **11–14:** Or, "and feed me," 1 Samuel 2:29. **15–20:** Numbers 32:7; Proverbs 5:19; Ezekiel 48:35: "The Lord is there." **25–26:** Literally, "to his mother's home." Song of Songs 3:4: "We rose and went to his mother's house," which allegorically was interpreted in the Targum and the rabbinic tradition as referring to the Temple. Genesis 49:15; Isaiah 9:3. **35–44:** Lamentations 1:14; Job 33:10, 35:16; Deuteronomy 3:26. **45–54:** Ezra 9:14; Genesis 23:8:

### THAT BITTER DAY

*SHIE*, #101; *HaShira*, #153:1. Like "The Dove," "Why Does Time Hound Me So" and "If You See Me," this poem was clearly written after the poet's forced and mysterious departure from Granada and his emigration to the far less cultured north. **Lines 1–2:** Habakkuk 1:6. **3–4:** Or, "I dwell among boors." Ezra 9:3; Psalms 142:5; Genesis 24:49; Isaiah 50:2.

### LET MAN REMEMBER

*SHIE*, #68; *HaShira*, #161:1. **Lines 5–6:** Psalms 18:11. Elitzur (*Shirat HaHol*, pp. 167–69) points out the subtle way in which the poet has loaded each pair of lines with antitheses, so that each positive thing is made to equal its opposite, and life itself is seen in this contemplative context as a gradual death.

## THE DOVE

*SHIE*, #154; *HaShira*, #151. Yosef Haim Yerushalmi comments on the way in which Ibn Ezra's poems from the north express a nostalgia "for the lost paradise of his beloved Granada" and a hope of return "at least as intense" as the expression of his longing for Zion in his liturgical poems ("Exile and Expulsion in Jewish History," in *Crisis and Creativity in the Sephardic World*, ed. Benjamin R. Gampel [New York, 1997], p. 16). Again, see Scheindlin on the conflation of personal longing and national restoration ("Moshe Ibn Ezra," in Menocal et al., *The Literature of al-Andalus*, p. 253). **Heading:** "And he said when he heard a dove cooing on a branch." **Lines 1–2:** Leviticus 12:6; Isaiah 17:6. **3–6:** Isaiah 58:11; Jonah 4:6; Deuteronomy 6:7; Judges 4:5. **7–10:** Isaiah 43:6; Deuteronomy 18:10–11. **11–12:** Ezekiel 32:18; Isaiah 35:2; Jeremiah 31:17; Proverbs 26:2. **13–14:** Psalms 55:7: "O that I had wings like a dove; then I might fly away and be at rest"; Psalms 102:15: "For Thy servants take pleasure in her [Zion's] stones, and love [cherish] her dust."

## WHY DOES TIME HOUND ME SO

*SHIE*, #36; *HaShira*, #152. **Heading:** "And he said when he was brought by the enemies' guile to a cliff on the highest mountain in Castile." It isn't clear why Ibn Ezra would have been imprisoned, but it may have had something to do with his having been associated with the ruling powers in Granada. **Lines 1–2:** Literally, "wake early." Proverbs 27:8; Judges 7:3; 2 Kings 21:8. **6:** Psalms 102:8: "I am become like a sparrow that is alone upon the housetop." **7–8:** For the most part, the untamed natural landscape held little fascination for the poets of Muslim Spain, and most of their "nature" poems (poems of description) concern a combination of the natural and the cultivated (Elitzur, *Shirat HaHol*, p. 433). Micah 1:8; Jeremiah 31:17–18. **9–10:** Micah 1:16: "Enlarge thy baldness as the vulture, for they are gone into captivity from thee"; i.e., even the vulture or eagle, seeing my state, would pull its hair out and enlarge its baldness out of sadness for me. "Cut themselves"—as a sign of mourning, as in Jeremiah 16:6; Deuteronomy 14:1. **11–14:** These lines echo the Arabic motif of shepherding the stars, and indicate both his utter solitude and his longing for his friends far away. Psalms 144:2, 139:3; Jeremiah 31:6; Genesis 22:17. **15–16:** I.e., the land of Christian Spain, as opposed to Granada and Muslim Spain. Isaiah 51:19; Psalms 20:9.

## ANCIENT GRAVES

*SHIE*, #152; *HaShira*, #161:8. **Lines 1–4:** Jeremiah 51:39, 57; Ecclesiastes 9:6.

## IF YOU SEE ME

*SHIE*, #210; *HaShira*, #161:9. **Lines 1–4:** Joshua 6:1. **5–6:** Daniel 10:8; Job 7:5, 21:26. **7–8:** Lamentations 4:8; Job 30:30. **9–10:** Psalms 69:9; Genesis 31:15. **13–14:** Ecclesiastes 2:14; Isaiah 10:25; Deuteronomy 12:5; Exodus 29:46. **15–16:** Job 18:13; Ecclesiastes 9:5. **17–18:** Ecclesiastes 6:3; Genesis 15:2; *Nedarim* 64b: "R. Joshua b. Levi said: A man who is childless is accounted as dead, for it is written, Give me children, or else I am dead [Gen 30:1]. And it was taught: Four are accounted as dead: a poor man, a leper, a blind person, and one who is childless."

## IVORY PALACES

*SHIE*, #90; *HaShira*, #161:6. **Lines 1–2:** Literally, "[All] who build homes of ivory. . . ." 1 Kings 22:39: "The ivory house that [Ahab] built"; Amos 3:15: "The ivory palaces shall be demolished"; Isaiah 2:16. **3–4:** 2 Chronicles 3:15. **5–6:** I.e., without an inhabitant. Jeremiah 9:10; Isaiah 24:12; Amos 6:8. **7–8:** Literally, "Say [you who hear me now], where are those who built and dwelled, and where are their souls and their bodies?" **9–10:** Job 27:8, 17:13–15: "I must look forward to Sheol as my home." **11–12:** 2 Kings 3:4; Genesis 22:10.

## THE WORLD

*SHIE*, #14; *HaShira*, #161:2. The poem presents the somewhat heretical implication that God set up man's instinct for transgression from the start. A similar suggestion is cunningly put forth in Ibn Gabirol's "Before My Being." The origin of the poem's central image is *Kalila and Dimna* and also appears in *Choice of Pearls*, trans. A. Cohen (New York, 1925), #522. **Lines 1–2:** Genesis 5:1–2; Ecclesiastes 3:11: "He hath set the world in their heart, so that man cannot find out the work that God hath done from the beginning to the end"; 2 Chronicles 35:25. **4:** *Ecclesiastes Rabbah* 1:3: "No man leaves the world with even half his desire in hand." **5–8:** Ezekiel 47:11; Jeremiah 10:13; Psalms 104:11.

## MY HEART'S SECRET

*SHIE*, #102; *HaShira*, #161:5. **Lines 1–2:** Malachi 1:9; Proverbs 25:9. **3–4:** Genesis 39:26; Habakkuk 2:18; 1 Samuel 18:23. **5:** The world of time and pleasure and materiality *(tevel)* is always feminine in the medieval Hebrew (and Arabic) context.

## I ROUSED MY THOUGHTS FROM SLUMBER

*SHIE*, #144; *HaShira*, #160. **Heading:** "And he said, consoling himself, as he turned toward asceticism." Scheindlin calls this a poem of "old age" and suggests that the poem presents a kind of spiritual autobiography—which happens to be remarkably similar to the one Browning presents in his "Rabbi Ibn Ezra" (though the latter is assumed to be about Avraham Ibn Ezra). **Lines 1–2:** The eyes are identified with desire. The life of desire in this scheme is a kind of slumber; the life of the mind and contemplation is wakefulness. Numbers 15:39. **3–4:** Ecclesiastes 2:3; Isaiah 41:22. **5–6:** Job 11:6. **7–8:** Job 11:6; Psalms 82:6. **9–12:** Numbers 24:4, 16; Exodus 17:7; Job 23:9. **13–18:** Proverbs 2:27, 6:22, 4:18; Psalms 119:105. **19–20:** Proverbs 20:27. **21–22:** Psalms 39:6. **25–26:** Ecclesiastes 12:14; *Ta'anit* 11a. **27–28:** Obadiah 1:3. **29–30:** Deuteronomy 25:9, where a widow's removal of a brother-in-law's shoe and spitting in his face acknowledges his (the brother-in-law's) formal refusal to marry her and "build up his brother's house." **31–36:** 2 Samuel 1:10; Isaiah 3:18; Job 38:32; Ezekiel 13:11. **37–38:** Ezekiel 43:8. **39–42:** Isaiah 5:18, 55:5; Ezekiel 7:11. **43–44:** Literally, "I said: I kissed him in peace, and they said: I bit him with my teeth." I.e., because they do not really know me (my character), even my gestures of friendliness are interpreted as underhanded schemes. The Hebrew plays on kiss (*nashaq*) and bite (*nashakh*), like the midrash on Jacob and Esau. Micah 3:5. **47–48:** Psalms 55:15. **51–52:** 1 Kings 9:3; Psalms 63:6. **55–56:** Psalms 87:7, where the word *ma'ayanai*—literally, "springs"—is usually translated as "thoughts," "roots," or "sources."

## Let Man Wail

*SHIE*, #128. **Lines 1–2:** Ezekiel 32:18; Psalms 31:11, 102:4; Exodus 19:18. **3–4:** Jeremiah 46:23.

## On the Death of His Son

From a series of eight poems he wrote after the death of his son Ya'aqov. **Heading:** "And he wrote short poems on the death of his small son." I. *SHIE*, #97. **Lines 1–4:** I.e., "my heart failed me," or "sank," as in Genesis 42:28.

II. *SHIE*, #237. **Line 4:** 2 Samuel 24:14, 1:26, 19:1.

III. *SHIE*, #211. **Line 2:** Job 41:6–7: "Who can open the door of his face? Round about his teeth is terror. His scales are his pride, shut up together as with a close seal" [NJPS: "binding seal"]. **3–4:** Job 18:14; Lamentations 2:22.

## The Blind

*SHIE*, #60. **Lines 1–2:** Genesis 27:1. **3–4:** *Megillah* 28a: "R. Nehunia b. HaQaneh was asked by his disciples: In virtue of what have you reached such a good old age? He replied: Never in my life have I sought respect through the degradation of my fellow." **5–6:** Jeremiah 22:28.

## The Gazelle's Sigh

*Moshe Ibn Ezra: Shirei Qodesh*, ed. S. Bernstein (Tel Aviv, 1958), #37 (hereafter *SQIE*); *HaShira*, #163:2. Even more than Ibn Gabirol, Ibn Ezra was known for his often remarkable incorporation of strategies and images from secular Hebrew and Arabic poetry into his poetry for the synagogue. The history of this poem testifies to that success: throughout the modern period it has been considered an *ahava*, that is, a liturgical poem attached to the part of the liturgy that speaks of God's love for Israel. Fleischer, however, notes that it appears in many manuscripts of the poet's (secular) diwan, and that Brody omitted it from his edition of the secular poems because he thought its content rendered it liturgical; that said, it appears in no prayer books, bears no acrostic signature or any other liturgical markers, and is in fact a secular poem that involves the poet's allegorical Judaification of an Arabic motif. As such, it perfectly straddles the border between four traditions (Hebrew and Arabic on the one hand, and secular and sacred on the other). **Lines 1–2:** The poem employs the motif of the *atlaal*, or abandoned site of a beloved's camp or dwelling, over which the lover weeps. The image is central to the early qasida of the Arabic tradition. Here the abandoned dwelling would be the Land of Israel, though the word Ibn Ezra uses for it *(ma'on)* associates it with the Temple. Deuteronomy 26:15; Psalms 26:8; Jeremiah 10:22. For a talmudic parallel, see also *Makkot* 24b. **3–4:** Amos 3:4. **5–6:** The gazelle here is the congregation of Israel (feminine: *Knesset Yisrael*) and Edom, as always in the context of medieval Hebrew verse, stands for Rome and Christianity. **7–8:** "The bridegroom of her youth" is God. Jeremiah 3:4; Proverbs 2:17. **9–10:** Song of Songs 2:5.

## GOLD

*SQIE*, #38; *HaShira*, #163:3. Acrostic: *Moshe*. An *ahava*. Again the poem begins with a scene that might easily be part of a secular love poem and continues in this fashion until the last two lines, where the loyalty expressed is completely out of keeping with the conventions of the secular love lyric. As Scheindlin notes, the passive religious attitude of the lover in this poem—known in Arabic as *tawakkul*, or complete trust, even surrender—is usually associated with individual piety (see, for instance, Yehuda HaLevi's, "You Knew Me"); here it applies to the entire people of Israel. **Lines 1–2:** As in the previous poem, the beloved is God and the lover is the congregation of Israel. 1 Kings 14:15. **4–5:** Jeremiah 2:2: "I remember for thee the affection of thy youth, the love of thine espousals; how thou wentest after me in the wilderness, in a land that was not sown"; Job 19:16; Psalms 119: 20, 40, 174. **6–7:** Job 13:15: "Though He slay me, yet will I trust in Him"; Deuteronomy 31:18. **8–9:** Lamentations 4:1.

## THE DAY TO COME

*SQIE*, #76; *HaShira*, #164. Acrostic: *Moshe*. A *seliha*, in the form of a *muwashshah*. Ibn Ezra was known as *HaSalah* (the penitent, or composer of penitential poems—*selihot*), and his collected liturgical works contain a great many such poems for the period leading up to the Jewish New Year and the Day of Atonement.

**Lines 1–8:** The day of one's death. Malachi 3:2. **16:** Psalms 146:4. **21:** Psalms 75:9. **32:** Deuteronomy 1:32. As in Ibn Gabirol's *Kingdom's Crown*, canto 27, the souls of the righteous ascend to the palace of wisdom and the throne of glory, where they dwell until the Day of Judgment.

## AT THE HOUR OF CLOSING

*SQIE*, #150. (A shorter version of the *piyyut* can be found in *The Language of Faith*, ed. N. Glatzer [New York, 1967], p. 298.) Acrostic: *Moshe Hazaq*. Ibn Ezra's most popular liturgical poem is found in many prayer books through the centuries, though Moshe Ibn Ezra was not always identified as its author. A *ne'ila*, the poem is recited as a prelude to the solemn conclusion near sunset of the Yom Kippur prayer service; it marks the annual "closing (*ne'ila*) of the gates" of heaven to prayers for repentance. The editor of Ibn Ezra's liturgical poems also calls it a *pizmon*, as the opening lines were recited after each stanza as a refrain. **26:** To Jerusalem and Samaria. Ezekiel 23:4, 11, 22, 36, and 44. See also Yehuda HaLevi's "Won't You Ask, Zion?" lines 55–56.

## YOSEF IBN TZADDIQ

### A WEDDING NIGHT'S CONSOLATION

*Shirei Ibn Tzaddiq*, ed. Y. David (New York, 1982), #33. The poem is addressed to the recently wedded Avraham Ibn Ezra, who found himself in a most uncomfortable situation when his bride's menstrual period began just after the wedding ceremony but before the marriage could be consummated. The biblically based Jewish laws of ritual purity forbid a husband from touching his wife for at least two weeks each month—seven days from the onset of bleeding and another seven days without any signs of blood. (Leviticus 15:19ff.: "And if a woman have an issue, and her issue in her flesh be blood, she shall be in her impurity seven days"; Leviticus 18:19: "Do not come near a woman during her period of uncleanness.") The second seven days were added by the rabbinic tradition, after which point ritual immersion in the *mikve* would render the woman "clean." (Later halakhic practices differed somewhat.) Ibn Tzaddiq, the *dayyan*, or religious judge, of Cordoba, teases his friend, who had no doubt been looking forward to his wedding night and now had to wait an additional two weeks to consummate the marriage. If the heading is understood as saying that Ibn Tzaddiq wrote on the seventh night after the wedding, then he might have been compounding the joke by writing just when a non-menstruating bride would, after the blood of the defloration, again be "clean" following her ritual immersion. (The two men were, however, not in the same city, and it would have taken at least a few days for the poem to reach Ibn Ezra, so he would not have received it on the seventh night.) In other words, what would normally be a second night to look forward to has become for Ibn Ezra simply another night of frustration. Ibn Ezra responds with "The Wedding Night, Continued" (below). **Heading:** "And R. Yosef Ibn Tzaddiq wrote this to one of his friends, our teacher and master Avraham (of blessed memory), seven days after his wedding [or during the week after his wedding], as the bride's menstrual period began before the deflowering, and he wrote in jest, saying." **Line 2:** "Bridegroom of blood" alludes to the circumcision incident of Exodus 4:25, where, after the circumcision of her son, Zipporah says: "You are truly a bridegroom of blood to me." The poem uses the scriptural citation to rub it in, as it were. **7:** Ezekiel 18:6: "neither hath [he] come near to a woman in her impurity." *Shulhan Arukh*, the most important medieval code of Jewish law (sixteenth century—but based on earlier compilations), explains: "Any kind of approach is forbidden; he should not play with her or indulge in foolery, or even speak words that may lead to sin" (*Hilkhot Niddah* 153; *Kitzur Shulhan Arukh*, trans. Judah Goldin [New York, 1961], 4:22). While stating that the menstrual period should be anticipated and weddings should be set while the bride is "clean," the *Shulhan Arukh* also accounts for cases in which "it happens that [the bride] becomes menstrually unclean after the wedding ceremony and before cohabitation." In these cases the bride and groom must be separated until she becomes clean. As we will see in Ibn Ezra's reply, the Spanish-Hebrew poets were much less strict about such things. **9:** Deuteronomy 19:11. **11–12:** I.e., the sperm. **13–14:** There are two readings for this line. The alternative reading has: "for a drop is already outside you." The rhetorical figure of contrasting elements suggests that the Hebrew should read *bitha* (safety i.e., if you stay outside, you'll be safe) rather than *tipa* (a drop). **16:** Job 20:8. **19–20:** Numbers 13:19. **21–22:** Isaiah 63:1: "Who is this that cometh from Edom, with crimsoned garments from Bozrah?" Ibn Ezra plays on this scriptural image of the deliverance to be brought by a divine being in crimson garments. According to rabbinic interpretation of this biblical verse, the being is a vision of God as a bloody warrior returning from His battle with Israel's enemy, whom He routed, bringing redemption to His people. **23:** Kahana's text of Ibn Ezra's reply, which also prints Ibn Tzaddiq's poem, reads: "my soul laments" (as in Isaiah 19:8). See notes to Avraham Ibn Ezra's "World Poetry." **25–26:** The precise meaning of these lines is uncertain, and they may be referring to elements of a previous conversation the two writers had. One possible reading is that the reference here is to the unclean state of the couple, as in *Menahot* 109a: "The priests who ministered in the Temple of Onias may not minister in the Temple of Jerusalem; . . . for it is written, Nevertheless the priests of the high places came not up to the altar of the Lord in Jerusalem, but they did eat unleavened bread among their brethren. Thus they are like those that had a blemish . . . they are not permitted to offer sacrifices." Kahana understands this to mean that Ibn Ezra is trapped in the worship of a woman (the high place, or altar)—though this isn't clear. **29–30:** "Roused" here is also uncertain, and most likely refers to the arguments that Ibn Tzaddiq recalls they would have over minor differences of opinion—the implication being that his friend knows Ibn Ezra's passionate nature and can imagine how hard the frustration must be for him. Given the context, however, it may also allude to the use of the same word (*mitgarim*) in *Sanhedrin* 45a: "Lest . . . the young priests conceive a passion for her." **31–32:** Psalms 68:36. **33–34:** Deuteronomy 28:43.

<h2 style="text-align:center">LADY OF GRACE</h2>

*Shirei Ibn Tzaddiq*, #17; *HaShira*, #245. Acrostic: *Yosef.* This most fluid of *muwashshahat* treats both Neoplatonic and popular beliefs concerning the linkage of soul and body. The Hebrew has an elaborate rhyme scheme, which adds a dense and perfectly symmetrical network of internal rhymes to the standard end-rhyme (*aa // bbb/aa // ccc/aa*, etc.) of the complex *muwashshah* stanza, yielding a full rhyme scheme that might be charted as follows: *abc/abc // def/def/def // agc/agc // hij/hij/hij // akc/akc*, etc. The translation echoes that movement through sound down the page, without trying to reproduce the rhyme scheme itself. The final two lines allude to the female voice of the secular *muwashshah's kharja* (final couplet or quatrain in the English) and indicate the poem's liturgical function as a prelude to the *nishmat* prayer. The poem is, liturgically, a *muharak* (a mover), that is, a strophic poem preceding the *reshut* to the prayer itself. **Line 1:** I.e., the soul. **4:** See Ibn Gabirol, *Kingdom's Crown*, canto 29. **5:** The rest of the poem responds to the questions posed in line 4. **13:** Proverbs 1:4. **20:** Jeremiah 23:28. **29:** The soul emanates from a divine source and is, therefore, eternal.

<h2 style="text-align:center">SHELOMO IBN TZAQBEL</h2>

Ibn Tzaqbel was also known as Shelomo Ibn Sahl and was a relative of the poet Yosef Ibn Sahl. For detailed discussion of the Hebrew *maqaama* and its conventions, see Schirmann, *Toldot* (1995), pp. 91ff.; M. Huss, "HaMagid beMaqaama HaQlassit," *Tarbiz* 65 (1996); and R. Drory, "The Maqama," in Menocal et al., *The Literature of al-Andalus*, pp. 190–210). The poems in this section are spoken by the (noble) woman at various points in the *maqaama*. First, while hiding behind a lattice she throws a perfumed apple inscribed with a poem down to the protagonist (Asher), who responds to this courtly gesture in apparently conventional but in fact presumptuous and somewhat vulgar fashion. The woman then seeks to teach him a lesson, gradually drawing him into both the palace and the ways of more refined courtly love. In the process, as she deceives and humiliates him through scenes of terror and "transvestite theater," there develops a contrast between what Raymond Scheindlin calls "fawns of the palace and fawns of the field" (see *Prooftexts* 6/3 [1986]), representing, respectively, courtly and uncourtly behavior in love. Tova Rosen, in related but not identical fashion, reads the *maqaama* and its lesson as a commentary on the patriarchal order and a story of the protagonist's "socialization, domestication, and sexual instruction" (*Unveiling Eve*, pp. 152–55).

### LINES INSCRIBED ON AN APPLE

*Yedi'ot HaMakhon leHeqer HaShira Ha'Ivrit* 2 (Berlin, 1936), p. 156; *HaShira*, #246, lines 30–31. **Line 2:** Song of Songs 2:17.

### NOTE TO A SUITOR NOW PERPLEXED

*Yedi'ot HaMakhon* 2:159; *HaShira*, #246, lines 104–6. **Line 5:** Literally, "How could I forget [how you behaved previously]?" I.e., how can I forgive you for being so diffident earlier on and showing interest in others instead of me?

### A FAWN WITH HER LASHES

*Yedi'ot HaMakhon* 2:161; *HaShira*, #246, lines 158–59. **Line 2:** 1 Kings 1:52. **3:** Proverbs 3:27. **4:** Psalms 77:10. The fawn is grammatically masculine (perhaps for the meter) in the Hebrew, but clearly refers to the girl.

## YEHUDA HALEVI

My comments here are based in part on Ross Brann's lucid examination of HaLevi's life and work, and the complex ways in which the poet is viewed in the literature. See *The Literature of al-Andalus*, pp. 265–81, and *The Compunctious Poet*, pp. 88–89, where Brann writes among other things of the social context of HaLevi's "war . . . waged against the cult of Arabic." Other views of HaLevi, he notes, treat his "renunciation of 'Greek wisdom'" and his "mystical rebirth." The poet's disillusionment with the situation of the Jewish courtiers is described in Schirmann, *Toldot* (1995), p. 437. On Jewish suffering at the hands of the Almoravids and the Christians, see note 47 to the introduction to this volume. Salo Baron's assessment is in "Yehuda HaLevi: An Answer to an Historic Challenge," *Jewish Social Studies*, July 1941, pp. 243–72. See also Yehuda Halevi, *Poems from the Diwan*, trans. Gabriel Levin (London, 2002), and the graceful introduction there. The chronology of HaLevi's emergence as a poet on the one hand and his departure from Spain on the other rely for the most part on Schirmann's version of these events in *Toldot* (1995), and in some cases on Ezra Fleischer's research, much of which draws from the documents preserved in the Cairo Geniza. Other scholars, however, have proposed alternative chronologies: Yosef Yahalom, for example, argues that HaLevi was born in the city of Toledo, c. 1085 (not 1075), and never met Ibn Ezra in Granada. Ibn Ezra, according to Yahalom, was already on the move, and by the time HaLevi made contact with him, the older poet was in

Estrella, near the northeast coast of the peninsula. After the two met there, HaLevi continued on to Granada alone. With regard to HaLevi's pilgrimage, Fleischer uses evidence from the Geniza letters to suggest that he had in fact planned to leave Spain some ten years earlier and may have gotten as far as North Africa, but for reasons that remain elusive, he turned back. Fleischer also has a different chronology for at least some of the sea poems, as noted below, and he suggests that a preliminary version of *The Kuzari* had been composed by the summer of 1129 (Ezra Fleischer and Moshe Gil, *HaLevi uVenei Hugo* [HaLevi and His Circle] [Jerusalem, 2001], pp. 67, 184).

"Extreme racialism" is how Baron characterized HaLevi's thought, as it was reflected in *The Kuzari* (though later in the essay he calls it, simply, "racism"). Specifically, Baron is responding to the views put forth in that volume, where the rabbi-scholar characterizes the (chosen) Jews as "a people natively different from, and superior to, all other peoples." In a long and somewhat complex and shocking passage, the rabbi-scholar claims in *The Kuzari* that Jews (but not converts to Judaism) have a kind of supersoul, which endows them with the gift of prophecy and supremacy (see cf. 1:103; also 1:27, 47, 95, and 115). As M. S. Berger puts it: "The Rabbi thus posits a fifth level of soul, higher than the rational faculty: the divine disposition or essence, of which only the Jews partake. . . . [This] sets the Jews apart from the rest of humanity in their very essence" ("Toward a New Understanding of Judah HaLevi's *Kuzari*," *Journal of Religion*, 1992, pp. 210–28). Baron, however, warns that these "racialist contentions" need to be read not in modern terms, but in the context of both HaLevi's argument about the centrality of Jewish powerlessness and the highly race-conscious nature of the Andalusian world. With regard to HaLevi's "proto-Zionism," Schirmann comments that "there is nothing in the poet's worldview remotely reminiscent of modern political Zionism." Schirmann goes on to say that HaLevi's relation to the Holy Land was purely visionary, and that he set out for it knowing full well that the Crusaders were there and that he was likely to die carrying out his mission (*Toldot* [1995], p. 464). That said, a more recent and perhaps culturally updated assessment is offered by David Hartman: "In Israel today" religious nationalists regard HaLevi rather than Maimonides or other medieval Jewish thinkers as the spiritual precursor of religious Zionism" (*Israelis and the Jewish Tradition* [New Haven, 2000], p. 26). For more on all of the foregoing, see Y. Yahalom, "Diwan and Odyssey," *Miscellania Estudios Arabica y Hebraica* 44 (1995): 23–45; Y. Yahalom, "Shira veHevra beMitzrayim, *Tzion* 45 (1980); Y. Yahalom, "Ginzei Leningrad ve-Heqer Shirat Hayyav shel R. Yehuda HaLevi," *Pe'amim* 46/47 (1991); Fleischer and Gil, *HaLevi uVenei Hugo*; Goitein, *A Mediterranean Society*, vol. 5, and "The Biography of R. Judah Ha-Levi in the Light of the Cairo Geniza Documents," *Proceedings of the American Academy for Jewish Research*, vol. 28 (New York, 1959), pp. 41–56. The Sufi background of the *Kuzari* is treated by Diana Lobel (*Between Mysticism and Philosophy* [Albany, 2000]), who notes that, while HaLevi doesn't mention the Sufis by name, "he is clearly aware of the power of the Arabic terms he chooses and uses them with ironic twists to draw in his Judaeo-Arabic readers. Like Maimonides in his *Eight Chapter on Ethics (Shemona Peraqim)*, HaLevi may be addressing Jews drawn to Sufi spirituality" (p. 159; see also pp. 4–5, 21, and 177).

All the poems in this selection were composed in the classical Andalusian styles, that is, as monorhymed or strophic poems employing quantitative meter.

## That Night a Gazelle

*Diwan: Yehuda HaLevi*, ed. H. Brody (Berlin, 1894–1930), 2:20 (hereafter *DYH*); *HaShira*, #175:4. **Line 3:** Song of Songs 4:1, 4. **4:** Her hair is *tzahov* (literally, "yellow") in the Hebrew, which in the medieval literary context (see, for instance, Ibn Janaah) suggests a reddish tint of one sort or another. The color of the ideal beloved's hair in the Arabic, and by extension Hebrew, tradition was of course black. But we know that blond or reddish hair was also prized. As HaLevi comes from the "Christian" north, it isn't surprising to find him celebrating the fairer-haired beauty as well. The Arabic author Ibn Hazm, HaNagid's peer, expresses a similar preference: "In my youth I loved a slave-girl who happened to be a blonde; from that time I have never admired brunettes, not though their dark tresses set off a face as resplendent as the sun." See A. J. Arberry, *The Dove's Neck Ring* (London, 1953/94), pp. 61, 64. **9:** Job 7:4.

## A Doe Washes

*DYH*, 2:12; *HaShira*, #175:6. **Heading:** "He improvised this when he passed by a stream where laundry was being done. And this is among his most beautiful works." (Or, "this is among the most beautiful things.") **Lines 1–2:** Ofrah is both a woman's first name and a word meaning "doe" or "fawn." **3–4:** Jeremiah 8:2.

## If Only Dawn

*DYH*, 2:45. This poem has also at times been attributed to Levi Ibn Altabbaan (see Pagis, *Shirei Ibn Altabbaan*, p. 166). Elitzur has a fine analysis of this poem (*Shirat HaHol*, pp. 101–3), wherein she notes the gradual lifting of the lover's gaze from line to line, from the wind to the clouds to the stars. At the same time, the presence or promise of the beloved grows closer and closer—from a caress mediated by the wind, to a softening of her heart, to the possibility of reaching her level, seeing her, and, perhaps, meeting on high. All of which only underscores the impossibility of their ever actually coming together. **Lines 3–4:** Psalms 72:3.

## That Day while I Had Him

*DYH*, 2:16; *HaShira*, #180:2. Essentially a translation of a poem by the great tenth-century Arabic poet al-Mutanabbi, which reads: "A Syrian woman, when I was alone with her,/saw her face in my eye;/and then she kissed my eye, and misled me,/for she was kissing there only her own mouth." HaLevi freely adjusts the situation to suit his needs, in the process changing the gender of the self-infatuated lover from female to male—something neither convention nor meter would necessarily call for. While poems such as this one don't necessarily confirm a poet's homosexual experience, they do provide further evidence that the Andalusian Hebrew poets were not merely using the Arabic convention of the homoerotic poem to disguise affection for the opposite sex. **Line 1:** Isaiah 66:12. **3:** Genesis 27:12.

## ANOTHER APPLE

*DYH*, 2:19. **Line 1:** Ezekiel 7:20. **4–8:** The poet's slight of hand is deftly executed from here until the end of the poem. Nothing he has seen has matched her grace, though the apple he's about to see (in his imagination) will be characterized in such terms as to recall precisely that grace. In other words, while no other woman is like her, she has the power to transform everything he sees into a reflection of her grace and beauty.

## TO IBN AL-MUʿALLIM

"Asher Ahaz beKenafot Ahava," ed. Y. Ratzhaby, *Itton 77*, no. 169 (1994). Now counted among the poet's finest works, this remarkably lush poem of friendship was discovered in the Firkovitch Leningrad collection and first published by M. Stern in *Romanica et Occidentalia*, ed. M. Lazar (Jerusalem, 1963), and then with a detailed commentary by Ratzhaby. The poem is addressed to Shelomo Ibn al-Muʿallim, a Seville-born close friend of the poet who had written to him with a poem of his own, probably from Morocco, where he practiced medicine. (Maimonides says that Ibn al-Muʿallim was court physician to ʿAli Ibn Yusef, the Almoravid ruler.) HaLevi was not in Granada to receive the letter and acknowledge the poem, and so his friend Moshe Ibn Ezra replied in his place; HaLevi then replied on his own when the letter finally reached him. The full qasida contains forty lines, which would be eighty in the translation. I have translated only an excerpt, from the erotic prelude (lines 1–2, 4–6 of the original) and lines 24–25. **Lines 1–2:** 2 Samuel 18:5: "Deal gently with the young man, for my sake." **3–4:** The attraction is "pure," i.e., Platonic; it isn't supposed to lead to consummation. Proverbs 5:19. **5:** Or, "Let me gather. . . ." **6:** I.e., the red of your blushing cheeks and the white of the face. The Hebrew employs the term for a prohibited mixture, *kilayyim* (Leviticus 19:19: "Thou shalt not sow thy field with two kinds of seeds"). **7–10:** That is, he would satisfy his desire (put out his fire) by taking in (seeing) the red glow of his cheeks, which also contain water that might put out the fire within his heart. The verb—translated here as "lift"—implies a withdrawal or scooping of the coals from the fires of the Temple offerings (*Yoma* 4:4: "Every day he would scoop out the cinders with a silver pan and empty them into a golden one; but today he would clear out the coals in a gold one, and in that same one he would bring the [glowing] cinders in[to the inner sanctuary]"). Isaiah 30:14: "To take fire from the hearth." **11:** Or: "I'd drain [suck] the lip." **13:** Song of Songs 4:3. **15–18:** The translation skips five Hebrew (ten English) lines in which the poet describes in extremely sensual terms the scroll on which Ibn al-Muʿallim's poem is written: "The rows of myrrh are a gown of gold, / like twilight spread across the noon. . . . / Across the scroll his hands have fashioned / colors not found in the face of the fawn." After that it skips twelve Hebrew lines (twenty four in English) in which HaLevi praises Ibn al-Muʿallim in extravagant fashion (he likens him to the sun that will shine with sevenfold strength during the age of the Messiah); he then addresses him directly and tells him how much he misses him. The rest of the poem describes the suffering that his parting caused. He closes with a blessing. **17:** Ratzhaby's manuscript has *hemah* (butter, as in Job 29:6); Stern has *homer* (clay), which makes more sense and which I have followed. In either case, the thrust is that the situation was comfortable for the poet, and he could do as he liked with Time, as the wheel of the sun turned like that of the potter.

## IF ONLY I COULD GIVE

*DYH*, 1:89. A *muwashshah*. In "If Only I Could Be," below, HaLevi employs the same form and similar motifs in a powerful liturgical poem. In this secular version, the images throughout are taken from the Arabic tradition. **Lines 1–4:** Job 29:2; Song of Songs 4:3. **8–10:** "Sun's brother"—an epithet for the beloved. **13–14:** Literally, "Love's hand joined me to him, and never led me astray." **15–16:** Genesis 16:5. **21:** The fine thread of cruel fate. **34:** Psalms 18:17. **35:** The poet now turns to tell of his new friend, David [Abu al-Hasan ben al-Dayyan], who made him forget his sorrow over separation from the "fawn." He dedicates this poem to him. **40:** Judges 29:9. **40:** Judges 9:29. **41–42:** Deuteronomy 32:42. **45–50:** The poet now lays the ground for the *kharja* of the poem. **51–54:** HaLevi here follows common practice with the secular *muwashshah* and places the lines of the *kharja* in the mouth of a female figure, who speaks in the local dialect—in this case a mixture of Arabic and Romance (written out in Hebrew letters). Usually this is a woman of a lower class; here it is a dove who sings like a young woman, and her song seems to be telling the protagonist that, with his new friend, he will overcome the obstacles Fate puts before him. According to Yosef Yahalom and Isaac Benabu ("The Importance of the Genizah Manuscripts for the Establishment of the Text of the Hispano-Romance Kharjas In Hebrew Characters," *Romance Philology* 40/2 (1986): 139–58), these lines should read: "venceray beni / el querer estaba beni // dexa al-zameni / con fillo [d'] Ibn al-Dayyeni."

### EPITHALAMIUM

*D.Y.H.*, 2:29. A wedding poem, a genre that combines elements of the encomium and the poem of desire, or love poem. It often incorporates elements of the poems of description as well (particularly descriptions of the garden). Other wedding poems are closer in spirit and form to liturgical poetry, and still others were intended to be recited as part of the liturgy. See, in this volume, Dunash's "Blessing for a Wedding." **Lines 1–2:** Genesis 14:3; Isaiah 24:21. **4:** Job 41:8: "One is so near another that not even a breath can enter between them. They are joined to one another [and] cannot be parted." A lovely image, of course, though in Job it refers to the scales on a dangerous mythological creature, modeled on the crocodile. **6:** The translation here is free. The lines read, literally, "and found a sun [the bride] among its daughters." **7:** Literally, "he set up a canopy of leafy boughs." The masculine subject here refers to the groom, though as the image of the final lines unfolds, readers who have the Psalms in mind will most likely also understand it as referring to—or at least suggesting— God. This ambiguity, however, is not central to the poem, which concentrates on the happy couple. "Leafy boughs" literally translates an obscure phrase from Leviticus 23:4; in the context of the poem, the various commentators note, it means "myrtle branches," as the wedding canopies were often decorated with branches from fragrant plants. The "myrtle canopy" is mentioned in *Ketubot* 17b. Myrtle and its fragrance are traditionally associated in this poetry (as in classical Western verse) with beauty and love; in the Hebrew context there is also a remote messianic dimension to the association, deriving from Zechariah 1:8–11. See Ibn Gabirol's "The Garden" and the notes to that poem. **8:** The image of the tent for the sun derives from Psalms 19:5: "He placed in them [in the heavens] a tent for the sun, who is like a groom coming forth from his chamber." Sun (*shemesh*) can be either masculine or feminine, grammatically. In the psalm it is masculine; in the poem it is analogous to the bride. The tent is like the heavens, in which the sun shines (and has dominion). In the modern context, the canopy will inevitably also be understood as shelter, and the translation preserves that possibility.

### WHEN A LONE SILVER HAIR

*DYH*, 2:316; *HaShira*, #178:2. **Line 4:** 1 Samuel 30:8: "And David inquired of the Lord, saying: 'Shall I pursue after this troop?'"

### IF TIME

*DYH*, 2:301. This poem also appears in Falaqera's *Book of the Seeker*.

## Inscriptions on Bowls

Two of several such inscriptions that are attributed to both HaLevi and Moshe Ibn Ezra. The practice of decorating bowls with lines of verse was taken over from the Arabic tradition. In both cases, the bowl itself is speaking.

*I.*

*DYH*, 2:312; *SHIE*, #48. The bowl speaks to the guest before it. The Hebrew mentions only a piece of "fine fat," implying a juicy piece of meat; the connotations of fat were entirely positive in the medieval context and implied bounty. **Heading:** "Among what he inscribed on gilded bowls."

*II.*

*DYH*, 2:215; *SHIE*, #165. **Heading:** As above. The bowl speaks to its host and, by implication, the guests who admire it. **Line 4:** Lamentations 2:19.

## Four Riddles

HaLevi had a distinct fondness for the riddle, and his diwan contains some forty-nine of them. Like all the medieval Hebrew (and Arabic) riddles, these rely on an often deliberately misleading presentation of apparent paradoxes and oppositions, the solution of which usually lies in unraveling the metaphorical code of the poem. Essentially descriptive epigrams, the best of them lose little from the revelation of their answers.

*I.*

*DYH* 2:195. The translation is somewhat free. Answer: A hand mirror.

*II.*

*DYH* 2:205; *HaShira*, #179:1. Answer: A pen.

*III.*

*DYH* 2:200. Answer: Seed.

*IV.*

*DYH* 2:209. Answer: A cloud. **Lines 3–4:** The Hebrew verb is *soheqet*, which might be variously translated as laughing, playing, teasing, being happy.

## Departure

*DYH*, 1:159. This is essentially HaLevi's translation, or adaptation, of an Arabic poem, whose author isn't mentioned. **Line 3:** Genesis 33:14, with reference to Jacob and Esau. **6:** Jeremiah 14:18.

ON FRIENDSHIP AND TIME

*DYH*, 1:154; *HaShira*, #185:1. This qasida was written to the poet's older friend and former mentor, Moshe Ibn Ezra, who was at the time living in "exile" in northern—Christian—Spain while HaLevi was still in the south. (For details on Ibn Ezra's departure from Andalusia, see the biographical introduction to his poems in this anthology.) It is one of the more moving poems of friendship in the entire canon. The long prelude treating separation (in this case philosophically) is followed by a transition (lines 25–28) to the poet's direct address to his friend and fond recollection of their friendship (lines 29–44). That in turn is followed by HaLevi's uncharacteristic complaint (lines 45–64)—reminiscent of Ibn Gabirol's "On Leaving Saragossa"—about the company he is now forced to keep. Finally the poet returns to the philosophical theme with which the poem began. **Lines 1–2:** Judges 5:21. **8–9:** Psalms 8:4. **9–10:** Psalms 77:11. **13–16:** Genesis 25:23, 11:1–9—the story of Jacob and Esau on the one hand, and the Tower of Babel on the other. **18:** Proverbs 3:8. **19–20:** Isaiah 8:21; Numbers 23:7–8. **21–22:** Job 21:13. **24:** Job 30:4. **27:** Exodus 40:35. **28:** Jeremiah 13:17. **31:** Genesis 44:30. **37–38:** Song of Songs 5:13; Isaiah 66:11. **39–40:** Song of Songs 2:17. **42:** Isaiah 9:4. **45:** HaLevi turns to his present state, surrounded by people who neither understand him nor have much patience with him. **46–48:** Jeremiah 9:7; Psalms 55:22. **50:** Isaiah 5:21. **59–60:** Genesis 37:7, and Joseph's dream of the sheaves. **62:** Proverbs 11:22. **66:** I.e., Time, or Fortune and Fate, are merely vessels, which will be shed when the soul passes on to the world to come. Daniel 3:27.

SLAVES OF TIME

*DYH*, 2:300; *HaShira*, #227. **Line 1:** *Qiddushin* 22b: "Why was the ear singled out from all the other parts of the body? The Holy One, blessed be He, said, This ear—which heard my Voice on Mount Sinai when I proclaimed, *For unto me the children of Israel are servants, they are my servants* (Leviticus 25:55), and not servants of servants, and yet this [man] went and acquired a master for himself—let it be bored." Also *The Kuzari: An Argument for the Faith of Israel*, trans. from the Arabic by Hartwig Hirschfeld, introduction H. Slonimsky (New York, 1964), 5:25: "I only seek freedom from the service of those numerous people whose favor I do not care for, and shall never obtain, though I worked for it all my life. Even if I could obtain it, it would not profit me—I mean serving men and courting their favor. I would rather seek the service of the One whose favor is obtained with the smallest effort, yet it profits in this world and the next. This is the favor of God, his service spells freedom, and humility before Him is true honor." **4:** Lamentations 3:24: " 'The Lord is my portion,' saith my soul."

HEAL ME, LORD

*DYH*, 2:294; *HaShira*, #233. **Heading:** "And he wrote this when he drank a potion." HaLevi, we recall, was a physician, and the "I" of this poem is clearly personal. All knowledge, even medical knowledge, is nothing without divine guidance. See *The Kuzari* 1:79, which states that the "conditions which render man fit to receive [the] divine influence do not lie within him." HaLevi then proceeds by way of analogy to compare the man who has prepared himself properly to receive the divine influence to a well-trained physician who is trained in the preparation of appropriate medicines and is able to explain to patients how they are to be administered. **Line 1:** Numbers 12:13. **5–6:** Job 10:7.

## True Life

*DYH*, 2:296; *HaShira*, #221. The transparency of this poem is representative of the transparency at the heart of HaLevi's mystical vision, a vision which involves the aspirant's surrender to the divine and his passive reception of God's presence. That said, this is apparently not a liturgical poem at all, and Brody classifies it with the secular poetry. The image of God appearing in a dream recalls the night-visitation of the lover in Arabic secular love poetry (see, for instance, Yosef Ibn Hasdai's "The Qasida," above) and adds a measure of passion and vulnerability to the poem. The final image of the poem recalls Raabi'a, the mystical Arabic woman poet who was known to shut the windows in spring, since, as Rumi put it in his version of her story, "the gardens and the fruits are inside, in the heart" (Schimmel, *Calligraphy and Culture*, p. 39, and Scheindlin, *The Gazelle*, p. 200). HaLevi comments in *The Kuzari*, 4:3: "But our intellect . . . cannot penetrate to the true knowledge of things, except by the grace of God, by special faculties which He has placed in the senses. . . . To the chosen among His creatures He has given an inner eye which sees things as they really are, without any alteration. . . . [The] prophets without doubt saw the divine world with the inner eye. . . . His sight reaches up to the heavenly host direct, he sees the dwellers in heaven, and the spiritual beings which are near God, and others in human form." **Lines 1–2:** Psalms 36:10. **3:** Exodus 33:22–23. **4:** "In a dream," i.e., with that "inner eye." **7–8:** Exodus 28:26.

## The Morning Stars

*Shirei Qodesh leRabbi Yehuda haLevi*, ed. D. Yarden (Jerusalem, 1978/86), #288. (hereafter *SQYH*); *HaShira*, #234. A *reshut*. Three levels of the cosmos praise God by mirroring His splendor in their own way: the stars, the angels, and the people of Israel, though the universalizing vision of Neoplatonic linkage (which we find, for instance, with Ibn Gabirol) gives way here to HaLevi's particularist vision, wherein the congregation gathered in the synagogue at dawn represents the elect human contingent in this chorus of praise. This medieval cosmic scheme is nonetheless very loosely based on Psalms 103:20, which exhort His angels, His heavenly hosts, and "His works in all places of His dominion" to bless the Lord. The three "dominions," "worlds," or "forces" are also mentioned in

Avraham Ibn Ezra's commentary to these psalmic verses and to Daniel 10:21, as well as in the mystical Hebrew work *Sefer HaBahir*. **Lines 1–4:** As above, so below, down through the levels of creation. Job 38:7: "When the morning stars sang together, and all the sons of God shouted for joy." **6:** Psalms 57:9.

## HIS THRESHOLDS

*SQYH*, #95; *HaShira*, #219. A *reshut* to the *nishmat*. Acrostic: *Yehuda*. Again, the notion of *tawakkul* is at the heart of HaLevi's religious experience. **Lines 1–2:** Psalms 22:21; Jeremiah 2:36; Isaiah 5:11, 21:4; Job 24:15. **9:** Scheindlin notes that the imperative here applies both literally (come to the synagogue) and figuratively (think of God always and trust in His way; but—and especially—just *be*, i.e., "imitate His unmoved serenity").

## WHERE WILL I FIND YOU

*SQYH*, #97, lines 1–2, 13–14; *HaShira*, #231. This poem is part of a longer *ofan* for the festival of Simhat Torah. To the best of my knowledge, it was first published as an independent lyric fragment in *Language of Faith*, ed. Nahum Glatzer (New York, 1974). While the full poem is also of interest, these verses seem to epitomize HaLevi's lyric faith and poetics, and so I present them in their fragmented form; they are among his most famous—and powerful—lines. **Lines 1–5:** Solomon's prayer in 2 Chronicles 6:18: "But will God in very truth dwell with me on the earth? Behold, heaven and the heaven of heavens cannot contain Thee; how much less this house which I have builded." Isaiah 6:3; Ezekiel 3:12; *Hagigah* 13b: "'Blessed be the glory of the Lord from His place'; accordingly, no one knows His place." **8–9:** Exodus 19:17: "And Moses brought forth the people out of the camp to meet God." Rashi comments on this verse: "This tells us that the Shekhina was going forth to meet them, as a bridegroom who goes forth to meet his bride"; also Rashi to Deuteronomy 33:2: "He (God) was Himself going forth facing them." See Septimus, *Divrei Hazal*, p. 611.

## YOU KNEW ME

*SQYH*, #68; *HaShira*, #229. A *reshut*. Acrostic: *Yehuda*. Reading this poem alongside Ibn Gabirol's "Before My Being," which takes up an almost identical poetic tack, highlights the essential difference between the two poets. Scheindlin: "[HaLevi's] religious stance is not the complex, bitter piety of [Ibn Gabirol's "Before My Being,"] but the accepting, tranquil mood of *tawakkul*" (*Gazelle*, p. 216). **Lines 1–2:** Jeremiah 1:5: "Before I formed thee in the belly I knew thee, and before thou camest forth out of the womb I sanctified thee; I have appointed thee a prophet unto the nations!" **5–6:** *The Kuzari*, 5:20. **8:** Psalms 5:13. **9–10:** The line refers both to any synagogue and the shrine in Jerusalem. As in "Where Will

I Find You" and other poems, HaLevi blends private and public religious concerns more thoroughly than any other poet of the period.

### A Doe Far from Home

SQYH, #330; HaShira, #190. An *ahava*. **Lines 1–4:** Again, the doe is Israel and the beloved is God. Edom is Christendom and Hagar is Islam. Proverbs 5:19; Genesis 18:13; Job 30:1; Lamentations 4:21; Genesis 34:8; Deuteronomy 10:15. **5–8:** Genesis 16:11–12; Song of Songs 8:5; *Megillah* 29a: "Come and see how beloved are Israel in the sight of God, in that to every place to which they were exiled, the Shekhina went with them." **9–10:** Song of Songs 8:7; Psalms 78:21.

### A Dove in the Distance

SQYH, #357; HaShira, #196. One of HaLevi's finest poems. Its genre isn't known; Schirmann tentatively classifies it as a *seliha*. Acrostic: *Yehuda Levi*. The dove in the Hebrew liturgical tradition is—by virtue of its tenderness and poignant cooing (which imply suffering)—associated with the beloved in the Song of Songs (2:14, 5:2, 6:9, and more), and by extension with the congregation of Israel. (See Hosea 11:11 and Isaiah 39:14, 60:8.) In the Andalusian context it also carries overtones of the spring garden and all that implies. The rhythm of the opening in Hebrew and English alike mimics the fluttering and flight of the dove. **Line 1:** Psalms 56:1: "Upon the silenced dove, of those that are far away" (*The Hirsch Psalms* [Jerusalem and New York, 1997]). In the Targum, the community of Israel far from its cities is likened to a silent dove. Also Psalms 55:7–8. **7:** It was thought that the redemption would come one thousand years after the destruction of the Temple, i.e., 1068 (calculated in the Jewish calendar from 68 C.E. rather than 70). **12:** Isaiah 53:12. **14:** Jeremiah 20:9: "And if I say: 'I will not make mention of Him, nor speak any more in His name,' then there is in my heart as it were a burning fire shut up in my bones." **24:** Job 14:21. **27:** Psalms 50:3.

### You Slept, Then Trembling Rose

DYH, 2: 302; HaShira, #202. This apocalyptic poem is included in the secular diwan, though its substance and field of reference are religious. It involves a dream-vision, most likely a reflection of the poet's deep-seated personal desire for collective deliverance and redemption, and the poem confirms the messianic background to his eventual pilgrimage. (The poet sees the fall of the Kingdom of Ishmael, which was predicted for 1130.) While HaLevi didn't embark on his voyage across the Mediterranean for another eleven years, recent scholarship (see above) indicates he did in fact attempt to leave Spain just before 1130, but his plans were dashed for reasons that remain obscure. **Line 2:** Genesis 37:10; the line is a verbatim quotation of Jacob's response to Joseph's having told him of his dream about the sun, the moon, and the eleven stars bowing down to him. It also echoes Daniel 2:3 and Nebuchadnezzar's question about his own dream, which Daniel eventually interprets, very much along the revolutionary lines and language of the vision in this poem. **7:** The Hebrew has "your mistress's child," i.e., Sarah's son (the people of Israel). Genesis 15:8, 17:2ff. **9:** Literally, "and the year 4890 [according to the Jewish calendar; 1129/30 C.E.] will come." Years, like numbers, in Hebrew are written out with letters standing for the numerals, so that the year 4890 is the same as the word meaning "to crush" or "pull down," as in Jeremiah 1:10: "See, I have set this day over the nations and over the kingdoms, to root out and to pull down, and to destroy and to overthrow." It appears elsewhere in Jewish medieval literature as well, prior to HaLevi (*Pirqei Heikhalot Rabbati* 40:1). **11:** Genesis 16:12. **13–18:** The remainder of the poem is largely in Aramaic, intensifying the allusion to and identification with the Book of Daniel's apocalyptic visions. The implicit equivalence is between Ishmael and the figures seen in Daniel's vision. Daniel 7:8, 21, 2:33, 34: "a stone which . . . smote the image upon its feet that were of iron and clay, and broke them in pieces"; Job 41:3.

## LOVE'S DWELLING

*SQYH*, #332; *HaShira*, #192. Again a fascinating blend of Arabic/Hebrew, Muslim/Jewish, and religious/secular concerns, compounded by the confusion of apparent tranquility and inner agony embodied in the poem. Previous commentators have noted the strangely foreign (non-Jewish) nature of the poem's sentiments, and this extreme expression of Israel's love for God was in fact revealed by scholar Israel Levin to be a translation (except for the final two lines) of an eighth/ninth-century secular Arabic poem by Abu-l-Shis, a contemporary of Abu Nuwas. Scheindlin points out that the Arabic poem was anthologized by the Andalusian Sufi and contemporary of HaLevi, Ibn al-'Arif, who interpreted it along religious lines. Scheindlin has an extensive discussion of all of the above elements of the poem (*Gazelle*, pp. 79–83). He compares it to Ibn Ghiyyat's "My Wandering" (above) and observes that Ibn Ghiyyat's poem expresses the fairly common pride of the martyr, while HaLevi's expresses the more radical, transformative pride of the mystic. See also *The Kuzari*, 1:115: "If we bear our exile and degradation for God's sake, as is meet, we shall be the pride of the generation which will come with the Messiah, and accelerate the day of the deliverance we hope for." **Line 1:** Proverbs 8:22. **2:** Ruth 1:16. **3:** For a sense of the secular Arabic tradition behind this poem, see Ibn Hazm's *The Ring of the Dove*, trans. A. J. Arberry, p. 96. **4:** 1 Samuel 2:30. **6:** Psalms 69:27. **10:** Deuteronomy 9:26; Psalms 111:9.

## LORD,

*SQYH*, #32; *HaShira* #228. A baqasha for Yom Kippur. **Line 1:** Psalms 38:10. **2:** Ezekiel 36:3. **3–4:** Psalms 30:6; Job 6:8. **5:** Psalms 31:6; Malachi 2:15. *The Kuzari*,

1:108. **6:** Jeremiah 31:25. **7–8:** Deuteronomy 11:22. *Berakhot* 18a–b, where wicked men are called dead while alive, and the righteous are called alive when they die. **9–10:** Exodus 10:26. **11:** Psalms 25:4. **12:** Literally, "prison of folly." Psalms 126:4. **15–18:** Job 7:20; Isaiah 1:14; Psalms 31:11. **21:** Genesis 23:4. **23–24:** Genesis 30:30. **25:** Ecclesiastes 3:11. **29–30:** Job 17:14. **31–32:** Ecclesiastes 7:14; Judges 19:9. **40:** *Avot* 1:14. **41–42:** Micah 1:8; Isaiah 61:10.

## If Only I Could Be

*SQYH*, #28; *HaShira*, #225. A *muharak*, in the form of a *muwashshah*. Acrostic: *Yehuda*. It is interesting to compare this poem with HaLevi's "If Only I Could Give," (above), which treats a similar situation in wholly secular fashion. **Lines 1–2:** Job 29:2, 31:15. **5–6:** Isaiah 49:5; Psalms 23:1, 139:13. **7–10:** Psalms 139:2–3, 23–24. **21–22:** Psalms 25:5. **24:** Job 10:2. **26:** Psalms 40:9. **29:** Numbers 12:13, where Moses asks that Miriam's leprosy be healed. **31–34:** Deuteronomy 29:27; 1 Kings 8:57; Psalms 71:9. **35–36:** Ezekiel 26:16. **37–40:** Micah 1:8; Jeremiah 51:18; Isaiah 53:5. **45–48:** Numbers 4:47; Proverbs 2:5. **51–54:** Isaiah 64:11, 11:11, 58:9.

## Won't You Ask, Zion

*SQYH*, #401; *DYH*, 2:155–58; *HaShira*, #208:1. A *qina*. Though the poem is classified as part of the poet's secular diwan, it has been incorporated into the Ashkenazic liturgy for the Ninth of Av, which commemorates the destruction of the Temples. It is now one of HaLevi's most well-known works. Gabriel Levin speaks of its "iconic" status: "Translated into numerous languages, it was appropriated by German Romantics, Haskalah reformists and Jewish nationalists who saw in its fervor and unrestrained longing for a homeland an echo of their own strivings for religious-national identity. After reading Johann Gottfried von Herder's translation, published in 1791, Goethe would write with admiration of the poem's rare 'fire of longing'" (*Poems from the Diwan*, p. 162). Fleischer and Gil suggest that the poem was most likely written in Egypt (*HaLevi uVenei Hugo*, p. 235). **Lines 1–2:** Those who are held like prisoners in Exile, "captive" to their longing. **6:** Isaiah 57:19. **8:** Zechariah 9:12: "Return to the stronghold, ye prisoners of hope." **11:** Psalms 133:3. **12:** Micah 1:8. **14:** Genesis 31:27. **16:** Genesis 32:3, 31. Peni'el, meaning "God's face," because Jacob wrestled with the angel and encountered the Lord there. Mahana'im refers to "God's camp," where Jacob was met by angels. **18:** The Shekhina, which figures prominently in *The Kuzari*, 2:14, 23. **19:** *The Kuzari*, 2:14 and 4:10. **20–21:** Isaiah 60:19. **26:** Jeremiah 3:17; Genesis 27:37, where Isaac refers to Esau and his descendants (i.e., Christianity) as Jacob's servants. **29–30:** Psalms 55:7–8; Song of Songs 2:17. **33–34:** The cave of Machpelah in Hebron, where according to tradition all the patriarchs and matriarchs except for Rachel are buried. Genesis 23:6, 19, 49:29–32, and 50:13. **35–36:** Isaiah 10:18. **37–38:** Mount Abarim is in Moab, but according to HaLevi also part of the Land of Israel. Mount Hor is the mountain where Aaron died. Numbers 20:25; Deuteronomy 32:48–50. The two great lights are Moses and Aaron. **39–40:** Exodus 30:23; *The Kuzari*, 4:17; Psalms 102:15. **41–42:** Isaiah 20:3. **44:** *Yoma* 52b: "In the days of Jeremiah the prophet the ark had already vanished." **45–46:** Jeremiah 7:29. **49–51:** Jeremiah 15:3; Ecclesiastes 11:7. The Hebrew plays on the word *'oravim* (ravens / crows), which is spelled the same as *'aravim* (Arabs), though the words are vocalized differently. **55–56:** Ezekiel 23:4: "Samaria is Oholah, and Jerusalem is Oholibah." They committed "harlotries." **57:** Lamentations 2:15. **67–68:** 1 Samuel 15:27; Song of Songs 7:9. **69–70:** Babylonia and Egypt. Literally, "Could their vanity [i.e., their sorcerers and the like] resemble your Urim and Tummim?" (Exodus 28:30 and 1 Samuel 28:6). Fleischer sees the mere raising of this comparison as an indication that the poem was written in Egypt, as part of an argument the poet was having with the local Jews, who tried to persuade him not to make the dangerous trip to the Holy Land, and to rest content with the "holy" sites of Egypt. A question of this sort, he says, would never have been raised in Andalusia (*HaLevi uVenei Hugo*, pp. 234–35). **74:** Proverbs 27:24; Isaiah 2:18. **76:** Psalms 65:5; Daniel 12:12. **82:** Ezekiel 16:55.


## My Heart Is in the East

*SQYH*, #402; *DYH*, 2:155; *HaShira*, #208:2. This is one of the most famous poems in all of Hebrew literature, and its theme and lyric concision have spoken to Jews throughout the Diaspora for centuries. On the whole, it is a song of antitheses, contrasting West and East, ease and hardship, waste and worth, and material and spiritual planes of existence. Its nationalist emphases apart, the poem also brings to mind the early Arabic poem by the first Spanish emir, the Damascene refugee Abd al-Rahmaan I (d. 788), who longed for his home in the East (see Cole, *Selected HaNagid*, p. xxvi). **Lines 1–2:** The Atlantic Ocean—or the Sea of Darkness—was considered the outer limits of the known world. **5–8:** Numbers 30:5–6. The poet is referring to his vow to abandon Spain and all it stands for and head for Jerusalem, then in Crusader hands. (The Crusaders, who conquered the city in 1099, forbade Jews to reside within its precincts.) "Arabia's chains" refers to Muslim rule in Spain and the entire Islamic ethos that went with it, but it also alludes to the Arabic meters, which HaLevi elsewhere refers to as "shackles." **12:** Psalms 28:2.


## How Long Will You Lie

*SQYH*, #10; *HaShira*, #218. *Reshut* to the *nishmat*. Acrostic: *Yehuda*. **Line 1–2:** Proverbs 6:9–10: "How long wilt thou sleep, O sluggard"; *Hagigah* 16a; Ecclesiastes 11:10. **4:** Proverbs 13:24. **5–6:** Isaiah 52:2; Song of Songs 5:2. **7:** Psalms 84:4. The word *dror* in the Hebrew means both "swallow" and freedom. **8–9:** Psalms 89:8; Jeremiah 31:11–12: "They shall come and shout on the heights of Zion, radiant over the bounty of the Lord."

## HEART AT SEA

*SQYH*, #407; *DYH*, 2:160; *HaShira* #212:1. From here on the poems in this section are all technically "nonliturgical poems"—that is, they are included in HaLevi's secular diwan, despite their explicitly religious content. Psalms 107:23 provides the literary background for this poem, which is essentially an imaginary voyage to the Holy Land. Like "My Heart Is in the East," "How Long Will You Lie," "Won't You Ask, Zion," and other poems, it may have been composed along the arc of HaLevi's self-preparation for his eventual abandonment of Spain and journey to the Land of Israel. For analysis of this poem see Andras Hamori, "Lights in the Heart of the Sea: Some Images of Judah Halevi's," *Journal of Semitic Studies* 30/1 (1985): 75–83. **Lines 3–4:** *The Kuzari*, 5:25. **6:** Literally, "and run after every desire." **7–8:** Judges 18:9; Genesis 25:29–34 and Esau's sale of his birthright to Jacob for a pot of lentils—i.e., reward in this world as opposed to the world to come. **9–10:** Proverbs 30:15–16; Ezekiel 47:12. **15–16:** Psalms 12:2; Numbers 24:1. Literally, "with a double heart." **17:** *Avot* 5:23: "Be bold as a leopard and light as an eagle and swift as a gazelle and strong as a lion to do the will of the father which is in Heaven." **19–20:** I.e., though the storms be such that they cause mountains to fall into the sea, or create waves that look like mountains, then crumble. Psalms 46:3: "though mountains be moved into the heart of the seas." **21–22:** Literally, "hands are like rags" and "cunning soothsayers," as in Isaiah 3:3. The word (*harashim*) can also be read as "workers" (Jeremiah 10:3, 1 Chronicles 4:14); Jeremiah 38:12. **25:** Isaiah 33:23. **30:** Leviticus 26:5. **35–36:** Genesis 6:14ff. **43–44:** Job 17:1. **52:** The poet turns to address himself. **54:** Exodus 14:21; Joshua 4:22–23. **58:** *Avot* 2:2. **63–64:** Psalms 89:10; "Thou rulest the proud swelling of the sea; when the waves thereof rise, Thou stillest them." 107:29–30; 1 Samuel 30:16. **71:** Genesis 1:26. **75:** *Sotah* 17a: "And the sea resembles heaven." **76:** Ezekiel 27:24ff. **78:** Psalms 89:10.

## MY SOUL LONGED

*SQYH*, #409; *HaShira*, #213. **Heading:** "On his emigration and his longing toward Jerusalem." **Line 1:** I.e., the sanctuary and the Temple shrine (as in the Jerusalem Talmud, Nazir 80:8). Psalms 84:3. **2:** Because of the difficult nature of the voyage. Exodus 15:15. **3:** 2 Samuel 14:20; Jeremiah 32: 18–19.

## HAS A FLOOD WASHED THE WORLD

*SQYH*, #417; *DYH*, 2: 169; *HaShira*, #214:8. The voyage on the small wooden vessels of the day would have taken an uncomfortable six weeks—a considerable risk for a man of HaLevi's age (he was at least sixty-five). In one of his other sea poems HaLevi makes it clear that, "buried alive in a wooden coffin [of the ship], . . ./he could sit—but not stand up on his feet,/lie down—but not stretch out." Gabriel Levin comments: "[The boats] were no more than seagoing barges, shaped like oversized nutshells and propelled by oars and stiff, square-rigged sails.

Passengers, who were expected to bring their own provisions, slept on deck, pressed against bales of merchandise" (*Poems from the Diwan*, p. 23). Levin also notes the dangers of starvation, illness, and piracy. Jews were separated from the other passengers. HaLevi's sea poems are, after HaNagid's (possibly fantastical) poem about his encounter with the sea monster, the only poems from the Spanish-Hebrew period that deal with the sea or sea travel. There is, it hardly needs to be said, given the conditions sketched above, nothing romantic about them. **Lines 1–2:** Genesis 6:17, 8:13; Ezekiel 30:12; Proverbs 17:1. **3–4:** Jeremiah 33:10; Genesis 7:21; Jeremiah 12:4; Psalms 73:19; Isaiah 50:11. **5–6:** Literally, "seeing a mountain or pit." Jeremiah 2:6. **9–10:** Job 40:25. **11–12:** Literally, "as though it (the craft) had been stolen by the hand of the sea." Schirmann notes that the image here is based on the vocabulary of pledge and trust, as in Leviticus 5:21: "When a person sins . . . by dealing deceitfully with his fellow in the matter of a deposit or pledge . . . ." The implication is that the craft is given to the sea as a pledge and should be returned (to land or safety) at the end of the voyage, but the sea seems to be reneging on that agreement and trying to swallow it up, or hide it in the swells. Hosea 9:2; Joshua 7:11. **13–14:** Jonah 1:15; Psalms 28:7; Leviticus 21:12.

## IN THE HEART

*SQYH*, #416; *DYH*, 2: 174; *HaShira*, #214:7. **Heading:** "And he said during a storm at sea." **Lines 1–2:** Psalms 93:3. **3–4:** Psalms 95:5; Daniel 6:27. **5–6:** Jeremiah 5:22.

## ABOVE THE ABYSS

*SQYH*, #415; *DYH*, 2: 174; *HaShira*, #214:6. **Heading:** "And he said at sea during a storm." **Lines 1–2:** Nahum 2:11. **3–4:** Psalms 107:27. **7–8:** Psalms 107:27, 116:19.

## TIME HAS TOSSED ME

*SQYH*, #420; *DYH*, 2: 182; *HaShira*, #216. Written while in Egypt, where he spent the winter, awaiting the second leg of his voyage. HaLevi's ship arrived two weeks late, reaching the port of Alexandria on September 9, 1140. **Heading:** "And he said concerning the Egyptian desert." **Lines 1–2:** Literally, "the desert of Noph," which is Memphis, south of Cairo. Isaiah 22:18: "He will violently roll and toss thee like a ball into a large country; there shalt thou die, there shall be the chariots of thy glory." Also Isaiah 19:13. **3–4:** An epithet for Jerusalem, as in Psalms 48:3: "Fair in situation, the joy of the whole earth; even Mount Zion, the uttermost parts of the north, the city of the great King." **5–6:** Based on the new JPS translation of Isaiah 22:18, and Gabriel Levin's note and translation in his *Poems from the Diwan*—and in keeping with the rhythmic emphases of the Hebrew—I have translated *etznof* as "whirl," though it can also be taken to mean "wrap" or "wind" [His glory or turban about me] or "exult and dance." The

Hebrew is likewise ambiguous. Psalms 48:3; Isaiah 59:17; Psalms 71:13; Leviticus 16:4; Isaiah 22:18 (NJPS): "He will wind you about Him as a headdress, a turban." The turban, or miter, was a sign of spiritual merit and exaltation.

## Be with Me

SQYH, #419; DYH, 2: 183; HaShira, #215:1. Written in Egypt. This poem is an indication of HaLevi's original plan, which was to take the desert route during the winter months. **Line 1:** The poet is addressing God. Tzo'an is a biblical name for Egypt; the holy mountain here is Sinai and the sea is the Red Sea. Psalms 78:12; Numbers 13:22; Exodus 13:18. **2:** A biblical town north of Jerusalem, Shiloh was a center of Israelite worship; the tabernacle was erected there during the time of Joshua. The poet says that he will follow the trail of the ark of the covenant through the desert and to the Land of Israel and the various places it passed through there, including Shiloh and Jerusalem's shrine. The ark was eventually lost and the place where it was hidden was never discovered (Yoma 52b and "Won't You Ask, Zion," lines 43–44). Joshua 18:1; Exodus 33:6; 1 Samuel 17:30; Genesis 49:10; Jeremiah 49:2. **3:** Joshua 3:6; Isaiah 49:23; Psalms 19:11. **5–6:** Israel is likened in the midrash to a dove; its enemies to crows or ravens. See "Won't You Ask, Zion," line 51; Song of Songs 1:5; Jeremiah 5:3, 50:6; Exodus 12:39; Leviticus 12:8; Psalms 147:9.

## Along the Nile

DYH, 1: 112; HaShira, #215:3. This lyric—which constitutes the descriptive opening section of a sixty-eight-line qasida—was written between October and December 1140, from Damietta, an important commercial city (eight miles from the Mediterranean) that served as a major link in the transference of goods from Europe to the East. It therefore had a prosperous Jewish community. The poem is part of a reply to a letter from HaLevi's friend in Cairo, Natan Ibn Shmu'el, who served as secretary to the Egyptian Nagid, Shmu'el ben Hananya. (The remainder of the poem praises his friend in conventional fashion and takes up the theme of his pilgrimage and praise of God.) The scene is the fields around the Nile which are covered with crops and flowers, and the poet describes the young men and women he sees on the banks and walkways along the river. The descriptive metaphors infuse this secular scene with a distinctive religious charge. **Lines 1–2:** These lines reverse the thrust of Ezekiel 26:16: "Then all the princes of the sea shall come down from their thrones, and lay away their robes, and strip off their richly woven garments; they shall clothe themselves with trembling." Also Genesis 27:15–16. **3–4:** Song of Songs 2:10; Isaiah 19:7; Exodus 5:13; Psalms 45:14. **5–6:** The Hebrew specifies Goshen, which might refer to the countryside of the northern delta, or to Egypt generally. The priestly breastplate and vest are from Exodus 28:4ff.: "And these are the garments which they shall make: a breastplate, and an ephod, and a tunic of checquer work . . . and they shall take the gold, and the blue, and the purple, and the scarlet, and the fine linen. And they shall make the ephod." **7–8:** Cities in upper Goshen, along the Nile. **9–10:** Ecclesiastes 2:8: "and women very many"—i.e., young women. **11–12:** Isaiah 3:20. **13:** Deuteronomy 11:16: "Take heed to yourselves, lest your heart be deceived, and ye turn aside and serve other gods, and worship them. . . . and the anger of the Lord be kindled against you . . . and ye perish quickly from off the good land which the Lord giveth you." **17–18:** Psalms 45:15: "All glorious is the king's daughter . . . her raiment is of chequer work inwrought with gold." **19–20:** A western breeze, a harbinger of the wind that would soon take him to the Holy Land.


## THIS BREEZE

*SQYH,* #413; *DYH,* 2: 171; *HaShira,* #214:4. HaLevi boarded his ship on May 7, but four days later it was still in port. All the boats heading west, for Spain, Tripoli, Sicily, and Byzantium had already sailed, one letter-writer noted, but HaLevi's ship had to wait for a wind that would take him northeast. Finally, after a week of tense anticipation, on May 14, 1141, on the first day of Shavu'ot, our letter-writer records that "The west wind has risen, the ship has sailed." This poem was probably written on board, outside the port of Alexandria, just as his boat was preparing to depart. HaLevi would have had time to give the poem to his friend, the businessman Abu Nasser Ibn Avraham, who had boarded the ship to say farewell. (Goitein, along with Fleischer and Gil, think that HaLevi wrote one other short lyric, not translated here, at this time. Other scholars believe this poem might have been written on the earlier leg of the voyage, from the east coast of Spain to Alexandria.) The trip to Acre normally took some ten days. (See Fleischer and Gil, *HaLevi uVenei Hugo,* p. 251.) If Fleischer, Gil, and Goitein are correct, this poem—which is one of his finest—may well be the last word we have from HaLevi. **Lines 1–2:** "We can defend *perfumed sea,*" says Guy Davenport—writing of Edgar Allan Poe's "Helen"—"which has been called silly, by noting that classical ships never left sight of land, and could smell orchards on shore, that perfumed oil was an extensive industry in classical times and that ships laden with it would smell better than your shipload of sheep" (*The Geography of the Imagination* [San Francisco, 1981], p. 7). **3–4:** Psalms 135:7: "He bringeth forth the wind out of His treasuries." **5–6:** As in "How Long Will You Lie?" (above), the words for "birds" and "freedom" are identical in the Hebrew. Jeremiah 34:17; Exodus 30:28; Song of Songs 1:13. **9:** Joshua 10:6. **11–12:** The hills of the Land of Israel. **13–14:** I.e., rebuking the East for the wind it sends. Psalms 106:9: "And He rebuked the Red Sea, and it was dried up"; Jeremiah 1:13. **15–16:** The poet is still addressing the wind, although he refers to it as, literally, "one who is held back by the Rock," i.e., the Lord. **18:** Amos 4:13: "For, lo, He that formeth the mountains, and createth the wind, and declareth unto man what is His thought, that maketh the morning darkness and treadeth upon the high places of the earth; the Lord, the God of hosts, is His name."

## CHRISTIAN SPAIN AND PROVENCE

### AVRAHAM IBN EZRA

The characterization of Ibn Ezra as a "great rebel" is Yosef Tubi's, in "Avraham Ibn Ezra's Poetry as a Link in the Transition of Hebrew Poetry in Spain from Its Islamic to Its Christian Period" (in *Abraham Ibn Ezra and His Age: Proceedings of the International Symposium,* ed. Fernando Díaz Esteban [Madrid, 1990]). In addition to breaking new thematic ground, Ibn Ezra was responsible for technical advances in the field, including a return to writing poems in the biblical style, with neither meter nor rhyme. On the whole, however, he maintained the Andalusian quantitative system of meters, though he employed strophic forms more often than his predecessors. He is also responsible for the incorporation of an allegorical strain into the rhymed-prose narrative. *Hai Ben Meqitz*—which was based in part on an Arabic tale by Ibn Sinna—is a long narrative work written before Ibn Ezra's departure from Spain; its two central figures, the author and his Virgil-like guide, soar over creation as they ascend through the elements and up through the spheres to the realm of wisdom.

### FORTUNE'S STARS

*Yalqut Avraham Ibn Ezra,* ed. I. Levin (Tel Aviv, 1985), hereafter *Yalqut,* #39, #40, and #38, line 5; *HaShira,* #250:1, 2. The suite gathered under this title in English comprises two discrete poems and the final verse from another poem on the same theme. Ibn Ezra wrote several important works on astronomy and astrology. As one writer has put it, for Ibn Ezra "true religion lies in recognizing the place assigned to the stars in the natural order that God has willed" (C. Sirat, *A History of Jewish Philosophy in the Middle Ages* [Cambridge and Paris, 1985/90], p. 106). While this poem is clearly in a light, humorous mode, it emerges from a lifelong preoccupation with the heavens and their influence. Ibn Ezra himself wrote, in his *Sefer HaMivharim:* "He who was born in a [stellar] configuration which is defective relative to the perfect thing cannot become like the one who was born in a perfect configuration. . . . He who has it in his configuration to be poor and without wealth cannot become rich, except for this: because man's soul comes from a place higher than all the stars, man can by means of his mind mitigate his misfortune somewhat." The notion of the stars veering off course derives from Ecclesiastes 1:15 and 7:13: "Who can make straight what He has made crooked?" In his commentary to the latter, Ibn Ezra writes: "The wise astrologers understand the verse [in Genesis 2:3], 'And God rested from all the work that he had done in creation,' that God delegated to the created [stars] governance of the sublunar world. Therefore if one's stellar configuration [at birth] is crooked [or thwarts him] in matters of wealth or other [misfortunes] there is no remedy for him" (*Twilight of a Golden Age*, ed. and trans. L. Weinberger [Tuscaloosa, 1997], pp. 66–67).

## How It Is

*Yalqut*, #41; *HaShira*, #249. See note to "Fortune's Stars." The poem is not found in the poet's diwan, but scholars generally attribute the poem to Ibn Ezra. **Line 1:** I.e., expecting a handout from the patron.

## A Cloak

*Yalqut*, #44; *HaShira*, #251. An excellent example of the "new realism," in which the subject matter is broadened and further personalized, this time in a self-mocking fashion. **Lines 4–6:** Job 3:4: "Neither let the light shine upon it." **8:** 2 Samuel 12:31. **13:** Isaiah 61:3: "the mantle of praise [glory/splendor] for the spirit of heaviness."

## The Flies

*Yalqut*, #43, *HaShira*, #252. Ibn Ezra most likely had Ibn Sahl's poem about the fleas in mind when he wrote this. In any event, he would have been familiar with it. The opening consciously employs the solemn trope and register of poems of lamentation or complaint (see, for example, Avraham Ben Shmu'el's "To Whom among the Avengers of Blood," or, for earlier instances, Ibn Gabirol's "On Leaving Saragossa"), thereby setting up his audience for more of the same. What follows is, of course, something very different. The contrast between the respective relation of man and God to the winged things that surround them plays in the final line on Psalms 99:1: "He [God] is enthroned upon the cherubim." In Jewish tradition God, or the presence of God, is said to rest between the two [winged] cherubim that lie over the synagogue ark in which the Torah is held.

## World Poetry

*Qovetz Hokhmat HaR. Avraham Ibn Ezra*, ed. D. Kahana (Warsaw, 1922), Part 1, #66 (hereafter *Qovetz Ibn Ezra*); *HaShira*, #255. Attributed to Ibn Ezra. **Line 1:** Literally, "love and pleasure"; "boasts," which has been interpolated for sound, picks up both on the Arabic poetic genre of *fakhr* (boasting) and the demonstrative nature of its bawdier poetry. In one of his liturgical poems, Ibn Ezra writes: "The songs of the nations are founded on nothing, and so I sing to the God of the chosen."

## All the Rest Is Commentary

### I. The Flood

*Qovetz Ibn Ezra*, #19. This poem, like the two that follow, serve as preludes to sections of Ibn Ezra's extensive biblical commentaries. See Genesis 9:11–17, for the story of the covenant of the rainbow; Isaiah 54:9: "For this to me is like the waters of Noah." This poem has also been attributed to Yehuda Alharizi (*Masei Yehuda*, ed. Y. Blau and Y. Yahalom [Jerusalem, 2002], #65).

II. Reading Exodus

1. Levin, *Avraham Ibn Ezra, Hayyav veShirato* (Tel Aviv, 1969), p. 219. This poem serves as the motto to Ibn Ezra's commentary to Exodus and the weekly reading, or *parasha*, beginning *Beshalah* (Exodus 13:17: "And it came to pass, when Pharaoh let the people go . . ."). The last line reads, literally: "Observe, you who are wicked, and take to heart the entire matter of Pharaoh and the *parasha* of Beshalah."

III. The Miracle (at Lehi)

N. Ben Menahem, "Tlunot HaRav Avraham Ibn Ezra 'al Ro'a Mazalo," *Sinai* 24 (1949): 71. Also in Levin, *Avraham Ibn Ezra, Hayyav veShirato*, p. 206. While the manuscript in question notes that this is by Ibn Ezra, the attribution is questionable. **Lines 3–4:** Genesis 26:19; Song of Songs 4:15; Judges 15:14–19, where Samson used the jawbone *(lehi)* of an ass to kill a thousand Philistines and then, when he complained of thirst, was rewarded by God: "And it came to pass . . . that he cast away the jawbone . . . and that place was called Ramath-lehi [Jawbone Heights]. . . . [And] God cleaved the hollow that is in Lehi, and there came water thereout."

Pleasure

*Qovetz Ibn Ezra*, #54. Attributed to Ibn Ezra.

In Place

*Qovetz Ibn Ezra*, #5. The repeated use of the word "place" in this poem plays on several rabbinic sayings and conventions. **Line 1:** *Ta'anit* 21b: "It is not the place that honors the man, it is the man who honors the place"; *Bekhorot* 30b: "Let the dignity of the elder lie undisturbed in its place." **5:** "The Place" *(HaMaqom)* is a common epithet for God, the Omnipresent. **6:** *Berakhot* 16b: "As they say to a man for his ox and his ass: 'May the Almighty replenish your loss.' "

The Wedding Night, Continued

*Qovetz Ibn Ezra*, #49. This poem is Ibn Ezra's reply—in the same Hebrew meter and with the same Hebrew rhyme—to Ibn Tzaddiq's poem sympathizing with his plight on his wedding night. (See the note to Ibn Tzaddiq's "A Wedding Night's Consolation" for details of the situation and the relevant laws of ritual purity.) Ibn Ezra's poem also contains the same number of lines and employs the same circular structure. Given the content of the two poems, it's all the more interesting to keep in mind that Ibn Tzaddiq was the *dayyan*, or religious judge, of Cordoba. **Line 11:** Genesis 18:13. "Rivers of Eden" here implies both the menstrual flow from the womb and pleasure *('edna)* lost. **14:** I.e, I'm blinded by the light;

I can look but not touch. There may also be a very distant echo here of the Mish-
naic term *saris hama*, "castrated of the sun," i.e., born castrated, castrated before
one saw the sun (*Yebamot* 8:4). **17:** The signs that the menstrual period is over and
there is no blood. In other words, Ibn Ezra took a lenient view of the laws of ritual
purity. After her period was over, but before she had waited an additional seven days
to be ritually immersed (after the period rabbinic law calls for seven days of *libun*,
cleaning or whitening, during which white, *lavan*, garments are worn), he engaged
in what sounds like the medieval version of heavy petting with his bride, i.e., sexual
contact short of intercourse. That he is boasting of this to his friend the religious
judge would seem to indicate that a certain laxity in the application of the law was
not uncommon. *Shabbat* 13a gives a sense of just how seriously these days of *libun*
were normally taken: "It is taught in the [midrash] *Tanna devei Eliyahu*: It once hap-
pened that a certain scholar who had studied much Bible and Mishna, and had
served scholars much, yet died in middle age. His wife took his *tefillin* and carried
them about in synagogues and schoolhouses and complained, 'It is written in the
Torah, *for that is thy life, and the length of thy days* (Deuteronomy 30:20): my husband
who read [Bible], learning [Mishna], and served scholars much, why did he die in
middle age?' And no man could answer her. On one occasion I [Elijah, the supposed
author of the text being cited], was a guest at her house, and she related the whole
story to me. Said I to her: 'My daughter! How was he to thee in thy days of men-
struation?' 'God forbid!' she rejoined; 'he did not touch me even with his little fin-
ger.' 'And how was he to thee in thy days of white [garments]?' 'He ate with me,
drank with me, and slept with me in bodily contact, and it did not occur to him to
do other.' Said I to her: 'Blessed be the Omnipresent for slaying him!' " **21:** Job 21:24.
**22:** Literally, "as a Nazarite goes around the vineyard [to avoid it]." *Avodah Zarah* 17a:
"Even mere approach is forbidden because we say to a Nazarite, 'Go, go—round
about; but do not approach the vineyard' "—to be on the safe side. The Nazarite, or
ascetic, has vowed to abstain from wine. **24:** That is, not yet having immersed her-
self in the ritual bath, which is filled with running water or rainwater. Ibn Ezra's
word here, *gushma*, seems to be derived from the root yielding *geshem*, rain, as in
Ezekiel 22:24: "You are an uncleansed land, not to be washed with rain," i.e., she's
pure according to the seven-day biblical standard, but not yet ritually immersed and
ready for intercourse. **27:** Another manuscript reads: "But what would any of this
be worth?" **30:** The Hebrew *'ad hormah* (to the point of total destruction) involves
an inversion of *rahma* (her womb) and implies penetration and defloration.


AN ANCIENT BATTLE

*Qovetz Ibn Ezra*, #118; *HaShira*, #259. One of three poems Ibn Ezra wrote about
chess, and possibly the earliest poetic record in European literature of the game,
which some say was introduced to Spain by Ziryaab (though this has never been
proven). Chess was a popular pastime for Jews in the Middle Ages, and it is men-
tioned by several prominent commentators. (Maimonides forbade playing for

money.) The medieval rules varied slightly from modern practice. See I. Abrahams, *Jewish Life in the Middle Ages* (Cleveland, New York, and Philadelphia, 1896/1958), pp. 388ff.; Weinberger, *Twilight of a Golden Age*, p. 128; and Ree Hans, "Ziryab the Musician," in *The Human Comedy of Chess: A Grandmaster's Chronicles* (Milford, CT, 1999). In Hebrew the poem rhymes in couplets—the equivalent of the quatrain in translation. **Lines 16–28:** Literally, "Cushites," or "black men," and "Edomites," which is derived from the biblical "Edom" and the word for "red" (*adom*); it always refers to Christians in the medieval Spanish context, and here it suggests skin color as well. In the Middle Ages, black opened the game, and the pawns, or foot soldiers, could move three spaces in any direction. **29:** The queen—who was known as the *paraz* (leader or ruler [Habakkuk 3:14])—was allowed to move only one space at a time, in any direction. **33:** The "bishop" was known as "the elephant" and could advance within a range of only three spaces. **37:** Literally, "the horse," which is what today's "knight" was called. **41:** Our word "rook" comes from the Persian (and Arabic) *rukh*, which in turn gave rise to the Hebrew *rokh*. **54:** I.e., if the opponent declares "Check!"

### LAMENT FOR ANDALUSIAN JEWRY

*Yalqut*, #35. The Hebrew is in syllabics, rather than quantitative meter, with regular internal rhyme as well as final monorhyme. A *qina*, or lament, for the Jewish communities of Spain and North Africa that were destroyed by the invading Almohads in 1146. This poem was written while Ibn Ezra was in the south of France, and the poet was, as Ross Brann points out, no doubt responding to reports that reached him from al-Andalus and North Africa. The plainness of the diction, imagery, and rhetorical figuration is in keeping with the grave nature of the situation described, and the poem is distinctive for its uncharacteristically physical and objective treatment of calamity and exile—at least until the final stanza and its confession. The standard medieval treatment of exile and loss in liturgical works was essentially metaphysical, moral, or psychological. See, for instance, Yehuda HaLevi's "A Doe Far from Home," "A Dove in the Distance," "You Slept, Then Trembling Rose," and Avraham Ben Shmu'el's "To Whom among the Avengers of Blood." While Ibn Ezra speaks here for the entire congregation of Israel, the poem wasn't included in North African prayer books and was probably not intended for recitation as part of the liturgy; contemporary editors of Ibn Ezra's poems place it among his secular works. For more detailed literary and historical analysis of this poem, see Cohen, *Under Crescent and Cross*, pp. 182–84; Brann, *Power in the Portrayal*, pp. 121–26, and "Tavni'ot shel Galut," in *Sefer Yisrael Levin*, pp. 51–54; and Weinberger, *Twilight of a Golden Age*, p. 99. **Lines 1–2:** Lamentations 1:16. Weinberger notes that the opening line is "an inversion of the rabbinic comment in Genesis Rabbah 51:3 that "nothing evil descends from above." Likewise, in contrast to the Jerusalem of Lamentations, Lucena is depicted as being innocent. **3:** Lamentations 4:3. For more on Lucena, see biographical notes on Ibn Mar Sha'ul and Ibn Ghiyyat. **5:** The approximate time passed since the destruction of the Second Temple. **6:** Lamentations 1:1. **10:** I.e., became a mosque. **12:** Jeremiah 8:23. Seville's Jewish community was almost completely destroyed. **15:** I.e, they were forced to convert to Islam. **16:** Lamentations 2:13. **23:** Psalms 58:8. **24:** Sijilmasa: a city in western Morocco. **30–32:** Telmesen is today in northwestern Algeria; Ceuta, in northern Morocco, on the Straits of Gibraltar; Meknes, also in northern Morocco. Der'a was an important Moroccan Jewish community. **33:** Psalms 79:3. **34:** At this point the *ubi sunt*–like catalogue of communities comes to an end, and the poet begins his confessional conclusion. See the penitential poem by Avraham Ben Shmu'el ("To Whom among the Avengers of Blood") for a similar gesture in the wake of loss. **38:** I.e, strayed from Spain, or possibly the Land of Israel, or both. Calling this the most fascinating line in the poem, Ross Brann notes how exile from Spain is merged into the larger exile from the Land of Israel, just as the personal voice of the exiled poet is blended with that of the community of Israel. Seeing their situation as part and parcel of the larger history of Israel, the new exiles would be strengthened and better able to bear the hardship of their circumstances. As such the confession of guilt at the end of the poem seeks to return to the metaphysical plane of redemption, without losing touch with the physical (or political) plane of actual exile and deliverance. **43–44:** Lamentations 1:2, 3:50. The handmaiden here alludes to Hagar, Ishmael's mother, i.e., the Muslims, and the Almohads in particular.

## ELEGY FOR A SON

*Yalqut*, #36. Scholarly readings of this poem differ markedly, with the majority understanding it as a powerful personal elegy for the poet's own son, Yitzhaq Ibn Ezra (see the biographical introduction to his poems, above, and the notes to that section). According to this personal reading, the poem was written three years after his son Yitzhaq's death, when news of his demise (in the East) finally reached Avraham. Some scholars have suggested that the poem is not about a physical death at all but about the son's conversion to Islam—though this has been a minority opinion. Ezra Fleischer, on the other hand, noting the oddness of the opening and the absence of any editorial comment about a personal context (*Toldot* [1995], pp. 82–85), says that this poem isn't about Avraham Ibn Ezra's son at all; it's a standard (traditional) eulogy, of the sort that Yehuda HaLevi and the other poets were often asked to write for their communities—(though this doesn't necessarily mean it is any less powerful). The opening, he says, is a kind of prelude, in which the poet summons the boy's father. Likewise, the end of the poem involves a return of the poet's voice, and a summation of the father's situation. The poem involves no mention of Yitzhaq's conversion because Yitzhaq converted (and died) after his father had already passed away. Furthermore, the Geniza records show that Avraham Ibn Ezra may have had more than one son (*HaLevi uVenei Hugo*, pp. 150, 420). I have adopted Fleischer's interpretation, which seems to rest on sound textual evidence, though earlier scholars' evaluation of the poem's merits still seem to me to apply. **Lines 1–4:** The poet calls to the father to come forward in his grief. Genesis 22:1ff., and the story of the sacrifice of Isaac. "And [the Lord] said unto [Abraham] . . . Take now thy son, thine only son, whom thou lovest, even Isaac." **5:** The father speaks. Lamentations 3:1: "I am the man who has seen affliction." **11–12:** Isaiah 65:23: "They shall not labor in vain, nor bring forth for terror; for they are the seed blessed of the Lord, and their offspring with them." **14:** Genesis 35:29. **15–16:** Lamentations 1:2; Micah 2:4. **19:** Isaac left Spain with Yehuda HaLevi and set sail for Egypt. There they parted ways, with HaLevi heading for Jerusalem and Isaac, it seems, for Baghdad. **21:** The circumstances referred to here are not clear. **24:** Genesis 25:21. **25:** The Hebrew is addressed to a single "friend" or "companion." **29:** 2 Samuel 14:7. **33:** Psalms 73:26; Genesis 27:30; Psalms 90:1. **35:** The father's speech has come to a close and the poet appeals on his behalf to God. **38:** Jeremiah 34:18. **44:** Genesis 24:14.

## My Hunger

*Shirei Qodesh shel R. Avraham Ibn Ezra*, ed. I. Levin (Tel Aviv, 1980), #32 (hereafter *SQA Ibn Ezra*). A *reshut*. Acrostic: *Avraham*. **Line 6:** 1 Samuel 2:1. **8:** I.e., to Muslims and Christians. **10:** A distinction is normally made in medieval Jewish thought between the three spiritual aspects of man: *nefesh*, *ru'ah*, and *neshama* (loosely: heart [or appetite], spirit, and soul).

## Sent Out from the Glory

*SQA Ibn Ezra*, #30; *HaShira*, #263:1. A *reshut* to the *qaddish*. Acrostic: *Avraham*. **Line 1:** In the Neoplatonic scheme the soul emanates from Intellect. **2:** The "four living creatures" of the chariot in Ezekiel 1:5ff., which bear the Throne of Glory, from which souls emanate and to which they return after death (*Shabbat* 152b). According to Ibn Ezra's commentary to Psalms 8:4, the tenth heavenly sphere (the sphere of Intellect) is the Throne of Glory. **4:** Ibn Ezra's commentary to Genesis 1:26 reads, in part: "He is the One. He made all. He is all. And this I cannot explain [or, I cannot explain any further]." See also Ibn Gabirol's "I Love You" for a similar suggestion of pantheism. **6:** Proverbs 20:27. **8:** Job 36:4. **9:** Implying perhaps the word of your prayer, but also more. **10:** Literally, "until His mercy brought you." **12:** The last line suggests that the poem leads into the recitation of the *qaddish*: "May His great name be exalted and hallowed."

## Lord, I Have Heard

*SQA Ibn Ezra*, #26. A *baqasha*. Acrostic: *Avraham*. **Lines 2–3:** The translation here is based on commentary by Israel Levin, who notes that the lines are obscure. **12:** Numbers 14:20: "And the Lord said: 'I pardon, as you have asked' " (NJPS).

## My God,

*SQA Ibn Ezra*, #27. A *reshut* for the festival of Shemini 'Atzeret. Acrostic: *Avraham*
**Line 1:** Psalms 24:4. **2:** The body in the Neoplatonic scheme (and the medieval
scheme generally—see, for example, HaNagid's "Earth to Man" and Ibn
Gabirol's "Heart's Hollow") is seen as a prison to the soul. **3–4:** See notes to "Sent
Out from the Glory," line 2 (above). **5–6:** In the Hebrew these lines are cast in the
third person. Psalms 40:6. **7–8:** Psalms 147:15ff.: "He sends forth His word to the
earth . . . He lays down snow like fleece, scatters frost like ashes" (NJPS). **9–10:**
God's "servants" (literally, "emissaries") would seem to refer to the cherubim of
Ezekiel 1:10, who bear the divine chariot and have a human face at the front, a
lion on the right, an ox on the left, and an eagle at the back. I. Levin also notes
that Ibn Ezra may be alluding to the signs of the zodiac in their spheres and the
influence they have over events on earth.

## To the Soul

*SQA Ibn Ezra*, #31. Acrostic: *Avraham Hazaq*. **Lines 1–2:** A description of the soul.
See notes to "Sent Out from the Glory" (below). **4:** Ecclesiastes 10:1: "So doth a lit-
tle folly outweigh wisdom and honor." **7:** "Its sleep" refers to the soul's time in the
body—human life, which is seen as illusive. **10:** I.e., exiled from its divine source, to
which it desires to return. Isaiah 49:21: "An exile, wandering to and fro." **11:** Knowl-
edge of the soul within will lead to knowledge of its source. **14:** 1 Samuel 25:29:
"The life of my lord will be bound up in the bundle of life in the care of the Lord;
but He will fling away the lives of your enemies as from the hollow of a sling."

## Blessèd Is He Who Fears

*SQA Ibn Ezra*, #254. A *seliha*. Acrostic: *Avraham Bar Me'ir Ben Ezrah Nehamato*. "In
a certain sense Ibn Ezra does not accept exterior revelation, only interior vi-
sion. . . . Perhaps the angel who speaks to the prophet is his own soul. . . . He
who speaks is man and he who listens is man" (Colette Sirat, *History of Jewish
Philosophy* [Cambridge, 1985], p. 108). **Line 1:** Psalms 1:1: "Happy [blessed] is the
man that hath not walked in the counsel of the wicked, nor stood in the way of
sinners." **2:** I.e., the voice that reminds him of all that follows. **4:** Isaiah 2:22: "Oh,
cease to glorify man, who has only a breath in his nostrils! For by what does he
merit esteem?" (NJPS). **5:** Psalms 78:39. **6:** Genesis 3:19: "Until you return to the
ground—for from it you were taken. For dust you are, and to dust you shall re-
turn" (NJPS). **7:** Isaiah 59:19: "For distress will come in like a flood, which the
breath of the Lord driveth." **13:** Nehemiah 2:6. **16–17:** Ecclesiastes 3:19: "For that
which befalleth the sons of men befalleth beasts . . . as the one dieth, so dieth the
other; yea, they have all one breath; so that man hath no preeminence above a
beast; for all is vanity [vapor]." Also Psalms 144:4: "For man is like unto breath."

**23:** The defilement and impurity that come with death. Numbers 19:11ff. and Leviticus 7:20. **29:** Ezekiel 2:10. **35–36:** Exodus 16:20. **47:** Zechariah 14:12: "Their flesh shall rot away . . . and the tongue shall rot away in their mouths." **53:** Ecclesiastes 12:3: "And the ladies that peer through the windows grow dim." **59:** Ecclesiastes 3:19: "All is vanity (*hevel*)" or "all amounts to nothing." *Hevel* in Hebrew literally indicates vapor. **61:** Literally, "Encompass him with your word." **65:** Job 2:6: "Only spare his life [soul]."

I Bow Down

*SQA Ibn Ezra*, #298; *HaShira*, #269. A *rehuta*. Acrostic: *Avraham Ezrah* (each letter twice). This poem is unique in Ibn Ezra's work, as it dispenses entirely with meter and rhyme, which are replaced here by a biblical-style prosody and parallelism—along with considerable internal rhyme. Schirmann notes that "indeed the spirit of biblical poetry hovers over [this poem]," which, he says, treats matters that are sublime and profound, and presents a curious mixture of emotional turbulence and seemingly restrained intellectual analysis. **Line 1:** Genesis 48:12; 1 Kings 1:23, and more. **3:** Psalms 9:3, 21:8. **4:** I.e., higher. **6:** Zechariah 4:6: "not by might or by power, but by my spirit"; Psalms 51:18–19: "the sacrifices of God are a broken spirit"; and Job 12:10: "[The Lord] in whose hand is the soul of every living thing." In Ibn Ezra's Neoplatonic worldview, the supernal soul is part of the divinity. **7–8:** The heart is considered the best, or purest, place in the body, for in a sense it is *not* physical: Ibn Ezra in his commentary to Genesis 1:1 calls it "the first chariot of the soul." (Soul here is not to be confused with the appetitive *nefesh*—also called "soul"—which appears in Arabic and Arabic-influenced medieval poetry). **8:** Isaiah 66:1–2; Deuteronomy 10:14. **18:** Psalms 60:13: "For vain is the help of man." **25–26:** Numbers 15:39: "Do not follow your heart and your eyes in your lustful urge." **29:** Jeremiah 49:16. **32:** Others understand the noun in question—*zil'afa*—to mean "rage" or "burning indignation" as in Psalms 119:53. **33:** Lamentations 1:20. **37:** Psalms 143:8. **40:** 1 Kings 8:32: "Then hear Thou in heaven."

Children of Exile

*SQA Ibn Ezra*, #232. A *seliha*. Acrostic: The first letter of each word runs through the alphabet and then the first letters of the next five words spell *Avraham*. **Line 1:** Lamentations 3:1. **4:** Habakkuk 1:2. **5:** *Baba Batra* 12b: "Since the Temple was destroyed, prophecy has been taken from prophets and given to fools and children." **9:** Psalms 88:16: "I suffer your terrors wherever I turn" (NJPS). **11:** Literally, "with the humble one's prayer we approach you." Numbers 12:3: "Now Moses was a very humble man" (NJPS). **12:** Literally, "against your people." Exodus 32:11: "But Moses implored the Lord, saying: 'Let not your anger blaze forth against your people'" (NJPS).

## I CALL TO HIM

*SQA Ibn Ezra*, #184; *HaShira*, #271. *Reshut* to the *qaddish*, in a strophic form. Acrostic: *Avram*. **Lines 1–2:** Daniel 11:36; Psalms 16:6. These lines echo the *qaddish* of the liturgy and indicate that this poem is a prelude to that prayer. "Magnified [exalted] and sanctified be the name of God throughout the world. . . . Exalted and honored be the name of the Holy One, blessed be He, whose glory transcends all praises, hymns [songs], and blessings that man can render unto Him." **6:** Cf. Ibn Ezra's commentary to Genesis 1:1 (above, note to "I Bow Down," line 8). **10:** Isaiah 40:17. **13–14:** Cf. Ibn Ezra's commentary to Psalms 8:4 and 103:21 on the structure of the spheres and the placement of the throne. **16:** Based on Psalms 104:3, the meaning of which has long been disputed. The biblical verse has traditionally been translated: "Who layest the beams of Thine upper chambers in the waters," but it has been (rightfully) argued that this image is blurred. My translation, then, is based on the Anchor Bible's understanding of the line. See *The Anchor Bible: Psalms III,* ed. Mitchell Dahood (Garden City, 1970), p. 34. **17:** Job 26:13: "By His breath the heavens are serene."

## YOU WHOSE HEARTS ARE ASLEEP

*SQA Ibn Ezra*, #237. *Tokheha*. Acrostic: *Avraham Ezrah Hazaq*. **Lines 3–4:** Avot 3:1: "Akabja ben Mahalel said: Keep in view three things and thou wilt not come into the power of sin. Know whence thou comest and whither thou goest and before whom thou art to give strict account." **7:** The soul descends from the Divine, and so contemplation of it will lead to knowledge of God. **8:** Job 19:26: "But I would behold God while still in my flesh" (NJPS). This highly charged verse in Job has been understood numerous ways, from the preceding Neoplatonic interpretation to a near-pantheistic reading. **9:** The microcosm of man and his soul, which is in the image of the macrocosm. This was a common medieval understanding, and Ibn Ezra mentions it explicitly in his commentary to Genesis 1:28: "The body of man is like a microcosm." **11:** Ibn Ezra's commentary to Genesis 1:1, where he states that the heart is the soul's first chariot." **13:** Literally, "Your head is the house *it/He* dwells in." The referent of the (masculine) pronoun in the Hebrew isn't clear. Grammatically it would seem to refer to God, or the "heart" of line 11. Levin notes that it stands for the Active Intellect (grammatically feminine), which emanates in the Neoplatonic scheme from God and contains, therefore, elements of the divine. In his commentary to Genesis 1:1, Ibn Ezra states: "The heavenly soul of man is called heart, although the heart is a body, and the soul [feminine] is incorporeal, since the heart is the principal seat [chariot] [of the Lord]" (M. Friedlaender, *Essays on the Writings of Abraham Ibn Ezra* [London, 1877], p. 20). The catalogue of body parts and the overall analogy resembles that of Ecclesiastes 12:3–4. **31:** The four elements combine in man along with the four humors (dryness, moisture, heat, and cold), and they are united only by means of the soul. **33:** I.e., the soul. **38:** In [the ruined body] you will see worms. **43:** Ecclesiastes

3:18–21. **50–51:** From Ibn Ezra's commentary to Exodus 20: "From the ways of the Name the learned man will know the Name." Also, his commentary to Exodus 31:28: "He will not know Him if He does not know his [own] soul and spirit and body." **52:** Job 36:22: "Who is a leader like unto Him?"

## YITZHAQ IBN EZRA

Ibn Ezra's character is sketched by Ezra Fleischer in *Toldot* (1997), pp. 71ff. The twelfth-century manuscript containing the poems that Yitzhaq wrote after his departure from Spain was purchased in Aleppo, Syria, by a collector and poetry lover, around 1902, but the new owner turned down various offers for it made by scholars in Berlin and Jerusalem, and what is known as the Silvera manuscript remained in Aleppo. During World War II and its aftermath all traces of it disappeared, and scholars assumed it was lost. It resurfaced with the Silvera family only in 1967, and scholars gained access to it in 1970. The poems themselves were published in a critical edition nine years later. A partial edition of Yitzhaq Ibn Ezra's work, based on other sources, had appeared in 1950.

### ON THE DEATH OF YEHUDA HALEVI

*Yitzhaq Ibn Ezra, Shirim*, ed. M. Schmelzer (New York, 1979), p. 20, lines 13–30. See also Fleischer and Gil, *HaLevi uVenei Hugo*, pp. 167–71. **Heading:** "And the speaker wrote to his father informing him of the death of his relative." While neither the heading nor the poem explicitly mention HaLevi, scholars agree that it is almost certainly about the great poet. The poem would, then, most likely have been written in Fustat (Old Cairo), sometime around late June or early July 1141, and sent to Avraham Ibn Ezra in Italy. Its elegiac opening (lines 1–12, not translated here) presents a picture of the world in mourning: the skies have gone dark, the sea is storm-tossed—like the speaker himself, who weeps. The translation picks up with the central section of the qasida, which describes the poet's solitude and explains the cause of his grief. Ibn Ezra had considerable trouble in Egypt after HaLevi's departure for Acre: he became embroiled in bitter quarrels and failed to find either patronage or employment. Soon he was lashing out at various community leaders in venomous poems. **Lines 1–2:** Lamentations 3:1; Job 20:8. **3–6:** Isaiah 44:14; Leviticus 6:6; 1 Samuel 20:41. Ibn Ezra also alludes directly to a poem of HaLevi's here (*Diwan*, 2:279, lines 15–19), one which is dedicated to the "brothers Ibn Ezra." The figure of the blood in one's tears is a standard Arabic image of powerful sadness: behind it lies the notion that the blood has risen from the heart to the eyes. **7–8:** Psalms 129:3; Genesis 37:7. **9–10:** Ecclesiastes 12:4; Jeremiah 8:7; Leviticus 26:36. **11–12:** Job 5:1; Psalms 139:7. **13–14:** Exodus 30:23, 25; Song of Songs 1:13; Ecclesiastes 10:1. **15–16:** Fate (or Time, in the medieval understanding) as the subject is implicit in the original. Ibn Ezra again quotes a poem by HaLevi here.

(See his poem to Moshe Ibn Ezra in this volume, "On Friendship and Time.")
The arm rings and jewels are indications of friendship. **17–18:** Joel 2:10; Numbers
24:3—though in this context the phrase means he is, figuratively, blind or lost,
without HaLevi's guidance. **19–20:** Daniel 1:10; Job 17:16, 26:6. It should be kept in
mind that Yitzhaq is writing here to his real father, Avraham. **21–24:** Proverbs
3:35; Daniel 12:9. **23:** Literally, "wisdom went still and turned to folly." **25–26:** Isa-
iah 24:9; Numbers 30:4. **27–28:** Job 31:18; Psalms 16:6: "The lines are fallen unto
me in pleasant places," i.e., my lot is pleasant. Fleischer calculates that Yitzhaq
most likely married HaLevi's daughter when he was eighteen, but, he adds, the
ties between the two families no doubt went back to Yitzhaq's childhood. **29–32:**
2 Kings 7:9; Psalms 34:5; Deuteronomy 6:11: "and houses full of all good things"
and 28:8: "The Lord will command the blessing with thee in thy barns." **33–34:**
Exodus 16:15; Job 30:4: "The roots of broom are their food." **35–36:** Job 5:1; Eccle-
siastes 7:26. These lines mark the transition to the final section of the qasida (not
translated here), in which the speaker turns to Avraham, his father, asking him
both to return to Spain to care for two people whom he does not mention
explicitly—possibly Yitzhaq's brothers, as Fleischer and Gil speculate in *HaLevi*,
p. 171—and to answer this poem and the letter it accompanies.

## OVER HIS BOY

*Shirim Hadashim min HaGeniza*, p. 281. This poem surfaced in the mid-sixties,
when it was published in Schirmann's collection of poems from the Cairo Ge-
niza, alongside two other poems by Avraham Ibn Ezra's son. It does not appear,
however, in the Silvera manuscript of poems, and the editor of the critical edi-
tion of Ibn Ezra's poems based on that manuscript places it in the section of po-
ems attributed to Ibn Ezra but of uncertain provenance (*Yitzhaq Ibn Ezra, Shirim*,
p. 146). Ezra Fleischer on the other hand, makes a strong case for removing the
attribution to Yitzhaq altogether *(Toldot* [1997], p. 75). The vivid depiction of the
old man and the boy caught in the act apart, the poem is of interest for what
seems to be its explicit condemnation of homosexuality (a trend that will de-
velop as the poetry moves out of Muslim Andalusia and into Christian lands).
That condemnation would seem to be at odds with the often stunning homo-
erotic poetry of the classical Andalusian period (beginning with Yitzhaq Ibn Mar
Sha'ul). Matti Huss notes, however, that the objection here is not necessarily
to homoeroticism per se, so much as to the combination of the ugly and the
beautiful, the young and the old, which violates the medieval aesthetic, with its
Platonic identification of the beautiful and the good, the ugly and the bad. Be
that as it may, the poem is also noteworthy as an example of the emergent new
realism in this work. See M. Huss, " 'Mahberet Shali'ah HaTzibbur: leShe'lat
Meqoroteiha veZiqatha leSifrut Ha'Ivrit HaHomoerotit beYemei HaBenayim,"
*Tarbiz* 72/1–2 (2003) pp: 219–20). For other poems treating homoeroticism as a
subject of controversy, see, in this volume, Yehuda Alharizi, "Boys: Two Poems."

**Lines 1–2:** Jeremiah 9:9: "From the mountains will I take up a weeping and a wailing, and from the pastures of the wilderness a lament." **3:** Micah 1:8: "I will make a wailing like a jackal." **7–8:** I.e., he tended to fall in with the wrong crowd. Proverbs 22:24. **11–12:** Psalms 14:1: "They have dealt corruptly, they have done abominably"; Proverb 20:2; Psalms 78:21; Proverbs 26:17. **13:** Jeremiah 20:8. **21:** Exodus 27:4. **26:** Genesis 49:27.

CONVERSION

*Yitzhaq Ibn Ezra, Shirim,* p. 147; *HaShira,* #287. Fleischer suggests that the conversion poem is most likely not by Ibn Ezra. A recent Geniza finding attributes it to a twelfth-century Eastern scholar, Barukh Ben Melekh (*Toldot* [1997], p. 79). Only one late manuscript attributes it to Ibn Ezra, and in most manuscripts there is no attribution at all. Schirmann's anthology, however, does attribute it to Ibn Ezra, and in the critical edition of Ibn Ezra's poems, it appears in the section of poems of uncertain provenance. **Line 2:** Zephaniah 3:13; 2 Chronicles 19:7. **3–8:** Genesis 49:9, 38:1; 2 Samuel 13:1 and more—all biblical episodes indicating that even the great figures of the Jewish people have erred at times and sinned. Amram's son is Moses. **11–12:** I.e., if I tell my fellow Jews that the Prophet (Muhammad) is a madman, but because of my circumstances am forced to acknowledge him with every blessing. . . . "Madman" was a common medieval epithet among Jews for Muhammad. Another possible reading of these lines is "if I say (in public) that a madman's a prophet, and with every blessing acknowledge him." **13–14:** The implication here is that the conversion was only outward—and perhaps performed under duress or simply in a moment of weakness—while inwardly the poet has continued to be (or gone back to being) a believing Jew. **15–16:** Literally, "I've returned . . . ."

YOSEF QIMHI

By "ordinary mysticism" I mean not qabbalistic speculation or vision but the sort of sacred linkage implied by the standard liturgy. See Max Kadushin, *Worship and Ethics* (New York, 1963), pp. 13–18, where he talks of the "normal mysticism of the common man."

LOVE FOR THE WORLD

*Sheqel HaQodesh,* ed. Hermann Gollancz (London, 1919), #96; *HaShira,* #288:1.

ALWAYS BE VIGILANT

*Sheqel HaQodesh,* #399; *HaShira,* #288:7.

### CONSIDER THIS

*Sheqel HaQodesh*, #376; *HaShira*, #288:6.

### SUFFER YOUR SORROW

*Sheqel HaQodesh*, #73.

### ON WISDOM

*Sheqel HaQodesh*, #33 and #49.

### IF YOU HEAR SOMEONE INSULT YOU

*Sheqel HaQodesh*, #61 and #62.

### WAIT AND BE SAVED

*Sheqel HaQodesh*, #161.

### WEALTH

*Sheqel HaQodesh*, #86 and #103.

### SILENCE AND SPEECH

*Sheqel HaQodesh*, #241 and #235. **Line 8:** I have translated Gollancz's text, though it doesn't suit the meter. A more metrical solution would yield *lasimo ben lehayayim* (to put it between the cheeks), but that would repeat the image of line 4.


## YOSEF IBN ZABARA

Schirmann points out that there is no hard evidence of Ibn Zabara's having gone to study in Narbonne. One of the town's sages, Yosef Qimhi (the poet, see above), mentions the opinions or readings of "the student R. Yosef Ibn Zabara" in his commentary to the biblical Book of Proverbs.

### SWEET AND SOUR

*Sefer Sha'ashu'im*, ed. Israel Davidson (Berlin, 1925), chapter 8, p. 90. This poem is unattributed and appears in the context of a discussion of eating habits and good health, in the course of which Plato, Galen, Diogenes, and many others are quoted alongside anonymous proverbs put in the mouths of a Roman, Indian, Babylonian, and Arab.

## MY EX

*Sefer Sha'ashu'im*, chapter 12, p. 141; *HaShira*, #310, lines 71–75. This is one of three poems in *Sefer Sha'ashu'im* that Davidson attributes to Ibn Zabara directly. In the narrative the poet's companion recites this poem, saying it is about his first wife. In the Hebrew the poem is cast in the present tense. The anatomical emphasis is characteristic of Ibn Zabara, the physician and physician's son. **Line 3:** Job 4:21. **8:** Isaiah 40:22. **9:** Job 6:3. **10:** Job 30:27, 41:23.

## LOOK AT THESE PEOPLE

*Sefer Sha'ashu'im*, chapter 6, p. 63. This chapter treats religious hypocrisy. **Line 3:** 1 Samuel 2:3. **8:** Judges 5:8; *Yebamot* 115a. **10:** Their only righteousness amounts to unctuous exaggerations of emphases at prayer. See Ibn Gabirol's "The Bee" for a discussion of how the Shema' should be recited. **12:** That is, until they're like Hevel (Abel in Hebrew), which also means "vapor."

## THE PHYSICIAN

*Sefer Sha'ashu'im*, chapter 10, p. 123. This poem also appears in Ibn Falaqera's *Book of the Seeker*.

## ANATOLI BAR YOSEF

While the name "Anatoli" is Greek in origin and hardly Jewish, it was given to more than a few Provençal Jews. It is a translation of the Hebrew "Zarhaya" (literally, the light bearer).

## THE TEST OF POETRY

*Shirei Anatoli Bar Yosef*, ed. E. Cohen, M.A. thesis, The Hebrew University of Jerusalem (Jerusalem, no date), #57. See also M. Stern, "A Twelfth-Century Circle of Hebrew Poets in Sicily," *JJS* 5 (1956): 112. **Heading:** "And Anatoli, of blessed memory, wrote to a man who turned to him with a weak poem." **Line 2:** Or, "in the furnace of form." **5:** Proverbs 20:5. **10:** Literally, "choose pure diction." **11:** Literally, "Don't weary yourself and pile up words." Ecclesiastes 1:8: "All things toil to weariness; man cannot utter it." **14:** Psalms 139:16. **15–16:** Psalms 41:2.

**17–18:** Literally, "What was sown there [or, its seed] were thirsty." Isaiah 61:11.
**19–20:** *Sheqalim* 2:4: "a minted coin"; *Baba Qama* 97a: "Where the government declared [a] coin obsolete it would be tantamount to its being disfigured . . . and the inhabitants of a particular province rejected it while it was still in circulation in another province." **27–28:** Proverbs 2:2, 4: "So that thou make thine ear attend unto wisdom, and thy heart incline to discernment; . . . If thou seek her as silver, and search for her as for hid treasures; then shalt thou understand the fear of the Lord, and find the knowledge of God."

Motto

*Shirei Anatoli*, #9. **Heading:** The book's motto [or, a dedication]. **Line 1:** Genesis 33:14: "I will journey on gently. . . ." **4:** I.e., he will fill the stanzas and lines of his poems with love and strong feeling.

YEHUDA IBN SHABBETAI

While the work is generally thought to have been written in 1188, Huss is of the opinion that in fact it was written in 1208. Detailed discussion of Ibn Shabbetai's life and work can be found in *Minhat Yehuda*, ed. M. Huss, Ph.D. thesis, The Hebrew University of Jerusalem (Jerusalem, 1991), hereafter *Minhat Yehuda*, a revised version of which is forthcoming in book form. For a feminist reading of the *maqaama*, see Tova Rosen's *Unveiling Eve*, which notes that, at the very least, *Minhat Yehuda* expresses "the qualms and ambivalence of the contemporary intellectual Jewish milieu" when it came to the sacred Jewish institution of wedlock (p. 123). See also her remarks about the associative (feminine) field that is built up around notions of, on the one hand, the world *(dunya/tevel)* and, on the other, the soul *(nafs/nefesh)* in Arabic and Hebrew.

FROM *THE OFFERING OF YEHUDA THE MISOGYNIST*

*I. Pharaoh's Wisdom*
   *Minhat Yehuda*, ed. M. Huss, lines 137ff.; *HaShira*, #303, lines 34–37. **Line 1:** Isaiah 28:29: "Wonderful is His counsel, and great His wisdom." **4:** Exodus 1:16: "And [the king of Egypt] said: 'When ye do the office of a midwife to the Hebrew women, ye shall look upon the birthstool: if it be a son, then ye shall kill him; but if it be a daughter, then she shall live.'"

*II. The Misogynist in Love*
   *Minhat Yehuda*, lines 532ff. **Line 2:** Habakkuk: 3:16: "Rottenness entereth into my bones." **6:** Genesis 19:33.

*III. A Raised Offering*

*Minhat Yehuda*, lines 540ff. **Line 2:** Song of Songs 6:4, 10: "You are beautiful, my darling, as Tirzah"; "Who is she that shines through like the dawn, beautiful as the moon, radiant as the sun?" **4:** Leviticus 10:15: "The thigh of heaving and the breast of waving shall they bring with the offerings of the fat made by fire" (NJPS: "elevation offering").

*IV. Two Things*

*Minhat Yehuda*, lines 628ff. **Line 4:** Hosea 12:13.

*V. The Sage Lies*

*Minhat Yehuda*, lines 293ff., version 2. **Line 1:** Genesis 23:6.

## YEHUDA ALHARIZI

The Arabic biography was discovered and published by Yosef Sadan in 1996 (*Pe'amim* 68: pp. 16–67). (At various points Ibn Gabirol speaks of himself in terms that have led scholars to say he was "short and ugly"—but that is description by inference; see *Toldot* [1995], p. 267.) In addition to having written the *Tahkemoni* and *Al-Rawda al-'Aniiqa*, Alharizi is the author of a medical treatise in meter and rhyme; a small body of liturgical poems; four collections of homonymic epigrams; several macaronic poems; a considerable body of poems in Arabic; possibly, an important book containing ethical proverbs, short poems, and unrhymed prose (*Sefer Pineni HaMelitzot*); and—it seems—a series of ten long philosophical-religious poems on the nature of God and existence (*The Divine Qasidas*; see E. Fleischer, "HaQasidot HaElohiyot," *Tarbiz* 66/1 [1997]). The most recent scholarly findings from Russian archives show Alharizi to be a Jewish poet who, while in the East, made a living writing in Arabic and translating from it. Apart from Al-Hariiri's *Maqaamaat* and his translations of Maimonides, Alharizi translated numerous other scientific and philosophical works from Arabic. In one bizarre case that testifies to the hunger for manuscripts at the time, Alharizi translated part of a work by Maimonides that turned out to have been originally translated from Maimonides' Arabic into Hebrew by Shmu'el Ibn Tibbon, and then translated back into Arabic by another translator; that Arabic translation then fell into Alharizi's hands, and he translated it into Hebrew once again! (See the introduction to this volume, final section.) For more on Alharizi, see *The Book of Tahkemoni*, trans. David Segal (Oxford, 2001); *The Tahkemoni*, trans. Victor E. Reichert, 2 vols. (Jerusalem 1965/73); and Yosef Yahalom's *Mas'ei Yehuda*, ed. Y. Blau and Y. Yahalom (Jerusalem, 2002).

### BORN TO BASENESS

*Mas'ei Yehuda*, #26; *Tahkemoni*, ed. Y. Toporowski (Tel Aviv, 1952). All citations of sources from the *Tahkemoni* are taken from Gate 50 unless otherwise noted. The translation follows the text of Blau and Yahalom, p. 393. "And I wrote this about a man in Kalneh [al-Raqqah—today's Syria], whom I praised, though he fled to Harran and hid himself from me." **Line 3:** "In two languages," i.e., in poems in both languages, or possibly a macaronic poem employing both Hebrew and Arabic. **5:** So he would reward me for my poem with payment. Song of Songs 3:1–2: "I sought him but found him not." **7–10:** In other words, he reserves the right to put his name in writing and make his character known. At the same time the poem serves as a warning to future patrons.

### The Hypocrite

*Mas'ei Yehuda*, #24; *Tahkemoni*, pp. 292–93. **Heading:** "And I wrote this about a man who sowed contention [Proverbs 6:19], when I saw him praying contritely." The white clothes suggest that the poem may be about a certain cantor. **Line 2:** Psalms 41:7.

### The Jerk

*Mas'ei Yehuda*, #48; *Tahkemoni*, p. 401; *HaShira*, #322:12. **Line 4:** Job 26:7: "He . . . who suspended earth over emptiness."

### A Miser in Mosul

*Mas'ei Yehuda*, #167; *Tahkemoni*, p. 429. **Line 1:** The poet was hoping for monetary compensation. **2:** Psalms 5:10. **3:** A vow to reward him. **14:** Song of Songs 1:16. **15–16:** The man justifies his refusal to pay by alluding to Scripture's commandment in Exodus 21:10 to support a female slave even if her owner marries another woman: "If he marries another, he must not withhold from this one her food [i.e., the slave's food], her clothing, or her conjugal rights." The original quotes the line from Scripture exactly; the English lowers the register to preserve the humor. M. Huss states that this is the only Hebrew text in which the suggestion is made—however ironically or humorously—that the obligations of the active partner and the rights of the passive partner in a homosexual relationship are equal to those of husband and wife in the context of heterosexual marriage. That said, in this poem and others by Alharizi, homosexual practice (as opposed to homoerotic pronouncement) is clearly denounced. See Huss, "Mahberet Shal-i'ah HaTzibbur," p. 221.

### The Miser

I.
   *Mas'ei Yehuda*, #19; *Tahkemoni*, p. 391. **Line 2:** Genesis 24:16.

*II.*

*Mas'ei Yehuda*, #25; *Tahkemoni*, p. 393. **Line 3:** The pipe here is a word of uncertain meaning, possibly a bagpipe-like instrument made from the bladder of an animal.

*III.*

*Mas'ei Yehuda*, #42; *Tahkemoni*, p. 399. The final line draws on a popular image from *Midrash Ma'aseh Torah*, where it is one illustration of a series of impossible conditions.

## On Zion's Holy Hill

*Mas'ei Yehuda*, #114; *Tahkemoni*, p. 417. **Line 1:** The man has been identified as R. Eliyahu HaMa'aravi, who headed one of the Jewish communities in Jerusalem. Alharizi describes him as "a man of charity and good works, though people said he was involved with wicked and ugly acts, and God knows all secrets" (*Mas'ei Yehuda*, p. 56). **2:** Leviticus 13:5–6. **3–4:** In the original the poem puns on the nickname "Rosh HaPe'or" (literally, the head of/peak of Pe'or). The word Pe'or in the place name puns on the word *pa'ar*, "to open widely" or "uncover oneself." Rosh Pe'or in Scripture (Numbers 23:28) is where Balak made a pagan offering with Balaam, hoping to get him to curse the Israelites. The Talmud (*Sanhedrin* 64a) states that the shrine of Pe'or was associated with "uncovering" oneself before the idol, with the implication being a defilement of a sexual sort, probably anal. Balaam, of course, is associated with an ass (Numbers 22:22ff.). Y. Ben Na'eh comments on this in "Mishkav Zakhar beHevra HaOthmanit," *Zion* 66 (2001): 194–95. Huss notes that the condemnation of homosexual acts here and in some of the other poems is all the more startling given the fact that in this same chapter Alharizi presents "classical" homoerotic poems he composed about the beauty of boys (e.g., "Measure for Measure").

## Boys: Two Poems

*I. If Amram's Son*

*Mas'ei Yehuda*, #124; *Tahkemoni*, p. 418. Alharizi often added his own headings to the poems, and this one reads: "One of 'Adina's/composed these scandalous poems/full of terrible things—/and this was among them." While the heading attributes the poem in the context of the *Tahkemoni*'s narrative to a resident of Baghdad ('Adina), rather than to Alharizi—and while there is evidence from other texts to support this claim—some scholars believe that this may simply be a fictional device. This poem is followed by ten replies, the first by the poet and the rest by nine other "men of intelligence, wisdom, integrity, and faith"; each condemns the man, his poem, and all it implies. **Line 1:** Amram's son is Moses. Cf. *Baba Metzi'a* 75b: "Had Moses our Teacher known that there was profit in this thing, he would not have prohibited it." While the talmudic text refers to usury, the poet, whether Alharizi or another, diverts the phrase for his own purposes in the poem. **4:** The law referred to is Leviticus 18:22: "Thou shalt not lie with mankind, as with womankind; it is abomination."

*II. An Answer*

 *Mas'ei Yehuda*, #130; *Tahkemoni*, p. 420. The punishment mirrors the active/passive dynamic of the sex.

## MASTERS OF SONG

*Mas'ei Yehuda*, p. 171; *Tahkemoni*, Gate 18, p. 183; *HaShira*, #312, lines 57–60. **Line 1:** Exodus 16:21. **3–4:** Literally, "And at a time when the sons of the East did not find a vision in song, the sons of the West prophesied." Lamentations 2:29.

## MEASURE FOR MEASURE

*Mas'ei Yehuda*, #94; *Tahkemoni*, p. 414.

## A LOVER WANDERED

*Mas'ei Yehuda*, #97; *Tahkemoni*, p. 396. **Line 5:** Literally, "in honor of the red-eyed one," as in Genesis 49:12: "His eyes shall be red with wine"—indicating someone who is always drunk with wine, or in this case, love.

## HOW LONG, MY FAWN

*Mas'ei Yehuda*, #160; *Tahkemoni*, p. 428. **Line 1:** Blau and Yahalom read *matay* (how long) instead of the *Tahkemoni's motee* (my death), and I have followed their reading. **4:** Exodus 22:5: "When a fire is started and spreads to thorns, so that the stacked, standing, or growing corn is consumed, he who started the fire must make restitution."

## CURSES' COMPOSITION

*I.*

 *Mas'ei Yehuda*, #27; *Tahkemoni*, pp. 393–94; *HaShira*, #312, lines 357–61. **Heading:** "And this I wrote of a man/who in Kalneh was the basest of oxen;/he was always making poems/that really were broken cisterns,/the waters of which were poison [bitter]." The man's name was, it seems, Berakhot (Barakat, in Arabic), which means "Blessings." Alharizi turns the name inside out, in keeping with the man's character. **Line 6:** Leviticus 19:20. **8:** Genesis 30:23.

*II.*

*Mas'ei Yehuda*, #28; *Tahkemoni*, p. 394. **Heading:** "And from him I borrowed a book—/his epigrams, not worth the look,/and as soon as he'd sent it on,/he came and took it home,/and I wrote this." Proverbs 26:11.

### A FLASHING SWORD

*Mas'ei Yehuda*, #105; *Tahkemoni*, p. 414. **Lines 1–4:** Proverbs 12:18; Isaiah 5:24: "As the tongue of fire devoureth the stubble, and as the chaff is consumed in the flame . . ."

### PALINDROME FOR A PATRON; OR, CAUTION: THIS DOOR SWINGS BOTH WAYS

*Tahkemoni*, p. 93. The rhymed prose leading up to this poem (i.e., the *maqaama*'s narrative) can also be read in reverse. The prose lines immediately preceding the poem weave in the loaded line from Deuteronomy 11:26: "Lo, I set before you this day the blessing and the curse."

### A POEM NO PATRON HAS EVER HEARD: WITH THE LETTER *R* IN EVERY WORD

*Tahkemoni*, p. 119. As with the preceding poem (the palindrome), the rhymed prose leading up to this metered poem duplicates the feat and contains the letter *r* in every word.

### ADMIRATION FOR THE PATRON AGAIN I'LL PROVE, AND THE LETTER *R* I'LL NOW REMOVE

*Tahkemoni*, p. 121. Again, the rhymed prose before the poem reproduces the constraint.

### TWO POEMS ON KARAISM

*Tahkemoni*, p. 175. These are the first two poems (in reverse order here) of a series in which the believer (*hama'amin*) debates the sectarian Karaite (*hamin*). Karaism was a serious threat to medieval Judaism at one point, and recent scholarship has proposed that its aggressive presence in Sa'adia Gaon's day may have spurred the development of biblical Hebrew along scientific lines and so, indirectly, the new Hebrew poetry in Spain. By Alharizi's time, the movement had waned in the East. The poet's own position vis-à-vis the group was tolerant (and influenced by Maimonides). He refers to members of the sect, however, as *minim*, heretics, or schismatics. See Segal, *The Book of Tahkemoni*, pp. 507–10; J. Rosenthal, "Karaites and Karaism in Western Europe" [Hebrew], *Mehqarim uMeqorot* 8 (1967): 238–44; and Lasker, "Karaism in Twelfth-Century Spain," *Journal of Jewish Thought and Philosophy* 1–2 (1992): 179–95.

### Virtue

*Tahkemoni*, p. 197. In Gate 19 seven poets debate which virtue is most prized by God. This is the first and, I believe, most interesting poem in that series, though Alharizi suggests that the final value, good-heartedness, is in fact most highly prized in the eyes of God, as it contains all the other values in it.

### I'll Set Out a Verse, and Lay the Foundation; Then You'll Add One for the Stanza's Completion

*Tahkemoni*, Gate 32, pp. 264, 268–70. These five poems are the product of a verse competition between a young man and one of the *Tahkemoni*'s main characters, Hever the Kenite. The narrator of the story says he witnessed the competition in his youth. While attending a gathering of intellectuals who were discussing poetry and other abstruse matters, an older man entered and boasted of his own poetic prowess. A young man in the crowd challenged him to a competition. The young man would first recite lines in rhymed prose, and then the old man would complete the thought, maintaining the rhyme. Then each would follow with a metrical poem on the same topic. The excerpts here are taken from twenty-one examples they produced. In each case the old man betters the younger by raising the additional verse to another level of complication or irony, and often by exploiting linguistic elements introduced by the former. In the process he implicitly puts the youth in his place.

*IV.*
    The pomegranate is veiled by its branches and leaves.

### YA'AQOV BEN ELAZAR

On the link to European sources, see Schirmann, *Toldot* (1997), pp. 233–40, and R. Scheindlin, "Sippurei Ha'ahava shel Ya'aqov ben Elazar: Ben Sifrut 'Aravit leSifrut Romans," *The Proceedings of the Eleventh World Congress of Jewish Studies*, division C, vol. 3 (Jerusalem, 1994). Schirmann and Scheindlin come down strongly on the side of at least *some* European influence, most likely one of the early romances. The link between the thirteenth-century anti-Maimunists and their beards is made by E. Horovitz in an article in *Pe'amim* 59 (1994): 124 ff.

### The Hypocrite's Beard

*Sipurei Ahava shel Ya'aqov Ben Elazar*, ed. Y. David (Tel Aviv, 1992/93), part 8, line 317. This poem is drawn from a chapter in which 'Akhbor, an eighty-year-old hypocrite with a long beard comes to town and wins the hearts of the wicked townspeople by posing as a righteous man and delivering a fiery sermon on evil—in particular the sins of greed and extortion. He implores his listeners to repent, in the process telling them tales about hard-hearted people who did not give to the needy. The crowd is won over and donations gathered for the preacher. Lemu'el, the narrator—who has chosen to wander in the world so as to come to know it as it really is, for better and for worse—smells a rat, follows 'Akhbor home, and discovers that he lives in a palace where he is waited on by four beautiful women who serve him a lavish meal, then play and sing wine-songs in the Andalusian tradition for him. After reciting some poems of his own about his desire, 'Akhbor dismisses them, calls out in a whisper, and a black woman comes into the room. The two are about to make love when the narrator, who can no longer tolerate what he's seeing (the woman's race, it seems, is the final straw), throws himself at the would-be lovers and strips them bare. After a brief argument with 'Akhbor, Lemu'el lets out a shout, the (white) servant girls enter, and Lemu'el tells them what their master has been up to. The girls recite poems—including the one presented here—that mock their master and in particular his beard; then they attack him viciously, pulling at the beard and beating the old man to death. Finally they toss his body into a pit. **Lines 1–4:** Literally, " 'Akhbor's beard, like a foolish shepherd's, has branches extending in every direction." Zechariah 11:15: "the gear of a foolish shepherd." I have translated freely here to account for the poem's removal from the narrative, where it is clear what 'Akhbor represents. (His name is biblical [Genesis 38:38, 2 Kings 22:14, and elsewhere] but may also carry the overtones of *'akhbar*, a mouse or rat.) The primary dictionary definition of "cant," it should be recalled, is "the hypocritical expression of pious sentiments; insincere religious or moralistic talk." In addition to the common usage—"words used to stock effect"—it is also "the secret jargon of thieves, gypsies, etc." The image of the branching beard appears to have been drawn from Ezekiel 31, where a positive depiction of the branches with animals among them (31:5–6) is reversed when punishment is rendered (31:10–15). There too everything in the branches of the fallen tree makes its way to the netherworld. In another beard poem, Ben Elazar writes that Akhbor's beard runs from his cheek to his rectum. Also Ezekiel 24:12. **8:** The Hebrew has "what seemed like a bird"; I have brought over the image of the night from line 11, where the word from Isaiah can mean both arrow-snake and a kind of night bird, possibly an owl. **10:** Song of Songs 2:15. **11:** Isaiah 34:15. **14:** Isaiah 32:17. **15:** Micah 4:4. Literally, "Each man beneath his fig tree, in the shadow of 'Akhbor's beard."

## Four Poems on Subtle Love

The "subtle love" here has often been referred to as spiritual love, though it should be pointed out that, at least in poems 2–4, the refinement of passion through sublimation is clearly a stage along the path to physical consummation. In *Sefer HaMeshalim*, poems 2–4 appear as part of the narrative of the love story of Sahar and Kima. I have grouped them together in keeping with the outline of that story, adding the short poem from the amatory allegory of book 1 at the start.

*I. The Doe*

*Sipurei Ahava*, part 1, line 47. In this scene the intellect, personified as a general, addresses its own eye, instructing it to gaze at the doe (i.e., the soul), whom he seeks in love. In Plato's *Phaedrus*, intellect is presented in similar terms (see Rosen, *Unveiling Eve*, pp. 95ff., for a full discussion, and *Phaedrus*, lines 250ff.). The conventions of the classical Andalusian erotic poem are jostled and blurred here. While the poem is presented as an erotic poem in that classical tradition, with the doe as the object of desire, the lover from the outset accepts separation from the beloved, as part of the new code of "spiritual love"; at the same time, the soul's desire to reciprocate by praising the intellect (line 4) subverts the conventional poetics of classical Andalusian secular love poetry (which call for the refusal of the lover's advances). That said, the poem does preserve the poetics of the erotic Andalusian epithalamia, which are also at work in the entire sequence: consummation of at least one sort is hinted at, though not depicted, when at the end of the complicated allegory of book 1, the poet's soul convinces him to escort her to the Garden of Delight, where they will encounter the General of Love—the intellect—with his mistress Wisdom, and—she imagines—make love to her. **Line 4:** Literally, "She [the object of the desire] will praise you every day." Psalms 119:175: "Let my soul live and it shall praise thee." **8:** I.e., writing this poem.

*II. A Kiss*

*Sipurei Ahava*, part 9, line 299. **Line 1:** The Hebrew speaks of the *malakh yedidim*—literally, the angel (or envoy) of friends (or lovers), i.e., her own hand, which the noble lady would, after elaborate and agonizing trials of courtship, kiss in his presence—"her eyes dancing and smiling, as though they embraced"—as a symbolic gesture to her suitor. Because the courtly convention calls for restraint (and because others are present—the "spies" of the literary convention), this distant, symbolic gesture is all she can offer her frustrated suitor—for now. (Kissing the back of one's own hand may also have been a traditional gesture of respect. See Elitzur, *Shirat HaHol*, 2:111–13) In this poem, the woman tells of an incident that reveals the man's impatience with this waiting game. **4:** Literally, "Is this the Law of the Gentle [or refined]?"

*III. A Lover's Transgression*

*Sipurei Ahava*, part 9, line 365. This poem is in response to Sahar's continued impatience and complaint that the fire within him has made him thirsty. He asks her to "please tilt your pitcher, so I can drink. . . ." **Line 3:** The word for "his jail" (*sohoro*) puns on the name Sahar. **6:** Literally, "that it [my heart] can't hear."

*IV. Spats and Squabbles*

*Sipurei Ahava*, part 9, line 393. This poem is spoken by the man. The happy end of this chapter has the two married, but Sahar applies the lesson he has learned in order to keep the tension in the marriage alive.

## AVRAHAM IBN HASDAI

### WATCH OUT

*Ben HaMelekh veHaNazir*, ed. A. M. Habermann (Tel Aviv, 1950), chapter 5, p. 44. This and the following two poems are recited by rivals of the king's assistant. In an attempt to undermine the king's confidence in him, they come before the king and accuse the assistant of lying and insubordination.

### PROPORTION

*Ben HaMelekh veHaNazir*, chapter 5, p. 50. Advice given to the king's assistant or second in command, in the wake of the rivals' attack, when he has fallen into disfavor with the king.

### AGE AS AUTHOR

*Ben HaMelekh veHaNazir*, chapter 6, p. 64; *HaShira*, #327, lines 126–29. This is part of the prince's reflections after his expedition.

### WHICH IS MORE BITTER

*Ben HaMelekh veHaNazir*, chapter 11, p. 91.

### THE LYING WORD

*Ben HaMelekh veHaNazir*, chapter 5, pp. 43–44.

### THE MONK'S ADVICE

*Ben HaMelekh veHaNazir*, chapter 12, p. 96.

### ADVICE FOR A FUTURE KING

*I. Wisdom's Mantle*
   *Ben HaMelekh veHaNazir*, chapter 27, p. 179.

*II. Don't Believe*
   *Ben HaMelekh veHaNazir*, chapter 30, p. 193.

*III. The Hyssop and the Cedar*
   *Ben HaMelekh veHaNazir*, chapter 30, p. 188; *HaShira*, #332:3. 1 Kings 15:13.

## MEIR HALEVI ABULAFIA

### PLEA FOR A TAX BREAK

*Yedi'ot HaMakhon leHeqer HaShira Ha'Ivrit* 2, ed. H. Brody (Berlin, 1936), p. 36. The Arabic heading is corrupt. Haim Brody, the editor of Abulafia's poems, provides what appears to be a composite rendition drawn from various sources: "And he addressed the vizier Abu 'Amar ben Shushan, at the behest of R. Avraham Ha-Yarhi, may his soul rest in Eden, seeking [tax] shelter, which he did not receive from him." **Line 2:** Lamentations 1:13. **4:** Jonah 1:13.

### (L)ATTITUDE

*Yedi'ot HaMakhon leHeqer HaShira Ha'Ivrit* 2, p. 22. **Line 1:** Psalms 33:11. **2:** Zephaniah 3:5; Psalms 17:2.

### FIGHTING TIME

*Yedi'ot HaMakhon leHeqer HaShira Ha'Ivrit* 2, p. 23; *HaShira*, #336. **Line 3:** Genesis 37:14. **5–6:** That is, only the best and brightest (the largest) of the heavenly hosts, the sun and the moon, must on occasion suffer eclipse, just as the best of creation—man, and among them the best of men—must contend against Time or Fate and sometimes fail. Isaiah 50:3. A note following the poem in manuscript indicates that this is a translation of a poem by the emir of Seville, al-Mu'atamid.

## YITZHAQ HASNIRI

### ON THE WORSHIP OF WOOD AND A FOOL

*Piyyutei R. Yitzhaq HaSniri*, ed. B. Bar-Tiqvah (Ramat Gan, 1996), #48. An *ofan*, for the second day of Passover, in the form of a *muwashshah*. Acrostic *Sniri*. **Line 1:** Qedar, one of Ishmael's sons (Genesis 25:13), is a standard epithet for Islam; "fool" refers to Muhammad (see Yitzhaq Ibn Ezra's "Conversion," above). This sort of disparagement was by no means uncommon, even in this culture of coexistence. Some Muslims, for instance, referred to Jews as "apes" or "monkeys." **3–6:** Edom is a standard epithet for Christianity. The Hebrew actually employs another epithet, *'utz* (Genesis 36:28: "The children of Dishan—'Utz and Aran"; Lamentations 4:21), which involves a play on the word for "wood" (*'etz*), implying that the pagan worship of wood is etymologically embedded in the history and ancestry of that religion. Isaiah 40:19–20: "To whom then will ye liken God? . . . The image perchance, which the craftsman hath melted, and the goldsmith spread over with gold? . . . A holm-oak is set apart; He chooseth a tree that will not rot. He seeketh unto him a cunning craftsman, to set up an image, that shall not be moved." **7**: Jeremiah 22:14. **9**: Isaiah 41:7: "So the carpenter encouraged the goldsmith. . . . And he fastened it with nails, that it should not be moved." **19**: Jeshurun is a standard epithet for Israel. **22**: "They" refers to the heavenly hosts of angels and links the *piyyut* to the liturgy. (See "ofan," in the glossary.)

## MESHULLAM DEPIERA

For more on Meshullam's work and the complex nature of his longer poems especially, see Brann, *Compunctious Poet*, pp. 141–43, and James H. Lehman, "Polemic and Satire in the Poetry of the Maimonidean Controversy," *Prooftexts* 1, 2 (1981): 133–51; also articles by Fleischer and Septimus (in the notes below to Moshe Ben Nahman). Fleischer (*Toldot* [1997], p. 321) observes that Meshullam managed his quiet (and almost entirely personal) revolution while maintaining all the outward trappings of Andalusian verse (its meters, rhyme scheme, and form). In the social context of Meshullam's day, he adds, neither the qabbalists nor the participants in the Maimonidean controversy found any great need for poetry, and Meshullam's innovations were never really developed—though he was looked up to by some of the later poets, especially in Shelomo DePiera's circle. Lehman proposes that the town of Piera might be in Burgundy rather than Catalonia.

### THE POET

*Yedi'ot HaMakhon leHeqer HaShira Ha'Ivrit* 4, ed. H. Brody (Berlin/Jerusalem, 1938), p. 92; *HaShira*, #344. This poem treats the notion that *meitav hashir kezavo* "the truest poetry is the most feigning," a maxim that the Hebrew poets adopted from Arabic, though James Lehman proposes that the language of the poem takes it well beyond the conventional approach. The Hebrew *ani hu . . . ani hu* ("It is I . . . I am"—as in *Numbers Rabbah* 10:5, and in the poem) is, says Lehman, "a rabbinic catch phrase for the constancy of God. . . . The poet, too, is a creator, but an inconstant and deliberately fickle one." Cf. HaNagid's epigram on the same theme, "He'll Bring You Trouble," above, and the notes to that poem.

### ON A NEW BOOK BY MAIMONIDES

*Yedi'ot HaMakhon leHeqer HaShira Ha'Ivrit* 4, p. 39. One of several, mostly long, poems by the poet concerning Maimonides; some 20 percent of Meshullam's extant output treats the controversy surrounding his philosophy. His critique here is directed at Ben Maimon's most famous book, *Guide for the Perplexed*, or *Guide of the Perplexed*, which applies Aristotelian philosophy to the understanding of Scripture and key Jewish concepts, including prophecy, sacrifice, and the resurrection of the dead. Maimonides called for an allegorical or figurative inter-pretation of Scripture and its miracles, and likened prophecy to dreaming. See, for example, *Guide of the Perplexed*, trans. and ed. S. Pines (Chicago, 1963), 3:50, 2:36–48. Some scholars feel that Meshullam softened his critique in the wake of Nahmanides' famous letter to the French rabbis, calling for a reconciliation; James Lehman (above) sees all of Meshullam's "conciliatory" gestures as being part of a satirical polemic against the rationalists. His loyalty to the qabbalists, says Lehman, never wavered. **Line 1:** The *shibbutz* here is compound, alluding to the assertion in *Sefer Yetzira*, "*blom pikha*," "bridle [or block] your mouth [from speaking]"—meaning that one should refrain from commenting on sacred mysteries—and also to Psalms 32:9: "Be ye not as the horse or as the mule, which have no understanding, whose mouth must be held in with the bit and bridle, that they come not near you." **2:** Literally, "These are things we have not heard before"—which expresses astonishment and skepticism, but might also indicate that they have no precedent in Scripture and therefore are lacking in authority, invalid, or worse. **4:** Jeremiah 23:28: "The prophet that hath a dream, let him tell a dream; but he that hath my word, let him speak my word faithfully" (*Guide of the Perplexed*, pp. 370ff.).

### Before You Take Up Your Pen

*Yedi'ot HaMakhon leHeqer HaShira Ha'Ivrit* 4, p. 39, #16, lines 9–10. These lines are taken from a much longer poem addressed to a friend who has given vent to his anger. The poet cautions him about putting such sentiments into circulation, as they can't be taken back. Isaiah 16:3; Genesis 22:6; Proverbs 30:14: "This is a gener-ation whose teeth are as swords, and their great teeth as knives."

### How Could You Press for Song

*Yedi'ot HaMakhon leHeqer HaShira Ha'Ivrit* 4, #16, lines 32–end. This excerpt is drawn from the same poem as "Before You Take Up Your Pen" and comprises the second part of the qasida. The first half of the qasida takes his friend to task for having given vent to his anger; the second part addresses his friend's request for poems and defends his own (apparently new or recently developed) inclina-tion to mystical religious study rather than poetry. This is one of the first of the Spanish-Hebrew poems to come out explicitly against secular learning involving the Hebrew language, and as such, it is of considerable importance. Study of He-brew grammar was an essential part of the Andalusian cultural revolution brought about in the tenth and eleventh centuries, and the emergence of the great poetry of the period is unthinkable without it. (See for example, Ibn Gabirol's hymn to the language in *Selected Ibn Gabirol*, p. 49, and in the original Hebrew, *SH*, #226.) Here, for the first time, we find a poet not only avoiding such study, but mocking it and its heroes outright. Fleischer comments that this attitude is a product of the poet's worldview and that of his circle, and that it testifies to the collapse of the traditional Andalusian-Hebrew value system (*Toldot* [1997], p. 296). **Line 1:** His friend is pressing him to write and send on new poems. **8:** The poet alludes specifically to the "order" of the Mishna known as *Ohalot* (Tents—as in Numbers 19:14: "Whoever dies in a tent"), which deals with the laws of purity and contact with corpses; I have generalized the allusion to refer to the Mishna generally. **9:** I.e., the tractate known as *Berakhot* (Blessings), chapter 5, which begins with the line the poet alludes to: "One may stand to pray only in a solemn frame of mind." **10:** I.e., *Baba Batra*, chapter 8, which treats the laws of ownership, property, and inheritance. **11–12:** *Sefer Yetzira* 1:2, which understands the mysteries of the cosmos through the mystical interpretation of language and, more precisely, Hebrew letters. The seven Hebrew letters which can be doubled are *bet, gimel, dalet, kaf, peh, resh,* and *tav*. At one time in Hebrew all could express two different sounds, depending on whether or not they were doubled (see line 23). **15:** In Hebrew, as in Arabic, the verb is normally based on a three-letter root, though sometimes four-letter roots occur as well. **16:** The expanses of circles, that is, their area. In other words, is grammar practical, like geometry? **23:** Hard and soft refer to certain Hebrew letters whose sound can be altered by the addition of a dot to the center of the letter, yielding, for example, either *v* or *b, f* or *p*, etc. **25:** Qimhi is David Qimhi (c. 1160–1235), known as Radaq, who wrote an important grammatical work and biblical dictionary, as well as a commentary that was printed in all subsequent major editions of the rabbinic Bible. He was firmly on Maimonides' side of the argument over scriptural interpretation. **26:** "The wise one of Fez" is Yehuda Hayyuj (c. 945–1000), one of the most important Hebrew grammarians. Born in Fez, he came to Cordoba in 960 and entered the fray in the violent grammar wars between Menahem Ibn Saruq and Dunash (see introduction). He is responsible for the major "discovery" of the three-letter root of the Hebrew verb, and all subsequent work on Hebrew language has been based on his ideas. **28:** "The winged one" is Yonah Ibn Janaah (whose name means "son of the wing" in Arabic), a Spanish-Hebrew grammarian and lexicographer from the first half of the eleventh century. His most important works are *Sefer HaRiqma* and *Sefer HaShorashim* (translated from Arabic by Yehuda Ibn Tibbon), a wide-ranging book on Hebrew grammar and a complete dictionary of biblical Hebrew, respectively. **29:** "Dots and lines," i.e., the Hebrew vowels beneath, above, and within the letters. **32:** Whether the word should have a masculine or feminine grammatical marker. **34:** Hebrew, like Arabic, has verbs that are classified as "full" or "hollow," "weak" or "strong," depending on which letters comprise the root. **35–36:** The poet concludes that he isn't interested in the dry study of grammar; he is concerned only with religious study and, it seems, his own immortality as a poet (based on previous work) or the sense of the eternal that study and engagement with the mysteries of creation and existence yield. The contradiction between his having stated at the start that he isn't interested in poetry and his having written a long poem to explain why (in which he also singles out the religious value of song) is also found in the work of other poets. (Ibn Gabirol, for instance, writes a poem about not being able to write poems, as do Todros Abulafia and Vidal Benvisite.)

### As One with the Morning Stars

*Yedi'ot HaMakhon leHeqer HaShira Ha'Ivrit* 4, p. 105, #45, lines 1–13; *HaShira*, #342. This is the opening (prelude) to a long poem to "Avraham HaNasi," who is most likely Avraham Ibn Hasdai, author of *The Prince and the Monk* (above). The repetition Meshullam employs here (e.g., lines 1–2, 14–15, 15–16) is characteristic, and he makes use of a variety of such repetitive strategies to strengthen the sense of linkage and unity in the poem, even as his ideas tend to strike out in seemingly contradictory directions. **Line 1:** Job 38:7: "When the morning stars sang together . . ." **6:** Others understand *yetzuray* (Job 17:7) as "feelings" instead of "limbs." **13:** Or: "And I broke out in song and began to strum." **18:** The poet takes the lack of reply from the surrounding world, including his own instruments, as a sign (see lines 23–26) that the people around him are not capable of hearing what he has to say in song and so it is pointless to continue singing or composing poems. The continuation of the poem explicitly castigates the "lowly generation" into which the poet and his friends, including Ibn Hasdai, were born. He then goes on to mention specific friends who are in fact worthy, and praises them all.

### MOSHE BEN NAHMAN (NAHMANIDES)

The combination of French heresy and papal pressure for increased restrictions on Jews led the Church to focus on Spain. The Dominican and Franciscan orders were founded to combat "religious nonconformity," and "the special mechanism of inquiry known as the Inquisition was established . . . [introducing] a new weapon, the so-called 'dialogue of controversy' " (Gerber, *The Jews of Spain*, p. 102). The Disputation at Barcelona was one of those "dialogues."

While Ben Nahman himself expressed a pronounced reluctance with regard to the inclusion of liturgical poetry in the worship service ("who adds to the hymns and songs acts improperly" [*Hidushim, Berakhot* 59a]), all but one of his extant poems are explicitly religious or liturgical; and religion, along with a powerful desire for individual salvation in the face of persecution, pervades even the one nonliturgical poem in his canon, "Me'a Batim" (One Hundred Verses). For more on Ben Nahman's poetry and influence, see E. Fleischer, "The Gerona School of Poetry," and B. Septimus, " 'Open Rebuke and Concealed Love': Nahmanides and the Andalusian Tradition"—both in *R. Moses Nahmanides: Explorations in His Religious and Literary Virtuosity*, ed. I. Twersky (Cambridge/London, 1983). The quote from his letter can be found in Chavel's edition of Nahmanides' work (see citation below), p. 368. DePiera had seen the Mongols as heralds of the messianic age. The Mongols were in Jerusalem itself for only three months, in 1260, but they caused considerable damage. See also M. H. Burgoyne, *Mamluk Jerusalem,* London, (1987), p. 58.

## BEFORE THE WORLD EVER WAS

*Kitvei Rabbeinu Moshe Ben Nahman,* ed. H. Chavel, (Jerusalem, 1963), 1: 392; *HaShira,* #352. A *seliha (mustajaab).* Acrostic: *Moshe Ben Nahman Yerondi Hazaq.* This *piyyut* treats the Day of Judgment and the soul's descent from on high to be reunited with the body. Schirmann notes that, at least at first glance, it contains the first true mixture of qabbalistic elements and the world of Andalusian poetry. He adds that while qabbalistic elements generally had a negative influence on the quality of medieval Hebrew verse, in this case the poem embodies the mystical elements quite naturally. Septimus also reads the poem in a qabbalistic light, noting that "the magnificent opening stanzas . . . in which the soul makes its descent through the world of the *sefirot, . . .* constitute a kind of qabbalistic *tiqqun* of the traditional Andalusian genre [of soul-poems having a tripartite structure and progression: the soul's origin in the upper world; its earthly exile; and ultimate reunion with its heavenly source]. . . . This 'return of all things to their original state' finally establishes the spiritual and literary symmetry required by Andalusian sensibility—but it establishes it on qabbalistic terms, as all things are in the end reabsorbed into the realm of the *sefirot*" ("Open Rebuke," pp. 28–29). Gershom Scholem translated the poem into German. (See Scholem in *Schocken Almanach* 5696 [Berlin, 1935/36], pp. 86ff.). Fleischer argues that previous scholars have read the poem incorrectly, and that in fact its imagery is purely Neoplatonic and not qabbalistic at all. For more on the Gerona qabbalists, see Scholem's *Origins of the Kabbalah* (Philadelphia and Princeton, 1987), pp. 365ff. **Lines 1–4:** The poem is preceded by the scriptural verse: "I say, My work is concerning a king"—or, in the NJPS version, "I speak my poem to a king" (Psalms 45:2), which is then sung as a refrain after each stanza. All subsequent quatrains of the poem end with the word "king." Proverbs 8:23; Daniel 11:3; Job 28:12; Nehemiah 13:6: "In the two and thirtieth year of Artaxerxes king of Babylon I went unto the king, and after certain days asked I leave of the king." **5–8:** Esther 3:9: "to bring it into the king's treasuries." **10:** Zechariah 4:3. Some commentators suggest that the image of left and right involves an allusion to qabbalistic concepts. **12:** Nehemiah 3:15: "and the wall of the pool of Shelah by the king's garden." This is sometimes understood to refer to Siloam's pool in Jerusalem, or simply an "irrigation pool." **13–16:** Psalms 139:15; Jeremiah 14:8; Nehemiah 2:6: "For the king said unto me . . . 'For how long shalt thy journey be? And when wilt thou return?'" **17–20:** Psalms 119:105; Proverbs 20:37; Job 30:15; Proverbs 24:21: "My son, fear thou the Lord and the King." **21–24:** Proverbs 16:11; Job 37:13; Psalms 44:14; 2 Samuel 3:37: "It was not by the king's will that Abner son of Ner was killed." **25–28:** Ezekiel 26:16; Psalms 32:5; Job 30:23, 16:8; Nehemiah 2:9: "I gave them the king's letters"—i.e., what the king has recorded. **29–32:** Hosea 13:5; Genesis 42:34; Numbers 11:34; Jeremiah 31:19; Ecclesiastes 8:2: "I counsel thee: Keep the king's command." **33–36:** I'll be judged for secret sins. Ecclesiastes 3:11, 12:14; Psalms 90:8; Daniel 1:10: "I fear my Lord the king." **37–40:** The subject is the now-penitent "heart" of line 33. Isaiah 66:2; Job 20:21; Proverbs 25:5: "Take away the wicked from before the king." **41–44:** *Sheqalim* 1:6–7; *Avot* 4:22: "Despite your wishes are you going to give a full accounting before the king of kings, the Holy One, Blessed be He." **45–48:** Psalms 62:13; Daniel 9:7; Psalms 130:4: Nehemiah 5:4: "money for the king's tribute." **49–52:** Psalms 71:6; 89:3; Isaiah 65:24; Ezra 8:22: "For I was ashamed to ask of the king." **53–56:** Literally, "the body in its prison" (i.e., the ground), as in Psalms 142:8. Micah 7:19; Psalms 57:2, 31:2; Proverbs 30:28: "Yet is she in the king's palace." **57–60:** "She" refers to the soul. Job 9:31; 1 Kings 3:28: "And all Israel heard of the judgment which the king had judged." **61–64:** Genesis 49:24; *Berakhot* 13a; Esther 2:9; 1:8; Nehemiah 2:8: "Asaph the keeper of the King's park."

### From "One Hundred Verses"

*Kitvei Ben Nahman*, p. 398. This hymn to old age is Nahmanides' only extant "secular" (nonliturgical) poem; it is also the only poem of his written in quantitative meter and monorhyme. In classical Andalusian verse old age is almost always cast in a negative light, while youth is celebrated. As such the thrust of the poem is consistent with the emphases of the Gerona school's counterpoetics, wherein the Andalusian aesthetic, or ethos, is challenged directly. For this excerpt from what would be a two-hundred-line English poem, I have woven together passages from three separate parts of the poem, emphasizing the rewards of age (i.e., truth, closeness to the divine) and the vision of the resurrection (rather than the more predictable, if elegant, elegy for lost youth). All this is described with tremendous passion. The metaphysical nature of the poem notwithstanding, it is couched in an utterly personal, intimate tone. The addressee is R. Yonah Gerondi, the poet's teacher and cousin. **Lines 1–4:** Hosea 8:2; Isaiah 24:14; Nehemiah 13:6; Job 38:12; Isaiah 47:11. **5–8:** Hosea 13:15; Esther 8:16. **9:** My reading follows Brody, who has *te'erav* (please) for *tir'av* (starve); cf. Proverbs 13:19: "The desire accomplished is sweet to the soul." **11:** The translation skips the next twenty-one lines of the Hebrew (lines 6–26, doubled in English), which continue the friends' elegy for the golden days of youth and all its pleasures, including wine, women, war, wealth, and the like. The translation picks up at the poet's reply, line 27 in the Hebrew, and continues through line 31 of the Hebrew, with the poet justifying the ways of God. **11–14:** Amos 6:13; Ecclesiastes 1:17; Proverbs 27:9; Isaiah 53:3. "A destiny" is literally "days have sought [against] and fallen [upon us]," as in Genesis 43:18. **15–18:** Nehemiah 13:31; Isaiah 28:17; Psalms 112:5; Song of Songs 6:5. **19–20:** I.e., time dressed you up and made you look good, for a while. Psalms 90:10: "Yet is their pride but travail and vanity"; 2 Kings 9:30: "And Jezebel painted her eyes"; Ezekiel 23:40: "for them you painted your eyes and put on your finery" (NJPS). **21:** The translation then skips Hebrew lines 32–55, which extend the description of youth as vanity, and drive home the point that only a fool could think one might hold on to its delights. The English resumes at lines 56–60, with the poet about to begin his praise of old age. **22–24:** Proverbs 4:19; Psalms 80:17, 37:20. **26–30:** Psalms 24:4, 69:22, 102:10. **31:** Lines 61–69 of the Hebrew, omitted here, extend the description of "those who go in fear of sin" and their service of God. The translation resumes at line 70 of the Hebrew and then continues without interruption to the poem's conclusion. Cf. *Hagigah* 13a, which implies that one should be fifty years old before taking up the mystical study of the Chariot, or the secrets and mysteries of the divine world, the Qabbala. Proverbs 18:12. **34:** Ezekiel 10:12; Exodus 3:2. **36:** Song of Songs 2:4. **38:** Habakkuk 3:4. **39–40:** Jeremiah 31:12. **44:** Job 40:22. **48–50:** Psalms 25:13; Isaiah 66:11; Ezekiel 28:16; 1 Samuel 25:29; Exodus 28:2; Psalms 50:2. **51–52:** Isaiah 2:19; *Ketubot* 111a: "to roll through the cavities"—the dead beyond the borders of Israel must "roll" through underground cavities that will be opened up so that the righteous may reach Israel before they can be brought back to life. **56:** Proverbs 3:35. **58–60:** Jeremiah 12:1; Psalms 17:5. **61:** Psalms 103:21. **63–66:** This seems to be alluding to a specific historical occurrence, but the allusion has remained obscure and may simply be general. Hosea 9:13; Micah 6:7; Psalms 127:3; Jeremiah 16:6. **69:** The line, based on Ezekiel 16:6, can also be translated: "Despite our blood, we live" (NJPS). **71:** Psalms 17:14. **73–74:** Psalms 17:15; *Sukkah* 45b. **75–76:** Isaiah 45:8; Job 2:3. **77–80:** Psalms 103:5; Job 33:25: "His flesh is tenderer than a child's; He returneth to the days of his youth"— i.e., he regains the strength and health of youth; Isaiah 26:19; Psalms 8:6, 145:5. They did not seek glory and splendor in their prayers, so much as righteousness and guidance. That is, they worshiped in purity, not for reward. **81–84:** Proverbs 16:15; Isaiah 24:23, 25:8. **85–90:** Proverbs 16:15; Jeremiah 51:56; Deuteronomy 32:35; Isaiah 59:18, 34:4; Psalms 104:30. **91–92:** Isaiah 26:4; Jeremiah 4:24.

## SHEM TOV IBN FALAQERA

See also *Falaqera's Book of the Seeker*, trans. and ed. M. Herschel Levine (New York, 1976). The epigram in the biographical note is from *Sefer HaMevaqesh* (below), p. 8. The characterization of the work as "a ritual exorcism or catharsis through which Falaqera hopes to purge his heart and mind of poetry" is Brann's (*Compunctious Poet*, p. 136). Falaqera valued the poetry of the Bible highly, but distinguished between the various degrees of poetry; the postbiblical, or Spanish, poets represent the lowest degree of achievement in his scheme. See also Adele Berlin, *Biblical Poetry through Medieval Eyes* [Bloomington, 1991], p. 97.

### Career Counseling

*Sefer HaMevaqesh* [no editor listed] (Warsaw, 1924), p. 41; *HaShira*, #354, lines 37–38. Doctors were an easy target in the ancient world and the Middle Ages, and poems about their malpractice are common (see Ibn Zabara's "The Physician," above). In other places, Falaqera and the other poets treat the profession respectfully, and it should be noted that it was a common occupation for Jews.

## A Mystery

*Sefer HaMevaqesh*, p. 53. Ecclesiastes 11:5: "As thou knowest not what is the way of the wind, nor how the bones do grow in the womb of her that is with child."

## On Poets and Poetry

*Sefer HaMevaqesh*, p. 79; *HaShira*, #356, lines 89–90. This poem comes toward the end of part 1 of *The Book of the Seeker*, which marks the formal renunciation of Falaqera's life as a composer of verse. The didactic material of part 2 of the book is entirely in prose. Tova Rosen writes that, after meeting with a poet, the seeker is "filled with disgust at the profession." Looking elsewhere in his work she notes the equivalence Falaqera implicitly draws between poetry and women with their seductive, and dangerous, charms. "This juncture between the hatred of women and the assault on poetry," she says, "is typical of the thirteenth century, the Aristotelian Century, not only in Jewish culture, but in Islam and in Christian Europe as well." At the heart of this juncture are Maimonides' (negative) views on poetry (*Unveiling Eve*, pp. 75–82). See also Fleischer's observations in *Toldot* [1997], p. 282, n. 15.

## Why God Made You

*Sefer HaMevaqesh*, p. 55. See *Choice of Pearls*, "On Patience," #147. Santob De Carrión casts the same notion in verse in his *Moral Proverbs*. For an adaptation of those proverbs, see my *Hymns & Qualms* (Riverdale-on-Hudson, 1998), pp. 92–105.

## The Fool Thinks

*Iggeret HaMusar* [The Book of Ethics], ed. A. M. Habermann, *Qovetz 'al-Yad*, n.s., 1 (1936): 57.
**Line 4:** Proverbs 18:14.

## Poverty's War

*Iggeret HaMusar*, p. 67; *Sefer HaMevaqesh*, p. 17.

## YITZHAQ IBN SAHULA

The reader of *Meshal HaQadmoni* may wonder why its otherwise qabbalistically inclined author chose to leave all traces of mysticism out of his work (though this is the first work in which *The Zohar* is mentioned). Raphael Loewe suggests that he did so for several reasons: (1) the work was intended for ordinary, not esoteric, readers; (2) Maimonides (who appears in the book in thinly disguised form) is the model of the ideal man for the author and his readers, and he came down—famously—on the nonmystical (i.e., rationalist) side of the medieval debate over faith; and (3) the denunciation of astrology in the work might have seemed to Ibn Sahula somehow at odds with a presentation of mystical doctrine. (See Ibn Sahula, *Meshal HaQadmoni: Fables from the Distant Past*, ed. and trans. Raphael Loewe (Oxford, 2004), pp. xxiii–xxiv.) The other curious detail of the qabbalistic matrix behind the book is that *The Zohar*'s principal author, Moshe de Leon, at one point identifies himself as the author of a work that is also called *Meshal HaQadmoni*. While it seems odd that two books, by two friends, would emerge from the same part of Spain with precisely the same title at roughly the same time, scholars have been unable to identify the book de Leon referred to, and the mystery of the "other" *Meshal HaQadmoni* remains unsolved.

### THE CYNIC SPEAKS

*Meshal HaQadmoni*, ed. Y. Zemora (Tel Aviv, 1952), vol. 1, chapter 4, pp. 22–23. **Line 7–8:** Ecclesiastes 2:10; Psalms 46:1. **11–12:** Isaiah 22:18.

### ON HUMILITY

*Meshal HaQadmoni*, vol. 4, chapter 60, p. 232. **Line 1:** Isaiah 18:3. **2:** Lamentations 4:6. **10:** 1 Samuel 18:8.

## AVRAHAM ABULAFIA

Just why there isn't more first-rate qabbalistic Hebrew poetry from Spain (or elsewhere, for that matter) has been a matter of some speculation. Gershom's Scholem's works are peppered with indications that he considers the subject of qabbalistic poetry a promising one for study, and he finds far more Qabbala in verse than do other scholars, such as Schirmann and Fleischer. Fleischer speculates that the paucity of qabbalistic poems may have something to do with the cerebral nature of Jewish mysticism on the one hand and the secular foundations of Spanish-Hebrew poetry on the other. Schirmann laments the fact that the qabbalists simply weren't good poets, or had a hard time expressing their complex thought and theories in poetry. More recently Moshe Idel has suggested that the qabbalistic emphasis on *mitzvot*, the observance of the commandments within a mystical framework, in many ways occupied the place in Jewish mysticism that poetry occupied in the mystical traditions of other faiths; that is, the mystical performance of the commandments cathected the psychic energy that might otherwise have gone into the making of poems.

## From *The Book of the Letter*

In making these selections from the some fourteen hundred lines of verse in *The Book of the Letter*, I have tried to give a sense of the poem's various modes (lyrical, narrative, apocalyptic) as well as its shifting rhythms and moods; I have not, however, included any of the most obscure language-centered passages, which are composed entirely of neologisms. Apart from the first section, the excerpts here are taken from the final 350 lines of the poem. My annotation is based on Moshe Idel's *The Mystical Experience in Abraham Abulafia* (Albany, 1988), pp. 95–105 and 157–58) and Scholem's lecture on Abulafia, published in *Major Trends in Jewish Mysticism* (New York, 1946), pp. 119–55. For more detailed summaries of Abulafia's thought, see Idel (above, and *Language, Torah and Hermeneutics in Abraham Abulafia* (Albany, 1989), and Colette Sirat's *History of Jewish Philosophy in the Middle Ages* (Cambridge, 1985). The speaker in this poem is one Zekharyahu, whose name is numerologically equivalent to "Avraham," and the book has also been called *Sefer Zekharyahu*.

*And the letter is longing:*

*Sefer ha'Ot: Apokalypse des Pseudo-Propheten und Pseudo-Messias Abraham Abulafia,* ed. A. D. Jellinek, in *Jubelschrift zum Sibzigsten Gebortstage des Prof. Dr. H. Graetz, Breslau, 1897,* section 4, p. 70; M. Idel's manuscript (given to this translator), p. 5a, lines 277–88. The Hebrew involves anagrammatic play on "the letter" *(ha'ot—heh, aleph, vuv, tav)* and "desire" *(ta'ava—tav, aleph, vav, heh),* both of which are formed from four letters: *heh, aleph, vuv, tav;* in the same way the poem plays with "sky" *(hashahaq)* and "desire" *(hahosheq—literally, "the one who desires"),* both of which employ *heh, het, vuv, shin, quf;* in both cases only the vocalization differs. To get a sense of that dimension one might translate the opening as: "And the sign sings,/and sky is key/to knowing the will."

*And YHVH spoke:*

Jellinek, section 6, p. 81; Idel MS, p. 17a. "The letter" (or "sign") in Abulafia's thought indicates Active Intellect. Kingdom and Law are one of several conflicting forces that appear in the poem, and in Abulafia's thought generally. "Your father and mother" here are most likely Adam and Eve. Throughout his work Abulafia makes extensive use of Hebrew numerology *(gematria);* here, for instance, "my father and mother" = 70 = blood and ink = Adam and Eve. "And ink" = 26 = YHVH, while the pronounced form of the divine name *(Yod Heh Vav Heh)* = 44 = blood. The Sabbath's triumph over the days of the week is the triumph of the sacred over the profane, but also of intellect over imagination, and life over death. In *Sefer HaMelitz*, Abulafia writes: "A line of life, a line of ink; and a line of death, a line of blood." Elsewhere he states plainly: " 'Adam and Eve' in numerology equals 'my father and mother,' and their secret is blood and ink, and this latter is proven by this name, YHWH, and one who merits it will have engraved upon his forehead a *tav* [the Hebrew letter]—for one a *tav* of blood, for the other a *tav* of ink." He goes on to derive the significance of that *tav* from its combination, when it is written out, with ink (*dyo*) in the word *yoledet* (she gives birth), as opposed to that of blood (*dam*) in *muledet* (she is born). In the former (*yoledet*), the letters *yod, lamed,* and *dalet* are combined with the *tav*; in the latter, the same three letters are combined with *mem* (as in blood). A follower of Abulafia's thought, Isaac of Acre (in the thirteenth–mid-fourteenth century) writes: "The blood alludes to the secret of the sacrifices and the prayers, while ink is like the writing of the Torah in ink upon a book." All of the above is drawn from Idel, *Mystical Experience in Abulafia,* pp. 96, 99, 155, and 158.

*The Lord showed me:*
Jellinek, section 7, p. 81; Idel MS, pp. 18a–b. The vision of the man and his army is met with fear on the part of the poet-seer, which, as Idel notes (*Mystical Experience,* p. 119), might be taken as either a Jungian fear of encounter with the inner Self or a Rudolph Otto–like dread and awe before the "wholly Other." Referring to another of Abulafia's works (*Sitrei Torah*) in which the poet-seer cites *Sefer Yetzira* 5:2—"the heart in soul [i.e., within man] is like the king in a battle"—Idel is convinced of the internal nature of the events described. The man himself is an external product of the "intellectual flow." The sign or letter on the man's forehead, which stands for the letters of the divine name, becomes the fount of seventy tongues, that is, the Active Intellect. "The Active Intellect is the potion of life for those who are able to receive its flux, while for those who are unable to do so it is the potion of death" (Idel, p. 97). Likewise, the transformation of the colors here—black to red and vice versa—is indicative of the dual potential of the letter. *Shabbat* 55a: "The Holy One, blessed be He, said to Gabriel: Go and record upon the forehead of the righteous a line of ink, that the angels of destruction may not rule over them; and upon the foreheads of the wicked a line of blood, so that the angels of destruction may rule over them." At the end of this section, the phrase "and turned into another man" alludes to 1 Samuel 10:7, where prophecy itself transforms Saul.

*And from the bow of knowing:*
Jellinek, section 7, pp. 82–83; Idel MS, pp. 20a–20b.

*And I lifted up my eyes:*
Jellinek, section 7, p. 83; Idel MS, pp. 22a–23b. "The stone that drew it" is in Hebrew *even zohelet* (the stone of Zohelet—literally, a creeping stone), from 1 Kings 1:9, where Adonijah slays sheep and oxen, but here Abulafia seems to be describing a "magnet." Later in the poem Abulafia says that the stone of Zohelet is the mind disturbed with terror and fear. "V.i.s.i.o.n" is marked (in the Hebrew) to indicate an acronym, most likely for *meshalim, remazim, aggadot, halakhot* (parables,

symbols, legends, and laws) = *marah* (vision). The old man in that vision, according to Idel, is Metatron (Prince of the Face or Presence), again the Active Intellect. What is central is that in this case, as with the previous vision, the encounter is between two men, in (Blakean) human form, not between disembodied intellectual capacities. The throne of judgment involves the "two attributes by which the word is led": judgment and mercy.

*The name of the first warrior-king is Qadari'el:*
    Jellinek, section 7, p. 84; Idel MS, pp. 24b–25a. The names of the kings would seem to reflect the powers they embody and might be understood as the East of God, the Word of God, the Rule of God, and the Era of God. Isaac of Acre describes the "four worlds" as emanation, creation, formation, and action. Yeho'el means, "God is willing" (Idel, *The Mystical Experience*, p. 105). Elliot Wolfson identifies Yeho'el as Metatron, Prince of the Countenance (Wolfson, *Abraham Abulafia, Kabbalist and Prophet* [Los Angeles, 2000], p. 101). "The year of mind" (or "spirit"—*shnat hamo'ah*) is the numerological shorthand (48) for the Hebrew year of 5048, or 1288 C.E., when he wrote the poem.


## AVRAHAM BEN SHMU'EL

### To Whom among the Avengers of Blood

*HaShira* #396. A *seliha* in the form of a *rehuta*. Acrostic: *Avraham Ben Shmu'el*. See *Genesis Rabbah* 18 for the full inventory of body parts. Y. Ratzhaby traces the ideas in the poem to a fifth- or sixth-century Persian literary source (Y. Ratzhaby, *MeGinzei Shirat HaQedem*, [Jerusalem, 1991], pp. 302–5.) **Line 1:** Numbers 35:21. **7:** Isaiah 54:16. **8:** *Sanhedrin* 7:4: "[These are the felons who are put to death by stoning . . . ] he who beguiles [others to idolatry], and he who leads a whole town to idolatry." **11:** Ecclesiasticus 9:3. **15:** Isaiah 30:16. **22:** Isaiah 49:17. **26:** The last two lines suggest that the poem could be read as part of the penitential service, leading into the standard prayer accompanying hymns of this sort, "God, King who sits on the throne of mercy, who acts with kindness, and pardons the sins of his people."


## YOSEF GIQATILLA

The spelling of the poet's name varies; most often it is Giqatilla, but one also encounters Chiqatilla and Giqatilia.


### The Nut Garden

*Sefer Ginat Egoz leRibi Yosef Giqatilla* (Jerusalem, 1989), p. 1.
    **Line 3:** "Its" refers to "feeling"—something that is explicit in the gendered Hebrew.

## TODROS ABULAFIA

The "parables and riddles" *(meshalim vehidot)* of the title of Todros's diwan are medieval synonyms for "poems and epigrams," or verse in the standard Hebrew mode of the day. The terms are taken from Proverbs 1:6: "To understand a proverb *(mashal)*, and a figure; the words of the wise, and their dark sayings *(hidot)*." Some of Todros's headings were in Arabic, and he also composed the prefaces to some of his shorter compilations in Arabic, especially those composed in his youth. The characterizations of Todros's work are wide-ranging. "One of the greatest of Hebrew poets" is Moses Gaster's, in the English foreword to his facsimile edition of Sha'ul 'Abdullah Yosef 's manuscript copy, *Sefer Gan HaMeshalim veHaHidot leHaSar Todros HaLevi Ibn Abu al-'Aafi'a, Kefi 'Ataqat Mar Shaul Yosef meHong Kong meKhtav Yado Mamash Ketavnito Ketzuro, 'Im Petah Davar* (London, 1926), 1:1. (This was the facsimile version from which Yellin worked to prepare his critical edition.) "A mediocre epigone" is how Schirmann sums up the opinions held by Brody and Yellin *(Toldot* [1997], p. 390). Schirmann himself writes in his anthology that, though Todros wasn't in the "front rank" of Hebrew poets, a careful selection of his work reveals his "unique personality"; he was, says Schirmann, an "interesting" poet, worthy of a full critical study. Brody and Yellin, he continues, were judging Todros by the wrong criteria, for "in his best and unconventional poetry," where Todros shocks the reader with his candor and personal approach, he is writing what Goethe called "fragments of a great confession" and in this respect is unmatched by any of the medieval Hebrew poets *(Toldot* [1997], pp. 389–90). In an earlier article, however, Schirmann had said that Todros was "superficial and repetitive," and that his poems were primarily valuable for the historical material they contain *(Encyclopedia Judaica* [1972], 1:195). Sha'ul 'Abdullah Yosef, for his part, calls Todros a "marvelous poet . . . unique among the poets of Israel," and he singles out his craftsmanship, which he says excels that of Ibn Gabirol and HaLevi! *(Gan HaMeshalim*, vol. 2, part 2, page xliv). Yellin, who quotes these lines from one of Yosef 's letters, explains that by "craftsmanship" Yosef no doubt meant word play, including puns and clever employment of biblical phrases. Yellin adds that Todros reflects a "new spirit" in Hebrew poetry, one in which content takes precedence over style, and that he excelled at description. Calling Todros's work egocentric (since it extended no further in its vision than the Jewish quarter of Toledo and was entirely lacking in national consciousness), historian Yitzhaq Baer adds: "God forbid that we should compare him to Ibn Gabirol or HaLevi!" Still, he says, Todros was a "real poet," who wrote out of a deep inner need ("Todros Ben Yehuda HaLevi uZemano," *Zion* 2, [1937]: 55; see also Baer, *A History of the Jews in Christian Spain*, 1: 123f.). Dan Pagis, however, held to the opinion that Todros was "one of the last great poets to appear in the Spanish school" *(Hiddush uMasoret beShirat haHol* [Jerusalem, 1976], p. 186). See also A. Doron, *Meshorer ba-Hatzer HaMelekh* (Tel Aviv, 1989), pp. 11–16. As Baer sees it, Todros's work offers a much fuller "autobiography" than anything we can find in the work of the troubadour poets. Fleischer has high praise for the poet's lyricism, which he considers a resurrection of the Andalusian model. Despite the return to that classical model, says Fleischer, Todros was hardly a neoclassical writer; on the contrary, his temperament was romantic through and through: "There wasn't a single Andalusian negative commandment ('Thou shalt not') that he didn't violate." On the whole Fleischer notes Todros's anxious and belated relation to his classical predecessors, whom he often treats ironically, and he appreciates the energy, dexterity, and sharpness of his work (*Toldot* [1997], pp. 396–97). It is also Fleischer who says that Todros was "a graphomaniac (if it is possible to ignore the negative connotations of the term)." That is, he continues, Todros was "a poet for whom it was hard *not* to write," and in this and other respects he resembles Shmu'el HaNagid (*Toldot* [1997], p. 391).

## I've Labored in Love

*Gan HaMeshalim veHaHidot*, ed. D. Yellin (Jerusalem, 1932), #723; *HaShira*, #379. (All subsequent indications of sources for Todros Abulafia's poems refer to Yellin; the headings in that collection were written by the poet himself.) **Heading:** "Of an Arab daughter whose love gave me pleasure,/when with other women I saw her,/as each was kissing her sister." For another medieval Hebrew expression of a man's desire to be a woman, see Qalonymos Ben Qalonymos's "On Becoming a Woman," below. **Line 8:** *Ketubot* 108b: "Admon laid down seven rulings: If a man dies and leaves sons and daughters, if the estate is large, the sons inherit it and the daughters are maintained [from it], and if the estate is small, the daughters are maintained from it, and the sons can go begging. Admon said, 'Am I to be the loser because I am a male?'"

## She Said She Wanted

*Gan HaMeshalim*, #123; *HaShira*, #376. **Line 8:** Job 35:3.

## The Day You Left

*Gan HaMeshalim*, #97. **Lines 5–6:** Lamentations 1:14: "The yoke of my transgressions . . . are come up upon my neck . . . the Lord hath delivered me into their hands, against whom I am not able to stand."

## That Fine Gazelle

*Gan HaMeshalim*, #89; *HaShira*, #374. **Line 4:** Literally, "My friend . . ." **6:** Literally, "Leave desire and you'll find relief."

## They Fight with Me over Desire

*Gan HaMeshalim*, #104. **Line 4:** Deuteronomy 13:6.

## That Girl Emerged

*Gan HaMeshalim*, #70. **Line 4:** Deuteronomy 32:13: "And he made him to suck honey out of the crag [rock]."

## May My Tongue

*Gan HaMeshalim*, #98. **Line 1:** Psalms 137:6. **4:** Genesis 24:2: "[Abraham] said to his servant, . . . 'Put, I pray thee, thy hand under my thigh.'" The biblical gesture accompanied a vow and may have involved touching the genitals.

## There's Nothing Wrong in Wanting a Woman

*Gan HaMeshalim*, #721; *HaShira*, #381. **Heading:** "I'll make mention of my sins/and of (on) *'alamot* I'll sing"—which plays on Genesis 41:9: "I must make mention today of my transgressions" and the heading to Psalms 46: "On *'alamot*, a song"—meaning either, (1) "with the musical instrument known as the *'alamot* I'll sing"; (2) in a whisper I'll sing; or (3) "of maidens I'll sing." In characteristic fashion, Todros turns what at first sounds like a confessional allusion on its head; as Brann notes, "the 'confession' is actually an avowal and the musical double-entendre is more like a celebration" (*Compunctious Poet*, p. 146). **Line 11:** Proverbs 9:13: "She is thoughtless and knoweth nothing." **16:** Psalms 45:14: "Her raiment is of chequer work inwrought with gold." **20:** Literally, "Alas," or "Ah," as in Ezekiel 6:11. **22:** Leviticus 20:15: "And if a man lie with a beast . . ."

## Strong Poet, Weak Poet

*Gan HaMeshalim*, #494. Part of a *tenso*-like exchange with a talented poet named Pinhas, about whom very little is known with any certainty. (*Tenso* is a Provençal term indicating a lyric poem of dispute or personal abuse.) He may in fact have been a member of a family of distinguished liturgical poets in Provence and northern Spain. The exchange seems to have begun in fraternity and ended in ac-rimony, after Pinhas slandered Todros in a long poem to Todros's patron, Yitzhaq (#396 in Yellin)—though here too we don't know for sure just when the thirty-five poems in the series were composed. **Heading:** "I laid him waste,/and from his own cup I gave him a taste." **Line 4:** Judges 4:21, where Ya'el sticks the tent pin, or stake, into Sisera's head. "Standards" translates *yated*, which is in this case a loaded word. It literally means "stake," but it is also the word used to im-ply part of the quantitative poetic meter, which is composed of *yated*s and *tenu'as* (short and long metrical feet); here, of course, it also means both "up-right pole" and "criteria." It picks up on an image from Pinhas's previous poem to Todros, where he says that the (sexual) power of his (Pinhas's) own poems are sufficient to satisfy (literally, "to stick in the stake for") two thousand women. Todros sets him straight with this reply. The passive partner in this context is considered an object of little worth at best, and shame at worst. The active partner is all virility.


### PLASTER AND PEARLS

*Gan HaMeshalim*, #500. Also from the exchange with Pinhas. **Heading:** "And I said: Could rubies resemble sand? Can't he distinguish between the sacred and the profane?" **Line 6:** Proverbs 24:31. **8:** Psalms 104:10. Literally, "Give me the valleys of your verse, my friend, and I will send forth springs into them." **9:** Psalms 104:25.


### NOTHING LEFT TO SAY

*Gan HaMeshalim*, #507. Also from the exchange with Pinhas, toward the end. The heading notes that he wrote this when Pinhas was slow in responding to another poem Todros had sent him. **Line 2:** *Sanhedrin* 97a: "The son of David will not come . . . until the last *peruta* (small coin) is gone from the purse." **4:** Ezekiel 21:33. **5:** Ruth 2:15–16. **8:** 2 Kings 4:10: "Let us make, I pray thee, a little chamber on the roof; and let us set for him there a bed, and a table." "Little chamber" in the Hebrew of 2 Kings is *'aliyat qir* (literally, an upper room with a wall), which Abulafia changes to *'aliyat shir* (an upper part of a poem, i.e., an opening stanza or line), as he puns on the notion of a stanza as a room (in Hebrew, a *bayit*, which means both a verse and a home).


### TEACHERS AND WRITERS

*Gan HaMeshalim*, #735. **Line 4:** Literally, "You teach, and the law is like the others [teach it]." Schirmann, basing his reading on talmudic usage, understands "others" to mean "the *goyim* (nations / non-Jews)." Yellin suggests that it means, "You teach, but your rulings and understandings are not in line with those of the sages" (see *Baba Batra* 96b). **7–8:** This alludes to the well-known Hebrew proverb: "Learn from writers (*soferim*), not from books *(sefarim)*."


### BEFORE THE KING

*Gan HaMeshalim*, #636. **Heading**: "When I went to the King to enter his service, I presented him with a cup—a work of fine craftsmanship, and on its brow I engraved [these verses] in a line." **Line 6:** Exodus 23:14–15: "And none shall appear before me empty-handed"—referring to the pilgrimage festivals, on which one "goes up" to Jerusalem.

MY KING

*Gan HaMeshalim*, #644. **Line 1:** The opening of the poem echoes the prayer from the morning liturgy—"May it be your will, Lord, . . . that you save me today . . . from brazen men"; the poet seems to be deliberately blurring sacred and secular realms (and concerns). **5–6:** *Hagigah* 15a. The translation is based on Davidson's reading (in Yellin). Also Isaiah 52:7; Genesis 42:35: "Every man's bundle of money was in his sack."

POEMS FROM PRISON

*I. As Love Lives*

*Gan HaMeshalim*, #649; *HaShira*, #392:2. **Heading:** "When the king imprisoned us in the pit with the other viziers, in the place where the king's prisoners are held, and we were given nothing to drink or eat—only foul water—and the lice and rodents gnawed at our flesh, and the bees pursued us, and no one went out and no one came in among our friends, I heard what sounded like the song of swifts and doves when the partridge is pursued in the hills, and in my distress I wrote these lines." **Line 1:** Amos 8:14. **12:** 1 Kings 17:6: "and the ravens brought [Elijah] bread and flesh."

*II. Treacherous Time*

*Gan HaMeshalim*, #655.

*III. The Filthy Lay in Darkness with Me*

*Gan HaMeshalim*, #831; *HaShira*, #392:1. Acrostic: *Todros*. This is an example of the *Todrosi'a* (pl. *Todrosi'ot*)—a form invented by the poet. See biographical note preceding the translations. Other *Todrosi'ot* follow below, where the acrostic *Todros* is noted. **Line 1:** Ezekiel 32:19. **5:** 1 Samuel 24:12. **6:** Psalms 51:14.

*IV. My Rings Have Fallen*

*Gan HaMeshalim*, #906; *HaShira*, #392:3. Acrostic: *Todros*. **Line 6:** *Shabbat* 157a.

*V. Is It the Lord*

*Gan HaMeshalim*, #686. One of several poems Todros wrote about his inability to compose. Medieval Hebrew poems about "writer's block" are extremely rare: in fact, the only other poet who seems to have treated this subject directly was Shelomo Ibn Gabirol, in "I've Made You My Refuge," above. (Shem Tov Ardutiel's *The Battles of the Pen and the Scissors* might also be addressing this topic.) See also other poems by Todros here, including "The Sea Casts Up Mire and Mud" (below). In contrast to the Golden Age poets, who continually boast of their literary powers, the later poets gradually reveal a dependency on the muse, and at times present themselves as helpless before her, rather than as masters of song. On the whole, however, Todros cannot be said to be lacking in confidence. **Line 4:** His legacy as a Levite (Todros *HaLevi* Abulafia). **5:** Jeremiah 17:14. **9–10:** Isaiah 58:9.

## Time Tries as I Drift

*Gan HaMeshalim*, #682. The poet compares his struggles to a sea (of trials) on which man floats or glides. The poem indicates that one of his sons had died.

## The Sea Casts Up Mire and Mud

*Gan HaMeshalim*, #855; *HaShira*, #392:7. Acrostic: *Todros*. **Line 1:** Isaiah 57:20. **3–4:** Psalms 12:9; Jeremiah 15:19. **8:** Literally, "one with wisdom toys with time, and entertains himself with 'maybe' and 'if only.'" Schirmann interprets this as "Takes comfort in the hope of change." **10:** Isaiah 40:15: "Behold, the nations . . . are counted as the small dust of the balance."

## On a Bible Written by Shmu'el HaNagid

*Gan HaMeshalim*, #691. **Heading:** "What he wrote on a Bible, written in the hand of Shmu'el HaNagid, which he bought in Seville." **Line 1:** I.e., Moses. **2:** Shmu'el HaNagid, the poet. Ibn Daud's *Book of Tradition* notes that HaNagid served as a scribe and counselor to King Habbuus, meaning that he both wrote documents and copied them. **4:** Betzalel, the biblical artist and craftsman; Exodus 28:39.

## Time Spreads Its Nets

*Gan HaMeshalim*, #770. **Line 1:** Ezekiel 26:5, 14: "She [Tyre] shall be a place for the spreading of nets." **3–4:** Psalms 75:6–8, 10:10. **10:** Psalms 16:6. **13–14:** Ecclesiastes 4:6. **16:** Genesis 6:9. **17–18:** Ecclesiastes 3:19. **19–20:** 1 Samuel 2:3. **22:** Ecclesiastes 11:5. **23–24:** Literally, "shouldn't be dwelt on." "Secret scroll" refers to talmudic matters (such as new halakhic rulings) that, while originally transmitted orally, were written down so as not to be forgotten—though they may not have been intended for wide distribution. See *Shabbat* 6b and *Baba Metzia* 92a. "Sealed words" are matters pertaining to the "end of days," as in Daniel 12:9: "These words are secret and sealed till the time of the end."

## Old Age Is Double-Edged

*Gan HaMeshalim*, #804. **Heading:** "The splendor of age's silver on the head I pronounced, but that 'old men's glory is the hoary beard' [Proverbs 20:29, with a change of vocalization] I denounced." **Line 1:** Literally, "Old age can be divided two ways, and this is how I make that division." Or: there are two aspects to aging. **4:** Psalms 133:2: "[To dwell together] is like precious oil upon the head, coming down upon the beard"; 1 Samuel 21:14.

PERVERSION'S PIGEONS

*Gan HaMeshalim*, #863. Acrostic: *Todros*. Lines 2, 4, and 6 in the original end with a homonym rhyme: *moreh*. **Line 1:** The Hebrew *'avel* might also be understood in this case as "falsehood." **9–10:** The Hebrew alludes to the mystical *Sefer Yetzira*'s (1:1) *sefer* (book, text, scripture) and *sippur* (story, telling, communication), which are of course sufficiently obscure in context, though the literal meaning is straightforward. It also refers to the midrashic texts *Sifra* and *Sifrei*—the implication being that the latter are even less well known.

MY THINKING WOVE

*Gan HaMeshalim*, #924. Acrostic: *Todros*. **Line 1:** Isaiah 59:5; Exodus 26:31. **2:** *Numbers Rabbah* 12:4: "Call it [the sun] purple, because the Lord, blessed be He, created it to weave manna for creation." In the logic of the midrashic image, which the poet adopts, the sun is called "purple" or "crimson" (Song of Songs 3:9–10) and sends rain that in turn yields the nectar and sweetness of fruit, or "manna"— so that the manna is, as it were, spun as an extension of the woven purple of the sun on its throne. **4:** Literally, "expressed in pleasant words"; Song of Songs 7:2. **6:** Hosea 2:1. **8:** Genesis 47:23. *Avot* 4:3: "Despise not any man and regard nothing as impossible; for you find no man who has not his hour, and no thing which has not its place."

THE LORD IS GOOD AND SO I'M TORMENTED

*Gan HaMeshalim*, #899. Acrostic: *Todros*. **Line 1:** The poem begins with a nearly direct quotation from Psalms 119:71. **5:** Isaiah 6:5. **9–10:** The Hebrew contains a complicated pun, an echo of which the English picks up in a slight departure from the literal reading. The line literally reads: "You who forgive and are good, I have only a verse [literally, 'house'] of the poem for you as an offering; take my verse which I have brought"—with the word for "verse" being identical to that for "house" (*bayit*), and with the two Hebrew words for "here-is my-verse" (*he veiti*), being identical to the Hebrew word for "I've brought" (*heveiti*).

DEFILED AND PURE ARE ONE

*Gan HaMeshalim*, #930. Acrostic: *Todros*. **Line 5:** Isaiah 22:2; Job 36:29. **6:** Jeremiah 48:44. **8:** Genesis 20:16: "You have been cleared." Yellin glosses: "See, and know." **10:** Joshua 1:9.

## On Hearing Church Bells

*Gan HaMeshalim*, #983; *HaShira*, #393. **Line 1:** The Hebrew opens: *"Hayaronu tzi'irim lasi'irim."* For *tzi'irim* here, some commentators read "villains," and others say it refers to the young monks of a specific order. It is also possible to read the word in the Arabic-influenced Andalusian pronunciation, wherein the Hebrew letter *tzadei* would be pronounced as an *s* instead of *tz*—so that *tzi'irim* (which normally means "young men")—would allude to their being "hairy" (*si'irim*), like the satyrs (also *si'irim*) they sing to. In any event, Christian practice here is likened to strange or heathen worship: Leviticus 17:7: "And they shall no more sacrifice their sacrifices unto the satyrs, after whom they go astray." "Satyrs" can also be understood as "demons," as in Rashi's commentary to the verse and R. David Qimhi's *Sefer Shorashim*. See also Isaiah 13:21. Schirmann glosses, "their gods"—the gods of the young men. **2:** Literally, "the God of creation." **3:** Psalms 119:62. **8:** Literally, "God of worlds on high and below, who brings down and exalts." **9–10:** The Hebrew plays on the image of crossing *yam suf* (the Red Sea or Sea of Reeds) and *yam tzuf* (the sea of honey), again confusing the *tz* and *s*—see line 1, above. Also 1 Samuel 9:5. **14:** Proverbs 3:15. **22:** I.e., they make honey and sting; Deuteronomy 1:44 and *Deuteronomy Rabbah* 1:6. (See Ibn Gabirol's "The Bee," above).

## I Take Delight in My Cup and Wine

*Gan HaMeshalim*, vol. 2, part 2, *muwashshah* 35; *HaShira*, #377:2. **Line 8:** Song of Songs 7:3. **23:** The daughter of Canaan, in this case, is most likely a Slavic girl. **39–40:** The lines treat the conventional figure of Arabic love poetry, the *'aadhil* (reprover or reproacher). In both Hebrew and Arabic poetry he almost always shadows a would-be male lover; here it seems he is watching a woman. Ibn Hazm writes of the reproacher in *The Ring of the Dove*: "Love has it various misfortunes: of these the first is the Reproacher. . . . There are diverse kinds. The original sort is a friend, between whom and yourself the burden of cautiousness has been let drop. . . . The second type . . . is the thorough-going scolder" (trans. Arberry, [1953; London, 1994], p. 96). **43–44:** The Arabic *kharja* reads, literally, "If a man [someone] is looking at me,/because of my thinness he wouldn't see me."

## NAHUM

### Winter Has Waned

*Shirei Nahum*, ed. Y. David (Jerusalem, 1974), #1; *HaShira*, #397. A *me'ora*, or "poem of light." Acrostic: *Nahum*. The strophes have been recast slightly in the English in the interest of flow and coherence. **Lines 11–14:** Isaiah 13:14; Song of Songs 8:2, 8:14. **18:** Song of Songs 7:3. Milk and wine represent discrete examples of love's pleasures; though the Hebrew has, literally, "wine with milk," the line isn't implying that they're drunk together. **21–22:** Song of Songs 5:13. **28:** Numbers 24:6. **30:** Numbers 28:10. **33:** Proverbs 31:7: "Let him drink and forget his poverty." **35:** Song of Songs 2:9. **36:** Song of Songs 7:4. The beloved himself in Song of Songs is likened to a "gazelle," so it is natural for it to graze with fawns. **40:** Psalms 61:3. **42:** Song of Songs 5:10. **41:** According to *Shabbat* 22b, the western lamp (or branch of the candelabra) of the Temple burned the longest. The miracle of its endurance testified to the Divine Presence in Israel. **43:** An epithet for God. Ezekiel 28:14, according to the Targum and Rashi: "who rules supreme." **44:** I.e., the light given by this lamp is the light, and hope, of redemption.

## AVRAHAM HABEDERSHI

### WHY THE POET REFUSES TO FIGHT

*HaShira*, #400:1. HaBedershi tries to avoid dealing with HaGorni, who has tirelessly, and loudly, sought the more established poet's support and approval. He begins with an ironic jab at HaGorni's honor, suggesting that quarreling with him isn't worth his (HaBedershi's) time. The poems allude to the legend, recorded in the Talmud and other rabbinic writings, about what the Amazons cleverly told Alexander in order to avoid a fight. *Leviticus Rabbah* 27:8, for instance, notes that immediately after the women said this to Alexander, "he turned away and departed. And then he wrote on the door of the gate of the city, 'I, Alexander of Macedon, a king, was a fool until I came to the town of Kartigna [i.e., of the Amazons] and learned wisdom from women.'" Also, *Tamid* 32a, *Pesiqta deRab Kahana* 9:74a), and elsewhere.

### YOUR MUSE

*HaShira*, #400:3. Soon the gloves are taken off and numerous poems are exchanged, including two that are ninety-eight and sixty-five Hebrew lines respectively. HaBedershi aims wherever he can, below the belt or for the poetic jugular. He wrote often of the mysterious *banot hashir* ("daughters of song," or Muses, as in Ecclesiastes 12:4), usually as an indication of what he felt were his own superior poetic gifts. The term could also refer simply to "your poem." **Line 2:** Literally, "if you don't choose the throng like whores," as in Psalms 55:15 ("he walketh with the throng"). "Troubadour" is in keeping with the cultural context of the time, especially that of the literary jousting with HaGorni. And as the biographical introduction notes, HaBedershi was at the very least aware of the Provençal troubadour poets. That he explicitly mentions Provençal poets who were known for their ethical and admonitory verse suggests that his acquaintance with their work was most likely more than superficial. **4:** Literally, "she became a concubine."

The Hebrew involves a complicated pun on one of the biblical names in Genesis 36:12.

## LAMENT FOR A FOE

H. Schirmann, "'Iyyunim beQovetz HaShirim shel Avraham HaBedershi," in *LeToldot HaShira veHaDrama Ha'Ivrit* (Jerusalem 1979), p. 418. Also in *Toldot* (1997), p. 490, note 100. These lines were excerpted from a longer poem (in manuscript only) and published by Schirmann in his essay on HaBedershi.

## THE POET'S DISTRESS

*HaShira*, #403. The context of this epigram isn't clear; but it seems to have been part of a separate exchange.

## YITZHAQ HAGORNI

### WOULD YOU TELL ME

*Shirei Avraham HaBedershi veYitzhak HaGorni veHugam*, ed. A. M. Habermann, (Jerusalem, 1969), p. 34. **Heading:** "When HaGorni told of all the great things he'd accomplished in the land where he dwelled, a valiant man approached him who thought there was something wrong with his song, and he said: 'I will listen, and look into [his song], and set it right,' but he couldn't."

### HAGORNI'S LAMENT

*Shirei HaBedershi*, p. 41; *HaShira*, #409. The somewhat obscure heading reads: "A *haluq* of HaGorni and his final words on desire and lust, and this while he was still in his prime, and had many years before him." According to Ezra Fleischer, the term *haluq* is derived from the French literary term *congé* (departure/separation), which in HaGorni's day indicated a lyrical poem treating the poet's departure from a city, friends, or life itself. In this case, the departure is from the licentious mode of life HaGorni led in the past. Fleischer reads it as a poem of penitence; Schirmann says it is distinctive for the grotesquery of the cultish practice it depicts and for its *lack* of true penitence. **Line 1:** Judges 11:4. **5:** Lamentations 5:15. **9:** Song of Songs 2:17. **19–20:** Daniel 10:8: "my comeliness [was turned in me into corruption]"; NJPS has "my vigor has been destroyed." **33–34:** Literally, "before they're made into images (*temunot*)"—that is, something that could be used for idolatrous worship or in amulets. At least *this* bit of him will be spared. The poet's boasting seems here to give way to the remorse of which Fleischer speaks, though that hardly diminishes the pride he takes in his sexual exploits.

## YEDAYA HAPENINI

Scholars assume that the poet's epithet refers to Perpignan, though no connection between the two words has been established. For Fleischer's characterization of Yedaya's book, see *Toldot* (1997), p. 530, n. 68.

### The World Is a Raging Sea

*Behinat 'Olam* (Vilna, 1879; reprinted Jerusalem, 1980), book 8; *HaShira*, #412. **Lines 1–2:** Jonah 1:15; Psalms 104:25. **6–7:** Proverbs 16:15; Job 33:30. **10–11:** *Pirqei Avot* 4:29. **17–18:** Job 28:22; Exodus 14:22. **19–20:** Ezekiel 22:14. **21–22:** Ecclesiastes 2:26. **25–28:** Daniel 11:10; Jonah 1:4. **36–38:** Literally, "from the juice of the pomegranates of your haughtiness"; Lamentations 1:19. **43:** Psalms 42:8. **40–41:** Job 38:16. **45–46:** Literally, "and none saith: Restore [him/it]"—as in Isaiah 42:22.

## AVNER [OF BURGOS?]

### The Last Words of My Desire

*Sefer Yovel leDoktor S. Federbush*, ed. A. M. Habermann (Jerusalem, 1961), section 2, pp. 176–77. The full poem has seven parts (pp. 175–99). Schirmann attributes the poem to Avner of Burgos; Habermann disagrees, claiming that Avner the apostate wasn't known as a penitent Jew—though of course that judgment involves a very limited reading of the poem. The vocalization of the Hebrew text is problematic in several places and has not always been followed in this translation. **Lines 1–9:** These lines involve a homophone inversion of 2 Samuel 23:1–3: "Now these are the last words of David; the saying of David the son of Jesse, and the song of the man raised on high, the anointed of the God of Jacob, and the sweet singer of Israel." Small changes of sound yield the opposite of Scripture's import: *ne'um David ben Yishai* (the saying of David the son of Jesse), for instance, becomes *ne'um day leha'vid ben shay* (the saying—speech/utterance—sufficient to wholly consume one who brings an offering, etc.). The original Hebrew is also obscure. **2:** Instead of *lo sharim*, read *le'asherim* (to idols). **5–7:** I.e., this is the utterance of a creature (desire, or "the evil impulse") which is anointed of alien gods and thrives on, or near, misfortune and ruin. Judges 10:6: "And the children of Israel again did that which was evil in the sight of the Lord, and served . . . the gods of Zidon, and the gods of Moab, and the gods of the children of Ammon." **8:** This line—*u'ne'im zarot el zar benei zenunim*—plays on *ne'im zemirot yisra'el* ("the sweet singer of Israel," again Samuel 23:1) and most likely alludes to Jesus. **10:** I.e., serve pagan gods and forces, not the Lord. Jeremiah 7:18: "The children gather wood, and the fathers kindle the fire, and the women knead the dough, to make cakes to the queen of heaven and pour out drink offerings unto other gods." There may also be an undercurrent of association with various New Testament passages that identify Jesus with that stone (e.g. Matthew 21:42 and 1 Peter 2:7). **13:** Proverbs 22:5. **14–15:** Psalms 118:22. **16–17:** Song of Songs 8:13. **18–19:** Psalms 50:16. **20–21:** Deuteronomy 32:17. **23–25:** *Sanhedrin* 82a; the Hebrew employs the acronym NasHGaz, referring to *nidda* (a menstruating woman), *shifha* (a non-Jewish maidservant), *goya* (a heathen woman), and *zona* (a whore)—all of whom are considered unclean and forbidden. Also Genesis 30:1. **26:** Isaiah 17:10: "For thou hast forgotten the God of thy salvation. . . . Therefore thou didst plant plants of pleasantness, and didst set it with the slips of a stranger [or: but it proved a disappointing slip]." A textual emendation by the editor notes that the Hebrew should have *na'manim* (as in Isaiah) instead of *ma'manim*. **28:** Jeremiah 5:8. **29–30:** These lines turn on its head the well-known passage from Proverbs 31:10, which enumerates the virtues of the "woman of valor" and the ideal wife. **33:** Proverbs 6:19. **35–36:** Isaiah 1:23. **38:** Isaiah 59:10. **39:** Lamentations 4:5. **40:** Isaiah 21:5. **41:** Isaiah 66:17. **43:** Proverbs 30:26. **45:** Habakkuk 2:16.


## QALONYMOS BEN QALONYMOS

Qalonymos appears in Immanuel's *Mahberot* in chapter 25. The carnivalesque reading of at least this section of *Even Bohan* is Tova Rosen's, in *Unveiling Eve*, pp. 168–86. She notes that Qalonymos's "assault on gender prejudices and his sympathy with the female sex is unequivocal. . . . Maleness is shown to be a competitive life track, an unwearied race after summits of intellectual fulfillment, a phallic arrow launched into the expanse of knowledge, an enormous intellectual odyssey. . . . That the journey ends with coming back home is of no wonder. . . . In contrast to the infinite and threatening male universe, the female space is delimited and warm, kind, and protected. . . . The vertical-phallic quest for the Logos takes place in an arid landscape, whereas woman's material sphere is horizontal and plentiful." Rosen notes that Qalonymos's critique goes well beyond the issue of gender, and *Even Bohan* includes "caricatures of Jewish social types," as well as "angry admonitions against gluttony, debauchery, gambling and fascination with clothes, and the satirist's joy in the human body, its needs, and laughter."


### ON BECOMING A WOMAN

*Even Bohan*, ed. A. M. Habermann (Tel Aviv, 1956), pp. 19–20; *HaShira*, #413:1, lines 27–40. **Line 4:** This alludes to a well-known legend, based on *Genesis Rabbah* 38, telling of how Abraham was saved from the fiery furnace into which the Chaldean king Nimrod had him thrown after he'd destroyed his father's idols. **6:** *Berakhot* 60a, where Leah (Dina's mother) was pregnant with a male child but asked God to turn the fetus into a female. **7:** Exodus 7:10. **8–9:** Exodus 4:3, 4:6,

14:16, 26ff. The Red Sea of the English Bible is literally, the Sea of Reeds (and most scholars now assume was it was an inlet of the Mediterranean). **10–11:** Psalms 66:6; Joshua 3:13–17. **14–15:** Psalms 114:8; Isaiah 58:11. **16–17:** The labor of men in this context would include religious and intellectual obligations. **20–22:** *Sanhedrin* 5b discusses "permanent defects" (or "irremovable blemishes"), as opposed to "passing defects" (or "removable blemishes"). The poem is of course referring to the penis. The section from which this excerpt has been drawn begins: "How defective [deformed/crippled/wounded] one is with an *etzba* (finger). And how much shame must he bear who was minted with the stamp of men." That line could also be understood as meaning "How much damage did he [God] do with a finger [i.e., his finger, with which he sent the plagues upon the Egyptians]." **28:** *Sanhedrin* 88a. **29:** *Berakhot* 9:3 and 5: "It is incumbent on man to bless [God] for the evil in the same way as for the good, as it says, 'Thou shalt love thy God with all thy heart'—with thy two impulses, the evil impulse as well as the good impulse." **30–31:** One of the regular morning benedictions said by men.


## YITZHAQ POLGAR

To Polgar's opening epigram, expressing disgust with Avner's treatise, Avner responds: "Every lion has its roar, and from afar/the weak at heart is seized with trembling./Hearing it, his two ears ring;/but what will he do on the Day of Reckoning?" Polgar responds to that as follows: "The lion's roar and cry of man/are both the bleating of goats to me. //But one who looks like a lion was scared,/and at the sound of my voice grew angry. //For all the world's great mysteries—/in my mind's eye I see. //I wasn't afraid, in fact I soared—/and all who heard, with me roared." (See A. Carmoli, *Literaturblatt des Orients* 16 (1840): 245.)


### FAITH'S PHILOSOPHY, PHILOSOPHY'S FAITH

*Ezer HaDat leR. Yitzhaq Poliqar*, ed. Y. Levinger (Tel Aviv, 1984), part 2, p. 71 and pp. 91–93; *HaShira*, #415, lines 45–49. Taken out of context, and given its vehemence, the first poem might seem to be referring to Avner; within the dialogue, however, the speaker is the elderly, conservative Torah scholar, who is attacking the younger good-looking philosopher for the introduction of doctrine foreign to Scripture. The second poem is spoken by the author.


## SHEM TOV ARDUTIEL (SANTOB DE CARRIÓN)

For an adaptation of Shem Tov's Spanish proverbs—which have survived in Hebrew transliteration—see my "Suite for Santob," *Hymns & Qualms*. For a full prose translation of the work with extensive commentary, see T. Perry, *The Moral Proverbs of Santob de Carrión: Jewish Wisdom in Christian Spain*, (Princeton, 1987). Machado's comments appear in Antonio Machado, *Selected Poems*, trans. A. True-blood (Cambridge, 1982), p. 10. The title of Shem Tov's narrative is sometimes cast in the singular: *Milhemet Ha'Et veHaMisparayim* (The Battle of the Pen . . . ). Susan Einbinder's study, "Pen and Scissors, A Medieval Debate," *Hebrew Union College Annual* 65 (1995), makes a convincing argument against the various one-to-one allegorical readings that have been proposed. Regarding the reading of the work as describing "the plight of a writer isolated, in what he considers extreme circumstances, from his community," she notes that Shem Tov's "desperate search for a new form of writing adequate for expressing his condition of crisis is depicted in his resort to an unnatural tool—the scissors—as the means to over-come silence and write." *The Battles of the Pen and the Scissors* is also known as *Ma'asei HaRav* (The Rabbi's Tale).

Einbinder comments further on the nature of the two types of writing: "The script of the Scissors, air cut into paper, is pure Form without Matter. The Pen, in contrast, fuses form and matter, shaping ink on the page. The Pen is also a phal-lic agent of the narrator, drawing from the inchoate matter of ink (grammati-cally feminine—and producing letters on the scroll *(megilla)* or letter *(iggeret)*—both also feminine words. In contrast, the self-sufficiency of the Scissors, a plural which is also one, is depicted by the Pen as unnatural and dangerous. Whatever extreme solution the Scissors' writing represents to Arudtiel, the frozen ink of the story and the dented tip of the Pen describe a situation of threatened po-tency in which the writer cannot write." Einbinder then quotes a line by the thirteenth-century Arabic "scissors poet" Humayd ibn 'Abd Allah al-Ansari al-Qurtubi: "Cutting reveals letters which have vanished./Amazing! A thing whose presence is its absence" ("Pen and Scissors," p. 272).

### From *The Battles of the Pen and the Scissors*

#### I. Writer, You Hold

*Ma'asei HaRav (Milhemet Ha'Et veHaMisparayim)*, ed. Y. Nini and M. Fruchtman (Tel Aviv, 1980), p. 41; *HaShira*, #417:1, lines 22–23. The action begins with the nar-rator's praise of his pen, which is summed up in this poem. **Line 2:** Nahum 3:3. **3:** Genesis 2:9. **4:** The allusion is to Moses' rod and the miracles or "signs" he pro-duces with it, as in Exodus 4:17 and elsewhere.

#### II. To Praise the Pen

*Ma'asei HaRav*, p. 45. The praise of the narrator's pen continues. **Line 2:** Liter-ally, "Is it excessive on the part of the single thing to both make mention of what was lost and preserve it?" **7–8:** *Shevu'ot* 20b: "[The commandments] 'Remember [the Sabbath day],' and 'Keep [the Sabbath day]' were pronounced in a single utterance—an utterance which the mouth cannot utter nor the ear hear"; Exodus 20:8: "Remember the Sabbath day"; Deuteronomy 5:12: "Observe the Sabbath day."

### III. Tomorrow I'll Write

*Ma'asei HaRav*, p. 53; *HaShira*, #417:2, lines 83–85. Meanwhile, the narrator has discovered that the inkwell has frozen solid and his pen is unable to crack the ice and withdraw any ink. He begins cursing his pen vehemently; the pen fights back and takes the narrator to task for his cruelty and for his having forgotten the pen's years of loyalty and service. Finally it suggests that the author try to crack the ice with his own finger instead of with the delicate nub of the pen. He tries, but the jagged ice cuts his finger and rips his fingernail. The narrator then admits that the elements have gotten the better of him, and he recites this poem. Machado refers to the town as "cold Soria." **Line 1:** *Omair emesh*—which might also be understood as "Yesterday he says" or "Last night he says." Genesis 31:29. **5–6:** Proverbs 27:1.

### IV. Enter the Scissors

*Ma'asei HaRav*, p. 57. The poet hears a voice which tells him to forget about the pen and the frozen ink, and think of other options. One could, for instance, write with scissors. And so begins a series of rhymed-prose lines in praise of the scissors and scissor writing, and then a series of metrical poems on the same subject. **Line 1:** I.e., the paper in which the scissors have cut out words. **2:** Job 13:28. Literally, "but this is among the written" (as opposed to the standard scriptural idiom, "among the living"). **3–4:** These lines employ the language of, and allude directly to, the morning prayer, "Blessed art Thou, Lord our God, King of the Universe, who has fashioned man with wisdom and created within him many cavities [hollows]."

### V. Work I Was Cut Out to Do

*Ma'asei HaRav*, p. 61. In the Hebrew the rhyme words are homonyms—*ru'ah*—meaning in this context "thought/spirit," "soul/spirit," and "wind." **Line 1:** The opening of the poem is missing in the Hebrew. **3–4:** Psalms 18:11 and 104:4.

### VI. The Pen Fights Back

*Ma'asei HaRav*, p. 63. **Lines 3–4:** Proverbs 13:12. **5–6:** I.e., your slow pace makes all who wait for you drowsy. Proverbs 19:15 and 23:21: "Drowsiness shall clothe a man in rags" ("in tatters" [NJPS]).

### VII. The Scissors Longed

*Ma'asei HaRav*, p. 80. The final word is given to the scissors, as the *maqaama* comes to a close with this poem, summarizing the scissors' desire. A twenty-two-line colophon follows in the voice of the author, thanking God for the powers He bestows, and noting that this poem too was written "without a pen and not with ink," toward the end of the month of Tammuz (approximately July), 1345.

## SHMU'EL IBN SASSON

For more on Ibn Sasson see R. Brann, A. Saenz-Badillos, and J. Targarona Borrás, "The Poetic Universe of Samuel Ibn Sasson, Hebrew Poet of Fourteenth-Century Castile," *Prooftexts* 16/1 (1996). They note that, while some scholars claim Ibn Sasson was raised or educated in Toledo, there is in fact no proof that he ever left Carrión de los Condes and Fromista. The rhymed-prose heading to "They Will Be Tried" appeared in poem 7 of the Chamiel edition (see below).

### Man's Peril

*Sefer Avnei HaShoham*, ed. H. Chamiel (Tel Aviv and Jerusalem, 1962), #28. **Line 4:** Ecclesiastes 7:26: "I find more bitter than death the woman whose heart is snares and nets"; Proverbs 27:8: "[The strange woman's] house is the way to the netherworld." In the original the final words of lines 2 and 4 are homonymous: *margalit* (pearl) and *mar galit* (bitterness you revealed).

### Why Most Poets Are Poor

*Avnei HaShoham*, #17; *HaShira*, #416. **Heading:** "I wrote this about the poets who are not rich." **Lines 3–4:** Genesis 43:32. **5–6:** Psalms 62:5. **9–10:** Job 4:13. **11–12:** *Ketubot* 103b: "cast bile among the students." **23–24:** Isaiah 47:13. **25–26:** Proverbs 23:19. **27–28:** Psalms 33:14. **29–30:** Job 38:41: "Who provideth for the raven his prey, when his young cry unto God, and wander for lack of food?" **31–32:** Isaiah 1:23. **37–38:** 1 Samuel 21:16: "Do I lack madmen, that you have brought this fellow?" In other words, writers and lunatics belong together. **39:** Alas, these fools know nothing. **43–44:** *Berakhot* 32a. **45–46:** Zephaniah 2:14. **47–48:** Nehemiah 12:46. **49–50:** Jeremiah 10:7.

### They Will Be Tried

*Avnei HaShoham*, # 8, lines 79ff. **Line 1:** Jeremiah 50:20. **2:** Literally, "and circumcised them." **4:** Psalms 49:7. **5:** Exodus 3:7. **9:** Jeremiah 51:51. **11:** Deuteronomy 6:5. **12:** Literally, "the Lord surely remembered them." Genesis 50:24. **12:** Zechariah 2:16. **13:** Exodus 2:23–24.

## MOSHE NATAN

The executive committee of the Barcelona conference asked the king to request that the Pope issue orders for the protection of the Jewish community. For more on the conference, see Baer, *A History of the Jews in Christian Spain*, pp. 25ff.

## PRISON

*Totza'ot Haim*, in Menahem di Lonzano, *Shtei Yadot* (Husyatin, 1909), part 29, p. 11b; *HaShira*, #418:2.

## From "THE TEN COMMANDMENTS"

*I.*

*Totza'ot Haim*, part 10, p. 7b; *HaShira*, #418:1. **Line 2:** Psalms 23:3.

*II.*

*Totza'ot Haim*, part 10, p. 7b. **Lines 1–2:** Genesis 4:10. **4:** I.e., "the killer of people" (literally, "of a person"). Numbers 31:19.

*III.*

*Totza'ot Haim*, part 10, p. 7b. **Line 2:** Literally, "Worship Him and you'll be free." See Yehuda HaLevi's "Slaves of Time" (above) for a superior treatment of the same theme.

## CLOTHES MAKE THE MAN

*Totza'ot Haim*, part 34, p. 12b; *HaShira*, #418:6. **Lines 1–2:** Jeremiah 25:38, 44:22. **4:** Amos 1:6.

## SHELOMO DEPIERA

The Saragossa group was also known by other names, including *Kat HaMeshorerim* and *Hevrat Nognim*. Regarding the quality of DePiera's (or DaPiera's) work, it is possible that his earlier work was superior to what has survived, though Vidal Benveniste's harsh criticism of his teacher would suggest otherwise. Don Shelomo's family also went by the Spanish name "de la Caballería," owing to the connection they maintained to the Templar order. "Frightening monotony" is Ezra Fleischer's characterization (*Toldot* [1997], p. 606). Raymond Scheindlin comments: "The contrast between the age of Todros Abulafia and that of Solomon DaPiera is palpable. Whereas, in the former it seems to be looking outward, in the latter, it seems to turn in on itself, even as the poems produced by DaPiera and his contemporaries habitually revert, in their last lines, to their openings" ("Fifteenth-Century Poetry in Spain," in *Crisis and Creativity in the Sephardic World*, ed. Benjamin R. Gampel [New York, 1997], pp. 34–36). (I have not translated any of DePiera's "circular" poems. See, instead, Benveniste's "The Tongue Speaks and the Hand Records," and Bonafed's "World Gone Wrong" and "Wherever You Go.") This inwardness, Scheindlin adds, can be explained in part as a response to the external threat presented by the events of

1391, which forced the Jewish writers to withdraw from the outside world and look back to the glories of the past, producing "a literature that was merely an extended homage to that past." But he also notes that there were more complex cultural factors at work, and that in fact the upper-class Jews were not at all cut off from the surrounding Christian/Spanish culture. So the Hebrew poets may in fact have looked outward, but imitation of what they found in the new court literature of the European vernaculars (which looked to the classical Latin and troubadour past in order to create something new in the stylized vernacular present) produced a very different effect in the context of Hebrew literature. For fourteenth- and fifteenth-century Hebrew was a classical language and not, like Romance or Provençal, a vernacular, and so the imitation of European trends in Hebrew resulted in the creation of a closed circuit, as it were, with the classical literature of the past being reflected in the classical language of the present. That, along with the gradually increasing distance from the Arabic root of Hebrew medieval poetry, brought about the attenuation of the four-teenth and fifteenth centuries. Lines of energy and poetic transfer were opened for Spanish-Jewish poets, by contrast, in Ladino, and for Italian-Hebrew poets, who would inject new blood into their poetry from the vernacular verse of their day.

### Thinkers with Thinking

*HaShira*, #429:3. **Line 3:** Numbers 22:23

### The Bee and the Grumbler

*HaShira*, #429:1. **Lines 4:** Literally, "and its mouth [the arrow's] . . ."

### Medieval Arthritis

*Diwan shel Shelomo Ben Meshullam DaPiera*, ed. S. Bernstein (New York, 1942), #129. **Line 4:** Exodus 1:16, where the "birthstools" are two stones the woman sits upon. 1 Samuel 4:19. **6:** Ezekiel 21:11: "Sigh, therefore, son of man, with the breaking of thy loins." (NJPS: "Sigh, on tottering limbs and bitter grief.")

### Winter in Monzón

*HaShira*, #427. **Heading:** "And one day I was sitting at home during a downpour, and the heavy cloud was releasing its torrent, and to make matters worse, the poet Don Vidal, whose poems 'hold up their hooves' [like a pig—to demonstrate that it is 'kosher,' i.e., of cleft hoof, while in fact demonstrating to all that it is, in fact, a pig—i.e., not kosher], seeming to honor my name but in his heart lying in wait for me (Jeremiah 9:7), as he has done in the past. And I too will not hold back, and I answered him." The excerpt translated here contains only the opening of DePiera's retort, the description of winter in the country. For the image of the pig holding up its hooves, see *Leqah Tov* 8: 29b and Jeremiah 9:7. **Line 2:** Deuteronomy 25:18. **4:** Leviticus 11:35. **10:** Isaiah 59:15. **11–12:** Jeremiah 36:22; Job 27:6. **15–16:** Isaiah 50:11; 2 Samuel 23:20. **17–18:** The language alludes to the story of the sacrifice (binding) of Isaac. **25:** Job 3:8.

### AFTER CONVERSION (TO VIDAL BENVENISTE)

*Shirei Don Vidal Benveniste*, ed. T. Vardi (M.A. thesis, The Hebrew University of Jerusalem, 1986), #15*. This poem was written after the poet's conversion to Christianity and sent to Don Vidal Benveniste, who responded with a particularly harsh poem of his own, using the same imagery. DePiera's use of the image of the whore may have emerged—consciously or not—from his guilt (over his conversion), but it also left him exposed, as it were, to Benveniste's brutal rejoinder ("To a Poet-Friend Too Much in Need," below). Schirmann comments that many of the "new Jews" who converted in 1391 and following the Disputation at Tortosa were particularly zealous in their adopted faith, while others took up the split life of secret Jews (known as *Conversos, Anusim,* or *Marranos*); still others converted out of convenience and were as apathetic to Christianity as they had been to Judaism (*Toldot* [1997], pp. 585–86). **Lines 3–6:** Isaiah 23:15: "Tyre shall be forgotten seventy years. . . . It shall fare with Tyre as with the song of the harlot; Take a harp, go about the city, thou harlot long forgotten. Make sweet melody, sing many songs, that thou mayest be remembered"; Job 28:27.

### TABERNACLES: A PRAYER

*Diwan Shirei Qodesh shel Shelomo Ben Meshullam DaPiera*, ed. S. Bernstein (Cincinnati, 1946), #4; *HaShira*, #431. A *reshut* for Sukkot. Acrostic: *Shelomo*. **Line 1:** "He" refers to the people of Israel (*'am Israel*). While "the congregation of Israel" (*knesset Israel*) is feminine, and most liturgical poems of this sort involve a feminine *knesset Israel* and a masculine deity, often in an allegorical situation of love and rejection, here the reference (*'am*) is grammatically and figuratively masculine. **2:** Deuteronomy 32:7, which mentions the "years of many generations" in which Israel dwelled as a self-sufficient and prosperous nation alone, guarded by God and not subjugated by another people. **3:** Job 4:5. **4:** In the original, "from calling your name I-Am" (Exodus 3:14). **6:** 2 Kings 8:10: "Thou shalt surely recover from this illness." **7:** Joel 1:8. **8:** Isaiah 4:6: "There shall be a pavilion for a shadow from the heat and for a refuge and a covert"; Jonah 4:6. The final line alludes to the holiday of Sukkot (the Feast of Booths, or Tabernacles).

## A Prayer for Rain and Sustenance

*Shirei Qodesh shel DaPiera*, #35. Acrostic: Within the opening line: *Shelomo*. Fleischer notes that the modern editor of DePiera's liturgical poems, S. Bernstein, separated elements that were originally parts of a *shivata* for rain, or a prayer in time of drought. (The *shivata* is a shortened form of the ancient *qerova*—which is a general term applied to all the composite hymns that ornament the *'amida*, the "standing prayer" at the heart of the liturgy.) This short poem was part of that larger sequence. The *shivata* and *qerova* were rarely taken up by the Spanish poets, with only Ibn Abitor, Ibn Gabirol, and Avraham Ibn Ezra having attempted them two to three centuries years earlier. Just what led DePiera to try his hand at this form remains a mystery. (Only parts of his poem are extant.) He may have written the prayer on demand, most likely at the request of the Ben Lavi family, which was close to the crown; the latter may have placed its request before the Ben Lavis. The prayers of the Jews in this respect were accorded unique power in Spain. This was also a way for the Jews to participate in what was a fairly widespread Catholic religious phenomenon (*Shevet Yehuda* [Hanover, 1874], p. 109). **Line 1:** Literally, "of the nations" (or "gentiles")—*Melekh hagoyim*, i.e., the Catholic monarch of Aragon.

## This Year's Wine: 1417

*HaShira*, #428:1. **Heading:** In the month of Shvat (January) I completed this poem, which I made in Monzón about the bad wines of the year 1417, and this is what I said." This is the latest recorded date for the poet. Each distich of the Hebrew (every other line of the English) contains a scriptural allusion or citation concerning wine and ends with the word itself. **Line 2:** Hosea 7:5: "The princes make him sick with the heat of wine"; Deuteronomy 32:33: "Their wine is the venom of serpents. **4:** Isaiah 28:1: "Woe to the crown of the pride of the drunkards of Ephraim, . . . which is on the head of the fat valley of them that are smitten down with wine!" **6:** Numbers 6:3: "The vow of a Nazarite . . . he shall abstain from wine and strong drink." **8:** Leviticus 23:13: "The drink-offering shall be of wine." **10:** Joel 4:3: "And they have . . . sold a girl for wine and have drunk." **12–14:** Proverbs 23:20, 30: "Be not among the winebibbers [those who guzzle wine] . . . They that tarry long at the wine." **16:** Isaiah 28:7: "The priest and the prophet reel through strong drink, they are confused because of wine." **18:** The poet is quoting the lying preacher of Micah 2:11, who says: "I will preach unto thee of wine and of strong drink." Jeremiah 23:26. **20:** Genesis 49:12: "His eyes shall be red with wine."

## VIDAL BENVENISTE

Shelomo Ben Lavi's grandson Yosef Ben Lavi was also known as Yosef (Vidal) Ben Benveniste Ben Lavi, and has therefore often been confused with his friend Vidal Benveniste, our poet. Yosef was Shelomo DePiera's student in the Ben Lavi household, where poetry was one of the subjects in the curriculum. A gifted student in all respects, especially in the field of philosophy, Yosef was also a talented poet and often exchanged poems with his teacher and in time with his friend Vidal, who, to confuse matters further, may have been Yosef's brother-in-law, but was also perhaps a distant blood relative. He too studied with Shelomo DePiera, though he was not nearly as close to him.

## ADVICE FROM WIVES

*Shirei Benveniste*, ed. T. Vardi (see DePiera's "After Conversion," above), #75; *HaShira*, #445. Precisely the opposite attitude toward a wife's advice is presented in the epilogue to *Melitzat 'Efer veDina*, where the repulsive old man, 'Efer, is rebuked by the narrator for not having listened to his wife, who in that tale's allegorical scheme represents "the wise, restorative soul which gives man success." **Line 3:** Psalms 133:1. **4:** Ezekiel 16:34.

## WHAT GIRLS WANT

*Melitzat 'Efer veDina*, ed. Matti Huss (Jerusalem, 2003), pp. 165–66, lines 169–72. The poem is in the first-person singular. **Line 1:** I.e., they run after males to mate. Jeremiah 2:23. **2:** Job 31:7. **8:** The verb that has been translated as "lie" can also mean "kneel," which of course would imply another sort of sexual encounter. However, in this context the verb is used as it is in Judges 5:27, where Sisera lies dead, fallen at the feet of Ya'el, who has slain him. *Yebamot* 103a, however, makes the sexual associations of the biblical verse clear: "That profligate [Sisera] had seven sexual connections on that day; for it is said, 'Between her feet he sunk, he fell, he lay; at her feet he sunk, he fell; where he sunk, there he fell down dead.'" The reference is clearly to the missionary position; oral sex was, it seems, not common, and certainly not written about in poems. The Talmud treats it in passing; see *Nedarim* 20a and b: "R. Johanan b. Dahabai said: The Ministering Angels told me four things: People are born lame because they [their parents] overturned their table [i.e., practiced 'unnatural' cohabitation]; dumb, because they kiss 'that place'. . . . R. Johanan said: The above is the view of R. Johanan b. Dahabai: but our Sages said . . . a man may do whatever he pleases with his wife: A parable: Meat which comes from the abattoir may be eaten, salted, roasted, cooked or seethed; so with fish from the fishmonger." (See also James Bellamy, "Sex and Society in Islamic Popular Literature," in *Society and the Sexes*, ed. Afaf Lutfi al-Sayyid-Marsot [Malibu, 1979], p. 34.)

## TO A POET-FRIEND TOO MUCH IN NEED

*Shirei Benveniste*, #15. Vidal Benveniste's response to Shelomo DePiera's poem after his conversion ("After Conversion," above). The poem answers DePiera directly, picking up on the aspects of the scriptural allusions around which Shelomo's poem pivots and using them against DePiera, thus rendering the retort doubly harsh and effective. As we've seen, this is not the first time Benveniste addressed his former teacher with harshness of this sort, and his attitude to Shelomo following the conversion wasn't necessarily shared by all their friends. Moshe Abbaas, for example, was far more understanding and gentle, and he sought to coax his friend back into the fold. **Heading:** "Don Vidal's reply to him: "Because of the oppressor's wrath, the doors to my song have closed, but now I'm forced by the poet, whose sins against his soul have come to my ears, and so the doorposts to the thoughts of my heart have been shaken and I have been moved to compose, for I will not suffer fools or men of iniquity." **Lines 1–2:** Isaiah 23:15 (see DePiera's poem). **3–4:** Hosea 4:16. **5–6:** Isaiah 23:15–16; Genesis 42:17. **7–8:** Isaiah 23:16; Judges 5:12; *Avodah Zarah* 17a: "Every harlot who allows herself to be hired will at the end have to hire." The Hebrew also has a particularly cruel twist, as the word *niskeret* (hired) involves the shifting of a single letter in the key word of DePiera's poem: *nizkeret* (recalled/remembered).

### Poems for a Doe in a Garden

These three poems are taken from a series (of five) that are prefaced by a prose passage describing the awakening of love. One day, the poet notes, he saw a young woman whose eyes were like a dove's and who charmed all who saw her. She held him in her spell and led him toward "sin[ning] with his skin [flesh]." She was "as beautiful as the clear moon and like the brightness of the horizon, her words split hearts, and she drowned her listeners in the sea of her love, and overcame the young men of Israel. . . . And so when I saw her I fell madly in love with her, and I sang her praises night and day."

I.
*Shirei Benveniste*, #66.

II.
*Shirei Benveniste*, #67. **Line 4:** Judges 5:31.

III.
*Shirei Benveniste*, #68; *HaShira*, #449:2, lines 6–11. This poem also appears in *Melitzat 'Efer veDina*, with some variants, and in a different context (lines 27–29). Huss comments there that the poem presents an ironic (nearly grotesque) take on the classical Andalusian erotic poem—as in the context of the *maqaama* it is obvious to all that the young woman has no desire whatsoever to "trap" the repulsive old man in her "net." On the contrary, he is the one who wants to do the trapping. It is also unusual that the doe calls out to the man. **Line 4:** Literally, "the lining of my heart (*segor libi*)"; cf. Ibn Janaah's *Sefer HaShorashim*, p. 333. **5:** Literally, "and bring me up with its hook."

## A Thank You Note

*Shirei Benveniste*, #77. To Ben-Lavi. The image of rain from the clouds is a conventional representation of the patron's bounty. In this case, however, it appears to be an expression of the poet's skill as a writer (and possibly calligrapher). Benveniste seems not to have had (or needed) a patron, and his poetry contains none of the conventional gestures of patron and patronized.

## Think about This

*Shirei Benveniste*, #82. **Line 1:** Proverbs 10:22. **4:** Ecclesiastes 5:12: "There is a grievous evil which I have seen . . . riches kept by the owner thereof to his hurt."

## Beyond Words

*Shirei Benveniste*, #88. **Line 2:** Isaiah 34:11: "He shall stretch over it the line of confusion and the plummet of emptiness." **3:** Literally, "without language, they thought they'd find the purest songs."

## My Son, before You Were Born

*Shirei Benveniste*, #71. One of four elegies written after the death of his son, Shelomo, whom he addressed by name in one of the longer poems. The tone of this recalls HaNagid's elegies for his brother, Isaac. **Line 1:** Genesis 25:22. **3:** 1 Samuel 1:27. **5–6:** Literally, "Now I would have preferred death to having given birth to you." Cf. Psalms 2:7.

## To One Who Said His Heart for Verse Was Adamant

*Shirei Benveniste*, #91. **Line 2:** Literally, "don't turn to devouring words," as in Psalms 52:6–7: "Thou lovest all devouring [pernicious] words, the deceitful [treacherous] tongue. . . . So God will tear thee down for good, will break thee." **3–4:** Jeremiah 17:1; Ezekiel 3:9: "As an adamant, harder than flint have I made my forehead"; Jeremiah 23:29.

## Clarity

*Shirei Benveniste*, #116. This minimalist gem stands in direct contrast to the conventional imagery of the Andalusian wine poem, which emphasizes the contrast between the cup (white, cool) and the wine (red, warm) inside it. Of note is the balance between all elements of the transparency the poet conjures—imagistic, tonal, and grammatical. That said, there is an Arabic precedent for it, in a poem by Abu Nuwas.

WHAT GOES AROUND COMES . . .

*Shirei Benveniste*, #128. **Line 2:** Psalms 79:12. **3:** Isaiah 44:18. **4:** Ecclesiastes 5:10.

THE TONGUE SPEAKS AND THE HAND RECORDS

*Shirei Benveniste*, #9. This poem was addressed and sent to Shelomo DePiera. It responds to a poem of DePiera's in which he suggests that Don Vidal has been slow in responding to a previous poem of his because his (Benveniste's) powers have waned. A letter follows the poem. Like many Hebrew qasidas in the thirteenth through fifteenth centuries, this one employs the circular structure in which the poem's opening line is repeated at the end. Scheindlin suggests that this new element of the qasida form may have arisen in Christian Spain when the open-ended classical qasida form was no longer familiar to audiences and had come to seem "formless." As the audience required some sort of marker indicating the end of the poem, this new device was called into service. (See Scheindlin, "The Hebrew Qasida in Spain," in *Qasida Poetry in Asia and Africa*, ed. S. Sperl and C. Shackle [Leiden, 1996], pp. 128–135). Whatever its origin, it became extremely common. For another example of it in this anthology, see Bonafed's "World Gone Wrong." **Lines 3–4:** Isaiah 2:21; Psalms 74:6. **5–6:** Deuteronomy 20:19; Job 38:36. **7–8:** Isaiah 51:9; 51:1–2. **9–10:** 1 Kings 7:29; Proverbs 26:13. **11–12:** The translation skips thirty-four Hebrew lines to the last part of the poem and Benveniste's central complaint. In the first sixteen Hebrew lines not translated, the poet praises his former teacher at length and in hyperbolic fashion for his erstwhile ways with the language; for the next eighteen he questions DePiera's choice of himself (Benveniste) to replace him as leader of the group of poets called '*Adat Nognim*, saying that Yosef Ben Lavi would have been the more appropriate choice, as he was the next in line and older than Benveniste. DePiera's judgment is clouded, he concludes. The translation picks up at line 39 of the original, with the closing section of the poem, in which Benveniste insults his former teacher. Psalms 40:13; 1 Samuel 12:33. **13–14:** Numbers 32:7. **15–16:** Psalms 140:6. **19–20:** Psalms 6:8. **23–24:** Literally, "My poem (or muse) is late and has been delayed." Psalms 94:17. **25–26:** Jeremiah 13:10. **29–30:** Job 41:11, 31. **31–32:** Deuteronomy 32:22. **35–36:** 1 Samuel 1:16. **39:** The Hebrew text is problematic, but appears to read *kebeitza o kekoteret*, alluding to Mishna *Orlah* 2:5 and the Jerusalem Talmud, *Baba Metzi'a* 7:4. **45–46:** Job 8:12, 15:32. Literally, "my spirit is like a lute."

## SHELOMO HALEVI (PABLO DE SANTA MARIA)

Shmu'el HaNagid and his son Yehosef were buried in the old cemetery near the Elvira gate, at a site that was marked and known to Granadans for several hundred years after their death, but we no longer know where that site is. (See *Toldot* [1995], p. 216, n. 170, and sources there, and Ibn al-Khatiib's *Al-Ihaatah fi Akhbaar Ghanaatah*.) For the information regarding the burial site of Pablo de Santa Maria, I am grateful to Professor Salvador Andrés Ordax, of the University of Valladolid, who sent on maps and explanations regarding the burial site and its history, including the relevant sections of B. Palacios's *Historia de la ciudad de Burgos* (1729), pp. 435–51; Professor Andrés Ordax's own volume, *Burgos Cathedral* (Leon, n. d.), was also extremely helpful. Yosef Haim Yerushalmi (in *Assimilation and Racial Anti-Semitism: The Iberian and the German Models*, Leo Baeck Memorial Lecture 26, [New York, 1982]) quotes the Spanish historian Americo Castro on the Jewish convert Pablo Santa Maria's influence: "From him stem all the theologians, jurists, and historians named Santa Maria, whose works fill fifteenth-century letters with distinction" (*The Structure of Spanish History* [Princeton, 1954], p. 537). For more on Shelomo/Pablo see Baer's *A History of the Jews in Christian Spain*, 2:139–50. On the talmudic injunction relating to drinking, see *Megillah* 7b.

### MEMORY'S WINE

*HaShira*, #436. The poem is a parody of a Sephardic liturgical form, the *mi kamokha* (who is like unto you), which surveys the history of the world from creation to the Exodus from Egypt. The parody surveys the history of wine from the time of Noah to the present. **Line 1:** Proverbs 23:31. **4:** Gifts of food are usually given on Purim, especially to the poor. **9–10:** Because wine was not known in the generation of Enosh, the people sinned and were punished by the flood. Genesis 4:22; 5:9. **11–12:** Noah—who is known in rabbinic literature as the World's Foundation—planted the first vine (Genesis 9:20); if not for that, another flood would have come upon humankind. **14:** Genesis 24:42. A feast is generally held on the afternoon of the holiday. **18:** Ecclesiastes 2:3: "I searched in my heart how to pamper [tempt] myself with wine."

### SHELOMO BONAFED

It is worth noting that the man who defended the integrity of the Jewish community with vehemence throughout his life was also known for his scandalous love affairs with much younger and not-necessarily-Jewish women. The stories around the poems he wrote about his love life are, however, more interesting than the poems themselves. They include one case in which the young woman's father ends up shipping the girl off to Sicily to protect her from the older Bonafed's wiles and grasp, and others in which he mentions the names of his beloveds. Malka/Reina, for example, rejected him, preferring the company of younger men.

## WORLD GONE WRONG

*HaShira*, #453. **Heading:** "One of the country's finest was deprived of all his property and possessions. His world was turned upside down, and changed like clay under the seal [Job 38:14] of Time, and where his lines had fallen in pleasant places, the sentence of days turned them to poison [wormwood]; for the meek of the age have become like the stars on high, and every fool now walks through the valley. And therefore I sent this poem to the exalted Anvidal Bonsegnor in Solsona, [having written it] when I was still young." The poem is a classic example of the topos of the inverted world and seems to be referring not only to the individual loss experienced by the poem's addressee but to the Spanish-Jewish community as a whole, which—in the wake of the events of 1391—was administered by unqualified and corrupt individuals from the working class (among them, weavers and leatherworkers). This, as Bonafed saw it, was contrary to the natural order of things. Bonafed wrote another poem, much later in his career, where he makes use of the same motif in attacking the corrupt members of the Saragossan Jewish community (see "A Vision of Ibn Gabirol," below). The topos of the inverted world was traditionally employed both to levy criticism at an existing social order and to lament change to a given order. (See E. Gutwirth, "The 'World Upside Down' in Hebrew," *Orientalia Suecana* 30 (1981): 141–47. This topos was especially popular in fifteenth-century Spanish literature. **Line 1:** Literally, "See, horses streak," or, "Look, horses streak." The poem opens with what Gutwirth calls "a series of *impossibilia*, as demanded by the conventions of the genre." **6:** Genesis 31:36. **9–10:** The impossible and/or unnatural situations of lines 1–8 are now revealed to be analogous to the unnatural state of things in the poet's world just now, where the "lower orders" of craftsmen have become too big for their britches and the community's leaders have proven themselves unworthy. Proverbs 2:15; Job 35:9. **11:** Psalms 31:13. **19–20:** Proverbs 26:18: "As a madman who casteth firebrands [sparks] . . . so is the man who deceiveth his neighbors." **23–24:** The Hebrew plays on the word *masekhet*, which means both "weave" (or "warp and woof") and "tractate"—as in a tractate of the Talmud. The implication is that he considers his work as sacred as Scripture. **25–26:** The tanner is known for the foul smell of the materials he works with and is generally considered repulsive. *Baba Batra* 16b: "Alas for him whose occupation is that of a tanner." **27–28:** Proverbs 18:23: "The answers of the rich are impudent [harsh]." **36:** Psalms 50:11. **37–38:** The betrayal of those who converted to Christianity. Isaiah 31:6. **42:** Exodus 29:2. **48:** Isaiah 35:6. **51:** Cherub—here a term of endearment and admiration. **52–53:** *Tosefta Bikurim* 2:16. Regarding the litany of craftsmen as part of a natural order gone wrong, E. Gutwirth points out that by the fifteenth century "contempt for the lower orders" of society, including manual laborers, craftsmen, and more, had become fairly widespread in elite Jewish circles. Gutwirth notes, for example, Profiat Duran's 1408 work on Hebrew language, in which the writer compares the days of Yehuda HaLevi and his own, praising the wealthy Jewish patrons who commissioned richly decorated manuscripts with thick, clear letters. But that, he notes, was in "those days, when they used to engage in Torah study in their thousands and tens of thousands, so much so that the artisans in their spare time did nothing but study, but nowadays, that there are more books than writers or readers, the artisans in their spare time . . . pursue vanity going to play dice, and the cause has vanished" ("Contempt for the Lower Orders in XV[th] Century Hispano-Jewish Thought," *Miscelanea de estudios y hebraicos* 29–30 [1981]). Manual labor is esteemed in classical rabbinic thought; the "contempt" here derives, Gutwirth notes, from its separation from study. (For another take on this, see Ibn Alahdab's "Renaissance Man.") **53–54:** I.e., if I ever abandon you, then the laws of nature will truly have been violated—not only by way of analogy, as in the opening. At the beginning of the poem these impossible situations are presented as metaphorical; at the close of the poem the impossibility is literal. That is, horses do *not* streak through the heart of the seas, and I will never abandon you. It is also possible, of course, to read the last line subversively and see an unconscious element (of disloyalty) in the friendship.

### A VISION OF IBN GABIROL

*HaPulmus shel Shelomo Bonafed beNikhbedei Saragossa*, ed. H. Schirmann (*Qovetz 'al-Yad* 4 [1946]:14), #4. **Heading:** "And another [poem] while I dwelled for a while with the pathetic Jews of Saragossa, who in their perversion made for themselves a golden calf and exchanged their glory for the likeness of kine, an evil man full of guile . . . one named Yosef Yeshu'a . . . who came from Sicily and didn't know how to disperse knowledge. This people that walked in darkness honored him with their silver and gold, and in setting him at their head they erred. And when I saw that this would come to a bitter end, I came out among them—for all they had was being lost, and fleeing before the Lord. And after I came to Belchite, the Lord happened to put before me the rhymes of the sage Shelomo Ibn Gabirol, which are more precious than gold, to rebuke this wicked community for having persecuted him long ago. The poem begins 'My throat is parched with pleading.' Then I awoke and said I will write like him, and make known throughout Israel their wickedness and the evil within the souls of these sinners. And after its likeness and image, and with the same meter, I composed this poem, which I sent to the sage Don Gonsalo Ibn Lavi, may his soul rest in Eden, and this is what I said." The poem is part of an extended series of epistles and short poems that Bonafed composed while in "exile" in the town of Belchite (roughly twenty-five miles southeast of Saragossa), railing against the nouveau-riche leaders of the Saragossan Jewish community, whom he considered coarse and wholly unworthy of their position. It was they who had let themselves be misled by the Sicilian rabbi Yeshu'a, whom Bonafed considered a pernicious boor and a fraud. Ibn Gabirol's poem is translated in full above (see, "On Leaving Saragossa"). Bonafed's poem, which is of a lesser order altogether—though not without power—is translated only in part (lines 19–37 of a seventy-line poem in Hebrew). **Line 4:** Habakkuk

3:11. **8:** Isaiah 45:24. **9:** The poet's full name is Shelomo Ben Reuben Bonafed. **23:** Both are "Shelomo."

WHEREVER YOU GO

A. Gross, "HaMeshorer Shelomo Bonafed," in *Sefer Zikaron leEfraim Talmedge* (Haifa, 1993), Appendix, p. 49, #1 ("an telkhi o tidrekhi iggeret"). The poem is one of several that the poet wrote to friends and colleagues who had converted. As Avraham Gross points out, these postconversion poems show just how central (Hebrew) poetry was to the group; it continued to bind them and exert its hold over them even after they'd been baptized. In lines 1–14 the poet is addressing the letter written by his baptized friend. **Lines 4–8:** Numbers 5:12; 1 Kings 14:3; Ezra 9:3–4; Proverbs 7:6. **12:** In Hebrew a pun: one of the constellations is known as "The Moth"—i.e., the surface of your letter is accomplished and impressive, but within it lies something destructive. **15–16:** Rimoq's letter itself is speaking here; it mentions the prefiguration of Jesus in Scripture, though the tone Bonafed lends the letter here is deeply ironic. Isaiah 63:1; Proverbs 9:14; Song of Songs 5:10. **17:** Proverbs 8:30. **20:** Isaiah 9:5, a verse that Christians read in Christological terms. **31–32:** The figure is hyperbolic, as though the spirit of poetry in him were the same spirit that inspired Deborah to sing and Barak to fight (Judges 4–5).

YITZHAQ ALAHDAB

Sicily became part of the House of Aragon after the great revolt against French colonization of 1282, when Peter III of Aragon became Peter I of Sicily. Following his reign, the island was ruled by a succession of Aragonese monarchs until 1412, when the crowns of Sicily and Aragon alike passed to Ferdinand I and the island came under direct Spanish rule. Fleischer sees Alahdab as a successor to Shmu'el Ibn Sasson and Shem Tov Ardutiel, and values him as well for the popular aspects of his work. Eliezer Gutwirth has written about the poet's focus on the "lower orders" or "trades" as an emblematic interest of a developing Hispano-Jewish bourgeois ideology (evident also in Moshe Natan's *Issues of Life*). The topos was increasingly prevalent in the European literature of the time. See E. Gutwirth, "Hispano-Jewish Bourgeois Ideology," in *Iberia and Beyond*, ed. Bernard Dev Cooperman (Delaware, 1998), pp. 154ff.

INFLATION

*Shirei Yitzhaq Ben Shelomo Alahdab*, ed. Ora Ra'anan (Lod, 1988), #38. **Lines 1–2:** Pesahim 102b. **4:** Deuteronomy 22:8, involving a pun on the word for "blood," *damim*, which can also in this plural form mean "money."

## Another Flea

*Shirei Alahdab*, #39.

**Line 4:** Or, "who bites the lion, whose blood he savors . . . and before their viziers show no favors."

## Security

*Shirei Alahdab*, #36.

## The Elderly Asked if the Doctors

*Shirei Alahdab*, #45. **Line 2:** Ecclesiastes 1:15.

## As Sorcerers Spread

*Shirei Alahdab*, #47. **Line 4:** Literally, "oven and stove" (Leviticus 11:35), which in *Ta'anit* 30a, b is understood as "a humble position or station."

## Being Poor

*Shirei Alahdab*, #66.

## State of the Art; or, Poetry Wails

*Shirei Alahdab*, #5; *HaShira*, #434. **Line 5:** Exodus 31:6; Isaiah 3:3. **8:** I.e., as they stood guard over poetry's standards. **9:** Shelomo Ibn Gabirol. Fleischer notes that HaNagid is conspicuously absent from the list of important poets; Alahdab most likely didn't know of his work. **10:** For more on the notion of "sacred currency," see the biographical introduction to Yosef Qimhi's poems and my comments there on the nature of *sheqel haqodesh*. "Sacred currency" had double value; here "currency" implies his language generally and, perhaps, the content of his liturgical poems. **12:** Job 37:18. **19:** Hosea 13:16. **21:** Moshe and Avraham Ibn Ezra. **22:** Genesis 46:29. **23:** 2 Kings 2:12. **24:** 1 Samuel 18:4. **30:** Ezekiel 12:13. **31:** Exodus 32:18. **33–34:** I.e., they announce themselves loudly and conspicuously. Leviticus 22:24. **36:** Exodus 7:29, 12:34: "So the people took their dough before it was leavened, their kneading bowls wrapped in their cloaks upon their shoulders"—i.e., everyone comes forth with what he has, whether or not the poems are ready and worthy.

## Renaissance Man

*Shirei Alahdab*, #13. In the original the poem is 177 lines long and contains thirty-six stanzas, including the introductory quatrain. They incorporate an alphabetical acrostic and, at the end, the acrostic *HaZaQ veEMaTZ* (be strong and of good courage). **Line 8:** Job 39:20. **9:** 1 Samuel 17:5. **10:** Literally, "an archer"; Genesis 21:20. **13:** Leviticus 26:36. **15:** Jeremiah 29:5. **22:** Jeremiah 22:14. **23:** Literally, "towers and delightful imagery"; Isaiah 2:16. **24:** Judges 6:2: "dens which are in the mountains" (Hebrew uncertain). **25:** The translation skips six Hebrew stanzas and resumes at stanza 10, line 43, of the original. **35:** Stanza 12, line 53, of the Hebrew. **45:** Stanza 22, line 103, of the Hebrew. **55:** Stanza 35, line 168, of the Hebrew. **62:** Some read the Hebrew here as: "I've grown tired, but soon I'll make my way to . . . ." **64–65:** Literally, "Then it was known that without me, all was a fraud,/and without me [i.e., my input] no one could lift a hand."

## MOSHE REMOS

Fleischer comments that the poem's heading doesn't mean that he was in fact executed the next day, but that—for some reason—the execution was delayed, with Remos adding the heading at a later point. (A comment by the Italian-Hebrew poet Moshe Rieti states that the execution did eventually take place, and it notes that Remos was buried outside Palermo, near the city wall.) Fleischer adds that Remos may well have had a European (and possibly folk) model in mind. Other famous later examples of poems written before execution, at least according to legend, are Chidiock Tichborne's "Elegy" of 1586, Sir Walter Raleigh's "The Pilgrimage," and Andre Chénier's late-eighteenth-century French poem from prison.

### Last Words

*Hebrew Ethical Wills*, ed. I. Abrahams (Philadelphia, 1926), pp. 238–48 (excerpts, as listed below); some of the translated passages can be found in *HaShira*, #459. An acrostic repeating the letters of the poet's name numerous times is woven through the poem. The Hebrew has no regular meter, and its quatrains rhyme *abab*, with the rhymes changing each quatrain. This quatrain form was quite popular in Hebrew medieval verse, though usually within a liturgical context; the secular use of it here is distinct. The excerpts here translate lines 1–12, 33–52, and 145–88 of the original. **Line 1:** Literally, "a learned man who seeks God." **2:** Psalms 14:2, 53:3. **3:** Jeremiah 11:19. **5–8:** *Ze'er Anpin* and *Ba'al haHotem*—literally, "the small countenance" and "the one with the nose": qabbalistic terms relating to divine anger and forbearance. **9–12:** These terms refer to the ten qabbalistic *sefirot*. **12:** Psalms 22:2. The translation skips twenty lines of the Hebrew at this point. **15:** Psalms 68:5; *Hagigah* 12b; *Guide to the Perplexed* 2. 4. **17:** Jeremiah 2:12: "Be astonished, O ye heavens, at this." **19:** Lines 19–32 enumerate the signs of the zodiac, all of which the poet mimics in his martyrdom. **27:** 1 Kings 12:11. **32:** The translation skips ninety lines of the Hebrew at this point. **36:** Jeremiah 22:19:

"He shall be buried with the burial of an ass, drawn and cast forth beyond the gates of Jerusalem." **45:** Isaiah 9:4: "For every boot stamped with fierceness." **46:** *Genesis Rabbah* 85:2. **50:** Or, "to give the heathens a beaker of reeling" (Isaiah 51:17). "Heathens" here is used in the biblical sense, indicating any "unclean" person, a non-Jew. **55:** Rabbi Akiva (c. 50–135 C.E.), one of the most famous sages of the talmudic period, who died at the hands of Roman torturers and approached his martyrdom as an opportunity to fulfill the commandments of the Shema'. *Berakhot* 61b: "Thou shalt love the Lord thy God with all thy heart and with all thy soul . . . even if you must pay for it with your life." **56:** Nehemiah 9:33. **60:** Literally, "I give my portion to the Living Rock, and 'the dead beast shall be his' " (Exodus 21:34). **64:** Lamentations 3:1. **66:** 1 Samuel 15:32. **69:** Ecclesiastes 12:13. **70:** The standard, ancient form of confession. *Yoma* 87b: "if he had said: 'Truly, we have sinned,' no more is necessary. . . . this was the main confession." **76:** Daniel 12:13; 1 Samuel 25:29: "The soul of my lord shall be bound in the bundle of life with the Lord"—i.e., in the care of the Lord.

## 'ELI BEN YOSEF [HAVILLIO?]

The attribution of the poems to Havillio was made by Yosef Tubi, who also commented on the unusual modesty of this epigram.

### WHO SOARS

" 'Eli Ben Yosef (Havillio?)—Meshorer 'Ivri min haDor haAharon biSefard," ed. Yosef Tubi, *Dapim leMehqar beSifrut* 7 (1991): 268, #5. **Line 1:** Judges 5:26. **4:** Job 20:24. **6:** Psalms 58:9; Deuteronomy 32:22.

## MOSHE IBN HABIB

Like the rest of the Jewish population in the western part of Iberia, Portugal's Jewish communities appear to have been small and impoverished at least up until near the end of the eleventh century, and we have little in the way of any records relating to their scholars and writers (Ashtor, *The Jews of Moslem Spain*, 2: 204; and A. Schippers, "Moshe Ibn Habib, Migrant and Poet," *Studia Rosenthaliana* 35/2 [2001]: 172–83). An independent Jewish community developed in Portugal over time, reinforced by the influx of tens of thousands of Spanish exiles after the Expulsion, who were given temporary asylum there before being expelled in 1497. As Yosef Haim Yerushalmi writes: "Portuguese Jewry . . . was cut off in its prime, perhaps even on the verge of greatness" ("A Jewish Classic in the Portuguese Language," intro. to *Consolação às Tribulações de Israel* [Lisbon, 1989], p. 24). Fleischer, in *Toldot* (1997), says that he left in 1497. Abravanel's poem is translated in full and discussed by Raymond Scheindlin in "Judah Abravanel to His Son," *Judaism*, 1992, and Constable, *Medieval Iberia*, pp. 357–63. The preface to *Darkhei No'am* reads, in part: "And I am Moshe . . . who has been humbled by time's trials and tribulations, which have uprooted me and my family, and the fighting surrounds me, and no one comes or goes, and I am here in Bitonto, for such it seems is my destiny, and harder than all is my poverty, for these three have given me over to this hole and cranny, far from the country of my birth, and the home of my father and my uncles." The three types of poetry that Habib discusses are drawn directly from the Arabic philosopher Al-Faraabi, who says that poetry is "of six kinds, three of which are praised and three blamed"; in terms closer to the Hebrew than those used by the *Encyclopedia Judaica* (which are quoted in the biographical introduction here), Adele Berlin describes the three types that Habib mentions as: "1) poems intended for the improvement of the intellect; 2) poems intended for the restoration of equilibrium when 'accidents of the soul,' such as anger and pride, threaten to overcome it; and 3) poems intended for the elevation of the soul from 'lesser accidents,' such as fear, pain, and cowardice" (Berlin, *The Bible through Medieval Eyes*, p. 116). The other three types of poetry that Habib says shouldn't be discussed involve the negation of the three positive types ("the opposites of the three which are praised"). See al-Faraabi, *Fusuul al-Madani: Aphorisms of the Statesman*, ed. and trans. D. M. Dunlop (Cambridge, 1961), pp. 49–50. See also M. B. Amzalak, *Portuguese Hebrew Grammars and Grammarians*, (Lisbon, 1928), pp. 10–12; R. Feingold, "'HaSiman haYehudi' bePortugal," *Pe'amim* 51 (1992): 70–80.

## Account

*Darkhei No'am 'im Marpei Lashon*, ed. V. Heidenheim, (Roedelheim, 1806), p. 12a; Schirmann, *HaShira*, #463a. **Line 1–2:** Ecclesiastes 5:10. **3–4:** The Hebrew *nihamti* is glossed by Schirmann as "regret"—at the sight of the flames coming forth from the account. The flames suggest what awaits the speaker.

## You Come to the House of God

*Darkhei No'am*, p. 17b. A homonym poem in the original. **Heading:** "About those who come to pray and bring their mouths but not their hearts." **6:** Exodus 30:23.

## SA'ADIA IBN DANAAN

The Jewish population of Granada is discussed by David Wasserstein in "Jewish Elites" (see introduction to this anthology, note 12). In the city itself (as opposed to the entire kingdom), there were by this time a mere five hundred and fifty Jews. He notes there that Ibn Danaan's date of death is listed in R. Arié, *L'Espagne musulmane*

*au temps des Nasrides, 1232–1492* (Paris, 1973), p. 336 (and n. 2), as December 11, 1492—
that is, a few months after the Expulsion. Others list his date of death as 1505 or af-
ter 1505 (see E. Hazan, *HaShira Ha'Ivrit beTzafon Afriqa* [Jerusalem, 1995], pp.
197–200), and the later date makes more sense. Hazan, whose anthology includes a
longer liturgical composition and a secular poem about misers, describes Ibn
Danaan's style as "light and winning," and he notes that in addition to the poet's
gentle and mischievous epigrams, he also wrote scores of both secular and liturgi-
cal poems. Davidson's *Thesaurus of Medieval Hebrew Poetry* (1933; New York, 1970),
4:455, lists sixty-two poems. See also A. Saenz-Badillos and J. Targarona Borrás, "Po-
emas de Se'adyah Ibn Danaan," ed. and trans. J. Targarona Borrás, *Sefarad* 46
(1990): 449ff. For prose and several other poems by Ibn Danaan, see also D. 'Ovadia,
*Fas veHokhmeiha* (Jerusalem 1979), 2: 1–91.

### ENMITY SMOLDERS

*Melekhet HaShir*, ed. Y. Neubauer (Frankfurt, 1865), p. 10.

### HORDES OF READERS

*Melekhet HaShir*, p. 8. **Line 3:** The sons of the biblical 'Ever, from which the word
'Ivrim (Hebrews) derives. Genesis 10:21: "And unto Shem, the father of all the
children of Eber. . . ."

### MIXED MESSENGER

*Melekhet HaShir*, p. 10; *HaShira*, #462:2. While this poem takes up the standard
trope of the dangerous woman and her smooth talk (with the final two lines pro-
viding a metaphorical explanation for the mixed message the woman sends), it
might—like many of Ibn Danaan's poems of desire—also be seen from this late
vantage point as an unconscious comment on the Arabized Hebrew poem itself.
As such, it recalls Dunash's "Eden" of Scripture and the "paradise grove" of Ara-
bic books. **Line 4:** Genesis 21:20: "And [Ishmael] became an archer."

### SHE TRAPPED ME

*Melekhet HaShir*, p. 8. **Lines 1–2:** Proverbs 9:17.

### CHIASMUS FOR A DOE

*Melekhet HaShir*, p. 8; *HaShira*, #462:1.

# ⊰ GLOSSARY ⊱

*The following notes relate only to terms mentioned in this anthology and are by no means exhaustive. Likewise, poems cited at the end of each entry illustrate the term under discussion but do not account for all the poems in this volume that demonstrate a given phenomenon.*\*

**acrostic:** While the vast majority of liturgical poems were written to be presented on behalf of a congregation of worshipers, and not as the personal expression of the individual poet, poets regularly "signed" their hymns with acrostics registering their names. Usually these acrostics ran down the spine of the poem, with the first letter of each line spelling out the poet's name. Sometimes the acrostic would include only the poet's first name, while at other times the full name in a variety of permutations would appear. Alternatively, particularly in longer composite poems, the poets employed alphabetical acrostics in a variety of (sometimes quite elaborate) arrangements.

*adab:* A central term in classical Arabic—and, by extension, Hebrew—literature, *adab* connotes both learning in its fullness as a way of life and the signature style of the cultured person. It refers at once to disciplines of the mind and soul, good breeding, refinement, culture, and belles lettres. Similar to the Greek notion of *paideia*.

*ahava:* A *piyyut*, or liturgical poem, that was originally part of the *yotzer*, a longer sequence of liturgical poems composed to accompany the recitation of the Shema' during the morning liturgy on Sabbaths and festivals. (*Yotzer* means "Creator" or "He who creates," as in the first benediction leading up to the recitation of the Shema': "Blessed art Thou, O Lord, Creator of the heavenly lights.") In Spain, it appears that the *yotzer* broke apart and its units became independent genres. The *ahava* was recited before the second benediction anticipating the Shema': "Blessed art Thou, O Lord, who in love *(be'ahava)* hast chosen Thy people Israel." Most of the Spanish *ahavot* are

---

\*Information for the glossary is drawn, for the most part, from Schirmann's two-volume history (see p. xxii, this anthology); *The Encyclopedia of Arabic Literature*, ed. Julie Scott Meisami and Paul Starkey (London/New York, 1998); Adonis, *Arabic Poetics*, trans. Catherine Cobham (Austin, 1990); Dan Pagis, *Secular Poetry and Poetic Theory: Moses Ibn Ezra and His Contemporaries* [Hebrew], (Jerusalem, 1970); Shulamit Elitzur, *Hebrew Poetry in Spain in the Middle Ages* [Hebrew] (Tel Aviv, 2004), vols. 1–3; *The Legacy of Muslim Spain*, ed. S. Jayyusi (Leiden, 1994); Michael Sells, *Desert Tracings* (Middletown, 1989); Neal Kozodoy, "Reading Medieval Hebrew Love Poetry," *AJS Review* 2 (1977); Proverbs/Ecclesiastes, ed. R.B.Y. Scott, *The Anchor Bible* (New York, 1965); Suzanne Stetkevych, *Abu Tammam and the Poetics of the Abbasid Age* (Leiden, 1991); Paul Fussell, *Poetic Meter and Poetic Form* (New York, 1965/79); and Raymond Scheindlin, *Wine, Women, and Death* (Philadelphia, 1986) and *The Gazelle* (Philadelphia, 1991).

strophic, rather than monorhymed, and they often incorporate elements from the Song of Songs. See Moshe Ibn Ezra's "Gold" and HaLevi's "A Doe Far from Home."

**badii'a:** An Arabic word that initially meant "something novel, original," but came to stand for a style of poetry. It derives from the root yielding, among many other things, the verb *abda'a* (to invent, to bring something new into creation) and one of the Islamic names for God, the Originator. In the history of Arabic literature, *badii'a* denotes the "new" poetry of the early Abbasid period (late eighth–early ninth century), one that employed more elaborate rhetorical figuration than did previous Arabic verse. In *Abu Tammam and the Poetics of the Abbasid Age* (Leiden 1991), Suzanne Stetkevych comments: "I would like to propose that *badii'a* poetry be defined not merely as the occurrence of this particular type of rhetorical device but rather that the *badii'a* style is first and foremost the intentional, conscious encoding of abstract meaning into metaphor. . . . The large number of . . . rhetorical devices in *badii'a* poetry is not a mere proliferation due to infatuation . . . but rather the product of a constant and ineluctable awareness of the logical and etymological relationship between words, and the intention to express this awareness" (pp. 8, 30). As the term "metaphysical" was originally a pejorative in the history of English poetry, so the root *b-d-'a* in Arabic yields the word for heresy (*bid'ah*), and Arabic literary history records very mixed feelings about the modern poets' inventiveness and break with tradition. Ibn Qutayba says that Muslim Ibn al-Waliid (d. 823) was the first Arab poet to employ the style, "the first to make meanings subtle and speech delicate" (Adonis, *Arab Poetics*, p. 50). Moshe Ibn Ezra referred to Ibn Gabirol as the first Hebrew poet to adopt the *badii'a* approach. Elements of it, however, are central to much of the Hebrew poetry composed in Andalusia. See Ibn Gabirol's "The Garden," Moshe Ibn Ezra's "A Shadow," Ibn Hasdai's "The Qasida," and HaLevi's "On Friendship and Time" and "Heart at Sea."

**baqasha:** There are two kinds of *baqashot* (liturgical poems of petition for the forgiveness of sins). The first is a long, comprehensive composition in powerfully cadenced nonmetrical lines that often rhyme. The second type, which appears to be an Andalusian phenomenon, is a shorter or medium-length monorhymed poem that usually repeats the poem's opening hemistich at the end. For the first type, see Ibn Gabirol's *Kingdom's Crown*; for the second, see Ibn Gabirol's "Before My Being" and HaLevi's "Lord, [All My Desire]."

**complaint, poems of:** The borders of this genre in Hebrew are not well defined. Generally speaking, poems of complaint are cast in the first person and reflect the poet's specific circumstances. The poem might treat a patron, an enemy, a disappointing friend or family member, a community as a whole, or even Fate or Time itself—but the perspective will always be personal and limited to the speaker. Poems of complaint often combine elements and strategies from a number of other genres, such as invective, boasting, rebuke, description, contemplation, or wisdom, and so forth. See Ibn Gabirol's "On Leaving Saragossa" (and "My Words Are Driven" in Cole, *Selected Ibn Gabirol*), Moshe Ibn Ezra's "The Dove" and "Why Does Time Hound Me So," Todros Abulafia's poems from prison, and Avraham Ibn Ezra's "A Cloak," "Fortune's Stars," and "How It Is."

**contemplative verse (wisdom poetry):** While Hebrew contemplative verse is in many ways modeled on the contemplative poetry of Arabic literature, the biblical tradition of wisdom literature in Hebrew also informs this genre, whose distinguishing feature is its universality. Other genres might treat a given moment (of a battle, at a party, in love, after a death), blending elements of the actual and the ideal, the personal and the conventional; but contemplative poems treat existence itself and speak from the perspective of Wisdom, which in this medieval scheme is suprapersonal and objective. Just as the biblical Book of Proverbs was used for instruction by Solomon the sage (who didn't necessarily write the proverbs there), so too the contemplative verse of medieval Hebrew Spain presents not so much personal insight as "instructional materials for the cultivation of personal morality and practical wisdom" (R.B.Y. Scott, Proverbs, *Anchor Bible,* introduction). It involves, in other words, a body of knowledge that would help one in the situations of living. Their objectivity notwithstanding, however, contemplative poems sometimes incorporate explicitly personal elements, which serve as a concrete illustration of the universal conclusion to be drawn from them. See HaNagid's "I Quartered the Troops for the Night," "The Market," and nearly all of his poems from *Ben Mishle* and *Ben Qohelet* (which make up the final third of the section devoted to him here), Ibn Gabirol's "If You'd Live among Men" and "Heart's Hollow," Moshe Ibn Ezra's "Ivory Palaces" and "The World," Yedaya HaPenini's "The World Is a Raging Sea," and later selections from the proverbs of Qimhi, and Moshe Natan.

*convivencia:* A term coined by modern Spanish scholars to refer to the culture of coexistence between Muslims, Christians, and Jews in both northern and southern Spain during the Middle Ages. The term itself means, literally, "dwelling together" and does not necessarily imply the sort of tolerance that we associate with coexistence today. Rather, as Thomas Glick writes, it "carries connotations of mutual interpenetration and creative influence, even as it also embraces the phenomena of mutual friction, rivalry, and suspicion." While religious communities were entirely distinct, and while political power was almost never shared, the marketplace and arena of culture brought the various ethnic groups together in a variety of fruitful ways. Medieval coexistence in Spain referred, then, to "a field of interaction" that was based on a deep-seated ethnic hierarchy involving protected and second-class citizens. In Muslim Spain these protected citizens (or *dhimmis*) were Christian and Jewish; in Christian Spain they included tolerated but often oppressed Jews and, to a lesser extent, Muslims. In both cases the situation was volatile, and political change often brought with it serious danger to minority populations. At its best, the culture gave Jews greater religious, social, economic, and intellectual freedom than they knew in any other medieval (non-Muslim) society; at its worst, it led to heavy taxation and serious oppression. When the bottom fell out of it, forced conversion, emigration, and slaughter weren't long in coming. Its limitations notwithstanding, *convivencia* has been described as the defining issue in the history of al-Andalus, and it resulted in a major renaissance of Arabic and Hebrew literature and learning, and in an early flowering of Spanish culture. See also note 70 to the introduction.

**descriptive verse:** Descriptive verse (*wasf* in Arabic) was one of the four categories of poetry that the medieval Arabic poet was expected to control—the other three being the boast (*fakhr*), the invective (*hijaa'*), and the elegy (*marthiya*). Probably deriving from the descriptions of the abandoned campsite and beloved in the ancient qasida's erotic prelude, and of animals and landscape in the journey section, or *rahiil*, it evolved into a genre of its own in Abbasid Baghdad and later in Spain. The tradition in Arabic was highly developed, with poets often devoting entire collections to elaborate treatments of single subjects, such as hunting animals, kinds of flowers, and specific objects. The Hebrew tradition tended to confine itself to a few central courtly topics: the garden, wine, nature in its more cultivated state, writing, beautiful young women and men, palace architecture and atmosphere, and the like. The riddle, too, was considered a kind of descriptive poem. While one might initially be inclined to take the genre of *wasf* poetry lightly—since it involves "mere" description—in fact an argument could be made for seeing this genre as, in some instances, central to the poetry of the period. To take but one example: as the garden is the place where members of the court society meet, and where visual, verbal, and musical aspects of its arts are combined, so the descriptive verse of the garden poems embraces and often addresses all of these constituent elements of Jewish-Andalusian society. See HaNagid's "Have You Heard How I Helped the Wise" (in Cole, *Selected HaNagid*), Ibn Gabirol's "Winter with Its Ink," "The Garden," "The Field," and (in Cole, *Selected Ibn Gabirol*) "The Palace," Moshe Ibn Ezra's "The Pen" and "A Shadow," HaLevi's "Four Riddles," and Shelomo DePiera's "Winter in Monzón."

**desire, poems of (or love poetry):** The Hebrew term *shirei hesheq* (literally, poems of desire or love), like the Hebrew term for the gazelle (*tzvi*—see below), derives from an Arabic parallel and involves a case of loan translation and linguistic slippage: one of the Arabic words for "passion" or "love" is *'ishq*, and a change of the initial letter brought poets to the biblical Hebrew *hesheq*.

Sometimes considered a subset of the wine poem (since the object of desire is often the cupbearer), the Hebrew poem of desire could adopt a variety of approaches, from overtly and powerfully sensual description of the beloved and the scene of the encounter, to wholly idealized portrayals of a refined situation, to humorous accounts of frustration and failure in the pursuit of experience. Strict if subtle conventions are adhered to, and knowing them and their social context helps distinguish the poetry's "purpose" and desired effect. The lover, for example, is usually miserable; the beloved is generally fickle and cruel; depictions of the beloved are stylized; and the poem implies no specific autobiographical experience (though neither does it rule any out). "It sometimes happens," writes Moshe Ibn Ezra, "that a poet can write of love without ever having loved" (*The Book of Discussion*, 143a). (For more specific criteria, see Cole, *Selected Ibn Gabirol*, pp. 287–88.) And, indeed, these poems comprise less a record of sexual adventure than what Andras Hamori has called "a badge of sensibility." As they celebrate a given moment and its qualities, the poems embody a sensitivity to beauty and a capacity for pleasure that are generalized (even polymorphous), and extend well beyond the confines of a given erotic situation. That said, they are at times powerfully sensual in every respect, and considerable controversy still surrounds the Hebrew poems of desire, particularly the homoerotic verse, with some scholars finding it impossible to square the explicit (homo)erotic atmosphere with the fact that the poets were ritually observant, learned Jews.

With regard to the question of homosexual *experience* and how it is that these pious Jews could possibly be "flouting" something so clearly prohibited by Scripture, the jury is still out. While we do not know whether any of the Jewish poets had homosexual experience, we do know that Andalusian court culture was *not* homophobic, and that homoerotic poems were both common and powerful. On the whole, the poems do not feel like the literary exercises some scholars make them out to be, and they might best be taken at face value—like the erotic poems of Emily Dickinson and Walt Whitman perhaps— with all the ambiguity that implies.

As the conventions of the poetry of desire, like wine poetry, were in the Arabic tradition adopted by the Sufis and subtly manipulated along religious lines, so too the Andalusian Hebrew poets brought the eroticism of secular poetry into the synagogue to create surprisingly (and at times stunningly) sensuous poems of devotion. Ibn Gabirol, Moshe Ibn Ezra, and HaLevi excelled at this sort of grafting.

See Ibn Khalfoun's "Love in Me Stirs"; HaNagid's "The Gazelle" and "In Fact I Love That Fawn"; Ibn Gabirol's "You Lie in My Palace"; Moshe Ibn Ezra's "Heart's Desire," "Gold," and "The Gazelle's Sigh"; HaLevi's "That Day while I Had Him," "A Doe Far from Home" and "Love's Dwelling"; Yehuda Alharizi's "Boys"; Todros Abulafia's "I've Labored in Love," "She Said She Wanted," and "There's Nothing Wrong in Wanting a Woman"; and Ibn Danaan's erotic epigrams.

**diwan:** A gathering of a given poet's poems, usually a "collected poems." The word is Persian in origin, and means—among other things—register, or record, as in Ibn Khaldun's famous pronouncement, "Poetry is the *diwan* of the Arabs," i.e., their historical record, or archive. Some of the *diwans* were compiled by the poets themselves, but most were put together by later (or contemporary) copyists and amateur lovers of poetry. The poems were often prefaced with headings describing the circumstances of composition or the poem's subject matter. The headings to the Hebrew Andalusian poems were always written in Judeo-Arabic; in Christian Spain, they were sometimes composed in Hebrew. Poems within the diwan were arranged either by chronology (to the extent that could be determined); alphabetically by their rhyme letter or the first word of the poem; by theme, genre, and meter; or in some cases by other, more complicated schemes. While the term *diwan* denoted a collection of secular verse, in fact most of the extant Hebrew *diwans* (in Arabic, *dawawiin*) contain some liturgical poems as well.

**encomia (poetry of praise):** According to Arabic tradition, it is possible to divide all of poetry and its genres into two overall categories: praise *(madiih)* and scorn *(dhamm)*. Along this line of thinking, the elegy involves praise for the dead; the erotic poem praise of beauty (male or female); the descriptive poem praise of nature; the boast poem praise of self; the wine poem praise of wine and drinking; the contemplative or gnomic poem praise of wisdom; poems of friendship praise for a leader, patron, prominent figure, or friend; and so forth. Satire or invective would then involve disparagement of a particular person (or his attributes); the poem of complaint scorn for one's own situation; poems of asceticism scorn for the world; and so on. Given the social circumstances of medieval Arabic and Hebrew poetry alike, where the poet sometimes depended on support from patrons or the extended court environment, it was natural that encomia constituted a considerable percentage of a poet's diwan. That said, many of the encomia are in fact poems addressed to friends rather than patrons, and celebrate either friendship itself or the qualities one admires in a peer—both potentially serious subjects for poetry. While there is a good deal of formulaic, panegyric verse among these poems of praise, the social occasion that called for them sometimes resulted in the composition of poems of true feeling and serious criticism (through subtle departure from accepted convention); sensuality (in the erotic prelude to the encomia); or meditation on value (elsewhere in the qasida—on which, see below). Not all encomia were odes; short poems of praise were written as well. On the whole, the poetry of praise should not be dismissed as a form of empty flattery (though it could be just that); it is rather what Julie Meisami describes as a complex literary vehicle for the presentation of cultural ideals. See Ibn Hasdai's "The Qasida," HaLevi's "On Friendship and Time," Alharizi's "A Poem No Patron Has Ever Heard," and, in Cole, *Selected Ibn Gabirol*, "The Palace."

**epigram:** Epigrams are extremely common in both Arabic and Hebrew medieval literature, and they need to be distinguished within the more general category of the *qit'a*, or short poem. As in classical Greek, Latin, and English literature, the Hebrew epigram is characterized by brevity, wit, and its point, or strong sense of closure. In the Arabic tradition, longer qasidas were often "ransacked" by anthologists for epigrammatic lines that would stand on their own, and this anthology contains several of these "detached" epigrams (the source of which is always listed in the notes to the poem). Epigrams ranged widely in theme, but gnomic, satirical, elegiac, and erotic epigrams abound.

*fakhr:* Literally, "pride" (Arabic); as a literary term it indicates self-vaunting poetry or a boast. Though sometimes considered as a genre of Arabic poetry, it is in fact an attitude or mode that finds expression in a variety of ways. In the oral culture of pre-Islamic Arabia, the poet was not only the spokesman of his tribe but a shamanlike figure who possessed magical powers and could help determine the fate of his people, by instilling them with strength-yielding confidence and demoralizing the enemy. The qasida or ode was one of their primary forms of communication in this respect, and in the pre-Islamic context the boast formed one of that poem's dominant elements, traditionally coming at the end of the three-part ode or in the body of the two-part ode. It was a common motif in subsequent Arabic and Andalusian Hebrew poetry as well. Originally the boast embodied either communal or personal virtues, especially those of *muruuwwa* (manliness), including generosity, heroism, fidelity, and self-control. While it is often hard for modern readers to relate to this self-satisfied or egoistical aspect of medieval Arabic and Hebrew work, it may help to see the boast poem on the one hand as a culture-bound vehicle for the transmission of value, and on the other as a Norman Mailer–like advertisement for oneself uttered in the highly competitive arena of literature—a literary analogue, perhaps, to the "trash talk" of contemporary athletes. Again, this element was less pronounced in the Hebrew poetry of the day than it was in the Arabic. See HaNagid's "On Fleeing His City" and (in Cole, *Selected HaNagid*) "Have You Heard How I Helped the Wise," and Ibn Gabirol's "I'm Prince to the Poem," "Truth Seekers Turn," "On Leaving Saragossa," "I Am the Man," "Prologue to *The Book of Grammar*," and (in *Selected Ibn Gabirol*) "The Palace" and "As the Roots of a Tree."

**gazelle:** Poets used several Hebrew terms to represent the figure of the beloved, including *tzvi* (f., *tzviyya*), *'ofer* (f., *'ofra*), and *ya'alat hen* (f.)—all of which can be translated variously as gazelle, hart, deer, fawn, hind, doe, roe, and more, depending on the circumstances of a given poem. The motif in Hebrew poetry evolved from both Song of Songs 2:9 ("Behold, my beloved is like a gazelle *[tzvi]* or a young hart [*'ofer ha'ayalim*]") and from the tradition of Arabic love poetry, which often likens the beloved to a gazelle *(ghazaal* or *zabi*—the Arabic cognate of the Hebrew *tzvi)*. As the Arabic word for the desirable young man or woman is a near-cognate—*sabi* or *sabiyya* (f.) (the root of which, as a verb, means "to feel sensual desire for," just as *tzvi* in Hebrew can also mean "beauty" or "glory" or "that which is desired")—an interesting opportunity for loan translation presented itself. Erotic poetry in Arabic is in fact known as *ghazal*, which also involves another case of linguistic slippage. The word derives from the verb *ghazala*, to spin, but assumed the associations of the gazelle early on. At times the feminine form of the animal will be used to represent a masculine beloved, or vice versa; at other times, the pronoun is a reliable indication of the beloved's gender. In the liturgical poetry the gazelle appears as an image of God (m.) or the congregation of Israel (f.). See Ibn Mar Sha'ul's "A Fawn Sought in Spain," HaNagid's "The Gazelle," Ibn Gabirol's "You Lie in my Palace," Moshe Ibn Ezra's "The Gazelle's Sigh," Alharizi's "Measure for Measure," Todros Abulafia's "She Said She Wanted," and many other poems. For more on the subject of erotic poetry and homoeroticism, see DESIRE, POEMS OF.

**genre:** Genres play a prominent role in medieval Hebrew poetry, and knowledge of the available generic options is necessary for proper reading of the work and appreciation of the ways in which poets manipulated their materials and at times transcended the period's conventions. Rather than viewing these conventions as impediments toward expression, one might first consider the ways in which generic assumptions and conventions live on and flourish in our own culture: in literature and drama (the fourth wall and the omniscient narrator); in rock and country songs (particularly about love); in films (through the sometimes contrived mechanisms propelling romantic comedies, murder mysteries, and road movies); in television shows, and elsewhere. As Paul Fussell has put it, "The notion that convention shows a lack of feeling, and that a poet attains 'sincerity' . . . by disregarding [convention], is opposed to all the facts of literary experience and history." See individual entries for encomia, wine poetry, erotic verse, contemplative verse, and so on.

*ge'ula:* Literally, [a poem of] "redemption," "salvation," or "deliverance." A liturgical poem that was originally part of the *yotzer* and treats Israel's exile and hopes for salvation. The *ge'ula* was recited on Sabbaths and festivals before the final benediction after the recitation of the Shema': "Blessed art Thou, O Lord, Redeemer (*go'el*) of Israel." In Spain, the *ge'ulot* were often strophic. See Ibn Ghiyyat's "My Wandering" and HaLevi's "If Only I Could Be."

*hijaa':* See INVECTIVE.

**invective:** One of the principle genres of Arabic poetry, invective (Arabic, *hijaa'*) is the inverse of the poetry of praise (see ENCOMIA, above). The Arabic word may originally have meant "casting a spell," and like the English word "spell" it also means "to write out." Both indicate a possible origin in magic, where the utterance of curses could destroy the honor of a person or tribe by articulating, and broadcasting, shameful attributes—sometimes as a prelude to, or substitute for, actual combat or violent confrontation. While the magical aspect of the enterprise eventually vanished, the destructive power of the utterance did not, and the Arabic and Hebrew medieval poets could be lethal in their verbal assaults. *Hijaa'* verse assumes a variety of forms, but it is particularly acute when loaded into the epigram, or concealed in a longer qasida of praise, where it would have ambushed its off-balance victim. The invective might be directed at a person or an entire group of people (e.g., a religion).

For all its ability to injure, however, the invective was also a source of amusement, humor, and—one assumes—catharsis. Again, the poem of invective was less common in Hebrew than it was in Arabic. See HaNagid's "The Critique," Ibn Gabirol's "The Altar of Song," Alharizi's "A Miser in Mosul" and "Born to Baseness," and Benveniste's "The Tongue Speaks and the Hand Records." Sometimes a single poem could be both a poem of praise and scorn: see, for example, Alharizi's "Palindrome for a Patron."

**kharja:**  The final couplet of the secular *muwashshah*, usually written out in the Arabic or Romance vernacular (or in a combination of the two) and spoken by a young woman or a creature of the poet's invention—such as a dove or the wind—from outside the masculine context of the poem, and sometimes outside its aristocratic environment. *Kharjas* were regularly drawn ready-made from Andalusian folk tradition, and the *muwashshah* would often be created around a given couplet from that tradition. In some instances they preserve the oldest known form of Spanish. The word itself is Arabic for "exit." Not all Hebrew *muwashshahat* contained the *kharja*. See HaLevi's "If Only I Could Give" and Todros Abulafia's "I Take Delight in My Cup and Wine."

**line:**  The principal Hebrew line *(bayit*—literally, "house"; plural, *batim)* taken over from Arabic comprised two generally symmetrical hemistiches, known as the *delet* (door) and the *sogair* (latch, or lock). In Arabic these were known as the *sadr* (chest, front) and the *'ajouz* (backside or rump). Each of these was normally end-stopped, but enjambment across the first hemistich was not uncommon. In both the shorter *qit'a* and the longer, polythematic qasida, the *sogair*, or second hemistich of each line, would maintain a single end-rhyme (monorhyme) throughout the length of the poem. It was also standard—but not required—for the opening hemistich (the initial *delet)* of the poem to rhyme with its *sogair.*

1) ---------------- a ---------------a
2) ---------------- x ---------------a
3) ---------------- x ---------------a

In printed editions of the poetry, and almost always in translation (particularly into an uninflected English, which is much less compact), the two parts of the line or *bayit* are sometimes printed on two separate lines.

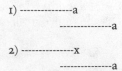

The lines of the qasida and *qit'a* alike were composed in one of the quantitative meters (and their variants) that were also adapted from Arabic prosody.

For other Hebrew forms of the line, see MUWASHSHAH and STROPHIC POEM, below.

**maqaama:** A rhymed-prose picaresque narrative that sometimes instructs as it entertains and is almost always interspersed with metrical poems illustrating developments in the story. It can tell a single continuous narrative or comprise a series of independent stories. The *maqaama*'s characters (who are usually given biblical names) include a narrator of solid social standing who wanders from place to place for business or pleasure and a restless, peripatetic protagonist who has fallen from grace and is now shameless in his quest for sustenance and personal gain. The protagonist also happens to be, by convention, a poet of remarkable gifts. The two men meet in nearly every chapter. The term *maqaama* is Arabic and implies a "place of assembly" or "public gathering," as the stories were almost always recited in such a forum. See Ibn Tzaqbel, Alharizi, Ibn Zabara, Ya'aqov Ben Elazar, and others.

**martial verse:** The only martial verse in the postbiblical Hebrew canon is by Shmu'el HaNagid. HaNagid's battle poems combine the Arabic tradition of *muruuwwa* (manhood or manliness) and the *hamaasa* (epic tradition) with sophisticated use of Hebrew biblical typologies. Often deriving his descriptions of a given battle from the tradition of Arabic martial verse, and mixing that with realia from the campaigns that he may himself have led (or administered), HaNagid then uses biblical elements to weave that compound into a full-fledged typological landscape. HaNagid himself, in that scheme, is seen as a David-like warrior-poet leading a kind of national renaissance, and his enemies (who were in fact the enemies of the Muslim Granadan army he led) become the incarnation of the ancient enemies of Israel. For all that, the poems are nonetheless highly personal. Several took the place of prayer on a given day, and some were written in commemoration of major Granadan victories, which are then elided into a triumph for the Jewish community as a whole. Other poems treat dream visions relating to battle. See HaNagid's "On Lifting the Siege" and "The War with Yaddayir" in this anthology; there are numerous other battle poems in Cole, *Selected HaNagid*.

**mehayyeh:** Literally, "He who revives." The *mehayyeh* is a liturgical poem that prefaces the second benediction of the central prayer of the Hebrew liturgy, the *'amida* (the standing prayer): "Blessed art Thou, O Lord, who callest the dead to life everlasting." See Ibn Gabirol's "Send Your Spirit." The *mehayyeh* is the second part of the *qedushta* (a larger Eastern composition of liturgical poems composed to be performed around the first two blessings of the *'amida* and its *qedusha*, or sanctification of the Lord of hosts).

**me'ora:** Literally, "[a poem of] light." Intended to ornament the first blessing leading up to the recitation of the Shema': "Blessed art Thou, O Lord, Creator of the heavenly lights." The *me'ora* usually treats the relationship between God and the congregation of Israel, and expresses hope in the coming redemption. See Nahum's "Winter Has Waned." Part of the *yotzer*.

**muharak:** A liturgical poem that prefaces the *nishmat kol hai* prayer ("The breath of every living being shall bless Thy name, O Lord"). The *muharak*, which is recited before the prayer and after the *reshut* to the *nishmat* (see RESHUT), is strophic, and often deals with the nature and qualities of the soul. The term is Arabic and means "mover" or "one which moves"; it was most likely connected to the way in which the *piyyut* was originally sung and performed in the synagogue. See HaLevi's "If Only I Could Be."

**mustajaab** (or **mustajiib**): A kind of *seliha* (see below), the *mustajaab* is a common Spanish-Hebrew strophic form beginning with a biblical verse that subsequently serves as a refrain throughout the hymn. (The term itself is Arabic and means "response.") The final lines of each strophe are also biblical and rhyme with the concluding word of the refrain. (Sometimes these rhyme words are identical.) See Ibn Gabirol's "He Dwells Forever" and Moshe Ben Nahman's "Before the World Ever Was."

**muwashshah:** An Andalusian Arabic strophic form, apparently developed from Romance folk poetry and adopted in the eleventh century by the Hebrew poets. In Hebrew, as in Arabic, the poem weaves together two (often elaborate) rhyme schemes, and sometimes two metrical schemes as well. The secular *muwashshah* usually closes with a *kharja* (see above). The *muwashshahat* were sung, and one often senses in the written texts the absence of the musical accompaniment and its shifting rhythms. The term itself has, unfortunately, been translated into English as "girdle poem" (no doubt as in the older meaning of that word—"belt"). In fact, the Arabic verb *washshaha* means to adorn or dress, and the noun *wushshaah* is "an ornamented sash or belt—in older times a doubled band with embedded gems worn sash-like over the shoulder (H. Wehr, *A Dictionary of Modern Written, Arabic* [1961; London and Beirut, 1980], pp. 1070–71)." One might, then, best think of the *muwashshah* as a poem in which the rhyming chorus winds about the various strophes of the poem as a gem-studded sash cuts across the body. Generally speaking, the *muwashshah* was considered a "nonclassical" form, and it was initially looked down upon in the Arabic tradition; *muwashshahat* were not usually included in a poet's *diwan*, and if they were, they were often relegated to the back of the manuscript and constituted a separate section. The earliest Arabic *muwashshahat* date from the end of the tenth century; in Hebrew the earliest extant *muwashshahat* are by Shmu'el HaNagid. The first liturgical *muwashshahat* are by Ibn Gabirol. In Hebrew, the *muwashshah* was absorbed more quickly into liturgical verse than it was into the secular dimension. For a telling example of the way in which this form could be adapted in Hebrew for either secular or liturgical use, see HaLevi's "If Only I Could Give" and "If Only I Could Be." Also Moshe Ibn Ezra's "Heart's Desire," Ibn Tzaddiq's "Lady of Grace," and Todros Abulafia's "I Take Delight in My Cup and Wine."

**nasiib:** The first and usually nostalgic section of the qasida. In the classical Arabic qasida, the *nasiib* is erotic and always refers to a relationship in the past. The poet comes across the ruins or traces (*atlaal*) of an abandoned campsite (*daar, manzil*), which trigger a series of memories of the beloved's beauty and the couple's time together. The poet laments the loss of that richness, but regains his composure and vows to move on. Sometimes the *nasiib* incorporates a night vision of the beloved (*khayaal, tayf*). Other motifs include the poet's watching the beloved's tribe prepare for departure. In the Hebrew qasida, as in the Arabic, the *nasiib* might be erotic (usually homoerotic), but at times it also faintly echoes the tradition of the abandoned campsite and embodies the theme of separation in any number of subtle ways. Transition from the *nasiib* to the body of the Hebrew poem is effected by means of the *takhallus* (literally, the "extrication" or "release"), a verse that tested the poet's skill and agility. See Yosef Ibn Hasdai's "The Qasida" and HaLevi's "To Ibn al-Mu'allim."

**ne'ila:** A penitential poem accompanying the fifth and final prayer session on the Day of Atonement. The Hebrew term means "closing," and the *ne'ila* is recited toward sundown, as the gates of heaven—which have been open during the festival—are shut until the following year. See Moshe Ibn Ezra's "At the Hour of Closing."

**nishmat:** See RESHUT.

**ofan:** The *ofan* is a section of the *yotzer* accompanying the part of the prayer service known as the *qedusha* (sanctification); it is recited between the *qedusha*'s two verses: "Holy, holy, holy, is the Lord of hosts; the whole earth is full of His glory" (Isaiah 6:3) and "Blessed be the glory of the Lord from His heavenly abode" (Ezekiel 3:12). The Hebrew term refers to the type of angels mentioned in the prayer that links these two verses: "And the celestial beings (*ofanim*) of the heavenly chariot, with great stirring, rise toward the seraphim and all together they respond with praise." The *ofan* tends to reflect that celestial "stirring" in its percussive cadence and dense, often alliterative weave. Generally speaking, it describes the holiness of the heavenly beings and their work. See Ibn Gabirol's "Angels Amassing" and HaSniri's "The Worship of Wood and a Fool."

**ornament:** A wide variety of rhetorical figures taken from Arabic poetry were employed in the composition of Hebrew verse, and numerous parallels to them can be found in Greek and Latin rhetoric. A very short list of important Hebrew and Arabic ornaments would include *shibbutz* or *iqtibaas* (quotation or inlay), *tajniis* (paronomasia, or word play of numerous sorts), *haqbalat hafakhim* or *mutaabaqa* (antithesis), *mubaalagha* (hyperbole), *mubaalagha maqbuula* (acceptable hyperbole), *istitraad* (digression), *isti'aara* (metaphor), *hitamemut* (feigned ignorance), and *husn al-ta'aliil* (fantastic etiology, or finding an interesting fictitious cause for a fact in reality). The categories of rhetorical figures are often extremely detailed and involve subtle distinctions between the varieties of figuration. Far from constituting a rote, prettifying application to an otherwise useful but plain facade, biblical inlay and the other ornaments of this poetry serve to highlight a given aspect of the verse by focusing attention on it and intensifying emphasis and effect. In a sense, the ornaments act like tiny turbines to the current of the verse, thousands of finely constructed stations-of-power set out along its flow.

**personal poem:** It is often hard for modern readers to understand the difference in the medieval context between "individuality" and "the personal" in poetry. While the Arabic and Hebrew traditions provided poets with a fixed set of genres and a host of conventions that they were expected to employ, the expression of individuality in verse was by no means ruled out. On the contrary, the conventions challenged the poet to place his stamp on the composition of the verse and the employment of the genres. While the poet's individuality does not necessarily manifest itself through "confession" or registration of the "personal" experience of which modern readers are so enamored, there is a good deal more of the personal in this verse than has often been acknowledged (see introduction, note 61), and poets often worked their own experience into the conventional parameters. Beyond that, some of their best poems involve the creation of a sui generis poetic mode, which scholars now refer to as the "personal poem." These poems treat singular and ephemeral, as opposed to the conventional, idealized, or essentialized situations of the classical genres. They detail the chronological, biographical, or experiential uniqueness of a given moment. And just as personal formulations and even personal experience might be worked into the conventional genres, so too conventional or idealized or general elements could be woven into the registration of the personal. See HaNagid's "On Lifting the Siege," Ibn Gabirol's "I Am the Man," Moshe Ibn Ezra's "The Dove" and "Why Does Time Hound Me So," HaLevi's sea poems, and Avraham Ibn Ezra's "A Cloak," "The Flies," and "The Wedding Night."

*pizmon:* The term itself means "refrain" and can refer to a wide variety of liturgical poems. In Spain, *pizmonim* tended to be strophic poems of an archaic cast with an introductory verse and refrain. See Ibn Avitor's "Hymn for the New Year." Refrains can also be found in Ibn Gabirol's "He Dwells Forever," Moshe Ibn Ezra's "At the Hour of Closing," and Nahmanides' "Before the World Ever Was."

*piyyut:* A liturgical poem. Both medieval and modern editions of medieval Hebrew poetry distinguish between *shirei hol* and *shirei qodesh*, that is, secular poems and sacred poems. In practice, however, the term *shirei qodesh*, and by implication *piyyut*, indicate poems written for incorporation into the liturgy. The term "secular poem" in this context simply means a poem for a nonliturgical setting: it may still involve religious and devotional concerns, without being a *piyyut*. The poet who composes *piyyutim* is called a *paytan*—both words deriving from the Greek *poietes* (maker).

*qasida:* An Arabic term indicating an ode, technically a polythematic poem of a certain length (in Hebrew, up to 149 lines) and written in monorhyme with a single classical quantitative meter. The qasida was developed by the fifth-century pre-Islamic Bedouin poets, who usually divided the ode into three overall parts (with many variable subdivisions): the *nasiib* (erotic prelude, which often included a "weeping over the abandoned campsite," or *atlaal*), the *rahiil* (journey across the desert, which included extensive description of the landscape's flora and fauna), and the *madiih* (encomium, or poem of praise, which often included a boast of some sort, advancing the values of the tribe or individual). Their respective themes might be summed up as "loss and longing," "setting out," and "celebration" or "condemnation." The term *qasida* is Arabic and derives, it seems, from the verb meaning "to intend" or "to aim." (Others feel that it refers to one of the ancient quantitative meters, which—like all the quantitative meters—early on were deployed in the two-part line, the distich, with monorhyme.) This intention—which came to expression in the encomium—could range widely from the tribal to the personal, but almost always involved the embodiment and presentation of critical cultural value. The seven great odes of the pre-Islamic tradition are known as the *Mu'allaqat* (the "hanging odes"), as legend, possibly grounded in historic fact, has it that they were hung on curtains draped over the pagan shrine of the Qa'aba (the Black Stone) at Mecca—a practice indicative of the central role that poetry has played in Arab society. In later Islamic periods and the courtly urban environments of Abbasid Baghdad, the qasida evolved in a variety of ways, gradually losing its central section (the *rahiil*) and taking on a bipartite form: *nasiib* and *madiih* (prelude and praise—with the praise often being followed by a request or message of some sort). In some poems, the erotic prelude was replaced by other subjects, and the encomium by its inverse: lampoon or invective *(hijaa')*. The Hebrew poets took up these developments and for the most part composed bipartite qasidas, though echoes of the three-part qasida can also be detected in certain instances (see, for instance, HaNagid's "On Fleeing His City"). In the two-part qasida the *nasiib* is—if all goes well—gracefully joined to the body of the poem by means of the *takhallus* (literally, the "extrication," i.e., transition), which, as it employs any number of possible rhetorical strategies, often mentions the name of the person being praised (in an encomium) and somehow links the parts thematically or in associative fashion. For a classic two-part qasida employing many of the Arabic motifs and figures, see Ibn Hasdai's "The Qasida." All the longer, non-strophic poems in this book are qasidas, though these long poems are sometimes broken down in translation into manageable English stanzas.

*qina* (**for the Ninth of Av**): There are two kinds of *qinot* in medieval Hebrew poetry. The first is a liturgical poem for the Ninth of Av, which commemorates the destruction of the First and Second Temples in Jerusalem. Liturgical poems of this sort were intended for recitation as part of the morning *qerova*, specifically, the part that ornaments the fourteenth benediction of the *'amida* on festivals ("Blessed art Thou, O Lord, [consoler of Zion], the builder of Jerusalem"), or on the evening of the holiday and the holiday itself.

*qina (elegy):* The second type of *qina* was simply a poem for the dead, an elegy (*marthiya* in the Arabic tradition), which could be deeply personal, written on commission, or provided for a member of the congregation. *Qinot* were also written for entire (destroyed) communities. Hebrew *qinot* (for the dead) go back to the Bible, the Talmud, and Eastern Jewish poetry. In Spain they developed as a secular subgenre modeled after monorhymed Arabic elegies, though in some cases (when they related to communities) they were later incorporated into the liturgy, for the Ninth of Av in particular. The Jewish poets also wrote strophic *qinot*, incorporating biblical elements, that mention the name of the deceased in the final line of each stanza. See Ibn Avitur's "Lament for the Jews of Zion," HaNagid's "On the Death of Isaac, His Brother," Ibn Gabirol's "See the Sun," HaLevi's "Won't You Ask, Zion," and Avraham Ibn Ezra's "Lament for Andalusian Jewry" and "Elegy for a Son."

*qit'a:* A short poem in the Arabic tradition, up to ten lines (twenty in English), treating a range of secular genres and themes. The *qit'a* (which means "fragment," or "piece") was for a long time thought to have "broken off " a larger composition (the qasida), but scholars now believe that they were also written as discrete, monothematic poems.

*rehuta:* An unrhymed *seliha* (penitential poem). The term itself derives from the root meaning "quick" or "smooth," as the poems are read rapidly and without any breaks or refrains. They also employ numerous scriptural references. Later poets imitated this form, which appears to have been introduced by Avraham Ibn Ezra. See his "I Bow Down" and Avraham Ben Shmu'el's "To Whom among the Avengers of Blood."

*reshut:* Originally a poetic prelude in which the *paytan* asked "permission" (*reshut*) from God and the congregation to recite a poem as part of the liturgy. In Spain the term indicated a short poem recited before part of the standard liturgy or before the Sabbath or festival prayer service as a whole. The *reshuyot* (plural) often employed the Arabized forms and motifs of secular poems and allowed for the individual expression of the *paytan* before the congregation and not simply in its name. As such, it stood in sharp contrast to the Eastern tradition of liturgical poetry and, not surprisingly, gave rise to some of the finest Spanish-Hebrew poems of devotion. *Reshuyot* to the *nishmat kol hai* prayer ("The breath of every living being shall bless Thy name, O Lord") were particularly popular and accomplished among the Spanish poets, though other liturgical stations were also ornamented with *reshuyot*. See Ibn Gabirol's "I Look for You," "Open the Gate," "The Hour of Song," and more; also Levi Ibn Altabbaan's "Utter His Oneness," HaLevi's "The Morning Stars" and "You Knew Me," Avraham Ibn Ezra's "Sent Out from the Glory" and "I Call to Him," and Shelomo DePiera's "Tabernacles: A Prayer."

*saj':* A term that is usually, if inadequately, translated as "rhymed prose," or "rhymed, rhythmic prose." Essentially belletristic, or formal, it is distinguished in the Arabic tradition from ordinary, unadorned prose. *Saj'* was used by pre-Islamic soothsayers for their oracular statements and incantations, and it is also employed extensively in the Quran. (See Michael Sells, *Approaching the Qur'án* [Ashland, 1999], for more on the way in which the "prose" of the Quran functions as poetry.) The Arabic word itself derives from the verb meaning "to coo," and evokes, as the lexicographer E. W. Lane illustrates it, "a pigeon continuing its cry uninterruptedly in one uniform way or manner . . . cooing and prolonging its voice." The origins of Hebrew *saj‘* can be traced to classical liturgical poetry from the East (from the sixth century on) and to rhymed epistolary prose, which emerges in the early tenth century. Ibn Gabirol's masterpiece, *Kingdom's Crown,* is also composed in *saj‘.* While in early eleventh-century Hebrew the form was most often reserved for episto-lary writing, in Ibn Gabirol's hands the *saj‘* is much closer to a kind of pulsing, symphonic free verse. All the Arabic and Hebrew *maqaama*s are written in *saj‘*, where it becomes a vehicle of entertaining and often humorous narrative. For more on the topic, see Cole, *Selected Ibn Gabirol,* pp. 289–90, and in this anthol-ogy, the selections from Ibn Gabirol's *Kingdom's Crown* and Qalonymos Ben Qalonymos' "On Becoming a Woman."

**seliha:** A general term describing poems written for fast days and days of peni-tence, especially those between the New Year and the Day of Atonement. The Hebrew term means "pardon" or "forgiveness" (i.e., a poem asking for for-giveness), and this overarching genre treats numerous subjects and includes a variety of subgenres, such as the *tokheha, vidu'i, qina, baqasha, mustajaab,* and more. The Spanish-Hebrew poets also composed some lyrical *selihot* of a per-sonal rather than communal cast. See Moshe Ibn Ezra's "The Day to Come," Avraham Ibn Ezra's "Blessèd Is He Who Fears," "To the Soul," and "Children of Exile," HaLevi's "A Dove in the Distance," and Moshe Ben Nahman's "Be-fore the World Ever Was."

**shibbutz:** The *shibbutz*—the use of recognizable scriptural verses or fragments of verses in poems—is one of the more well-known ornaments in medieval He-brew literature. It consists of at least three biblical words, not necessarily in the order in which they appear in Scripture, and can take several forms. The "neutral *shibbutz*" (by far the most common kind) employs scriptural elements but does not consciously involve the original context of the biblical phrase or substantially affect the interpretation of the poem. ("Neutral" here is a relative term; the fact that the words are drawn from Scripture lends them, from the start, a valence and prestige that are anything but "neutral.") "Charged *shib-butzim*" use implants that deliberately play off the original context of the scriptural fragment, adding substantially if subtly to the associative field of the poem. This kind of *shibbutz* was employed in a wide variety of ways and its ef-fect ranged widely. It might convey information essential to our understand-ing of the poem as a whole and our appreciation of its beauty, or merely per-tain to a certain aspect of the poem; and it could use the scriptural verse in ironic or wholly irreverent fashion, or radically alter its meaning. And finally, full-fledged biblical allusion acts like any literary allusion to a classical text. While implants of this sort were employed in earlier Hebrew verse, their role was enhanced with the Andalusian Jewish poets' return to a pure biblical diction, and the possibilities that *shibbutzim* offered for the subtle shading of meaning—and for surprise—were exploited. That said, the *shibbutz* should not, for the most part, be treated as a "key" to the poem's meaning.

The term itself is somewhat misleading and in fact reflects a development in nineteenth-century German scholarship (where it was known as *mussivstil*). The Hebrew term *shibbutz* means "setting" or "inlay," as in the craft of the jeweler or mosaicist, and relies on a metaphor that misses the dynamic action of the scriptural force in the poem. Like most of the rhetorical ornaments of this poetry, the use of scriptural fragments in the weave of the verse was, in part, brought over from Arabic literature, where it was based on the Quran and was known as *iqtibaas*, "the lighting of one flame from another." Far from implying a static effect, it suggested a source of power and transfer of energy. That effect, however, is usually local and has been described as lights flashing on and off for different periods of time and at different levels of strength and intensity.

Another compelling explanation of this rhetorical device is offered by Neal Kozodoy: "We might think of the poem," he writes, "as a garment woven with great skill from costly and colorful material. Into this fabric have been twined threads of pure gold, beaten down from a single golden bar, the Bible; . . . [These threads] call attention to themselves, first, inviting us to hold up the work, tilting it at a variety of angles and planes in an attempt to perceive whether they might not form some hidden pattern. At the same time, they impart real depth and brilliance to the surfaces surrounding them, and as we study those surfaces we become struck by the impression of motion, as the presence of the pure gold subtly alters the values and intensities of the surrounding hues."

**strophic poem:** A poem that employs rhymed strophes rather than the bipartite, monorhymed line of the qasida and the *qit'a*. Among the forms of strophic poetry in Hebrew are the *shir me'ain eizori* or *shir me'ain eizor* (semi-*muwashshah*) and the *muwashshah*. In fact, the Hebrew strophic poems may have evolved from an entirely separate Hebrew tradition, which existed in the East prior to the development of the Arabic *muwashshah* in Andalusia. The strophic poem can employ a wide variety of stanzaic structures and rhyme schemes, including a refrain, and might be written in syllabic or quantitative meter, or with no meter at all. See Ibn Gabirol's "He Dwells Forever."

*tokheha:* Literally, "admonition." A subgenre of the *seliha,* it originated in the early stages of the Eastern *piyyut* and was still written during the Spanish period. Alone among all the penitential genres it is not addressed to God and like certain *reshuyot* does not speak in the name of the people or the nation. Instead, the *paytan* turns to the individual worshiper and implores him to repent

and confess his sins. At times the *paytan* will also turn to God and ask for for-
giveness, while detailing man's weakness and worthlessness. The genre was
popular among the Spanish poets, as it dealt with the soul and its fate, both
important subjects for them. They were often recited alongside the *vidu'i*
(poem of confession) and on the Day of Atonement. See Avraham Ibn Ezra's
"You Whose Hearts Are Asleep" and, in Cole, *Selected Ibn Gabirol*, "Forget
Your Grief."

**'Udhri poetry:** Elegiac poetry treating unrealized love in the early Arabic tradi-
tion. The term derives from the Yemeni Banu 'Udhra, two of whose poets
wrote powerfully of devotion to the beloved and a willingness to undergo
hardship in love. Famous tragic lovers of the 'Udhri tradition, such as Majnun
and Layla, are separated but remain faithful and eventually die of sorrow. The
tradition was developed further in Abbasid and Sufi contexts, and the Hebrew
poets adopted various elements of it, especially in their religious verse. See
Ibn Ghiyyat's "My Wandering" and HaLevi's "Love's Dwelling."

**vidu'i:** A section of the liturgy recited on fast days and days of penitence, espe-
cially those between the New Year and the Day of Atonement. Sometimes in-
corporated into larger *piyyutim*. See, for example, Ibn Gabirol's *Kingdom's
Crown* and Avner's "The Last Words of My Desire."

**wasf:** See DESCRIPTIVE VERSE.

**wine poetry:** Generally speaking Hebrew poetry adopts the conventions of the
Abbasid wine poem *(khamriyya)*, which in turn traces its origin to the classical
qasida. The Hebrew wine poems share numerous motifs that are freely em-
ployed: an imperative, urging others to drink; lush descriptions of the wine's
color, scent, age, effect, and provenance; description of the (male or female) cup-
bearer (the *saqi*); and description of the site where the drinking takes place—
along a river, in a garden or palace, or indoors during the winter; and the con-
ventional rebuke of fault-finders, who chastise the speaker for indulging in drink
when they should be weeping over the abandoned campsite (Arabic) or the de-
struction of the Temple in Jerusalem (Hebrew)—or simply avoiding licentious-
ness and sin (both). The wine's power to overcome grief is often noted, and
sometimes religious, meditative, or even ethical dimensions are blended with
the wine poem. The perspective of the poem almost always *appears* to be per-
sonal, though it is usually more stylized than, say, a poem of complaint. Like the
Hebrew poems of desire, the Hebrew wine poems are not about indulgent or li-
centious behavior, but about sophisticated pleasure, perception, sensation, and
company.

    See HaNagid's "Mixed in Spain," "Your Years Are Sleep" and—in *Selected Po-
ems of Shmuel HaNagid,* "Have You Heard How I Helped the Wise"; also Ibn
Gabirol's "I'd Give Up My Soul Itself," Moshe Ibn Ezra's "Bring Me a Cup"
and "A Shadow," and Shelomo DePiera's "This Year's Wine."

**wit and entertainment, poems of—also riddles:** This category covers a variety
of poems that might also be subsumed under other generic headings. Some

riddles, for instance, are descriptive, some of the poems of wit involve invective, and the poems of entertainment could treat any number of categories, from wine to invective to description. Most but not all of these poems were cast in epigrammatic form. See HaNagid's "The Apple" and HaLevi's "Inscriptions on Bowls" and "Four Riddles" (as well as the notes to them).

*George Seferis: Collected Poems (1924–1955)*, translated, edited, and introduced by Edmund Keeley and Philip Sherrard

*Collected Poems of Lucio Piccolo*, translated and edited by Brian Swann and Ruth Feldman

*C. P. Cavafy: Selected Poems*, translated by Edmund Keeley and Philip Sherrard and edited by George Savidis

*Benny Andersen: Selected Poems*, translated by Alexander Taylor

*Selected Poetry of Andrea Zanzotto*, edited and translated by Ruth Feldman and Brian Swann

*Poems of René Char*, translated and annotated by Mary Ann Caws and Jonathan Griffin

*Selected Poems of Tudor Arghezi*, translated by Michael Impey and Brian Swann

*"The Survivor" and Other Poems*, by Tadeusz Rózewicz, translated and introduced by Magnus J. Krynski and Robert A. Maguire

*"Harsh World" and Other Poems*, by Angel González, translated by Donald D. Walsh

*Ritsos in Parentheses*, translated and introduced by Edmund Keeley

*Salamander: Selected Poems of Robert Marteau*, translated by Anne Winters

*Angelos Sikelianos: Selected Poems*, translated and introduced by Edmund Keeley and Philip Sherrard

*Dante's "Rime,"* translated by Patrick S. Diehl

*Selected Later Poems of Marie Luise Kaschnitz*, translated by Lisel Mueller

*Osip Mandelstam's "Stone,"* translated and introduced by Robert Tracy

*The Dawn Is Always New: Selected Poetry of Rocco Scotellaro*, translated by Ruth Feldman and Brian Swann

*Sounds, Feelings, Thoughts: Seventy Poems by Wislawa Szymborska*, translated and introduced by Magnus J. Krynski and Robert A. Maguire

*The Man I Pretend to Be: "The Colloquies" and Selected Poems of Guido Gozzano*, translated and edited by Michael Palma, with an introductory essay by Eugenio Montale

*D'Après Tout: Poems by Jean Follain*, translated by Heather McHugh

*Songs of Something Else: Selected Poems of Gunnar Ekelöf*, translated by Leonard Nathan and James Larson

*The Little Treasury of One Hundred People, One Poem Each*, compiled by Fujiwara No Sadaie and translated by Tom Galt

*The Ellipse: Selected Poems of Leonardo Sinisgalli*, translated by W. S. Di Piero

*The Difficult Days*, by Robert Sosa, translated by Jim Lindsey

*Hymns and Fragments*, by Friedrich Hölderlin, translated and introduced by Richard Sieburth

*The Silence Afterwards: Selected Poems of Rolf Jacobson*, translated and edited by Roger Greenwald

*Rilke: Between Roots*, selected poems rendered from the German by Rika Lesser

*In the Storm of Roses: Selected Poems by Ingeborg Bachmann*, translated, edited, and introduced by Mark Anderson

*Birds and Other Relations: Selected Poetry of Dezso Tandori*, translated by Bruce Berlind

*Brocade River Poems: Selected Works of the Tang Dynasty Courtesan Xue Tao*, translated and introduced by Jeanne Larsen

*The True Subject: Selected Poems of Faiz Ahmed Faiz*, translated by Naomi Lazard

*My Name on the Wind: Selected Poems of Diego Valeri*, translated by Michael Palma

*Aeschylus: The Suppliants*, translated by Peter Burian

*Foamy Sky: The Major Poems of Miklós Radnóti*, selected and translated by Zsuzsanna Ozváth and Frederick Turner

*La Fontaine's Bawdy: Of Libertines, Louts, and Lechers*, translated by Norman R. Shapiro

*A Child Is Not a Knife: Selected Poems of Göran Sonnevi*, translated and edited by Rika Lesser

*George Seferis: Collected Poems, Revised Edition*, translated, edited, and introduced by Edmund Keeley and Philip Sherrard

*C. P. Cavafy: Collected Poems, Revised Edition*, translated and introduced by Edmund Keeley and Philip Sherrard and edited by George Savidis

*Selected Poems of Shmuel HaNagid*, translated from the Hebrew by Peter Cole

*The Late Poems of Meng Chiao*, translated by David Hinton

*Leopardi: Selected Poems*, translated by Eamon Grennan

*Through Naked Branches: Selected Poems of Tarjei Vesaas*, translated and edited by Roger Greenwald

*The Complete Odes and Satires of Horace*, translated with introduction and notes by Sidney Alexander

*Selected Poems of Solomon Ibn Gabirol*, translated by Peter Cole

*Puerilities: Erotic Epigrams of The Greek Anthology*, translated by Daryl Hine

*Night Journey*, by María Negroni, translated by Anne Twitty

*The Poetess Counts to 100 and Bows Out*, by Ana Enriqueta Terán, translated by Marcel Smith

*Nothing Is Lost: Selected Poems*, by Edward Kocbek, translated by Michael Scammell and Veno Taufer, and introduced by Michael Scammell

*The Complete Elegies of Sextus Propertius*, translated with introduction and notes by Vincent Katz

*Knowing the East*, by Paul Claudel, translated with introduction and notes by James Lawler

*Enough to Say It's Far: Selected Poems of Pak Chaesam*, translated by David R. McCann and Jiwon Shin

*In Hora Mortis / Under the Iron of the Moon: Poems*, by Thomas Bernhard, translated by James Reidel

*The Greener Meadow: Selected Poems*, by Luciano Erba, selected, introduced, and translated by Peter Robinson

*The Dream of the Poem: Hebrew Poetry from Muslim and Christian Spain, 950–1492*, translated, edited, and introduced by Peter Cole